Nutrition in Infancy and Childhood

PEGGY L. PIPES, R.D., M.P.H.

Assistant Chief, Nutrition Section, Clinical Training Unit,
Child Development and Mental Retardation Center;
Lecturer, Parent and Child Nursing, School of Nursing,
University of Washington, Seattle, Washington

THIRD EDITION

with 76 illustrations

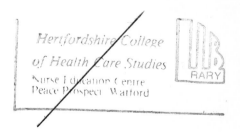

TIMES MIRROR/MOSBY College Publishing

St. Louis • Toronto • Santa Clara   1985

Editor: Nancy K. Roberson
Manuscript editor: Margaret R. Weeter
Designer: Diane M. Beasley
Production: Margaret B. Bridenbaugh

Cover photo by Four by Five Inc.

THIRD EDITION

Copyright © 1985 by Times Mirror/Mosby College Publishing

A division of The C.V. Mosby Company
11830 Westline Industrial Drive, St. Louis, Missouri 63146

Previous editions copyrighted 1977, 1981

Printed in the United States of America

Library of Congress Cataloging in Publication Data

Pipes, Peggy L.
  Nutrition in infancy and childhood.

  Includes bibliographies and index.
  1. Children—Nutrition. I. Title. [DNLM: 1. Child
Nutrition. 2. Infant Nutrition. 3. Nutrition—in adolescence. WS 115 N985]
RJ206.P56 1985   613.2′088054   84-9870
ISBN 0-8016-3938-7

TS/VH/VH 9 8 7 6 5 4 3 2 1   03/D/335

Contributors

JUDITH BUMBALO, M.S.
Doctoral student, Wayne State University, Detroit, Michigan

MIRIAM E. LOWENBERG, Ph.D.
Professor Emerita, Pennsylvania State University, University Park, Pennsylvania; Consultant, Seattle, Washington

BETTY LUCAS, M.P.H.
Lecturer, Parent and Child Nursing, School of Nursing; Nutritionist, Child Development and Mental Retardation Center, University of Washington, Seattle, Washington

L. KATHLEEN MAHAN, M.S., R.D.
Teaching Associate, Department of Pediatrics; Nutritionist, Pulmonary Training Program, University of Washington, Seattle, Washington

MARY O'LEARY, M.S.
Neonatal Nutritionist and Teaching Associate, Department of Pediatrics, University of Washington, Seattle, Washington

SALLY M. O'NEIL, Ph.D.
Associate Dean, Undergraduate Program, School of Nursing, University of Washington, Seattle, Washington

PEGGY L. PIPES, R.D., M.P.H.
Assistant Chief, Nutrition Section, Clinical Training Unit, Child Development and Mental Retardation Center; Lecturer, Parent and Child Nursing, School of Nursing, University of Washington, Seattle, Washington

ROBIN PRITKIN, M.S., O.T.R.
Occupational Therapist, Childrens Orthopedic Hospital, Seattle, Washington

JANE MITCHELL REES, M.S.
Teaching Associate, Department of Pediatrics, School of Medicine; Nutritionist, Adolescent Clinic, Child Development and Mental Retardation Center, University of Washington, Seattle, Washington

CRISTINE M. TRAHMS, M.S.

Teaching Associate, Department of Pediatrics, School of Medicine; Nutritionist, Child Development and Mental Retardation Center, University of Washington, Seattle, Washington

BONNIE WORTHINGTON-ROBERTS, Ph.D.

Professor of Nutrition, Department of Epidemiology/Pediatrics; Chief, Nutrition Section, Child Development and Mental Retardation Center, University of Washington, Seattle, Washington

Preface

Nutrition in Infancy and Childhood has, from its inception, focused on the application of nutrition information for infants and children. This approach has been continued in the third edition. Because a number of disciplines play a role in the provision of nutrition infromation to mothers and children, pediatric, occupational therapy, and maternal-child nursing students as well as nutrition students should find the information supportive of their practice.

Parents are concerned about their children receiving an adequate nutrient intake, about the effect of specific nutrients and foods on behavior and learning, and about the long-term effect of nutrient intake during childhood. The information included on hyperactivity, vegetarian diets for children, megavitamins for the developmentally delayed, and special concerns of nutrient intake can prepare students to answer the questions of concerned parents.

OBJECTIVES

This edition, like the first two, has been prepared to provide a clinical approach to current nutrition information to students who seek careers in the delivery of health care services to mothers and children. My goals are three: (1) that students have information to identify nutrition concerns and counsel parents; (2) that they understand that some nutrition concerns are based on behavioral prob-lems, oral motor incoordination, and other factors and that they seek appropriate consultation from other disciplines; and (3) that they gain an appreciation of the value of the interdisciplinary approach in the delivery of nutrition services.

NEW IN THIS EDITION

Two chapters have been added. Because of interest in nutrient support of premature and sick infants and the need for health care professionals prepared to select and develop formulas and methods for optimum nutrition for these babies, a chapter prepared by a neonatal nutritionist has been added. Its case studies describe how some of these infants have been fed. A brief review of new studies on the development of food patterns in children also has been added to complement the original chapter prepared by Miriam E. Lowenberg, a pioneer in the study of nutrition and feeding of young children. The information included was obtained from her many years of work with and study of feeding patterns of young children. The chapter on adolescent nutrition has been expanded to include a broader discussion of eating disorders. To aid students in applying the information, suggested learning activities have been added at the end of each chapter.

New line drawings and case studies have been added when appropriate to clarify information presented.

The three chapters on nutrients have been compiled into one, which focuses only on nutrient needs of children. Students who apply this information in clinical settings often need a quick reference to the derivation of recommended nutrient intakes.

ACKNOWLEDGMENTS

Many have been supportive and helpful during this revision. The staff and students of the Child Development and Mental Retardation Center at the University of Washington continue to suggest the addition of information they feel is useful in clinical practice. Clients seen in this setting have provided clues as to how to present useful and usable nutrition information for children. Researchers have graciously provided published tables and charts and additional information that permitted expansion of some of the subjects discussed. The pub-

lisher and reviewers, Marjorie V. Dibble, M.S., Syracuse University, and Deborah A. McNeill, Ph.D., Wayne State University, provided many helpful suggestions.

To the many friends and family members who have been supportive and helpful during this effort, I am particularly grateful. Ruth Boyd, who typed the manuscript, has taken a keen interest in preparing a readable manuscript, and in the production of this book has dedicated many of her days off to this effort. All contributors have maintained a pleasant outlook and continued effort despite frequent prodding to finish their chapters. Marie Hanak, photographer, and Greg Owens, graphic artist, have promptly provided the pictures and line drawings needed.

My parents have provided the interest and continuing support that made possible the completion of the revision.

Peggy L. Pipes

Contents

Nutrition: Growth and Development

1

A normal, healthy child grows at a genetically predetermined rate that can be compromised or accelerated by undernutrition, imbalanced nutrient intake, or overnutrition. Progress in physical growth is one of the criteria used to assess the nutritional status of populations and of individual children. It is, therefore, important that persons concerned with nutrition and feeding of infants and children be familiar with the process and parameters of growth as well as the charts and grids used to measure it.

There are many excellent reviews on growth and development. For a comprehensive review, the reader is referred to a standard textbook.[1,2] Although every aspect and component of growth is thought to be influenced by nutrition, this discussion will focus on those parameters with which persons concerned with a child's food intake will be dealing.

NUTRITION AND PHYSICAL GROWTH

Children who suffer from undernutrition are shorter and weigh less than their well-nourished peers. The rate of gain in weight is more affected than is the rate of gain in height, but if the nutritional deficit is severe enough and continues long enough, linear growth will be retarded or may cease and/or pubertal maturation and epiphyseal closure will be delayed. Linear growth will be more delayed when energy intake is adequate but protein intake is deficient. Weight will be affected when energy intake is deficient.[3,4] Overnutrition results in taller, heavier, more mature children.

During and after World War II several studies were conducted in Europe to determine the effect of war-induced shortages of food on the growth of children.[5-7] Prewar heights of children were found to be consistently greater than those recorded during the war years. The differences were most pronounced in adolescents except in the case of 16-year-old girls in Paris. The average heights of this age group were greater during the war than before it because most of the girls in this age group had worked on farms during vacations and had obtained better food.

Children from low-income families consume less food and, therefore, less energy and total nutrients than children from families with greater financial resources. Nutritional status studies have shown that children from these families are shorter and weigh less than children whose families are more affluent. Differences in stature are greater than those in weight. In fact, several studies have found that children who live under conditions of marginal food supplies are shorter yet appear fatter than those who have an abundant supply of food available.[8,9] Results of studies to determine the effect of nutritional supplementation during the third trimester of pregnancy through the third year of life on poverty children in Colombia, South America "at risk" of malnutrition show that children who received supplements were taller and heavier than those in a nonsupplemented control group at 18 and 36 months of age. They, however, remained smaller than Colombian children from higher socioeconomic families who probably had more food available.[10] Children at nutritional risk who have received Women's, Infants', and Children's supplemental food packages that include iron-fortified cereal, iron-fortified infant formula or milk, cheese, eggs, and fruit and vegetable juices have experienced increased rates of growth in height and weight.[11]

Growth patterns of children of racial groups whose members have been believed genetically small have been found to increase under conditions of improved nutrition. Especially striking is the change in the growth pattern of Japanese children born since World War II. In 1962 boys at 14 years of age were found to be 7.6 cm taller and girls at 11 years of age 6.6 cm taller than prewar children of the same ages. The change in growth patterns has been credited to an increase in the intake of animal protein.[12] A 1960 survey of children in Japanese orphanages whose food budgets were limited found heights to be significantly less than those of the national averages for children of the same age and sex. Adolescents were shorter as compared with their age group average than were younger children. During the subsequent 10 years the provision of 180 gm milk and one egg daily and increases in food budgets resulted in improvements in the quality and quantity of protein as well as in the amount of total nutrients consumed. Increases in average stature were greater than expected. A 1970 survey found that only teenage boys were significantly below the national averages for height.[13]

CHARACTERISTICS OF GROWTH

Growth may be defined as an increase in the physical size of the body as a whole or as an increase in any of its parts associated with an increase in cell number and/or cell size. Development is defined as the acquisition of function associated with cell differentiation and maturation of individual organ systems. Growth and development are affected by genetic, hormonal, environmental, and behavioral factors that interact to determine an individual's growth pattern. Individual children have their own genetically predetermined growth patterns. Growth and development, however, proceed in an orderly and predictable sequence. Each organ and organ system has its own period of rapid growth marked by rapid cell differentiation, changes in form, and susceptibility to physical and environmental influences.

Critical Periods of Growth

Increases in physical size are achieved by increases in both the number and size of cells. Cell growth in any organ proceeds in three stages: *hyperplasia*, in which an increase occurs in cell number; *hypertrophy* and *hyperplasia*, in which increases occur in both the size and number of cells; and *hypertrophy*, in which only the size of the cells increases. Growth in both the number and size of cells can be assessed by calculation of the rates of weight to deoxyribonucleic acid (DNA) or of protein to DNA.

Enesco and Leblond[14] determined the number of cells in each organ of the rat at different ages throughout growth by measuring the DNA content of the organ. Knowing the weight of the organ, they then estimated the size of the cells. Winick and Noble,[15] using the same method for rat studies, found that there is a time when cell division stops before the organ attains its final size. There is a phase when cell number is not increasing but cell size is. Some tissues like the brain reach a full adult complement of DNA sometime in the second year, whereas others, such as muscle, continue to increase in DNA throughout adolescence.

Winick and Noble[16] found that rats malnourished by restriction of total food intake during the period of increase in cell number but given normal diets during later growth had a reduction in the number of brain cells, whereas those malnourished in later life and rehabilitated had a normal number as well as size of cells. Elliott and Cheek,[17] in studies of muscle and liver cells of rats, found that restriction of calories resulted in fewer cells, whereas restriction of protein and calories resulted in a decrease in cell size and number. Winick and Noble[18] have also found that overnutrition during a period of hyperplasia resulted in larger animals with a larger number of cells in the organs. The period of hyperplasia, the time when cell number is increasing, is the time the organ is most vulnerable to compromised nutrition and can be considered *critical* to an individual's acquisition of a normal complement of cells.

Growth in Height and Weight

The birth weight is determined by the mother's pre-pregnancy weight and weight gain during pregnancy. After birth genetic influences are "target seeking." A period of "catch-up" or "lag-down" growth may occur. The majority of infants who are genetically determined to be longer shift channels of growth during the first 3 to 6 months. However, many infants born at or below the 10th percentile who are determined to be of average height may not achieve a new channel until 1 year of age. Larger infants whose genotypes are for smaller size tend to grow at their fetal rates for several months before the lag-down in growth becomes evident. Often a new channel is not apparent until the child is 13 months of age.[19]

Immediately after birth there is a weight loss, but birth weight is usually regained by the tenth day. Thereafter, weight gain in infancy proceeds at a rapid but decelerating rate. By 4 months of age most infants have doubled their birth weights, and by 12 months of age their birth weights have usually tripled. Males double their birth weights earlier than do females, and smaller newborns double their birth weights sooner than do heavier infants. The weight increment during the second year is slightly less than the birth weight. The normal newborn infant who weighs 3.5 kg at birth, for example, can be expected to weigh 7 kg at 4 to 6 months, 10.5 kg at 1 year, and 13 kg at 2 years of age. Thereafter, the yearly increments in weight proceed at a slower but constant rate averaging 2.3

kg/year until the ninth or tenth year, when the rate of gain shows a steady increase. This rate continues until adolescence, when a rapid increase in the rate of gain occurs.

As shown in Tables 1-1 and 1-2, annual increments in height decrease from birth until adolescence, when a spurt in growth occurs. Infants usually increase their lengths by 50% by 1 year of age, double them by 4 years of age, and triple them by 13 years of age. The average birth length of 50 cm increases to 74 to 76 cm at 1 year of age, 100 to 105 cm at 4 years of age, and 150 to 155 cm in the preadolescent years. During adolescence the rapid rate of linear growth is most pronounced in the earliest period of acceleration preceding menarche in females. Acceleration of growth generally occurs 2 years later in males than in females. The adolescent growth spurt occurs in every individual; however, it varies in age of onset, intensity, and duration. Growth continues after adolescence but at a very slow rate until the epiphyses close and linear growth ceases.

Racial differences have been noted in rates of growth. Amercan black infants are smaller than American white infants at birth. They grow more rapidly during the first 2 years and from that age through adolescence are taller than American white boys and girls of the same age groups. Asian children tend to be smaller than black children and white children.[20]

Changes in Body Proportions

Increases in height and weight are accompanied by changes in body proportions. The head at birth accounts for approximately one fourth of the total body length, but one eighth of the total body length when growth has ceased. Leg length increases from approximately three eighths to one half of the total body length between birth and adulthood (Fig. 1-1).

Body Composition

Changes occur not only in height and weight during growth but also in the components of the tis-

Table 1-1. NCHS percentiles for length and weight

Age	Percentiles, Boys			Percentiles, Girls			Measurement
	10th	50th	90th	10th	50th	90th	
Birth	47.5	50.5	53.4	46.5	49.9	52.0	Length (cm)
	2.8	3.3	3.8	2.6	3.2	3.6	Weight (kg)
4 months	60.2	63.7	67.1	58.7	62.0	65.3	Length (cm)
	5.4	6.7	7.9	5.1	6.0	7.1	Weight (kg)
8 months	67.7	71.0	74.5	65.7	69.1	72.6	Length (cm)
	7.6	8.8	10.1	7.0	8.2	9.4	Weight (kg)
12 months	72.8	76.1	79.8	70.8	74.3	78.0	Length (cm)
	8.8	10.2	11.5	8.2	9.5	10.9	Weight (kg)
18 months	78.7	82.4	86.6	77.2	80.9	85.0	Length (cm)
	9.9	11.5	13.0	9.3	10.8	12.3	Weight (kg)
24 months	83.5	87.6	92.2	82.5	86.5	90.8	Length (cm)
	10.9	12.6	14.3	10.3	11.9	13.6	Weight (kg)
30 months	88.2	92.3	97.0	87.0	91.3	95.6	Length (cm)
	11.8	13.7	15.5	11.2	12.9	14.8	Weight (kg)
36 months	92.4	96.5	101.4	91.0	95.6	100.0	Length (cm)
	12.7	14.7	16.7	12.1	13.9	16.0	Weight (kg)

From National Center for Health Statistics, Health Resources Administration, Department of Health, Education and Welfare, Hyattsville, Md.

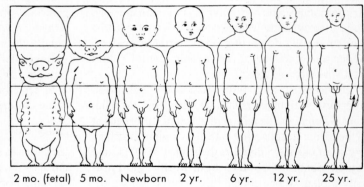

Fig. 1-1. Changes in body proportions from second fetal month to adulthood. (From Robbins, W.J., and others: Growth, New Haven, Conn., 1928, Yale University Press.)

2 mo. (fetal) 5 mo. Newborn 2 yr. 6 yr. 12 yr. 25 yr.

sues. Increases in height and weight and skeletal maturation are accompanied by changes in body composition—in adiposity, lean body mass, and hydration. Estimates of the changes in body composition have been made from chemical analysis of human bodies and of individual tissues, from indirect measurements of water and electrolyte levels, from excretions of creatinine and hydroxyproline, and from estimates of fatness. Indirect measurements of body fat have been attempted by several methods, including measurements of the density of the whole body, measurements of total body weight minus lean body mass, use of fat-soluble gases, measurement of the thickness of fat by roentgenographic studies, and measurements of subcutaneous fat layers. Although there is much

Table 1-2. NCHS percentiles for length and weight

Age	Percentiles, Boys			Percentiles, Girls			Measurement
	10th	50th	90th	10th	50th	90th	
2 years	83.5	86.8	92.0	82.1	86.8	92.0	Stature (cm)
	10.96	12.34	14.38	10.3	11.80	13.58	Weight (kg)
3 years	90.3	94.9	100.1	89.3	99.1	99.0	Stature (cm)
	12.58	14.62	16.95	12.26	14.1	16.54	Weight (kg)
4 years	97.3	102.9	108.2	96.4	101.6	106.1	Stature (cm)
	14.24	16.69	19.32	13.84	15.96	18.93	Weight (kg)
5 years	103.7	109.9	115.4	102.7	108.4	113.8	Stature (cm)
	15.96	18.67	20.14	15.26	17.66	21.23	Weight (kg)
6 years	107.7	116.1	121.9	106.6	114.6	120.8	Stature (cm)
	16.93	20.69	24.31	16.05	19.52	23.89	Weight (kg)
7 years	115.0	121.7	127.9	113.6	120.6	127.6	Stature (cm)
	19.53	22.85	27.36	18.39	21.84	27.39	Weight (kg)
8 years	118.1	127.0	133.6	118.7	126.4	134.2	Stature (cm)
	20.4	25.3	31.06	20.45	24.84	32.04	Weight (kg)
9 years	125.2	132.2	139.4	123.9	132.2	140.7	Stature (cm)
	23.33	28.13	35.57	22.92	28.46	37.6	Weight (kg)
10 years	130.1	137.5	145.5	129.5	138.3	147.2	Stature (cm)
	25.52	31.44	40.80	25.76	32.55	43.7	Weight (kg)
11 years	135.1	143.3	152.1	135.6	144.8	153.7	Stature (cm)
	28.17	35.30	46.57	28.9	36.95	49.96	Weight (kg)
12 years	140.3	149.7	159.4	142.3	151.5	160.0	Stature (cm)
	31.46	39.78	52.73	32.53	41.53	55.99	Weight (kg)
13 years	145.8	156.5	167.0	148.0	157.1	165.3	Stature (cm)
	35.6	44.95	59.12	36.35	46.10˙	61.45	Weight (kg)
14 years	148.8	163.1	173.8	151.5	160.4	168.7	Stature (cm)
	38.22	50.77	65.57	40.1	50.28	66.04	Weight (kg)
15 years	158.2	169.0	178.9	153.2	161.8	170.5	Stature (cm)
	46.06	56.71	71.91	43.38	53.68	69.54	Weight (kg)
16 years	163.9	173.5	182.4	154.1	162.4	171.1	Stature (cm)
	51.16	62.1	77.97	45.78	55.89	71.68	Weight (kg)
17 years	167.7	176.2	184.4	155.1	163.1	171.2	Stature (cm)
	55.28	66.31	83.58	47.04	56.69	72.38	Weight (kg)
18 years	168.7	176.8	185.3	156.0	163.7	173.6	Stature (cm)
	57.89	68.88	88.41	47.47	56.62	82.47	Weight (kg)

From National Center for Health Statistics, Health Resources Administration, Department of Health, Education and Welfare, Hyattsville, Md.

yet to be learned about body composition, there is an important body of data that can be related to physical growth and nutrient needs.

Determinations of total body water alone or in combination with other measurements such as density or potassium have been used as a basis for estimations of lean body mass. Total body water as a percentage of body weight decreases throughout infancy from approximately 70% at birth to 60% at 1 year of age. Reduction of body water is almost entirely extracellular. Extracellular water decreases from 42% of body weight at birth to 32% of body weight at 1 year of age. This change results from decreases in the water content of adipose tissue, increases in adipose tissue, and relative increases in lean body mass.[21] The percentage of weight of water in lean body mass at any age is relatively stable. In other words, there is a direct relationship between total body water and lean body mass. Water is estimated to be responsible for 80% of the weight of fat-free mass at birth and 72% to 73% of the weight of fat-free mass of an adult. Fomon and others[21] estimated the percentage of water in fat-free mass of the male reference as 77.9% at 4 months, 79.0% at 12 months, 77.5% at 3 years, and 75.1% at 10 years of age. They estimated the percentage of water in fat-free mass of the reference female to be 79.7% at 4 months, 78.8% at 12 months, 77.9% at 3 years, and 76.9% at 10 years of age. Adipose tissue contains about 15% water.

Using data on total body water and total body potassium and knowledge of the concentration of potassium in extracellular and cellular water as well as mineral content of the body, Fomon and others[21] have estimated the body composition of children between birth and 10 years of age (Table 1-3).

Since potassium is found predominantly within the cells of lean tissue and ^{40}K in a fixed relationship to total body potassium, measurements of ^{40}K give an estimate of lean body mass in older children and adults. The concentration of potassium in lean body mass of newborn infants is less than in the adult, and it increases during infancy and early childhood. Because of these changes ^{40}K is not, at present, considered a reliable indicator of lean body mass in young children. It is considered, however, to be a valid measure of lean body mass in the older child and adolescent.

Anderson and Langham[22] found that potassium concentration (gram per kilogram of body weight) increases from the first year of life, reaches a maximum at 8 or 9 years of age, and then declines sharply. After this decline sex differences become apparent. Potassium concentration showed a sec-

Table 1-3. Body composition of reference children

Age	Length (cm)	Weight (gm)	Fat (gm)	Fat (%)	FFBM (gm)	Protein	Components of FFBM (% of body weight)					
							Water			Minerals		Carbohydrate
							TBW	Extracellular Water	Cellular Water	Osseous	Non-osseous	
Boys												
Birth	51.6	3545	486	13.7	3059	12.9	69.6	42.5	27.0	2.6	0.6	0.5
1 mo	54.8	4452	671	15.1	3781	12.9	68.4	41.1	27.3	2.6	0.6	0.5
2 mo	58.2	5509	1095	19.9	4414	12.3	64.3	38.0	26.3	2.4	0.6	0.5
3 mo	61.5	6435	1495	23.2	4940	12.0	61.4	35.7	25.8	2.3	0.6	0.5
4 mo	63.9	7060	1743	24.7	5317	11.9	60.1	34.5	25.7	2.3	0.5	0.4
5 mo	65.9	7575	1913	25.3	5662	11.9	59.6	33.8	25.8	2.3	0.5	0.4
6 mo	67.6	8030	2037	25.4	5993	12.0	59.4	33.4	26.0	2.3	0.5	0.4
9 mo	72.3	9180	2199	24.0	6981	12.4	60.3	33.0	27.2	2.3	0.6	0.5

12 mo	76.1	10150	2287	22.5	7863	12.9	61.2	32.9	28.3	2.3	0.6	0.5
18 mo	82.4	11470	2382	20.8	9088	13.5	62.2	32.3	29.9	2.5	0.6	0.5
24 mo	87.2	12590	2456	19.5	10134	14.0	62.9	31.9	31.0	2.6	0.6	0.5
3 yr	95.3	14675	2576	17.5	12099	14.7	63.9	31.1	32.8	2.8	0.6	0.5
4 yr	102.9	16690	2656	15.9	14034	15.3	64.8	30.5	34.2	2.9	0.6	0.5
5 yr	109.9	18670	2720	14.6	15950	15.8	65.4	30.0	35.4	3.1	0.6	0.5
6 yr	116.1	20690	2795	13.5	17895	16.2	66.0	29.6	36.4	3.2	0.6	0.5
7 yr	121.7	22850	2931	12.8	19919	16.5	66.2	29.1	37.1	3.3	0.6	0.5
8 yr	127.0	25300	3293	13.0	22007	16.6	65.8	28.3	37.5	3.4	0.6	0.5
9 yr	132.2	28130	3724	13.2	24406	16.8	65.4	27.6	37.8	3.5	0.6	0.5
10 yr	137.5	31440	4318	13.7	27122	16.8	64.8	26.7	38.0	3.5	0.6	0.5
Girls											
Birth	50.5	3325	495	14.9	2830	12.8	68.6	42.0	26.7	2.6	0.6	0.5
1 mo	53.4	4131	668	16.2	3463	12.7	67.5	40.5	26.9	2.5	0.6	0.5
2 mo	56.7	4989	1053	21.1	3936	12.2	63.2	37.1	26.1	2.4	0.6	0.5
3 mo	59.6	5743	1366	23.8	4377	12.0	60.9	35.1	25.8	2.3	0.6	0.5
4 mo	61.9	6300	1585	25.2	4715	11.9	59.6	33.8	25.8	2.3	0.5	0.4
5 mo	63.9	6800	1769	26.0	5031	11.9	58.8	33.0	25.9	2.2	0.5	0.4
6 mo	65.8	7250	1915	26.4	5335	12.0	58.4	32.4	26.0	2.2	0.5	0.4
9 mo	70.4	8270	2066	25.0	6204	12.5	59.3	32.0	27.3	2.3	0.5	0.4
12 mo	74.3	9180	2175	23.7	7005	12.9	60.1	31.8	28.3	2.3	0.5	0.5
18 mo	80.2	10780	2346	21.8	8434	13.5	61.3	31.5	29.8	2.4	0.6	0.5
24 mo	85.5	11910	2433	20.4	9477	13.9	62.2	31.5	30.8	2.4	0.6	0.5
3 yr	94.1	14100	2606	18.5	11494	14.4	63.5	31.3	32.2	2.5	0.6	0.5
4 yr	101.6	15960	2757	17.3	13203	14.8	64.3	31.2	33.1	2.5	0.6	0.5
5 yr	108.4	17660	2949	16.7	14711	15.0	64.6	31.0	33.6	2.5	0.6	0.5
6 yr	114.6	19520	3208	16.4	16312	15.2	64.7	30.8	34.0	2.6	0.6	0.5
7 yr	120.6	21840	3662	16.8	18178	15.2	64.4	30.3	34.1	2.5	0.6	0.5
8 yr	126.4	24840	4319	17.4	20521	15.2	63.8	29.6	34.2	2.5	0.6	0.5
9 yr	132.2	28460	5207	18.3	23252	15.1	63.0	28.9	34.1	2.5	0.6	0.5
10 yr	138.3	32550	6318	19.4	26232	15.0	62.0	28.1	33.9	2.5	0.6	0.5

From Fomon, S.J., and others: Am. J. Clin. Nutr. **35:**1169, 1982. ©Am. J. Clin. Nutr. (American Society for Clinical Nutrition).

ond increase in males between 14 and 16 years of age and another decline at 16 years of age. The potassium concentration in the female continued to decline during adolescence.

At any age taller children of the same sex have a greater amount of lean body mass than their shorter peers. During adolescence the rate of deposition of lean body mass per centimeter of height is much greater than during the preadolescent years; adolescent males accumulate lean body mass at a much faster rate than do females. The height at which one enters the adolescent growth spurt and the rate of gain in length influence the rate at which lean body mass is acquired.

Forbes,[23] in studies of persons 7.5 to 20.5 years of age, found, with a ^{40}K counter, a linear relationship between height and lean body mass at any age and an exponential relationship between lean body mass, height, and age groups. Sex differences in lean body mass and height ratios were noted in the earlier years, although they were not found great enough to be significant. Males had greater amounts of lean body mass per centimeter of height than did females. After 12.5 years of age the lean body mass : height ratio increased rapidly in the male, whereas the increase was more gradual in the female. The female's lean body mass : height ratio maximum, which was about two thirds that of the male maximum value, appeared to be attained at 16 years of age, 3 years earlier than in the male. At 20 years of age males had one and a half times more lean body mass per centimeter of height than did females.

Fat is found in adipose tissue, in sites in the bone marrow, in phospholipids in the brain and the nervous system, and as a part of cells. It is the component of the body in which the greatest differences between children, age groups, and sexes are seen. The fat content of the body increases slowly during early fetal development, then increases rapidly in the last trimester. Widdowson and Spray found total body fat of the newborn infant to have a mean value of 16%.[24] Fat accumulates rapidly during infancy until approximately 9 months of age.

Between 2 and 6 months of age the increase in adipose tissue is more than twice as great as the increase in the volume of muscle.[21] Sex-related differences appear in infancy, the female depositing a greater percentage of weight as fat than the male.

During childhood the yearly increments for fat show a steady decrease. In many children there is a prepubertal fat spurt occurring before the true growth spurt. When growth proceeds most rapidly in height, adipose tissue increases least rapidly in the female. In the male there is an actual decrease and loss of fat during high velocity periods of growth.[25]

Examples of Growth in Special Systems

Brain and adipose cellular development have been intensively studied in relation to nutrition and nutrient intake. Although the long-term physiological and behavioral effects have yet to be clarified, events during early growth of these two systems are thought by many investigators to be important to an individual's growth and development.

Brain growth. The most rapid and critical period of brain growth in humans begin 9 months before birth and continues into the second year. During this time there is rapid cell multiplication and increasing differentiation. Thereafter, there is an increase only in cell size and a resulting increase in mass. A study comparing brain growth of marasmic and normal infants who died in the first year of life demonstrated significant reductions in wet weight, dry weight, total protein content, and total DNA in the cerebrum, cerebellum, and brain stems of marasmic children. The brain stem was less affected.[26] Brains of children thought to be adequately fed in the first year of life but malnourished at an older age have been found to have a normal complement of DNA but reduced brain weight. This indicates a normal cell number but reduced cell size, further defining the critical period of increase in cell number of the brain.[27]

Dobbing and Sands[28] believe that there are two

periods of rapid growth of total DNA in the brain—one at approximately 18 weeks gestation, thought to represent neuronal multiplication, and one at 3 months after birth thought to be glial replication.

Brasel and Gruen[29] have concluded that most neuronal cell division, at least in the cerebrum, occurs prenatally during the second trimester. They believe that glial cell division is a postnatal event that peaks at 3 months of age. Growth in DNA in the total brain and its two major regions continues into the second year of postnatal life, probably reaching a plateau at approximately 18 months of age.

The rapid increase in brain mass is accompanied by rapid increases in head circumference. The head grows rapidly prenatally and during the first year of life. Head circumference achieves two thirds of its postnatal growth by 24 months of age.[30] Head circumferences of malnourished children have been found to be smaller than those of their well-nourished peers.[31]

Malnourished children have been reported to perform less well on a variety of intelligence tests than those who are well nourished. But it must be recognized that children who are so nutritionally deprived that they experience brain growth retardation usually come from environments that may also compromise a child's development. The interaction of these two variables make the permanent effects of nutrition on mental development difficult to ascertain.

It has been well documented that children who have been subjected to malnutrition prenatally because of war-induced famine or during infancy because of disease or anomalies and who have been discharged to middle class families that provided sufficient food and stimulating environments were able to make up any nutritionally induced intellectual deficits.[31-34]

It has also been reported that children at "nutritional risk" who were provided food supplements performed better on tests of infant behavior at 4, 6, 12, 18, 24, and 36 months of age than their non-supplemented peers, an effect more pronounced in females than in males. The effect was most noticeable on motor tasks. The effect of the supplementation, however, appeared to be contemporaneous. There was no difference in the performance of children whose supplementation was stopped at 6 months of age and a control group never supplemented on tests administered after supplements ceased.[35] The fact still remains that some children who were malnourished in later life who have returned to environments of poverty, questionable sanitation, limited stimulation, and undernutrition have performed as well or almost as well on intelligence tests as their peers, whereas some children who were malnourished at earlier stages of development who have returned to the same type of environments have not been able to perform as well.

Adipose cell size and number. The study of the development of adiposity has suffered for several reasons. The number and size of fat cells is estimated by biopsy of surgical specimens. Cell size is estimated by microscopic examination and/or after collagenase digestion, precipitation of stromal tissue, and osmium fixation of free adipose cells. Cell number is defined by determining the weight of lipid in the average cell and estimating how many cells are in the weight of the body.

Adipose tissue is distributed throughout the body. There is, however, a range of cell size at any site that varies from one site to another. Estimates of fat, number, or size based on a single biopsy may not be representative of body fat. The method of Hirsh and Gillian requires a given amount of lipid in the cell to make it float. Only cells with that amount of lipid can be identified. Those that are depleted cannot be identified and counted.[36]

Studies of obesity in adults have shown that obesity may be associated with an increase in adipose cell number and in cell size or with only an increase in the size of the cell. Weight reduction in adults results only in a decrease in the size of adipose cells, not a reduction in the number of adipose cells. Studies of 21-year-old obese subjects who had a history of childhood obesity before and after weight reduction showed a larger number of adipose cells as compared with nonobese adults. Reduction in weight of the subjects was associated with a reduction only in cell size, not in cell number.[37]

Brook[38] found that the number of adipose cells of children who became obese in the first year of life was higher than the number of adipose cells of children who became obese in later childhood. He also found that those children who were light for their age and who suffered an insult to growth in infancy had a profound deficit in adipose cell number.

In spite of the limitations of methodology, a body of comparable data from a number of researchers lead some to believe that there are periods when the development of adiposity may have implications in the development and prognosis of future obesity. These periods are thought to be from birth to 2 years of age and during the preadolescent and adolescent growth spurt.

Knittle[39] has studied children throughout growth and reports data on children and adolescents 2 to 16 years of age. He found that obese children had significantly more fat cells at 2 years of age than nonobese children and that this persisted through all ages studied. Obese children showed increases in cell number at all ages. Nonobese children experience no change in cell number between 2 and 10 years of age, but a significant increase after 10 years of age.

Obese children had significantly larger fat cells than nonobese children of the same age between 2 and 10 years of age. After that age differences in fat cell size were not significant. Nonobese children experienced an increase in the size of their cells between 10 and 16 years of age that was not experienced by obese children.[36]

Brook[38] noted in older nonobese children little change in cell size during childhood and hypothesized that the increase in body fat during childhood must be a result of a gradual increase in number of adipose cells and that variations in body fatness must be caused by differences in cell size. He

believes that the adipose organ increases by increases in both cell size and number during childhood and that increases in cell number do not occur after puberty.

The results of a study of 18 grossly obese girls 8.4 ± 1.2 years of age compared with nonobese control subjects show that the obese girls have an increase in cell number and size. This increase in cell numbers remained after "more or less" successful weight reduction but was unchanged in the nonobese group. No difference was noted in fat cell number between those who had early onset or later onset obesity.[40]

Whether an increased adipose cell number at any age predisposes a child to later obesity and has an influence on the prognosis for weight reduction and maintenance of normal weight remains hypothetical. There is, however, evidence that obesity in school-age years is likely to continue into adolescence and adulthood and that early onset obesity is much more resistant to therapy than onset of obesity in later life.[41] The accumulation of excessive numbers of adipose cells or larger cells at any age is to be discouraged at any age.

METHODS OF ASSESSMENT

It is important that persons concerned with a child's nutrient intake be aware of how growth is progressing. Assessments are made by periodic determinations of height, weight, and head circumference. The measurements must be determined accurately, and they must be interpreted in relation to the child's current stage of growth. Individual children whose growth does not appear to be proceeding normally may require additional methods of assessment such as bone age and fatfold measurements.

Growth Standards

Growth standards for height, weight, and head circumference make it possible to visualize how a child's growth is proceeding. Standards for bone age permit an estimate of physiological maturity.

Fatfold and arm circumference standards provide a basis for determining obesity versus overweight.

Height, weight, and head circumference. Standards for growth have been devised from studies in which large numbers of healthy, normal children of the same race and socioeconomic group were carefully measured at various ages and the data ranked in percentiles, the number in the percentile indicating the position that a measurement would hold in a series of 100.[39-42] Data from these studies have been presented in tables, charts, and graphs. Growth curves and grids have been designed to measure how far the child has grown (distance curves) or how fast the child has grown (velocity curves). These growth grids are used in health evaluation to give some indication of how a child is growing, and are often used in the assessment of nutritional status.

The grids are prepared so that age values lie along the axis, whereas height or weight values or changes in height or weight values are plotted along the abscissa. Height and weight values plotted for one age give information as to how children rank in size in relation to other children of the same sex, age, and ethnic background and information as to the relationship of weight to height as compared with other children. Several measurements of height and weight at different ages plotted on the grids enable one to visualize if the child's growth is progressing as might be expected. Most children stay in approximately the same percentile during growth. Growth, however, does not proceed in a smooth curve as the charts might be interpreted to indicate. Children grow in spurts, and changes may not adhere to the normal curve. A child may have no gain one month but considerable gain the next. During adolescence the growth patterns of many individuals will change in percentile, the early maturer moving to a higher percentile and the later maturer to a lower percentile. Both patterns usually return to the original percentiles by the time growth is complete. It is for this reason that maturational stages become important in adolescence.

Velocity grids give an indication of how fast a child is growing.[43,44] Children tend not to stay at a given velocity percentile nearly as closely as they do to a distance percentile. However, change does signal an important acceleration or deceleration. These grids are particularly useful in adolescence when children and parents often become concerned about height and weight in relation to peers and about final stature.

The most commonly used growth grids in North America are those prepared by an expert committee for the National Center for Health Statistics (NCHS).[42] Data from the Fels Research Institute was used to determine the standards for children from birth to 36 months of age. The committee used data from the Health Examination Surveys and the Health Nutrition Examination Survey to prepare grids for children from 2 to 18 years of age.

These charts depict physical growth of United States children better than the grids constructed 30 to 40 years ago that were based on growth of Northern European Boston children and Iowa children.

In addition to graphs that reflect gains in weight and height, the committee constructed body weight for length or stature graphs that are appropriate for plotting values for prepubescent boys and girls.

Appropriate use of these charts requires that measurements be made in the same manner in which the reference data were secured. Weight values for the child less than 36 months of age should be obtained while the child is nude, using calibrated beam balance scales. Length values should be of recumbent length, not of upright height (Fig. 1-2). The charts for children between 2 and 18 years of age use measurements of children in stocking feet and standard examination clothing (Fig. 1-3).

Fig. 1-4 shows the effect of undernutrition on a female infant subjected to inadequate calorie intake because of a dilute formula. The mother of this infant was concerned because the baby was spitting up. A neighbor suggested that she add additional water. When the baby continued to spit up, the mother diluted the formula even more. When a nutrition evaluation was requested at 10 weeks of age it was found that the child had gained only 460 gm since birth. Her weight was increasing at a very slow rate, dropping from the 10th to the 3rd percentile. Her linear growth continued in the 50th percentile. She was consuming an incredible amount of formula, but only 190 to 225 kcal/day, approximately 50 kcal/kg. A change to a concentrated formula that provided 24 kcal/oz resulted in a gain of 500 gm the first week and 240 gm the second week. The rapid rate of gain continued until she reached the 25th percentile, where she has remained.

Fig. 1-5 shows the effect of a restriction in food intake on the growth of a preschool boy because of a sudden change in income and the parents' inability to buy the quantity of food they had previously provided. Catchup occurred when the family applied for and received food stamps and the child was given his normal ration of food.

Fig. 1-6 shows the drop in weight percentile of an obese adolescent who was sufficiently motivated to lose weight that she adhered to a low-calorie diet. This grid, prepared by Tanner and others[43,44] in England, is frequently used in clinics serving adolescents. The graphs shown differ in that the first two examples present data on children living in the United States, whereas the last graph presents data on children living in England.

Growth grids for premature and low birth weight infants have been prepared by Gairdner and Pearson[45] (Fig. 1-7). These grids use the concept of conceptual age, that is, chronological age as corrected to the expected date of delivery.

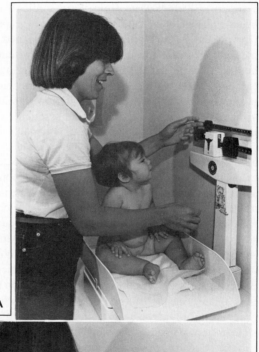

Fig. 1-2. A, Infant is weighed nude on calibrated-beam balance scale. **B,** Recumbent length is measured with a suitable measuring board.

Measurements of head circumference are made in health examinations by passing a metal, cloth, or paper tape measure over the most prominent part of the occiput and just above the supraorbital ridges (Fig. 1-8).

The NCHS growth grids include data on changes in head circumference from birth to 36 months of age in percentiles. Nellhaus[30] prepared a graph of head circumference measurements from birth to 18 years of age. His graph reflects weighted averages of variance from records of fourteen reports in the world's literature and shows standard deviations.

Most clinics use the NCHS head circumference grid for children less than 36 months of age and the Nellhaus grid for children over 3 years of age. Sequential measurements plotted on these grids

(Fig. 1-9) can be used to identify children whose cranial growth is deviating from normal. A rapid increase in the rate of growth may indicate hydrocephalus. A slowdown or arrest in the rate of growth may indicate a condition that will cause developmental delays. Such slowdowns and arrests have been noted in children who were subjected to severe undernutrition.

Skeletal maturation. Fusion of the epiphyses and the appearance of ossification centers occur first in one bone and then in others in a predictable order. As a result, skeletal maturation can be assessed by observation of the various centers of ossification and the fusion of the epiphyses on roentgenographic studies. Standards of bone age have been devised from longitudinal roentgenographic stud-

Text continued on p. 22.

Fig. 1-3. A, Four-year-old is weighed on beam balance scale. **B,** The child is measured with heels, buttocks, shoulders, and head touching the wall.

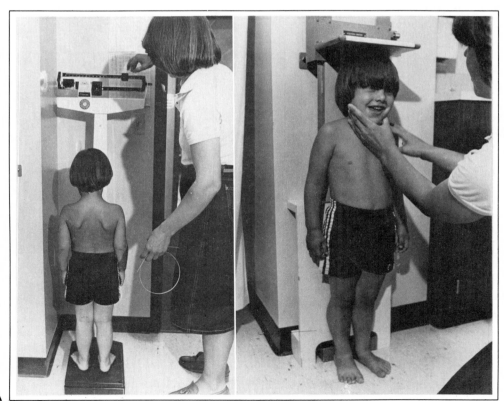

A   B

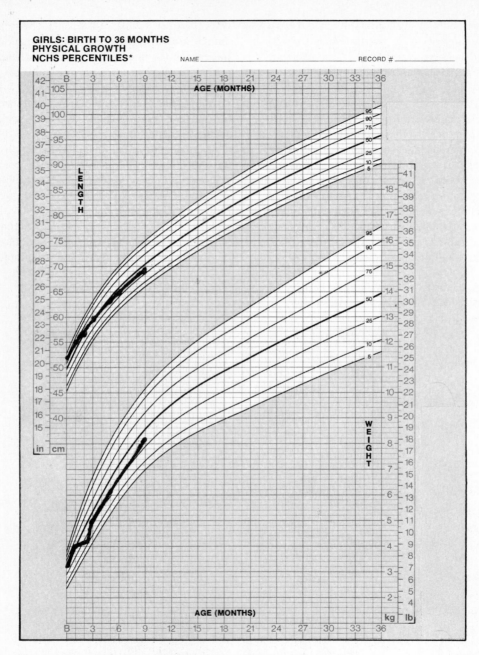

Fig. 1-4. Growth chart for infant girls. (Courtesy Ross Laboratories.)

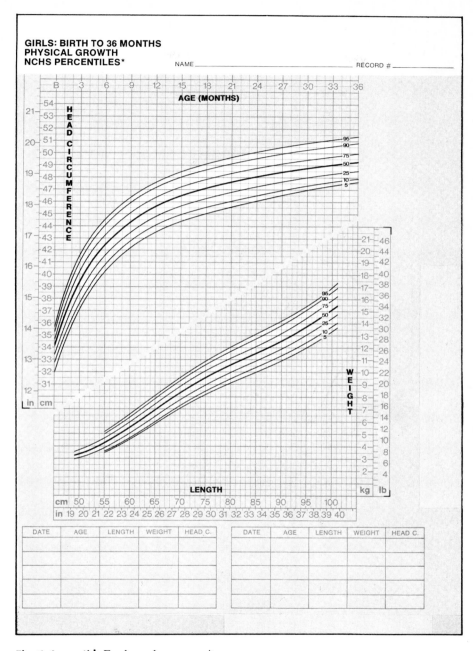

GIRLS: BIRTH TO 36 MONTHS
PHYSICAL GROWTH
NCHS PERCENTILES*

NAME _____ RECORD # _____

Fig. 1-4, cont'd. For legend see opposite page.

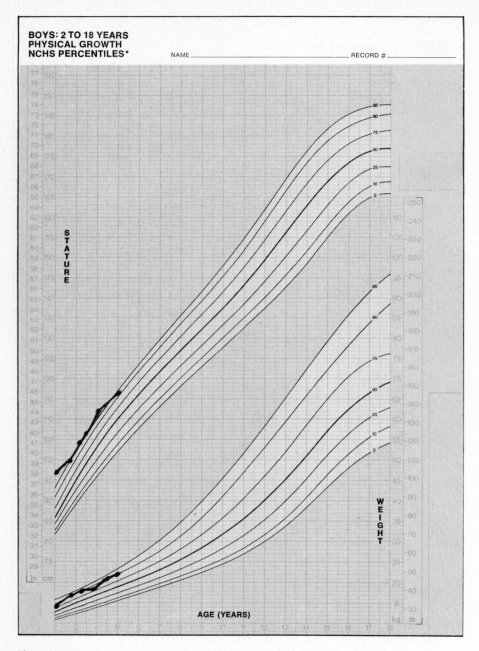

Fig. 1-5. Growth chart for boys aged 2 to 18 years. (Courtesy Ross Laboratories.)

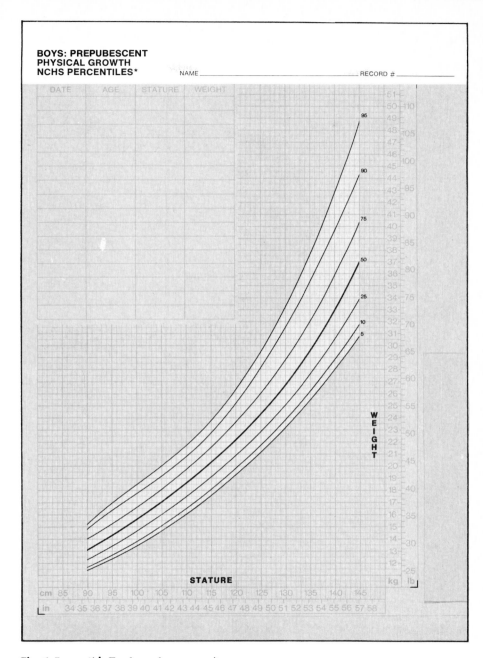

Fig. 1-5, cont'd. For legend see opposite page.

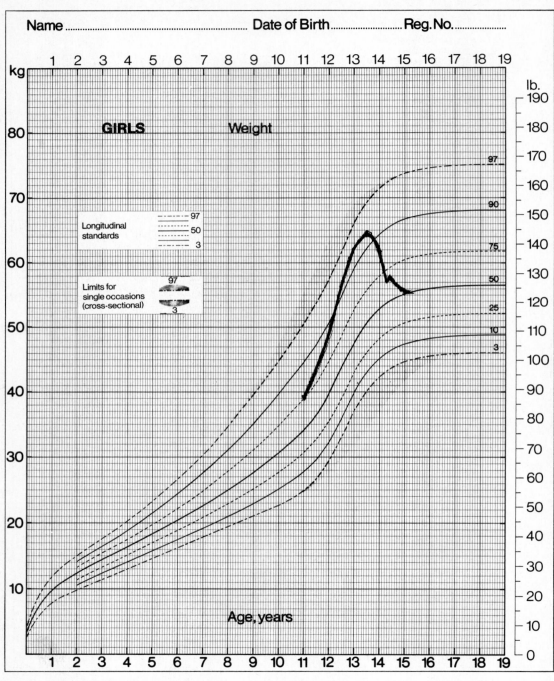

Fig. 1-6. Growth charts for girls. (From Tanner, S.M., and Whitehouse, R.N.: Clinical longitudinal standards for height, weight, height velocity, and stages of puberty, Arch. Dis. Child. **51:**170, 1976.)

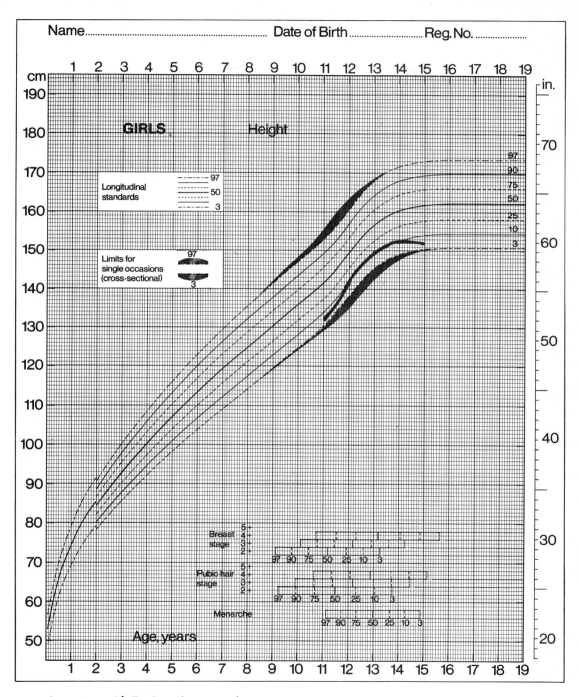

Fig. 1-6, cont'd. For legend see opposite page.

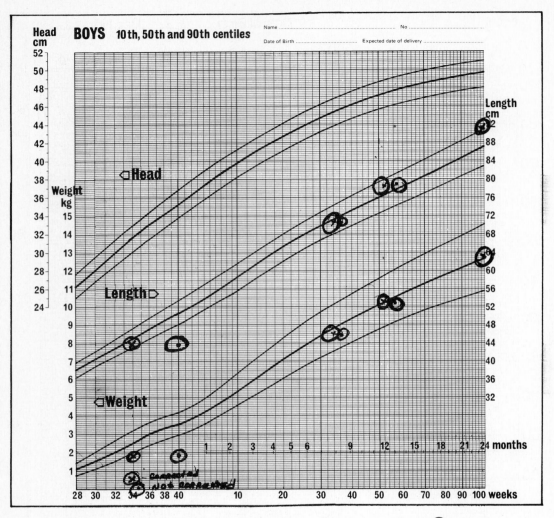

Fig. 1-7. Heights and weights of a male infant born at 34 weeks' gestation. ⊗ denotes plottings when corrected for gestational age. ⊙ denotes plottings by chronologic age. The infant caught up to the 95th percentile by age 24 months. (From Gairdner, D., and Pearson, J.: A growth chart for premature and other infants, Arch. Dis. Child. **46**:783, 1971. Copyright Castlemead Publications.)

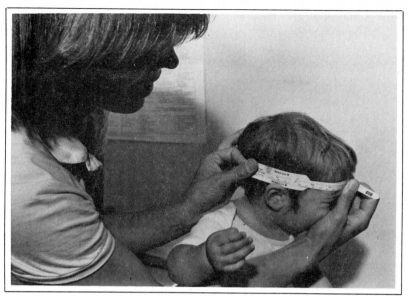

Fig. 1-8. Head circumference is measured over the most prominent part of the occiput and just about the supraorbital ridges.

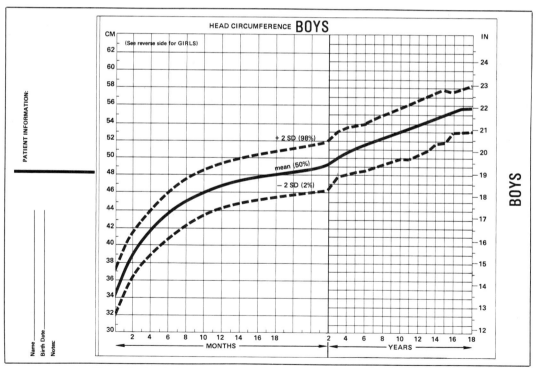

Fig. 1-9. Head circumference charts. (From Nellhaus, G.: Composite international and interracial graphs, Pediatrics **41**:106, 1968.)

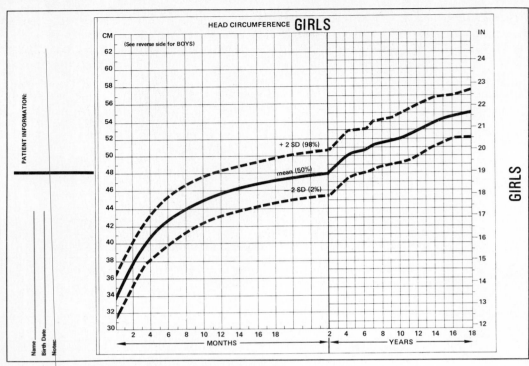

Fig. 1-9, cont'd. For legend see p. 21.

ies of hands and wrists of children. The most commonly used standards are those of Greulich and Pyle, which were based on 100 hand films of children who were examined periodically from birth to 18 years of age.

Bone age is often used to assess the physiological maturity of a child whose linear growth appears to be proceeding at a very slow or very rapid rate. It is an especially useful tool in adolescence when parents and/or children become concerned about late and early maturation. Bone age correlates with secondary sex characteristics and with mature height.

Undernutrition will retard skeletal ossification. Insufficient calorie intakes slow bone growth and delay calcification of the ossification centers. Also, the bone appears normal but often is thinner. Protein malnutrition, caused by either an insufficient intake of protein or an intake of poor quality protein or both, results not only in a reduction in bone growth but also in delays in appearance of ossification centers and possible alterations in the sequence of ossification.[46] Obese children have been found to have advanced skeletal ages.

Fatfold thickness. Since approximately half of the total body fat is deposited in subcutaneous adipose tissue, the fatness of an individual can be estimated by measuring the thickness of the fatfold at selected sites with special calipers that have been calibrated to provide a constant tension. It is important that proper calipers be used. Plastic calipers are not generally adequate.[47] In general one truncal (subscapular) measurement and one limb (triceps) measurement are advised. If only one measurement is to be used, measurement of the triceps is preferred. The triceps is the easiest site to

Table 1-4. Percentiles for triceps skinfold (mm^2) for whites of the United States: Health and Nutrition Examination Survey I of 1971 to 1974

Age group	Males								Females							
	n	5	10	25	50	75	90	95	n	5	10	25	50	75	90	95
1-1.9	228	6	7	8	10	12	14	16	204	6	7	8	10	12	14	16
2-2.9	223	6	7	8	10	12	14	15	208	6	8	9	10	12	15	16
3-3.9	220	6	7	8	10	11	14	15	208	7	8	9	11	12	14	15
4-4.9	230	6	6	8	9	11	12	14	208	7	8	8	10	12	14	16
5-5.9	214	6	6	8	9	11	14	15	219	6	7	8	10	12	15	18
6-6.9	117	5	6	7	8	10	13	16	118	6	6	8	10	12	14	16
7-7.9	122	5	6	7	9	12	15	17	126	6	7	9	11	13	16	18
8-8.9	117	5	6	7	8	10	13	16	118	6	8	9	12	15	18	24
9-9.9	121	6	6	7	10	13	17	18	125	8	8	10	13	16	20	22
10-10.9	146	6	6	8	10	14	18	21	152	7	8	10	12	17	23	27
11-11.9	122	6	6	8	11	16	20	24	117	7	8	10	13	18	24	28
12-12.9	153	6	6	8	11	14	22	28	129	8	9	11	14	18	23	27
13-13.9	134	5	5	7	10	14	22	26	151	8	8	12	15	21	26	30
14-14.9	131	4	5	7	9	14	21	24	141	9	10	13	16	21	26	28
15-15.9	128	4	5	6	8	11	18	24	117	8	10	12	17	21	25	32
16-16.9	131	4	5	6	8	12	16	22	142	10	12	15	18	22	26	31
17-17.9	133	5	5	6	8	12	16	19	114	10	12	13	19	24	30	37
18-18.9	91	4	5	6	9	13	20	24	109	10	12	15	18	22	26	30
19-24.9	531	4	5	7	10	15	20	22	1060	10	11	14	18	24	30	34

From Frisancho, A.R.: Am. J. Clin. Nutr. **34**:2540, 1981. © Am. J. Clin. Nutr. American Society for Clinical Nutrition.

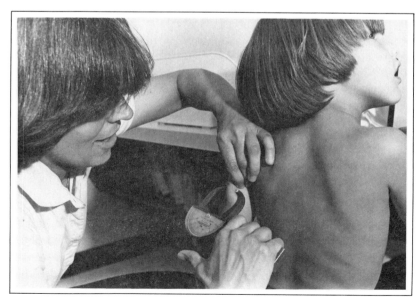

Fig. 1-10. Triceps fatfold measurements are taken midway between the acromion and olecranon processes.

measure and is representative of body fatness (Fig. 1-10).

The triceps measurement is taken midway between the acromion and olecranon processes. The client stands with the back to the measurer, arm relaxed with palm facing the lateral thigh. The tips of the acromial process and olecranon are palpated, and a point halfway between is marked on the skin. The skinfold is picked up over the posterior surface on the triceps muscle 1 cm above the mark on a vertical line, and the jaws of the caliper are applied to the marked level.[48] The jaws of the caliper are permitted to exert full pressure as the trigger level of the caliper is released. The dial is read to the nearest 0.5 mm. Measurement error can be minimized by averaging three measurements.

Standards for triceps fatfold measurements have been published.[49] Triceps fatfold measurements have been compiled from a cross-sectional study of white subjects from 1 to 75 years of age and are included in the Health and Nutrition Examination Survey I (1971-1974) (Table 1-4). Such measurements are very useful as a complement to standard growth charts in the evaluation of children's growth and in the decision as to the necessity to modify calorie and/or nutrient intake. Athletic, muscular children may appear overweight or obese if only height and weight are used as criteria for judgment. On the other hand, handicapped children with poor muscle tone often plot in a lower percentile for weight than height even though they have an adequate amount of adipose tissue.

It must be noted that all data in these norms are derived from white children. Racial differences have been noted in measured fat thicknesses. Puerto Ricans have greater fat measurements than do North American whites and blacks. Black children have a greater deposition of adipose tissue from infancy through 4 years of age than do their white peers. After 4 years of age, the differences are reversed.[50] Group norms and genetic differences must be considered in interpreting fatfold measurements.

Mid–upper arm circumference. Measurement of mid–upper arm circumference combined with triceps fatfold is one method used to estimate muscle and fat bulk. The measurement, as the triceps fatfold, is made at the midpoint of the upper part of the left arm. A paper insertion tape is used most often (Fig. 1-11). The subject is positioned with

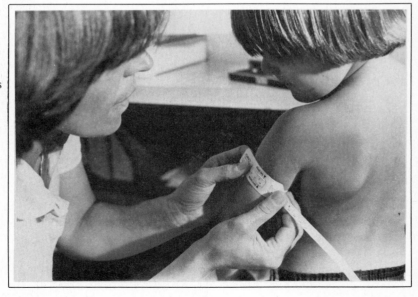

Fig. 1-11. Mid–upper arm circumference is measured with paper insertion tape that touches skin but does not compress the tissue.

the left arm completely relaxed and extended by the side. A mark is drawn on the lateral side of the arm midway between the acromion and the olecranon. The tape is passed around the arm so that it is touching the skin but not compressing the tissue. It is important to ensure that the tape is in a plane perpendicular to the long axis of the arm.[48] Arm circumference is measured to the nearest 0.1 cm. Arm muscle diameter may be estimated by the following formula:

$$\text{Arm muscle diameter (mm)} = \frac{\text{Arm circumference (mm)} - \text{triceps fatfold (mm)}}{\pi}$$

Standards for arm muscle diameter and arm circumference have been derived from the Health and Nutrition Examination Survey I (see Table 1-4).

Some researchers have developed weight-height indexes of relative body weight. Several that are reliable for adults are not applicable for children. Durant and Linder[51] found that the weight-length index calculated by the following formula was the most appropriate for children:

$$\text{WLI} = \frac{A}{B} \times 100$$

$$A = \frac{\text{actual weight (kg)}}{\text{actual height (cm)}}$$

$$B = \frac{\text{50th percentile expected weight (kg) for age}}{\text{50th percentile expected height (cm) for age}}$$

The normal range for children is between 90 and 109. Those who score below 89 can be considered lean, over 110 overweight, over 120 obese. The method does classify muscular children as overweight. However, fatfold measures can validate or negate the assumption.

Potassium 40. Research centers may be equipped to estimate body composition by measuring the amount of ^{40}K emitted from an individual by radioactive counting. The gamma rays of ^{40}K are counted by using NaI crystals as detectors or in a liquid scintillation chamber. Both of these instruments, which measure ^{40}K, must be accurately calibrated, are relatively expensive, and are rarely

available for clinical evaluation of individual children. Neither instrument offers the potential for any hazard or trauma to the individual other than claustrophobia, which may be experienced in the steel chamber that is used when ^{40}K radiation is measured with NaI. The length of time the individual must remain in the counter ranges from several minutes to several hours.

When the ^{40}K content of the body has been determined, the fat-free or lean body mass is calculated by dividing the total ^{40}K content of the body by the known ^{40}K content of lean body mass.

$$\text{LBW} = \frac{^{40}K \text{ (gm)}}{\text{gm of } ^{40}K/\text{kg of lean body weight}}$$

Forbes and Lewis[52] estimated that there are 2.66 gm of ^{40}K/kg of lean body weight. Behnke and Wilmore[53] calculated the ^{40}K content of lean body weight to be 2.46 gm/kg for males and 2.28 gm/kg for females.

FAILURE TO THRIVE

If inadequate growth in height or weight occurs in the absence of disease or other medical concerns, environmental and/or nutritional deprivation is suspected. Some researchers believe that nonorganic failure to thrive results from endocrinological changes in children who do not have adequate mothering. Others believe that mothers with unmet needs of their own have distorted perceptions of how much food their children need to eat and do not offer their children sufficient food. These children are often viewed as having had feeding problems in infancy and difficulty in accepting semisolid foods. They frequently will consume more food for their fathers than for their mothers. When placed in an environment that provides adequate mothering and stimulation, such as a foster home, the children consume large quantities of food. They catch up in height and weight, and their rates of growth become appropriate.

Therapy for this failure to thrive must be directed to correction of the psychosocial difficulties that caused the disturbed mother-child relationship.

CATCH-UP GROWTH

During recovery from undernutrition or illness that has ceased or depressed growth, a child grows at a rate above that expected for his or her age. As the more rapid growth proceeds, the child catches up toward his or her growth curve. Prader, Tanner, and von Harnack[54] have termed this growth rate *developmental canalization*. Gain in weight proceeds very rapidly until the child reaches the correct weight for height, then proceeds at a slower rate as height and weight increase together. During the second phase, growth proceeds at a height-expected rather than age-expected rate.[55]

When an insult such as malnutrition occurs to growth, the timing, severity, nature, and duration of the insult will influence the degree of deficit observed in growth and has been thought to influence the potential for catch-up. Early researchers reported that malnutrition sufficient to cause hospitalization during the first year of life results in permanent stunting in linear growth and head circumference of these children when compared with children of their same age and racial group.[56]

However, several studies of children rehabilitated from malnutrition have shown that catch-up growth is possible. Garrow[57] showed that Jamaican children who were malnourished in infancy caught up or grew larger than their siblings on examination 2 to 8 years after discharge from the hospital. Children in Peru who had been hospitalized for malnutrition between 3 and 15 months of age and were then discharged to foster homes, adoptive parents, or relatives of higher socioeconomic status than their parents were able to catch up in both height and head circumference at a time when catch-up growth of most malnourished children had decelerated.[58] Stoch and Smythe[59] found that African adolescents nutritionally deprived in infancy caught up in height by 15 to 18 years of age when compared with control subjects of the same

age group. Differences in head circumference increased over time.

Although there is evidence that low birth weight infants are at a greater risk for short stature than are other infants, the premature infant seems to have a better chance to catch up to his or her normal growth channel than does the infant who is small for gestational age.

Several researchers have studied catch-up growth in children known to be malnourished in infancy because of illness or physical anomalies that had been corrected by medical therapy or surgery or were uncorrectable. Barr, Shmerling, and Prader[60] studied patients with celiac disease for 3 years after the institution of a gluten-free diet between 9 and 15 months of age. At the time of diagnosis height, weight, bone age, metacarpal cortex, and diameter were all retarded significantly. In 3 years all parameters except metacarpal diameter demonstrated complete catch-up.

Ellis and Hill[61] found that children with cystic fibrosis who received adequate medical care and who had and had not suffered from severe malnutrition in infancy caught up in height and weight for age when evaluated at 7 to 10 years of age.

SUMMARY

Children grow at their individual predictable rates; the range of growth rates at any age is large. When plotted on growth grids, measurements of growth provide information as to whether children are expressing their genetic potential for growth. Fat-fold measurements taken with calibrated instruments provide important information when children are suspected to be undernourished or overfat. If children are not growing as expected, the adequacy of their energy and nutrient intake should be investigated.

That catch-up growth is possible has been demonstrated in a number of children malnourished in early life because of chronic disease or physical anomalies who were rehabilitated. On the other hand, Eid[62] conducted a follow-up study on children who failed to thrive in the first year of life because of chronic disease or physical anomalies to determine if a treated group and an untreated group were able to achieve heights and weights equal to siblings who were used as control subjects. He found that failure to thrive in the first year caused significant growth retardation in both treated and untreated children. His conclusion was that the duration of illness and undernutrition and the interaction of these factors were the most significant causes of permanent growth retardation. There is much yet unknown about the ability of an undergrown child to catch up. The initial period of rapid gain in weight and height is common among all children during rehabilitation. It appears that some children almost or do completely catch up, whereas some do not catch up but remain stunted.

SUGGESTED LEARNING ACTIVITIES

1. Obtain heights and weights of a child over several years from a school health record or medical chart, plot them on a growth grid, and interpret the curves on the grid.
2. Describe how one would interpret to a school-age boy and his parents the physical growth of a child growing at the 10th percentile whose neighbor of the same age and sex is growing at the 95th percentile.
3. Calculate the weight-height index of a child suspected to be a growth failure.
4. Describe measuring devices and scales that provide valid information.
5. Demonstrate how to correctly measure mid–upper arm circumference and triceps fatfold thickness.

REFERENCES

1. Lowrey, G.H.: Growth and development of children, ed. 7, Chicago, 1978, Year Book Medical Publishers, Inc.
2. Falkner, F., and Tanner, J.M., editors: Human Growth, vols. 1-3, New York, 1978, Plenum Publishing Corp.
3. Driezen, S., Spirakis, C.N., and Stone, R.E.: A comparison of skeletal growth and maturation in undernourished and well-nourished girls before and after menarche, J. Pediatr. **70**:256, 1967.
4. Kulin, H.F., and others: The effect of chronic childhood malnutrition on pubertal growth and development, Am. J. Clin. Nutr. **36**:527, 1982.
5. Stuart, H.C.: Studies of the nutritional state of children in unoccupied France in the fall of 1942, J. Pediatr. **25**:257, 1944.
6. LaPorte, M.: Effects of war-imposed dietary limitations on growth of Paris school children, Am. J. Dis. Child. **71**:244, 1946.
7. Ellis, R.W.B.: Growth and health of Belgian children during and after German occupation, Arch. Dis. Child. **20**:97, 1945.
8. Committee to Review the Ten-State Nutrition Survey, American Academy of Pediatrics: The ten-state survey: a pediatric perspective, Pediatrics **51**:1095, 1973.
9. Adrianzen, T.B., Baertl, J.M., and Graham, G.G.: Growth of children from extremely poor families, Am. J. Clin. Nutr. **26**:926, 1973.
10. Mora, J.O., and others: The effects of nutritional supplementation on physical growth of children at risk of malnutrition, Am. J. Clin. Nutr. **34**:1885, 1981.
11. Edozien, J.C., Switzer, B.R., and Bryan, R.B.: Medical evaluation of the special supplemental food program for women, infants, and children, Am. J. Clin. Nutr. **32**:677, 1979.
12. Mitchell, H.S.: Nutrition in relation to stature, J. Am. Diet. Assoc. **40**:521, 1962.
13. Mitchell, H.S., and Santo, S.: Nutritional improvement in Nokkaido orphanage children—1960-1970, J. Am. Diet. Assoc. **72**:506, 1978.
14. Enesco, M., and Leblond, C.P.: Increase in cell numbers as a factor in the growth of the organs of the young male rat, J. Embryol. Exp. Morphol. **10**:530, 1962.
15. Winick, M., and Noble, A.: Quantitative changes in DNA, RNA, and protein during prenatal and postnatal growth in the rat, Dev. Biol. **12**:451, 1965.
16. Winick, M., and Noble, A.: Cellular growth in rats during malnutrition at various ages, J. Nutr. **89**:300, 1966.
17. Elliott, D.A., and Cheek, D.B.: Muscle and liver cell growth in rats with hypoxia and reduced nutrition. In Cheek, D.B., editor: Human growth, body composition, cell growth, energy, and intelligence, Philadelphia, 1968, Lea & Febiger.
18. Winick, M., and Noble, A.: Cellular response with increased feeding in neonatal rats, J. Nutr. **91**:179, 1967.
19. Smith, D., and others: Shifting linear growth during infancy: illustration of genetic factors in growth from fetal life through infancy, J. Pediatr. **89**:225, 1976.
20. Smith, D.W.: Growth and its disorders, Philadelphia, 1977, W.B. Saunders Co.
21. Fomon, S.F., and others: Body composition of reference

children from birth to 10 years, Am. J. Clin. Nutr. **35:**1169, 1982.

22. Anderson, E.C., and Langham, W.H.: Average potassium concentration of the human body as a function of age, Science **130:**713, 1959.

23. Forbes, G.B.: Relation of lean body mass to height in children and adolescents, Pediatr. Res. **6:**32, 1972.

24. Widdowson, E.M., and Spray, C.M.: Chemical development in utero, Arch. Dis. Child. **26:**205, 1951.

25. Tanner, J.M.: Growth at adolescence, Oxford, Blackwell Scientific Publications, 1962.

26. Winick, M., Rosso, P., and Waterlow, J.: Cellular growth of cerebrum, cerebellum, and brain stem in normal and marasmic children, Exp. Neurol. **26:**393, 1970.

27. Winick, M.: Nutrition and nerve cell growth, Fed. Proc. **29:**1510, 1970.

28. Dobbing, J., and Sands, J.: Quantitative growth and development of the human brain, Arch. Dis. Child. **48:**757, 1973.

29. Brasel, J.A., and Gruen, R.K.: Cellular growth, brain, liver, muscle, and lung. In Falkner, F., and Tanner, J.M., editors: Human growth, vol. 2, New York, 1978, Plenum Publishing Corp.

30. Nellhaus, G.: Head circumference from birth to 18 years, Pediatrics **41:**106, 1968.

31. Stoch, M.B., and Smythe, P.M.: The effect of undernutrition during infancy on subsequent brain growth and intellectual development, S. Afr. Med. J. **41:**1027, 1967.

32. Stein, Z., and others: Nutrition and mental performance, Science **178:**708, 1972.

33. Valman, H.B.: Intelligence after malnutrition caused by neonatal resection of ileum, Lancet **1:**425, 1974.

34. Lloyd-Still, J.D., and others: Intellectual development after severe malnutrition in infancy, Pediatrics **54:**306, 1974.

35. Waber, D.P., and others: Nutritional supplementation, maternal education, and cognitive development of infants at risk of malnutrition, Am. J. Clin. Nutr. **34:**807, 1981.

36. Knittle, J.L., and others: Childhood obesity. In Suskind, R.M., editor: Textbook of pediatric nutrition, New York, 1981, Raven Press.

37. Brook, C.G.D.: Cellular growth: adipose tissue. In Falkner, F., and Tanner, J.M., editors: Human growth, vol. 2, New York, 1978, Plenum Publishing Corp.

38. Brook, C.G.D.: Cell growth in man, Am. Heart J. **86:**571, 1973.

39. Knittle, J.L.: Obesity in childhood: a problem in adipose tissue cellular development, J. Pediatr. **81:**1048, 1972.

40. Hager, A., and others: Adipose tissue cellularity in obese school girls before and after dietary treatment, Am. J. Clin. Nutr. **31:**68, 1978.

41. Committee on Nutrition, American Academy of Pediatrics: nutritional aspects of obesity in infancy and childhood, Pediatrics **68:**880, 1981.

42. National Center for health Statistics: NCHS growth charts, 1976, Monthly vital statistics report, vol. 25, no. 3, Suppl. (HRA) 76-1120, Rockville, Md., 1976, Health Resources Administration.

43. Tanner J.M., Whitehouse, R.H., and Takaishi, M.: Standards from birth to maturity for height, weight, height velocity, and weight velocity: British children, 1965. Part I. Arch. Dis. Child. **41:**454, 1966; Part II. Arch. Dis. Child. **41:**613, 1966.

44. Tanner, J.M., and Whitehouse, R.H.: Clinical longitudinal standards for height, weight, height velocity, and stages of puberty, Arch. Dis. Child. **51:**170, 1976.

45. Gairdner, D., and Pearson, J.: A growth chart for premature and other infants, Arch. Dis. Child. **46:**783, 1971.

46. Greulich, W.W., and Pyle, S.I.: Radiographic atlas of skeletal development of the hand and wrist, Stanford, Calif., 1959, Stanford University Press.

47. Gray, G.E., and Gray, L.K.: Anthropometric measurements and their interpretation: principles, practices, and problems, J. Am. Diet. Assoc. **77:**534, 1980.

48. Cameron, N.: The methods of auxological anthropometry. In Falkner, F., and Tanner, J.M., editors: Human growth, vol. 2, New York, 1978, Plenum Publishing Corp.

49. Frisancho, A.R.: New norms of upper limb fat and muscle areas for assessment of nutritional status, Am. J. Clin. Nutr. **34:**2540, 1981.

50. Garn, S.M., Clark, D.C., and Guire, K.E.: Growth, body composition, and development of obese and lean children. In Winick, M., editor: Childhood obesity, New York, 1975, John Wiley & Sons, Inc.

51. Durant, R.N., and Linder, C.W.: An evaluation of five indexes of relative body weight for use with children, J. Am. Diet. Assoc. **78:**35, 1981.

52. Forbes, G.B., and Lewis, A.M.: Total sodium, potassium, and chloride in adult man, J. Clin. Invest. **35:**596, 1956.

53. Behnke, A.R., and Wilmore, J.H.: Evaluation and regulation of body build and composition, Englewood Cliffs, N.J., 1974, Prentice-Hall, Inc.

54. Prader, A., Tanner, J.M., and von Harnack, G.A.: Catch-up growth following illness or starvation, J. Pediatr. **62:**646, 1963.

55. Davies, T.F., and Parkin, J.M.: Catch-up growth following childhood malnutrition, East Afr. Med. J. **40:**672, 1972.

56. Graham, G.G.: Effect of infantile malnutrition on growth, Fed. Proc. **26:**139, 1967.

57. Garrow, J.S.: The long-term prognosis of severe infantile malnutrition, Lancet **1:**1, 1967.

58. Graham, G.G., and Adrianzen, T.B.: Late "catch-up" growth after severe infantile malnutrition, Johns Hopkins Med. J. **131**:204, 1972.
59. Stoch, M.B., and Smythe, P.M.: fifteen-year developmental study on effects of severe undernutrition on subsequent physical growth and intellectual functioning, Arch. Dis. Child. **51**:327, 1976.
60. Barr, D.G.D., Shmerling, D.H., and Prader, A.: Catch-up growth in malnutrition, studied in celiac disease after institution of gluten-free diet, Pediatr. Res. **6**:521, 1972.
61. Ellis, C.E., and Hill, D.E.: Growth, intelligence, and school performance in children with cystic fibrosis who have had an episode of malnutrition during infancy, J. Pediatr. **87**:565, 1975.
62. Eid, E.E.: A follow-up study of physical growth following failure to thrive with special reference to a critical period in the first year of life, Acta Paediatr. Scand. **60**:39, 1971.

ADDITIONAL READINGS

Baertl, J.M., Adrianzen, T.B., and Graham, G.G.: Growth of previously well-nourished infants in poor homes, Am. J. Dis. Child. **130**:33, 1976.

Beardslee, W.R., and others: The effects of infantile malnutrition on behavioral development: a follow-up study, Am. J. Clin. Nutr. **35**:1437, 1982.

Brozek, J.: Human body composition, Oxford, 1965, Pergamon Press, Ltd.

Burgert, S.L., and Anderson, C.R.: A comparison of triceps skinfold values as measured by the plastic McGaw caliper and the Lang caliper, Am. J. Clin. Nutr. **32**:1531, 1979.

Cheek, D.B.: Human growth, body composition, cell growth, energy, and intelligence, Philadelphia, 1968, Lea & Febiger.

Cronk, C.E., and Roche, A.F.: Race and sex-specific reference data for triceps and subscapular skinfolds and weight/stature, Am. J. Clin. Nutr. **35**:347, 1982.

Dugdale, A.E., and Griffiths, M.: Estimating fat body mass from anthropometric data, Am. J. Clin. Nutr. **32**:2400, 1979.

Garrow, J.S.: New approaches to body composition, Am. J. Clin. Nutr. **35**:1152, 1982.

Graham, G.G.: Environmental factors affecting the growth of children, Am. J. Clin. Nutr. **25**:1184, 1972.

Graham, G.G., and others: Growth standards for poor urban children in nutrition studies, Am. J. Clin. Nutr. **32**:703, 1979.

Hamill, P.V.V., and others: Physical growth: National Center for Health Statistics percentiles, Am. J. Clin. Nutr. **32**:607, 1979.

Hicks, L.E., Langham, R.A., and Takenaka, J.: Cognitive and health measures following early nutritional supplementation: a sibling study, Am. J. Public Health **72**:1110, 1982.

Himes, J.H., Roche, A.F., and Webb, P.: Fat areas as estimates of total body fat, Am. J. Clin. Nutr. **33**:2093, 1980.

Klein, P.S., Forbes, G.B., and Nadar, P.R.: Effect of starvation in infancy (pyloric stenosis) on subsequent learning abilities, J. Pediatr. **87**:8, 1975.

Krzywicki, H.J., and others: A comparison of methods for estimating human body composition, Am. J. Clin. Nutr. **27**:1380, 1974.

Mann, M.D., Bowie, M.D., and Hansen, J.D.L.: Total body potassium estimations in young children: the interpretations of results, Pediatr. Res. **8**:879, 1974.

Neumann, C.G., and Alpaugh, M.: Birthweight doubling time: a fresh look, Pediatrics **57**:469, 1976.

Novak, L.P., and others: Total body potassium in infants, Am. J. Dis. Child. **119**:419, 1970.

Owen, G.M.: The assessment and recording of measurements of growth of children: report of a small conference, Pediatrics **51**:461, 1973.

Roche, A.F., and Himes, J.H.: Incremental growth charts, Am. J. Clin. Nutr. **33**:2041, 1980.

Sheng, H.P., and Huggins, R.A.: A review of body composition studies with emphasis on total body water and fat, Am. J. Clin. Nutr. **32**:630, 1979.

Williams, J.P.G., Tanner, J.M., and Hughes, P.C.R.: Catch-up growth in female rats after growth retardation during the suckling period, comparison with males, Pediatr. Res. **8**:157, 1974.

Williams, J.P.G., Tanner, J.M., and Hughes, P.C.R.: Catch-up growth in male rats after growth retardation during the suckling period, Pediatr. Res. **8**:149, 1974.

Wingerd, J., and Schoen, E.J.: Factors influencing length at birth and height at 5 years, Pediatrics **53**:737, 1974.

Winick, M.: Malnutrition and brain development, New York, 1976, Oxford University Press, Inc.

Collecting and Assessing Food Intake Information

2

PEGGY L. PIPES
JUDITH BUMBALO
ROBIN PRITKIN

Nutrition screening, evaluation and/or counseling, and education have become integral parts of many health care, public health, and supplemental food programs that provide services to infants and children. In addition, children perceived as having feeding problems, those who must consume therapeutic diets, and those whose parents are concerned about the adequacy of their food intakes are frequently referred for a team management approach. Plans for modifying food intake in childhood should be based on information more comprehensive than that which identifies excesses or deficits in energy and nutrient intakes and cultural food practices. Health care professionals must work jointly to synthesize information and establish programs that can be carried out by children and/or their parents. Goals for change in food intake should be identified and periodically reassessed. It is imperative, therefore, that health care professionals recognize the necessity of accurate data collection in relation to the nutrient intake from the food consumed, the developmental level of feeding behavior (oral motor screening), psychosocial issues that affect behavior, and mother-child interactions that affect food and nutrient intake.

It is important to recognize that an assessment of food intake is not an assessment of nutritional status. The latter requires anthropometric data and

biochemical and clinical evaluations as well as dietary intake data. Adequately collected food intake data can, however, provide information on which judgments of the adequacy of a child's current food intake can be made and plans for resolving concerns of food and nutrient intake can be designed and assessed. It is important for individuals who collect this information to be aware of the variety of methods of collecting food intake information and to develop skills for screening oral motor difficulties of feeding and psychosocial factors that compromise a child's nutrient intake.

TOOLS FOR COLLECTING DIETARY INTAKE DATA

Health care professionals in clinical settings use a variety of tools for collecting dietary data, each tool having limitations and varying degrees of reliability. The choice of tool will depend on the purpose of the interview, the time commitment of the professional, and cooperation of the child and/or parents. Information sought will vary with the problem. For example, detailed documentation of an early feeding history may be important for counseling parents of young children with feeding problems, whereas this would be inappropriate if the patient were an obese adolescent. Only one tool will be used in some instances, whereas a combination of tools is appropriate at other times. It is important to recognize that valid methods for assessing the dietary intake of groups vary with those designed to collect information on one child for whom plans for nutrition education and counseling are to be developed. The tools most often used in the clinical setting are the 24-hour recall, the dietary history, and the 3- and 7-day food records. Food frequencies have been considered to be applicable in some circumstances.

The interview is the most important aspect of any of the tools used, the validity of the information obtained being dependent on the client's understanding of the reasons for the interview and the information sought, the client's comfort with the interviewer, and the interviewer's skills at probing for and validating information. Whether the child or parents should be interviewed depends on several developmental and psychosocial factors. Beal found that with few exceptions girls under 12 years of age and boys under 13 to 14 years of age were unlikely to give reliable nutrition histories.[1] However, if there is considerable conflict between a preadolescent and the parents about food intake, it may be important to interview the child individually as well as with the parents so that an appropriate counseling relationship can be established.

It must be remembered that assessment data is only as valid as the child's or parents' willingness to share information with the interviewer. It is important that they feel comfortable with the interview and the individual conducting the assessment. A friendly greeting and clear definition of the purpose of the interview and the reasons for the questions asked aid in establishing rapport with the client. Providing an adequate diet for children is a very important aspect of mothering. Parents may feel threatened when questioned about a child's food intake. In addition, the interviewer must have reasonable expectations for the respondent. The mother of seven children cannot be expected to give information as precisely for one child as does a mother who devotes her time to an only child. A number of meals and/or snacks may be consumed outside the home in a day-care center or at school, and parents may not know what children receive in these settings.

During the interview the interviewer must be careful to avoid suggesting time, meals, food, or amounts consumed. For example, the question When does your child first have something to eat or to drink? is appropriate, whereas the question When does your child first eat breakfast? is inappropriate. The tone of voice is also important. Neither approval nor disapproval should be expressed verbally or nonverbally by facial expression. Food preferences of the interviewer should never be indicated. Silences must be accepted with comfort, and parents should be permitted time to formulate answers to questions and to ask questions of their own.

24-Hour Recall

The most common method used for collecting dietary data to characterize the nutrient intake of populations is the 24-hour recall, often used in combination with 1-, 3-, or 7-day food records. The 24-hour recall has also been used successfully to screen children at nutritional risk and can give some indication as to compliance with a dietary regimen during clinical follow-up. It cannot be substituted for more intensive methods when judgments regarding the adequacy of an individual child's food intake are to be made.

Parents or the child are asked to relate every food in portion sizes that the child has consumed for the past 24 hours. Errors in the 24-hour recall have been reported to result from inability of the parents or children to remember exactly what was eaten, difficulties in estimating portion sizes, and lack of commitment of the individual who is being interviewed.[2] There is no assurance that the recall of the day selected is typical of other days. The accuracy with which portion sizes are reported can be increased by the use of food models and by skillful probing.

Food Diary for Infants
(Birth to 1 Year)

Instructions

1. Record *all* formula, milk, and food that the baby consumes immediately *after* each feeding.
2. If your baby is breast-fed, record the time of day the baby is fed and how long the baby feeds.
3. If your baby is formula-fed, record the time of day the baby eats, the kind of formula the baby is fed, and the amount actually consumed.
   Infant formula preparation:
   Is the formula iron fortified?
   ☐ Yes   ☐ No
   Formula (brand name): _____
   _____ oz liquid *or*
   _____ tbsp powder
   Water
   _____ oz
   Other (describe): _____
   _____ oz
   _____ tbsp
   Total prepared formula
   _____ oz
4. If the baby spits up or vomits, estimate the amount.
5. Measure the amounts of any other foods carefully in terms of ounces of liquid (e.g., 2 oz apple juice), level tbsp (e.g., 2 tbsp dry rice cereal), or portions of commercially prepared or home prepared foods (e.g., ½ of a 4.7 oz jar or level tablespoon of strained peaches).
6. Does the baby take a vitamin supplement? ☐ Yes   ☐ No
   If yes, what kind? _____

Day 1

Date _____ Day of week _____

Most recent weight _____ on (date) _____.

Time	Food or Formula	Amount	Time	Food or Formula	Amount

Adapted from Food Diary for Infants used at the Child Development and Mental Retardation Center, University of Washington, Seattle, Wash.

Food Diary for Children

Instructions

1. Record all foods and beverages immediately after they are consumed.
2. Measure the amounts of each food carefully with standard measuring cups and spoons. Record meat portions in ounces or as fractions of pounds, e.g., 8 oz of milk; 1 medium egg; ¼ lb of hamburger; 1 slice of bread, white; ½ of small banana.
3. Indicate method of preparation, e.g., medium egg, fried; ½ cup baked beans with a 2-inch slice of salt pork; 4 oz of steak, broiled.
4. Be sure to record any condiments, gravies, salad dressings, butter, margarine, whipped cream, relishes, e.g., ¾ cup of mashed potatoes with 3 tbsp of brown gravy, ¼ cup of cottage cheese salad with 2 olives, ½ cup of cornflakes with 1 tsp of sugar and ⅓ cup of 2% milk.
5. Be sure to record all between-meal foods and drinks, e.g., coffee with 1 oz of cream, 12 oz of cola, 4 sugar cookies, 1 candy bar (indicate brand name).
6. If you eat away from home, please put an asterisk (*) in the food column beside the food listing.

Day 1

Date _____ Day of week _____ Weight _____

Time	Food	Amount	How Prepared

Adapted from Record of Food Intake used at the Child Development and Mental Retardation Center, University of Washington, Seattle, Wash.

Todd, Hudes, and Calloway[2] compared the 24-hour recall and 30-day recorded food intakes by graduate students and found that a single recall did not give an accurate assessment of the intake for that day nor for the 30-day mean. There was, however, no consistent bias. Some subjects overestimated their intake, and others underestimated it.

3- and 7-Day Food Records

The 3- or 7-day food record or a written diary of all food and beverages consumed is a tool commonly used to characterize current intakes of individual children (see Food Diary for Children, p. 32, and Food Diary for Infants, p. 33). Parents are instructed to measure or weigh portions of food offered and amounts not eaten and record the amounts consumed. Parents report that measuring and weighing pose no problems but that they find the rigidity of recording each time the child eats difficult. Sometimes they forget foods that are added to other foods; catsup, butter, jelly, and the like may be unintentionally omitted from the record. Therefore, careful instruction as to how to record food intake is important.

McHenry, Ferguson, and Gurland[3] found that records covering less than 20 consecutive meals or 7 days may not provide valid information.

Stuff and others[4] compared 1-, 3-, and 7-day records of food intake with food frequency records and found that 3-day records did not provide good individual estimates of nutrient intake compared with 7-day records but did provide an estimate of the general quality of the diet.

A study comparing calculated nutrient intake of weighed and estimated portion sizes recorded in food diaries found intraindividual variations smaller for weighed food records than diary estimates. However, weighing food was reported to be tedious for the client and expensive for the investigator because scales were provided.[2] The provision of casette recorders, which made it possible for individuals to record their intake on tape, seems to have alleviated some of this difficulty in the study with graduate students.[2]

Dietary History

Another method to review dietary intake in retrospect is the research dietary history method developed by Burke[5] and modified and redescribed by Beal.[1] By interview the investigator obtains an estimate of the frequency and amounts of food and nutrient supplements consumed in a specified period, usually 1 to 6 months. Parents are questioned about the child's food likes and dislikes. If parent-child interaction or early feeding experiences are suspected to be etiological in the nutrition concern, information will be elicited on the early feeding history. The interview is often cross-checked with a 24-hour recall and/or 3-day record of food consumed.

This methodology requires a skilled interviewer. The dietitian/nutritionist must gain the confidence of the parent or child, make good estimates, and judge if the answers are reliable. It is time consuming and cannot be adequately completed in less than 1 hour. The finding that dietary histories administered to 5-, 9-, and 13-year-old children could not be replicated is not surprising in view of previous studies and emphasizes the need to include parents in obtaining food intake information for young children.[6]

Several researchers have cautioned against using this tool as the sole source of data. Huenemann and Turner[7] compared the research-type dietary history with 10- to 14-day weighed food records for a group of subjects 6 to 16 years of age and found that no history agreed within 20% for all constituents; the greatest deviations were for vitamins A and D, calories, riboflavin, and thiamine. Other investigators compared dietary histories with 7-day food records and 24-hour recalls and found that dietary histories gave distinctly higher values than 7-day food records and 24-hour recalls for groups.[8] Trulson[9] compared 7-day food records, an average of three or more 24-hour recalls, and dietary histories of clinic patients 7 to 12 years of age. She found no proof that one method was more reliable than another, but she preferred the interview method since it might reveal long-range dietary practices. The 7-day food records and detailed dietary histories gave results showing closest similarity, but findings were not consistent.

Food Frequency Questionnaires

Several researchers have developed food frequency questionnaires. Clients are asked to estimate the portion size and frequency with which they currently consume specified foods and mixed dishes. Since the format is computer compatible, it can be keypunched and calculations quickly returned.

Abramson, Slome, and Kosovsky[10] found the food frequency was a simple and economical method of detecting differences in the usual diet patterns among groups. Stuff and others[4] found that this method provided estimates of intake higher than the 7-day food record.

When collecting food intake information the interviewer must keep in mind that dietary history and food frequency methods yield higher intakes then 3- or 7-day food intake records. Using both the dietary history and a record of food intake is likely to add credibility to the assessment. The interviewer must, however, recognize the life-style demands of the respondent and negotiate a reasonable approach for both the client and health care professional. If parents are literate, concerned, and motivated, they may be happy to keep the food records. Day-care workers and preschool teachers are generally very agreeable about keeping records in their setting. However, it may be necessary to accept a 3-day rather than a 7-day record from a working mother with a large family. If the parents clearly do not want to keep the diet diary, the interviewer must be satisfied with the dietary history, but recognize its limitations.

ASSESSING DIETARY INTAKE INFORMATION

When the dietary intake information has been collected, an assessment of the adequacy of nutrients in the foods consumed is performed. The decision as to the method of evaluation and which nutrients will be calculated will be based on the precision and reliability of the information collected, the foods that appear in the dietary records, the interviewer's knowledge of foods as sources of nutrients, and the problem presented for evaluation.

In some instances intake data may be compared to food groups; other times knowledge of foods that are present or absent in the dietary history as sources of nutrients may give sufficient indication of the presence or absence of problems of nutrient intake. If precise and complete information has been collected, hand or computer calculations of nutrients in the foods consumed may be compared with a standard.

When parents are unable or unwilling to give information that can be quantitated, such as when they report intake as bites of meat instead of one fourth of a 2-oz hamburger patty or when cross-checks reveal inconsistencies, the analysis of food groups or foods as sources of nutrients seems appropriate. If, however, the child is underweight or overweight, or if food sources of a particular nutrient appear on the record only occasionally, calculations of nutrient intake are important. Several computer programs are available. Coding foods consumed and calculations by computer can yield information on a greater number of nutrients more efficiently and quickly than can hand calculation (Table 2-1).

When calculations are complete, the data must be compared with a standard. All standards formulated are intended to be used to interpret data on groups of people and are not intended to be used for evaluating the adequacy of nutrient intakes of individuals. The National Research Council's recommended daily dietary allowances for children are generally based on studies of adults from which extrapolations were made for children. A margin of safety above the average requirement is applied to each nutrient. This margin is not standard but varies for each nutrient.

Some programs define children at nutritional risk as those who consume less than two thirds or three fourths of the recommended daily dietary

Table 2-1. One-day food record and nutrient intake of a 2-year-old girl, 82.40 cm, 14.50 kg

Food description	Amount (gm)	Calories	Protein (gm)	Calcium (mg)	Iron (mg)	Thiamine (mg)	Riboflavin (mg)	Niacin (mg)	Vitamin C (mg)	Folate (µg)	Vitamin A (IU)	Vitamin D (IU)
Eggs, chicken, hard cooked	48.00	77.28	6.14	25.92	1.10	0.04	0.13	0.05	0.00	23.52	249.60	22.08
Bread, white, enriched (3%–4% nonfat dry milk)	25.00	67.50	2.18	21.00	0.63	0.06	0.05	0.60	Unknown	8.75	Unknown	Unknown
Cow's milk, whole (3.5% fat)	360.00	234.00	11.74	428.40	0.18	0.11	0.61	0.30	3.60	18.00	504.00	147.60
Rice, white enriched	50.00	54.50	1.00	5.00	0.45	0.06	0.04	0.50	0.00	8.00	0.00	Unknown
Frankfurters, cooked	50.00	153.50	7.00	2.50	0.75	0.08	0.10	1.25	0.00	Unknown	0.00	0.00
Orange juice, frozen concentrate, diluted	240.00	108.00	1.68	21.60	0.24	0.22	0.02	0.72	108.00	132.00	480.00	Unknown
Macaroni and cheese, baked, enriched	125.00	268.75	10.50	226.25	1.13	0.13	0.25	1.13	Unknown	Unknown	537.50	Unknown
Beans, green, canned, drained solids	45.00	10.80	0.63	20.25	0.68	0.01	0.02	0.14	1.97	18.00	211.50	Unknown
Chicken, fryer, drumstick, fried	35.00	82.25	11.41	5.25	0.81	0.02	0.14	2.49	Unknown	Unknown	49.00	Unknown
Tortilla	30.00	63.00	1.50	60.00	0.90	0.04	0.02	0.30	0.00	Unknown	6.00	Unknown
TOTALS		1119.58	53.78	816.17	6.85	0.76	1.39	7.47	113.57*	208.27*	2037.60*	169.68*

Cal/cm: 13.59
Cal/kg: 77.21
Prot/cm: .65
Prot/kg: 3.71

*Indicates incomplete data in the computer.

allowances of any nutrient and include these children and their families in intensive nutrition follow-up. It may also be important for these children to have a more intensive nutrition evaluation, including biochemical evaluation of their nutritional status.

Anthropometric measurements (height, weight, fatfold measurements) can give indications of the appropriateness of the child's energy intake. If rates of weight gain are excessive or inadequate, calculations of the child's energy intake provide important data on which plans for adjustments in energy intake can be made.

SCREENING CHILDREN AT NUTRITIONAL RISK

The objective of screening is to identify infants and children who appear to have nutritional problems that require further investigation. The interview is brief and information sought is qualitative. It is often performed by paraprofessionals (e.g., community health workers, nutrition aides), nurses, or other professionals who assume the role of case manager. The 24-hour recall screening questionnaires or questionnaires filled out by parents may be used. (See Screening Questionnaire for Infants, pp. 38-39, and Screening Questionnaire for Young Children, pp. 40-41.)

Anthropometric data plotted on growth grids are also used in screening. In general, when children's growth patterns plot at less than the 10th percentile, when they are underweight or overweight for their lengths (Chapter 1), or when interviews show patterns of intake that indicate a nutrient consumed in short supply, the children are referred for more intensive counseling.

From information on the screening questionnaire, parents of infants and children who need further evaluation and/or counseling can also be identified. A "red flag" could be raised from the infant screening questionnaire if an infant were offered over- or underdiluted formulas, if homogenized milk were offered to infants under 6 months of age,

or if nonfat or 2% milk were offered any time in the first year. Other infants who may be identified as "at risk" include those who receive semisolid foods before 4 months of age and those who are bottle fed as they go to sleep.

As the child ages, the quantity of milk consumed and the frequency with which the listed food groups are eaten can identify older children at risk.

All infants or children who require a modified diet to control chronic disease or whom parents perceive as having a feeding problem will need further assessment.

DIETARY ASSESSMENT

Parents and children referred for intensive evaluation of nutrient and energy intake will anticipate a more extensive interview. Even so, the dietitian/nutritionist should carefully explain the purpose of the questions to be asked and reasons for the continuing "how much and how often" questions. Decisions regarding which tool will be used may be made after the parents and/or children arrive and express their concern or lack of concern.

The dietary history, in combination with a 7-day food record, is the preferred tool currently available for dietary assessment in a clinical setting. These procedures require a skilled nutritionist and are costly in time, and not all parents and/or children can respond with validity even though they may wish to do so.

Some programs use a food frequency questionnaire and 24-hour recall, a method that requires less time and is less taxing on the client but yields less valid and useful information.

During this interview the nutritionist collects information about family interactions that affect a child's food intake (e.g., family members present at mealtimes, the use of food as rewards), the food budget and money spent for food, the frequency with which family and children eat away from home, and the family's use of community resources that provide food or nutrition education (Fig.2-1).

Screening Questionnaire for Infants

	Yes	No
Infants (from birth to 1 year of age)		
1. Is the baby breast fed?	☐	☐
If yes, does he/she also receive milk or formula?	☐	☐
If yes, what kind? _____		
2. Does the baby receive formula?	☐	☐

      If yes ☐ Ready-to-feed
           ☐ Concentrated liquid
           ☐ Other: _____

      How is formula prepared (especially dilution)?

_____

_____

	Yes	No
Is the formula iron fortified?	☐	☐
3. Does the baby drink milk?	☐	☐

      If yes ☐Whole milk
           ☐ 2% milk
           ☐ Skim milk
           ☐ Other: _____

4. How many times does he/she eat each day, including milk or formula? ___

	Yes	No
5. Does the baby usually take a bottle to bed?	☐	☐

    If yes, what is usually in the bottle?_____

6. If the baby drinks milk or formula, what is the usual amount in a day?
      ☐ Less than 16 oz
      ☐ 16 to 32 oz
      ☐ More than 32 oz

7. Please indicate which (if any) of these foods the baby eats and how often:

	Never or Hardly Ever (Less than Once a Week)	Sometimes (Not Daily but at Least Once a Week)	Every Day or Nearly Every Day
Eggs	☐	☐	☐
Dried beans or peas	☐	☐	☐
Meat, fish, poultry	☐	☐	☐
Bread, rice, pasta, grits, cereal, tortillas, potatoes	☐	☐	☐
Fruits or fruit juices	☐	☐	☐
Vegetables	☐	☐	☐

8. If the baby eats fruits or drinks fruit juices every day or nearly every day, which ones does he/she eat or drink most often (not more than three)? _____

_____

9. If the baby eats vegetables every day or nearly every day, which one does he/she eat most often (not more than three)? _____

Screening Questionnaire for Infants—cont'd

10. Does the person who cares for the baby have use of a
    Stove?   ☐   ☐
    Refrigerator?   ☐   ☐
    Piped water?   ☐   ☐
11. Does the baby take vitamin or iron drops?   ☐   ☐
    If yes, how often? _____
    What kind? _____
12. Is the baby on a special diet now?   ☐   ☐
    If yes, what is the reason?
    Allergy—specify type of diet: _____
    Weight reduction—specify type of diet: _____
    Other—specify type of diet: _____
    Who recommended the diet? _____
13. Does the baby eat clay, paint chips, dirt, or anything else that is not usually considered ☐   ☐
    food?
    If yes, what? _____
    How often? _____
14. Do you think the child has a feeding problem?   ☐   ☐
    If yes, describe: _____

From Fomon, S.J.: Nutritional disorders of children: prevention, screening, and follow up, Publication No. 76-5612, Rockville, Md., 1976, Department of Health, Education, and Welfare.

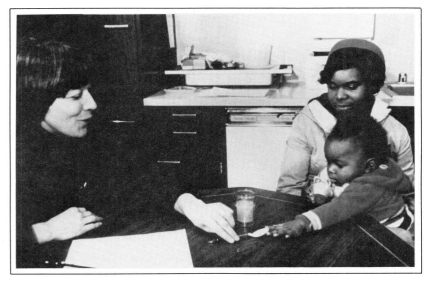

Fig. 2-1. Nutritionist evaluates the nutritional adequacy of a preschooler's food intake.

Screening Questionnaire for Young Children

Preschool children and young school-age children　　　　　　　　　　　　　　　**Yes**　　**No**

1. Does the child drink milk?　　　　　　　　　　　　　　　　　　　　　　　□　　□
   If yes □ Whole milk
   　　　□ 2% milk
   　　　□ Skim milk
   　　Other: _____
   If yes, how much?
   　　□ Less than 8 oz
   　　□ 8 to 32 oz
   　　□ More than 32 oz

2. Does the child drink anything from a bottle (for children less than 4 years of age)?　□　　□
   If yes □ Milk
   　　　□ Other: _____

3. Does the child take a bottle to bed?　　　　　　　　　　　　　　　　　　　□　　□
   If yes, what is usually in the bottle? _

4. How many times a day does the child usually eat (including snacks)? _____

5. Please indicate which (if any) of these foods the child eats and how often:

	Never or Hardly Ever (Less than Once a Week)	Sometimes (Not Daily but at Least Once a Week)	Every Day or Nearly Every Day
Cheese, yogurt, ice cream	□	□	□
Eggs	□	□	□
Dried beans, peas, peanut butter	□	□	□
Meat, fish, poultry	□	□	□
Bread, rice, pasta, grits cereal, tortillas, potatoes	□	□	□
Fruits or fruit juices	□	□	□
Vegetables	□	□	□

6. If the child eats fruits or drinks fruit juices every day or nearly every day, which does he/she eat or drink most often (not more than three)?_____

_____

7. If the child eats vegetables every day or nearly every day, which one does he/she eat most often (not more than three)? _____

8. Does the child usually eat between meals?　　　　　　　　　　　　　　　　□　　□
   If yes, name the 2 or 3 snacks (including bedtime snacks) that the child has most often: _____

9. Does the person who cares for the child have use of a
   Stove?　　　　　　　　　　　　　　　　　　　　　　　　　　　　　　□　　□
   Refrigerator?　　　　　　　　　　　　　　　　　　　　　　　　　　　□　　□
   Piped water?　　　　　　　　　　　　　　　　　　　　　　　　　　　□　　□

Screening Questionnaire for Young Children—cont'd

10. Does the child take vitamin or iron drops or tablets?   ☐   ☐
    If yes, how often? _____
            What kind? _____
11. Is the child on a special diet now?   ☐   ☐
    If yes, what is the reason? _____
        ☐ Allergy—specify type of diet: _____
        ☐ Weight reduction—specify type of diet: _____
        ☐ Other—specify reason for diet and type of diet: _____
    Who recommended the diet? _____
12. Does the child eat clay, paint chips, dirt, or anything else that is not usually considered ☐   ☐
    food?
    If yes, what? _____
            How often? _____
13. How would you describe the child's appetite?
        ☐ Good
        ☐ Fair
        ☐ Poor
        ☐ Other: _____

From Fomon, S.J.: Nutritional disorders of children: prevention, screening, and follow-up, Publication No. 76-5612, Rockville, Md., 1976, Department of Health, Education and Welfare.

The case of a 13-month-old girl referred for dietary assessment because of inadequate weight gain may clarify the process. This girl was the unplanned child of the second marriage of a couple who also had teenage children in their home. All medical reasons for failure to thrive had been ruled out. The interview with both father and mother proceeded as follows:

Interviewer: Let's begin with the early feeding history. Was the baby breast- or bottle-fed?

Mother: She was and still is breast fed. I do not want her to drink formula or cow's milk. I have given her a little goat's milk from a cup.

Interviewer: Did she have any problems sucking at the breast?

Mother: None at all until she was 6 months. Then she wouldn't take much at a time but wanted to feed often. I want to breast-feed her as long as she wants to.

Interviewer: When was she introduced to foods other than milk?

Mother: I gave her cereal when the doctor told me to, about 5 months, then vegetables and fruits, and I think meat about 9 months. I made them for her from only fresh pure foods. I give her only "natural foods" now.

Interviewer: When did she begin finger-feeding?

Mother: About 6 months, I think. She feeds herself rice crackers.

Interviewer: When did she eat table foods that were not pureed?

Mother: I began mashing up vegetables and grinding meat when she was 8 months old.

Interviewer: Does she drink from a cup?

Mother: She has a little goat's milk from a cup, but I have to help her hold it.

Interviewer: Does she try to feed herself?

Mother: She tries to get the spoon, but I can't stand the mess she makes so I feed her.

Interviewer: Now I would like for you to tell me how she lives her day with food. When does she first have something to eat or drink?

Mother: Well, she wakes about 3:00 or 4:00 in the morning and breast-feeds.

Interviewer: Then when does she have something to eat or drink again?

Mother: Well, she wakes again about 8:00, and I give her rice cereal from the health food store.

Interviewer: How much does she eat?

Mother: She's not too interested. Maybe ¼ cup.

Interviewer: Do you put anything on the cereal?

Mother: A little goat's milk.

Interviewer: How much?

Mother: An ounce or so.

Interviewer: Do you put anything else on the cereal?

Mother: Nothing else.

Interviewer: How often (out of 7 days) does she have rice cereal?

Mother: Oh, she has it 7 days at breakfast.

Interviewer: When does she have something else to eat or to drink?

Mother: She usually breast-feeds sometime in the morning.

Interviewer: How long does she stay at the breast?

Mother: About 10 minutes. She's learning to bite.

Interviewer: And when does she have something to eat again?

Mother: Between 11:00 and 12:00 I give her lunch. She likes yogurt and sardines. Sometimes I give her a cracker with sunflower seed butter on it or if I have leftovers from the night before, I may give them to her.

Interviewer: What's next?

Mother: She usually breast-feeds after lunch and again midafternoon, and she has a bottle of pear juice sometime in the afternoon.

Interviewer: How much pear juice does she drink?

Mother: Six or seven ounces.

Interviewer: How often does she have the juice?

Mother: Three or four times a week. If she doesn't have juice, she gets half of a small banana.

Interviewer: When does she eat again?

Mother: She eats with us about 7:00.

Interviewer: What does she usually eat?

Mother: I offer her fish, or yogurt, or cottage cheese, but she won't eat much. If we have hamburger or a vegetable she'll eat, I'll give her that.

Interviewer: How much does she eat?

Mother: About a tablespoon of two or three foods.

Interviewer: What do you do when she does eat?

Mother: I offer her more.

Interviewer: What do you do when she refuses to eat?

Mother: I try to find something else for her to eat or try to get her to eat another bite.

It became apparent during the interview that the mother was unable to give information that could be quantitated so a 7-day record of the child's food intake was requested. A sample of the record received is shown in the box below. Quantitation

---

Food Intake Record

4:30 AM	Breast fed
8 AM	Rice bran, 2 tsp
	Rice puffs, 1 tbsp
	Goat's milk, ½ oz
9 AM	Breast fed
10:15 AM	Banana, ¾ small
11:30 AM	Wheat grain crackers, ⅓
	Goat's milk, 2 oz
	Raw sunflower butter, 1 tsp
	Alfalfa sprouts, 1 tsp
	Mozarella cheese, grated, 1 tsp
	Beets, 1 tsp
	Sardines, 3
	Goat's milk yogurt, 2 tbsp
1 PM	Breast fed
4:30 PM	Pear juice, 6 oz
5:30 PM	Sardines, 2
	Brown rice cracker, 1
	Sprouts, taste
7:50 PM	Goat's milk yogurt, 2 tbsp
8 PM	Breast fed

of the 7-day food record showed an intake of 500 kcal/day or less in addition to the breast milk consumed. On this basis, inadequate energy and nutrient intake was diagnosed to be the cause of the infant's inadequate weight gain.

Therapy for this family involved much more than nutrition counseling. Psychosocial and parenting issues had to be dealt with as well.

If children are overweight, activity patterns are explored. Discussions about the consumption of vending machine food and the effects of television on eating patterns may also provide important information.

It may be necessary to discontinue the detailed probing necessary for dietary history and use only a cross-check if parental tolerance for the continued questions is limited. It is also important to recognize that it may not be possible to obtain sufficient information during one interview; several follow-up clinic or home visits may be necessary to obtain a true picture of the child's feeding history and food intake.

Preschool teachers and public health nurses often provide information about a child's food intake at school and family food patterns.

When dietary data have been collected, an assessment is made of:

1. Parental knowledge of nutrition and appropriate foods for children
2. The adequacy of nutrients provided by the food offered to the child
3. The adequacy of the diet consumed by the child
4. Parental knowledge of and use of community resources to improve the nutritional status of the child
5. Delays in feeding skills that affect food and nutrients consumed
6. Real or potential behavior patterns that can or do compromise a child's nutrient intake
7. The motivation of parents and the child to change the patterns of food intake

If this assessment indicates that adjustments need to be made only in the kinds of food or size of portions offered to and/or consumed by the child or if a therapeutic diet is indicated, plans for modifying the child's food intake should be made with the child and/or parents. The counselor should be aware of community resources that help with the provision of food such as the Supplemental Food Program for Women, Infants, and Children, which provides foods such as iron-fortified formula milk or cheese, eggs, iron-fortified cereals, and vitamin C–containing juices to pregnant women and children under 5 years of age who qualify for the program; the food stamp program, which provides funds that can be spent for foods in the grocery store; and school lunch programs. Clients may need help in contacting agencies that administer the programs. Plans for modifying food intake should be communicated to teachers, school lunch personnel, and others in the child's food environment.

If it appears that the child has delays in feeding skills or eating patterns or that parent-child interactions are also operative in problems presented, the investigator may need to screen for these specific problems so that appropriate referrals can be made.

ORAL MOTOR EVALUATIONS

Children who are developmentally delayed and those who have abnormal muscle coordination may have difficulty with the various skills needed for the process of eating. These skills are normally learned or are already present so early in life that they are taken for granted. A knowledgeable therapist should be involved in the evaluation and planning for any person with motor feeding problems. Infants and children with these problems, however, are often identified during a dietary intake interview and observation of feeding behavior.

Motor coordination problems may be identified by interview with parents and by observation of children as they eat food and drink liquid. It is important to observe the degree of assistance assumed by parents, as well as the child's abilities. The observer may offer food textures with which the child is not familiar to determine if oral developmental delays are caused by a lack of oral motor skills or a lack of opportunities for a more mature performance. For example, more tongue, jaw, and lip movement may be seen when a piece of cheese is placed between the molars than when pureed spoon food is offered (Fig. 2-2).

When making the transition to solid foods, the child will initially attempt to use oral patterns that are familiar and habitual, even though they may not be effective. Loss of food from the mouth may be caused by immature tongue movement and should not be interpreted as dislike for the food. Placement of food at the side of the mouth reduces food ejection caused by immature tongue movement. Occasional choking and coughing are not unusual during the transition period from pureed spoon foods to soft table foods. Hiding lumps of solid food within pureed or strained food will not help in making the transition. For a child with primitive oral patterns, it will be much more difficult to handle a multitextured food that requires the sorting out of the pieces that require chewing from the pieces that can be swallowed without chewing. Gradual introduction of increasingly more textured

and drier foods is a better approach to making the transition from pureed foods to table foods. It is most important not to get upset when a child chokes. Ordinarily, the child can handle choking without assistance. If there is no coughing or breathing, the evaluator can quickly perform the Heimlich maneuver or bend the child forward and tap sharply between the shoulders. Fortunately few genuine emergenices arise, but it is important to be prepared by knowing how to handle emergencies. When asking a parent to try new food textures, one needs to assure them that simple choking is not life threatening if one knows how to deal with it.

The Screening of Eating Abilities form (pp. 45 to 49) can be used by the dietitian or nutritionist during the dietary assessment when the child has not yet been seen by a skilled therapist or no therapist is available. This screening tool was developed at the Child Development and Mental Retardation Center of the University of Washington to be used by their comprehensive child evaluation teams. The form can serve as a guideline on which to record information. When completed, the evaluator should be able to determine if the child's eating problems are caused by difficulties in body and

Fig. 2-2. Occupational therapist evaluates oral motor patterns of child with cerebral palsy.

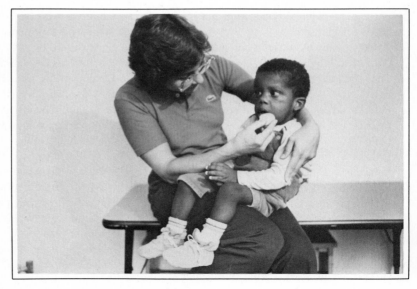

Screening of Eating Abilities

Child's name: _____ ID#: _____ B.D.: _____
Medical diagnosis, if known: _____
Name of evaluator: _____
Name of parent or caregiver: _____ Phone: _____
Other agencies involved: _____

I. Questions to ask of parent or caregiver
   A. What are your greatest concerns in regard to feeding?
   B. What are the food likes and dislikes of your child in relation to texture, temperature, color, and flavor?
   C. Are some foods more difficult for your child to eat than others?
   D. Are there any foods that your child cannot eat?
   E. Does he/she take any medication or food supplements?
   F. When does he/she have meals and snacks?
   G. Does he/she eat with the family?
   H. Who assists at mealtimes (home, school, other)?
   I. How much assistance is given?
   J. What textures are usually eaten (thin liquid, thick liquid, soft spoon food, soft chewy food, ground food, chopped food, crunchy food—see list below)?

II. Tactile sensitivity
   These stimuli are applied toward the beginning of the evaluation before offering food but after the child has had some opportunity to adjust to you as a stranger. Tell the child what you are going to do before applying the stimuli. Be cautious in overinterpreting inappropriate responses that may be social or behavioral and not necessarily tactile.
   First, lightly stroke the front and back of each of the child's hands. Then stroke the front aspect of the skin on each arm. Finally, stroke the face, lips, and gums with firm pressure of your fingertips.

APPROPRIATE	QUESTIONABLE APPROPRIATENESS
Neutral or positive response to touch	Muscle tension, moving away from stimulus, or vocal protest
☐ Hand, arm	☐ Hand, arm
☐ Face	☐ Face
☐ Gums, outside teeth, when stroked with a fingertip	☐ Gums, outside teeth, when stroked with a fingertip

Questionable appropriate responses may be caused by situational variables, but if caregiver reports consistent negative responses, a therapy referral is indicated.

III. Food offered
   These foods are listed in sequence according to difficulty and are grouped into three levels of corresponding normal developmental skills. Ask the caregiver to first offer foods commonly eaten at

Continued.

Adapted from Carman, P.: Screening of eating abilities, Occupational Therapy Department, Child Development and Mental Retardation center, WJ-10, Seattle, 1980, University of Washington.

Screening of Eating Abilities—cont'd

home, then to try some of the other textures at more difficult levels. Watch carefully for amount of chewing, movement of food within the mouth, and tendency to choke. Small amounts of food are offered from each category appropriate to the child's developmental level so that satiation does not occur too quickly. Thin liquid is offered to every child, but soft spoon foods or soft chewy foods should be omitted when the child has demonstrated higher level skills. Thick liquid is offered only when thin liquids are difficult (evidenced by choking, liquid running out of mouth).

A. *Child less than 5 months of age developmentally* (needs head and trunk support while eating, i.e., needs to be held in adult's arms, infant seat, special support chairs).
  ☐ Thick liquid (optional, offered when thin liquid is taken with difficulty): milkshake, thinned applesauce, thinned yogurt
  ☐ Thin liquid: milk, water, fruit juice
  ☐ Soft spoon food: applesauce, pudding, yogurt
  ☐ Soft chewy food: cheese, fish, vienna sausage

B. *Child 5 to 12 months of age developmentally* (good head control, needs some trunk support while eating, sits upright in chair).
  ☐ Ground solid food: "junior foods," ground table foods (dry consistency)
  ☐ Crunchy food that dissolves readily: cracker, potato stick
  ☐ Oblong finger food (easier to grasp): potato stick, green bean
  ☐ Small finger food (harder to grasp): Cheerio, puffed cereal
  ☐ Hard crunchy food: melba toast, bread stick

C. *Child more than 12 months of age developmentally* (with good head and trunk control and tongue mobility, lateralization).
  ☐ Chopped table foods
  ☐ Bite-sized table foods: raisins
  ☐ Multitexture foods (solid plus liquid): apple, celery, soup
  ☐ Chewy food: chicken, hamburger, small pieces of well-cooked meat
  ☐ Hard foods that break into diffuse pieces: carrots, nuts (if older than 2 years of age)

IV. Observations of child eating

Caregiver is asked to feed the child in the usual way. Ask whether any particular equipment or furniture is used that may not be present for this observation.

Mark NA (not applicable) if child is younger than stated age. Asterisks indicate posture or movement that is always abnormal; other activity of questionable appropriateness may be caused by neurological immaturity or other factors.

A. Positioning

APPROPRIATE	QUESTIONABLE APPROPRIATENESS
☐ Held by caregiver (if younger than 1 year of age) within 30° of upright	☐ Held by caregiver (lying back, asymmetrical, or otherwise unusual)
☐ Within 30° of upright, propped, or special seat (hips flexed 90° in usual sitting angle)	☐ Held by caregiver (older than 1 year of age)
☐ High chair	☐ Lying on flat surface
☐ Other: _____	☐ Other: _____

Screening of Eating Abilities—cont'd

The health professional may wish to discuss alternative means of positioning if the usual method is questionably appropriate. If the child has abnormal muscle tone, appropriate positioning is much more difficult to achieve. Consultation with a physical therapist or occupational therapist should be obtained. Any of the following behaviors under the "questionable" column indicate need for a consultation or a therapy program.

B. *Posture and movement*

APPROPRIATE

☐ Head in alignment with body
☐ Head control stable (expected by 4 or 5 months of age)
☐ Arms forward, hands midline (frequent by 4 to 6 months of age)
☐ Hands, legs, and feet move freely, without stiffness
☐ Hips flex easily for sitting, knees spread apart spontaneously for wide sitting base
☐ Trunk straight when sitting (expected by 5 to 6 months of age)

QUESTIONABLE APPROPRIATENESS

☐ Head frequently back or to one side, rotated to one side
☐ Lack of head stability, excess motions, floppy, pushes back, falls forward (older than 5 months of age)
☐ Arms frequently retracted at shoulders, hands do not come together (older than 4 to 5 months of age)
☐ Legs and feet seem stiff, seldom move, or move in stereotyped patterns
☐ Hips resist bending or intermittently extend; narrow sitting base, knees pull together
☐ Trunk tilted, slumped, rotated, or arched backwards (older than 5 months of age)

C. *Oral motor coordination*

APPROPRIATE

JAW

☐ Jaw opens and closes easily, controlled to receive food
☐ Jaw stabilized with little movement
☐ Jaw moves up and down with slight lateral movements when chewing ("rotary")

QUESTIONABLE APPROPRIATENESS

☐ Jaw opens too wide or with tension
☐ Delayed jaw opening response to receive food
☐ Jaw moves up and down while drinking from a cup so liquid is lost (older than 12 months of age)
☐ Jaw clamps down intermittently (older than 2 years of age)
☐ Lack of up and down movement with solid food

APPROPRIATE

TONGUE

☐ Tongue stays within mouth while drinking
☐ Tongue stays within mouth with foods
☐ Tongue lateralized, food placed at side (6 months of age); food placed midline (9 months of age)

QUESTIONABLE APPROPRIATENESS

☐ Tongue protrudes past border of lips while drinking
☐ Tongue protrudes with spoon foods
☐ Tongue moves forward and backward when solid foods are placed at side of mouth or presented midline, no lateral movement

Screening of Eating Abilities—cont'd

LIPS
- ☐ Lips seal on nipple or cup rim
- ☐ Lips close on and clean spoon
- ☐ Lips move actively while chewing

- ☐ Liquids not retained well by lips with nipple, with cup (older than 24 months of age)
- ☐ Spoon foods not retained well by lips (older than 8 months of age)
- ☐ Passive lips while chewing

SWALLOW
- ☐ Swallows readily
- ☐ Swallows liquids, no choking
- ☐ Swallows solids, seldom chokes

- ☐ Delayed swallow, slows eating
- ☐ Chokes two or more times when drinking liquid from a cup
- ☐ Chokes two or more times when drinking liquids other than from a cup (bottle, etc.)
- ☐ Chokes two or more times when solids are fed

GAG REFLEX
- ☐ Normal gag reflex (readiness to vomit when pressure applied to pharyngeal wall, soft palate, posterior tongue)

- ☐ Gag reflex hyposensitive (slow or absent)
- ☐ Gag reflex hypersensitive (occurs to pressure on middle or front of tongue or at sight of certain food)

SALIVA CONTROL
- ☐ Swallows salive (doesn't drool)

- ☐ Drools when not eating (older than 24 months of age) and when not teething

D. *Prehension*

Grasping of objects starts with a reflexive closing when the palmar surface of the hand is stimulated; the grasp becomes voluntary with maturity and is gradually refined to use of opposed fingertips. Any observations of questionable quality or prolonged primitive skill level should be cause for further evaluation.

APPROPRIATE
- ☐ Reflexive grasp (fading by 3 months of age)
- ☐ Raking grasp, whole hand (by 6 months of age)
- ☐ Thumb to side of fingers (8 months of age and older)
- ☐ Thumb to fingertips of index and/or middle fingers

QUESTIONABLE APPROPRIATENESS
- ☐ Wrist flexed, hand often in awkward position
- ☐ Hand usually fisted (older than 3 months of age)
- ☐ Hand usually limp or grasp weak
- ☐ Grasps food too tightly
- ☐ Raking, use of whole hand (older than 12 months of age)
- ☐ Difficulty releasing grasp (older than 12 months of age)

Screening of Eating Abilities—cont'd

E. *Hand and arm movement*

A child must have head and upper trunk control before the hand can be used for purposeful reaching. At first the hand and arm movements appear to be random. Purposeful movements are first seen as a child brings the hands to the mouth and the hands together at midline. Reaching for toys and bringing them to the mouth precedes finger-feeding. As control of the trunk improves, arm and hand use matures. A child will usually grab the spoon and help bring it to the mouth long before he or she is able to control it independently. The effort of holding a cup is seen initially as the cup is pushed tightly against the mouth to stabilize it; it is difficult at this stage to stop drinking and put a partially full cup back to the table without spilling. Abnormal muscle tone or lack of head and trunk stability interferes with the quality and effectiveness of hand use.

APPROPRIATE
- ☐ Hand to mouth
- ☐ Hands to midline, hands together
- ☐ Hand touches object purposefully
- ☐ Toy to mouth
- ☐ Holds bottle or drinks from cup (hands may be on cup, adult controls)
- ☐ Self-feeds finger foods
- ☐ Helps with spoon
- ☐ Independent with spoon, spills
- ☐ Independent with spoon, no spills
- ☐ Holds cup with some assistance
- ☐ Independent with cup

QUESTIONABLE APPROPRIATENESS
- ☐ Arms tight, limited movement
- ☐ Hands usually fisted (older than 2 to 3 months of age)
- ☐ Hand frequently misses object, overshoots (older than 6 months of age)
- ☐ No attempt to reach for food or spoon, even when hungry and food is within reach (older than 6 months of age)
- ☐ Uses spoon with much extraneous movement and spilling
- ☐ Other: _____

F. *Cooperation*

APPROPRIATE
- ☐ Motivated to eat
- ☐ Accepts food passively
- ☐ Participates to best of ability
- ☐ Socially appropriate behavior

QUESTIONABLE APPROPRIATENESS
- ☐ Does not seem to care about eating
- ☐ Actively resists eating (turns mouth away or slow to open mouth)
- ☐ Physical skills not used to potential for self-assistance
- ☐ Socially disruptive, attention seeking

Any observations of questionable cooperation would tend to reduce the validity of other observations. A more thorough evaluation of parent-child interaction during mealtime may be indicated and may be the primary need of the child.

oral coordination and if further appropriate resources are necessary. It should be noted that when age guidelines are mentioned they are intended to be lenient in recognition of the normal range for acquisition of skills. Morris[11] provides more detailed description of the age range at which various oral skills are acquired and provides more examples of guiding questions that can be used during a parent interview.

If the oral motor screen identifies delays in feeding behavior in the absence of abnormal movement patterns, changes in the diet can be suggested to support development progress as outlined in Chapter 13. If abnormal oral and movement patterns are identified, however, referral to a specialized therapist is important. When motor control problems and abnormal muscle tone are observed throughout the body as well as the mouth, an occupational or physical therapist who specializes in pediatrics or neurological disorders should be contacted. If the problem seems to be primarily oral, a speech therapist may be the first contact. Resources for names of treatment centers or private therapists are the United Cerebral Palsy Association in each state, the local Easter Seal Society, or the Neurodevelopmental Treatment Association.[12]

When specialized services are not immediately available, initial steps may be attempted to improve the quality of food intake by using the basic principles of positioning discussed in Chapter 13. It is important to use a problem-solving approach that includes feedback from client and caregiver. The rationale for suggested changes should be thoroughly explained and expectations for follow-through must be reasonable. It may take more time to feed a child in the desired position, especially at first, so parents could be asked to try the new procedure at the beginning of each meal or at the meal that is the least stressful. Consideration of the client's and caregiver's comfort, feelings, and opinions should be clearly communicated.

When the caregiver does not want to make any changes in the feeding procedure, a compromise suggestion may be to allow a therapist to use the new procedures for a while, until the client is more comfortable and successful. Changes in motor control may be slow to achieve, but changes in the feeding environment are not as difficult to achieve and may have great significance in the long-term social, nutritional, and physical development of the individual.

CONSIDERATION OF PSYCHOSOCIAL FACTORS

Whenever and wherever the nutrition of a child is discussed, consideration must also be given to factors that have no direct relationship on the feeding process. Eating behavior serves as a sensitive barometer of the general adjustment of child, parent, and family. For this reason intrapersonal and interpersonal factors that influence food intake should also be taken into consideration when collecting and assessing information.

Since parents are primarily responsible for providing infants and children with both food and the environment in which it is consumed, attention should be given to the parents' psychosocial well-being, adaptation to the parenting role, and general level of parenting skills. Because patterns of food intake, even in young children, can be altered by emotional status, screening should also consider the socioemotional development of the child. When appropriate food is available and there is no evidence of biological or organic problems in the child, it is not unusual to find that the cause of a disturbance in food intake is within the psychosocial/emotional category. Such problems can manifest themselves in a variety of ways, for instance parent or child dissatisfaction with the feeding or mealtime situation, parental neglect or overconcern with food or feeding, anorexia or vomiting, and food aversions or food gorging.

Level of Stress/Family Coping

Infants and children are sensitive to the feelings and attitudes of parents, particularly at feeding time or bedtime. Research by Brandon[13] on the

Screening Questionnaire for Family Stress

	Yes	No
1. During the past year have any of the following occurred in your immediate family?		
Family moved?	☐	☐
Death, divorce, separation, loss of family member?	☐	☐
Marriage, reconciliation, pregnancy, new family member?	☐	☐
Serious injury or illness, problem with aging relative?	☐	☐
Loss of work, change of job, retirement?	☐	☐
Frequent or serious arguments or fights?	☐	☐
Money problems?	☐	☐
Drug or drinking problems?	☐	☐
Trouble with the law?	☐	☐
Some other serious problem?	☐	☐
If yes, what? _____		
2. During the past year:		
Has anyone in your family been seriously upset, depressed, or moody?	☐	☐
Have you been generally happy with your family's way of life?	☐	☐
Have you often felt lonely or cut off from other people?	☐	☐
Have you and your mate had serious differences that you feel may be related to differences in religion, race, nationality, family background?	☐	☐
3. Have you and your children been separated for more than 1 day in the past year?	☐	☐
Do you have someone reliable to take care of your children when you need it?	☐	☐
Are your children cared for daily by someone outside the family?	☐	☐
If yes, has it been the same person for the past year?	☐	☐

Adapted from Metz, J.R., and others: Pediatrics **58**:4, 1976. Copyright American Academy of Pediatrics, 1976.

epidemiology of childhood eating disturbances found that the parents of the maladjusted group, as compared with the control group, were younger, more dependent on relatives, regarded as unstable or suffering from mental problems, reported unhappy childhoods, experienced marital conflict, or were regarded as showing disturbed relationships with their children. It is reasonable to hypothesize that parents who are anxious or distressed somehow communicate these states to their babies and young children, which in turn affects feeding behavior. Older children are also quick to identify tension or conflict between adults at the dinner table and to respond accordingly. Reality stressors

like a job or financial worries, recent change of domicile, and illness or injury of child or parent are additional factors that can disrupt routines and can be associated with temporary symptoms related to food or feeding behavior. Personal problems of adult family members, for instance, marital discord, unresolved grief, depression, drug use, or lack of self-esteem, also may influence the feeding situation involving children. When the feeding problem appears to be nonorganic, it is appropriate to ask parents a few simple questions to determine the emotional climate in the home. This can be done selectively in an interview or by using a questionnaire as a routine part of the assessment process (see Screening Questionnaire for Family Stress on p. 51).

Parental Feelings of Competence and Satisfaction

Clinical observations indicate that parental *feelings* of competence and satisfaction or dissatisfaction with the parental role are psychological factors that also have an influence on the food intakes and feeding behaviors of children. When an individual, for whatever reason, experiences minimal feelings of success in carrying out the activities associated with parenting, the opportunity for experiencing satisfaction decreases proportionately and the stage is set for problems in parent-child interaction. If the parent does not feel adequate in handling child care activities outside the feeding sphere, lack of confidence or feelings of incompetence can eventually be manifested in a dysfunctional feeding situation. The mother who reported the following impressions was trying to deal with a 3-year-old boy whose diet consisted only of olives, avocados, and salmon:

I'll never forget what I felt like when he was 2 weeks old and I had to care for him completely on my own. It wasn't at all what I expected. I was scared to death and sure that every time he cried I must have done something wrong. There were half-filled bottles all over the house because I worried that the milk might spoil if Gary didn't drink it in 10 or 15 minutes. My mother-in-law didn't help. She is still always giving me suggestions for a better way to do something.

In early infancy the close relationship to and dependence on the mother, in particular, often become linked with the feeding process. For this reason many individuals equate successful mothering with a well-nourished infant or child and a nonproblematic feeding situation. The comments of the mother of a developmentally delayed toddler with congenital heart disease (still on a diet of pureed foods) are illustrative:

I couldn't do anything about his heart, but I did pretty well at feeding him by that nasogastric tube. Nobody else could do it as well as I did. Now when he doesn't eat I fix

a special high-calorie pudding for him so that he doesn't lose weight. He really gobbles it down!

Factors like past experience, age, knowledge of child growth and development, and the input of significant family members or professionals are important determinants of parental feelings of competence.[14] The standards of performance or values that parents hold for themselves, along with their more general feelings of self-esteem, are also related to perceptions of competence. But probably the most significant influence on parental feelings of success or satisfaction is the responsiveness of the child; that is, does the child show developmental and social evidence of a positive response to parenting? With these determinants in mind the following questions can serve as guidelines for eliciting data on the adjustment to parenting and its associated emotional responses:

1. As you were growing up, did you observe or assist with the upbringing of younger children such as brothers or sisters, relatives, friends, or neighbors?
2. How would you rate your maternal feelings on a scale of 1 to 5 with 1 being very maternal and 5 being nonmaternal?
3. What has been the biggest surprise or thing you least expected about being a parent?
4. How satisfied are you with your child's physical growth and development?
5. How satisfied do you feel with your child's social adjustment?
6. How much influence does your spouse have on your ideas about child rearing? Do you usually agree or disagree on child-rearing concerns?
7. Who or what has had the most influence on your ideas about child rearing? Books, magazines, or the media? Religion? Friends, neighbors, or relatives? Professionals? Formal education or parenting classes?
8. When you and your child are getting along as you usually do, how does your relationship with your child make you feel as a parent?

9. How competent do you feel about how you handle your life in general?
10. How competent do you feel as a parent?
11. How competent a parent do you think you are *from the viewpoint of others* who know you well?
12. Before you had your own family, how did you feel about children?

Parent-Child Interaction

An integral component of assessment and data collection related to food intake is consideration of the interaction between child and parent. To have an indication of the effects of food and the feeding situation on the parent-child dyad, such data should be based on observation of both mealtime and non-mealtime situations. It is important to determine if food-related parent-child problems are situation specific or part of a more basic discord. Ideally, the assessment should be done in the home setting during mealtime *and* free-play situations. If this is not possible, every attempt should be made to simulate natural conditions in the clinic, office, or hospital environment.

Several research methodologies and standardized tools have been developed to evaluate parent-child interaction, for instance, Verbal Interaction Record,[15] Mutual Problem-Solving Task,[16] Nursing Child Assessment Feeding Scales,[17] and Nursing Child Assessment Teaching Scales.[18] Some practitioners may want to obtain training in the use of standardized assessment techniques; however, less formalized methods can also be helpful in collecting data. Using the concepts of affectional ties, propensity to interact, and feedback and reciprocity as organizers, it is possible to identify the essential elements of most interaction between parents and children.

1. **Affectional ties** (refers to the emotional attachment and degree of psychological involvement between parent and child)
   A. Appropriate interview questions
      1. Do you believe in such a thing as "unconditional mother love"? Would you ever use such a term to describe your feelings about _____ ?
      2. How old was _____ when you really felt that he/she was *your* child?
      3. How does _____ know that you love and care about him/her?
      4. How do you know that _____ loves you?
      5. Who or what is _____ most attached to?
      6. Have you ever regretted the decision to become a parent? Occasionally? Frequently?
   B. Direct observation
      1. Attentiveness of parent to child's distress; physical comforting
      2. Use of expressions of love or special designations to refer to child *or* use of negative terms to refer to child; no reference to child by name
      3. Evidence of parental pleasure when child is complimented or comments are made regarding parent-child physical resemblances
      4. Evidence of strong mutual need for togetherness and a maximum avoidance of separation *or* parent or child tendency/preference for isolated activity
      5. Willingness to "relinquish child" to care of a stranger

II. **Propensity to interact** (refers to the ability and desire of parent or child to give and receive communication)
   A. Appropriate interview questions
      1. When _____ is not around, do you ever find yourself thinking of something you want to do with him/her or something you want to tell him/her?
      2. Have you been (or are you ever) so preoccupied with adult worries or concerns that you don't have any energy left to interact with _____ ?
      3. Can you identify any person, thing, or situation that interferes with your rela-

tionship or communication with
_____ ?

4. How would you describe your relationship with _____ ?

B. Direct observation
   1. Evidence of physical intactness (especially sensory and perceptual) of parent and child
   2. Evidence of emotional intactness of parent and child
   3. Presence or absence of reality stressors (as per Family Stress Questionnaire)

III. **Feedback and reciprocity** (refers to chains of response between parent and child; activity of one that occurs as a direct result of stimuli from the other)

A. Appropriate interview questions
   1. How does _____ let you know that he/she needs something or wants your attention? What is your usual response to this?
   2. Who or what usually initiates the interaction between you and your child?
   3. What do you do for _____ ? What does _____ do for you?

B. Direct observation
   1. Efforts on the part of either parent or child to remain "in touch" (physically or verbally) that are successful
   2. Conversation, singing, laughing, or smiling that maintains an extended interaction (one partner answers the other, the latter responds in turn, and so on)
   3. Presence or absence of eye contact between parent and child
   4. Presence or absence of caregiving activity on the part of the parent in response to behavior (e.g. cry, yawn, request)
   5. Manner in which infant or young child is held
   6. Attention of parent to cues in the feeding situation (e.g., satiation, hunger, pacing)

When data indicate that the cause of a child's feeding or food intake problem is most likely psychosocial, intervention must be planned accordingly. The primary focus of treatment will most likely be on strategies to alleviate stress and support family coping abilities, on increasing parental knowledge and skill regarding child rearing, or on facilitating the parent-child relationship. In some situations these goals may be accomplished within the context of the feeding situation; however, in the majority of instances more specific treatment is indicated. Reality-based family needs demand rapid provision of concrete services to relieve situational demands. For this reason referral to a public or private family service or social welfare agency may be appropriate. Those situations that require supportive counseling or education and anticipatory guidance may be handled in a variety of ways, for instance, with family therapy, enrollment in parenting classes, referral to a parent group, or one-to-one work with a qualified professional.

The variety of concerns presented about infant's and children's food intake clearly indicates that information sought must be based on the problems presented and the health care professional's judgment. In some instances dietary intake data may provide sufficient information to design plans with parents and children to modify energy and nutrient intakes. In many instances if plans are to be effective the behavioral and psychosocial influences on a compromised food intake must be investigated. Parents of children with oral motor and self-feeding delays may need help in identifying specific foods to support developmental progress. Those with abnormal motor patterns will need therapy.

Screening procedures may identify children with "feeding problems" of multiple etiology for whom an interdisciplinary assessment is appropriate. Factors that must be considered are adequacy of nutrient intake, structural abnormalities of the oral cavity, oral tissue health, medical status, speech development, living environment, social environment, and neurological integrity (including sensation). The collective data provide a base on which the cause of the problem may be determined, effective treatment plans may be designed, and progress may be assessed.

The team approach facilitates identification of priorities for treatment and use of a logical step-by-step approach. Periodic reevaluations of identified concerns indicate the effectiveness of programs designed.

SUMMARY

Several studies have attempted to assess dietary methodologies. Most of these studies have found that children who provide information are not as reliable as adults. Even so, all methodologies have inherent limitations that should be recognized. The results of diet histories have not agreed with those of weighed food records when applied to individual children. Most studies have indicated that diet histories of children overestimate intake by individuals compared with 3- and 7-day food records. Children who have delays in feeding skills should be screened to determine whether the delays are because of abnormal motor patterns or because of an overall delay, which should determine the need for an occupational or physical therapy evaluation. Because many feeding difficulties in childhood have their etiology in parent-child interactions, it may be necessary to evaluate the family level of stress and coping and the interaction between parent and child.

SUGGESTED LEARNING ACTIVITIES

1. Interview parents of a preschool child to collect a diet history. Assess the validity of the information collected.
2. Keep a 7-day record of all food and beverages consumed. Assess the difficulty in keeping such a record.
3. Assess stress in the family of a preschool child whose parents consider him/her to have a feeding problem.
4. Observe a comprehensive nutrition/feeding

evaluation of a child who has oral motor feeding delays. Using appropriate tools, record dietary intake information, eating abilities, and the level of family stress.

REFERENCES

1. Beal, V.A.: The nutrition history in longitudinal research, J. Am. Diet. Assoc. **51**:426, 1967.
2. Todd, K.S., Hudes, M., and Calloway, H.: Food intake measurements: problems and approaches, Am. J. Clin. Nutr. **37**:139, 1983.
3. McHenry, E.W., Ferguson, H.P., and Gurland, J.: Sources of error in dietary surveys, Can. J. Public Health **36**:355, 1945.
4. Stuff, J.E., and others: A comparison of dietary methods, Am. J. Clin. Nutr. **37**:300, 1983.
5. Burke, B.S.: The dietary history as a tool in research, J. Am. Diet. Assoc. **23**:1041, 1947.
6. Räsänen, L.: Nutrition survey of Finish rural children. VI. Methodological study comparing the 24-hour record and the dietary history interview, Am. J. Clin. Nutr. **32**:2560, 1979.
7. Huenemann, R.I., and Turner, D.: Methods of dietary investigation, J. Am. Diet. Assoc. **18**:562, 1942.
8. Young, C.M., and others: A comparison of dietary study methods. I. Dietary history vs 7 day record, J. Am. Diet. Assoc. **28**:124, 1952.
9. Trulson, M.F.: Assessment of dietary study methods. I. Comparison of methods for obtaining data for clinical work, J. Am. Diet. Assoc. **30**:991, 1954.
10. Abramson, J.N., Slome, C., and Kosovsky, C.: Food frequency tool as an epidemiological tool, Am. J. Public Health **53**:1093, 1963.
11. Morris, S.E.: The normal acquisition of oral feeding skills: implications for assessment and treatment, New York, 1982, Therapeutic Media, Inc.
12. Neurodevelopmental Treatment Association Inc., Executive Secretary, P.O. Box 14613, Chicago, IL 60614.
13. Brandon, S.: An epidemiological study of eating disturbances, J. Psychosom. Res. **14**:253, 1970.
14. Sutherland, S.: An exploratory study of the factors which contribute to a material sense of competence among mothers of children in preschools, parenting classes and a day care center, Unpublished masters thesis, Seattle, 1980, University of Washington.
15. Lambie, D.L., Bond, J.T., and Weikart, D.P.: Verbal interaction record, monograph 2, High Scope Monograph Series, Home teaching with mothers and infants. The Ypsilanti-Carnegie infant education project: an experiment, Ypsilanti, Mich., 1974, High Scope Press.
16. Epstein, A., and Weikart, D.P.: Mutual problem-solving task, monograph 6, High Scope Monograph Series. The

Ypsilanti-Carnegie infant education project: longitudinal follow-up, Ypsilanti, Mich., 1980, High Scope Press.

17. Nursing child assessment feeding scales. In Barnard, K.E., and Eyres, S.J., editors: Child health assessment, part 2: the first year of life, Publication No. HRA 79-25, Washington, D.C., June 1979, U.S. Department of Health, Education and Welfare.

18. Nursing child assessment teaching scales. In Barnard, K.E., and Eyres, S.J., editors: Child health assessment, part 2: the first year of life, Publication No. HRA 79-25, Washington, D.C., June 1979, U.S. Department of Health, Education and Welfare.

ADDITIONAL READINGS

Balogh, M., Kahn, H.A., and Medalie, J.H.: Random repeat 24-hour dietary recalls, Am. J. Clin. Nutr. **24**:304, 1971.

Beaton, G.H., and others: Sources of variance in 24-hour dietary recall data: implications for nutrition study design, Am. J. Clin. Nutr. **32**:2546, 1979.

Emmons, L., and Hayes, M.: Accuracy of 24-hour recalls of young children, J. Am. Diet. Assoc. **62**:409, 1973.

Frank, G.C., and others: Adapting the 24-hour recall for epidemiologic studies for studies of school children, J. Am. Diet. Assoc. **71**:26, 1977.

Krantzler, N.J., and others: Methods of food intake assessment, J. Nutr. Educ. **14**:108, 1982.

Rush, D., and Kristal, A.R.: Methodologic studies during pregnancy: the reliability of the 24-hour recall, Am. J. Clin. Nutr. **35**:1259, 1982.

Shapiro, L.R.: Streamlining and implementing nutritional assessment—the dietary approach, J. Am. Diet. Assoc. **75**:230, 1979.

Smith, M.A., editor: Guide for nutritional assessment of the mentally retarded and the developmentally disabled, Memphis, Tenn., 1976, Child Development Center, University of Tennessee.

Young, C.M.: The interview itself, J. Am. Diet. Assoc. **35**:677, 1959.

Nutrient Needs of Children

3

Children must consume sufficient high-quality protein, vitamins, minerals, and energy in their diets if acceptable growth is to occur. Energy generated from the metabolism of fats, carbohydrates, and proteins provides the fuel that supports the maintenance of bodily functions and covers the cost of activity and growth. Protein provides amino acids for the synthesis of new tissues and nitrogen for the maturation of existing tissue in early childhood.

Vitamins function in a variety of metabolic processes that make protein synthesis and energy metabolism possible. Their requirements are, therefore, determined by intakes of energy, protein, and other nutrients. Minerals are essential components of body tissue. Their requirements are influenced by rates of growth and the interrelationships they share with other nutrients.

Many factors determine a child's needs for nutrients including body size, rates of growth, physical activity, basal energy expenditure, and reserves acquired in utero by the infant and by dietary intake in the older child.

ENERGY

Energy requirements. The energy expended by any child is determined primarily by body size and composition, physical activity, and rate of growth. In infancy a higher basal metabolic demand is thought to be caused by a larger loss of heat because of a relatively greater body surface and by a larger proportion of metabolic tissue.[1] Measurements of basal metabolic rates in older children have determined that males expend greater amounts of basal energy than do females. The differences are small during the preadolescent years and become pronounced during adolescence.

Maintenance requirements approximate 1.5 the basal metabolic expenditure, since some movement occurs even during sleep, and the specific dynamic action is estimated to be 6% of ingested energy. Energy costs of growth have been estimated to approximate 4.4 to 5.7 kcal/gm of tissue gained.[2-4] Decreasing rates of growth result in decreasing requirements for energy per unit of size (kcal/kg). In other words, as children grow older they need greater numbers of calories because of larger body sizes, but their need for energy per unit of size decreases.

The contribution of physical activity to total energy expenditure is quite variable among children and in individual children from day to day. At all ages, activity patterns among children show wide ranges both in the time spent in the various activities and the intensity of the activities. Some infants, for example, may be quiet, cuddly, and satisfied to explore their environment with their eyes, but others may expend more energy in crying, kicking, and physical movement to see the world around them. Some older children may engage in such sedentary activities as looking at

Table 3-1. Recommended energy intakes for children of various ages

	Age	Weight (kg)	Height (cm)	Energy needs (kcal)	Ranges
Infants	0.0-0.5	6	60	kg × 115	(95-145)
	0.5-1.0	9	71	kg × 105	(80-135)
Children	1-3	13	90	1300	(900-1800)
	4-6	20	112	1700	(1300-2300)
	7-10	28	132	2400	(1650-3300)
Males	11-14	45	157	2700	(2000-3700)
	15-18	66	176	2800	2100-3900)
Females	11-14	46	157	2200	(1500-3000)
	15-18	55	163	2100	(1200-3000)

From Food and Nutrition Board: Recommended dietary allowances, rev. ed. 9, Washington, D.C., 1980, National Academy of Sciences, National Research Council.

Table 3-2. Selected foods as sources of energy

Food	Energy	
	kcal/oz	kcal/tbsp
Milk		
Human milk	24	12
Commercially available infant formula	20	10
Whole cow's milk	20	10
Commercially Available Infant Foods (Average Value)		
Dry infant cereals	105	9
Strained and junior fruits	16	8
Strained and junior vegetables	11	5
Strained and junior meats	32	16
Strained egg yolks	58	29
Strained and junior dinners		
Vegetables with meat	15	7.5
High meat dinners	24	12
Strained and junior desserts	22	10

Adapted from Gebhardt, S.E., Cutrufelli, R., and Matthews, R.H.: Composition of foods, baby food, raw, processed, prepared, Agriculture Handbook No. 8-3, Washington, D.C., 1978, U.S. Department of Agriculture.

books or watching television, whereas their peers may be engaged in physical activities that demand running, jumping, and general body movements.

Spady[8] estimated the energy expenditure of activity of fourth and fifth grade schoolchildren to be 31.2% and 25.3% of total energy expenditure for males and females, respectively.

Energy requirements, which are greatest per unit of size in infancy, decline until adolescent growth is complete. During adolescence the energy expen-

Table 3-3. Selected foods as sources of energy

Food	Portion Size	Average kcal
2% milk with 2% nonfat milk solids	½ cup	72
Meat, poultry, or fish	1 oz	80
Egg	1 medium	80
Peanut butter	1 tbsp	94
Cheese	½ oz	57
Legumes, cooked	¼ cup	90
Enriched bread	½ slice	35
Ready-to-eat cereals (not sugar coated)	¾ cup	70
Cooked cereal	½ cup	55
Saltine crackers	1	12
Rice, macaroni, spaghetti, cooked	¼ cup	50
Potato (boiled)	½ medium	45
Potato chips	5	55
Green beans	¼ cup	6
Carrots		
Cooked	¼ cup	15
Raw	2 medium sticks	14
Apple	1 small	80
Banana	1 small	80
Orange	1 small	50
Orange juice	½ cup	60
Sugar	1 tsp	16
Jam or jelly	1 tsp	20
Butter, margarine, oil, mayonnaise	1 tsp	35
Cookies, assorted	1	40-50
Ice cream	¼ cup	70

Adapted from Adams, C.F.: Nutritive value of American foods in common units, Agriculture Handbook No. 456, Washington, D.C., 1975, U.S. Department of Agriculture.

diture will be a reflection of the adolescent growth spurt. Since adolescents enter the growth spurt at different ages, requirements established for a given age must be applied with caution.

During a period of catch-up growth, the requirement for energy and nutrients will be greatly increased. Intakes of 150 to 250 kcal/kg of body weight have been recommended for children of preschool age. An intake of 200 kcal/kg/day should produce a weight gain of 20 gm/kg/day.[5,6]

The energy needs of individual children of the same size, age, and sex vary. Reasons for these differences remain unexplained. Differences in physical activity, in the metabolic cost of minimal and excessive protein intakes at equivalent levels of energy intake, and in the efficiency with which individuals utilize energy have all been hypothesized to exert an influence.[7] Recommended daily dietary allowances (RDA) established by the Food and Nutrition Board are given in Table 3-1. These allowances give a wide range of recommended energy intakes in each age group. It is hypothesized that 50% of these calories will be expended for maintenance, 25% for activity, and 25% for growth during infancy.

Table 3-4. Foods that provide appropriate energy for various age groups

Age	Weight (kg)	Recommended Energy Intake (kcal)	Examples of Foods that Provide RDA for Energy
2 months	5	575	28-32 oz human milk or infant formula
10 months	9.5	1000	24 oz homogenized milk or infant formula
			8 tbsp dry infant cereal
			14 tbsp junior fruit
			8 tbsp junior vegetable
			4 tbsp junior meat
			½ slice toast
			1 oz chopped chicken
			1 tbsp mashed green beans
			1 small banana
			2 tbsp ice cream
			2 arrowroot biscuits
4 years	18	1530	24 oz milk
			6-8 oz fruit juice
			3 slices bread
			½ to ¾ cup dry cereal
			2 tbsp peanut butter
			1 tsp jelly
			1 frankfurter
			¼ cup macaroni and cheese
			¼ cup green beans
			⅓ cup ice cream
			1 graham cracker
			1 medium apple
			1 small banana

Recent studies suggest that children are consuming less energy than recommended, with 6- to 11-year-old children consuming more than 20% less than the suggested intake.[9] Spady[8] found that although the total energy expenditures of fourth and fifth grade boys approximated the recommended allowances, girls expended only 80% of the recommended allowances. The recommended allowances are often used to establish energy needs of groups. In combination with growth data, the allowances can provide a basis for estimations of appropriate ranges of energy intakes of individual children.

In 1930 an expert committee, after reviewing energy intake data in relation to physical parameters, stated that height appeared to be the most appropriate criterion on which to base studies of energy needs.[10] The observation was never used. In estimating energy needs of children, body surface or weight has continued to be used as a reference for suggested energy intakes of children. Energy per cm of height has been proved clinically, however, to be a useful reference in estimating energy needs and designing diets for individual children. It is an especially useful reference for children who are genetically short. For example, preschool children with Prader-Willi syndrome maintain their weight in growth channel consuming 10 to 11 kcal/cm of height as compared with 14.7 to 15.4 kcal/cm of height, the 50th percentile of intake of normal males, and 12.9 to 13.8 kcal/cm of height, the 50th percentile of intake of normal females of the same age.[11,12] Culley and others[13] found that although children with Down's syndrome consumed considerably less energy than their age group peers to maintain their weight in growth channel, their intakes per cm of height were similar. Males with Down's syndrome consumed 16.1 kcal/cm of height and females 14.3 kcal/cm of height.

Food sources. Energy values of foods commonly consumed in infancy and childhood are given in Tables 3-2 and 3-3. To demonstrate food intakes that support appropriate energy intakes for several age groups, data for 2-month-old, 10-month-old, and 4-year-old children are given in Table 3-4.

PROTEIN AND AMINO ACID REQUIREMENTS

Protein provides calories but also serves a more important and complex function. Protein is the basic component of the protoplasm in the cells; therefore, an adequate intake of protein is essential if normal growth is to occur.

Amino acid requirements of infants have been estimated by Holt and Snyderman[14] from studies in which pure amino acids were supplied in proportions of amino acids of human milk. The requirement of an amino acid was defined as the least amount required to maintain satisfactory nitrogen retention and weight gain when nitrogen levels and other amino acids were held constant. Fomon and Filer[15] and Fomon and others[16] have estimated amino acid requirements from intakes of infants between 8 and 112 days of age who were fed whole protein in cow's milk formulas and soy formulas. Satisfactory linear growth and weight gain, nitrogen balance, and serum concentrations of albumin equivalent to those of normal breast-fed infants were used as criteria of adequacy.

The FAO/WHO expert committee has suggested that a composite of the lower estimates of the data from the studies of Holt and Snyderman[14] and from

Fomon and Filer[15] would provide estimates of the upper range of the requirement of infants 0 to 6 months of age[17] (Table 3-5).

Estimates of amino acid requirements of 10- to 12-year-old preadolescents based on studies by Nakagawa and others[18] are given in Table 3-6. These investigators found amino acid requirements for 10- to 12-year-old children to be two to three times greater than those for adults. Requirements of males in all cases exceeded those of females.

Protein needs for growth expressed as percentages of requirement decrease as rates of growth decline. The 50% of protein need used for growth in the first 2 months of life declines to 11% at 2 to 3 years of age and is gradually reduced to 0% after an increase during the adolescent growth spurt. Amino acids required for growth differ from those required for maintenace. Factorial calculations based on patterns of growth indicate that the suggested amino acid requirements after infancy have been overestimated.[19]

Recommended intakes. The recommendations for daily protein intakes for infants and children given in Table 3-7 assume an adequate intake of energy. These recommendations are based on ingestion of milk protein in infancy and a mixed diet that provides protein that has an efficiency of utilization of 75% in older children.

The RDA for protein for children has decreased since 1958. Some authorities believe the decrease has been to a level too low to meet the needs of American children. For example the RDA for 7- to 10-year-old children has been reduced from 60 gm to 34 gm, 5.7% of the total average energy intake. For preschool children protein is 7.1% of mean energy intake. Based on nitrogen balance studies, Abernathy and Ritchey[20] conclude that a more appropriate protein allowance for 7- to 10-year-old children would be 45 gm or more per day. Reported protein intakes of children in the United States have shown actual protein intakes to be 10% to 15% of kilocalories consumed. During periods of catch-up growth, protein requirements increase.

Table 3-5. Estimated amino acid requirements of infants

| | Estimated requirements | | |
Amino acid	Holt and Snyderman[14] (mg/kg/day)*	Fomon and Filer[15] (mg/kg/day)†	Composite of Lower Values (mg/kg/day)‡
Histidine	34	28	28
Isoleucine	119	70	70
Leucine	229	161	161
Lysine	103	161	103
Methionine plus cystine	45 plus cys	58§	58
Phenylalanine plus tyrosine	90 plus tyr	125§	125
Threonine	87	116	87
Tryptophan	22	17	17
Valine	105	93	93

From Energy and Protein Requirements, Report of a Joint FAO/WHO Ad Hoc Committee, World Health Organization Technical Report Series No. 522, FAO Nutr. Meet. Rep. No. 52, Geneva, 1973, World Health Organization.
*Requirements estimated when amino acids were fed or incorporated in basal formulas. The values represent estimates of maximal individual requirements to achieve normal growth.
†Calculated intakes of amino acids when formulas were fed in amounts sufficient to maintain good growth in all the infants studied; the amino acids were not varied independently.
‡Based on a safe level of 2 gm protein/kg/day, the average of suggested levels for the period 0 to 6 months of age.
§The values for cystine and tyrosine were estimated on the basis of the methionine: cystine and phenylalanine: tyrosine ratios in human milk.

Table 3-6. Estimated amino acid requirements of schoolchildren 10 to 12 years of age

Amino acid	Observed Requirement* (mg/kg/day)
Histidine	0
Isoleucine	30
Leucine	45
Lysine	60
Methione plus cystine	27
Phenylalanine plus tyrosine	27
Threonine	35
Tryptophan	4
Valine	33

From Energy and Protein Requirements, Report of a Joint FAO/WHO Ad Hoc Committee, World Health Organization Technical Report Series No. 522, FAO Nutr. Meet. Rep. No. 52, Geneva, 1973, World Health Organization.
*Based on Nakagawa, I., and others. The values represent estimates of the upper range of individual requirements for the achievement of positive nitrogen balance in boys.

Intakes of 3.2 gm of milk protein/kg when energy intakes are adequate have been suggested.[21]

Fomon and others[16] have suggested that during infancy amino acid and protein requirements expressed per unit of calories consumed reflecting both size and rate of growth would be more meaningful than expressions of requirements on the basis of body weight alone. They estimate the protein requirement to be 1.6 gm/100 kcal for children 1 to 4 months of age and 1.4 gm/100 kcal for children 8 to 12 months of age.

The Committee on Nutrition of the American Academy of Pediatrics[22] has set minimum standards for infant formula of 1.8 gm/100 kcal with a protein efficiency ratio equal to that of casein.

The protein requirement for any child depends on the rate of growth and the quality of protein in the diet. This implies that evaluation of a child's protein intake must be approached on the basis of the adequacy of the rate of growth, the quality of

Table 3-7. Recommended daily intakes of protein for children

	Age (years)	Protein (gm/kg)
Infants	0-0.5	2.2
	0.5-1	2.0
Children	1-3	1.8
	4-6	1.5
	7-10	1.2
Males	11-14	1.0
	15-18	0.8
Females	11-14	1.0
	15-18	0.8

From Food and Nutrition Board: Recommended daily dietary allowances, ed. 9, Washington, D.C., 1980, National Academy of Sciences, national Research Council.

Table 3-8. Approximate protein contents of various milks and foods fed to infants

Food	Protein (gm/oz)
Human milk	0.3
Commercial formulas	0.5
Homogenized milk	1.1
Evaporated milk prepared 1:1	1.1
Infant cereals, high protein	10.2
Infant cereals, rice	2.0
Strained chicken noodle dinners	0.6
Strained split pea, vegetable, and ham or bacon dinners	1.1
Strained beef and vegetable dinners	1.6
Strained turkey and vegetable dinners	1.6
Strained egg yolk	2.8
Strained beef	3.9
Strained veal	3.8

From Gebhardt, S.E., Cutrufelli, R., and Matthews, R.H.: Composition of foods, baby foods, raw, processed, prepared, Agriculture Handbook No. 8-3, Washington, D.C., 1978, U.S. Department of Agriculture.

protein in the foods ingested, the combinations of foods that provide amino acids consumed together, and the adequacy of those nutrients (minerals and vitamins) and energy that are necessary for protein synthesis to proceed.

Food sources. Protein of high quality is available to most infants in developed countries as human milk and modified cow's milk formula. Infants whose parents are unwilling to feed them cow's milk formulas or infants who have allergic reactions to cow's milk are often fed formulas prepared from water-soluble soy isolates. As discussed in Chapter 4, commercially prepared formulas are prepared so that all nutrients are provided in the appropriate amounts. Home preparation of soy formulas should be discouraged because parents may not be careful to heat the milk sufficiently to achieve inactivation of the trypsin inhibitor and may discard the residue of soy material from which the milk was made. In so doing, much of the protein and many of the other essential nutrients are discarded.

Table 3-8 lists foods commonly consumed in infancy that contribute protein.

As children grow older and accept table food they receive additional foods that provide high-quality protein. Examples of foods acceptable to preschoolers that provide high-quality protein are given in Table 3-9.

Examples of combinations of foods that meet the recommended allowances for protein for 2-month-old, 10-month-old, and 4-year-old children are given in Table 3-10. The examples given include much less protein than most children consume. In fact, it would be very difficult to provide sufficient energy in the diet if protein intakes were restricted to only the recommended amounts and milk and small amounts of other animal protein were included in the diet. For example, 4-year-old children who consume the food listed would receive approximately 500 kcal/day from these sources, leaving 1000 kcal that need to be met totally from vegetables, fruits, fat, and sweets, without protein from meats, breads, nuts, other cereal grains, or cheese (Table 3-9).

The protein intakes of some children are a matter of concern. Kwashiorkor (severe protein deficien-

Table 3-9. Selected foods as sources of protein for preschool children

Food	Portion size	Protein (gm)
Yogurt, made from whole milk	½ cup	3.7
Cheddar cheese	1 oz	7.1
Hamburger patty	2 oz	15.4
Chicken drumstick	1	12.2
Peanut butter	1 tbsp	4.0
Egg	1 medium	5.7
Liverwurst	1 oz	4.6
Tunafish	¼ cup	11.5
Frankfurter, 5″ by ¾″	1	5.6
Nonfat milk solids, dry	1 tbsp	1.52

From Adams, C.F.: Nutritive value of American foods in common units, Agricultural Handbook No. 456, Washington, D.C., 1975, U.S. Department of Agriculture.

Table 3-10. Foods that provide recommended protein for children

Age	Weight (kg)	Recommended Protein Intake (gm)	Examples of Foods that Provide RDA for Protein
2 months	5	11	33 oz human milk *or* 22 oz commercially manufactured infant formula
10 months	9.5	19	18 oz homogenized milk
4 years	18	27	16 oz milk 1 tbsp peanut butter 1 medium egg

cy) has been reported in infants whose parents purposely withheld milk after episodes of vomiting and/or diarrhea treated with clear liquids and in children from families who live in extreme poverty where there was marked restriction of protein intake.[23,24] Children with multiple allergies who have learned to control parents by refusing all protein-rich foods have been known to experience catch-up growth when their parents learned to reinforce their acceptance of the meats and soy milk to which they had no allergic reactions. Children who are hypersensitive in the oral area frequently refuse all meat and eggs and will consume very limited amounts of milk and dairy products if unlimited amounts of carbohydrates such as starches and sugars are available to them. Limited financial resources restrict the amounts of high-quality protein parents can purchase for their children. Without very careful planning the quality of a child's protein intake may be compromised.

FAT

Fat, the most calorically concentrated nutrient, supplies between 40% and 50% of the energy consumed in infancy and approximately 40% of the energy consumed after infancy by individuals in developed countries. Because it is calorically concentrated, it may be very important in the diet of children who are lean and physically active and have a small appetite or in the diet of children with oral motor problems who can consume only a limited volume of food. However, chunky, passive children should limit the quantity of fat they consume to keep from gaining weight too rapidly.

Essential fatty acids. Polyunsaturated linoleic acid has been conclusively proven to be an essential nutrient for both children and adults. Although arachidonic acid performs some of the same functions, it is not essential because it can be synthesized from linoleic acid.

Some investigators consider linolenic acid also essential even though no specific deficiency of linolenic acid has been reported in humans.

One of the earliest manifestations of fatty acid deficiency recognized in animals was an increased basal metabolic rate.[25] Infants who are fed formulas low in the essential fatty acid consume greater numbers of calories than do those who consume adequate quantities of linoleic acid to maintain normal growth. Caloric utilization has been reported to vary with intakes of linoleate up to 4% to 5% of the calories.[26] It has been suggested that the ratio of triene:tetraene fatty acids in the blood serum can be used in assessing nutritional status of linoleic acid. A triene:tetraene ratio of 0.4 or less is considered indicative of normal fatty acid status, and a ratio greater than 0.4 is indicative of an insufficient intake of essential fatty acid.[26] Such biochemical evidence of deficiency appears when linoleic acid is fed as less than 1% of the total calories. On this basis the minimal requirements for linoleic acid are considered to be approximately 1% of the calories consumed, and an optimal intake is thought to be 4% to 5% of the calories consumed.

Recommended intakes. No recommendations for intakes of fat have been made. However, if less than 30% of energy intakes are derived from fat, a dry and unpalatable diet may result.

Fomon[27] suggests that diets that provide less than 30% of total calories or greater than 50% of total calories as fat should be avoided.

Food sources. Human milk, cow's milk, and commercially available infant formulas provide approximately 50% of the calories as fat. Approx-

Table 3-11. Foods as sources of fat for infants

Food	Fat (gm/oz)
Infant cereal, dry (11-13 tbsp/oz)	0.8-2.2
Vegetable and meat dinners	0.1-1.1
Meat and vegetable dinners	0.6-1.6
Strained and junior meats	1.1-2.7
Strained egg yolks	4.9

From Gebhardt, S.E., Cutrufelli, R., and Matthews, R.H.: Composition of foods, baby foods, raw, processed, prepared, Agriculture Handbook No. 8-3, Washington, D.C., 1978, U.S. Department of Agriculture.

Table 3-12. Foods as sources of fat for preschool children

Food	Portion size	Fat (gm)
Cooking fat	1 tbsp	12.5
Mayonnaise	1 tbsp	11.2
Butter	1 tsp	3.8
Cheddar cheese	1 oz	7.1
Peanut butter	1 tbsp	8.1
Frankfurter, 5″ by ¾″	1	11.5
Broiled hamburger patty	2 oz	15.4
Chicken drumstick	1	12.2
Egg	1 medium	5.1
Tuna, drained	¼ cup	3.3
Ice cream	¼ cup	3.5
Potato chips	10	8.0

From Adams, C.F.: Nutritive value of American foods in common units, Agriculture Handbook No. 456, Washington, D.C., 1975, U.S. Department of Agriculture.

imately 4% of the total calories in human milk and 1% of the calories in cow's milk are provided by linoleic acid. Commercially available infant formulas contain blends of vegetable oils and contribute greater amounts of linoleic acid.

The Committee on Nutrition of the American Academy of Pediatrics[22] has recommended that infant formulas contain a minimum of 300 mg of 18:2 fatty acids/100 kcal (1.7% of the energy content).

Prepared infant foods are relatively low in fat as compared with foods consumed by older children. Tables 3-11 and 3-12 list the amounts of fat provided by foods commonly consumed by infants and children.

CARBOHYDRATES

Carbohydrates supply between 40% and 50% of the energy consumed by most infants and children in North America.

Recommended intakes. Since glucose can be synthesized from amino acids and the glycerol moiety of fat, no specific recommendations for intake have been made. The Food and Nutrition Board of the National Research Council suggests minimum intakes of 50 to 100 gm/day.

Current interest in dietary fiber as a means to prevent diverticular disease, cancer of the colon, coronary heart disease, obesity, and irritable bowel syndrome in later life has caused many professionals to recommend a high-fiber diet. The Committee on Nutrition of the American Academy of Pediatrics[28] has stated that more work must be done on the effect of a high-fiber diet on mineral status before firm recommendations can be made. However, the committee recommends a substantial amount of fiber to ensure normal laxation. The inclusion of whole grain cereals, breads, fruits, and vegetables in the diet of preschool, school-age, and adolescent children is important.

Food sources. The predominant carbohydrate in the young infant's diet is lactose, found in human milk and cow's milk. It has become a common practice for parents to add starch (in the form of prepared cereals and ingredients of commercially prepared infant foods) and sucrose (which they add to fruits and vegetables) to the infant's diet at 4 to 6 months of age (Table 3-13).

Some foods contain carbohydrate and few other nutrients, whereas others contribute carbohydrate and, in addition, other essential nutrients. Candy, cookies, and potato chips, for example, provide primarily calories, whereas cereal grains are

Table 3-13. Carbohydrates in foods for infants

Food	Carbohydrate (gm/oz)
Human milk	2.9
Prepared infant formulas	2.1
Homogenized milk	1.5
Infant cereals, dry	16.4-22.8
Strained and junior desserts	3.7-6.1
Strained and junior vegetable and meat dinners	1.9-3.2
Strained and junior meat and vegetable dinners	1.2-5.3
Strained and junior fruit	2.9-6.1
Strained and junior vegetables	1.6-4.6

From Gebhardt, S.E., Cutrufelli, R., and Matthews, R.H.: Composition of foods, baby foods, raw, processed, prepared, Agriculture Handbook No. 8-3, Washington, D.C., 1978, U.S. Department of Agriculture.

important sources of the B vitamins; potatoes contribute vitamin C; and legumes offer amino acids, iron, and B vitamins as well as carbohydrates. Therefore, careful attention to the nutrients carried by the carbohydrate-containing foods is important in planning diets for children.

Most children prefer "sweet foods." In fact, infants at birth appear to distinguish sugar water from plain water. They accept larger quantities of sugar-sweetened solutions than unsweetened mixtures.[29] Indiscriminate consumption of candy, cookies, carbonated beverages, and other sweetened drinks dulls the appetite for other foods and should be discouraged. The impact of these sucrose-containing foods on the incidence of dental caries is discussed in Chapter 9.

WATER

Even more essential to the body than food is water. It functions as an essential component of body structure and as a solvent for minerals and other physiologically important compounds. It transports nutrients to and waste products from the cells and helps to regulate body temperature.

The percentage of body weight provided by water decreases from approximately 75% at birth to 60% at 1 year of age (see Chapter 1). After 1 year of age intracellular water accounts for approximately 60% and extracellular water for 40% of total body water.

Recommended intakes. Water is lost by evaporation through the skin and respiratory tract (insensible water loss) and through perspiration when the environmental temperture is elevated and by elimination in the feces and in the urine. During growth a positive water balance is necessary since additional water is obligated as a constituent of tissue and for increases in the volume of body fluids. The amount of water required for growth, however, is very small at all ages.

Water lost by evaporation in infancy and early childhood accounts for more than 60% of that needed to maintain homeostasis, as compared with 40% to 50% in the adult. At all ages approximately 24% of the basal heat loss is by evaporation of water through the skin and respiratory tract.[30] This amounts to 45 ml of insensible water loss per 100 kcal expended. Fomon[27] estimates evaporative water loss at 1 month of age to average 210 ml/day and at 1 year of age, 500 ml/day. Adult losses by evaporation average 800 to 1050 ml/day under ordinary circumstances. Evaporative losses increase with fever and increased environmental temperature. Increases in humidity decrease respiratory loss. Loss of water in the feces averages 10 ml/kg/day in infancy.[31]

The volume of urine in general reflects fluid intake. It includes both water required to concentrate the solutes presented to the kidney for excretion and water requirement is determined by the diet and by the concentrating power of the kidney.

Ziegler and Fomon have developed a method for estimating the renal solute load by calculating the amount of dietary sodium, chloride, potassium, and urea (estimated to be 4 mOsm/gm of protein). The urinary water requirement can then be estimated from the sum of these values. The National

Table 3-14. Water requirements of infants and children

Age	Water requirement (ml/kg/day)
10 days	125-150
3 months	140-160
6 months	130-155
1 year	120-135
2 years	115-125
6 years	90-100
10 years	70-85
14 years	50-60

From Laupus, W.E.: Nutrition and nutritional disorders. In Vaughan, V.C., McKay, R.J., and Nelson, W.E., editors: Nelson textbook of pediatrics, ed. 10, Philadelphia, 1975, W.B. Saunders Co.

Research Council recommends an intake of 1.5 ml/kcal/day for the infant, 1.0 ml/kcal/day for the adult.[33] Balance studies of 5-year-old children showed intakes of 1100 ml/day; metabolic water contributed an additional 200 ml/day. Water intakes averaged 0.7 ml/kcal/day[34] Ranges of average water requirements of infants and children are given in Table 3-14.

Food sources. Fluid in liquids and food consumed are the primary source of water. In addition, metabolic water is created from the metabolism of protein, fat, and carbohydrate: 1 gm protein produces 4.1 ml water, 1 gm carbohydrate produces 5.5 ml water, and 1 gm fat produces 1.07 ml water. Table 3-15 gives the water content of representative foods consumed in infancy and early childhood. When milk is boiled the liquid evaporates and protein and electrolytes are concentrated. Boiled milk is an inappropriate feeding for infants.

Because of a relatively greater demand for insensible water and a renal concentrating capacity that may be less than that of the adult, the infant is vulnerable to water imbalance. Under normal environmental conditions infants do not need additional water. Difficulties arise when formulas are improp-

Table 3-15. Percentage of water in selected foods

Food	Water (%)	Food	Water (%)
Human milk	85.2	Strained carrots	92.3
Cow's milk	87.4	Hamburger patty	68.3
Infant cereals, high protein	6.1	Chicken, cooked, dark meat	64.4
Infant cereals, rice	6.7	Egg, hard boiled	73.7
Strained macaroni and cheese	87.1	Oatmeal, cooked	83.6
Strained chicken with vegetables	90.0	Bread, white, enriched	35.6
Strained beef with vegetables	85.4	Carrots, cooked	91.2
Strained applesauce	88.6	Peas, canned	81.5
Strained peaches	80.1	Banana	75.7
Strained beef	80.6	Pears, canned	91.1
Strained peas	87.5		

From Gebhardt, S.E., Cutrufelli, R., and Matthews, R.H.: Composition of foods, baby foods, raw processed, prepared, Agriculture Handbook No. 8-3, Washington, D.C., 1978, U.S. Department of Agriculture.

erly prepared (see Chapter 4), when infants ingest limited volumes of milk during illness, and when extrarenal losses are greater than usual, such as during episodes of vomiting and diarrhea.[34] To ensure adequate water intakes infant formula should not be concentrated to more than 100 kcal/100 ml.

As children grow older the concentrating power of the kidney increases. Children learn to communicate and ask for water when they become thirsty. Difficulties in achieving water balance are unlikely in the absence of vomiting or diarrhea.

MINERALS

Although minerals contribute only 3% to 4% of body weight, they play important roles in the regulation of body fluids, acid base balance, and metabolic processes. The Food and Nutrition Board of the National Research Council has established allowances for three major and three trace minerals (Table 3-16). Insufficient information exists on many of the trace minerals to make recommendations for daily intake. Ranges of intake, however, have been suggested and are given in Table 3-17.

Calcium and Phosphorus

Calcium and phosphorus occur in the body in three systems. Bone contains 99% of body calcium; the remaining 1% is found in body fluids and striated muscle. Bone contains 80% of body phosphorus; the remaining 20% is found in striated muscle and blood serum. Plasma calcium and phosphorus levels are higher in children than in adults. Serum concentrations of the minerals are highest during early childhood, then decrease, paralleling decreases in the parathyroid hormone. The levels stabilize between 6 and 12 years of age and decline during adolescence to adult values.[35]

The calcium content of the body reflects both sex and stature. The body of the adult female contains approximately three fourths as much calcium as the body of the adult male. The skeletons of blacks tend to be larger than those of whites. The amount of calcium accumulated during growth depends on the rate of growth and final stature attained. It has been estimated that the fetus acquires an average of 97 mg of calcium/day.[36] Shaw[37] estimates the placental transfer at term to be 150 mg/kg/day.[39] The body of the full-term newborn infant has been estimated to contain approximately 27 gm of calcium, that of the adult

Table 3-16. Recommended daily dietary allowances for minerals

	Age (years)	Calcium (mg)	Phosphorus (mg)	Iodine (μg)	Iron (mg)	Magnesium (mg)	Zinc (mg)
Infants	0.0-0.5	360	240	40	10	50	3
	0.5-1.0	540	360	50	15	70	5
Children	1-3	800	800	70	15	150	10
	4-6	800	800	90	10	200	10
	7-10	800	800	120	10	250	10
Males	11-14	1200	1200	150	18	350	15
	15-18	1200	1200	150	18	400	15
Females	11-14	1200	1200	150	18	300	15
	15-18	1200	1200	150	18	300	15

From Food and Nutrition Board: Recommended dietary allowances, rev. ed. 9, Washington, D.C., 1980, National Academy of Sciences, National Research Council.

Table 3-17. Estimated safe and adequate daily dietary intakes of selected trace minerals and electrolytes

	Age (years)	Copper (mg)	Manganese (mg)	Fluoride (mg)	Chromium (mg)	Selenium (mg)	Molybdenum (mg)
Trace minerals							
Infants	0-0.5	0.5-0.7	0.5-0.7	0.1-0.5	0.01-0.04	0.01-0.04	0.03-0.06
	0.5-1	0.7-1.0	0.7-1.0	0.2-1.0	0.02-0.06	0.02-0.06	0.04-0.08
Children	1-3	1.0-1.5	1.0-1.5	0.5-1.5	0.02-0.08	0.02-0.08	0.05-0.1
and	4-6	1.5-2.0	1.5-2.0	1.0-2.5	0.03-0.12	0.03-0.12	0.06-0.15
adolescents	7-10	2.0-2.5	2.0-3.0	1.5-2.5	0.05-0.2	0.05-0.2	0.1-0.3
	11+	2.0-3.0	2.5-5.0	1.5-2.5	0.05-0.2	0.05-0.2	0.15-0.5
		2.0-3.0	2.5-5.0	1.5-4.0	0.05-0.2	0.05-0.2	0.15-0.5

	Age (years)	Sodium (mg)	Potassium (mg)	Chloride (mg)
Electrolytes				
Infants	0-0.5	115-350	350-925	275-700
	0.5-1	250-750	425-1275	400-1200
Children	1-3	325-975	550-1650	500-1500
and	4-6	450-1350	775-2325	700-2100
adolescents	7-10	600-1800	1000-3000	925-2775
	11+	900-2700	1525-4575	1400-4200
		1100-3300	1875-5625	1700-5100

From Food and Nutrition Board: Recommended dietary allowances, rev. ed. 9, Washington, D.C., 1980, National Academy of Sciences, National Research Council.

female 770 to 920 gm of calcium, and that of the adult male 950 to 1290 gm of calcium.

Skeletal requirements for calcium and phosphorus depend on body size and rates of growth. Requirements are greatest for taller, more rapidly growing children at any age.

Garn[38] has estimated gains in skeletal weight and amounts of calcium and phosphorus retained in bone from longitudinal and cross-sectional roentgenographic studies of the second metacarpal.

Christiansen, Rödbro, and Neilsen[39] have measured bone density of school-age children at different ages by photon absorption. Other investigators have analyzed skeletal weights and percentages of skeletal ash of individuals from infancy to adulthood.[40]

Leitch and Aitken[41] have estimated skeletal calcium requirements from analysis of the calcium content of analyzed bodies and rates of growth.

Garn estimates an average skeletal retention in males of 90 mg of calcium/day and 43 mg of phosphorus/day in the first year of life. Leitch and Aitken suggest skeletal calcium increments during the same period to average 150 mg/day. Both investigators estimate a decline in skeletal retentions of the minerals between the first and fourth years, after which the skeletal retentions gradually increase. Garn estimates that during the adolescent growth spurt males retain an average of 275 mg of calcium and 132 mg of phosphorus/day. Leitch and Aitken suggested that between 15 and 17 years of age skeletal requirements for calcium average 375 to 400 mg/day. The Committee on Nutrition of the American Academy of Pediatrics[36] estimates a retention of 290 to 400 mg of calcium/day in males and 210 to 240 mg of calcium/day in females during their peak growth spurts. Skeletal retentions of the two minerals are less in females than in males except between the tenth and twelfth years when rates of growth of females are greater than those of males.

Recommended intakes. Attempts to establish recommended intakes of calcium have caused considerable controversy for many years. Populations that have adapted to intakes of 200 to 400 mg/day without adverse effects have been identified.[42] However, rickets has been reported in one full-term infant who for 10 months consumed a lamb-base formula deficient in calcium but adequate in vitamins.[43] Osteomalacia, which improved rapidly with calcium supplements, has been identified in three black children, a 4-year-old girl, and 6- and 13-year-old boys in South Africa.[44] The recommended daily dietary allowances (Table 3-16) were planned to meet the needs of formula-fed infants who retain 25% to 30% of the calcium consumed in cow's milk.[33] Although breast-fed infants ingest less calcium, they retain approximately two-thirds of intake. Recommendations for children are set at 800 mg/day, since growing children may need two to four times as much calcium as adults. The higher recommended intakes of 1200 mg/day during preadolescence and puberty were designed to provide for maximum calcium retention.

Recommended intakes of phosphorus are the same as for calcium except during infancy, when a calcium:phosphorus ratio in the diet of 1.5:1 is recommended.

Food sources. Milk and dairy products are the richest sources of calcium in the North American diet. Table 3-18 shows the contribution of selected milk and dairy products. Egg yolks and most dark green leafy vegetables also contribute appreciable amounts of calcium.

Phosphorus is found in combination with calcium in dairy products but also occurs in foods that contain little calcium. It occurs in most protein-rich foods such as meats, eggs, nuts, and legumes and is also found in grains. Phosphate-containing additives are ingredients of many carbonated beverages, processed meats, cheese, and refrigerated bakery goods.

Neonatal hypocalcemia. Plasma concentrations of calcium and phosphorus are greater in cord blood than in maternal blood. During the first 2 to 3 days of life the levels of calcium fall significantly.[45] The decline is greatest in premature infants, infants of abnormal pregnancies and deliveries,

Table 3-18. Calcium in milk and dairy products

Food	Household Measure	Calcium (mg)
Human milk	4 oz	40
Cow's milk	4 oz	144
Powdered milk, nonfat, instant dry	⅓ cup	293
Cheddar cheese	1 oz	213
Yogurt	½ cup	147
Custard, baked	½ cup	148
Chocolate pudding, cooked with milk	½ cup	133
Chocolate pudding, instant	½ cup	187
Ice cream	½ cup	97

From Adams, C.F.: Nutritive value of American foods in common units, Agriculture Handbook No. 456, Washington, D.C., 1975, U.S. Department of Agriculture.

infants with asphyxia, and infants of diabetic mothers.[46,47] In normal, full-term infants the decline is greatest in those who are formula-fed and least in those who receive human milk. The fall in plasma calcium levels is accompanied by a rise in plasma inorganic phosphorus levels.[48]

After the initial decline, plasma calcium levels stabilize and tend to rise by the tenth day of life, the level being dependent on the phosphorus content or the calcium:phosphorus ratio of milk.[49] Serum calcium concentrations in breast-fed infants are greater than those in formula-fed infants. Serum concentrations of phosphorus reflect the phosphorus content of the milk consumed, being significantly less in breast-fed infants than in formula-fed infants.[48,50] Breast-fed infants generally show an increase in serum calcium concentration by 5 to 7 days of age. Snodgrass and others[48] noted no increase in levels of plasma calcium in formula-fed infants between the first and sixth to eighth day of life. They noted a fall in serum calcium concentrations in one third of formula-fed infants during the first week of life; in 9% of infants the levels fell below 7.5 mg/100 ml, a level at which hypocalcemia is defined by many and at which the infant is at risk of tetany.

There are two periods when hypocalcemia is detected in the neonate. Early neonatal hypocalcemia occurs in the first 24 to 48 hours and is thought to be the result of depressed levels of parathyroid hormone as a result of transient functional hypoparathyroidism.[51] It occurs most frequently in infants of diabetic mothers, infants who have experienced asphyxia, and low birth weight infants.[52] Some investigators have suggested that a continuous prophylactic infusion or oral supplements of calcium and magnesium lactate be given to all low birth weight infants.[53,54] Late neonatal hypocalcemia occurs in association with hyperphosphatemia in otherwise normal, full-term infants between the fifth and eighth day of life. It is rarely seen in breast-fed infants but occurs more often in infants who receive a high dietary intake of phosphorus. Phosphorus consumed in excess of that which can be excreted by the kidney elevates serum phosphate levels. It has been hypothesized that elevated serum phosphorus levels depress serum calcium levels by causing deposition of calcium in bone. A normal response would be an increased output of parathyroid hormone, causing solubilization of bone mineral, phosphate diuresis, and blockage of tubular resorption. The neonatal infant with an immature parathyroid gland may not be able to respond with the normal homeostatic mechanism, and serum calcium levels may fall. Irritability and convulsions often, although not inevitably, occur when serum levels fall below 7 mg/100 ml.

One of the striking differences between human milk and cow's milk is the content of calcium and phosphorus. Cow's milk contains more than three times as much calcium and six times as much phosphorus as does human milk. There is less calcium relative to phosphorus in cow's milk than in human milk. Gittleman and Pincus[55] in 1951 found that newborn infants who were given a high-phosphate diet as represented by evaporated milk or whole cow's milk mixtures responded with hyperphosphatemia and a tendency toward hypocalcemia. In 1952 Gardner[56] suggested that excess dietary phosphorus in the face of limited kidney function had profound effects on the renal tissue as well as on the parathyroid gland, causing hypertrophy of the parathyroid gland and renal lesions.

Manufacturers of infant formulas have reduced the quantity of phosphorus in cow's milk formulas. Isolated cases of neonatal hypocalcemic tetany, however, continue to be reported. Pierson and Crawford[57] reported two cases of neonatal hypocalcemia resulting in tetany that occurred on the eighth and ninth days of life. One infant received a high-phosphate load from a soybean formula preparation, the other from the addition of cereal to the formula. Monitoring the amount of phosphorus consumed by infants in the early neonatal period continues to be important.

Magnesium

Magnesium is the fourth most abundant mineral in the body and the second most abundant intercellular cation. Approximately 50% of the body's magnesium is deposited with calcium and phosphorus in bone, 25% is in muscle, and the remained is found in soft tissue.

Recommended intakes. The recommended daily dietary allowances for infants have been estimated from the magnesium content of human milk and cow's milk (Table 3-16). Allowances for children and adolescents are stated to be only estimates

intended to allow for increasing needs during bone growth.[33]

Harris and Wilkinson[58] state that the newborn infant needs to retain 10.2 mg/day of magnesium to satisfy the requirement for growth. Fomon[27] estimates the requirement to be 16.5 mg/day during the first 4 months and suggests an intake of 25 mg/day. Laupus[59] suggests intakes of 40 to 70 mg/day for infants, 100 to 150 mg/day for children 1 to 3 years of age, 200 to 300 mg/day for children 3 to 12 years of age, and 350 to 400 mg/day for adolescents 12 to 18 years of age.

Food sources. Magnesium is found in many foods. Nuts, soybeans, whole grains, legumes, and shellfish are excellent sources. It exists in all green plants as a component of chlorophyll. Human milk contains approximately 4 mg of magnesium/100 ml and cow's milk contains 12 mg of magnesium/100 ml.

Iron

Iron is the most abundant trace mineral in the body, accounting for approximately 75 mg/kg of the full-term newborn infant, 50 mg/kg of the adult male, and 35 mg/kg of the adult female.[60]

The concentration of hemoglobin at birth averages 17 to 19 gm/100 ml of blood. During the first 6 to 8 weeks of life it decreases to approximately 10 to 11 gm/100 ml because of a shortened life span of the fetal cell and decreased erythropoiesis. After this age there is a gradual increase in hemoglobin concentration to 13 gm/100 ml at 2 years of age. During adolescence a sharp increase occurs in males at the time of the growth spurt.

Iron deficiency is the most common nutritional deficiency in North America. It occurs most frequently in 4- to 24-month-old infants, in adolescent males, and in females during their childbearing years. It may result from inadequate iron intakes, impaired absorption, a large hemorrhage or repeated small hemorrhages. Microcytic hypochromic anemia is the final stage of deficiency, occurring only after iron stores are depleted and there has been a fall in plasma iron and transferrin satura-

Table 3-19. Selected food sources of iron

Food	Household Measure	Iron (mg)
Iron-fortified formula	8 oz	3.0
Infant cereals, high protein	1 tbsp	1.8
Infant cereals, rice	1 tbsp	1.8
Strained split peas with ham	1 oz	0.1
Strained chicken with vegetables	1 oz	0.1
Strained beef with vegetables	1 oz	0.1
Strained beef	1 oz	0.4
Strained liver	1 oz	1.5
Hamburger, cooked	2 oz	1.8
Chicken, dark meat	1 oz	0.5
Liver, beef	1 oz	2.5
Liver, chicken	1 liver	2.1
Liverwurst	1 oz	1.7
Frankfurter, 5″ by ¾″	1	0.9
Egg	1 medium	1.0
Pork and beans	¼ cup	1.5
Peanut butter	1 tbsp	0.3
Bread, enriched white	1 slice	0.7
Macaroni, enriched, cooked	¼ cup	0.4
Carrots, cooked	¼ cup	0.2
Orange	1 medium	0.6
Canned pears	¼ cup	0.1

From Adams, C.F.: Nutritive value of American foods in common units, Agriculture Handbook No. 456, Agriculture Research Service, Washington, D.C., 1975, U.S. Department of Agriculture; and Gebhardt, S.E., Cutrufelli, R., and Matthews, R.H.: Composition of foods, baby foods, raw, processed, prepared, Agriculture Handbook No. 8-3, Washington, D.C., 1978, U.S. Department of Agriculture.

tion. Iron deficiency is diagnosed when transferrin saturations fall below 16%[61]; anemia is diagnosed when hemoglobin concentrations fall below 11.0 gm/100 ml and hematocrits fall below 33%.[62]

Iron is accumulated in utero in proportion to body size. Premature and low birth weight infants have limited reserves at birth that are quickly depleted during rapid growth. Even with the advantage of full-term iron stores, the rapidly growing infant is at risk of iron deficiency.

Recommended intakes. The recommended dietary allowances of the National Research Council assume 10% absorption and are planned to meet variations in individuals (Table 3-16). Iron requirements of individual children vary with rates of growth and increasing blood volumes, iron stores, variations in menstrual losses of iron of adolescent females, and the timing of the growth spurt of adolescents. Larger, more rapidly growing children have the greatest requirement for iron at any age.

During menstruation iron loss varies widely among females but is consistent from month to month in individuals. Average losses of blood of 15-year-old girls in a Swedish study were 33.8 ml/period, equivalent to an iron loss of approximately 0.5 mg of iron/day.[63]

Food sources. Diets in North America have been estimated to provide 6 mg of iron/1000 kcal. Organ meats, shellfish, and muscle meats provide the richest and most usable sources. Other food sources include nuts, green vegetables, whole wheat flour, and bread.

Of the iron in pork, liver, and fish, 30% to 40% is in the form of heme iron, and of the iron in beef, lamb, and chicken, 50% to 60% is in the form of heme iron. Obviously, these foods are sources of nonheme iron also, as are greens, vegetables, grains, legumes, and eggs.[64] Human milk and cow's milk contain 0.5 to 1.0 mg of iron/liter. During infancy, iron-fortified formulas and cereals fortified with reduced iron are primary food sources. Table 3-19 lists representative sources of iron for infants and children.

Iron absorption from food. The percentage of iron absorbed from food depends on the presence of heme iron and/or nonheme iron, the combinations of food consumed together, and the iron reserves of the individual. Individuals with inadequate iron stores absorb approximately 35%; those with adequate iron stores absorb 25% of heme iron consumed. Individuals with deficient iron reserves may absorb as much as 20% of nonheme irone, whereas iron-replete individuals may absorb as little as 2%. The presence of meat, which offers heme iron and ascorbic acid, increases the absorption of nonheme iron. Absorption is decreased by the inclusion of dairy products, eggs, calcium phosphate salts, or tea in the foods consumed at the same time.[64] Forty-nine percent of the iron in human milk, 19% of the iron in cow's milk, and 3% of the iron in iron-fortified formula is absorbed.[65] The addition of strained vegetables to the infant's diet significantly reduces the availability of iron from human milk.[66]

Many foods are fortified with iron salts. Of particular importance to persons concerned with iron intakes of infants and children are those iron salts used to fortify the commercially prepared infant formulas, cereal grains, and cereals consumed so abundantly by children. Iron-fortified formulas contain 12 mg of iron/quart as ferrous sulfate. Cereals and baked products may be fortified with reduced iron, sodium iron pyrophosphate, or ferric orthophosphate.

Ferrous sulfate is the most available of the iron salts, but it is seldom used to fortify food because of difficulties in manufacturing. The percentage of absorption of reduced iron will depend on the particle size, surface area. and porosity of the salts, which in turn determines the extent to which the particles dissolve in the acid of the stomach.[67]

Some pediatricians believe it may be advantageous for infants over 6 months of age to receive one feeding that does not include milk but iron-fortified cereal, vegetables, and/or fruit and vitamin C–containing fruit juice.

Adolescents are at risk for iron deficiency because of the high demands for iron during the adolescent growth spurt and the onset of menses.

A desirable iron status can be compromised by a low-calorie diet, poor selection of foods, or any dietary extremes. Assuming that a well-chosen diet contains approximately 6 mg of iron/1000 kcal, adolescents dieting to lose weight will be receiving minimal iron intakes. In addition to this, the common practice of choosing foods such as yogurt and cottage cheese as primary protein foods in a reducing diet results in an even lower dietary iron intake.

Regular monitoring of iron status should ideally be provided for infants and adolescents, especially those having limited high-iron foods available or those practicing various dietary extremes or restrictions.

Iodine

Of the iodine in the human adult, 70% to 80% is concentrated in the thyroid gland, which synthesizes its only functional compounds, thyroxine and triiodothyronine. The remaining iodine in the body is distributed in the blood, skin, and other tissues.

Recommended intakes. The Food and Nutrition Board of the National Research Council recommends an intake of 40 µg of iodine/day during the first 6 months of life, gradually increasing to 150 µg/day in adolescence (Table 3-16). The breast-fed infant will receive 10 to 20 µg of iodine/100 kcal from an adequately fed lactating mother. It has been suggested that requirements for 8- to 16-year-old children may not be much greater than 56 µg/day.[27] Average intakes of iodine in the United States are five to ten times the recommended amounts. However, wide variations in iodine intakes may be experienced by individuals, depending on sources of food and geographical locations.

Food sources. Iodized salt, bread made with iodate as a dough conditioner, milk, and seafood are excellent sources of dietary iodine. The fact that the iodine content of food is determined by the soil in which it is grown is no longer of significance in the etiology of iodine deficiency. Food consumed in one area is often transported from another. The iodine content of milk and dairy products depends on whether the cattle have been given iodine-supplemented feed or iodized salt blocks. Milk iodine may be as high as 450 µg/liter.

The amounts of iodine absorbed from environments polluted by the combustion of fossil fuels and organic matter can be significant. Many therapeutic drugs also contain large amounts of iodine.[68]

Zinc

Zinc is distributed throughout all cells and tissues. The fetus contains approximately 20 mg/kg, whereas the adult has 30 mg/kg of fat-free tissue.[69] It leaves the hair only when the hair is shed.

Hambidge and others[70] reported low concentrations of zinc in hair in 10 of 132 children over 4 years of age from middle- and upper-income families that were studied in Denver, Colorado. The children had histories of poor appetite, consumed small amounts of meat, and had diminished taste acuity. Nine of the ten children had heights that plotted at or below the 10th percentile. Increased appetite, taste acuity, and growth occurred after zinc supplementation.

It appears that many preschool and school-age children from low- and middle-income families may be ingesting inadequate amounts of zinc.

Studies in Denver of Headstart children 3.5 to 6 years of age whose heights were less than the 3rd percentile revealed that 40% had low concentrations of hair zinc and 69% had low plasma and/or hair zinc concentrations.[71] Supplements of zinc sulfate that provided 0.2 mg zinc/kg given to five schoolchildren with hypogeusia and low levels of zinc in hair resulted in normalization of taste perception and substantial increases in hair zinc content.[72]

Recommended intakes. Recommendations for intake have been made from studies of zinc intakes of apparently well-nourished individuals and from studies of zinc balance.

The infant is born without zinc stores and rapidly becomes dependent on an adequate supply of biologically available zinc. Normal breast-fed infants have been noted to be in negative balance at 1 week of age. One study comparing hair zinc concentration of breast-fed and formula-fed babies during the first 6 months found that only male formula-fed infants experienced a significant decline in hair zinc concentrations, suggesting that males have a higher requirement for zinc during the period studied.[72] Variations in plasma zinc concentrations during growth reflect the continual utilization and depletion of body stores of zinc. Declines occur during periods of most rapid growth. The steepest decline appears to occur at 10 to 11 years of age in the female and at 12 to 13 years of age in the male.[73] Breast-fed infants receive 0.7 to 5 mg/day, approximately 0.2 to 1.2 mg/kg.[74] Intakes of children 1 to 3 years of age have been estimated to average 5 mg/day, those of children 3 to 5 years of age 5 to 7 mg/day, and those of adolescents 13 mg/day.[75] Balance studies of Engel, Miller, and Price[76] suggest that 6 mg/day is adequate for preadolescent children. Studies by Tribble and Scoular[77] indicate that 12 mg/day is adequate for college students.

The Food and Nutrition Board of the National Academy of Sciences has based its recommended intake on the above studies (Table 3-16).

Food sources. Seafoods and meats are rich

Table 3-20 Selected food sources of zinc

Food	Household Measure	Zinc (mg)
Cow's milk	4 oz	0.5
Ground beef, cooked	2 oz	2.5
Chicken drumstick	1	1.4
Liver, beef, cooked	2 oz	2.9
Liverwurst	1 oz	0.8
Frankfurter	1	0.9
Egg	1 medium	0.5
Oatmeal, cooked	½ cup	0.6
Bread, white	1 slice	0.2
Bread, whole wheat	1 slice	0.5
Green beans, canned	¼ cup	0.2
Spinach	½ cup	0.6
Banana	½ medium	0.2
Orange	1 medium	0.3

Adapted from Murphy, E.W., Willis, B.W., and Watt, B.K.: J. Am. Diet Assoc. **66:**345, 1975.

sources of available zinc. Cereals and legumes also contain significant amounts.[78] The bioavailability ranges from 20% to 30%. Estimates of zinc in human milk and cow's milk range from 3 to 5 mg/liter.[79] Picciano and Guthrie[80] found ranges of 0.14 to 3.95 mg/liter in milk of 50 lactating women. Colostrum contains 20 mg/liter, three to five times as much as later milk. Levels of zinc in human milk decline after 2 months of lactation and may fall below 1 mg/liter. Infant formulas are supplemented and contain 3 to 4 mg of zinc/liter. Animal studies suggest a bioavailability of 59.2% of zinc in human milk, 43% to 53.9% of zinc in cow's milk, and 26.8% to 39.5% of zinc in infant formula.[81] Table 3-20 gives the zinc content of representative foods consumed by infants and children.

Fluoride

Fluoride in the body is concentrated in the bones and teeth. The concentration in bones increases linearly with increased intakes.

The role of fluoride as an essential trace mineral lies in its ability to reduce the incidence of dental caries. It has not been proved essential to survival. Epidemiological studies have repeatedly proved that there is a close relationship between tooth decay and the amount of fluoride ingested during tooth development.[82] When the fluoride content of community drinking water has been adjusted to a level of 1 ppm (1 mg/liter), the incidence of dental caries has been reduced 40% to 60%.[83] Although the effect is especially important during tooth development, fluoride has also been shown to be beneficial to adults.[84]

Recommended intakes. The Committee on Nutrition of the American Academy of Pediatrics[85] recommends that supplemental fluoride dosages be adjusted to the fluoride content of the water supply (Table 3-21). In communities with less than 0.3 ppm of fluoride in the water supply, supplements of 0.25 mg of fluoride/day are recommended from 2 weeks to 2 years of age, 0.5 mg/day between 2 and 3 years of age, and 1.0 mg/day after 3 years of age. It is suggested that children whose drinking water contains between 0.3 and 0.7 mg of fluoride ppm receive 0.25 mg between 2 and 3 years of age and 0.50 mg between 3 and 16 years of age.

Food sources. All foods and water contain very small amounts of fluoride. Seafood and tea are exceptions and contain greater amounts. Food produced and prepared in areas in which the water is fluoridated reflect the fluorine content of the water. Cow's milk contains 0.03 to 0.1 μg of fluoride/liter; human milk contains less than 0.05 mg/liter.[86] There is an increasing concentration of fluoride in the food chain. Processing food with fluoridated water significantly increases its fluoride content. The fluoride content of ready-to-drink fruit juices increases five to twenty times when fluoridated water is used in processing. The fluoride content of infant cereals is influenced by the fluoride content of the water in which they were produced. Mechanically deboning meat increases the fluoride content of the end products, because bone chips are incorporated during processing.[87] Infant formula is no longer manufactured with fluoridated water.

Table 3-21. Supplemental fluorine dosage schedule (mg/day*)

	Concentration of Fluoride in Drinking Water (ppm)		
Age	<0.3	0.3-0.7	>0.7
2 weeks to 2 years	0.25	0	0
2 to 3 years	0.50	0.25	0
3 to 16 years	1.00	0.50	0

From Committee on Nutrition: Pediatrics **63:**150, 1979. Copyright American Academy of Pediatrics 1979.
*2.2 mg of sodium fluoride contains 1 mg of fluoride.

Mottling and fluorosis of tooth enamel. When the fluoride concentrations of drinking water increase above 2 ppm, mottling (a brown stain on the teeth) during tooth development occurs. The incidence and severity of the manifestation increase as the fluoride content of the water increases. At levels of 8 ppm almost all individuals who have consumed water during tooth development have extensively mottled teeth.[83] In areas with a high natural concentration of fluoride, it has become a practice to dilute fluoride to no more than 1.2 ppm. In warmer climates and during periods of elevated environmental temperatures when the intakes of water are increased, suggested levels for fluoridation of water are 0.6 to 0.7 ppm.[88]

Fluorosis, usually manifested as opaque spots or streaks on the enamel of permanent teeth, has been noted in 63% of children by the time they were 7 to 12 years of age in a community without fluoridated water when the use of fluoride supplements was common. Levitt[87] suggests that the definition of the optimum concentration of fluoride in community water supplies needs to be reassessed.

Remaining trace elements

The fact that only safe and adequate intakes have been recommended for the remaining trace minerals—copper, manganese, chromium, selenium, and molybdenum—indicates the lack of information necessary to define needs during the life cycle.

Less than adequate intake during infancy and childhood may occur in cases of generalized malnutrition or in infants maintained on low copper formulas. Infants and children who consume a variety of foods are likely to consume appropriate quantities of these nutrients.

VITAMINS

The function of vitamins in metabolic processes makes the requirement determined by intakes of energy, protein, and saturated fats. Exact needs are difficult to define.

Most vitamins cross the placenta and accumulate in the fetus at greater concentrations than in the mother. Maternal hypovitaminemia will be reflected in the fetus.[89]

Vitamins A, E, and β-carotene concentrations are lower in the newborn infant's blood than in the mother's. The concentration of water-soluble vitamins in the blood of the neonate is higher than that of the mother.

Recommended intakes. Fat-soluble vitamins in excess of need are not excreted but are stored. Reserves can be accumulated. The toxicity of excessive intakes of vitamins A and D is well documented.

In contrast to vitamins A, D, E, and K, the water-soluble vitamins are stored in small amounts and deficiencies can be expected to occur in a relatively short period if the nutrient is absent from dietary intake.

Recommended dietary allowances of vitamins from birth to 18 years of age, as prepared by the Food and Nutrition Board of the National Research Council, are given in Table 3-22.

Because available information is not sufficient to make recommendations for intakes of vitamin K, biotin, and pantothenic acid, amounts that are safe and adequate have been estimated.

The RDA for most vitamins is interpolated from infant and adult allowances or calculated on the basis of energy or protein allowances.[27]

The allowance for vitamin A for infants is based

Table 3-22. Recommended daily dietary allowances of vitamins

Age (yr)		Fat Soluble			Water Soluble						
		Vitamin A RE* (µg)	Vitamin D (µg)	Vitamin E (mgα-TE)	Thiamine (mg)	Riboflavin (mg)	Niacin (mg)	Vitamin B₆ (mg)	Folacin (µg)	Vitamin B₁₂ (µg)	Ascorbic acid (mg)
Infants	0.0-0.5	420	10	3	0.3	0.4	6	0.3	30	0.5	35
	0.5-1.0	400	10	4	0.5	0.6	8	0.6	45	1.5	35
Children	1-3	400	10	5	0.7	0.8	9	0.9	100	2.0	45
	4-6	500	10	6	0.9	1.0	11	1.3	200	2.5	45
	7-10	700	10	7	1.2	1.4	16	1.6	300	3.0	45
Males	11-14	1000	10	8	1.4	1.6	18	1.6	400	3.0	50
	15-18	1000	10	10	1.4	1.7	18	1.8	400	3.0	60
Females	11-14	800	10	8	1.2	1.3	15	1.8	400	3.0	50
	15-18	800	10	8	1.1	1.3	14	2.0	400	3.0	60

From Food and Nutrition Board: Recommended dietary allowances, rev. ed. 9, Washington, D.C., 1980, National Academy of Sciences, National Research Council.

on the average retinol content of human milk. Recommendations for children and adolescents are interpolated from infant and adult male allowances.

Although 100 international units (IU) per day of vitamin D prevents rickets and ensures adequate absorption of calcium and normal mineralization of bone in the infant, better calcium absorption and some increase in growth has been noted with intakes of 400 IU/day, the RDA. Vitamin D can be formed by the action of sunlight on the skin. The amount formed depends on several variables, and amounts formed cannot be readily measured.

Requirements for vitamin E are related to the polyunsaturated fatty acid content of cellular structures. An assumption is made that requirements increase with body weight until maturity. An intake of 5 IU at 9 kg increasing to 12 IU at 40 kg of body weight should be satisfactory in diets providing 4% to 7% of kilocalories as linoleic acid.

The allowances for thiamine and riboflavin are calculated on the basis of energy intake. Studies suggest that the minimum requirement of thiamine of infants is approximately 0.27 mg/1000 kcal.[90,91] One study indicated that 3 mg/1000 kcal was adequate for preadolescent children.[92] Another study of 14- to 17-year-old males indicated that 0.38 ± 0.059 mg/1000 kcal[93] meets their minimum requirement. The RDA is calculated on the basis of 0.5 mg/1000 kcal.

Urinary excretion of riboflavin is low in adults and in children maintained on diets containing up to 0.5 mg/1000 kcal and increases as riboflavin intakes increase up to 0.75 mg/1000 kcal.[94] The RDA is based on 0.6 mg/1000 kcal.

The fact that tryptophan is converted to niacin makes basic requirements for niacin difficult to determine. The RDA for infants is based on 8 niacin equivalents per 1000 kcal, about two thirds of which will be converted from tryptophan. For children over 6 months of age, the RDA is based on 6.6 niacin equivalents per 1000 kcal.[27]

The recommended intake of 0.3 mg of vitamin B₆ per day for young infants and 0.6 mg of B₆ per

Table 3-23. Selected foods as sources of vitamin A

Food	Household Measure	Vitamin A (IU)
Cow's milk	8 oz	350
Human milk	8 oz	560
Cheddar cheese	1 oz	370
Egg	1 medium	520
Liver, beef	1 oz	15,112
Liver, chicken	1 liver	3080
Liverwurst	1 slice, ⅓ oz	650
Butter	1 tsp	160
Apricots, canned	¼ cup	1125
Orange	1 medium	280
Peach	1 medium	1330
Watermelon	½ cup diced	470
Carrots	¼ cup	3808
Acorn squash	¼ baked and mashed	718
Sweet potatoes, mashed	¼ cup	5038
Green peas	¼ cup	280
Spinach	¼ cup cooked	3645
Tomatoes, canned	¼ cup	542

From Adams, C.F.: Nutritive value of American foods in common units, Agriculture Handbook No. 456, Washington, D.C., 1975, U.S. Department of Agriculture.

Table 3-24. Selected food sources of vitamin C

Food	Household Measure	Vitamin C (mg)
Human milk	8 oz	16
Cow's milk	8 oz	2
Broccoli	1 spear	22
Brussels sprouts	¼ cup	31
Cabbage, raw, chopped	¼ cup	11
Cabbage, cooked, wedge	¼ cup	10
Cantaloupe, diced	½ cup	27
Grapefruit	½	37
Orange	1 medium	66
Orange juice	½ cup	62
Potato, boiled (2½ inch)	½	11
Strawberries	1 cup	88
Tomato, raw (2⅛ inch)	1	42
Tomatoes, canned	½ cup	20
Tomato juice	½ cup	20

From Adams, C.F.: Nutritive value of American foods in common units, Agriculture Handbook No. 456, Washington, D.C., 1975, U.S. Department of Agriculture.

Table 3-25. Foods as sources of riboflavin

Food	Household Measure	Riboflavin (mg)
Human milk	8 oz	0.08
Cow's milk	8 oz	0.41
Prepared infant formula	8 oz	1.48-2.80
Cheddar cheese	1 oz	0.13
Infant cereals, high protein	1 tbsp	0.06
Infant cereals, rice	1 tbsp	0.06
Farina	½ cup	0.035
Oatmeal	½ cup	0.025
Macaroni, enriched	¼ cup	0.03
Liver, beef	1 oz	1.18
Liver, chicken	1 liver	0.67
Broccoli	1 spear	0.03
Green peas	¼ cup	0.03
Spinach	¼ cup	0.06

From Adams, C.F.: Nutritive value of American foods in common units, Agriculture Handbook No. 456, Washington, D.C., 1975, U.S. Department of Agriculture.

day for older infants is based on experience with proprietary formulas. The allowance for older children is calculated on the basis of 0.02 mg of vitamin B_6 per gram of expected dietary protein intake.[27]

The requirement for folacin in infancy has been estimated to be 5 µg/kg of body weight, the basis for the RDA.[95] For older children and adults, folacin needs are extrapolated from those of infants.

The B_{12} allowance is based on that in the milk of a lactating woman with adequate serum B_{12} and a margin of safety. For formula-fed infants, the Committee on Nutrition of the American Academy of Pediatrics[22] recommends an intake of 0.15 µg/100 kcal. The RDA for older infants and children has been calculated on this same basis.

An intake of 10 mg/day of vitamin C is adequate to prevent and cure scurvy in humans. It does not, however, provide for acceptable reserves. Newborn infants consuming 7 to 12 mg of vitamin C have been protected from scurvy.[96,97] An intake of 35 mg/day should provide an adequate margin of safety. On the basis of body weight the vitamin C requirement of older children is higher than that of

adults. The 45 mg/day for children to 11 years of age and 60 mg thereafter is thought to provide for that need and the margin of safety.

Food sources. Vitamins reported to be most often consumed in less than appropriate amounts by preschool and school-age children are vitamins A, C, B_6, and riboflavin.[98-100] Food sources of these vitamins are given in Tables 3-23 through 3-26. Because goat's milk is folate deficient, attention must be given to that vitamin if infants are fed goat's milk.

Vitamin supplements. A prophylactic intramuscular dose of 0.5 to 1 mg of vitamin K or an oral dose of 1.0 to 2.1 mg of vitamin K is usually given to infants at birth as a protection against hemorrhagic disease of the newborn.[101] After receiving this dose, human beings are able to synthesize vitamin K from the bacteria in their gut. Vitamin K supplement is needed only for children who malabsorb fat.

The importance of appropriate vitamin supplementation of breast-fed infants is discussed in Chapter 4. After infancy, the percentage of children who are given vitamin supplements declines;

Table 3-26. Selected food sources of vitamin B_6

Food	Household Measure	Vitamin B_6 (mg)
Cow's milk	1 cup	0.1
Human milk	1 cup	0.02
Infant cereals, high protein	1 tbsp	0.01
Infant cereals, rice	1 tbsp	0.007
Infant dinners, split peas and bacon	1 oz	0.014
Infant dinners, vegetables and liver	1 oz	0.036
Strained beef	1 oz	0.056
Strained liver	1 oz	0.227
Beef liver, uncooked	3½ oz	0.84
Chicken liver, uncooked	3½ oz	0.75
Beef, uncooked	3½ oz	0.33
Chicken, canned	1 oz	0.084
Peanut butter	1 tbsp	0.053
Egg	1 medium	0.055
Whole wheat bread	1 slice	0.05
White bread	1 slice	0.011
Green peas, canned	¼ cup	0.008
Tomatoes, canned	¼ cup	0.054
Squash, frozen	¼ cup	0.055
Banana	1 small	0.71
Orange juice	½ cup	0.05
Strawberries	½ cup	0.040

Adapted from Orr, M.L.: Pantothenic acid, vitamin B_6 and vitamin B_{12} in foods, Home Economics Research Report No. 36, Washington, D.C., 1969, U.S. Department of Agriculture.

however, over half of preschool and school-age children receive multi–vitamin-mineral preparations.[102]

Because Cook and Payne[102] found the use of vitamin supplements significantly increased the percentage of second and sixth grade children who meet 67% of the RDA compared with nonsupplemented children, they consider vitamin supplementation advisable. However, Breskin[103] noted no significant differences in biochemical indices with the exception of RBC folate of children who consumed supplements compared with those who did not, even though mean intakes of vitamin B_6 of the nonsupplemented group were 30% below the RDA. Many of the nonsupplemented children did not ingest two thirds of the RDA of folate. All values were in the normal range of accepted standards.

The Committee on Nutrition of the American Academy of Pediatrics[102] has defined four groups of children who are at particular risk and for whom vitamin supplementation may be appropriate: children from deprived families, especially those who suffer from parental neglect or abuse; children who have anorexia, poor and capricious appetites, poor eating habits, and who are on regimens to manage obesity; pregnant teenagers; and children who consume vegan diets.

Vitamin supplementation of diets of older children should be recommended only after careful evaluation of the child's food intake. Diets of children who restrict their intake of milk because of real or imagined allergies, lactose intolerance, or for psychosocial reasons should be monitored for riboflavin and vitamin D. Diets of infants and children receiving goat's milk should be carefully monitored for food sources of folacin. Diets of children who consume limited amounts of fruits and vegetables should be checked for sources of vitamins A and C.

Vitamin supplements, especially those that are colored and sugar coated, should be stored in places inaccessible to young children.

SUMMARY

The nutrient needs of individual children vary at any age depending on body size, patterns of activity, and rates of growth. They are greatest per unit of body size in infancy and decline with age.

The recommended dietary intakes during childhood are extrapolated from needs of infants and adult males or are calculated on the basis of presumed energy or protein intake. Intakes of individual children should be evaluated not in relation to the total amounts listed on the RDA chart but on the same basis the RDA was calculated.

Studies indicate that intakes of protein are generally adequate in North America. Nutrients most likely to be consumed in low or deficient amounts are calcium, iron, and vitamins A and C.

Children at risk for nutrient inadequacies are those from deprived families; those who have an excessive appetite, poor eating habits, or anorexia, or those on regimens to manage obesity; pregnant teenagers; and those who consume vegan diets.

SUGGESTED LEARNING ACTIVITIES

1. Calculate the energy intake of two children of the same age and sex whose height are in 10th and a 90th percentile. Compare this with the RDA on the basis of total calories, calories per kilogram, and calories per centimeter.
2. Calculate the grams of protein provided by a preschool and school lunch. What percentage of the RDA does this provide?
3. Discuss the bioavailability of iron and zinc in foods acceptable to preschool children. How can one ensure an adequate intake?
4. Compare the content of a popular children's vitamin-mineral supplement with an adult vitamin-mineral supplement.
5. Compare the cost of the vitamins available in drug stores, health food stores, or sold door-to-door by individuals.
6. Compare the cost of meeting the RDA for vitamins with food or with vitamin-mineral supplementation.

REFERENCES

1. Snyderman, S.E.: Nutrition in infancy and adolescence. In Goodhart, R.S., and Shils, H.E., editors: Modern nutrition in health and disease, ed. 6, Philadelphia, 1980, Lea & Febiger.
2. Brooke, O.G., Alvear, J., and Arnold, M.: Energy retention, energy expenditure, and growth in healthy immature infants, Pediatr. Res. **13:**215, 1979.
3. Ashworth, A.: Growth rates in children recovering from protein-calorie malnutrition, Br. J. Nutr. **23:**835, 1969.
4. Spady, D.W., and others: Energy balance during recovery from malnutrition, Am. J. Clin. Nutr. **29:**1073, 1976.
5. Spady, D.W., Hill, A.A., and Waterlow, J.C.: Energy cost of catch-up growth in malnourished children, Nutr. Metab. **21:**224, 1977.
6. Ashworth, A.: Ad lib feeding during recovery from malnutrition, Br. J. Nutr. **31:**109, 1974.
7. Hegsted, D.M.: Energy needs and energy utilization, Nutr. Rev. **32:**33, 1974.
8. Spady, D.W.: Total daily energy expenditure of healthy, free ranging school children, Am. J. Clin. Nutr. **33:**766, 1980
9. Food and nutrient intakes of individuals in 1 day in the United States, Spring, 1977, U.S.D.A. Nationwide Food Consumption Survey, 1977-1978, Preliminary Rep. No. 2, Washington, D.C., 1980, Science and Education Administration.
10. White House Conference on Child Health and Protection: Growth and development of the child. III. Nutrition. Report of the Committee on Growth and Development, New York, 1932, Century House, Inc.
11. Pipes, P., and Holm, V.A.: Weight control of children with Prader-Willi syndrome, J. Am. Diet. Assoc. **62:**520, 1973.
12. Beal, V.A.: Nutritional intake. In McCammon, R.W., editor: Human growth and development, Springfield, Ill., 1970, Charles C Thomas, Publisher.
13. Culley, W.J., and others: Calorie intake of children with Down's syndrome (mongolism), J. Pediatr. **66:**772, 1965.

14. Holt, L.E., Jr., and Snyderman, S.E.: The amino acid requirements of infants, J.A.M.A. **175**:100, 1961.

15. Fomon, S.J., and Filer, L.J.: Amino acid requirements for normal growth. In Nyhan, W.L., ed.: Amino acid metabolism and genetic variations, New York, 1967, McGraw-Hill Book Co.

16. Fomon, S.J., and others: Requirements for protein and essential amino acids in early infancy, Acta Paediatr. Scand. **62**:33, 1973.

17. Report of a Joint FAO/WHO Ad Hoc Expert Committee: Energy and protein requirements, World Health Organization Technical Series No. 522, FAO Nutr. Meet. Ser. No. 52, Geneva, 1973, World Health Organization.

18. Nakagawa, I., and others: Amino acid requirements of children: nitrogen balance at the minimal level of essential amino acids, J. Nutr. **83**:115, 1964.

19. Lozy, M., and Hegsted, D.M.: Calculation of the amino acid requirements of children at different ages by the factorial method, Am. J. Clin. Nutr. **28**:1052, 1975.

20. Abernathy, R.P., and Ritchey, S.J.: Position paper on RDA for protein for children, Adv. Med. Biol. **105**:1 1978.

21. Whitehead, P.G.: Protein and energy requirements of young children living in developing countries to allow for catch-up growth after infections, Am. J. Clin. Nutr. **30**:1545, 1977.

22. Committee on Nutrition, American Academy of Pediatrics: Commentary on breastfeeding and infant formula, Pediatrics **57**:278, 1976.

23. John, T.J., and others: Kwashiorkor not associated with poverty, Pediatrics **90**:730, 1977.

24. Chase, H.P., and others: Kwashiorkor in the United States, Pediatrics **66**:972, 1980.

25. Wesson, L.G., and Burt, G.O.: The metabolic rate and respiratory quotients of rats on a fat deficient diet, J. Biol. Chem. **91**:525, 1931.

26. Holman, R.J., Caster, W.O., and Weise, H.F.: The essential fatty acid requirement of infants and the assessment of their dietary intake of linoleate by serum fatty acid analysis, Am. J. Clin. Nutr. **14**:70, 1964.

27. Fomon, S.J.: Infant nutrition, ed. 2, Philadelphia, 1974, W.B. Saunders Co.

28. Committee on Nutrition, American Academy of Pediatrics: Plant fiber intake in the pediatric diet, Pediatrics **67**:572, 1981.

29. Maller, O., and Desor, J.A.: Effect of taste on ingestion by human newborns. In Bosma, J.F., editor: Oral sensation and perception, Publication No. (NIH) 73-546, Bethesda, Md., 1973, Department of Health, Education and Welfare.

30. Hey, E.N., and Katz, G.: Evaporative water loss in the newborn baby, J. Physiol. **200**:605, 1969.

31. Pratt, E.L., Bienvenu, B., and Whyte, M.M.: Concentration of urine by young infants, Pediatrics **1**:181, 1948.

32. Ziegler, E.E., and Fomon, S.J.: Fluid intake, renal solute load, and water balance in infancy, J. Pediatr. **78**:561, 1971.

33. Food and Nutrition Board: Recommended dietary allowances, rev. ed. 9, Washington, D.C., 1980, National Academy of Sciences, National Research Council.

34. Stolley, H., and Schlage, C.: Water balance and water requirement of preschool children, Nutr. Metab. **21**(suppl. 1):15-17, 1977.

35. Arnaud, S.B., and others: Serum parathyroid hormone and blood minerals: interrelationships in normal children, Pediatr. Res. **7**:485, 1973.

36. Committee on Nutrition, American Academy of Pediatrics: Calcium requirements in infancy and childhood, Pediatrics **62**:826, 1978.

37. Shaw, J.C.L.: Evidence for defective skeletal mineralization in low birth weight infants: the absorption of calcium and fat, Pediatrics **57**:16, 1976.

38. Garn, S.M.: The earlier gain and the later loss of cortical bone in nutritional perspective, Springfield, Ill., 1970, Charles C Thomas, Publisher.

39. Christiansen, C., Rödbro, P., and Neilsen, C.T.: Bone mineral content and estimated total body calcium in normal children and adolescents, Scand. J. Clin. Lab. Invest. **35**:507, 1975.

40. Trotter, M., and Hixon, B.B.: Sequential changes in weight, density, and percentage ash weight of human skeleton from the early fetal period through old age, Anat. Rec. **179**:1, 1974.

41. Leitch, I., and Aitken, F.C.: The estimation of calcium requirements: a re-examination, Nutr. Abstr. Rev. **29**:393, 1959.

42. Walker, A.R.P.: The human requirement of calcium: should low intakes be supplemented? Am. J. Clin. Nutr. **25**:518, 1972.

43. Kooh, S.W., and others: Rickets due to calcium deficiency, N. Engl. J. Med. **297**:1264, 1977.

44. Marie, P.J., and others: Histological osteomalacia due to dietary calcium deficiency in children, New. Engl. J. Med. **307**:584, 1982.

45. David, L., and Anast, C.S.: Calcium metabolism in newborn infants, the interrelationship of parathyroid function and calcium, magnesium, and phosphorus metabolsim in normal, "sick," and hypocalcemic newborns, J. Clin. Invest. **54**:287, 1974.

46. Tsang, R.C., and Oh, W.: Neonatal hypocalcemia in low birth weight infants, Pediatrics **45**:773, 1970.

47. Tsang, R.C., and others: Hypocalcemia in infants of diabetic mothers, J. Pediatr. **80**:384, 1972.

48. Snodgrass, G.J.A.I., and others: Interrelations of plasma

calcium, inorganic phosphate, magnesium, and protein over the first week of life, Arch. Dis. Child. **48:**279, 1973.

49. Barltrop, D., and Oppe, T.E.: Dietary factors in neonatal calcium homeostasis, Lancet **2:**1333, 1970.

50. Oppe, T.E., and Redstone, O.: Calcium and phosphorus levels in healthy newborn infants given various types of milk, Lancet **1:**1045, 1968.

51. Tsang, R.C., and others: Possible pathogenic factors in neonatal hypocalcemia of prematurity, J. Pediatr. **82:**423, 1973.

52. Schedewh, H.K., and others: Parathormone and perinatal calcium homeostasis, Pediatr. Res. **13:**1, 1979.

53. Salle, B.L.: Prevention of early neonatal hypocalcemia in low birth weight infants with continuous calcium infusion: effect on serum calcium, phosphorus, magnesium, and circulating immunoreactive parathyroid hormone and calcitonin, Pediatr. Res. **11:**1180, 1977.

54. Moya, M., and Domeneax, E.: Calcium intake in the first five days of life in the low birth weight infant, Arch. Dis. Child. **53:**784, 1978.

55. Gittleman, I.F., and Pincus, J.B.: Influence of diet on the occurrence of hyperphosphatemia and hypocalcemia in the newborn infant, Pediatrics **8:**778, 1951.

56. Gardner, L.: Tetany and parathyroid hyperplasia in the newborn infant: influences of dietary phosphate load, Pediatrics **9:**534, 1952.

57. Pierson, J.D., and Crawford, J.D.: Dietary dependent neonatal hypocalcemia, Am. J. Dis. Child. **123:**472, 1972.

58. Harris, I., and Wilkinson, A.W.: Magnesium depletion in children, Lancet **2:**735, 1971.

59. Laupus, W.E.: Nutrition and nutritional disorders. In vaughan, V.C., McKay, R.J., and Nelson, W.E., editors: Nelson's textbook of pediatrics, ed. 10, Philadelphia, 1975, W.B. Saunders Co.

60. Widdowson, E.M., and Spray, C.M.: Chemical development in utero, Arch. Dis. Child. **26:**205, 1951.

61. Smith, N.J., and Rios, E.: Iron metabolism and iron deficiency, In Schulman, I., editor: Advances in pediatrics, Chicago, 1974, Year Book Medical Publishers, Inc.

62. World Health organization: Nutritional anaemias, Report of a World Health Organization Scientific Group Technical Report Series No. 405, Geneva, 1968, World Health Organization.

63. Hallberg, L., and others: Menstrual blood loss—a population study, Acta Obstet. Gynecol. Scand. **45:**320, 1966.

64. Monsen, E.R., and others: Estimation of available dietary iron, Am. J. Clin. Nutr. **31:**134, 1978.

65. McMillan, J.A.: Iron absorption from human milk, simulated human milk, and proprietary formulas, Pediatrics **60:**896, 1977.

66. Saarinen, U.M.: Iron absorption from breast milk, cow's milk, and iron-supplemented formula: an opportunistic use of changes in total body iron determined by hemoglobin, ferritin and body weight in 132 infants, Pediatr. Res. **13:**143, 1979.

67. Waddell, J.: The bioavailability of iron sources and their utilization in food enrichment, Fed. Proc. **33:**1779, 1974.

68. Cullen, R.W., and Oace, S.M.: Iodine: current status, J. Nutr. Educ. **8:**101, 1976.

69. Widdowson, E.M.: Chemical analysis of the body. In Brozek, J., editor: Human body composition, Oxford, 1965, Pergamon Press, Ltd.

70. Hambidge, K.M., and others: Low levels of zinc in hair, anorexia, poor growth, and hypogeusia in children, Pediatr. Res. **6:**868, 1972.

71. Hambidge, K.M., and others: Zinc nutrition of preschool children in the Denver Headstart Program, Am. J. Clin. Nutr. **29:**734, 1976.

72. MacDonald, L.D., Gibson, R.S., and Miles, J.E.: Changes in hair zinc and copper concentrations of breast fed and bottle fed infants during the first six months, Acta Paediatr. Scand. **71:**785, 1982.

73. Butrimovitz, G.P., and Purdy, W.C.: Zinc nutrition and growth in children, Am. J. Clin. Nutr. **31:**1409, 1978.

74. Schlage, C., and Wortberg, B.: Zinc in the diet of healthy preschool and school children, Acta Paediatr. Scand. **61:**421, 1972.

75. Cavell, P.A., and Widdowson, E.M.: Intakes and excretions of iron, copper and zinc in the neonatal period, Arch. Dis. Child. **39:**496, 1964.

76. Engel, R.W., Miller, R.F., and Price, N.O.: Metabolic patterns of preadolescent children. XIII. Zinc balance. In Prasad, A.S., editor: Zinc metabolism, Springfield, Ill., 1966, Charles C Thomas, Publisher.

77. Tribble, H.M., and Scoular, F.I.: Zinc metabolism of young college women on self-selected diets, J. Nutr. **52:**209, 1954.

78. Underwood, E.J.: Trace elements in human and animal nutrition, New York, 1977, Academic Press, Inc.

79. Johnson, P.E., and Evans, G.W.: Relative zinc availability in human milk, infant formulas, and cow's milk, Am. J. Clin. Nutr. **31:**416, 1978.

80. Picciano, M.F., and Guthrie, H.A.: Copper, iron, and zinc contents of mature human milk, Am. J. Clin. Nutr. **29:**242, 1976.

81. Burch, R.E., Hahn, H.K., and Sullivan, J.F.: Newer aspects of the roles of zinc, manganese, and copper in human nutrition, Clin. Chem. **21:**501, 1975.

82. Dean, H.T., Arnold, F.A., and Elvove, E.: Domestic water and dental caries. V. Additional studies of the relation of fluoride domestic water to dental experience in

4425 white children, Public Health Rep. **57:**1155, 1942.

83. Nizel, A.E.: Nutrition in preventive dentistry: science and practice, ed. 2, Philadelphia, 1983, W.B. Saunders Co.

84. Russell, A.L., and Elvove, E.: Domestic water and dental caries. VII. A study of the fluoride-dental caries relationship in the adult population, Public Health Rep. **66:**1389, 1951.

85. Committee on Nutrition, American Academy of Pediatrics: Fluoride supplementation: revised dosage schedule, Pediatrics **63:**150, 1979.

86. Dirks, O.B., and others: Total and free ionic fluoride in human and cow's milk as determined by gas-liquid chromatography and the fluoride electrode, Caries Res. **8:**181, 1974.

87. Leverett, D.H.: Fluorides and the changing prevalance of dental caries, Science **217:**26, 1982.

88. Galagan, D.J., and Vermillion, J.R.: Determining optimum fluoride concentrations, Public Health Rep. **72:**491, 1957.

89. Baker, H., and others: Vitamin profile of 174 mothers and newborns at parturition, Am. J. Clin. Nutr. **28:**59, 1975.

90. Knott, E.M., Kleiger, S.C., and Schultz, F.W.: Is breast milk adequate in meeting thiamine requirements in infants? J. Pediatr. **22:**43, 1943.

91. Knott, E.M., Kleiger, S.C., and Torres-Bracamonte, F.: Factors affecting the thiamine content of milk, J. Nutr. **25:**49, 1943.

92. Boyden, R.F., and Erikson, S.E.: Metabolic patterns of preadolescent children: thiamine utilization in relation to nitrogen intake, Am. J. Clin. Nutr. **19:**398, 1966.

93. Dick, E.C., and others: Thiamine requirement of eight adolescent boys, as estimated from urinary thiamine excretion, J. Nutr. **66:**173, 1958.

94. Sebrell, W.H., and others: Human riboflavin requirement estimated by urinary excretion of subjects on controlled intake, U.S. Public Health Rep. **56:**510, 1941.

95. Sullivan, L.W., Lubby, A.L., and Streitt, R.R.: Studies of daily requirement of folic acid in infants and the etiology of folate deficiency in goat's milk megaloblastic anemia, Am. J. Clin. Nutr. **18:**311, 1966.

96. Goldsmith, G.A.: Human requirements for vitamin C and its use in clinical medicine, Ann. N.Y. Acad. Sci.**92:**230, 1961.

97. Rajalakshmi, R., Doedhar, A.D., and Ramakrishnan, C.V.: Vitamin C secretion during lactation, Acta Paediatr. Scand. **54:**375, 1965.

98. Abraham, S., and others: Dietary intake finding, United States 1971-1974, DHEW Publication No. (HRA) 77-1647, Washington, D.C., 1977, U.S. Government Printing Office.

99. Centers for Disease Control: Ten-state nutrition survey, DHEW Publication No. (HSM) 72-8130-34, Washington, D.C., 1972, U.S. Department of Health, Education and Welfare, Health Services and Mental Health Administration.

100. Fries, M.E., Christey, B.M., and Suskill, J.A.: Vitamin B_6 status of a group of preschool children, Am. J. Clin. Nutr. **34:**2706, 1981.

101. Committee on Nutrition, American Academy of Pediatrics: Vitamin and mineral supplement needs in normal children in the United States, Pediatrics **66:**1015, 1980.

102. Cook, C.C., and Payne, I.R.: Effect of supplements on the nutrient intake of children, J. Am. Diet. Assoc. **74:**130, 1979.

103. Breskin, M.W., and others: Water soluble vitamins: intakes and indices in children, J. Am. Diet. Assoc. (In press.)

ADDITIONAL READINGS

Alfin-Slater, R.B., and Aftergood, L.: Essential fatty acids reinvestigated, Physiol. Rev. **48:**758, 1968.

Almroth, S.G.: Water requirements of breast-fed infants in a hot climate, Am. J. Clin. Nutr. **31:**1154, 1978.

Ashworth, A.: Energy balance and growth experience in treating children with malnutrition, Kidney Int. **14:**301, 1978.

Beal, V.A.: Calcium and phosphorus in infancy, J. Am. Diet. Assoc. **53:**450, 1968.

Beal, V.A., Meyers, A.J., and McCammon, R.W.: Iron intake, hemoglobin, and physical growth during the first two years of life, Pediatrics **30:**518, 1962.

Berenberg, W., Mandell, F., and Fellers, F.X.: Hazards of skimmed milk, unboiled and boiled, Pediatrics **44:**734, 1969.

Bowering, J., Sanchez, A.M., and Irwin, M.I.: A conspectus of research on iron requirements of man, J. Nutr. **106:**985, 1976.

Bozkowa, K., and Gornicke, B.: Studies on the influence of diets on the metabolism of infants, Bibl. Nutr. Dieta **20:**114, 1974.

Bruck, E., Abal, G., and Aceto, T., Jr.: Pathogenesis and pathophysiology of hypertonic dehydration with diarrhea, Am. J. Dis. Child. **115:**122, 1968.

Burman, D.: Haemoglobin levels in normal infants aged 3 to 24 months, and the effect of iron, Arch. Dis. Child. **47:**261, 1972.

Castile, R.G., Marks, L.J., and Stickler, G.B.: Vitamin D deficiency, rickets, two cases with faulty infant feeding practices, Am. J. Dis. Child. **129:**964, 1975.

Chopra, J.G., Forbes, A.L., and Habicht, J.P.: Protein in the US diet, J. Am. Diet. Assoc. **72:**253, 1978.

Coble, Y.D., Schulert, A.R., and Farid, Z.: Growth and sexual development of male subjects in an Egyptian oasis, Am. J. Clin. Nutr. **18:**421, 1966.

Coble, Y.D., and others: Zinc levels and blood enzyme activities in Egyptian male subjects with retarded growth and sexual development, Am. J. Clin. Nutr. **19:**415, 1966.

Cockburn, F., and others: Neonatal convulsions associated with primary disturbances of calcium, phosphorus, and magnesium metabolism, Arch. Dis. Child. **48:**99, 1973.

Colle, E., Ayoub, E., and Raile, R.: Hypertonic dehydration (hypernatremia): the role of feedings high in solutes, Pediatrics **22:**5, 1958.

Committee on Amino Acids, Food and Nutrition Board: Improvement of protein nutriture, Washington, D.C., 1974, National Academy of Sciences, National Research Council.

Committee on Nutrition, American Academy of Pediatrics: Relationship between iron status and incidence of infection in infancy, Pediatrics **62:**246, 1978.

Committee on Nutrition, American Academy of Pediatrics: Water requirement in relation to osmolar load as it applies to infant feeding, Pediatrics **19:**339, 1957.

Committee on Nutrition, American Academy of Pediatrics: Zinc, Pediatrics **62:**408, 1978.

Coodin, F.J., Gabrielson, I.W., and Addiego, J.E.: Formula fatality, Pediatrics **47:**438, 1971.

Cook, J.D., and others: Serum ferritin as a measure of iron stores in normal subjects, Am. J. Clin. Nutr. **27:**681, 1974.

Crawford, M.A., Hassam, A.G., and Rivers, J.P.W.: Essential fatty acid requirements in infancy, Am. J. Clin. Nutr. **31:**2181, 1978.

Czajka-Narins, D.M., Haddy, T.B., and Kallen, D.J.: Nutritional and social correlates in iron deficiency anemia, Am. J. Clin. Nutr. **31:**955, 1978.

Daily fluoride supplements and dental caries, Nutr. Rev. **36:**329, 1978.

Dirks, O.B.: The relation between the fluoridation of water and dental caries experience, Int. Dent. J. **17:**582, 1967.

Dresher, A.N., Barnett, H.L., and Troupkou, V.: Water balance in infants during water deprivation, Am. J. Dis. Child. **104:**366, 1962.

Evans, E., and Whitty, R.: An assessment of methods used to determine protein quality, World Rev. Nutr. Diet. **32:**1, 1978.

Evans, G.W., and Johnson, P.E.: Determination of zinc availability in foods by the extrinsic label technique, Am. J. Clin. Nutr. **30:**873, 1977.

Fomon, S.J., and others: Calcium and phosphorus balance studies with normal full-term infants fed pooled human milk or various formulas, Am. J. Clin. Nutr. **12:**346, 1963.

Fomon, S.J., and others: Excretion of fat by normal full-term infants fed various milks and formulas, Am. J. Clin. Nutr. **23:**1299, 1970.

Fomon, S.J., and others: Food consumption and growth of normal infants fed milk based formulas, Acta Paediatr. Scand. Suppl. 223, 1971.

Food and Agriculture Organization of the United Nations: Calorie requirements report of the Second Committee on Calorie Requirements, FAO, Italy, 1972.

Food and Nutrition Board: Iodine nurture in the United States, Washington, D.C., 1970, National Academy of Sciences, National Research Council.

Galli, C., Jacini, G., and Pecile, A., editors: Dietary lipids and post natal development, New York, 1973, Raven Press.

Gibson, R.S., Anderson, B.M., and Scythes, C.A.: Regional differences in hair and zinc concentrations: a possible effect of water hardness, Am. J. Clin. Nutr. **37:**37, 1983.

Gregor, J.L., and others: Calcium, magnesium, phosphorus, copper, and magnesium balance in adolescent females, Am. J. Clin. Nutr. **31:**117, 1978.

Hahn, P.: Lipid metabolism and nutrition in the prenatal and postnatal period. In Winick, M., editor: Nutrition and development, New York, 1972, John Wiley & Sons, Inc.

Hallberg, L., and Solvell, L.: Absorption of hemoglobin iron in man, Acta Med. Scand. **181:**335, 1967.

Harvey, D.R., Cooper, L.V., and Stevens, J.F.: Plasma calcium and magnesium in newborn babies, Arch. Dis. Child. **45:**506, 1970.

Hegsted, D.M.: Protein needs and possible modifications of the American diet, J. Am. Diet. Assoc. **68:**317, 1976.

Hegsted, D.M.: Theoretical estimates of protein requirements of children, J. Am. Diet. Assoc. **33:**225, 1957.

Henkin, R.I., and others: Idiopathic hypogeusia with dysgeusia, hyposmia and dysosmia: a new syndrome, J.A.M.A. **217:**434, 1971.

Hennon, D.K., Stookey, G.K., and Muhler, J.C.: Prevalence and distribution of dental caries in preschool children, J. Am. Dent. Assoc. **79:**1405, 1969.

Hennon, D.K., Stookey, G.K., and Muhler, J.C.: Prophylaxis of dental caries: relative effectiveness of chewable fluoride preparations with and without added vitamins, J. Pediatr. **80:**1018, 1972.

Herbert, V.: The five possible causes of all nutrient deficiency: illustrated by deficiencies of vitamins B_{12} and folic acid, Am. J. Clin. Nutr. **26:**77, 1973.

Hoglund, S., and Reizenstein, P.: Studies in iron absorption. V. Effect of gastrointestinal factors on iron absorption, Blood **34:**496, 1969.

Horwitt, M.K.: Vitamin E: a reexamination, Am. J. Clin. Nutr. **29:**569, 1976.

Hunter, R.E., and Smith, N.J.: Hemoglobin and hematocrit values in iron deficiency in infancy, J. Pediatr. **81:**710, 1972.

Irwin, M.I., and Hegsted, D.M.: A conspectus of research on amino acid requirements of man, J. Nutr. **101:**535, 1971.

Irwin, M.I., and Hegsted, D.M.: A conspectus of research on protein requirements of man, J. Nutr. **101**:385, 1971.

Keen, J.H.: Significance of hypocalcaemia in neonatal convulsions, Arch. Dis. Child. **44**:356, 1969.

Kidd, P.S., and others: Sources of dietary iodine, J. Am. Diet. Assoc. **65**:420, 1974.

Kimber, C., and Weintraub, L.R.: Malabsorption of iron secondary to iron deficiency, N. Engl. J. Med. **279**:453, 1968.

Lindquist, B.: Nutritional needs in preschool and school age. In Blix, G., editor: Nutrition in preschool and school age, Symposium of the Swedish Nutrition Foundation VII, Uppsala, 1969, Almqvist & Wiksell.

London, W.T., Vought, R.L., and Brown, F.A.: Bread—a dietary source of large quantities of iodine, N. Engl. J. Med. **273**:381, 1965.

London, W.T., and others: Epidemiologic and metabolic studies of a goiter endemic in eastern Kentucky, J. Clin. Endocrinol. Metab. **25**:1091, 1965.

Malvaux, P., Beckers, C., and De Visscher, M.: Iodine balance studies in non-goitrous children and adolescents on low-iodine intake, J. Clin. Endocrinol. Metab. **29**:79, 1969.

Martinez-Torres, C., Renzi, M., and Layrisse, M.: Iron absorption by humans from hemosiderin and ferritin: further studies, J. Nutr. **106**:128, 1976.

McBean, L.D., and Speckman, E.W.: A recognition of the interrelationships of calcium with various dietary components, Am. J. Clin. Nutr. **27**:603, 1974.

McCormick, D.B.: Biotin, Nutr. Rev. **33**:97, 1975.

McWhirter, W.R.: Plasma tocopherol in infants and children, Acta Paediatr. Scand. **65**:446, 1975.

Meiners, C.R., and others: The relationship of zinc to protein utilization in the pre-adolescent child, Am. J. Clin. Nutr. **30**:879, 1977.

Monsen, E.R., and Cook, J.D.: Food iron absorption in human subjects. IV. The effects of calcium and phosphate salts on the absorption of nonheme iron, Am. J. Clin. Nutr. **29**:1142, 1976.

Moran, J.R., and Green, H.L.: The B vitamins and vitamin C in human nutrition. I. General considerations and obligatory B vitamins. II. Conditional B vitamins and vitamin C, Am. J. Dis. Child. **133**:308, 1979.

Murphy, E.W., Willis, B.W., and Watt, B.K.: Provisional tables on the zinc content of food, J. Am. Diet. Assoc. **66**:345, 1975.

Oaski, F., and Landaw, S.A.: Inhibition of iron absorption from human milk by baby food, Am. J. Dis. Child. **134**:459, 1980.

Owen, G.M., and others: Nutritional status of preschool children: plasma vitamin A, J. Pediatr. **78**:1042, 1971.

Pecoud, A., Donzel, P., and Schelling, J.L.: Effect of food stuffs on the absorption of zinc sulfate, Clin. Pharmacol. Ther. **17**:469, 1975.

Rivlin, R.S., editor: Riboflavin, New York, 1975, Plenum Publishing Corp.

Soderhjelm, L., Weise, H.F., and Holman, R.T.: The role of polyunsaturated fatty acids in human nutrition and metabolism, Prog. Chem. Fats Other Lipids **9**:555, 1970.

Srikantia, S.G.: Human vitamin A deficiency, World Rev. Nutr. Diet. **20**:184, 1975.

Sterner, R.T., and Price, W.R.: Restricted riboflavin: within subject behavioral effects in humans, Am. J. Clin. Nutr. **26**:150, 1973.

Van der Horst, R.L.: Scurvy in a 4 year old child, Am. J. Dis. Child. **126**:712, 1973.

Wait, B., Blair, R., and Roberts, L.J.: Energy intakes of well nourished children and adolescents, Am. J. Clin. Nutr. **22**:1383, 1969.

Williams, M.L., and others: Calcium and fat absorption in neonatal period, Am. J. Clin. Nutr. **23**:1322, 1970.

Winberg, J.: Determination of renal concentration capacity in infants and children without renal disease, Acta Paediatr. Scand. **48**:318, 1959.

Ziegler, E.E., and others: Nitrogen balance studies with normal children, Am. J. Clin. Nutr. **30**:939, 1977.

Infant Feeding and Nutrition

4

At no time in the life cycle will as many changes in relation to food and nutrient intake be observed as during the first year of life. Influenced by a rapid but declining rate of physical growth and maturation of the oral, fine, and gross motor skills and relationships established with their parents, infants prepared at birth to suck liquids from a nipple are at 1 year of age making attempts to feed themselves table food with culturally defined utensils. The need for nutrients and energy depends on the infant's requirement for maintenance, physical growth, and energy expenditure. The foods offered to infants reflect culturally accepted practice. Infants' acceptance of food is influenced by neuromotor maturation and by their interactions with their parents. A variety of combinations of foods and milks will be consumed by well-nourished children at any month during infancy.

MATURATION OF DIGESTION AND ABSORPTION

The newborn is a functionally immature organism. Although the normal neonate is well prepared to digest and absorb human milk and cow's milk or soy formulas at birth, maturation of many of the enzyme systems occurs during and after the first year.

The stomach capacity of infants increases from 10 to 20 ml at birth to 200 ml by 12 months of age. The rate of emptying depends on the size and composition of the meal. During the first weeks after birth, gastric acidity decreases. For the first few months it remains lower than in the adult.

Proteolytic activity of duodenal juice is as great in infancy as in adulthood. However, the total quantity of protein that can be digested per hour is less during infancy and childhood and increases with age.[1]

A greater percentage of fat is absorbed in later life than in infancy. Approximately 95% of ingested fat is absorbed by adults. Newborns absorb approximately 85% to 90% of the fat provided by human milk. Many infants absorb less than 70% of the fat in cow's milk.[2] Mixtures of vegetable oils in commercially prepared infant formulas are well absorbed, although the reason for the degree of absorption of those containing oleo oil remains unclear.[2] Absorption of fat begins to reach adult levels between 6 and 9 months of age.

Pancreatic lipase activity is low in the newborn, especially the premature infant. The bile acid pool, although present, is reduced. When compared with an adult on the basis of body surface, the newborn, although able to synthesize bile, has a bile acid pool one half that of the adult.[3]

During infancy the position the saturated fatty acid occupies on the glycerol molecule influences absorption. Stearic acid is poorly absorbed in any position. Free palmitic acid hydrolyzed from positions 1 and 3 is poorly absorbed, whereas palmitic acid, which occupies position 2 on the glycerol molecule, remains as a monoglyceride and appears to be well absorbed.[4]

Maltase, isomaltase, and sucrase activity reach adult levels by 28 to 32 weeks gestation. Lactase, present at low levels at 28 weeks gestation, increases near term and reaches adult levels at birth.[5] Salivary and pancreatic amylase are low during the first months after birth. Concentrations of salivary amylase rise to adult values between 6 months and 1 year of age.[6] Concentrations of pancreatic amylase increase from birth through the preschool years. Hadorn and others[7] found that output of amylase per kg in children less than 6 months of age was two to four times less than in children 1 year of age. There also appears to be an increase in output of amylase from preschool to school-age years.

Because pancreatic amylase is low in infancy, the early introduction of large quantities of starches may result in loss of calories provided by those foods in the stools or in abnormally loose stools. A 4-month-old infant who failed to gain normally and who had copious, loose, frequent stools as a result of absent amylase activity has been reported by Lillibridge and Townes.[8] When starch was removed from the diet, the infant experienced catch-up growth despite a reduction in calorie intake. There was improvement in stool consistency, volume, and frequency. At 12 months of age the child had low amylase activity but was able to consume a completely liberalized diet and maintain normal growth.

DeVizia and others[9] concluded from balance studies on infants 1 to 3 months of age who were fed cooked wheat, corn, tapioca, potato, and rice starch and on children 1 to 2 years of age who were fed cooked wheat and potato starch that although pancreatic amylases are low in infancy there may be sufficient amounts to digest 10 to 23 gm of dietary starch per day in infants 1 to 3 months of age or that digestion of starch may be provided at least in part by the activity of maltase, which splits starch and dextrins directly into glucose. Fomon[2]

suggested, however, that bacterial digestion of starch in the colon could explain the absence of starch in the feces. He believes increases in blood glucose after starch feeding are more reliable for determining digestion of starch.

Measurements of blood glucose levels of infants 2½ to 3½ days of age who were fed starch orally showed only small increases in blood sugar levels that were delayed in timing of occurrence when compared with rises in blood glucose levels of the same infants fed glucose, maltose, and detrimaltose.[10] Husband, Husband, and Mallinson[11] showed that starch empties more rapidly from the stomachs of infants 4 to 60 days of age than does an equal amount of glucose. A slow but sustained rise in the blood glucose level over 2½ hours suggested that starch hydrolysis was slow.

RENAL FUNCTION

The newborn has a functionally immature kidney. The ratio of glomerular surface area to tubular volume in an infant's kidney is high, compared with the kidney of an adult.[12] The glomerular filtration rate is low. The concentrating capacity of some neonates has been reported to be as limited as 700 mOsm/liter, and for others it is as great as that of older children and adults, 1200 to 1400 mOsm/liter. Infants, therefore, are vulnerable to water imbalance.[13,14]

MILK IN THE INFANT'S DIET

That human milk from adequately nourished lactating mothers offers nutritional, immunological, and psychosocial benefits to infants has never been questioned. Even so, the incidence of breast-feeding of the newborn infant fell to 18% in 1966. Renewed interest in promoting breast-feeding and supporting the lactating mother caused the incidence of breast-feeding during hospitalization to increase to 57.6% in 1981. However, many infants are breast fed for only a few months. At 3 to 4 months of age, 35.2% were breast fed; by 5 to 6 months of age, only 26.8% of infants continued to be breast fed in 1981. The incidence of breast-feeding in the hospital was highest among mothers who had some college education, were not employed outside the home, and who had just delivered their first infant. It was higher in upper-income families than among those with lower incomes. Mothers from higher-income families maintained a higher incidence of breast-feeding when their infants were 6 months of age. More multiparous mothers had maintained breast-feeding than primiparous mothers.[15]

Most normal full-term infants who are not breast fed receive a cow's milk–base formula; very few receive fresh cow's milk. Milk-free formulas such as soy, meat base, or a hydrolyzed casein formula are fed to infants who do not tolerate milk.

Colostrum and Transitional Milk

For the first few days after birth, the breast-fed infant ingests a yellowish, transparent fluid called colostrum. Human colostrum contains more protein but less fat, carbohydrate, and energy than does mature human milk. Concentrations of sodium, potassium, and chloride are greater in colostrum than in later milk. Between the third and sixth day colostrum changes to a milk that, compared with mature milk, has a high protein content. By the tenth day the breast-fed infant receives mature milk.

Comparison of Nutrient Compositions of Human Milk and Cow's Milk

Nutrients secreted in human milk vary and reflect individual biochemical variability among women, the diet consumed, the stage of lactation, and the length of time the mother has breast fed.[16] When milk is analyzed for nutrient content, the time of day the milk was expressed and whether foremilk or hindmilk is analyzed influenced its nutrient composition. Therefore, wide ranges of many vitamins and minerals have been reported. Table 4-1 lists average nutrients contained in pooled human

Table 4-1. Nutrient content of human milk and cow's milk

Constituent (per liter)	Human milk	Cow's milk
Energy (kcal)	690	660
Protein (gm)	9	35
Fat (gm)	40	38
Lactose (gm)	68	49
Vitamins		
Vitamin A (IU)	1898	1025
Vitamin D (activity)	40	14
Vitamin E (IU)	3.2	0.4
Vitamin K (μg)	34	170
Thiamine (μg)	150	370
Riboflavin (μg)	380	1700
Niacin (mg)	1.7	0.9
Pyridoxine (μg)	130	460
Folic acid (μg)	41-84.6	2.9-68
Cobalamine (μg)	.5	4
Ascorbic acid (μg)	44	17

Data from Hambreaus, L.: Pediatr. Clin. North Am. **24**:17, 1977; Blanc, B.: World Rev. Nutr. Diet. **36**:1, 1981; Jensen, R.G., Haggerty, M.M., and McMahon, K.E.: Am. J. Clin. Nutr. **31**:990, 1978; Jansson, L., Akesson, B., and Holmberg, L.: Am. J. Clin. Nutr. **34**:8, 1981; Reeve, L.E., Chesney, R.W., and DeLuca, H.F.: Am. J. Clin. Nutr. **36**:122, 1982; Cooperman, J.M., and others: Am. J. Clin. Nutr. **36**:576, 1982; Keimpulainen, J., and Vuori, E.: Am. J. Clin. Nutr. **33**:2299, 1980; Siimes, M.A., Vuori, E., and Kuitunen, P.: Acta Paediatr. Scand. **68**:29, 1979; Vuori, E.: Acta Paediatr. Scand. **68**:571, 1979; Vuori, E., and Kuitunen, P.: Acta Paediatr. Scand. **68**:33, 1978; and Nayman, R., and others: Am. J. Clin. Nutr. **32**:1279, 1979.

milk and minimum federal standards for homogenized milk.

Both human and cow's milk are complex liquids containing more than 200 components in the fat- and water-soluble fractions. There are, however, considerable differences in the quantity and availability of the nutrients to the human infant in the two milks. Differences are thought to reflect species specific nutrient needs to support individual maintenance and growth needs of the offspring. This hypothesis is further supported by the fact that

Table 4-1. Nutrient content of human milk and cow's milk—cont'd

Constituent (per liter)	Human milk	Cow's milk
Minerals		
Calcium (mg)	241-340	1200
Phosphorus (mg)	150	920
Sodium (mg)	160	506
Potassium (mg)	530	1570
Chlorine (mg)	400	1028
Magnesium (mg)	38-41	120
Sulfur (mg)	140	300
Iron (mg)*	0.56-0.3	0.5
Iodine (mg)	200	80
Manganese (μg)+	5.9-4.0	20-40
Copper (μg)	60	110
Zinc (mg)‡	4-.5	3-5
Selenium (μg)	20	5-50
Fluoride (mg)	0.05	0.03-0.1
Chromium (μg)	4	2

*Median values at 2 weeks and 5 months of lactation.
+Median values at 2 weeks and 5 months of lactation, after which time the manganese content of human milk tends to increase.
‡Median values at 2 weeks and 37 weeks of lactation.

there are changes in the nutrient composition of human milk during lactation. For example, the concentration of iron, copper, and zinc decline between 2 weeks and 5 to 9 months of lactation.[16,17] Protein concentration decreases from the first week through 6 to 9 months of age and then rises slightly, reflecting the infant's declining needs during declining rates of growth.[18]

Human milk and cow's milk provide similar amounts of water and approximately the same quantity of energy.[19] The nutrient sources of the energy are, however, different. Protein supplies approximately 7% of the calories in human milk and 20% of the calories in cow's milk; the carbohydrate lactose supplies approximately 42% of the calories in human milk and 20% of the calories in cow's milk. The percentage of calories supplied by fat is similar in both milks.

The protein content of human milk approximates 0.9 gm/100 ml, compared with 3.5 gm/100 ml in cow's milk. Nonprotein nitrogen accounts for 25% of total nitrogen in human milk, 5% of total nitrogen in cow's milk. During lactation protein levels decrease. Anderson, Atkinson, and Bryan[20] noted a linear decrease in protein nitrogen content of milk during the first 4 weeks of lactation. Chavalittamrong and others[21] found a decrease from 1.56 gm/100 ml at 1 to 7 days to .60 gm/100 ml at 180 to 270 days, then a gradual increase at 270 days in milk of the mothers.

Casein and whey constitute the protein in both milks. Amounts of whey protein are similar in each. Cow's milk contains six to seven times as much casein as does human milk, and differences in the casein/whey ratios of the two milks are great. The casein/whey ratio of human milk is 40:60, whereas the casein/whey ratio of cow's milk is 82:18. β-Lactoglobulin, the dominant whey protein in cow's milk, is absent in human milk, in which α-lactoglobulin and lactoferrin are the predominant whey proteins.

During digestion in the stomach the protein of milk mixes with hydrochloric acid. The result of this process is the formation of curds from the casein and calcium and of a liquid that contains the whey. Because of its lower casein content, human milk forms a soft, flocculent, easy-to-digest curd in the infant's stomach. The increased casein content of fresh cow's milk causes it to form a tough, cheesy, hard-to-digest curd. Homogenization, boiling, and dilution of cow's milk modify the curd and prevent the formation of the hard curds in the stomach so that it is easily digested by the infant.

The amino acid composition of human milk meets the needs of the neonate with an immature enzyme system, whereas that of cow's milk may be inappropriate. The newborn has a limited ability to metabolize phenylalanine to tyrosine. Human milk has a low content of tyrosine and phenylalanine compared with cow's milk. Cystathionase, an enzyme that catalyzes the transulfuration of methionine to cystine, is low in the neonate. Taurine and cystine are present in much higher concentrations in human milk than in cow's milk.

The total fat content of human milk and cow's milk is similar. Saturated fatty acids predominate in cow's milk. The fatty acid pattern of human milk resembles that of the maternal diet. About 98% of the fat in human milk is triglycerides in which palmitic acid is in position 2, enhancing its absorbability. The average content of linoleic acid is 10% of fat, but ranges of 1.0% to 43.0% have been reported. Linoleic acid provides an average of 4% of the calories in human milk but only 1% of the calories in cow's milk. The cholesterol content of human milk averages 20 mg/100 ml, but there is considerable variability. Values up to 47 mg/100 ml have been reported. Cow's milk contains 7 to 25 mg/100 ml of cholesterol.[22] Diurnal variations occur in human milk, the fat content being higher in early mornings. The content of short-chain fatty acids is greater in cow's milk. Human hindmilk has a higher percentage of fat than foremilk.

Both cow's milk and human milk contain lipoprotein lipase in the cream fraction that is stimulated by serum and inhibited by bile salts. Human milk contains an additional lipase that is stimulated by bile salts and contributes significantly to the hydrolysis of milk triglycerides. These enzymes contribute significantly to a higher percentage absorption of human milk fat as compared with butter fat.

The concentration of lactose is greater in human milk than in cow's milk. This nutrient is incorporated into galactolipids in the brain and spinal cord. Trace amounts of glucose, galactose, glucosamines, and other nitrogen-containing carbohydrates are also present in both milks. Human milk contains L-bifidus factor, a nitrogen-containing carbohydrate, in concentrations 40 times greater than in cow's milk. This carbohydrate is required by the bacteria *Lactobacillus* for growth.

Human milk from adequately nourished mothers is a reliable source of fat-soluble vitamins A and E and the water-soluble vitamins. Human milk contains 40 to 50 IU/liter of vitamin D activity.

Although human milk does provide calcium and phosphorus to the neonate in a form usable by the neonate without the presence of vitamin D, the provision of other sources of vitamin D becomes increasingly important as the infant grows older.[23]

Cow's milk is a reliable source of vitamin A and the B vitamins. It contains less vitamin E and more vitamin K than human milk. Most dairies fortify homogenized, 2%, and nonfat milk with vitamin D. Evaporated milk that is reconstituted with equal amounts of water is fortified with 400 IU/quart. The milk is low in vitamin C.

Cow's milk contains four times as much vitamin K as human milk. In breast-fed infants the prothrombin level is 20% to 50% of that of the adult in the first few days. Hemorrhagic disease of the newborn may occur if vitamin K is not given. A prophylactic dose of .5 to 1.0 mg is usually given to breast-fed infants at birth.

The increase in home deliveries with subsequent breast-feeding has caused concern. O'Connor and others[24] describe two infants delivered at home who were not given vitamin K and required hospitalization at 4 to 5 weeks because of vitamin K deficiency. Women who plan to have home deliveries should be counseled about the infant's need for vitamin K prior to delivery.

Inadequate amounts of water-soluble nutrients in the maternal diet will be reflected in the milk produced for the infant. Infantile beriberi is well known in East Asians when maternal intakes of thiamine are inadequate. Vitamin B_{12} deficiency has been reported in a breast-fed infant whose mother had been a vegan for 8 years before her pregnancy and in the infant of a mother who had pernicious anemia.[25] Supplementation of a folate-deficient woman resulted in a prompt increase in her milk folate.[26]

The mineral content of cow's milk is several times greater than that of human milk. Cow's milk contains more than three times as much calcium and six times as much phosphorus as does human milk. The high phosphate load and calcium/phosphate ratio have been implicated as etiological factors of late hypocalcemic tetany of the neonate.

The iron content of human milk declines from .5 to .3 mg/100 ml between 2 weeks and 5 months of age; that of cow's milk remains at .5 mg/100 ml. It has been reported that 5- to 7-month-old infants absorbed 49% of the iron in human milk but only 10% of iron in cow's milk.[27] However, Garry and others[28] believe that exclusively breast-fed infants are not receiving sufficient iron to meet their needs after 3 months of age. They found that as infants adjust to their feedings they experience a reduction in percentage of iron retained. They noted that exclusively breast-fed infants, regardless of whether they had received iron supplements or been solely breast fed, had greater total body iron than infants fed formula with or without iron at 3 months of age. However, exclusively breast-fed infants who did not receive iron supplements after 3 months experienced a negative total body iron increment during 4 to 6 months of age, utilizing their reserves. They think that if no additional source of iron is given breast-fed infants after 6 months of age, they will rapidly deplete their reserves.

Human milk contains less zinc than does cow's milk. In cow's milk zinc binds strongly to casein, but very little is bound to the whey. The zinc-binding capacity of human milk protein is assumed to be minimal. As the stomach acid secretion is low in early infancy, ingested zinc may not be released from casein or its curd, making zinc from cow's milk inaccessible to infants.[29] Studies suggest that the bioavailability of zinc in human milk is 59%, in cow's milk 43% to 51%.[30]

Plasma fluoride is poorly transferred to breast milk, and breast-fed infants receive almost no fluoride.

The high protein and mineral content of cow's milk places a much greater osmolar load on the kidney of the infant and obligates a greater amount of water for excretion. The margin of safety is smaller. Cow's milk may not supply sufficient amounts of water when the environmental temperature is high. Neither milk may provide adequate amounts of water when requirements are increased by fever, vomiting, or diarrhea.

Anti-infective Characteristics of Human Milk

In addition to nutrients, human colostrum and milk contain antibodies, enzymes, and other factors absent or present in only minute amounts in cow's milk—factors that provide infants with protection against enteric infections.[31] Table 4-2 gives the antibacterial and antiviral factors that are present in breast milk.

Lactobacillus microorganisms in the gastrointestinal tract, whose growth is dependent on L-bifidus factor, produce acetic and lactic acids. The resulting acidic environment interferes with the growth of certain pathogenic organisms such as *Escherichia coli* and *Shigella* and provides a medium in which lysozymes are stable. Lysozymes exert their effect by destroying bacterial cell membranes after the organisms have been inactivated by peroxides and ascorbic acid also present in human colostrum and milk.

Immunoglobulins (antibodies) to many different types of organisms, including pertussis, staphylococci, *E. coli,* and *Salmonella,* have been identified in colostrum and, in smaller amounts, in mature human milk. Since these immunoglobulins are not absorbed, they exert an effect only through the gastrointestinal tract. Infants who are breast fed by mothers with high titers of antibodies to poliomyelitis are resistant to infection with orally administered polio vaccine. It is, however, believed that human milk does not completely inhibit the effectiveness of the vaccine. Lactoperoxidase, an enzyme present in human milk and saliva, aids in killing streptococci and may act on other organisms.

Large amounts of lactoferrin and small amounts of transferrin (iron-binding proteins) in human milk exert a bacterial effect. Lactoferrin is less than 50% saturated with iron. In fact, Fransson and Lönnerdahl[32] found the iron saturation of lactoferrin to be only 1% to 4%. It is bacteriostatic because

Table 4-2. Antibacterial and antiviral factors in breast milk

Factor	Shown in Vitro to be Active Against
Antibacterial factors	
L. bifidus growth factor	Enterobacteriaceae, enteric pathogens
Secretory IgA	*E. coli*, *E. coli* enterotoxin, *C. tetani*, *C. diphtheriae*, *D. pneumoniae*, *Salmonella*, *Shigella*
C1-C9	Effect not known
Lactoferrin	*E. coli*, *C. albicans*
Lactoperoxidase	*Streptococcus*, *Pseudomonas*, *E. coli*, *S. typhimurium*
Lysozyme	*E. coli*, *Salmonella*, *M. lysodeikticus*
Lipid (unsaturated fatty acid)	*S. aureus*
Milk cells	By phagocytosis: *E. coli*, *C. albicans*
	By sensitized lymphocytes: *E. coli*
Antiviral factors	
Secretory IgA	Polio types 1,2,3, Coxsackie types A9, B3, B5; ECHO types 6, 9; Semliki Forest virus, Ross River virus, rotavirus
Lipid (unsaturated fatty acids and monoglycerides)	Herpes simplex; Semliki Forest virus, influenza, dengue, Ross River virus, Murine leukemia virus, Japanese B encephalitis virus
Nonimmunoglobulin macromolecules	Herpes simplex; vesicular stomatitis virus
Milk cells	Rotavirus; induced interferon active against Sendai virus; sensitized lymphocytes? phagocytosis

Modified from Welsh, J.K., and May, J.T.: J. Pediatr. **94:**1, 1979.

it deprives bacteria of the iron-containing environment necessary for their normal cell growth.[31]

Because of the presence of these and other anti-infective factors, infants who receive human milk have a lesser incidence of gastrointestinal and other infections than those fed other milks. This is true of those who live in well-santized environments as well as those who live under constant risk of environmental contamination.[33]

Antiallergenic Characteristics of Human Milk

The intestine of the newborn infant is permeable to macromolecules. Secretory IgA in human milk promotes closure of the gut and, therefore, decreases the permeability of allergens. Cow's milk protein β-lactoglobulin and serum bovine albumin are the most common allergens in infancy.

Breast-feeding is the best prophylaxis for food allergy during infancy.

Modified Cow's Milk Formula for Infants

Modified, commercially manufactured formulas prepared from nonfat cow's milk are readily available and are generously used for feeding in early infancy. Cow's milk is modified to reduce the solute load by reduction of the protein and mineral content. The curd tension is reduced by homogenization and heat treatment to produce an easily digested protein.

Three manufacturers (Wyeth, Mead Johnson, and Ross Laboratories) combine demineralized whey with nonfat milk to produce a product with a whey/casein ratio similar to that of human milk. Minerals removed from the whey by electrodialysis

Table 4-3. Nutrient levels of infant formulas (per 100 kcal)

Nutrient	CON 1976 recommendations		
	Minimum		Maximum
Protein (gm)	1.8		4.5
Fat			
(gm)	3.3		6.0
(% cal)	30.0		54.0
Essential fatty acids (linoleate)			
(% cal)	3.0		—
(mg)	300.0		—
Vitamins			
A (IU)	250.0	(75 μg)*	750.0 (225 μg)*
D (IU)	40.0		100.0
K (μg)	4.0		—
E (IU)	0.3	(with 0.7 IU/gm lin- oleic acid)	—
C (ascorbic acid) (mg)	8.0		—
B_1 (thiamine) (μg)	40.0		—
B_2 (riboflavin) (μg)	60.0		—
B_6 (pyridoxine) (μg)	35.0	(with 15 μg/gm of protein in formula)	—
B_{12} (μg)	0.15		—
Niacin			
(μg)	250.0		—
(μg equiv)	—		—
Folic acid (μg)	4.0		—
Pantothenic acid (μg)	300.0		—
Biotin (μg)	1.5		—
Choline (mg)	7.0		—
Inositol (mg)	4.0		—
Minerals			
Calcium (mg)	50.0+		—
Phosphorus (mg)	25.0+		—
Magnesium (mg)	6.0		—
Iron (mg)	0.15		—
Iodine (μg)	5.0		—
Zinc (mg)	0.5		—
Copper (μg)	60.0		—
Manganese (μg)	5.0		—
Sodium (mg)	20.0	(6 mEq)‡	60.0 (17 mEq)‡
Potassium (mg)	80.0	(14 mEq)‡	200.0 (34 mEq)‡
Chloride (mg)	55.0	(11mEq)‡	150.0 (29 mEq)‡

From Committee on Nutrition, American Academy of Pediatrics: Pediatrics **57**(2):278, 1976. Copyright American Academy of Pediatrics, 1976.
*Retinol equivalents.
+Calcium to phosphorus ratio must be no less than 1.1 nor more than 2.0.
‡Milliequivalent for 670 kcal/L of formula.

Table 4-4. Nutrient content of commercially available cow's milk–base formula

	Similac	Similac with Whey	Enfamil	S.M.A.
Nutrient source				
Protein	Casein	Lactoalbumin, casein	Reduced mineral whey, casein	Demineralized whey, casein
Fat	Soy oil, coconut oil, corn oil	Soy oil, coconut oil	Soy oil, coconut oil	Oleo; soybean, safflower, and coconut oils
Carbohydrate	Lactose	Lactose	Lactose	Lactose
Nutrients per 100/ml—Normal Dilution				
Energy (kcal)	68	68	67	67
Protein (gm)	1.5	1.5	1.5	1.5
Fat (gm)	3.6	3.6	3.8	3.6
Carbohydrate (gm)	7.2	7.2	6.9	7.2
Vitamin A (IU)	25	25	21	26
Vitamin D (IU)	40	40	42	42
Vitamin E (IU)	2	2	2	1
Vitamin C (mg)	5.5	5.5	5.5	5.8
Thiamine (μg)	65	65	53	71
Riboflavin (μg)	10	10	11	11
Niacin (mg) (equiv.)	.7	.7	.8	1.0
Pyridoxine (μg)	40	40	42	40
Vitamin B_{12} (μg)	.15	.15	.16	.11
Folic acid (μg)	5	10	10.5	5.3
Calcium (mg)	51	40	46	44
Phosphorus (mg)	39	30	31.7	33
Magnesium (mg)	4	5	4	5
Iron (mg)	tr.	1.2	tr.	tr.
Zinc (mg)	.5	.5	.5	.37
Copper (μg)	60	60	63.4	48
Iodine (μg)	10	10	10.5	7

are added to concentrations similar to that of human milk, resulting in simulated human milk.

Combinations of vegetable oils, a high percentage of which are absorbed in infancy, are added, and carbohydrate is added to increase the caloric concentration to approximately that of human milk and cow's milk. Vitamins and minerals are added. Formulas are marketed both with and without ferrous sulfate in amounts that provide 12 mg of iron/quart.

Formulas for Infants

The Committee on Nutrition of the American Academy of Pediatrics, concerned about the composition of proprietary infant formulas, issued a policy statement on standards for these products.[34] These standards are based on the composition of milk from a healthy mother and are given in Table 4-3. The minimum amount for each nutrient is close to that of human milk and thus is the preferable quantity. The maximum amount is given for

Table 4-5. Nutrient content of soy formulas and other milk substitutes for infants

	Prosobee	Isomil	Meat-base Formula	Nutramigen	Progestimil
Nutrient Source					
Protein	Soy protein	Soy protein	Beef hearts	Casein hydrolysate	Casein hydrolysate
Fat	Soy oil	Coconut oil, soy oil	Sesame oil	Corn oil	Corn oil, medium-chain triglycerides
Carbohydrate	Corn syrup solids	Sucrose, Corn syrup solids	Modified tapioca, sucrose	Modified tapioca, sucrose	Corn syrup solids, modified tapioca starch
Nutrients per 100 ml—Normal Dilution					
Energy (kcal)	67	68	66	67	68
Protein (gm)	2.0	2.0	2.6	2.2	1.9
Carbohydrate (gm)	3.6	3.6	3.2	2.6	2.7
Vitamin A (IU)	21	25	17	17	21
Vitamin D (IU)	42	40	39	42	42
Vitamin E (IU)	1	2	.7	1	2
Vitamin C (mg)	5.5	5.5	5.7	5.5	5.5
Thiamine (μg)	52.8	40	55	53	53
Riboflavin (μg)	63.4	60	95	63.4	63.4
Niacin (mg) (equiv.)	.8	.9	.4	.8	.8
Pyridoxine (μg)	42	40	80	42	42
Vitamin B_{12} (μg)	.2	.04	.8	.2	.2
Folic acid (μg)	10.5	10	2.5	10.5	10.5
Calcium (mg)	63	70	95	64	64
Phosphorus (mg)	50	50	63	48	48
Magnesium (mg)	7.4	5	3.8	7.4	7.4
Iron (mg)	1.3	1.2	1.3	1.3	1.3
Zinc (mg)	.5	.5	.3	.4	.4
Copper (μg)	63	50	40	63	63
Iodine (μg)	6.8	10	3.2	4.8	4.8

formulas intended for low birth weight or sick infants who take less formula and, therefore, need the higher nutrient content.

Nutrients provided by commonly used formula preparations are given in Table 4-4.

Hypoallergenic Formulas

The most commonly used products for infants who have conditions that contraindicate the use of cow's milk are the soy milks. The most frequently used formulas are constructed of protein isolated from soy meal fortified with methionine, corn syrup and/or sucrose, and soy or vegetable oils to which vitamins and minerals have been added. The trypsin inhibitor in raw soybean meal is inactivated during heat processing. The goitrogenic effect of soy is diminished by heating and the addition of iodine.

Other formulas are marketed for infants who do not tolerate either soy or cow's milk. Nutramigen, prepared from a casein hydrolysate and corn oil, and Progestimil, which contains a casein hydrolysate and medium-chain triglycerides, are commonly used when infants do not tolerate cow or soy milk. A meat-base formula prepared from strained beef hearts, tapioca, and sucrose is also available for use in such cases. Those formulas made from casein hydrolysate have an unpleasant odor and taste and are rarely accepted by infants if not introduced before 8 to 9 months of age. Meat-base formula has a brownish color not pleasant to many mothers. The composition of non-cow's milk–base formulas is given in Table 4-5.

Feeding infants formulas made from recipes that have not been proved to support adequate nutrition should be strongly discouraged. Malnutrition has been observed in infants fed a barley water, corn syrup, and whole milk formula.[35] Kwashiorkor has been reported in infants fed a nondairy creamer as a substitute for milk.[36]

Formula Preparation

Manufacturers market formulas as liquid concentrates to be prepared for feeding by mixing equal amounts of the liquid and water. Ready-to-feed formulas that require no preparation are available in an assortment of sizes (4-, 6-, 8-, and 32-oz bottles and cans). Powdered formula that is prepared by mixing 1 level tbsp of powder in 2 oz of water is also available. One recommended evaporated milk formula is prepared by mixing 13 oz (one can) of evaporated milk with 2 tbsp of corn syrup and 18 oz of water. All of the formulas, when properly prepared and adequately supplemented, provide the nutrients important for the infant in an appropriate caloric concentration and present a solute load reasonable for the normal full-term infant. Errors in dilution caused by lack of understanding of the proper method of preparation, improper measurements, or the belief of the parents that their child should have greater amounts of nutritious food can lead to problems.

Result of errors in formula preparation. Failure to gain appropriately in height and weight has been observed as a result of dilution of ready-to-feed formulas in the manner concentrates are prepared. Mothers have been known to add extra water to formula in the belief that more dilute formula might reduce spitting up by their infants.

Feeding undiluted concentrated formula increases calories, protein, and solutes presented to the kidneys for excretion and may predispose the young infant to hypernatremia and tetany as well as obesity. Problems of improper formula preparation have most frequently been reported with the use of powdered formula and occur most often when an increased need for water caused by fever or infection is superimposed on consumption of an already high-solute formula. Infants fed concentrated formula during such illnesses may become thirsty, demand more to drink, or refuse to consume more liquid because of anorexia secondary to illness.[37] When presented with more milk concentrated in the protein and solutes, the osmolality of the blood increases and hypernatremic dehydration may result. Cases of cerebral damage and gangrene of the extremities have been reported to be the result of hypernatremic dehydration and metabolic acidosis.[38,39] The feeding of undiluted evaporated milk for 5 days after an illness during infancy has been reported to be the cause of gangrene resulting in the loss of limbs in a 6½-week-old infant.[40] Infants who have been fed improperly prepared concentrated and ready-to-feed formulas with less dramatic long-term effects have been noted by many who counsel parents of very young infants.

Overdiluting formula or offering water as a substitute for milk or as a pacifier can lead to serious consequences. Water intoxication resulting in hyponatremia, irritability, and coma has been reported in several infants fed 8 oz of water after each feeding or water as a substitute for milk because of financial inability of parents to buy more formula.[41,42]

Anticipatory guidance of parents of young infants should include information on the variety of formulas available with which to feed their infants, differences in methods of preparation of each product, and the dangers of overdiluted formula and excessive water intake.

Sterilization of formulas. Although terminal sterilization is recommended for infant formulas, many parents do not follow this practice but prepare formulas by the clean technique, one bottle at each feeding time, and immediately feed the infant. Several researchers have found no differences in incidence of illness or infection of infants fed formulas prepared by the clean technique or by terminal sterilization regardless of socioeconomic background or housekeeping practices.[43,44] Formulas prepared by both methods result in milk that produces aerobic bacteria.

If formulas are to be prepared by the clean technique, it is important that the hands of the person preparing the formula are first carefully washed. All equipment to be used during preparation, including the cans that contain the milk, the bottles, and the nipples, must be thoroughly washed and rinsed. Once opened, cans of formula must be covered and refrigerated. The formula is prepared immediately before each feeding. After the formula has been heated and the infant has been fed, any remaining milk should be discarded. Warm milk is an excellent medium for bacterial growth.

Milk Consumed by Older Infants

Homogenized cow's milk is offered to many infants by 5 to 6 months of age. Some parents feed their infants 2% milk, and a few parents concerned about weight gain and prevention of atherosclerosis give their infants nonfat milk. Others, convinced that goat's milk offers advantages, feed either fresh or evaporated goat's milk. Neither 2% nor nonfat milk is appropriate for infants in the first year of life. They are frequently fortified with nonfat milk solids, which increase the protein and mineral content of the milk and increase the solutes that must be excreted by the kidney. It can be anticipated that infants fed nonfat milk will receive an excessive percentage of their calories from protein and that their intakes of calories may be sufficiently

reduced that normal increments in weight gain may not be achieved. Studies of male infants who were fed nonfat milk with added linoleic acid between 4 and 6 months of age revealed that these infants increased their volume of intake of both milk and infant foods. However, since energy intakes were insufficient to meet requirements for growth, fat reserves were depleted, as demonstrated by reductions in fatfold thickness.[45] Fresh or pasteurized goat's milk offers the same disadvantages as cow's milk. All goat's milk is deficient in folacin and should not be offered without a food source and/or supplement of this nutrient.

Enteric blood loss as a result of intakes of more than a quart of homogenized milk per day was believed to be one factor responsible for as great as 50% of the iron deficiency in infancy.[46]

Fomon and others[47] found that infants fed whole cow's milk between 112 and 140 days of age had more guaiac-positive stools than did those fed a commercially prepared formula. Infants who had been fed soy protein isolates between 8 and 112 days of age had more fecal blood loss than did those fed a cow's milk–base formula the first 112 days. However, between 140 and 196 days of age there was no difference in the number of guaiac-positive stools between infants fed a whole cow's milk or a heat-treated formula. Therefore it is clearly inappropriate to offer infants milk that is not heat treated during the first 6 months of age. The Committee on Nutrition of the Academy of Pediatrics has stated there is no convincing evidence that feeding whole milk after 6 months of age is harmful if adequate supplementary feedings are given.[48]

One manufacturer (Ross Laboratories) markets a formula for the older infant that consists of nonfat milk, corn oil, and sucrose, the caloric concentration of which is reduced to 16½ kcal/oz as compared with 20 kcal/oz in standard formulas. The formula is fortified with both iron and vitamins. Infants fed this milk and pureed foods have been noted to increase their volume of intake, so that when compared with infants consuming a standard formula supplying 20 kcal/oz energy intakes are similar.[49]

Economics of Infant Feeding

Several attempts have been made to compare the economic impact of the provision of energy and nutrients to support human lactation with the use of prepared infant formula. Investigators have reported both disadvantages to breast-feeding and to formula-feeding.

It must be remembered that the numbers of foods that supply important nutrients for lactation are large. Therefore, the economic impact can range from a minimal increase to a sizeable increase over basic food costs.

Young infants who consume a whole milk or evaporated milk formula prepared with added carbohydrate are hypothesized to be receiving the least expensive feeding. However, many infants malabsorb as much as 34% of butterfat ingested. Any savings may be lost in the feces. The cost of commercially prepared formula varies with packaging. Concentrated formulas are the least expensive; ready-to-feed formulas are the most costly. The nutrient support for breast-feeding cost about 50% to 60% as much as the ready-to-feed formula.[50]

Feeding the infant human milk can be less expensive or more expensive than commercially prepared formula, depending on the parents' food purchasing practices and selection of foods. The many advantages of human milk far exceed any small monetary advantage to the use of prepared formula. Money saved can be obligated by additional medical care when the resistance factors are not present in the young infant's diet. Parents may need help in the selection of appropriate low-cost foods, but breast-feeding should never be discouraged on an economic basis.

Bonding

Klaus and Kennell[51] have shown that the first few minutes and hours of life are important to maternal-infant bonding. This leads to attachment, the unique relationship between two people that is special and lasts forever. Mothers who have immediate skin contact with their infants shortly after birth have significantly more attachment behaviors. Breast-feeding facilitates this attachment.

FOODS IN THE INFANT'S DIET

In spite of the fact that no nutritional advantage can be expected from the early introduction of semisolid foods, many families feed them in the first month of life. Semisolid foods are introduced by parents on the advice of physicians, neighbors, and friends and because parents think that it is time for their infants to eat foods other than milk. Some parents add semisolid foods in the hope that they will encourage their infants to sleep through the night, a commonly held belief that has been proved to be untrue.[5] Other parents feed semisolid foods because they think that their infants are hungry or because they consider the acceptance of these foods a developmental landmark.

Many infants receive table food by the time they can sustain a sitting posture. After infants begin to finger feed, increasing amounts of table food are included in their diets.

Semisolid Foods

The age of introduction of semisolid foods to infants in the United States declined from 1920, when these foods were seldom offered before 1 year of age, to 1960 to 1970, when they were frequently offered in the first weeks and months of life. Concern that this early introduction of semisolid foods predisposed infants to obesity and allergic reactions caused many health care professionals in the pediatric community to reexamine the appropriate age for the introduction of these foods. It is currently recommended that the feeding of semisolid foods be delayed until the infant's consumption of food is no longer a reflexive process and the infant has the fine, gross, and oral motor skills to appropriately consume them, i.e., at approximately 4 to 6 months of age. Even so, many parents are

Table 4-6. Suggested ages for the introduction of semisolid foods and table foods

Food	Age (months)		
	4 to 6	6 to 8	9 to 12
Iron-fortified cereals for infants	Add		
Vegetables		Add strained	Gradually delete strained foods, introduce table foods
Fruits		Add strained	Gradually delete strained foods, introduce chopped well-cooked or canned foods
Meats		Add strained or finely chopped table meats	Decrease the use of strained meats, increase the varieties of table meats
Finger foods such as arrowroot biscuits, oven-dried toast		Add those that can be secured with a palmar grasp	Increase the use of small-sized finger foods as the pincer grasp develops
Well-cooked mashed or chopped table foods, prepared without added salt or sugar			Add
Juice by cup			Add

reported to continue to offer semisolid foods in the first month of life. Table 4-6 gives suggested guidelines for the introduction of semisolid foods to normal infants.

It appears to make little difference whether fruits or vegetables are introduced first. New foods should be added singly at intervals of no more than every 3 days. The introduction of nitrate-containing vegetables (e.g., carrots, beets, and spinach) is usually delayed until the infant is at least 4 months of age, because the nitrate can be converted to nitrite in the stomach of the young infant. This can result in methemoglobinemia.

Infant's acceptance of semisolid foods. Parents report both immediate acceptance and rejection of semisolid foods, a fact that may relate to the mother's skill in feeding and her attitudes and feelings about these foods. Some parents who believe that the use of semisolid foods is important add them to the formula, cut a larger hole in the nipple, and feed the semisolid foods in this manner. One manufacturer markets a syringe with a plunger and a nipple with which mothers can force feed their babies by pushing the strained food through the nipple. These practices increase the energy and nutrient composition of the formula and may deprive the infant of experiences that are important in the development of feeding behavior.

Commercially prepared strained and junior foods are offered to many infants. Some mothers prefer to make their own with a blender or strainer. Ready-to-serve single-grain dry cereals such as rice cereal are commonly the first food offered to infants because rice is considered the least allergenic of the cereal grains and because most cereals are fortified with iron. Parents are reported to mix milk with cereal until it is almost liquid. Fruits are commonly reported as favorites. Vegetables appear to be accepted without problems. Preferences have been suggested for yellow vegetables, green beans, and peas; spinach and beets are often reported to be rejected. Strained meats, especially liver, are frequently rejected by infants. Parents state that the infants reject the sticky, granular texture rather than the taste of meats. Older infants are, as a result, often fed strained and junior vegetable and meat mixtures and high-meat dinners.

Food additives and fortification in semisolid foods. Concern that intakes of sodium in the first year might predispose infants to later hypertension has resulted in the deletion of salt from commercially prepared infant foods. Sugar is added only to desserts. All cereals are fortified with niacin, thiamine, riboflavin, calcium, and phosphorus. All dry infant cereals are fortified with electrolytically reduced iron. If fortified with iron, strained jarred cereals with fruit are fortified with ferrous sulfate. High-meat and mixed dinners are prepared with rice or wheat flour or tapioca to increase shelf-life. Modified corn or tapioca starch is included in some

desserts. Fruits and fruit juices are enriched with vitamin C.

Home preparation of semisolid foods (Fig. 4-1). It is both possible and economical for parents to prepare semisolid foods for their infants with a food grinder, blender, or strainer. The foods should be carefully selected from high-quality fresh, frozen, or canned fruits, vegetables, and meats and should be prepared so that nutrients are retained. The area in which the foods are prepared and the utensils used in preparation should be meticulously cleaned. Salt and sugar should be used sparingly, if at all. When the food has been cooked, pureed, and strained, it should be packaged in individual portions and refrigerated or frozen so that a single portion can be heated and fed

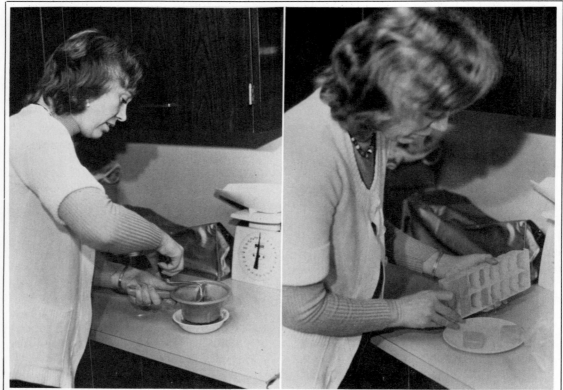

Fig. 4-1. A, Mother prepares food for her infant. **B,** After the food is frozen in icecube trays, she removes the cubes and stores them in individual portions for later use.

without compromising the quality and bacterial content of the entire batch. Directions for preparation of infant foods are given in the box below.

Home-prepared infant foods have a greater energy content than commercially prepared foods and many have a higher salt content. One study found that home-prepared infant foods had 1005% more salt than commercially prepared food.[53]

Fruit juice. When a high percentage of infants were fed evaporated milk formulas, vitamin C–containing fruit juices were commonly introduced in the first month of life. The widespread use of vitamin-fortified formula and vitamin supplements made this practice unnecessary. Because a sucrose-containing liquid consumed as infants go to sleep sometimes results in extensive dental caries (see Chapter 10), it is generally recommended that the introduction of fruit juice be delayed until it can be consumed from a cup.

Nutrients in semisolids. Ranges of nutrients found in any group of foods for infants are sizeable (Table 4-7).

Strained and junior fruits contribute one third more calories, only a fraction of the vitamin A, but twice as much vitamin C as do vegetables when fed in equal amounts. Vegetables contribute small but important amounts of iron. Fruit juice is fortified with abundant amounts of vitamin C.

Strained and junior meats contribute significant amounts of protein and iron. High-meat dinners contribute less than half as much protein as pure meat; vegetables and meat contribute less than one fifth as much protein as pure meat. Strained and junior meats and high-meat dinners contribute similar amounts of iron; strained vegetables and meat contribute much less iron. Strained vegetables and meat provide slightly less than half as many calories as meat; high-meat dinners provide 75% as many calories as pure meat. Strained egg yolks have the highest calorie concentration of the prepared infant foods.

Directions for Home Preparation of Infant Foods

1. Select fresh, high-quality fruits, vegetables, or meats.
2. Be sure all utensils, including cutting boards, grinders, knives, etc., are thoroughly clean.
3. Wash your hands before preparing the food.
4. Clean, wash, and trim the foods in as little water as possible.
5. Cook the foods until tender in as little water as possible. Avoid overcooking, which may destroy heat-sensitive nutrients.
6. Do not add salt. Add sugar sparingly. Do not add honey to foods for infants less than 1 year of age.*
7. Add enough water so that the food has a consistency that is easily pureed.
8. Strain or puree the food using an electric blender, a food mill, a baby food griner, or a kitchen strainer.
9. Pour puree into ice cube tray and freeze.
10. When food is frozen hard, remove the cubes and store in freezer bags.
11. Unfreeze and heat in serving container the amount of food that will be consumed at a single feeding (in water bath or microwave oven).

From Pipes, P.L.: Nutrition in infancy. In Krause, M.V., and Mahan, L.K.: Food, nutrition, and diet therapy, ed. 7, Philadelphia, 1984, W.B. Saunders Co.

*Botulism spores have been reported in honey, and young infants do not have the immune capacity to resist this infection.

Table 4-7. Ranges of selected nutrients per ounce in commerically prepared infant foods

Food	Energy (kcal)	Protein (gm)	Iron (mg)	Vitamin A (IU)	Vitamin C (mg)
Dry cereal	102-114	2.0-10.2	17.0-21.0	0-20	0-1.4
Strained and junior fruits	11-23	0.0-0.2	0.0-2.0	3-206	0.2-35.3
Strained and junior vegetables	7-18	0.2-1.0	0.1-0.4	9-3348	0.6-3.6
Strained and junior meats	27-42	3.6-4.4	.3-1.5	8-10811	.3-.7
Strained egg yolks	58	2.8 .	0.8	355	0.4
Strained and junior meat and vegetable dinners	20-33	1.6-2.6	0.0-0.3	22-237	0.1-0.5
Strained and junior vegetables and meat dinners	9-70	0.1-1.5	0.1-0.3	4-1114	0.2-1.2
Strained and junior desserts	17-25	0.0-0.8	0.0-0.1	4-71	0.2-8.9

From Gebhardt, S.E., Cutrufelli, R., and Matthews, R.H.: Composition of food, baby foods, raw, processed, prepared, Agriculture Handbook No. 8-3, Washington, D.C., 1978, U.S. Department of Agriculture

Table 4-8. Nutrient content of selected table foods commonly fed to infants

Food	Portion size	Energy (kcal)	Protein (gm)	Iron (mg)	Vitamin A (IU)	Vitamin C (mg)
Cooked cereal (farina)	¼ cup	26	0.8	Dependent on level of fortification		
Mashed potato	¼ cup	34	1.1	0.2	10	5
French fried potato	3, 1″ to 2″	29	0.4	0.2		
Spaghetti	2 tbsp	19	0.6	0.2		
Macaroni and cheese	2 tbsp	54	2.1	0.2	107	
Liverwurst	½ oz	45	2.1	0.8	925	
Hamburger	½ oz	41	3.4	0.5	5	
Eggs	1 medium	72	5.7	1.0	520	
Cottage cheese	1 tbsp	5	1.9		23.7	
Green beans	1 tbsp	3	0.15	0.2	43	1
Cooked carrots	1 tbsp	2.81			952	
Banana	½ small	40	0.5	0.35	90	5
Pudding	¼ cup	70	2.2	Trace	102	
Lollipop	1 oz hard candy	109				
Saltine crackers	1	12	0.2			
Vanilla wafer	¼″ thick, 1¾″ diameter	18	0.2			
Cheese strips	¼ oz	28	1.78		92	

From Adams, C.F.: Nutritive value in American foods in common units, Agriculture Handbook No. 456, Washington, D.C., 1975, U.S. Department of Agriculture.

Strained and junior desserts are rich in carbohydrate and calories. A few are fortified with vitamin C. All have a sweet taste, and indiscriminate use of these items should be discouraged.

Table Food

Food from the family menu is introduced at an early age in the diets of many infants. The age of introduction and type of food offered will reflect cultural practice. For example, crumbled cornbread mixed with pot liquor (liquid from vegetables) may be fed to infants in the southern states by 3 months of age, ''sticky'' rice may be fed to Oriental infants in the Pacific Northwest by 6 to 7 months of age, mashed beans are often given to Latin American infants at 2 to 4 months of age, and mashed potatoes are offered to many infants by 3 to 4 months of age.

Honey, sometimes used as a sweetener for home-prepared infant foods and formulas and recommended for use on pacifiers to promote sucking in hypotonic infants, has been implicated as the only food source of spores of *Clostridium botulinum* during infancy. These spores are extremely resistant to heat and are not destroyed by present methods of processing honey. Botulism in infancy is caused by ingestion of the spores, which germinate into the toxin in the lumen of the bowel. Honey should not be fed to infants less than 1 year of age.[54]

Stages of development of feeding behavior indicate readiness to progress in textures of food and will be discussed in the section on development of feeding behavior. The energy and nutrient composition of foods offered must also be considered. Examples of table foods often offered and their contribution to an infant's dietary intake are given in Table 4-8.

INTAKES OF INFANTS

Volume of intake and energy consumption is influenced not only by the infant's requirements for maintenance, growth, and activity but also by the parents' sensitivity to and willingness to accept cues of hunger and satiety, parental eagerness for the infant to feed, and the parents' skill at feeding. The caloric concentration of the formula is also a determinant of the volume of intake, calorie intake, and growth in early infancy.[55,56]

Infants feed differently, and mothers vary in their sensitivity to the child's cues. Thoman[57] found that primiparous mothers spent more time stimulating their infants during feeding than did multiparous mothers, yet their infants spent less time sucking during breast-feeding and consumed less from bottles at feeding than did infants of multiparous mothers in the newborn period. Primiparous mothers stimulated their infants during pauses between sucking. The stimulation prolonged the pause and reduced the total consumption of food.

Growth Response to Feeding

Normal breast-fed infants regulate their intakes of milk to meet their needs for normal growth and development. Formula-fed infants have been reported to regain their birth weights more rapidly than breast-fed infants.[58] Weight gains of formula-fed infants have been found to be equal to or slightly greater than those of breast-fed infants in the first 4 months of life.[59,60] Beal[59] reports that infants in her study who were breast fed longer than 6 months had greater increments in weight gain at 1 year of age and were heavier for length at that time than formula-fed infants.[60]

Energy Intakes

Per unit of size, infants consume the greatest number of calories between 14 and 28 days of age, a time known to many pediatricians as the hungry period.[55] Mothers who are breast-feeding often find it necessary to provide supplemental bottles at the end of a breast-feeding when the breasts are emptied for several days during this hungry period, after which lactation adjusts to increased intakes and breast-feeding alone can be resumed. After this time, although total quantity and energy intakes increase, intakes per unit of size decrease. Infants

Table 4-9. Ranges of volume of intake and energy consumption of normal infants

Age (months)	Denver studies (calories/kg/day)	Boston studies (calories/kg/day)
2-3	89-141	90-159
5-6	75-139	82-163
9-12	74-152	75-152

From Rueda-Williamson, R., and Rose, H.E.: Pediatrics **30:**639, 1962.

Table 4-10. Fiftieth percentile of male and female infants in Denver study of normal infants

Age (months)	Male (calories/kg/day)	Female (calories/kg/day)
0-1	115	115
1-2	131	131
2-3	116	115
4-5	101	104
9-12	101	97

From Beal, V.A.: Nutritional intake. In McCammon, R.W., editor: Human growth and development, Springfield, Ill., 1970, Charles C Thomas, Publisher.

consume greater amounts of food and nutrients as they grow older but less and less per unit of body size.

Wide ranges of volume of intake and energy consumption throughout the first year of life have been noted in formula-fed infants by several researchers.[61,63] Table 4-9 gives ranges reported in Boston and Denver studies.

The 50th percentile of intake of male and female infants in the Denver studies is given in Table 4-10.[64] Between 5 and 12 months of age, the 50 percentile of intake remained at 100 or 101 kcal/kg/day in males and gradually declined from 104 to 97 kcal/kg/day in females.

Studies by Fomon and others[55] have shown that the caloric concentration of the formula influences calorie intake during the first 41 days of life. Female infants who were fed formulas calorically concentrated to 100 kcal/100 ml (30 kcal/oz) reduced their volume of intake but consumed greater numbers of calories, whereas those who were fed formulas calorically diluted to 54 kcal/100 ml (16.5 kcal/oz) increased their volume of intake but consumed fewer calories, as compared with infants who were fed formulas of normal caloric concentration. After this period, adjustments in volume of intake were sufficient so that calorie intakes were similar for the entire 111-day study period. Infants who were fed the calorically concentrated formula were, however, heavier for their lengths at 111 days of age than were infants who had been fed the calorically dilute formulas.[56] Male infants who were fed formulas concentrated to 133 kcal/100 ml (40 kcal/oz) reduced their volume of intake but consumed greater numbers of calories during the first 84 days of life and experienced "supernormal" rates of growth in both length and weight during the first 42 days of life, as compared with infants who were fed formulas providing 67 kcal/100 ml (20 kcal/oz).[55]

FEEDING BEHAVIORS

Defining developmental readiness for changes in textures of food and the acquisition of self-feeding skills is important in establishing realistic goals for normal and handicapped infants and children. Illingworth and Lister[65] have defined a "critical or sensitive" period of development in relation to eating, a time at which a specific stimulus, solid food, must be applied for the organism to learn a particular action, that of accepting and eating table food, which is more difficult to masticate. They point out that an infant learns to chew at about 6 or 7 months of age, thus he or she is, at this point, developmentally ready to consume food. If solid foods are withheld until a later age, the child will have considerably more difficulty in accepting them.

In 1937 Gesell and Ilg[66] published observations of their extensive studies of the feeding behavior of infants. Their observations are as valid today as they were then. Cineradiographic techniques developed since then have permitted more detailed descriptions of sucking, suckling, and swallowing.[67,68]

Development of feeding behavior depends on the maturation of the central nervous system, which controls the acquisition of fine, gross, and oral motor skills, each of which influences the child's ability to consume food and the manner in which he or she suckles, sucks, chews, and swallows. Normal development proceeds in an orderly and predictable cephalocaudal sequence. Likewise, the sequence of acquisition of feeding skills occurs in a predictable order influenced by the acquisition of function and behavior.

It is important to recognize that even though the normal neonate is well prepared to suck and swallow at birth, the physical and neuromotor maturation during the first year alter both the form of the oral structure and the methods by which the infant extracts liquids from a nipple. Each of the parameters of change influences the infant's eating skills. At birth the tongue is disproportionately large in comparison with the lower jaw and essentially fills the oral cavity. The mandible is retruded relative to the maxilla, the maxilla protruding over the mandible by approximately 2 ml.[69] When the mouth is closed, the jaws do not rest on top of each other, but the tip of the tongue lies between the upper and lower jaws. There is a "fat pad" in each of the cheeks. It is thought that these pads serve as a prop for the buccinator muscle, maintaining rigidity of the cheeks during suckling.[70] The lips of the neonate are also instrumental in sucking and suckling and have characteristics appropriate for their function at this age. A mucosal fold on the free edge of the gums in the region of the eye tooth buds of both jaws is instrumental in sealing off the oral cavity as the lips close around a nipple. The mucosal fold disappears by the third or fourth month, when the lips have developed muscular control to seal the oral cavity.[70]

The sucking, swallowing, and respiratory centers are located in close proximity within the brain stem. The rhythmic functions must be coordinated to allow for the crossing of the alimentary and respiratory pathways in the pharynx.[71] The newborn infant coordinates sucking, breathing, and swallowing.

The newborn infant sucks reflexively, the young infant (beginning at 2 to 3 weeks of age) suckle, and as the infant grows older he or she learns mature sucking. Some description of the two processes, therefore, seems important.

Suckling

Cineradiographic studies by Ardran, Kemp, and Lind[67] have shown that the processes of breast suckling and bottle suckling are similar. The nipple of the breast becomes rigid and elongated during breast feeding so that it closely resembles a rubber nipple in shape, and both assume a similar position in the infant's mouth. The infant grasps the nipple in his or her mouth. The oral cavity is sealed off by pressure from the median portions of the lips assisted by the mucosal folds in the jaws. The nipple is held in the infant's mouth with the tip located close to the junction of the hard and soft palates.

During the first stage of suckling, the mandible and tongue are lowered while the mouth is closed, thus creating a negative pressure. The tip of the tongue moves forward. The mandible and tongue are next raised, compressing the anterior end of the nipple. The compression is moved anteroposteriorly as the tip of the tongue withdraws, thus stroking or milking the liquid from the nipple. The retruded position of the mandible maximizes the efficiency of the stroking action.[67,68] As the tongue moves back, it comes in contact with the tensed soft palate, thus causing liquid to squirt into the lateral food channels. The location of the larynx is much higher during infancy than it is in adulthood, and the larynx is further elevated by muscular contractions during swallowing. The epiglottis functions as a breakwater during swallowing. As the liquid is squirted back in the mouth, the epiglottis is positioned so that it parts the stream of liquid, thus passing it to the sides of the larynx instead of over it. Thus liquid does not pass over the laryngeal entrance during early infancy because of the relatively higher position of the larynx and parting of the stream of liquid by the epiglottis (Fig. 4-2).[70]

Sucking

Mature sucking is an acquired feature of the orofacial muscles. It is not a continuous process. Upon accumulation of sufficient fluid in the mouth, sucking and breathing are interrupted by a swallowing movement. The closure of the nasopharyngeal and laryngeal sphincters in response to the presence of food in the pharynx is responsible for the interruption of nasal breathing.[71]

During swallowing the food lies in a swallow preparatory position on the groove of the tongue. The distal portion of the soft palate is raised toward the adenoidal pad in the roof of the epipharynx. The tongue is pressed upward against the nipple so that the bolus of milk follows gravity down the sloping tongue reaching the pharynx. As the bolus moves downward, the posterior wall of the pharynx comes forward to displace the soft palate toward the dorsal surface of the tongue and the larynx is elevated and arched backward. The bolus is expressed from the pharynx by peristaltic movements of the pharyngeal wall toward the back of the tongue and the larynx. The bolus spills over the pharyngoepiglottic folds into the lateral food channels and then into the esophagus.[68]

The tonsils and lymphoid tissue play an important role as infants swallow; they assist in keeping the airway open and in keeping food away from the

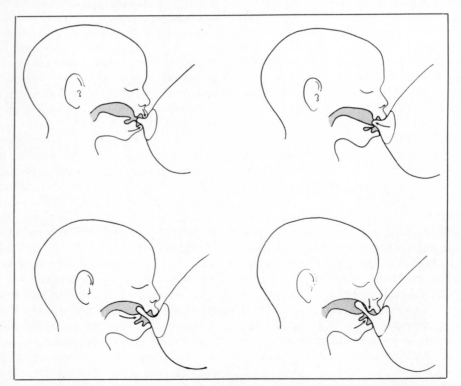

Fig. 4-2. During suckling the infant grasps the nipple. The tongue moves forward, and the mandible and tongue compress the anterior end of the nipple. The compression is moved anteroposteriorly as the tip of the tongue milks the fluid from the nipple.

Table 4-11. Sequence of development of feeding behavior

Age	Reflexes	Oral, Fine, Gross Motor Development
1-3 months	Rooting and suck and swallow reflexes are present at birth Tonic neck reflex present	Head control is poor Secures milk with a suckling pattern, the tongue projecting during a swallow By the end of the third month, head control is developed
4-6 months	Rooting reflex fades Bite reflex fades Tonic neck reflex fades by 16 weeks	Changes from a sucking pattern to a mature suck with liquids Sucking strength increases Munching pattern begins Grasps with a palmar grasp Grasps, brings objects to mouth and bites them
7-9 months	Gag reflex is less strong as chewing of solids begins and normal gag is developing Choking reflex can be inhibited	Munching movements begin when solid foods are eaten Rotary chewing begins Sits alone Has power of voluntary release and resecural Holds bottle alone Develops an inferior pincer grasp
10-12 months		Reaches for a spoon Bites nipples, spoons, and crunchy foods Grasps bottle and foods and brings them to the mouth Can drink from a cup that is held Tongue is used to lick food morsels off the lower lip Finger feeds with a refined pincer grasp

Modified from Gessell, A., and Ilg, F.L.: Feeding behavior of infants, Philadelphia, 1937, J.B. Lippincott Co.

posterior pharyngeal wall as the infant is fed in a reclining position, thus delaying nasopharyngeal closure until food has reached the lower pharynx.[65]

As the infant grows older the oral cavity enlarges so that the tongue no longer fills the mouth. The tongue grows differentially at the tip and attains motility in the larger oral cavity. The elongated tongue can be protruded to receive and pass solids between the gum pads and erupting teeth for mastication. Mature feeding is characterized by separate movements of the lip, tongue, and gum pads or teeth.[70]

Sequence of Development of Feeding Behavior

The sequence of development of feeding behavior is given in Table 4-11, and Fig. 4-3.

Newborn infants can neither focus their eyes nor direct their hands, yet they find nourishment. The "rooting reflex" caused by stroking of the perioral skin including the cheeks and lips causes an infant to turn toward the stimulus, so that the mouth comes in contact with it. Stimulus placed on the lips causes involuntary movements toward it, closure, and pouting in preparation for sucking.[72] These reflexes thus enable the infant to suck and receive nourishment. Both rooting and suckling can be elicited when the infant is hungry but are absent when the infant is satiated.[73] During feeding the neonate assumes a tonic neck position, the head rotated to one side and the arm on that side extended while the other is fisted. The infant seeks the nipple by touch and obtains milk from the nipple with a rhythmic suckle.[66] Semisolid foods, introduced at an early age into the diets of many infants fed by spoon, are secured in the same manner as is the milk, by stroking movements of the tongue with the tongue projecting as the spoon is with-

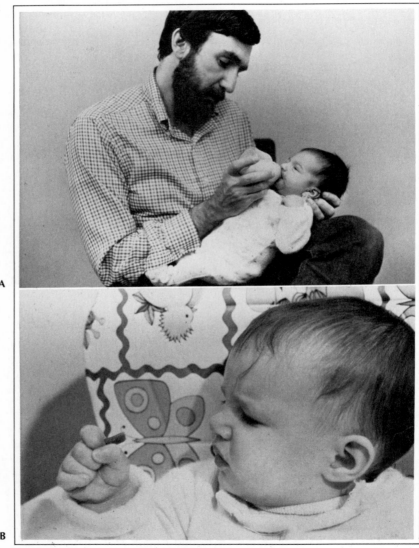

A

B

Fig. 4-3. Sequence of development of feeding behaviors. **A,** Infant sucks liquids. **B,** Five-month-old infant begins to finger feed.

drawn. Frequently, food is expelled from the mouth.

By 5 weeks of age the infant can focus the eyes on faces, and by 12 weeks of age the gaze can be shifted. At 10 weeks of age the infant is able to recognize the breast or bottle as the source of food.

By 16 weeks of age the more mature sucking pattern has become evident, with the tongue moving back and forth as opposed to the earlier up-and-down motions. Spoon feeding is easier because the infant can draw in the lower lip as the spoon is removed. The tonic neck position has faded, and

C

D

Fig 4-3, cont'd. Sequence of development of feeding behaviors. **C,** Eight-month-old infant is fed table food. **D,** Eleven-month-old infant begins to feed herself.

the infant assumes a more symmetrical position with the head at midline. The hands close on the bottle.[66] By 20 weeks of age the infant can grasp on tactile contact with a palmar squeeze. By 24 weeks of age he or she can reach for and grasp an object on sight. In almost every instance the object goes into the mouth.

Between 24 and 28 weeks of age the beginning of chewing movements, an up-and-down movement of the jaws, occurs. This, coupled with the ability to grasp and the hand-to-mouth route of grasped objects, as well as sitting posture, indicates a readiness of the infant to finger feed. Infants at this age grasp with a palmar grasp. Therefore,

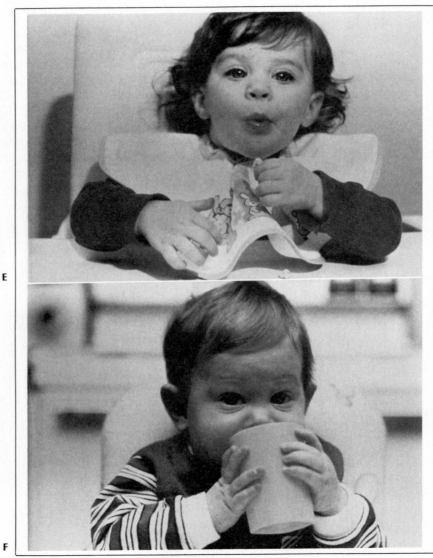

Fig. 4-3, cont'd. Sequence of development of feeding behaviors. **E,** Ten-month-old infant purses her lips. **F,** Twelve-month-old infant drinks from a cup.

the shape of the food presented for the child to finger feed is important. Cookies, melba toast, crackers, and teething biscuits are frequently introduced at this stage (Fig. 4-4).

Between 28 and 32 weeks of age the infant gains control of the trunk and can sit alone without support. The sitting infant has greater mobility of the shoulders and arms and is freer to reach and grasp. The grasp is more digital than the earlier palmar grasp. The infant is able to transfer items from one hand to another and learns to voluntarily release and resecure objects. The beginning of chewing patterns (up-and-down movements of the jaws) is demonstrated. The tongue shows more maturity in regard to spoon feeding than to drinking. Food is received from the spoon by pressing the lips against the spoon, drawing the head away, and drawing in the lower lip. The infant is aware of a cup and can suck from it. Milk frequently leaks from corners of the mouth as the tongue is projected before swallowing.[66]

The introduction of soft mashed (but not strained) foods is appropriate at this stage of development. In fact, it is at this stage of development that Illingworth and Lister[64] believe it is critical to introduce the infant to harder-to-masticate foods.

Between 6 and 12 months of age the infant gradually receives greater amounts of food from the family menu and less and less of the pureed and strained items. Foods should be carefully selected and modified so that they are presented in a form that can be manipulated in the mouth without the potential of choking and aspiration, as may occur with small grains of rice or corn. Many parents mash well-cooked vegetables and canned fruits and successfully offer them to their infants. Well-cooked ground meat dishes such as ground meat in gravies or sauces appear to be easily accepted, as are liverwurst, minced chicken livers, and drained tuna fish. Custards, puddings, and ice cream soon become favorites.

By 28 weeks of age infants are able to help themselves to their bottle in sitting postures, although they will not be able to tip the bottle adaptively as it empties until about 32 weeks of age. By the end of the first year they can completely manage bottle feeding alone.

By 32 weeks of age infants bring their heads forward to receive the spoon as it is presented to them. The tongue shows increased motility and allows for considerably increased manipulation of food in the mouth before swallowing. At the end of

Fig. 4-4. Six-month-old-infant demonstrates readiness to finger feed.

the first year, infants are able to manipulate food in the mouth with definite chewing movements.

During the fourth quarter of the first year, the child develops an increasingly precise pincer grasp. The bottle can be managed alone and can be resecured if it is lost. Infants at this age are increasingly conscious of what others do and often imitate the models set for them.[66] By 1 year of age the patterns of eating have changed from sucking to beginning rotary chewing movements. Children understand the concept of the container and the contained, have voluntary hand-to-mouth movements and a precise pincer grasp, and can voluntarily release and resecure objects. They are thus prepared to learn to feed themselves, a behavior they learn and refine in the second year (Fig. 4-5).

FEEDING THE INFANT

Presented with the breast of an adequately fed lactating mother or the nipple on a bottle of properly prepared formula, the hungry infant receives both biochemical and psychosocial nurturance. Although studies of Holt and others[73] have indicated that infants accept cold formula, most mothers warm the milk to body temperature.[74] The infant held in a semireclining position who is offered the nipple sucks and receives the major portion of nourishment in 20 minutes (Fig. 4-6). Most physicians recommend a flexible self-demand schedule. Newborn infants will initially feed six to eight times a day at intervals of 2 to 4 hours and will consume 2 to 3 oz at a feeding. By 2 weeks of age most infants will have increased the amount of milk consumed at a feeding and reduced the number of feedings to six. By 2 months of age most infants are fed five times a day and sleep through the night. By 6 months of age most consume three meals and four milk feedings a day.

Infants swallow air as well as formula during feeding. Holding the child in an upright position and gently patting the back encourages expulsion of swallowed air and prevents distention and discomfort.

Difficulties in Infant Feeding

During feeding both the mother and infant receive satisfaction and pleasure. The infant is pleased because hunger is satiated, the mother because she

Fig. 4-5. Ten-month-old infant becomes interested in feeding himself.

has fulfilled the needs of her newborn infant. Infants learn that they can trust their mothers to feed them and that they please their mothers by eating. Successful feeding provides the basis for the warm, trusting relationship that develops between infants and their mothers.

Difficulties in feeding resulting from a weak suck, maternal difficulty in establishing adquate lactation, improper equipment such as firm nipples with small holes, or other causes are frustrating to both infants and their mothers. Hungry infants cry more frequently, demand to be fed more often, and may create anxiety in conscientious and concerned mothers.

Since infants have not yet learned to separate themselves from others in the environment, they perceive the feelings of others as their own immediate feelings in any particular situation. Thus they are easily susceptible to parental anxieties and may

Fig. 4-6. Mother feeds her 3-week-old infant in semireclining upright position.

reflect these by crying and not eating well. When the infant does not eat well, parental anxieties may increase. Thus the cycle can begin. It is possible that such bottle-fed infants will feed more easily when presented the bottle by a less intense person. However, when the infant is successfully fed by another, the parent's feelings of inadequacy and anxiety may be increased.

To achieve successful mother-child feeding experiences, it is important to work directly with the mother. It may be necessary for the professional to determine any problems with equipment used and positioning, then to model a calm, relaxed feeding situation for the mother. Care should be taken not to usurp the mother's role, thus increasing her feelings of inadequacy. An approach that seems to be beneficial to all concerned is to (1) model a feeding, (2) sit beside the mother and talk her through a feeding while showing her how to use a relaxed position, (3) reinforce her mothering behaviors, and (4) help her to become aware of cues from the infant that he or she is relaxed.

This method may need to be used for several feedings until the mother and infant can achieve a successful, relaxed experience. Even then, parents may need further support in their continuing efforts to create a relaxed and warm relationship with their infants during feeding.

Several cases of malnutrition and failure to thrive have been reported in breast-fed infants secondary to an inadequate milk intake, and thus an energy and nutrient intake.[75,76] Most of the mothers were primiparous women who seemed intelligent and mature. They appeared to not be aware that their babies were not gaining or were losing weight or that their milk production was inadequate. Mothers should be supported in breast-feeding. However, when the infant is not satisfied after feeding at both breasts or has not gained adequately, temporary use of supplemental feedings is appropriate. Mothers should be counseled to have the baby nurse at both breasts at each feeding and to then offer a supplemental formula. When adequate lactation is established, the supplemental bottles can be discontinued.

It is important for parents to recognize that newborn infants demonstrate a pattern of crying in early life and that a crying infant is not a symptom of inadequate mothering. The amount of time an infant cries increases from 2 weeks of age to approximately 6 weeks of age, when it peaks. After this time crying decreases. The major concentration period is from 6 to 11 PM. Other periods of crying occur in the morning from 4 to 7 AM and 9 to 11 AM. By 10 weeks of age most infants become more quiet.[77] Seldom is this crying a symptom of allergy, and it is no indication for formula change.

Parents of colicky babies—those who are otherwise healthy and well fed but who cry constantly for several hours, draw their legs onto their abdomens and pass large amounts of gas—often request changes in the infants' formulas. This rarely resolves colic, and frequent change in formulas should be discouraged. It has been suggested that colic in some breast-fed infants may be resolved by eliminating milk from the mothers' diets.[78,79] A casein hydrolysate formula may alleviate symptoms in some but not all bottle-fed infants.[80]

Both spitting and regurgitation can occur in infants and usually causes concern for parents. During the early months of life some otherwise healthy infants spit a small amount of any milk or food digested at each feeding. Although the infants do not fail to thrive, parents may seek help in resolving this situation. There is no therapy. The problem usually resolves itself by the time the infants can sustain sitting. Regurgitation, the effortless expulsion of gastric contents, is a symptom that demands medical evaluation. The most common cause of persistent regurgitation is gastrointestinal reflux, the result of decreased pressure in the lower esophageal sphincter. Positioning in an infant seat at a 45° to 60° angle may help, but it will not decrease the amount of contact of gastric acid on the esophageal mucosa. Surgery may be indicated.[81]

Some infants are easily distracted by noise or by other influences in the environment. Such infants feed more easily at the night feeding. Presentation of the bottle in a quiet and partially darkened room by a rested mother may promote successful feeding for both the mother and her infant.

Many parents perceive their infants as having feeding problems. Problems in order of frequency have been reported to be refusal of a particular food because of taste or texture, dissatisfaction with amount consumed, spitting up, and developmentally related problems such as refusing the bottle or refusing to be fed and only finger-feeding.[82] Such difficulties are usually of short duration and rarely compromise an infant's nutrient intake or physical growth. Parents, however, may need reassurance that their infant's development is normal and that their food-related behaviors are not of nutritional concern.

Recognizing Cues of Satiation and Readiness to Progress

Successful infant feeding is generally regarded in our society as a measure of competent parenthood. As such, it is a reinforcing experience to parents. They must learn to recognize and to accept their infant's cues, as the infant uses a variety of cries and vocalizations to express needs. Frequently, parents, for one reason or another, cannot always discriminate their infant's cries. Consequently, they give food to satisfy all types of infant discomforts. The infant, in turn, may not learn to discriminate hunger from other discomforts and may learn to rely on eating to satisfy a wide variety of needs. Parents must learn to recognize satiation of hunger in infants and be willing to accept their infant's expressions of satisfaction, to set limits on amounts of food offered to eager eaters, and to decline the natural inclination to overfeed infants who please others by accepting more food. Satiety behavior of infants is given in Table 4-12. Parents who are eager for their infant to empty the bottle encourage excessive intakes of food and can reinforce eating to the extent that obesity may result. Infants may be offered food and formula by many people: parents, baby-sitters, aunts, siblings, and others. Mothers

Table 4-12. Satiety behaviors in infants

Age	Behavior
4-12 weeks	Draws head away from nipple
	Falls asleep
	When nipple is reinserted, closes lips tightly
	Bites nipple, purses lips, or smiles and lets go
16-24 weeks	Releases nipple and withdraws head
	Fusses or cries
	Obstructs mouth with hands
	Increases attention to surroundings
	Bites nipple
28-36 weeks	Changes posture
	Keeps mouth tightly closed
	Shakes head as if to say "no"
	Plays with utensils
	Hands become more active
	Throws utensils
40-52 weeks	Behaviors of above period typical
	Sputters with tongue and lips
	Hands bottle or cup to mother

From Pipes P.L.: Health care professionals. In Garwood, G., and Fewell, R.: Educating handicapped infants, Rockville, Md., 1982, Aspen Systems. With permission by Aspen Systems Corp.; modified from Gessell, A., and Ilg, F.L.: Feeding behavior of infants, Philadelphia, 1937, J.B. Lippincott Co.

who are dissatisfied with the infant's food intake may find that the infant has reduced the intake to compensate for food offered by others.

Additional cues that parents must recognize are those that indicate the infant's readiness for increasingly independent feeding experiences. The infant's ability to put objects to his or her mouth and to chew on them indicates a readiness to use increasingly solid foods and to begin finger-feeding. Anticipatory guidance to parents during this period about developmental changes is an important factor in their acceptance of and adaptation to their infant's behavior.

Recognizing Needs for Nutrients and Energy in the Infant's Diet

Most infants consume foods that provide nutrients in excess of recommended amounts, with the exception of iron. Human milk, cow's milk, and formula provide the major source of protein and calcium and important sources of vitamin A and the B vitamins in early life. Breast-fed infants should receive supplements of iron, vitamin D, and fluoride. Iron-fortified formulas contribute appreciable amounts of iron in early infancy. When enriched cereals are introduced into the diet, another important source of iron is available.

Because of the great variability in calories and nutrients provided by foods offered to infants, selection of foods and the amounts offered should be based on the infant's rate of gain in height and weight as well as on nutrient needs. The introduction and acceptance of iron-containing foods before the time homogenized milk replaces iron-fortified formula or iron supplements are discontinued is important, because the infant must continue to consume foods that provide this nutrient as it is deleted from milk or supplements. Fruit juice offers sources of vitamin C when vitamin-containing formulas are no longer consumed. It seems reasonable to encourage parents of infants whose gains in weight are more rapid than gains in length to feed the lower-calorie infant foods such as vegetables and dinners. Parents of infants whose increments of weight gains are small should be encouraged to feed greater amounts of the higher-calorie strained meats and fruits. Amounts of semisolid foods offered to infants should be adjusted to their appetites and rates of weight gain. Experiences with a variety of flavors and textures are thought to be conducive to acceptance of a variety of foods in later life.

SUMMARY

Infants can be adequately nourished consuming a variety of combinations of milks, supplements, and semisolid foods. Maturation of the oral and fine motor skills indicate appropriate stages for the introduction of semisolid and solid foods. Current recommendations include breast-feeding by an adequately nourished mother and the introduction of semisolid foods at 4 to 6 months of age and of finger foods when the infant reaches out, grasps, and brings items to his or her mouth.

If the mother is unable or unwilling to breast-feed, a variety of properly constructed infant formulas are marketed that have been proved to support normal growth and development in infants. It is to the formula-fed baby's advantage to receive a formula with iron.

Infants should be permitted to establish their own feeding schedule and fed to satiety. When they develop a voluntary mature sucking pattern, the introduction of semisolid foods is appropriate. When munching and rotary chewing begin, the introduction of soft-cooked table food is appropriate. Infants can begin to drink from a cup with help between 9 and 12 months of age.

Difficulties in infant feeding that indicate a need for intervention include inadequate milk production by the mother, poor suck, improper formula preparation, and parental anxiety about feeding their infants.

SUGGESTED LEARNING ACTIVITIES

1. Investigate the incidence of breast-feeding in the maternity unit of your local hospital.
2. Investigate local agencies in your community that provide support for the lactating mother.
3. Describe formula products available for feeding infants in your community.
4. Compare the cost of homemade and commercially available foods for infants.
5. Describe how useful mothers find the nutrition information found on commercially prepared baby food container labels.
6. Observe infants feeding at 2, 4, 7, and 9 months of age and describe changes in the way babies secure their food.
7. Describe appropriate therapy for breast-fed babies who are thought to be gaining weight too fast.

REFERENCES

1. Lindberg, T.: Proteolytic activity in duodenal juice in infants, children, and adults, Acta Paediatr. Scand. **63:**805, 1974.
2. Fomon, S.J.: Infant nutrition, ed. 2, Philadelphia, 1974, W.B. Saunders Co.
3. Watkins, J.B.: Bile acid metabolism and fat absorption in newborn infants, Pediatr. Clin. North Am. **2:**501, 1974.
4. Filer, L.J., Mattson, F.H., and Fomon, S.J.: Triglyceride configuration and fat absorption by the human infant, J. Nutr. **99:**293, 1969.
5. Bayless, T.M., and Christopher, N.L.: Disaccharidase deficiency, Am. J. Clin. Nutr. **22:**181, 1969.
6. Rossiter, M.A., and others: Amylase content of mixed saliva in children, Acta Paediatr. Scand. **63:**389, 1974.
7. Hadorn, B., and others: Quantitative assessment of exocrine pancreatic function in infants and children, J. Pediatr. **73:**39, 1968.
8. Lillibridge, C.B., and Townes, P.L.: Physiologic deficiency of pancreatic amylase in infancy: a factor in iatrogenic diarrhea, J. Pediatr. **82:**279, 1973.
9. DeVizia, B., and others: Digestibility of starches in infants and children, J. Pediatr. **68:**50, 1975.
10. Anderson, T.A., Fomon, S.J., and Filer, L.J.: Carbohydrate tolerance studies with 3-day-old infants, J. Lab. Clin. Med. **9:**31, 1972.
11. Husband, J., Husband, P., and Mallinson, C.N.: Gastric emptying of starch meals in the newborn, Lancet **2:**290, 1970.
12. Nash, M.A., and Edelmann, C.M.: The developing kidney, Nephron **11:**71, 1973.
13. Edelman, C.M., Barrett, H.L., and Troupkon, V.: Renal concentrating mechanisms in newborn infants. Effects of dietary protein and water content, role of urea and responsiveness to antidiuretic hormone, J. Clin. Invest. **39:**1062, 1960.
14. Polacek, E., and others: The osmotic concentrating ability in healthy infants and children, Arch. Dis. Child. **40:**291, 1965.
15. Martinez, G.A., and Dodd, D.A.: 1981 milk feeding patterns in the United States during the first 12 months of life, Pediatrics **71:**166, 1983.
16. Blanc, B.: Biochemical aspects of human milk, World Rev. Nutr. Diet **36:**1, 1981.
17. Siimes, M.A., Vuori, E., and Kuitunen, P.: Breast milk iron—a declining concentration during the course of lactation, Acta Paediatr. Scand. **68:**29, 1979.

18. Vuori, E., and Kuitunen, P.: Concentrations of copper and zinc in human milk, Acta Paediatr. Scand. **68**:33, 1978.

19. Hambraeus, L.: Proprietary milk versus human breast milk in infant feeding, Pediatr. Clin. North Am. **24**:17, 1977.

20. Anderson, G.H., Atkinson, S.A., and Bryan, M.H.: Energy and macronutrient content of human milk during early lactation from mothers giving birth prematurely and at term, Am. J. Clin. Nutr. **34**:258, 1981.

21. Chavalittamrong, B., and others: Protein and amino acids of breast milk from Thai mothers, Am. J. Clin. Nutr. **24**:1126, 1981.

22. Jensen, R.G., Hagerty, M.M., and McMahon, K.E.: Lipids of human milk and infant formulas: a review, Am. J. Clin. Nutr. **31**:990, 1978.

23. Reeve, L.E., Chesney, R.W., and De Luca, H.F.: Vitamin D of human milk: identification of biologically active forms, Am. J. Clin. Nutr. **36**:122, 1982.

24. O'Connor, M.E., and others: Vitamin K deficiency and breast feeding, Am. J. Dis. Child. **137**:601, 1983.

25. Higginbottom, L., Sweetman, L., and Nylan, W.L.: A syndrome of methylmalonic aciduria, homocystinuria, megaloblastic anemia, and neurological abnormalities of a B_{12} deficiency in an infant strictly breast-fed by a mother with latent pernicious anemia, J. Pediatr. **100**:917, 1982.

26. Cooperman, J.M., and others: The folate in human milk, Am. J. Clin. Nutr. **36**:576, 1982.

27. Saarinen, U.M., Siimes, M.A., and Dallman, P.R.: Iron absorption in infants: high bioavailability of breast milk iron as indicated by the extrinsic tag method of iron absorption and by the concentration of serum ferritin, J. Pediatr. **91**:36, 1977.

28. Garry, P.J., and others: Iron absorption from human milk and formula with and without iron supplementation, Pediatr. Res. **15**:822, 1981.

29. Harzer, G., and Kauer, H.: Binding of zinc to casein, Am. J. Clin. Nutr. **35**:981, 1982.

30. Johnson, P.E., and Evans, G.W.: Relative zinc availability in human breast milk, infant formulas, and cow's milk, Am. J. Clin. Nutr. **31**:416, 1978.

31. Welsh, J.K., and May, J.T.: Anti-infective properties of breast milk, J. Pediatr. **94**:1, 1979.

32. Fransson, G.B., and Lönnerdal, B.: Iron in human milk, Pediatrics **96**:380, 1980.

33. Larsen, S.A., and Homer, D.R.: Relation of breast- versus bottle-feeding to hospitalization for gastroenteritis in a middle-class U.S. population, J. Pediatr. **92**:417, 1978.

34. Committee on Nutrition, American Academy of Pediatrics: Commentary on breast-feeding and infant formulas, including proposed standards for formulas, Pediatrics **57**:279, 1976.

35. Fabius, R.J., and others: Malnutrition associated with a formula of barley water, corn syrup, and whole milk, Am. J. Dis. Child. **135**:615, 1981.

36. Sinatra, F.R., and Merritt, R.J.: Iatrongenic kwashiorkor in infants, Am. J. Dis. Child. **135**:21, 1981.

37. Chambers, T.L., and Steel, A.E.: Concentrated milk feeds and their relation to hypernatraemic dehydration in infants, Arch. Dis. Child. **50**:610, 1975.

38. Macaulay, D., and Watson, M.: Hypernatraemia in infants as a cause of brain damage, Arch. Dis. Child. **42**:485, 1967.

39. Comay, S.C., and Karabus, C.D.: Peripheral gangrene in hypernatraemic dehydration of infancy, Arch. Dis. Child. **50**:616, 1975.

40. Abrams, C.A.L., and others: Hazards of overconcentrated milk formula, J.A.M.A. **232**:1136, 1975.

41. Partridge, J.C., and others: Water intoxication secondary to feeding mismanagement, Am. J. Dis. Child. **135**:38, 1981.

42. Schulman, J.: Infantile water intoxication at home, Pediatrics **66**:119, 1980.

43. Hargrove, C.B., Temple, A.R., and Chinn, P.: Formula preparation and infant illness, Clin. Pediatr. **13**:1057, 1974.

44. Kendall, N., Vaughn, V.C., and Kusakeroglu, A.: A study of preparation of infant formulas, Am. J. Dis. Child. **122**:215, 1971.

45. Fomon, S.J., and others: Skim milk in infant feeding, Acta Paediatr. Scand. **66**:17, 1977.

46. Woodruff, C.W., Wright, S.W., and Wright, R.P.: The role of fresh cow's milk in iron deficiency. II. Comparison of fresh cow's milk with a prepared formula, Am. J. Dis. Child. **124**:26, 1972.

47. Fomon, S.J., and others: Cow milk feeding in infancy: gastrointestinal blood loss and iron nutritional status, J. Pediatr. **98**:540, 1981.

48. Committee on Nutrition, American Academy of Pediatrics: The use of whole milk in infancy, Pediatrics **72**:253, 1983.

49. Fomon, S.J., and others: Recommendations for feeding normal infants, Pediatrics **63**:52, 1979.

50. Lamm, E., Delaney, J., and Dwyer, J.T.: Ecomony in the feeding of infants, Pediatr. Clin. North Am. **24**:71, 1977.

51. Klaus, M.H., and Kennell, J.H.: Maternal-infant bonding: the impact of early separation or loss on family development, St. Louis, 1976, The C.V. Mosby Co.

52. Beal, V.A.: Termination of night feeding in infancy, J. Pediatr. **75**:690, 1969.

53. Kerr, C.M., Reisinger, K.S., and Plankey, F.W.: Sodium concentration of homemade baby food, Pediatrics **62**:331, 1978.

54. Arnon, S.S., and others: Honey and other environmental risk factors for infant botulism, Pediatrics **94**:331, 1979.

55. Fomon, S.J., and others: Relationship between formula concentration and rate of growth of normal infants, J. Nutr. **98**:241, 1969.

56. Fomon, S.J., and others: Influence of formula concentration on caloric intake and growth of normal infants, Acta Paediatr. Scand. **64**:172, 1975.

57. Thoman, E.B.: Development of synchrony in mother-infant interaction in feeding and other situations, Fed. Proc. **34**:1587, 1975.

58. Fomon, S.J., and others: Food consumption and growth of normal infants fed milk-based formulas, Acta Paediatr. Scand. Suppl. 223, 1971.

59. Fomon, S.J., and others: Growth and serum chemical values of normal breast fed infants, Acta Paediatr. Scand. Suppl. 202, 1970.

60. Beal, V.A.: Breast and formula feeding of infants, J. Am. Diet. Assoc. **55**:31, 1969.

61. Beal, V.A.: Nutritional intake of children, I. Calories, carbohydrate, fat and protein, J. Nutr. **50**:223, 1953.

62. Rueda-Williamson, R., and Rose, H.E.: Growth and nutrition of infants: the influence of diet and other factors on growth, Pediatrics **30**:639, 1962.

63. Fomon, S.J., Owen, G.M., and Thomas, L.N.: Milk or formula volume ingested by infants fed ad libitum, Am. J. Dis. Child. **108**:601, 1964.

64. Beal, V.A.: Nutritional intake. In McCammon, R.W., editor: Human growth and development, Springfield, Ill., 1970, Charles C Thomas, Publisher.

65. Illingworth, R.S., and Lister, J.: The critical or sensitive period with special reference to certain feeding problems in infants and children, J. Pediatr. **65**:839, 1964.

66. Gesell, A., and Ilg, F.L.: Feeding behavior of infants, Philadelphia, 1937, J.B. Lippincott Co.

67. Ardran, G.M., Kemp, F.H., and Lind. J.: A cineradiographic study of breast feeding, Br. J. Radiol. **31**:156, 1958.

68. Ardran, G.M., Kemp, F.H., and Lind, J.: A cineradiographic study of bottle feeding, Br. J. Radiol. **31**:11, 1958.

69. Subtelny, J.D.: Examination of current philosophies associated with swallowing behavior, Am. J. Orthod. **51**:161, 1965.

70. Peiper, A.: Cerebral function in infancy and childhood, New York, 1963, Consultant's Bureau.

71. Gwynne-Evans, E.: Organization of the oro-facial muscles in relation to breathing and feeding. Br. Dent. J. **91**:135, 1952.

72. Bosma, J.F.: Maturation of function of the oral and pharyngeal region, Am. J. Orthod. **49**:94, 1963.

73. Ingram, T.T.S.: Clinical significance of the infantile feeding reflexes, Dev. Med. Child Neurol. **4**:159, 1962.

74. Holt, L.E., and others: A study of premature infants fed cold formula, J. Pediatr. **61**:556, 1962.

75. O'Connor, P.A.: Failure to thrive with breast-feeding, Clin. Pediatr. **17**:833, 1978.

76. Roddey, O.F., Martin, E.S., and Swetenburg, R.L.: Critical weight loss and malnutrition in breast-fed infants, Am. J. Dis. Child. **135**:597, 1981.

77. Brazelton, T.B.: Crying in infancy, Pediatrics **29**:579, 1962.

78. Jakobsson, I., and Lindberg, T.: Cow's milk proteins cause infantile colic in breast-fed infants: a double blind cross-over study, Pediatrics **71**:268, 1983.

79. Jakobsson, I., and LIndberg, T.: Cow's milk as a cause of infantile colic in breast-fed infants, Lancet **2**:437, 1978.

80. Lothe, L., Lindberg, T., and Jakobsson, I.: Cow's milk formula as a cause of infantile colic, Pediatrics **70**:7, 1982.

81. Cohen, S.: Developmental characteristics of lower esophageal sphincter dysfunction: a possible mechanism for infantile chalasia, Gastroenterology **67**:252, 1974.

82. Harris, L.E., and Chan, J.C.M.: Infant feeding practices, Am. J. Dis. Child. **117**:483, 1969.

ADDITIONAL READINGS

Ahn, C.H., and McLean, W.C.: Growth of the exclusively breast-fed infant, Am. J. Clin. Nutr. **33**:183, 1980.

Almrath, S.G.: Water requirements of breast-fed infants, Am. J. Clin. Nutr. **31**:1154, 1978.

Beal, V.A.: Dietary intake of individuals followed through infancy and childhood, Am. J. Public Health **51**:1107, 1961.

Beal, V.A.: On the acceptance of solid foods, and other food patterns of infants and children, Pediatrics **20**:448, 1957.

Berenberg, W., and others: Hazards of skim milk, unboiled and boiled, Pediatrics **44**:734, 1969.

Breast feeding and avoidance of food antigens in the prevention and management of allergic disease, Nutr. Rev. **36**:181, 1978.

Chan, G.M., and others: Growth and mineralization of normal breast-fed infants and the effects of lactation on maternal mineral status, Am. J. Clin. Nutr. **36**:438, 1982.

Committee on Nutrition, American Academy of Pediatrics: On the feeding of supplemental foods to infants, Pediatrics **65**:1178, 1980.

David, R.D., Ellis, D., and Gartner, J.C.: Water intoxication in normal infants: role of antidiuretic hormone in pathogenesis, Pediatrics **68**:349, 1981.

Fomon, S.J., and others: Influence of fat and carbohydrate content of diet on food intake and growth of male infants, Acta Paediatr. Scand. **65**:136, 1976.

Hambraeus, L.: The significance of mothers milk and breast-feeding for development and later life, Bibl. Nutr. Dieta. **31**:1, 1982.

Jimenez, R., and others: Vitamin K–dependent clotting factor in normal breast-fed infants, J. Pediatr. **100**:424, 1982.

Johnson, G.N., Purvis, G.A., and Wallace, R.D.: What nutrients do our infants really get? Nutr. Today **16:**4, 1981.

Larson, B.L., and Smith, V.R., editors: Lactation, a comprehensive treatise, vol. III, Nutrition and biochemistry of milk/maintenance, New York, 1974, Academic Press, Inc.

Lebenthal, E.: Use of modified food starch in infant nutrition, Am. J. Dis. Child. **132:**850, 1978.

Paxson, C.L., Adcock, E.W., and Morris, F.H.: Osmolalities of infant formulas, Am. J. Dis. Child. **131:**139, 1977.

Pipes, P.: When should semisolid foods be fed to infants? J. Nutr. Educ. **9:**57, 1977.

Thomas, M.R., and others: The effects of vitamin C, vitamin B_6, vitamin B_{12}, folic acid, and riboflavin on the breast milk and maternal status of well-nourished women at 6 months postpartum, Am. J. Clin. Nutr. **33:**2151, 1980.

Nourishing the Premature and Low Birth Weight Infant

5

MARY J. O'LEARY

The past decade has seen many advances in neonatal intensive care. New technologies, better understanding of pathophysiology, and cooperative interactions to regionalize the delivery of perinatal care have all contributed to the increased survival of newborns requiring intensive care. As the prognosis for survival of low birth weight (LBW) neonates improves, attention is being focused on the nutritional support of these infants. Adequacy of postnatal nutrition affects the clinical course of critically ill babies and may influence their long-term developmental outcome. This chapter describes current methods of nutritional support and suggests guidelines for nutritional assessment and management of LBW infants who require intensive care.

NUTRITION SERVICES IN NEONATAL CARE

Delivery of Neonatal Care

Practical considerations of limited economic, technical, and human resources prohibit the availability of intensive care facilities in all hospitals. However, so that all infants may be provided equal access to the highest quality care, a regionalized system of perinatal services has evolved over the past decade.

□Parts of this chapter are modified from O'Leary, M.J.: Nutritional care of the low birth weight infant. In Krause, M.V., and Mahan, L.K., editors: Food, nutrition, and diet therapy, ed. 7, Philadelphia, 1984, W.B. Saunders Co.

The regional perinatal network encompasses three levels of neonatal care. The system of classifying nurseries as level I, II, or III, based on the type of care they are capable of providing for newborn infants, has been described in several recent publications.[1-3]

Level I nurseries provide uncomplicated neonatal care for healthy infants who are products of normal, full-term pregnancies. In addition, level I nursery personnel are trained in early detection of potential complications and use coordinated mechanisms for referral and transports of high-risk infants to level II or level III units. When unexpected problems arise suddenly after birth, care provided on level I nurseries usually consists of stabilization until the infant can be safely transferred.

Level II nurseries also provide a full range of services for normal newborns and expertise in screening and referral of high-risk infants. But these nurseries are also prepared to care for sick neonates who are moderately ill or convalescing babies whose immaturity or medical risks preclude discharge.

In contrast level III nurseries are specifically staffed and equipped to cope with the most serious types of neonatal illnesses and abnormalities. Critically ill infants usually require intensive care and are hospitalized in neonatal intensive care units of level III tertiary care centers. A level III neonatal intensive care unit often assumes a leadership role within its region of influence by setting standards of clinical care, developing educational materials, and providing consultative services to other nurseries. The nutrition specialist on such a unit may, in turn, have a similar opportunity and responsibility to serve as a regional resource for improvement in nutritional care of high-risk newborns.

Role of the Nutritionist

The skills required of the pediatric nutritionist vary according to the clinical status of the newborn infants at each level of neonatal care. The National Research Council Committee on Nutrition of the Mother and Preschool Child has identified specific skills required to provide clinical services at each of the three levels of neonatal care.[4] In general, these skills should enable the nutrition consultant to screen for the various nutrition problems, monitor and assess nutritional progress, and develop and implement management plans.

It is important that nutrition services be coordinated with the physicians, nurses, and pharmacists also involved in the clinical care of these infants. Providing adequate nutrition to intensive care neonates is a challenge that requires the skillful input of several disciplines. Many nutritionists function as members of nutrition support teams that facilitate development of guidelines for safe and effective nutritional management of critically ill neonates.[5]

LBW INFANTS REQUIRING INTENSIVE CARE

Characteristics

The infants cared for in Level III intensive care units typically include those at high medical risk, critically ill babies with serious pediatric or surgical problems, or infants suffering from congenital abnormalities. Many of these infants weigh less than 2500 gm (5½ pounds) at birth, and are therefore classified as LBW infants. Increasing numbers of infants weighing less than 1500 gm (3½ pounds) are being admitted to Level III intensive care units.

These tiny babies are frequently referred to as very low birth weight (VLBW) infants. The medical status of larger infants may also warrant intensive care. However, the discussion in this chapter will focus on the particular problems and nutritional needs of LBW and VLBW infants who require Level III intensive care (Fig. 5-1).

Infants may be LBW because of a shortened period of gestation, which means that they are premature, or because of a retarded rate of growth, which makes them small for gestational age. Whereas the full-term infant is born between 37 and 42 weeks' gestation, a premature infant is born before 37 weeks' gestation. Infants born before 25 weeks' gestation rarely survive. Although the management of VLBW infants who require intensive care has improved dramatically during the past decade, medical science is still unable to meet the metabolic and medical needs of most infants born before the third trimester of pregnancy (earlier than 26 weeks' gestation).

Accurate assessment of gestational age is important in establishing nutritional goals for individual infants and in differentiating the short gestation infant from the small for gestational age infant. This differentiation is determined by the date of the last menstrual period, fetal ultrasound, and clinical assessment. Clinical parameters fall into two broad groups: (1) a series of neurological signs, dependent mainly on postures and tone, and (2) a series of external characteristics that reflect the physical maturity of the infant.[6]

LBW infants may have a variety of clinical problems in the early postnatal period. These problems vary in type and severity depending on such factors as the intrauterine health of the fetus, degree of prematurity, birth-related trauma, and functioning of immature or stressed organ systems. Although a wide range of medical problems may complicate the neonatal course of LBW infants, certain problems occur with such frequency as to be considered typical problems of prematurity. Small, immature infants are at risk for development of the problems listed in Table 5-1. Not all premature infants do, in

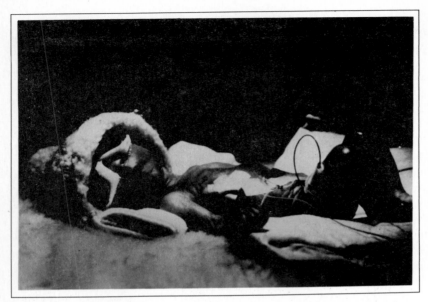

Fig. 5-1. Little girl born at 26 weeks' gestation, weighing 650 gm. Her eyes are covered for protection from the photography lights.

Table 5-1. Examples of problems common to premature or LBW infants in the neonatal period

System	Problem
Respiratory	Hyaline membrane disease, also known as respiratory distress syndrome
Cardiovascular	Patent ductus arteriosus
Renal	Fluid and/or electrolyte imbalance
Neurological	Intracranial hemorrhage
Metabolic	Hypoglycemia; hypocalcemia
Gastrointestinal	Hyperbilirubinemia; feeding intolerance; necrotizing enterocolitis
Hematological	Anemia
Immunological	Sepsis; pneumonia; meningitis

fact, develop clinical signs of these potential problems. However, medical and nutritional management of high-risk infants must anticipate their occurrence so that preventive measures can be taken or effective treatment modalities employed.

Metabolic Reserve

The inevitable interruption in influx of water, energy, and nutrients that occurs at the time of birth presents a greater hazard for the premature infant than for the full-term infant.[7] The premature infant has a smaller metabolic reserve and is physiologically less well prepared to maintain homeostasis. Fat stores are limited because most fetal fat is deposited during the last 6 weeks of gestation. In the premature infant weighing 1000 gm, fat contributes only 1% of total body weight; in contrast, the body of the full-term infant (3500 gm) is about 16% fat.[8] Glycogen reserves are particularly small and are rapidly depleted. Babies who weigh 1000 gm have a glycogen and fat reserve of approximately 110 kcal/kg.[9] With basal metabolic needs of about 50 kcal/kg/day, it is obvious that these babies will rapidly run out of fat and carbohydrate fuel unless adequate nutritional support is established. Depletion time will vary between 2 and 4 days, depending on the volume and concentration of parenteral dextrose that can be tolerated. Obviously, depletion time will be even shorter for premature babies who weigh less than 1000 gm at birth. Energy reserves are depleted most quickly by tiny infants who suffer from intrauterine growth retardation.

It is often difficult, however, to provide adequate nutritional intake during the first several days of life because of immaturity of the organ systems and severe medical problems. When adequate dietary intake cannot be achieved and fat and glycogen reserves have been exhausted, the infant will begin to catabolize vital body protein tissue for energy. Heird and others[9] have theoretically estimated the survival time of starved and semistarved infants. Their estimates assume depletion of all glycogen and fat and about one third of body protein tissue at a rate of 50 kcal/kg/day with fluids as intravenous water (no exogenous calories) or 10% dextrose solution. Even at the expense of significant protein tissue catabolism, the projected survival times shown in Table 5-2 are alarmingly short. These numbers are estimates and lack empirical precision, but they do serve to demonstrate the disadvantage of the small infant when faced with inadequate nutritional support.

Premature babies with small metabolic reserves are particularly vulnerable to the hazardous consequences of protein-energy malnutrition. Inadequate intake for even a few days may adversely affect their clinical course. For example, immature infants suffering from pulmonary disease may experience weakening of the respiratory muscles, depression of ventilatory drive, and increased difficulty in weaning from mechanical ventilation when protein-energy malnutrition complicates their clinical status.[10] The relationship between protein-energy malnutrition and decreased immune competence is well known and results in increased risk of infection.[11] Cardiac performance of malnourished patients may be depressed, resulting in decreased ability to withstand episodes of stress such as surgery.[12]

Furthermore, malnutrition in critically ill infants may compromise their long-term outcome. There is suggestive evidence from animal[13] and human[14] studies that protein-energy malnutrition at the crit-

Table 5-2. Duration of survival expected in starvation (H_2O only) and semistarvation ($D_{10}W$)

Birth Weight (gm)	Estimated Survival Time (Days)	
	H_2O only	$D_{10}W$
1000	4	11
2000	12	30
3500	32	80

From Heird, W.C., and others: J. Pediatr. **80**:351, 1972.

ical period of rapid brain growth results in irreversible impairment of brain growth and function. Damage from protein-energy malnutrition includes reduction in the number and size of brain cells. Therefore neonates in general, and LBW infants in particular, are at risk of suffering damaging consequences when protein-energy malnutrition complicates their clinical course.

Need for Fluid, Glucose, and Electrolytes

Because most LBW infants who require intensive care are unable to tolerate enteral feedings in the early neonatal period, intravascular delivery of fluid, glucose, and electrolytes must be established to maintain fluid balance and promote metabolic homeostasis. Immature newborns have an immediate need for fluid to replace ongoing water losses. Since most of these babies are unstable at birth and deprived of oral intake, intravenous (IV) fluid therapy is usually required to prevent dehydration or fluid imbalance. Premature infants become rapidly dependent on an exogenous source of glucose because of limited glycogen stores and decreased capacity for gluconeogenesis. To prevent hypoglycemia and to spare protein tissue, an IV solution containing a measured amount of dextrose is infused as soon as primary postnatal demands for resuscitation and stabilization have been completed. In addition to fluid and glucose administration, most premature newborns require sodium, chloride, and potassium to replace daily losses. In practice, electrolytes are not usually added to the IV solution until the second day of life.

PARENTERAL NUTRITION

Parenteral nutrition is broadly defined as the delivery of nutritive material by some means other than through the intestinal canal. Common usage of the term parenteral nutrition, however, usually refers to the parenteral delivery of a hyperalimentation solution containing dextrose, amino acids, electrolytes, minerals, vitamins, and trace elements. The osmolarity of this solution increases in proportion to the concentration of dextrose in the infusate and can be markedly hyperosmolar. Infusion of an isoosmolar lipid emulsion may accompany the delivery of the hyperalimentation solution.

Hyperalimentation fluids can provide all essential nutrients as the sole means of nutritional support. In this case, the term total parenteral nutrition is used to signify that no enteral feeds are being given and that all nutritional support occurs by means of a vascular route. In contrast, partial parenteral nutrition refers to the administration of hyperalimentation fluids as a supplement to limited enteral intake. Such a regimen is advantageous for LBW infants who are unable to tolerate full enteral feedings or who are being "weaned" from total parenteral nutrition to a program of complete enteral nutrition.

Route of Administration

It is possible to provide complete nutritional support to LBW infants by either central or peripheral vascular routes. Using the technique of catheter placement in a central blood vessel, it is possible to provide LBW infants with adequate caloric intake to permit positive nitrogen balance and allow normal growth and development.[15,16] Because blood flow through central vessels such as the superior vena cava is very rapid, hyperosmotic hyperalimentation fluids are quickly diluted and inflammation in the wall of the blood vessel is prevented. It is also possible to meet the nutritional needs of some LBW infants by peripheral delivery of parenteral nutrition. When isotonic lipid emulsions are appropriately used, their high caloric density decreases the need for hyperosmotic glucose solutions, such that the osmolarity of the solution entering the peripheral blood vessel is low enough to prevent damage to the vein.

Selecting the peripheral versus the central route of administration involves several considerations that should be individualized according to the unique circumstances of each infant. The principal factors to consider in choosing one technique over another are: (1) the caloric needs of the infant,[17] and (2) the projected duration of need for parenteral support.[18] Peripheral vein hyperalimentation solutions are usually not as calorically dense as central vein solutions. Peripheral veins are limited to dextrose concentrations of less than 10% to 15%, compared with central veins that can tolerate concentrations of 20% to 25%. This means that infants who receive central vein nutrition can potentially receive more calories to promote positive nitrogen balance and growth. In the critically ill infant for whom prolonged parenteral therapy is projected and improved physical growth is possible, central vein nutrition is usually the treatment of choice.[18] If minimal stress is present and vessel access is good, the peripheral route of administration is often preferred.[18] This is most desirable for infants who are expected to receive less than 2 to 3 weeks of parenteral nutrition therapy or for those infants who receive parenteral nutrition as a temporary supplement to a progressive enteral intake.

Consideration of certain practical advantages and potential disadvantages also plays a role in selecting the preferred method of delivery for individual infants. Several of these advantages and disadvantages are listed in Table 5-3. In general, there are more serious technical and infectious complications encountered in central compared with peripheral delivery, but both routes have characteristic problems related to the method of administration. Although strict adherence to aseptic technique and to established guidelines for catheter care and maintenance markedly decrease the incidence of these complications, neither method of delivery is benign. Therefore candidates for parenteral nutrition should be carefully selected on the basis of

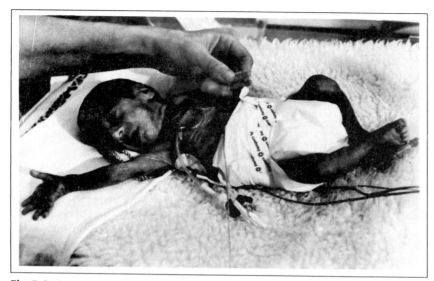

Fig. 5-2. A central venous catheter has been surgically implanted in the superior vena cava. This type of catheter permits delivery of hyperalimentation by a central venous route.

Table 5-3. Advantages and disadvantages of central compared with peripheral vein parenteral nutrition

	Advantages	Disadvantages
Central	Stable catheter	Infection of blood by means of catheter
	Concentrated dextrose solutions used allowing smaller infusion volume	Venous thrombosis
	Long-term	Hypoglycemia if abruptly discontinued
		Catheter must be surgically placed
		Requires frequent dressing changes
		Catheter dislodgment and infusion of fluid into thoracic cavity
Peripheral	Not surgically placed	Catheter unstable; repeated attempts to restart IV may be stressful
	Infection less likely	Depletion of venous access
		Interruption of nutrition when IV out of patient
		Larger volume of infusion

Modified from Dolcourt, J.: Pediatric parenteral nutrition manual, Salt Lake City, Utah, 1983, Primary Children's Medical Center.

need and the potential benefits of the nutritional support weighed against the risks inherent to the methods of delivery before initiating therapy. The decision to begin parenteral nutrition in infants should occur on an individualized rather than on a routine basis.

Indications

The need for parental nutrition is clear for those infants who have gastrointestinal problems that preclude or severely limit the use of the intestine for nutritional support. Infants with congenital anomalies of the enteric canal are usually unable to receive enteral nutrition until corrective surgical procedures occur. Total parenteral nutrition is indicated for these infants soon after birth and should be continued until recuperation is sufficient to permit oral feedings.[19] The use of total parenteral nutrition in surgical gastrointestinal disorders such as gastroschisis, omphalocele, tracheoesophageal fistulas, intestinal atresias, malrotation, and volvulus has been shown to greatly decrease the rate of morbidity and mortality in this vulnerable group of babies.[20-22]

Infants with ischemic disease of the intestinal mucosa, such as necrotizing enterocolitis, are also candidates for parenteral nutrition support. If necrotizing enterocolitis results in intestinal resection, total parenteral nutrition meets the infant's nutritional needs until the remaining intestine demonstrates returned function. According to Kerner,[18] a gradual transition from parenteral to enteral feeding can then begin. Partial parenteral nutrition provides supportive therapy while the intestine adapts and gradually compensates for the rapid transit, diminished digestive mass, and inadequate absorptive surface area.[18] Most of these infants are eventually able to tolerate a program of complete enteral nutrition.

Parenteral nutrition may also be indicated for repletion of a malnourished infant.[23] In clinical situations in which prolonged starvation is anticipated, parenteral nutrition may be started prophylactically (e.g., postoperative support).[24] Older infants with intractable diarrhea may be successfully rehabilitated with parenteral feedings as well.[25] In addition, certain situations that do not involve the gastrointestinal tract warrant the use of parenteral nutrition, for example, renal failure, hypermetabolic states, and malignancies.[26]

The need for parenteral nutrition in infants with the aforementioned conditions is clearly indicated. When the technique is applied with proper care, the morbidity and mortality associated with these clinical problems can be significantly reduced. Other clinical situations, however, are not as clearly indicative of the need for parenteral nutrition support. Deciding whether or not to give hyperalimentation solutions to a LBW infant for whom feeding is risky rather than prohibitive is a process that is more often ambiguous than clear.

Many VLBW infants demonstrate poor tolerance to enteral feedings in the first few days or even weeks of life. This is related in part to the inadequate mechanical and digestive function of their immature gastrointestinal tract. Mechanical limitations such as poor coordination of intestinal motility and delayed gastric emptying contribute to delayed introduction and slow progression of enteral feeds in VLBW infants.[18] The digestive capacity of the gastrointestinal system is also limited, although it is usually adequate when human milk or specialized formula products are appropriately selected. VLBW infants may also have medical problems that limit their ability to ingest and use enteral nutrients.[18] In general, infants who are medically unstable are often precarious in their tolerance of enteral feeds as well. When medical and gastrointestinal problems are imposed on LBW infants, some projection of the extent to which they will delay the progression of enteral feeds is important in determining whether or not parenteral nutrition is appropriate.

Parenteral nutrition in LBW infants is usually indicated when the projected duration of need for parenteral support exceeds the metabolic reserve of the infant. This period varies, as does the metabolic reserve, according to the birth weight and gestational age of the infant, the adequacy of intrauterine growth, and any metabolic stress that is superimposed on basal energy needs. For VLBW infants whose metabolic reserves are severely limited, it is imperative that efforts are made to provide early nutritional support. As shown in Table 5-2, survival time under conditions of starvation and semistarvation diminishes in proportion to decreasing birth weight and gestational age. Because malnutrition complicates the clinical course of these tiny infants and may have irreversible developmental consequences, parenteral nutrition may be indicated for VLBW infants who are unable to tolerate enteral feedings after as little as 2 to 3 days. Even if small amounts of enteral feeds are introduced in the first couple of days of life, immaturity of organ systems and coexisting medical stress often slow oral advancement substantially enough to warrant partial parenteral nutrition as a supplement to enteral feedings until the premature infant can tolerate full enteral volume and calories. When early introduction of any oral feeding is prohibited, the nutritional benefits and potential risks associated with parenteral nutrition should be considered and total parenteral nutrition started if the infant's condition permits catheter placement.

Larger LBW infants with correspondingly larger metabolic reserves may be able to tolerate a slightly longer delay before the need for parenteral nutrition becomes imminent. Still, these infants will begin to catabolize vital body protein tissue and deplete reserves of other essential nutrients within the first week of life if adequate nutritional support is not provided. Assuming somewhat larger stores of fat and glycogen in this population, the key factor in determining whether or not to begin parenteral nutrition is the predicted time lapse before there is adequate enteral intake. For example, a stable infant weighing 2000 gm who is hospitalized to rule out the possibility of sepsis (systemic infection) may initially receive IV fluid, glucose, and electrolytes but may not require hyperalimentation fluids if enteral feeds can be initiated within the first 4 to 5 days of life and can then be rapidly advanced. However, another infant of similar size and metabolic reserve who suffers episodes of clinical instability and associated feeding setbacks may benefit from partial parenteral nutrition until enteral feedings are sufficient to maintain homeostasis and promote growth.

Energy Needs

The energy needs of LBW infants who receive parenteral nutrition are usually less than those of infants who are enterally fed because absorptive loss does not occur when nutritional intake bypasses the intestinal tract. Whereas most LBW infants who are enterally fed need approximately 120[27] to 130[7] kcal/kg/day to grow, premature neonates demonstrate adequate growth with parenteral energy intakes of about 70 to 90 kcal/kg/day.[28]

Published studies of LBW infants generally show values for resting caloric expenditure to be about 50 kcal/kg/day, provided that measurements are made under thermoneutral conditions and that the infants are relatively inactive.[29] Provision of 60 kcal/kg/day plus 2.5 gm protein/kg/day is apparently adequate to meet resting metabolic needs as well as supporting some degree of tissue protein synthesis.[30] However, higher energy intakes are required for optimal nitrogen retention and growth. In a recent study of premature infants receiving total parenteral nutrition, intakes averaging 80 kcal/kg/day compared with 50 kcal/kg/day resulted in higher daily nitrogen retention and weight gain.[31] Nonprotein energy intakes providing greater than 70 kcal/kg/day and protein intakes of 2.7 to 3.5 gm/kg/day resulted in nitrogen accumulation growth rates similar to intrauterine values.[31]

It is often difficult, however, to provide sick LBW infants with adequate energy and other nutrients in the first several days of life. Many of these infants are severely stressed in the early postnatal period and may be fluid restricted to permit normal diuresis and to support medical management. These factors can limit energy intake to as little as 30 to 40 kcal/kg/day.[32] Until the infant's medical condition has stabilized, the goal of nutritional management should be the prevention of tissue catabolism and maintenance of metabolic homeostasis. This can usually be accomplished when energy intakes approximate 50 to 60 kcal/kg/day. An individual approach to the estimation of energy needs is helpful, because actual requirements can vary depending on factors such as gestational age, physiological stress, and thermal stability.

Hyperalimentation Solutions

Hyperalimentation fluids are complex solutions that must be carefully managed to derive maximum nutritional benefit without exceeding metabolic limitations. These fluids are capable of providing all essential nutrients to promote positive nitrogen balance and growth but must be tailored in their composition to meet the unique needs of each LBW infant. The theoretical and practical considerations involved in the management of hyperalimentation in pediatric patients have been expertly summarized by Kerner.[33]

Fluid. Parenteral fluid therapy is required by LBW infants who are unable to tolerate an adequate enteral volume. Infants deprived of a normal oral intake continue to lose basal amounts of fluid and require water replacement.[34] Water requirements are therefore estimated by the sum of the predicted losses. A major route of water loss in LBW infants occurs by evaporation of water through the skin and respiratory tract; this insensible water loss is highest in the smallest and least mature babies.[35] Reasons for the inverse correlation between birth weight and insensible water loss include increased permeability of the skin epidermis to water, larger body surface area relative to body weight, and greater skin blood flow relative to metabolic rate.[36] Water loss through the skin of LBW infants occurs mainly by evaporative heat loss, since sweating is limited in premature infants. Measurements of insensible water loss using direct weighing techniques show that insensible losses vary from about 10 to 60 ml/kg/day, with the higher losses occurring in the smallest babies.[37]

Excretion of urine is another important route of water loss for LBW infants. The range of urine volume that can be excreted is determined by the solute load presented to the kidneys for excretion and by the ability of the kidneys to concentrate the urine.[38] Immature infants are limited in their ability to regulate water balance by means of antidiuretic hormone control and do not achieve maximal concentration or dilution mechanisms until some time after birth.[36] Urine excretion by LBW babies normally varies between 60 and 125 ml/kg/day, with loss occurring at a rate of about 2 to 5 ml/kg/hour.[39] Fecal water loss on the other hand is small and relatively constant. The stool accounts for only about 10 to 15 ml/kg/day of water lost.[39]

There are two other factors to consider in the estimation of water requirements for LBW infants. First, there is a net loss of fluid when water is retained by tissues during growth. Second, there is a net gain in fluid when water is produced as a by-product of oxidative metabolism. Because the net loss and gain of these fluid components is roughly equal, they do not usually have practical importance in the calculation of actual water requirements for LBW infants.[39]

Several factors can either increase or decrease the fluid requirements of LBW infants by altering fluid losses. For example, radiant warmers[40] and phototherapy lights[41] markedly increase water requirements by increasing insensible fluid losses. On the other hand, heat shields[35] and thermal blankets[42] help to decrease the evaporative water losses of LBW infants. To determine total water requirements, the various environmental and physiological factors that alter fluid losses should be taken into account and the appropriate additions or subtractions should be made according to individual circumstances.

Because of the many variables affecting fluid losses and because of differences among babies depending on birth weight and medical status, it is difficult to establish routine guidelines for fluid management of LBW infants.[34] Many nurseries prefer to determine fluid needs based on individualized criteria. After initial fluid administration of 40 to 80 ml/kg/day, subsequent needs are determined by clinical examination of the patient. Clinical parameters and laboratory data such as urine output and specific gravity, serum electrolyte and blood urea nitrogen, blood pressure, peripheral circulatory status, mucous membrane moisture, and skin turgor aid in individualized fluid management.[39] In addition, serial body weights should be determined on a routine daily basis or more often as clinically indicated. According to the guidelines of Hodson and Truog, total daily fluid administration is generally increased by 10 to 15 ml/kg/day depending on clinical status, laboratory data, and estimates of insensible water loss.[39] Most LBW infants receive 100 to 200 ml of fluid/kg/day by the second week of life, with intakes averaging 120 to 160 ml/kg/day.

The consequences of inadequate fluid intake in LBW infants are serious and include such problems as dehydration, electrolyte imbalances, and hypotension.[43] Fluid excess on the other hand can also be dangerous for the LBW infant. If too much fluid is administered, edema and congestive heart failure with opening of the ductus arteriosus may ensue.[44,45] There are also some indications that intraventricular hemorrhage and bronchopulmonary dysplasia are related to excessive fluid administration in the first few days of life.[46,47]

Appropriate fluid intakes in premature infants should allow for normal transition of body fluids from fetal to neonatal status. Premature infants have relatively more total body water than do full-term infants, and a greater percentage of this total is present as extracellular fluid (Table 5-4). A contraction of extracellular water normally occurs in all newborn infants in the first few days of life but appears to be particularly important for LBW infants.[48] This reduction is accompanied by a normal loss of body weight (10% to 15%)[37] and by an improvement in renal function.[49] Failure of changes in fluid dynamics and lack of diuresis in the early neonatal period may complicate the course of the respiratory disease in LBW infants.[50]

Carbohydrate. Although LBW infants are metabolically dependent on the availability of glucose, there is no absolute parenteral or enteral requirement for carbohydrate. Glucose can be produced in the body through gluconeogenic pathways or by catabolism of glycogen stores. Enzymes for the endogenous production of glucose are present in LBW infants, but the high incidence of hypoglycemia in these babies when exogenous intake is poor indicates that gluconeogenic mechanisms are immature and that glycogen stores are limited in premature infants.

Dextrose (D-glucose) is the carbohydrate typically chosen for infants receiving parenteral nutrition. Glucose is a good source of energy, providing 3.4 kcal/gm. Tolerance to glucose infusions, how-

Table 5-4. Body water compartments of preterm and full-term infants (expressed as percent of body weight)

	Preterm	Full-term
Total body water	85-90%	80%
Extracellular fluid	50-55%	45%

From Hodson, W.A., and Truog, W.E.: Fluid and glucose administration. In Hodson, W.A., and Truog, W.E., editors: Critical care of the newborn, Philadelphia, 1983, W.B. Saunders Co.

ever, is variable in newborns and is limited in premature infants. Glucose intolerance characterized by hyperglycemia is common among LBW infants and is most frequently encountered in very immature babies.[51] The reasons for the limited glucose tolerance are still unclear, but possible causes include inadequate insulin production or function and immature hepatic enzyme systems.[52] It is interesting to note that hyperglycemia does not occur as often in LBW infants who are receiving an IV infusion of dextrose plus amino acids, compared with LBW infants receiving dextrose alone.[53] Kerner[52] has suggested that the amino acids may exert a stimulatory effect on the release of insulin, but concentrations of insulin in plasma under controlled circumstances have not yet been measured. Other hormonal systems may also play a role in the glucose metabolism of LBW neonates.[52] For example, the higher incidence of hyperglycemia among stressed infants may be associated with the stress-induced release of catecholamines and glucagon.[54]

Hyperglycemia is a hazardous condition for the LBW infant. When serum glucose levels exceed 150 mg/100 ml, glucosuria may follow. Glucosuria causes an osmotic diuresis, which may lead to dehydration, increased serum osmolarity, and potential complications.[54] Administration of glucose is usually monitored by frequent evaluation of serum glucose levels and by checking glucose oxidase reagent tests (using Dextrostix or Chemstrips) of blood and urine every 8 hours or as needed.

The first step toward preventing hyperglycemia in LBW infants is the administration of an amount of glucose that can be adequately metabolized without exceeding the infant's glucose tolerance. The amount of glucose supplied to the infant is determined not only by the concentration of the solution, but also by the rate at which it is administered. It is important to realize that the glucose load, and not the dextrose concentration alone, determines the amount of glucose that is delivered to an infant. Glucose load may be calculated using the following formula:

$$\text{Glucose load} = \text{mg/kg/minute} = \text{mg glucose/ml} \times \text{ml/kg/minute}$$

This formula can be used to adjust fluid volume and dextrose concentration without changing the glucose load.

According to Kerner[52]

Infants weighing less than 1000g at birth should initially receive no more than 6 mg glucose/kg/min, and those weighing between 1000 g and 1500 g should not recieve more than 8 mg/kg/min. Even with these low glucose loads, hyperglycemia could conceivably occur. After the infant has stablilized and is able to tolerate the initial infusion, the glucose load can be increased slowly with careful monitoring.

This can be accomplished either by advancing the concentration of the dextrose solution or by increasing the fluid volume. Most stable VLBW infants will tolerate daily increments in glucose load of approximately 1.5 to 2.0 mg/kg/minute,[54] but individual infants can demonstrate considerable variation in glucose tolerance. Dextrose infusion in larger LBW and full-term infants can usually be initiated at a rate of 7 to 8 mg/kg/minute and then rapidly increased to 12 to 14 mg/kg/minute without difficulty.[52] The maximum glucose load is determined either by the infant's glucose tolerance or by limitations in fluid volume (e.g., patent ductus arteriosus) and dextrose concentration (e.g., peripheral veins).

Glucose intolerance in LBW infants occasionally persists to such an extent that it severely limits caloric intake. Because nutrition is of vital importance to these babies and because hyperglycemia associated with glucose intolerance can have damaging consequences, attempts have been made to provide calories using alternative carbohydrate sources. Experimental use of galactose has produced potentially favorable results. In a study of premature infants who were intolerant to glucose infusions alone, Sparks and others[55] were able to avoid hyperglycemic episodes and increase caloric intake by infusing a solution containing carbohydrate as half glucose and half galactose. This success may be explained by the fact that galactose metabolism neither requires nor stimulates a substantial insulin release[56] and that the rate of galactose metabolism in the perinatal liver in vivo is faster than the rate of glucose metabolism.[57] No clinical or biochemical evidence of galactose toxicity was noted in the Sparks study; however, blood galactose levels in the parenterally fed infants averaged 15 mg/100 ml. This can be compared with blood galactose levels in infants fed lactose-containing formulas (0.8 to 4.2 mg/100 ml) or in infants with untreated galactosemia (60 to 150 mg/100 ml). Although parenteral galactose therapy may be beneficial in glucose-intolerant babies, further studies must be completed before recommendations for the use of galactose can be assured to be safe. Alcohol has also been used to improve the caloric intake of LBW infants.[58] Adverse reactions are uncommon among infants given small quantities of alcohol parenteral nutrition infusions; however, there is concern that even moderately increased levels of alcohol in the blood may jeopardize the developing central nervous system of premature infants.[52] Thus, the use of alcohol in parenteral nutrition of LBW infants is not usually recommended.

Preliminary reports indicate that insulin can be effective for use in premature infants in whom glucose intolerance persists despite conservative glucose intake. In a study in which small quantities of insulin were continuously infused to hyperglycemic, VLBW infants, the glucose tolerance and caloric intake significantly improved, while blood glucose levels normalized.[59] Other reports, however, show a highly variable response to insulin administration by LBW infants. Whereas one study reported resistance to the effects of insulin by four VLBW infants,[60] another study demonstrated that even tiny amounts of insulin can rapidly provoke hypoglycemia in some babies.[61] Because LBW infants are variable in their response to exogenous insulin and because the effects can range from hyperresponsiveness to insulin resistance, insulin should be administered with caution until further data are available to establish safe guidelines for clinical use.

Whereas hyperglycemia is a common problem among LBW infants, hypoglycemia is a relatively uncommon phenomenon after the first few days of life. Under normal circumstances, it is a concern only when the glucose infusion declines precipitously, which may occur because of complications in delivery such as infiltration at the peripheral intravenous site.[52] Rapid weaning from IV dextrose may also precipitate a hypoglycemic response if adequate energy is not provided by enteral feedings. The dextrose concentration can usually be decreased by 5 mg/100 ml decrements at 12-hour intervals without significant hypoglycemia, e.g., $D_{15}W$ to $D_{10}W$ to D_5W. When a decrease is ordered, Dextrostix estimations should be made hourly for at least 3 hours, since rebound hypoglycemia usually occurs within that period.[54]

Dextrose solutions are notoriously hyperosmotic. Because of their high osmolarity, subcutaneous infusions of solutions exceeding 10% to 15% dextrose have a high incidence of skin sloughs. Therefore, dextrose used in peripheral vein parenteral nutrition should not exceed this concentration. Although central vein parenteral nutrition concentrations greater than 25% dextrose can be used, concentrations above 25% are usually not necessary. Table 5-5 lists various dextrose concentrations, with their corresponding osmolarities and caloric densities. Since the osmolarity of human

Table 5-5. Osmolarity and caloric density of dextrose solutions

Dextrose Solution	Calculated Osmolarity (mOsm/L)	kcal/ml
D_5W*	252	0.17
$D_{7.5}W$	378	0.25
$D_{10}W$	505	0.34
$D_{15}W$	758	0.51
$D_{20}W$	1010	0.68
$D_{25}W$	1263	0.85

*D_5W = 5% dextrose = 5 gm/100 ml. Since hydrated dextrose provides 3.4 kcal/gm, 5 gm/100 ml × 3.4 kcal/gm = 0.17 kcal/ml

blood is approximately 300 mOsm/L, it is apparent that most dextrose solutions are comparatively hyperosmotic.

Protein. The first protein solutions available for IV use were hydrolysates of fibrin and casein. These products successfully supported positive nitrogen balance and growth in infants but were also characterized by certain problems. The protein hydrolysate solutions contained several amino acids as chloride salts. This contributed to the development of hyperchloremic metabolic acidosis in infants receiving parenteral nutrition. Furthermore, the amino acid composition of the protein hydrolysate solutions was inconsistent.[62] During the process of hydrolysis, only about half of the whole proteins were broken down to free amino acids; the remaining nitrogen was present as peptides that were incompletely utilized.[63]

Protein hydrolysates have now largely been replaced by crystalline amino acid solutions. These solutions mimic the amino acid composition of naturally occurring proteins with high biological values, such as casein or egg albumin. Since the amino acid composition of these solutions is known, protein intake is more consistent when free amino acids are infused. Furthermore, the crystalline amino acid solutions are more easily tailored for special conditions that predispose to difficulties in nitrogen utilization. Metabolic studies comparing crystalline amino acids and protein hydrolysates generally show better nitrogen utilization of the amino acid solutions.[64] For these reasons, crystalline amino acid solutions are currently the most common and often the only IV preparations in use on intensive care nurseries.

Several amino acid solutions are on the market; the products identified in Table 5-6 are among those frequently chosen for use in parenteral nutrition of LBW infants. These solutions were originally designed for use in adults, and although they are acceptable for LBW infants, they are not ideal. These products contain lesser amounts of certain amino acids than are theoretically required and may contain excessive quantities of others. Infusion of mixtures containing high amounts of gly-

cine, for example, may result in plasma glycine levels approximately four times normal postprandial values.[65] Since glycine is a potent neurotransmitter inhibitor, hyperglycinemia may have adverse effects on the developing central nervous system. In addition, these products contain little tyrosine and cysteine; these amino acids may be required by premature neonates. In studies in which either cysteine or tyrosine was removed from the diets of premature infants, there was a decreased level of that amino acid in the infant's plasma, as well as impaired nitrogen retention and growth.[66] In the case of cysteine, this may be explained by the low hepatic cystathionase activity of immature infants, such that there is inadequate conversion of methionine to cysteine.[67]

Table 5-6. Concentrations of amino acids adjusted to 2% solutions and compared to recommendations of amino acid requirements

Amino acid	Solution					
	Snyderman[73] (mg/kg/day)	GF-1[74] (mg/kg/day)	Travasol (mg/100 ml)	Freamine II (mg/100 ml)	Aminosyn (mg/100 ml)	Freamine III (mg/100 ml)
L-Leucine	240	400	124	181	188	181
L-Phenylalanine	144	100	124	113	88	113
L-Methionine	72	15	116	106	80	106
L-Lysine	168	120	116	205	144	205
L-Isoleucine	180	200	96	139	144	139
L-Valine	168	200	92	132	160	132
L-Histidine	58	50	88	56	60	56
L-Threonine	144	60	84	80	104	80
L-Tryptophan	36	30	36	31	32	31
L-Alanine	444	100	415	141	256	141
L-Arginine	122	250	207	73	196	191*
L-Proline	192	50	84	224	171	224
L-Tyrosine	144	12.5	8	—	18	—
L-Cysteine	72	85	—	<5	—	<5
L-Taurine	—	—	—	—	—	—
L-Serine	166	100	—	118	84	118
L-Glycine	396	100	415	400	256	280*
L-Glutamate	48	12.5	—	—	—	—

From Kerner, J.A., Jr.: Protein requirements. In Kerner, J.A., Jr., editor: Manual of pediatric parenteral nutrition. Copyright © 1983, John Wiley & Sons, Inc., New York.
*Note the two changes in Freamine III compared with Freamine II.

Since taurine is synthesized from cysteine, it too may be required by premature infants. Although the role of taurine has not been fully elucidated, this sulfonic amino acid is involved in a number of physiological functions.[68] For example, taurine is important in neural transmission, and in retinal, cardiac and muscle function in laboratory animals, and possibly in humans as well.[68] It is important to note, however, that although LBW infants may require cysteine, tyrosine, and taurine, many of these infants have received long-term parenteral nutrition with the amino acid preparations listed in Table 5-6 without evidence of nutrient deficiency.

Given the importance of parenteral nutrition for LBW infants, it seems reasonable that efforts would be made to develop amino acid mixtures that are more appropriate for immature infants. Such research is, in fact, now underway, and new solutions will probably be available in the near future. Although the ideal standard for the composition of these solutions is unknown, the amino acid profile of human milk[70] and the minimum requirement of amino acids for premature infants based on oral feeding studies[71,72] have been suggested as guidelines. Both Snyderman[73] and Ghadimi[74] have suggested amino acid mixtures that may be preferred for use in premature infants. Table 5-6 gives their recommendations and compares them with currently available amino acid solutions.

Several metabolic problems can occur in association with parenteral administration of amino acid solutions. Premature infants are at risk of developing metabolic acidosis while receiving parenteral nutrition.[69] Seashore[75] attributes this to the excess of cationic amino acids in most protein solutions. Metabolism of these positively charged amino acids can lead to production of hydrogen ions in excess of the buffering capacity of small, sick infants. Careful administration of a modest amount of protein and frequent monitoring of serum electrolytes and blood pH help to protect against the development of metabolic acidosis. Premature infants receiving crystalline amino acids are also at

risk of developing hyperammonemia; this may be related to hepatic immaturity or to hepatic dysfunction that occurs as a result of hepatocellular damage.[76,77] Since the blood ammonia concentration is directly related to the amount of protein infused, protein intake should be reduced when blood ammonia levels are high.[75] Azotemia, characterized by elevated blood urea nitrogen values, may also occur if the amount of protein delivered to an infant is excessive.

Plasma amino acid patterns reflect the amino acid composition of IV protein solutions.[78] Because the currently available amino acid mixtures are not ideal, LBW infants receiving parenteral nutrition do not have normal plasma amino acid profiles.[69] Abnormal plasma aminograms may be etiologically related to the hepatic dysfunction mentioned earlier. Cholestatic jaundice is one of the most serious complications of hepatic dysfunction[79]; this subject has been recently reviewed by Sinatra.[80] Although the causes of cholestasis are not completely understood, studies indicate that risk factors include prematurity, the duration of total parenteral nutrition, and the absence of enteral feedings.[81] In addition, the amount of protein infused during total parenteral nutrition may contribute to hepatic dysfunction.[82] Many nurseries respond to rising direct bilirubin fractions and abnormal liver function tests by decreasing the amino acid load.

The amount of protein delivered to an infant is determined by the protein load, which is a function of both the concentration of the amino acid solution and the rate at which it is administered. For example, if a 1.5% amino acid solution (i.e., 1.5 gm protein/100 ml) is infused at a rate of 120 ml/kg/day, then the infant actually receives 1.8 gm protein/kg/day. Although the initiation and advancement of protein in parenteral nutrition varies with individual circumstances, protein is usually added to the IV solution in the first 2 to 5 days of life and is increased every other day or as tolerated. Factors such as glucose tolerance, venous access, and medical condition may influence the decision to start or to advance protein intake. Kerner[69] recommends an initial protein load of 0.5 to 1.0 gm/kg/day. This may be gradually increased to a maximum of 2.0 to 2.5 gm/kg/day. Under normal circumstances and with adequate caloric intake, LBW infants achieve positive nitrogen balance at protein levels of 2.0 to 2.5 gm/kg/day.[83] Provision of protein in excess of actual requirements is discouraged, as the additional protein offers no apparent advantage and greatly increases the risk of metabolic complications.[54] Older infants and children may tolerate somewhat higher intakes of protein, but most investigators agree that more than 3 gm/kg/day is not necessary.[69]

Lipid. The first IV fat emulsion (Lipomul) was removed from the market in 1965 because of its association with a "fat-overloading syndrome."[84] There was no IV replacement until 1975 when Intralipid (Cutter Laboratories) was approved for use in the United States. There are now two additional fat emulsions available for IV use: (1) Liposyn (Abbott Laboratories), and (2) Travamulsion (Travenol Laboratories). The fat-overloading syndrome has not been associated with any of these newer products.[84]

The composition of these products is shown in Table 5-7. It is apparent that these products have different oil bases; this affects the fatty acid composition of the emulsions. All three products contain ample linoleic acid to meet the essential fatty acid needs of LBW infants.[84] However, it is possible that Liposyn, which is made from safflower oil, does not provide enough linoleic acid for infants receiving long-term total parenteral nutrition.[85,86] Recent evidence documenting differences in triglyceride clearance also favors the use of soybean oil–base as compared with safflower oil–base emulsions.[87] Most of the clinical experience with IV fat has come from Intralipid use; positive experience makes this preparation the one most commonly used in pediatric parenteral nutrition.

The emulsified fat particles of IV fat emulsions are cleared from the bloodstream in a manner similar to chylomicron metabolism. As summarized by Gryboski and Walker,[26] the enzyme lipoprotein lipase hydrolyzes the IV lipid to free fatty acids. These free fatty acids either circulate, bound to albumin, and are utilized as an energy source or are reesterified to triglycerides and stored in adipose tissue. If the rate of IV fat administration exceeds the infant's ability to adequately clear the free fatty acids and triglycerides from the bloodstream, hyperlipidemia occurs. Elevated triglyceride and

Table 5-7. Ten percent intravenous fat emulsions

	Intralipid	Liposyn	Travamulsion
Base	Soybean oil	Safflower oil	Soybean oil
Fatty acids			
Linoleic*	54%	77%	56%
Oleic	26%	13%	23%
Palmitic	9%	7%	11%
Linolenic*	8%	<0.5%	6%
Glycerin	2.25%	2.5%	2.25%
Egg phospholipids (emulsifier)	1.2%	1.2%	1.2%
Osmolarity	280 mOsm/L	300 mOsm/L	270 mOsm/L
Caloric value	1.1 cal/ml	1.1 cal/ml	1.1 cal/ml

Modified from Kerner, J.A., Jr.: Fat requirements. In Kerner, J.A., Jr., editor: Manual of pediatric parenteral nutrition. Copyright © 1983, John Wiley & Sons, Inc., New York.
*Major differences between Liposyn and the other two products.

free fatty acid levels may cause visible lactescence. Although the ability of newborn infants to clear lipid is variable, most infants born at term have clearance rates similar to those of adults.[88] Premature infants, however, often experience impaired lipid tolerance.[89] Infants at particular risk for hyperlipidemia include those who are (1) very premature (less than 32 weeks' gestation), (2) born weighing less than 1500 gm, (3) small for gestational age, (4) septic or acutely ill, or (5) nutritionally depleted.[84] Intravenous fat emulsions may be given to these infants after the first week of life, but careful monitoring and cautious advancement are required.

Heparin stimulates the release of the enzyme lipoprotein lipase and has been used to improve lipid tolerance in LBW infants.[84] One study showed that single bolus doses of heparin decreased blood lipid levels in premature infants, but this effect appeared to be transient.[89] Larger doses of heparin are needed to achieve a longer effect; however, these are not recommended because of possible bleeding problems.[90] A subsequent study showed that continuous heparin infusion increased lipolytic activity and decreased concentrations of blood triglycerides.[90] Although serum free fatty acid concentrations increased in response to heparin administration, the higher levels did not seem to interfere with albumin-bilirubin binding.[90] The use of heparin in premature babies is potentially beneficial, but further investigations are needed before routine recommendations can be made.

The impaired lipid tolerance characteristic of many LBW infants may be related in part to a lack of exogenous carnitine. Carnitine facilitates the mechanism by which fatty acids are converted to acyl carnitine derivatives to permit transport across the mitochondrial membrane. Once inside the mitochondria, B-oxidation of the fatty acids can occur. There is no carnitine in any of the solutions currently used in total parenteral nutrition regimens, and plasma levels of carnitine rapidly decrease in premature newborns if exogenous carnitine is not given[91] (e.g., no human milk or cow's milk–base formula). Although clinical problems secondary to a lack of carnitine have not yet been reported in LBW infants receiving total parenteral nutrition[84] the likelihood that carnitine will improve lipid tolerance in these babies encourages further research.

One important reason for administering IV fat emulsions to LBW infants is to provide energy in a concentrated form. The caloric density (1.1 kcal/ml) of the 10% emulsions allows a substantial number of calories to be delivered with only a moderate increase in fluid volume. Intralipid and Liposyn are also available as 20% solutions (2.0 kcal/ml), but use of these concentrated products should be limited to infants who are severely fluid restricted.[84] The low osmolarities of these preparations (shown in Table 5-7) make it possible, in some cases, to deliver sufficient calories for growth by a peripheral route rather than obligating a central mode of delivery.

Another significant reason for IV fat administration is to prevent essential fatty acid deficiency. The essential fatty acid needs of humans are usually expressed as the requirement for linoleic acid. Daily requirements are estimated to be 1% to 2% of total calories[92]; infants receiving Intralipid (containing 54% linoleic acid), therefore, require about 2% to 4% of total calories as Intralipid. Premature infants who do not receive exogenous fat can quickly develop essential fatty acid deficiency. Biochemical evidence of essential fatty acid deficiency has been noted in neonates as early as 2 days after initiating fat-free total parenteral nutrition;[93] clinical signs of the deficiency do not appear until somewhat later. Under normal circumstances, LBW infants should receive 0.5 to 1 gm/kg/day of an IV fat emulsion by the beginning of their second week of life to prevent essential fatty acid deficiency.[94] Attempts to meet essential fatty acid needs by infusion of plasma[93] or by cutaneous application of oils rich in polyunsaturated fatty acids[95] are probably not effective.

Intravenous fat emulsions can be administered

separately by peripheral vein, or they can be infused along side the hyperalimentation solution through a "Y" or a "T" connector placed close to the peripheral or central vein infusion site.[96] Under no circumstances should other solutions or medications be mixed with the IV fat, since this will result in instability of the fat droplets. Generally, these products should be infused over 24 hours,[84] and the rate of infusion should not exceed 0.15 gm/kg/hour.[97]

Some nurseries recommend that a dose of IV fat be given to check for allergic reactions, fever, and the like.[84] However, hypersensitivity reactions are rare in pediatric patients, and this testing may not be necessary.[96] In general, 0.5 to 1 gm/kg/day may be used as an initial load for LBW infants and may be increased as tolerated by 0.25 to 0.5 gm/kg/day to a maximum of 3 gm/kg/day.[84] In general, the lipid load should not exceed 40% to 50% of the total calories. Rate of advancement and maximal total dose are determined by the infant's ability to metabolize the IV lipid preparation. Tolerance should be monitored by periodic measurements of serum triglyceride and free fatty acid levels.[98] If these levels are elevated, the IV fat load must be adjusted accordingly.

It is important that hyperlipidemia be prevented or rapidly ameliorated in LBW infants receiving IV fat emulsions. If allowed to persist, the elevated blood lipids may provoke the following potential complications: (1) displacement of albumin-bound bilirubin by plasma free fatty acids, and (2) alteration of pulmonary function.

First, free fatty acids released during the hydrolysis of IV fat emulsions can compete with bilirubin for albumin binding sites. If bilirubin is displaced, the increase in free or unbound bilirubin can potentiate the risk of kernicterus.[99] In practice, this is an uncommon problem when IV fat administration is started during the second week of life when the bilirubin level is less than half the potential exchange level for the individual infant and when the lipid is infused slowly over 24 hours.[84] In a study at Stanford University where these condi-

tions were applied to 29 premature infants, the fatty acid/serum albumin molar ratio was well below 6.0,[100] which is considered to be the safe limit for LBW neonates.[101]

Second, hyperlipidemia resulting from the infusion of IV fat emulsions has been reported to affect pulmonary function. Reports of fat accumulation in pulmonary capillaries, macrophages, and alveolar cells[102] and lipid deposits in pulmonary arteries[103] are cause for concern although the clinical consequences are still unknown. Another report demonstrated hypoxemia associated with IV fat infusion; there was a significant decrease in arterial oxygen tension (PO_2) in premature infants given IV fat during the first week of life.[104] The association between lipid infusion and pulmonary changes is notable, but there is as yet no clear evidence to prohibit or even discourage the use of IV fat emulsions in LBW infants with respiratory disease. In fact, there is some indication that IV fat, in addition to dextrose solutions, may benefit the infant with respiratory disease. Parenteral nutrition regimens that include half the nonprotein calories as fat have lower carbon dioxide production and minute ventilation compared with regimens in which dextrose alone is the nonprotein calorie source.[105] High glucose loads may aggravate ventilator weaning or precipitate pulmonary failure.[106]

Carbohydrate loads that are proportionately high compared with poor intakes of fat and protein are also associated with fatty infiltration of the liver.[84] This kwashiorkor-like picture improves when fat is included in the diet. In a study of total parenteral nutrition in protein-depleted rats, fatty infiltration of the liver was avoided when a regimen of 75% carbohydrate and 25% fat was used.[107]

Electrolytes. Sodium, potassium, and chloride are supplied by total parenteral nutrition solutions; the usual requirements for these elements are listed in Table 5-8. Actual requirements, however, are variable depending on such factors as clinical status, renal function, state of hydration, and the use of diuretics.[108] Very immature infants may be limited in their ability to conserve sodium and may

Table 5-8. Recommended daily intakes of electrolytes for parenteral nutrition solutions

Element	Daily amount
Sodium	2-4 mEq/kg
Potassium	2-3 mEq/kg
Chloride	2-3 mEq/kg

From Poole, R.L.: Electrolyte and mineral requirements. In Kerner, J.A., Jr., editor: Manual of pediatric parenteral nutrition. Copyright © 1983, John Wiley & Sons, Inc., New York.

require up to 9 mEq/kg/day to maintain a normal serum sodium concentration (135 to 140 mEq/L).[109] Although 2 to 3 mEq/kg/day is the usual amount of potassium needed to maintain a normal serum level (3.5 to 5.0 mEq/L),[108] occasionally VLBW infants require as much as 8 to 10 mEq/kg/day of potassium.[110] Excess chloride intake is more common than inadequate intake; hyperchloremia in infants is manifested as metabolic acidosis.[108] The incidence of this acidosis can be decreased by altering the amounts of chloride salts in parenteral nutrition solutions; for example, sodium and potassium can be supplied as acetate or phosphate salts, rather than exclusively as chloride salts.[108] Serum electrolyte levels should be routinely monitored; they are checked initially on a daily basis and later 2 to 3 times per week. Urine sodium and specific gravity may be helpful tests if there is a serum abnormality.[39]

Minerals. The recommended magnesium intake for an LBW infant on a parenteral nutrition regimen is 0.25 to 0.5 mEq/kg/day at some centers,[108] and 0.5 to 1.0 mEq/kg/day at others.[39] Although most infants are able to maintain homeostasis at this level of intake, some infants who have problems such as impaired renal function, inflammatory bowel disease, or losses related to diuretic use may have increased magnesium needs.[108]

Calcium and phosphorus are important components of pediatric parenteral nutrition regimens. Recommended intakes for full-term infants vary from 0.5 to 2.0 mmol phosphorus/kg/day, and requirements for calcium vary from 0.5 to 2.5 mEq/kg/day.[108] Premature infants, however, may have higher calcium and phosphorus needs. During the final weeks of gestation, the fetus normally receives 120 to 160 mg/kg/day of elemental calcium by means of active transport mechanisms across the placenta.[111] Phosphorus is delivered to the fetus in approximately a 2:1, calcium/phosphorus ratio. Since 1 mEq of calcium is equivalent to about 20 mg of elemental calcium, it is apparent that premature infants on typical parenteral nutrition regimens receive less than one third the amount that would have been received in utero.

Low intakes of calcium and phosphorus by LBW infants receiving total parenteral nutrition can result in poor bone mineralization.[112] Several cases of rickets have been reported in premature infants receiving total parenteral nutrition.[113,114] Rickets is most likely to occur in infants born very prematurely who receive parenteral nutrition for long periods.

The calcium and phosphorus requirements of growing premature infants receiving total parenteral nutrition are not precisely known. Usual total parenteral nutrition regimens with 1 to 2 mEq calcium/kg/day may be inadequate when the growth rate of premature infants is rapid. LBW infants receiving 3 mEq/kg/day, with or without adequate vitamin D intake, have been reported to have developed rickets.[113] The demand for calcium by premature infants who are growing at intrauterine rates may approximate intrauterine requirements[114]; these are estimated to be approximately 6 to 8 mEq/kg/day (i.e., 120 to 160 mg elemental calcium/kg/day).[112]

In the past, it has been difficult to provide enough IV calcium and phosphorus to approach intrauterine accretion rates without precipitation of the minerals.[112] However, recent studies have shown that the concentrations of calcium and phosphorus can be increased without precipitation by favorably altering certain properties of the hyperalimentation solution, i.e., pH, temperature, amino acid product and concentration, type of calcium salt, dextrose concentration, and the order in which calcium and phosphate are added to the solution.[115-118] Up to 120 mg calcium/kg/day and 55 mg phosphate/kg/day can be successfully delivered by selected parenteral nutrition solutions.[115] Although this is possible for many premature infants, the concentrations of calcium and phosphorus needed to achieve such intakes by VLBW infants who are fluid restricted may exceed the limit of solubility.[116]

Calcium and phosphorus should be added to the parenteral nutrition solutions of LBW infants on an ongoing basis; they should not be discontinued simply because serum calcium levels are normal. Serum calcium levels can be maintained in a normal range at the expense of bone demineralization. Also, these levels can be normal or even high when hypophosphatemia is present.[116] It is generally recommended that premature infants receiving total parenteral nutrition be followed for the development of osteopenia or rickets by monitoring serum calcium, phosphorus, and alkaline phosphatase levels, as well as by radiographical bone studies.

Vitamins. Multivitamin preparations for IV administration are essential for use in total parenteral nutrition therapy.[119] They are required for the prevention of vitamin deficiency states, for maintenance of good nutritional status, and in some cases, for rehabilitation of patients with vitamin depletion. Although IV vitamin administration is clearly necessary, the specific requirements for vitamins in total parenteral nutrition are not well known. Because precise data describing IV vitamin needs of preterm infants are not yet available, the Recommended Dietary Allowances (which provide standards for vitamin intake for healthy, full-term infants who are enterally fed) are currently used as general guidelines. It is likely, however, that premature infants have higher needs for some vitamins because they have smaller body stores, greater losses, and higher intrinsic needs compared with full-term infants. Furthermore, the parenteral vitamin needs of LBW infants are probably different from their enteral requirements.

Kerner[120] has summarized several reasons why parenteral vitamin requirements might differ from oral recommendations. First, there are potential interactions between vitamins in multivitamin preparations or between vitamins and the amino acid or dextrose components of hyperalimentation solutions that may alter the effectiveness of specific vitamins.[118,120] Second, parenteral nutrients are generally infused from plastic or glass containers containing room air; thus, vitamins may adhere to tubing and containers or may be subject to oxidative destruction.[120-122] Other factors that might affect parenteral vitamin requirements include degradation of vitamins secondary to phototherapy or sunlight exposure,[123] increased urinary excretion,[124] underlying disease states,[120] and impaired synthesis, activation, or storage of vitamins related to bypassing the enteric canal.[120] In general, these factors act to increase parenteral vitamin requirements. Needs for water-soluble vitamins have been estimated at two to three times the oral RDA; when these amounts are infused, neither deficiencies nor toxicities have been observed.

Biotin is present in some IV multivitamin preparations (e.g., MVI-Pediatric and MVI-12) but is not included in others (e.g., MVI-concentrate). Deficiency can occur in infants who receive biotin-free total parenteral nutrition if endogenous synthesis by intestinal bacteria is suppressed by antibiotic therapy.[125] Parenteral administration of a multivitamin preparation containing biotin is preferred for LBW infants.

Whereas problems associated with parenteral administration of the water-soluble vitamins are primarily associated with deficient intake, inappropriate administration of fat-soluble vitamins may result in toxicity as well. Because the fat-soluble vitamins can be stored in body tissues, intakes of these vitamins should be closely monitored.

The amount of vitamin A delivered to an LBW infant receiving total parenteral nutrition should probably not be less than about 1500 IU/day nor more than 3000 IU/day.[126] This recommendation assumes that there is a substantial loss of vitamin A from hyperalimentation solutions because of adherence of the vitamin to the IV container and tubing, and to a lesser extent, because of photodegradation and oxidation.[127,128] Thus the infant actually receives a considerably smaller quantity of vitamin A. Further studies are needed to establish more precise recommendations for vitamin A intake by parenterally fed infants.

It is possible to argue that the vitamin D requirements of parenterally fed infants are less than those of enterally fed infants because there is little intestinal absorption of calcium during total parenteral nutrition. Although this argument may apply to adults,[129] it apparently does not apply to premature infants. These rapidly growing babies need vitamin D in addition to adequate amounts of calcium and phosphorus to prevent rickets. In a study of premature infants who had radiographical evidence of rickets while receiving total parenteral nutrition, bone mineralization improved after the quantity of parenterally delivered vitamin D was increased.[130] Vitamin D–resistant rickets may have occurred as a result of immaturity of the vitamin D hydroxylating enzyme systems. Current recommendations for parenteral intake of vitamin D range from 400 to 600 IU/day.

The vitamin E stores of LBW infants are substantially lower than those of full-term infants (e.g., 3 mg vitamin E in a 1 kg infant compared with 20 mg vitamin E in a 3 kg infant.)[131] Depletion of vitamin E stores is accelerated by excessive intake of iron and polyunsaturated fatty acids and can result in hemolytic anemia in susceptible infants.[132] Precise requirements for vitamin E by LBW infants receiving parenteral nutrition are not clearly established. Bell and Filer[132] have suggested that infants on total parenteral nutrition who receive vitamin E from an IV multivitamin preparation and from IV fat emulsions will consume adequate amounts of vitamin E.

Vitamin K is required for the synthesis of coagulation factors in the blood. Normally, it is derived from the diet and is synthesized by intestinal bacteria. Although bacterial synthesis of vitamin K may be adequate for some infants receiving total parenteral nutrition, other infants may experience changes in gut flora, especially while receiving antibiotic therapy, that render vitamin K synthesis inadequate.[133] LBW infants receiving total parenteral nutrition plus antibiotic therapy should either receive an IV multivitamin preparation that contains vitamin K or receive supplemental vitamin K.[120]

Some of the IV multivitamin preparations currently available are identified in Table 5-9. When MVI concentrate is used, supplemental folate, vitamin B_{12}, and vitamin K are recommended.[120] These vitamins can be added to the hyperalimentation solution or administered separately by an intramuscular or IV route.

Trace elements. LBW infants receiving total parenteral nutrition require the addition of trace elements to their hyperalimentation solutions. The small quantities of trace elements that are present as contaminants in hyperalimentation solutions or as normal components of blood products (which may be transfused into some babies receiving total parenteral nutrition) cannot be depended on to meet trace element needs. Premature infants are at particular risk for development of trace element deficiency states because of low body stores and increased requirements for growth.[134]

Although further research is needed to establish precise requirements of all trace elements in total parenteral nutrition, the recommendations of an expert panel of the American Medical Association[135] are currently used as guidelines (Table 5-10). Larger quantities of certain trace elements may be required in some cases. For example, the quantity of zinc may need to be increased if there are large volumes of intestinal fluid loss, since a large portion of zinc is excreted through the gastrointestinal tract.[136] Furthermore, a recent study by Zlotkin and Buchanan[137] showed that premature infants required intakes of 438 μg zinc/kg/day and 63 μg copper/kg/day to achieve intrauterine accumulation rates. These dosages are significantly higher than the AMA recommendations.

The iron requirements of preterm and full-term infants are discussed on p. 73. It is not common to

Table 5-9. Vitamin content of selected multivitamin preparations compared with the AMA/NAG* recommendations for children under 11 years of age*

Vitamin	AMA/NAG Recommendations	MVI Concentrate (per 1 ml)	MVI-12 (per 5 ml vial 1 + 5 ml vial 2)	MVI-Pediatric (per 5 ml)
A (IU)	2,300	2,000	3,300	2,300
D (IU)	400	200	200	400
E (IU)	7	1	10	7
K (mg)	0.2	—	—	0.2
C (mg)	80	100	100	80
Thiamine (mg)	1.2	10	3	1.2
Riboflavin (mg)	1.4	2	3.6	1.4
Pyridoxine (mg)	1	3	4	1
Niacin (mg)	17	20	40	17
Pantothenic acid (mg)	5	5	15	5
Folic acid (μg)	140	—	400	140
B_{12} (μg)	1	—	5	1
Biotin (μg)	20	—	60	20

From American Medical Association, Nutrition Advisory Group: J. Parent. Ent. Nutr. **3**:260, 1979. Copyright © 1979, The American Society of Parenteral and Enteral Nutrition.
*Product Information, USV Laboratories, Tuckahoe, N.Y., 1982.

Table 5-10. Suggested daily intake of essential trace elements

Trace Element	Daily Amount* (mg/kg)
Zinc	300†
	100‡
Copper	20
Chromium	0.14-0.2
Manganese	2-10

From Nutrition Advisory Group of the American Medical Association, Department of foods and Nutrition: J.A.M.A. **241**:2051, 1979. Copyright 1979, American Medical Association.
*Limited data are available for infants weighing less than 1500 gm. Their requirements may be higher because of low body stores and increased requirements for growth.
†Premature infants up to 3000 gm body weight. Thereafter the recommendations for full-term infants apply.
‡Full-term infants and children up to 5 years old.

add iron to total parenteral nutrition solutions because of concerns that allergic reactions may occur and because of reports of incompatibility between iron-dextran preparations and hyperalimentation solutions.[134] However, recent reports have shown that iron can be both safely and effectively added to hyperalimentation solutions.[138] Although effective, this practice should be limited to situations in which IV iron is clearly needed. Intravenous administration of iron may be indicated for LBW infants who have inadequate muscle mass for intramuscular injection and who require 2 or more months of total parenteral nutrition.

CASE 1

A 26-week-gestation infant weighing 750 gm at birth was admitted to a neonatal intensive care unit shortly after birth. The baby developed severe hyaline membrane disease and required assisted ventilation with oxygen needs of 85% to 90%. An umbilical arterial catheter was placed to aid in ventilatory management; fluid, glucose, and electrolytes were also infused through this line. The initial solution contained 10% dextrose; this was started at a rate of 70 ml/kg/day and was increased to 12.5% dextrose at a rate of 110 ml/kg/day by day 3 of life. Dextrostix measurements simultaneously increased from 60 to 80 mg/100 ml to 180 to 240 mg/100 ml; serum glucose measurements confirmed hyperglycemia. The dextrose infusion was subsequently reduced to 9% dextrose at a rate of 110 ml/kg/day. Blood sugar levels normalized, and the glucose load was then gradually increased without further difficulty. Because the serious nature of the infant's medical condition prohibited the introduction of enteral feedings in the first week of life and because metabolic reserves were presumed to be meager, parenteral nutrition was started on day 4 of life. At this time, the infant had lost 80 gm and weighed 10% less than birth weight. The initial hyperalimentation order included (1) rate: IV + hyperalimentation = 4.2 ml/hour (IV at keep-open rate of 1.5 ml/hour and hyperalimentation at rate of 2.7 ml/hour), (2) 8% dextrose, and (3) amino acid: 0.5 gm/kg/day. All electrolytes, minerals, vitamins, and trace elements were added to the 250-ml bottle in quantities that provided appropriate amounts to be delivered in 96 ml/kg/day of hyperalimentation solution. Intralipid was ordered on day 8 of life at an initial load of 0.5 gm/kg/day. Tolerance to all components of the hyperalimentation solution were routinely monitored as intake was advanced.

TRANSITION FROM PARENTERAL TO ENTERAL NUTRITION

The transition from parenteral to enteral nutrition should occur slowly. According to Kerner,[139] advancing enteral feedings too quickly may overtax the previously inactive gastrointestinal tract and can result in significant setbacks.

Infants who received total parenteral nutrition have a relatively low digestive mass and delayed gastrointestinal growth compared with infants who receive enteral stimuli. Studies in animals and humans have documented pancreatic hyposecretion, intestinal mucosal atrophy, and decreased parietal cell mass during total parenteral nutrition.[140,141] These effects are reversible on resumption of enteral feedings. Advancement of enteral feedings should, however, be gradual to allow time for adaptive increases in enzymes involved in digestion and metabolism and for establishment of mechanisms necessary for absorption of nutrients.[142,143]

Substituting enteral nutrients for parenteral nutrients is often more difficult than maintaining an infant on total parenteral nutrition. During the interval of transition, it is easy to deliver either excessive or insufficient amounts of fluid and nutrients. This period also presents the challenge of selecting an enteral feeding regimen that is tailored to the specific needs and capacities of each infant. Deciding when, what, and how to feed an LBW infant is complicated by problems in assessing intestinal function, and empirical choices are frequently required.

Guidelines

Levy, Winters, and Heird[94] have suggested guidlines for the initiation and advancement of enteral feedings in infants who have been maintained solely on total parenteral nutrition. They begin enteral feedings in small amounts (30 to 40 ml/kg/day) without changing the composition or infusion rate of parenteral nutrients. If the initial small volumes of enteral feedings are tolerated, Levy, Winters, and Heird[94]

slowly increase the volume of enteral feedings and decrease the volume of the parenteral infusate attempting to maintain an IV amino acid plus oral protein intake of approximately 3 g/kg/day, a total energy intake of 120 to 130 kcal/kg/day, and a total fluid intake of 150-160 ml/kg/day. Once an enteral intake providing 2.0 to 2.5 g protein/kg/day and more than 100 kcal/kg/day is tolerated, they discontinue infusion of the HA solution, and substitute a solution of 10% dextrose. The dextrose is decreased to 5 percent and subsequently discontinued when the infant is clearly tolerating the enteral feeding regimen and is gaining weight with enteral nutrients alone.

Nurseries vary in their approach to initiating enteral feeding. Some units introduce small volumes of dilute feedings and gradually increase the concentration while maintaining a constant volume. When full-strength feedings are tolerated, the volume is slowly advanced. Other nurseries start out with full-strength feedings but restrict initial enteral volumes to smaller amounts. The smallest infants usually require the most conservative approach to enteral feeding. Infants weighing less than 1000 gm may not tolerate an initial enteral volume of more than 20 ml/kg/day. The period of introduction of enteral feedings should be one of caution for tiny infants and should progress very slowly. Larger LBW infants are often able to tolerate larger intital volumes and can advance more rapidly.

During the transition from parenteral to enteral nutrition, feeding difficulties are common, but they are not well understood. Intolerance to enteral nutrients, requiring a change in the feeding regimen or a change in the method of delivery, may prolong the transition period.[139] Whereas uncomplicated infants can achieve full enteral nutrition within a week, babies with problems such as the short bowel syndrome may require a month or more to wean completely off parenteral nutrition.

CASE 2

An infant born at 28 weeks' gestation developed necrotizing enterocolitis during his fourth week of life. The necrotic damage to the small intestine necessitated surgical removal of 30 cm of bowel, encompassing the distal ileum and the ileocecal value. After 8 days of total parenteral nutrition, it was decided that enteral feedings could be introduced and cautiously advanced. An elemental formula (e.g., Pregestimil) was chosen to facilitate digestion and absorption of nutrients. The initial volume was 1 ml/hour fed by oral gastric gavage on a continuous drip schedule; this provided 25 ml/kg/day, given a body weight of 960 gm. The composition and infusion rate of the parenteral nutrients remained unchanged until day 3 of enteral feedings when the oral volume was increased to 2 ml/hour. At this point, the volume of the parenteral infusate was decreased to provide a total daily volume of 150 to 160 ml/kg/day. The concentrations of parenteral nutrients were adjusted to meet the goals of the nutritional therapy, e.g., to provide 2.5 to 3.0 gm protein/kg/day and at least 90 kcal/kg/day. Enteral volume was slowly increased in small amounts to allow time for morphological and functional adaptation of the remaining small bowel and to guard against the volume-induced dumping syndrome. Full enteral volume was not achieved until 28 days after the reintroduction of enteral feeds; at this time the infant weighed 1150 gm and was able to tolerate a continuous orogastric infusion of 8 ml/hour.

ENTERAL NUTRITION

Nutrient Requirements

Essential nutrients should be supplied to LBW infants in quantities sufficient to maintain homeostasis without unnecessary weight loss or tissue catabolism and yet not excessively to avoid potential toxicity and superfluous fat deposition.[144] The exact quantities of nutrients required to meet these goals are still being defined. In general, the nutrient requirements of premature infants are higher than those of full-term babies because a greater portion of the total nutrient intake is necessary for the synthesis of new tissue (i.e., growth).[144]

Energy. Sinclair and others[27] have estimated that 75 kcal/kg/day are required to meet maintenance energy needs, compared with 120 kcal/kg/day to provide adequate energy for growth as shown in Table 5-11. However, energy needs may be

Table 5-11. Energy requirements of low birth weight infants

	kcal/kg/day
Basal metabolic rate	50
Activity	15
Cold stress	10
TOTAL MAINTENANCE	75
Specific dynamic action	8
Fecal loss	12
Growth	25
TOTAL ADDITIONAL REQUIREMENTS	45
TOTAL ENERGY NEEDS FOR GROWTH	120

From Sinclair, J., and others: Pediatr. Clin. North Am. **17**:863, 1970.

increased by stress and rapid growth or decreased in a neutral thermal environment and when absorptive loss is eliminated with parenteral nutrition. To estimate the energy needs of individual infants, it is important to consider the dynamic biological and environmental factors that alter their needs (Table 5-12). To evaluate the accuracy of the estimate, it is important to consider the infant's growth progress in relation to their average energy intakes. Some premature infants may require at least 130 to 150 kcal/kg/day to sustain an appropriate rate of growth, especially during their catch-up growth phase (p. 26). To achieve these caloric intakes in babies with limited capacities to tolerate large fluid volumes, it is often necessary to concentrate the feedings to provide more than 20 kcal/oz.

Protein. Gastric, pancreatic, and intestinal enzymes responsible for protein hydrolysis are present in neonates, including premature babies.[145]

Active transport of amino acids in the small intestine of the infant has not been studied, but in view of the presence of active transport in fetal life, such mechanisms are presumed to be well developed.[145] Feeding studies corroborate the biochemical finding that neonates can digest and absorb an adequate quantity of dietary protein.[146]

Although much attention has been directed toward determining the protein requirement of LBW infants, this is still a controversial subject. At the core of the controversy are basic questions concerning optimal postnatal growth and tissue composition changes of premature babies. Answers to these questions and data from direct clinical investigations are needed to establish precise protein requirements.

One approach to estimating the protein needs of preterm infants considers the goal to be the intrauterine rate of protein accumulation.[7] A reference

Table 5-12. Factors to consider in estimating the energy requirements of LBW infants

Factor	Comment

Weight	Small babies may have:
	   High absorptive losses
	   High heat losses caused by a lack of subcutaneous fat insulation and a large body surface area

Classification	Small for gestational age infants often have:
	   High basal metabolic rate
	   Rapid growth rate

Postnatal age	Energy requirements may diminish with increasing postnatal age.

Physiological stress	Infants who experience:
	   Hypermetabolic states (e.g., fever).
	   Malabsorptive problems (e.g., short gut syndrome)
	   Labored breathing (e.g., chronic lung disease)
	 will have increased energy needs.

Environmental stress	Circumstances that increase:
	   Fluid losses (e.g., radiant warmers)
	   Energy expenditure (temperature instability)
	 will also increase energy needs.

Type of feeding	Enterally fed babies require more calories than parenterally fed infants. Inappropriate selection of a formula can increase absorptive loss.
Method of feeding	Some LBW infants expend more energy while learning to nipple feed.
Growth	Energy intake must be increased to support rapid catch-up growth.

fetus model is used to determine the amount of protein that would need to be ingested to match the quantity of protein that is deposited into newly formed fetal tissue.[147] To achieve these fetal accretion rates, additional protein must be supplied to compensate for intestinal losses and obligatory losses in urine and skin. Table 5-13 shows the advisable intakes for protein using this factorial method. Obviously, the advisable protein intake for enterally fed infants (3.5 to 4.0 gm/kg/day) exceeds the recommendation for parenterally fed babies (2.0 to 2.5 gm/kg/day). Although 3.5 to 4.0 gm/kg/day of protein is apparently well tolerated by stable infants who are growing rapidly, there are no clinical data to prove that this much protein is needed. In fact, this quantity may exceed the metabolic capacity of very immature babies or may stress the sick infant.

Another approach to estimating the protein needs of preterm infants considers the effect that the quality or type of protein fed may have on the quantitative requirement. Whey-predominant proteins of high biological value for the preterm infant (e.g., human milk protein) support sustained growth in quantities less than advisable intake estimates.[148] LBW infants who ingest adequate calories and whey-predominant protein at 2.25 mg/kg/day show steady gains in weight and length,[149] although their rate of growth may be slower compared with intrauterine growth curves.[150] It can be argued that a slower rate of growth is normal for preterm infants living in an extrauterine environment.

Several studies have shown that premature infants tolerate whey better than casein. Premature babies fed whey-predominant proteins experience less metabolic acidosis and have more normal plasma amino acid patterns than those fed casein-predominant proteins.[149,151-153] Whey protein is also more soluble in gastric acid secretions and may be more easily digested by the premature infant. Avoiding gastric curd formation probably averts the potential for lactobezoar development.[154] Furthermore, the amino acid composition of whey protein differs from that of casein and may be more appropriate for the premature infant. The premature infant has a limited ability to convert methionine to cystine as a result of little or no activity of the enzyme cystathionase. Whey protein contains more cystine and less methionine than does casein and may be more suitable for the immature baby during the first weeks of life. Because of the preference by preterm infants for whey protein, more whey (in the form of β-lactaglobulin) has been added to the premature formulas to simulate the amount present in human milk, resulting in a 60:40 whey/casein ratio.

In addition to the amount and type of protein, the distribution of protein calories (relative to carbohydrate and fat) affects the protein requirement. It is desirable that protein comprise 7% to 16% of total calories.[155] Feedings with less than 7% may limit

Table 5-13. Estimated requirements and advisable intakes for protein (grams) as derived by the factorial method

Body Weight of Infant	Tissue Increment (per day)	Dermal Loss (per day)	Urine Loss (per day)	Intestinal Absorption (% intake)	Estimated Requirement (per day)	Advisable Intake (per day)	(per kg)*	(per 100 kcal)†
800-1200 gm	2.32	0.17	0.68	87†	3.64	4.0	4.0	3.1
1200-1800 gm	3.01	0.25	0.90	87	4.78	5.2	3.5	2.7

From Ziegler, E.E., Biga, R.L., and Fomon, S.J.: Nutritional requirements of the premature infant. In Suskind, R.M., editor: Textbook of pediatric nutrition. Copyright 1981, Raven Press, New York.
*Assuming body weight of 1000 and 1500 gm, respectively, for the 800-1200 and 1200-1800 gm infants.
†Assuming energy intake of 130 kcal/kg/day.

growth; those with more than 16% may cause azotemia and acidosis.

Lipid. LBW infants need an adequate amount of dietary fat to help meet the high energy needs of growth, to provide essential fatty acids, and to assist in absorption of other important nutrients such as the fat-soluble vitamins and calcium. However, neonates in general and premature and small for gestational age infants in particular are relatively inefficient in digestion and absorption of lipid.

Fat digestion is compromised by low levels of lipase, the pancreatic enzyme responsible for the hydrolysis of dietary fats.[156] In addition, LBW infants, especially those who are very premature, have a relatively low concentration and an altered composition of bile salts. Their bile acid pool falls below the critical micellar concentration and is therefore insufficient to solubilize most long-chain lipids for absorption.[157] Because medium-chain triglycerides require few or no bile salts for absorption, these fats have been added to the new premature formulas in varying quantities. When medium-chain triglycerides are added to vegetable oils, there is improved fat absorption in LBW infants, resulting in alleviation of steatorrhea, increased weight gain, enhanced calcium absorption, and improved nitrogen retention.[158]

The composition of dietary fat also plays a role in the digestion and absorption of lipid. Full-term and preterm infants show better digestion and absorption of fats from human milk than from cow milk or standard infant formulas, in part because of the presence of two human milk lipases[159] and in part because of the unique fatty acid composition of human milk fat. Furthermore, vegetable oils are absorbed more efficiently by LBW infants than saturated animal fats.[160]

Vegetable oils containing polyunsaturated fatty acids contain linoleic acid; medium-chain triglyceride oil does not. Adequate intake of this essential fatty acid is important; at least 3% of the total enteral calories is required.[161] However, an excessively high intake of polyunsaturated fatty acids may have adverse effects. Because the fatty acid composition of the red blood cell membrane is primarily determined by the fatty acid composition of the diet, infants fed large amounts of polyunsaturated fatty acids have increased erythrocyte susceptibility to oxidative destruction. It is recommended that commercial formulas fed to LBW infants not contain more than about 12% linoleic acid to prevent hemolytic anemia.

The percentage of total calories as fat relative to carbohydrate and protein is another important consideration. It is desirable that fat comprise 30% to 55% of total calories;[155] fat intake greater than 60% of calories may lead to ketosis. Furthermore, a diet high in fat and low in protein may yield more fat deposition than is desirable for the growing LBW infant.

Carbohydrate. Lactose is the predominant carbohydrate in almost all mammalian milks. There is physiological concern that the premature infant's ability to digest lactose may be marginal; intestinal lactase activity develops during the third trimester of gestation but does not achieve maximal activity until term.[162] Premature infants fed high-lactose formulas or human milk might be expected to experience fermentative diarrhea secondary to incomplete lactose digestion and absorption; however, in practice, this is an infrequent problem.[163] Sucrose is another disaccharide commonly found in commercial infant formula products. Because sucrase activity is present at 70% of newborn levels early in the third trimester,[162] sucrose is well tolerated by most premature infants. Both sucrase and lactase are sensitive to changes in the intestinal milieu, however, and babies afflicted by diarrhea, receiving antibiotic therapy, or suffering from undernutrition may develop a temporary intolerance to lactose and sucrose.

Glucose polymers are an increasingly common carbohydrate in the diets of LBW infants. The polymers, composed mainly of chains of 5 to 9 glucose units linked together, are used to achieve the iso-osmolality of certain specialized formulas. Few data are available concerning the metabolism of glucose polymers in premature infants, although the polymers appear to be well digested and utilized.[164]

Human milk and standard infant formulas contain approximately 40% of the total calories as carbohydrate. An appropriate intake of carbohydrate is desirable; 35% to 65% of total calories as carbohydrate is the recommended range.[155] Too little carbohydrate may lead to hypoglycemia, while too much carbohydrate may provoke an osmotic diuresis or loose stools.

Vitamins and minerals. Premature infants require all of the vitamins and minerals that are essential for full-term infants; however, LBW babies have increased requirements for several of these as a result of poor body stores and physiological immaturity.

Premature infants who are growing rapidly require increased intakes of calcium, phosphorus, and vitamin D for optimal bone mineralization. As discussed on p. 68, the fetus accumulates 120 to 160 mg calcium/kg/day and about 75 mg phosphorus/kg/day during the final weeks of gestation; the premature infant is deprived of this important intrauterine mineral deposition. Inadequate dietary intakes can result in osteopenia of prematurity.[165]

This disease is characterized by undermineralization of growing bones and is documented by radiological evidence of "washed-out" bones in preterm infants. Very immature babies are particularly susceptible to osteopenia and may develop fractures or florid rickets[166] if dietary deficiency is prolonged.

The etiology of osteopenia of prematurity has been attributed to deficiency of calcium, phosphorus, and vitamin D, but the pathophysiology of the disease is not completely understood. It is known, however, that intakes of calcium and phosphorus from human milk and standard infant formulas are far below intrauterine accretion values. Table 5-14 compares the advisable intakes for calcium and phosphorus (based on intrauterine accretion rates) with the amounts contained in human milk, standard infant formulas, and specialized premature infant formula products. It is apparent that human milk and standard infant formulas do not provide enough calcium and phosphorus to match advisable intake recommendations. Since intestinal absorption of calcium from standard formulas can be as low as 40% to 60% of intake levels in LBW infants, the amount of calcium retained by the pre-

Table 5-14. Advisable intakes for calcium, phosphorus, protein, sodium, and vitamin D compared with selected feedings

	Advisable intake		Human Milk		Standard	Premature		
	1 kg body Wt.	1.5 kg body Wt.	Preterm	Mature	Enfamil Similac SMA	Enfamil Premature	Premie SMA	Similac Special Care
Calcium (mg/100 kcal)	160	140	40	43	66-78	117	92	178
Phosphorus (mg/100 kcal)	108	95	18	20	49-66	58	49	89
Protein (gm/100 kcal)	3.1	2.7	2.3 (range 1.9-2.8)	1.5	2.2	3.0	2.5	2.7
Sodium (mEq/100 kcal)	2.7	2.3	1.5 (range 0.9-2.3)	0.8	1.0-1.8	1.7	1.7	1.9
Caloric density (kcal/100ml)			73	67	81	81	81	81
Vitamin D (IU/day)*	600	600	?	4	70-75	75	76	180

Data from Brady, M.S., and others: Formulas and human milk for premature infants, J. Am. Diet. Assoc. **81:**547, 1982; and Lemons, J.A., and others: Pediatr. Res. **16:**113, 1982.

*At 120 kcal/kg/day for an infant weighing 1 kg.

mature infant may only be one fourth to one fifth of that which would have been received in utero. Calcium and phosphorus supplementation of human milk and standard infant formulas results in greater mineral retention as well as better bone mineralization.[167] In addition, rickets associated with human milk feedings resolves solely with the provision of supplemental calcium and phosphorus.[168] Thus, regardless of the vitamin D requirements of the LBW infant, it is apparent that many of the reported problems of osteopenia result from inadequate intake of calcium and phosphorus alone.

Specialized premature formulas now being marketed for LBW infants have a higher calcium and phosphorus content than human milk or standard infant formulas precisely for this reason. Premature infants weighing more than 1200 gm who are fed these high-mineral formulas achieve bone mineralization comparable to that observed during intra-uterine growth[169]; consequently, no additional calcium and phosphorus supplementation is needed. The specialized premature formulas have not, however, been tested in infants who weigh less than 1200 gm at birth; the cumulative calcium deficit may be higher in these tiny babies compared with larger LBW infants.[170] In contrast, premature infants fed human milk or standard infant formulas do require supplementation (refer to recommendations on p. 158).

It has been suggested that LBW infants have immature vitamin D hydroxylation pathways and that this may contribute to the development of osteopenia of prematurity. However, in a study of preterm infants of 32 to 37 weeks gestation, the administration of oral vitamin D_3 increased serum 1,25-dihydroxyvitamin D concentrations at 5 days of age[171]; this finding indicates that vitamin D is well absorbed and metabolized in preterm infants. Furthermore, serum 1,25-dihydroxyvitamin D levels were found to be elevated in LBW infants with rickets.[172] After feeding a standard infant formula supplemented with calcium and phosphorus, there was resolution of the rickets and serum 1,25-dihydroxyvitamin D concentrations fell to normal lev-

els.[172] These findings appear to show that rickets of prematurity is caused by calcium and phosphorus deficiency, rather than by a deficiency in vitamin D metabolism, and that the elevation of 1,25-dihydroxyvitamin D reflects a compensatory mechanism to achieve maximal calcium and phosphorus absorption.[112] In contrast, there has been one report of rickets in preterm infants in whom 1,25-dihydroxyvitamin D levels were low despite adequate intakes of vitamin D_3.[173] Since resolution of the rickets was achieved with 1,25-dihydroxyvitamin D supplementation, it is possible that a relative unresponsiveness of the intestine to the action of vitamin D may be an additional factor contributing to rickets of prematurity.[173]

Available data are not yet sufficient to establish a precise requirement for vitamin D. Although 400 IU/day may be adequate, rickets has been reported in some LBW infants consuming this amount of vitamin D.[174] Ziegler, Biga, and Fomon[7] have suggested an advisable intake of 600 IU of vitamin D per day. Although the specialized premature formulas contain more vitamin D than either standard infant formulas or human milk, the volume of milk consumed each day by LBW infants may be so small that the actual intake of vitamin D from any of these milks often falls below recommended levels. Vitamin D is frequently supplemented as part of a multivitamin (pp. 162-163).

Iron. LBW infants are particularly susceptible to iron deficiency because they have reduced iron stores associated with premature birth. Although iron stores are sufficient to permit expansion of the blood volume to nearly twice its initial size (i.e., until birth weight has doubled), they drop rapidly after about 2 months of age as active erythropoiesis resumes. Iron deficiency anemia may develop by 3 months postnatal age if iron supplementation is not provided. In contrast, full-term infants do not usually deplete their proportionately larger iron stores until after 4 to 6 months of age.

The iron intake currently recommended for premature infants is 2 mg/kg/day; this is twice the amount recommended for term infants.[175] It is possible that VLBW infants, especially those weighing less than 1000 gm, may require somewhat more iron; however, data are not yet available for specific recommendations.[176] Specialized premature formulas contain low levels of iron (less than 0.5 mg/kg/day when providing 120 kcal/kg/day). LBW infants fed these products need iron supplements by about the time they are 2 months of age. Similarly, the iron content of human milk does not meet the requirements of the premature infant, despite the enhanced absorption of iron from human milk. For infants receiving human milk or premature formula, oral ferrous sulfate drops are an effective supplement. Larger premature infants (weighing 2 kg or more) who are fed standard formula fortified with iron receive 1.8 to 2.0 mg elemental iron/120 kcal and do not require additional supplementation.

Most authorities agree that iron supplementation in LBW infants should be initiated by at least 2 months of age. However, whether or not to introduce iron supplements at an earlier time has been a controversial issue. The controversy has focused on two principal concerns: (1) hemolytic anemia, and (2) decreased host resistance to infection. Hemolytic anemia rarely occurs if an appropriate amount of iron is ingested by an infant whose vitamin E intake is adequate and whose polyunsaturated fatty acid intake is controlled. In vitro studies have indicated that exogenous iron may decrease host resistance to infection through saturation and inactivation of certain antibacterial, iron-binding proteins in serum and human milk.[177] However, in vivo studies do not support in vitro findings that ordinary iron supplementation predisposes infants to infection.[178]

Lundstrom, Siimes, and Dallman[179] suggest that iron supplements of 2 mg/kg/day, started at 2 weeks of age, are both safe and effective for LBW infants. Therefore, current recommendations for iron supplementation in LBW infants permit iron as early as 2 weeks of age, but not later than 2 months of age.

LBW infants may require more vitamin E than full-term infants, which has been assumed to be a result of poor absorption of vitamin E in the face of low body stores. Impaired absorption of vitamin E by premature infants was described in the early 1970s[175]; however, fat blends in current premature formulas are markedly improved, resulting in better absorption of both fat and vitamin E. In spite of this, the premature infant is born with poor vitamin E stores relative to the full-term baby. When supplemented with 30 IU vitamin E per day, most premature infants show plasma tocopherol levels within the desired range.[7] By comparison, nonsupplemented infants are more likely to demonstrate biochemical signs of vitamin E deficiency, e.g., lower hemoglobin concentrations, higher reticulocyte counts, and more fragile red cells in weak solutions of hydrogen peroxide. The advisable intake of vitamin E in LBW infants is 30 IU per day.[7]

An important function of vitamin E is its protection of biological membranes against oxidative breakdown of lipids. Requirements for vitamin E increase when the level of polyunsaturated fatty acids in the diet is high. The polyunsaturated fatty acids gradually produce a change in the composition of the fatty acids in cellular and intracellular membranes. The membranes then become more susceptible to oxidative damage, which increases the requirement for the antioxidant effect of vitamin E. Because iron is a biological oxidant, a diet high in either iron or polyunsaturated fatty acids increases the risk of vitamin E deficiency. A premature infant suffering from vitamin E deficiency may experience oxidative destruction of red blood cells or hemolytic anemia.

Several studies in the early 1970s indicated that premature infants were at high risk for developing hemolytic anemia.[175] However, the formula products used in these studies were high in polyunsaturated fatty acids and iron and contained fat blends that resulted in poor absorption of vitamin E. The combination of high polyunsaturated fatty acid content and high levels of the oxidant iron in the face of vitamin E deficiency resulted in red blood cell hemolysis by membrane destruction. Since that time, the composition of premature formulas has been favorably changed to correct these problems. Therefore, hemolytic anemia associated with vitamin E deficiency is rarely a problem today when careful attention is paid to the composition of the diet.

Since the dietary requirement for vitamin E depends on the polyunsaturated fatty acid content of the diet, the recommended intake of vitamin E is commonly expressed as a ratio of vitamin E to polyunsaturated fatty acids. The Committee on Nutrition of the American Academy of Pediatrics recommends that milk fed to premature infants provide at least 0.6 mg D-α-tocopherol per gram of polyunsaturated fatty acid (or 1 IU vitamin E per gram of polyunsaturated fatty acid).[162] Both human milk and the new premature formulas have vitamin E/polyunsaturated fatty acid ratios well above this recommendation.

The use of "pharmacological" doses of vitamin E for the prevention of diseases related to oxygen toxicity is an area of much speculation. Pharmacological doses of parenteral vitamin E protect against oxygen-induced retinopathy in kittens, an animal model of the acute proliferative phase of human retrolental fibroplasia.[180] Preliminary clinical data in infants also suggest that high doses of vitamin E (i.e., 100 mg/kg/day) may help to decrease the incidence of severe retrolental fibroplasia.[181,182] In addition, the beneficial effect of high doses of vitamin E for the prevention of pulmonary oxygen toxicity in infants at risk for developing bronchopulmonary dysplasia has also been suggested.[183] A subsequent study, however, could not demonstrate such an effect.[184] The appropriate use of pharmacological doses of vitamin E in preterm infants has not been documented as yet and must be weighed in terms of potential benefit and possible toxicity.[185] Thus, while available facts reinforce the need to provide supplemental vitamin E to LBW infants in quantities sufficient to produce normal blood levels (30 IU per day), the routine use of higher doses (100 IU or more per day) to produce supranormal blood levels of vitamin E should be regarded with caution.

Premature infants seem to have higher folic acid needs than full-term infants. Although serum folate levels are high at birth, they decrease dramatically soon thereafter.[186] This may be a reflection of the high utilization of folic acid by the premature infant for DNA and tissue synthesis. Because the preterm baby grows at a more rapid rate than the full-term infant, he or she may have a higher intrinsic need for folic acid.

A mild form of folic acid deficiency manifested by low serum folate concentrations and hypersegmentation of neutrophils is not unusual in premature infants. Megaloblastic anemia is much less commonly observed. A daily supplement of 50 to 70 μg is effective in preventing neutrophil hypersegmentation and low serum folate concentrations.[186] Ziegler, Biga, and Fomon[7] recommend an advisable intake of 60 μg per day.

The minimum daily sodium requirement for LBW infants has been estimated to be approximately 1.6 mEq/kg/day.[187] However, actual sodium requirements may be much higher for LBW infants who experience excessive sodium losses. LBW infants, especially those born at less than 33 weeks gestation, have immature renal systems and are consequently limited in their ability to conserve sodium. Below this gestational age, the glomerular filtration rate exceeds the limited tubular sodium resorption capacity, and excess sodium is lost.[188] Actual sodium needs of immature infants may be as high as 5 mEq/kg/day during the first 2 weeks of life for infants of less than 30 weeks' gestation and 4 mEq/kg/day for those born between 30 and 35 weeks' gestation.[188] Infants who suffer additional sodium losses through the gastrointestinal tract (e.g., diarrhea or malabsorption related to extreme immaturity)[189] or as a result of diuretic therapy may have sodium needs as high as 8 to 9 mEq/kg/day.[109]

High renal and gastrointestinal losses of sodium contribute to the susceptibility of LBW infants to hyponatremia in the neonatal period. Up to 30% of infants weighing less than 1300 gm at birth may by hyponatremic during the first weeks of life.[190] Other factors that contribute to the development of hyponatremia include increased sodium needs related to rapid rates of growth and poor dietary

Table 5-15. Factors to consider before feeding by an enteral route

Factors to consider	Comments
Perinatal	
Perinatal asphyxia	If severe, enteral feedings should be withheld during the first 48 hours of life and possibly longer, depending on respiratory status.
Apgar scores	Although both the 1-minute and 5-minute apgar scores are of concern when they are very low, a poor 5-minute score is more worrisome.
Respiratory status	
Ventilated baby with RDS	May consider feedings when: Ventilatory settings are consistent and show improvement. Blood gases are adequate. Episodes of apnea and bradycardia are mild and relatively infrequent. Low risk for pneumothorax.
Medical status	
Vital signs	Heart rate, respiratory rate, temperature, blood pressure, color, and tone should be adequate for each infant.
Acute illness (such as sepsis)	Acutely ill babies are medically unstable and less likely to tolerate enteral feedings. Once the acute phase has passed and the infant is responding to treatment, enteral feedings should be reconsidered.
Gastrointestinal tract	
Anomalies	Certain anomalies prohibit the use of enteral feedings (e.g., gastroschisis, omphalocele) until surgically repaired.
Patency	The inability to pass a feeding tube or the occurrence of vomiting or distention in response to enteral feedings may indicate inadequate patency of the gastrointestinal tract. Intestinal obstructions (e.g., atresia, stenosis, volvulus) may prohibit enteral feedings before surgical relief.
Functioning	Signs that indicate a functioning gastrointestinal tract should be present (e.g., normal bowel sounds, ability to pass stools).
Risk of necrotizing enterocolitis	Factors that may increase the risk for necrotizing enterocolitis include: Immaturity (<32 weeks gestation) VLBW (<1500 gm) Episodes of hypoxia (asphyxia, respiratory disease) Inadequate perfusion of the gastrointestinal tract Patent ductus arteriosus Presence of an umbilical arterial catheter (UAC-line)
Equipment/procedures	Intubation, extubation, etc., may be temporary barriers to enteral feedings. Any procedure that is stressful to the infant may warrant *temporary* withholding of enteral feedings.

intake resulting from consumption of small volumes of milk.

Although LBW infants are clearly vulnerable to hyponatremia, routine sodium supplementation of enterally fed infants is not recommended.[161] Individual infants vary in their ability to conserve sodium, and it is difficult to predict whether babies will become hyponatremic or maintain normal serum sodium levels. However, it is important to monitor the sodium status of all LBW infants by frequent assessment of serum and urinary sodium concentrations. Milks can be supplemented with sodium if repletion becomes necessary.

When to Begin Enteral Feedings

The decision to begin enteral feeding in LBW infants is often difficult and involves consideration of the degree of prematurity, history of perinatal insults, current medical condition, functioning of the gastrointestinal tract, and several other individualized concerns. Because of the complexity of these factors, the choice of optimal timing of feeding must be personalized for each LBW infant and altered according to the variable course of each baby. Consideration of the factors listed in Table 5-15 may facilitate the decision to start or to delay enteral feedings.

Methods of Feeding

Once it has been decided that enteral feedings will be initiated, one must select the optimal enteral feeding technique. LBW infants are usually fed either by gastric gavage (Fig. 5-3) or by nipple (Fig. 5-4). The methods of feeding LBW infants are the subject of an excellent review by Benda.[191]

Techniques. Oral gastric gavage feeding is often chosen for infants unable to suck because of immaturity or insults to their central nervous system. Infants of less than 32 to 34 weeks gestational age, regardless of birth weight, may be expected to have poorly coordinated sucking and swallowing activity related to their developmental immaturity and are consequently unable to nipple feed.[191] The major risks of the oral gastric gavage technique include aspiration and gastric distention. Because of weak or absent cough reflexes and poorly developed respiratory muscles, the tiny baby may not be able to dislodge milk from the upper airway, causing reflex bradycardia or airway obstruction. However, with electronic monitoring of vital functions and proper positioning in the infant during feeding, the danger of aspiration from regurgitation of stomach contents is minimized. Gastric distention and vagal nerve stimulation with resultant bradycardia are potential problems when oral gastric feedings are delivered on an intermittent bolus schedule.[191] Elimination of the distention and vagal bradycardia may occasionally require the use of an indwelling tube for continuous gastric gavage feedings, instead of the usual intermittent technique. Continuous drip feedings may benefit the tiny, immature infant whose small gastric capacity and slow intestinal motility sometimes impede the tolerance of larger volume bolus feeds. Nasogastric tubes are more stable in their replacement than oral gastric tubes and are preferred for babies on continuous drip feeding with tube changes every 8 hours. But because newborns are obligate nose breathers, more frequent replacement of nasogastric tubes may compromise the nasal airway in LBW infants with associated deterioration in respiratory function.

In the past, transpyloric gavage feeding was occasionally used for LBW infants. The goal of this method was to circumvent the often slow gastropyloric motility of the immature infant by passing the feeding tube through the stomach and pylorus and locating its tip within the duodenum or jejunum. Advantages to transpyloric feeding included the elimination of the pylorus as a barrier for adequate propulsion of milk and a reduced chance of aspiration. But there were several disadvantages as well. Transpyloric feedings were associated with decreased fat absorption, diarrhea, dumping syndrome, alteration of the intestinal microflora, contamination of the feeding system, intestinal perforation, and bilious fluid in the stomach.[192] Trans-

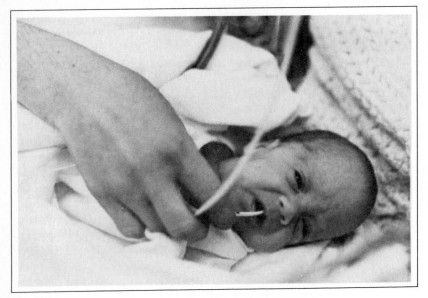

Fig. 5-3. Growing premature infant is being fed by oral gastric gavage.

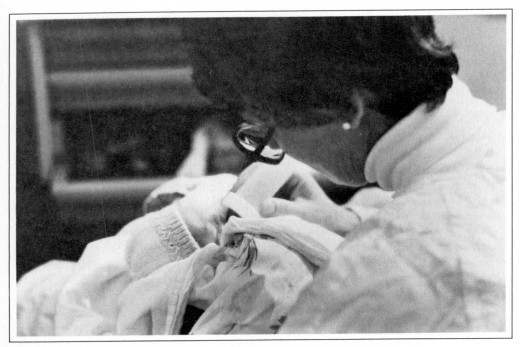

Fig. 5-4. A mother feeds her premature infant using a small, soft ''premie'' nipple.

pyloric tubes also required considerable expertise in their placement and x-ray films to determine the location of the catheter tip. Because of the problems inherent in using this technique, transpyloric feeding is now rarely used to feed LBW infants.

Nipple feeding may be attempted in infants whose gestational age is greater than 32 to 34 weeks.[191] The ability to nipple feed is usually indicated by evidence of an established sucking reflex and sucking motion. Because sucking requires considerable effort by the infant, any stress from other causes will diminish sucking ability.[191] Nipple feeding, therefore, should only be offered when the infant is minimally stressed and has sufficient maturity and strength for a sustained sucking effort. A soft ''premie'' nipple may facilitate early nippling attempts; when a gestational age of 35 weeks is reached, a regular nipple is usually tolerated.

Volume and schedule. The appropriate amount of milk to be fed to LBW infants depends, in part, on their estimated stomach capacity. The undistended stomach volume varies with the size of the infant and may be as small as 2 to 3 ml in the 800-gm newborn or about 40 ml in the 4000-gm newborn. The gastric capacity of neonates increases with postnatal age; therefore, this is of greatest concern during the early period of introduction to enteral feeds. Another important consideration in determining enteral volume is the gastrointestinal motility of LBW infants. This is perhaps the most limiting factor and may be a persistent problem for some premature infants. Because individual babies vary in their ability to move food through the gastrointestinal canal, all premature infants receiving enteral feeds must be monitored by regular measurements of gastric residuals. A suggested feeding schedule is shown in Table 5-16; these recommendations should be tailored to meet the fluid needs and feeding tolerances of individual infants.

Tolerance of Feedings

LBW infants are susceptible to feeding intolerance. Their esophageal motility is poor, and their gastro-

Table 5-16. Enteral feeding schedule for low birth weight infants

Feeding Fluid		Up to 1000 gm		1001-1500 gm		1501-2000 gm		2000-2500 gm	
		Amount	Frequency	Amount	Frequency	Amount	Frequency	Amount	Frequency
First feeding	Sterile water	1 ml	1 hr	2-3 ml	2 hr	4-5 ml	2 hr	10 ml	3 hr
Subsequent feedings (12-72 hr)	Human milk or formula	Gradually increase by 0.5-1.0 ml to maximum 3-5 ml	2 hr	Gradually increase by 1.0 ml to maximum 7-10 ml	2 hr	Gradually increase by 2.0 ml to maximum 12-15 ml	2-3 hr	Gradually increase by 5.0 ml to maximum 20 ml	3 hr
Final feeding schedule	Human milk or formula	6-12 ml	2 hr	18-28 ml	3 hr	28-37 ml	3 hr	37-50 ml	3-4 hr
Total volume (ml/kg/day)		120-150		150		150		150	

From Avery, G.B., and Fletcher, A.B.: Nutrition. In Avery, G.B., editor: Neonatology: pathophysiology and management of the newborn, Philadelphia, 1981, J.B. Lippincott Co.

esophageal sphincter is relatively incompetent, resulting in frequent regurgitation of food into the esophagus. Small gastric capacity, delayed gastric emptying time, and poorly coordinated intestinal motility may be additional problems. The overall result of this mechanical immaturity is a tendency, most apparent in the smallest infants, toward frequent abdominal distention, gastric residuals, and regurgitation, even in the absence of any recognized food intolerances or systemic illness.[191]

All LBW babies receiving enteral nutrition should be consistently monitored for signs of feeding intolerance; these indicators of feeding intolerance have been reviewed by Benda.[191] Vomiting of feedings usually signals the inability of the infant to retain that amount of milk. When not associated with other signs of a systemic illness or obstruction, vomiting may indicate a too rapid increase in feeding volumes or excessive volume for the infant's size and maturity.[191] It is possible that simply reducing the volume will eliminate the vomiting. However, if vomiting persists despite a reduction of intake, or if it is apparent that the infant is ill, it may be advisable to interrupt the feedings until the infant has stabilized.

Abdominal distention may be caused by feeding of excessive volumes, bowel obstruction, excessive swallowing of air, mask ventilation, paralytic ileus, or sepsis.[191] Clinical examination, as well as intermittent measurement of abdominal circumference, will aid in the early detection of distention. A distended abdomen often indicates the need for interruption of feeding until the cause of the distention is determined and the abdomen is once more soft and nondistended.

Gastric residuals are measured by aspiration of the stomach contents and should be routinely checked before each bolus gavage feeding and intermittently in all continuous drip feedings.[193] Whether or not a residual is significant depends in part on its volume in relation to the total volume of the feeding; a residual whose volume is more than about 20% of the total feeding might be a sign of feeding intolerance. When interpreting the significance of a gastric residual, however, it is important to consider that residual in light of other concurrent signs of feeding intolerance and the pattern of residuals established for that infant. Gastric residuals that are bloody or bilious are more alarming than those that appear to be undigested milk.

The frequency and consistency of bowel movements require constant attention when feeding LBW infants. Furthermore, routine testing of stools for reducing substances is a useful procedure that promptly detects incomplete absorption of sugars by the intestine. Although the presence of gross blood can be detected by simple inspection, occult blood is not always visible and should be investigated by a specific assay to detect small amounts of blood in the stool.

Necrotizing enterocolitis. Several authors have suggested that aggressive enteral feedings in the early days of life may be an etiological factor in the development of necrotizing enterocolitis. Necrotizing enterocolitis is a disease of complex multifactorial pathogenesis related to gut hypoperfusion, ischemia, and/or mucosal damage. Early enteral feedings in susceptible infants, especially when volumes are rapidly increased and hypertonic forumlas are fed, may predispose to necrotizing enterocolitis by contributing to mucosal damage.[194] When bacteria invade the damaged mucosa of the infant's intestine, bowel necrosis may result. Feedings may also provide substrate for intestinal bacterial growth.

Although enteral feedings may play a part in the pathogenesis of necrotizing enterocolitis, evidence concerning the role of feeding is primarily circumstantial, particularly as the disease has been reported in a number of infants before enteral feeding was begun.[195] Other factors associated with the development of necrotizing enterocolitis include birth asphyxia, arterial hypoxemia from respiratory disease, gut ischemia secondary to a patent ductus arteriosus, or aortic catheters. Enteral feeding is not singularly responsible for the pathogenesis of necrotizing enterocolitis; however, a conservative approach to enteral feeding may be warranted in

LBW infants, particularly when other risk factors for the development of the disease are present.

Composition of Feedings

Human milk. Although human milk is considered to be the ideal food for healthy, full-term infants,[196] there has been controversy over what constitutes the optimal diet for premature neonates.[197] Some studies have demonstrated that LBW infants fed banked human milk do not grow as rapidly as LBW infants fed infant formulas.[198,199] However, banked human milk, collected during the mature stage of lactation from mothers who have delivered full-term infants, does not provide enough protein and minerals to support intrauterine rates of growth in preterm infants.[200]

More recent studies show that premature infants fed their own mothers' milk grow much more rapidly than infants fed banked milk. When adequate volumes of milk from mothers who deliver early are fed to their healthy LBW infants, these babies are able to attain intrauterine rates of weight gain.[201,202] Furthermore, nutritional status as measured by plasma total protein and albumin concentrations is better in LBW infants fed their own mother's milk compared with those fed banked breast milk.[203] This is accomplished without indications of stress to the developing metabolic or excretory systems. Whether or not resumption of the intrauterine rate of weight gain is appropriate is a separate issue; the fact remains that milk from mothers who deliver early can support rates of growth similar to those achieved by enriched infant formulas.[200]

The different rates of growth in premature infants fed preterm versus mature human milk can be attributed to the unique nutrient composition of preterm human milk. During the first month of lactation, the milk from mothers who deliver prematurely appears to contain more energy and higher concentrations of protein and certain minerals than milk from a more mature stage of lactation.[204-207] It has been suggested that preterm milk more closely approximates the nutritional needs of LBW infants than does other breast milk.[208] Although several studies support the belief that preterm milk is uniquely suited to premature infants, one recent study did not find significantly different concentrations of nutrients in preterm compared with full-term breast milk.[209] These investigators suggest that the differences reported in previous studies may be related to differences in 24-hour expressed milk volumes.[209]

In addition to nutrient concentration, several other factors contribute to the widely held opinion that preterm mothers' milk for her own infant is the feeding choice for LBW babies. Human milk contains certain growth factors that exert a trophic effect on the developing intestinal epithelium of premature infants.[210] The presence of prostaglandins and other hormones in human milk has also been documented, but their physiological role is not yet clear.[211] Human milk protein is whey predominant, with an amino acid composition that favors the LBW infant. The presence of lipase and amylase[212] in human milk contributes to the premature infant's ability to digest fat and carbohydrate and to derive the maximum caloric benefit of the feeding. The renal solute load of human milk is appropriately low (90 mOsm/liter) and does not interfere with water balance in the LBW infant.

Two anti-infective factors in human milk favor its choice for immature babies: (1) maternal immune factors, notably secretory IgA, lysozyme, and leucocytes,[213-215] and (2) antibacterial factors that cause acidification of the infant's gut and promote the establishment of a vigorous lactobacillus flora.[216] These agents may provide protection from infection for the developing gut mucosa.[217] Although human milk does not prevent necrotizing enterocolitis,[218] there is a widespread clinical impression that necrotizing enterocolitis is less common in VLBW infants fed human milk versus infant formula products. There is also experimental evidence in a rat model that human milk macrophages protect against the development of necrotizing enterocolitis following an anoxic insult to the gut.[219]

Two potential problems are associated with feeding human milk to LBW infants. First, human milk, whether preterm, term, or mature, probably does not meet the calcium and phosphorus needs for normal bone mineralization in infants born prematurely.[220] Despite increased calcium retention found in preterm infants receiving human milk, the total calcium content of the milk may be deficient for the growing infant and may lead to a decrease in bone mineralization.[221] Calcium and phosphorus supplements are recommended for rapidly growing LBW infants fed predominantly human milk (p. 139).

A second problem can occur when LBW infants with high energy needs are fluid restricted such that the volume of human milk ingested is not adequate to support rapid growth. In this event, the addition of Human Milk Fortifier to breast milk may be beneficial. This powdered supplement contains protein and carbohydrate and increases the caloric density of human milk to about 24 kcal/oz without diluting the concentration of protein. Human Milk Fortifier also contains certain minerals, including calcium and phosphorus; when this fortifier is added to human milk, no additional calcium and phosphorus supplements are needed.

Providing breast milk for a premature infant can be a positive experience for a mother, who is otherwise confronted by the many stresses associated with separation from her baby in intensive care (Fig. 5-5). Since most preterm infants are neither strong enough nor mature enough to suckle at their mothers' breasts in the neonatal period, mothers usually express their milk for a considerable period before nursing can be established. Several factors related to the technique of expression, storage, and transport of milk must be considered to ensure that the breast milk provided is appropriate for feeding. Because of the ready access of most medications to human milk[222] and the risk of transmission of infection, both mothers and milk should be carefully screened.

Formulas. New formula preparations have been developed to meet the unique nutrient and physio-

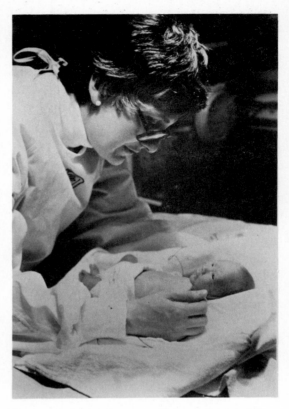

Fig. 5-5. A mother interacts with her premature infant, who is now 10 weeks old.

logical needs of growing LBW infants. The quantity and quality of nutrients contained in these products promote growth at intrauterine rates. When fed to stable premature infants who are growing rapidly, these specialized formulas are usually tolerated without metabolic consequences. Studies of stable babies weighing 1200 gm or more indicate that these formulas are safe and promote weight gain, fat absorption, nitrogen retention, and bone mineralization.[167] When fed to VLBW babies who are stressed and have not yet sustained a steady weight gain, premature formulas should be used cautiously. Because weight gain frequently does not occur in these small babies until after the first couple of weeks of life, premature formulas are sometimes introduced by diluting with water to half strength (12 kcal/oz) and fed in very small quantities. There is no proven advantage to prolonged dilute feeds[223]; therefore, concentration can usually be increased to 24 kcal/oz during the first 12 to 48 hours of enteral feeding, with a subsequent, gradual increase in volume over several days. The concentration of the premature formulas to 24 kcal/oz at full strength more easily meets LBW infants' energy needs in the face of fluid tolerance limitations.

The specialized new premature formulas differ in many aspects from standard cow's milk–base formulas. Table 5-17 summarizes these differences and identifies some of the advantages of feeding premature formulas to LBW infants. Refer to Table 5-18 for a summary of the composition of human milk and that of premature and standard infant formulas.

Selection of Feedings

Choice of an optimal feeding for an LBW infant is complicated by the fact that no ideal feeding exists. The extrauterine environment represents an abrupt change for the preterm infant, and most of these babies require a period of adjustment before tolerance to any enteral feeding can be established.

There may be some advantage in feeding sterile water as the first feeding after birth, since animal evidence indicates that pulmonary damage from aspiration of water is less than that of either 5% glucose in water or milk.[224] Following the first feeding, human milk or formula may be introduced in slowly increasing amounts.

During the initial period of feeding, premature infants are often still adjusting to enteral nutrition and may be experiencing concurrent stress, weight loss, and diuresis. The primary goal of enteral feeding during this initial period is to facilitate tolerance to the milk provided. Aggressive nutritional support from the onset of enteral feeding often meets with failure, as babies appear unable to assimilate a large volume and concentration of

Table 5-17. Comparison of premature versus standard formulas for feeding low birth weight infants

Element	Premature Formulas*	Standard Formulas†
	Designed, tested in premature infants	Designed, tested in full-term infants
Energy	24 kcal/oz	20 kcal/oz
Protein	Whey-casein; 60:40	Whey/casein; 60:40‡
Fat	Part medium-chaintriglycerides; part long-chain fats	100% long-chain fats
Carbohydrate	Part glucose polymers; part lactose	100% lactose
Calcium and phosphorus	Fortified to meet needs of premature	*Not* fortified to meet needs of premature
Iron	Not fortified	Available with or without added iron
Osmolality	Iso-osmolar (300 mOsm/kg H$_2$O)	Iso-osmolar

From O'Leary, M.J.: Nutritional care of the low birth weight infant. In Krause, M.V., and Mahan, L.K., editors: Food, nutrition, and diet therapy, ed. 7, Philadelphia, 1984, W.B. Saunders, Co.
*Enfamil Premature (Mead Johnson), Premie SMA (Wyeth Laboratories), and Similac Special Care (Ross Laboratories).
†Enfamil (Mead Johnson), Similac with Whey (Ross Laboratories), and SMA (Wyeth Laboratories).
‡Similac (Ross Laboratories) is also available with whey-casein; 18:82. Although the other standard formulas contain whey-casein; 60:40, they are not designed to meet the other unique nutrient and physiological needs of LBW infants.

nutrients until adjustment has been established. Supplementation of enteral feedings with parenteral fluids is often required until adequate oral volume is tolerated.

Selection of a milk with the characteristics listed

Table 5-18. Composition of Human Milk, Premature Formulas, and Standard Formulas

		Protein		Carbohydrate		Fat			Calcium	Potassium	Renal	Gastrointestinal
	Caloric density	Whey/casein	Total calories (%)	Type	Total calories (%)	Type	Total calories (%)		Calcium (mg/L)	Potassium (mg/L)	Renal (mOsm/L)	Gastrointestinal (mOsm/kg H₂o)
Human Milk												
Mature	20 kcal./oz. (0.67 kcal./ml.)	60:40	7	Lactose	38	Human milk fat	55		340	169	75	300
Premature	22 kcal./oz.) (0.73 kcal./ml.)	60:40		Lactose		Human milk fat			293	134		300
Standard Formula												
Similac	20 kcal./oz.	18:82	9	Lactose	43	Coconut and soy oils	48		510 520	390 438	110-120	285
Humanized Standard Formulas												
SMA	20 kcal./oz.	60:40	9	Lactose	41-43	Corn, coconut, and/ or soy, oleo, safflower oils	48-51		420	310	105	250
Similac PM 60/40	20 kcal./oz.	60:40	9	Lactose	41				400	200	92	260
Enfamil	20 kcal./oz.	60:40	9	Lactose	41				460	345	97	285
Similac with whey	20 kcal./oz	60:40	9	Lactose	43				400	300	104	300

Premature Formulas

Similac Special Care	24 kcal./oz. (0.81 kcal./ml.)	60:40	11	Lactose/ glucose poly- mers 50:50	42	MCT/corn/ coconut 50:30:20	47	1440	702	208	300
Enfamil Premie	24 kcal./oz.	60:40	12	40:60	42	40:40:20	44	940	470	220	300
SMA	24 kcal./oz	60:40	10	50:50	42	Coconut/saf- flower/ oleo/soy/ MCT 27:25: 20:18:10	48	750	400	175	300

From O'Leary, M.J.: Nutritional care of the low birth weight infant. In Krause, M.V., and Mahan, L.K., editors: Food, nutrition, and diet therapy, ed. 7, Philadelphia, 1984, W.B. Saunders Co.

on p. 162 may facilitate tolerance to enteral feedings during this initial period of adjustment. Feedings that meet these criteria include (1) human milk, (2) premature formula, or (3) a low-protein, low-mineral formula such as Similac PM 60/40 (Ross Laboratories).

When the mother who delivers early expresses milk for her own infant, it is the feeding of choice. Premature formulas were designed for the LBW infant; however, they should be used with caution during the initial period of enteral feeding. The low renal solute load of such formulas as Similac PM 60/40 may be of initial advantage to the stressed, immature infant experiencing obligatory water loss. However, the low protein and mineral concentrations in this formula are likely to be disadvantageous to the stable infant once growth is established.

After the initial period of adjustment, the goal of enteral feeding changes to provide complete nutrition to promote growth and rapid organ development. All essential nutrients should be provided in quantities that support sustained growth in all parameters. For this effect, the following feeding choices are appropriate: (1) human milk, (2) premature formula, or (3) standard infant formula.

Human milk continues to be the feeding of choice for the rapidly growing LBW infant. If fluid limitations exist, the volume of human milk ingested may be less than that needed to support adequate growth; Human Milk Fortifier (Mead Johnson) or a formula supplement (24 kcal/oz or more) may be desirable until fluid intake can be liberalized.

In general, infants weighing less than about 2 kg require special attention with respect to their nutritional needs and level of maturity. When human milk is not available, premature formulas are the usual choice for infants weighing less than 2 kg; standard formulas are more appropriate for larger babies. The decision to change from premature to standard formula will vary in timing depending on such factors as the infant's growth history, energy requirements, volume limitations, and discharge plans.

Criteria Which Promote Tolerance to Initial Enteral Feedings

1. Nutrient composition that is readily digestible and absorbable
2. Whey/casein 60:40
3. Low renal solute load
4. Iso-osmolality (300 mOsm/kg water)

From O'Leary, M.J.: Nutritional care of the low birth weight infant. In Krause, M.V., and Mahan, L.K., editors: Food, nutrition, and diet therapy, ed. 7, Philadelphia, 1984, W.B. Saunders Co.

Dietary Manipulations

It is occasionally desirable to increase the energy content of the formulas fed to small infants. This may be appropriate when the infant is not growing at a desirable rate and is already ingesting a maximum volume of fluid.

Concentration of formulas. One approach to providing hypercaloric formulas is to subtract water, thereby concentrating all nutrients, including energy. Concentrated infant formulas (24 kcal/oz or more) are available to hospitals as ready-to-feed nursettes. When using such concentrated formulas, however, it is important to consider the infant's fluid intake and fluid losses in relation to the renal solute load of the concentrated feeding to ensure that positive water balance is maintained.[225]

Caloric supplements. Another approach to increasing the energy content of formulas is the use of caloric supplements such as medium-chain triglyceride oil (Mead Johnson) and glucose polymers such as Polycose (Ross Laboratories). These supplements increase the caloric density without marked alterations in solute load or osmolality; however, they do alter the relative distribution of total calories from protein, carbohydrate, and fat. Because adding even small amounts of medium-chain triglyceride oil and/or Polycose adversely dilutes the percentage of protein calories while altering the percentage of calories from fat and carbohydrate, adding these supplements to human milk or standard 20 kcal/oz formula is not advised.

When a high-energy formula is appropriate, first add medium-chain triglyceride oil to a 24 kcal/oz base (either full-strength premature formula or a concentrated standard formula), to a maximum of 60% of total calories as fat and a minimum of 7% of total calories as protein. If more energy is needed for sustained growth, Polycose may then be added. The guidelines on p. 163 are recommended for use of medium-chain triglyceride oil and Polycose in LBW infants.

Vitamin and Mineral Supplementation

The vitamin and mineral requirements of preterm infants are not precisely known. Estimates (called advisable intakes) take into account intrauterine accretion rates, full-term infants' needs, and the unique physiological demands of LBW infants. Although these advisable intakes lack precision, they do serve as guidelines until more precise empirical data are available. Ziegler, Biga, and Fomon[7] have reported advisable intakes for vitamins and minerals by premature infants. Table 5-19 compares the vitamin recommendations for premature versus full-term babies.

Although human milk contains a full complement of vitamins and premature formulas have been fortified to better meet the needs of the LBW infant, most tiny babies consume such small volumes of milk that a multivitamin supplement is usually recommended. The type, quantity, and frequency of supplementation varies with individual body weight and predominent feeding (Table 5-20).

Recommendations for Use of MCT Oil* and Polycose† by Low Birth Weight Infants

1. To a 24 kcal/oz formula base, add: 0.4 ml MCT oil/oz formula = 27 kcal/oz formula
2. Then add: 1.5 ml liquid Polycose/oz formula = 30 kcal/oz formula
3. Increase volume of feeding as tolerated and wean off MCT oil and Polycose

From O'Leary, M.J.: Nutritional care of the low birth weight infant. In Krause, M.V., and Mahan, L.K., editors: Food, nutrition, and diet therapy, ed. 7, Philadelphia, 1984, W.B. Saunders, Co.
*MCT oil (Mead Johnson).
†Polycose (Ross Laboratories).

Table 5-19. Advisable intakes of vitamins for preterm compared with full-term infants

Vitamin	Preterm	Full-term (up to 12 Months)
Vitamin A (IU)	500	500
Vitamin D (IU)	600	400
Vitamine E (IU)	30	4
Vitamin K (μg)	15	15
Vitamin C (mg)	60	20
Thiamine (mg)	0.2	0.2
Riboflavin (mg)	0.4	0.4
Niacin (mg)	5	5
B_6 (mg)	0.4	1.5
B_{12} (μg)	1.5	—
Folic acid (μg)	60	50
Pantothenic acid (mg)	2	—
Biotin (μg)	12	—

From Ziegler, E.E., Biga, R.L., and Fomon, S.J.: Nutritional requirements of the premature infant. In Suskind, R.M., editors: Textbook of pediatric nutrition. Copyright, 1981, Raven Press, New York.

Oral vitamin and mineral supplementation should be delayed until the infant has tolerated full-strength formula or breast milk for at least 48 hours at a volume sufficient to provide calories for maintenance and growth. Because common liquid vitamin preparations have very high osmolarities, it is suggested that the supplements be administered in divided doses and mixed with the iso-osmolar milk before feeding. This minimizes the adverse side effects of vitamin supplementation such as increased gastric residuals and regurgitation.

CASE 3

Infant John was a 30-week gestation baby who weighed 1080 gm at birth. He was admitted to the neonatal intensive care unit with severe respiratory disease; although he was weaned from the ventilator by 4 weeks of age, he developed chronic lung disease and continued to require oxygen by hood. After 2½ weeks of total parenteral nutrition through an umbilical arterial catheter, John's respiratory status was stable enough to permit the introduction of enteral feeds. Premature formula feedings were initiated at full strength, but in small amounts, and John was gradually weaned from the hyperalimentation solution to a regimen of complete enteral nutrition by 6 weeks of age. At this time, he weighed 1360 gm and received 17 ml of 24 kcal/oz premature formula every 2 hours. This provided a total enteral volume of 150 ml/kg/day and a total caloric intake of 120 kcal/kg day. Vitamin supplements appropriate for a preterm infant were started after John was tolerating full enteral volume; iron supplements were also initiated at this time. Daily measurements of body weight and weekly measurements of occipital frontal circumference and length were plotted on a growth grid on an age-corrected basis. During the next 2 weeks, bolus feedings were increased as the infant grew to maintain a total enteral volume of 150 ml/kg/day and a caloric intake of 110 to 120 kcal/kg/day. However, John failed to grow at an adequate rate, and his growth curves were slow as compared with the standards on the growth grid. John was a fussy chronic lung baby, and he obviously expended considerable energy in his labored effort to breathe. Furthermore,

Table 5-20. Suggested schedule for vitamin/mineral supplementation based on body weight and predominant feeding

	Human Milk	Premature Formulas		Standard Formulas
		Similac Special Care (Ross)	Premature Enfamil With Whey (Mead Johnson)	Similac, Enfamil
<2000 gm Infant				
Premature vitamins compound* (0.6 cc t.i.d.)	Yes	Yes	Yes	Yes
Calcium (as gluceptate) (1.5 cc = 27 mg Ca)	Yes	No	No	Yes
Phosphorus (as KPO_4) (0.2 cc = 18 mg P)	Yes	No	No	Yes
Iron (2 mg/kg/day)	Prematures: Yes, when (1) body weight has doubled, and/or (2) infant is 2 weeks to 2 months of age			No, if receiving formula with iron
>2000 gm Infant				
Polyvisol (1.0 cc q.d.)†	No	(Not fed to infants >1200 gm body weight)		Yes
Vitamin D (as D_3) (400 IU q.d.)	Yes			No
Iron 1 mg/kg/day (full-term)	Full-term: yes, by 4 months of age			No, if receiving formula with iron

From O'Leary, M.J.: Nutritional care of the low birth weight infant. In Krause, M.V., and Mahan, L.K., editors: Food, nutrition, and diet therapy, ed. 7, Philadelphia, 1984, W.B. Saunders Co.
*In-house preparation based on Ziegler's advisable intakes for prematures.[7]
†Infants who weigh >2500 gm and ingest about ½ liter per day receive 0.5 cc per day.

John received Theophylline (a medication that increases basal metabolic rate). Because of John's high energy expenditure and his extra energy needs for catch-up growth, it was decided to increase his total caloric intake. Volume was limited to 150 ml/kg/day; thus, it was decided to add medium-chain triglyceride oil and Polycose to the formula to achieve a total caloric intake of 140 kcal/kg/day. This modification of the formula was tolerated by John, and his rate of growth increased. By 16 weeks of age, John's age-corrected growth curves were approaching the 50th percentile standard and his rate of gain was beginning to taper off. The caloric density of his formula was gradually decreased to 24 kcal/

oz. John continued to be followed by regular anthropometric measurements to ensure that his energy intake adequately met his needs for normal growth and development.

NUTRITIONAL ASSESSMENT

Growth

All neonates typically lose some weight after birth. This is particularly true for LBW infants who are born with more extracellular water than full-term infants and who may benefit from some degree of fluid loss. However, postnatal weight loss should not be excessive. LBW infants who lose more than about 15% to 20% of their birth weight can be expected to suffer from dehydration as a result of inadequate fluid intake or tissue wasting as a result of poor energy intake.

Weight is presently the most useful anthropometric determinant of nutritional status in the neonatal period. During this first month of life, the growth grid of Dancis, O'Connell, and Holt[226] is commonly used to assess weight progress. This grid has the advantages of depicting daily weight changes and actual growth curves; disadvantages include a small sample size to generate growth data that are now nearly 40 years old. The curves should not, therefore, be interpreted to represent optimal growth, particularly for VLBW infants in modern neonatal intensive care units.

Intrauterine growth curves have also been developed using birth weight data of infants born at successive weeks of gestation.[227] These curves do not depict the initial period of postnatal weight loss and are probably unrealistic goals for VLBW infants in the early neonatal period. Once the infant's condition stabilizes and full nutrient intake is possible, many infants are able to grow at a rate that parallels these curves (i.e., gain of 20 to 30 gm/day).

Although weight is the only convenient and reliable anthropometric parameter by which to assess nutritional status during the early neonatal period, serial measurements of length and head circumference should be taken once the infant is stable. Growth curves such as those shown on p. 20 in Chapter 1, are useful to evaluate the adequacy of growth in all parameters. Measurements of fatfold thickness or laboratory indicators of positive growth are still largely experimental for use in assessment of LBW infants.

During the first year of life, the healthy premature infant who is appropriate for gestational age grows at approximately the same rate as the fullterm infant of the same postconceptional age. Growth progress is comparable as long as the premature infant's age is corrected for prematurity.

For example, at 3 months postnatal age, the growth parameters of a premature infant born at 32 weeks gestation can be compared with those of a 1 month-old baby born at term. After discharge from a neonatal intensive care nursery, standard growth grids from the National Center for Health Statistics (refer to pp. 14-17 in Chapter 1) can be used to evaluate growth of a premature infant, providing corrected age is used until at least 1 year of age.

Infants who have suffered severe medical stress or undernutrition in the early postnatal period and infants who are small for gestational age often require a period of catch-up growth to fulfill their genetic potential. High energy intakes with appropriate concentrations of essential nutrients are frequently needed to potentiate catch-up growth. The catch-up period is characterized by the acceleration of the rate of growth in all parameters; once the infant has caught up, the rate of growth should slow to follow the normal channel for that child.

A small for gestational age infant whose intrauterine weight gain was poor, but whose linear and head growth are appropriate for gestational age (i.e., between the 10th and 90th percentiles on the intrauterine growth grid), has experienced asymmetrical intrauterine growth retardation. A small for gestational age infant whose length and occipital frontal circumference are also below the 10th percentile standards is said to be symmetrically growth retarded. Symmetrical intrauterine growth retardation usually reflects early and prolonged intrauterine deficit and is apparently more detrimental to later growth and development.[228,229]

Laboratory Indices

Several laboratory measurements have been used as indicators of nutritional status in children and adults. However, these measurements are difficult to interpret in premature infants. For example, serum albumin has a half-life of 20 days; thus, serum albumin is not as sensitive an indicator of protein status as are proteins with shorter half-lives, such as retinol-binding protein,[230] complement, and transferrin.[231] But according to Gryboski and Walker, no standard values from large populations of newborns exist for these latter proteins.[26] Although serum albumin and total protein values provide some information regarding protein status, these measurements may be unreliable when there are unusual losses from the gastrointestinal tract, or when albumin has been replaced with a parenteral transfusion.[26]

Antigenic skinfold testing is probably not useful in LBW infants because deficiencies in immunological capabilities are normal in newborns and particularly so in immature newborns.[26] A total lymphocyte count of less than 1500 is always abnormal, but it is not specific for malnutrition and may occur with overwhelming infection.[26] Therefore, because laboratory indices are difficult to interpret and because standards do not yet exist for populations of premature infants, anthropometric measurements are currently the principal means of evaluating the nutritional status of LBW infants.

NEURODEVELOPMENTAL OUTCOME

From the preceding discussion it is apparent that we are now able to meet the metabolic and nutritional needs of premature and LBW infants in a manner sufficient to sustain life and to promote growth and development. With adequate nutritional support and recent advances in neonatal intensive care technology, more tiny, immature infants are surviving than ever before. Survival for infants of 1001 to 1500 gm birth weight improved significantly during the 1970s.[232] During this same period, survival rates nearly doubled for extremely small babies of 501 to 1000 gm birth weight.[232] With increased survival of LBW infants, there is increased concern for the short- and long-term neurodevelopmental outcome for these babies. Many questions are asked about the quality of life awaiting infants who received neonatal intensive care.

Surviving LBW infants, particularly those with birth weights less than 800 gm, have an increased risk of developing central nervous system handicapping conditions of varying severity and functional impairment.[233] But in spite of this risk, the

Fig. 5-6. Same child as in Fig. 5-1. Here she is a healthy 2½-year-old.

majority of these premature babies reach school age without evidence of any disability (Fig. 5-6). It is not always apparent which infants will be undamaged and which will suffer major or minor handicapping conditions. The sometimes poor correlation, in an individual case, between neonatal course and developmental outcome makes neonatal survival decisions extemely difficult.[233] All premature and LBW infants merit personalized and sensitive screening and assessment, with intervention strategies employed as appropriate.

SUMMARY

Both parenteral and enteral nutrition can be effective in nourishing premature and LBW infants. The selection of one technique over another and the choice of specific nutritional goals should follow general guidelines such as those suggested in this chapter. However, these guidelines must be flexible to accommodate the range of individual variation. Clinical judgment of the unique needs of a particular infant may warrant a more tailored approach.

SUGGESTED LEARNING ACTIVITIES

1. Review the chart of an infant in a neonatal intensive care unit who is receiving total parental nutrition. Describe the condition that made total parenteral nutrition the appropriate method of feeding. Calculate the energy and nutrient intake for the past 24 hours.
2. Describe how the transition is made from total parental nutrition to enteral feeding in a premature infant.
3. Discuss the advantages and potential problems of human milk as the sole feeding for a premature infant.
4. Describe differences in commercially prepared formulas for full-term and those for premature infants.
5. Describe appropriate vitamin supplementation for the premature infant on enteral feedings.
6. Investigate the long-term prognosis for growth and development of premature and low birth weight babies.

REFERENCES

1. Committee on Perinatal Health: Toward improving the outcome of pregnancy, New York, 1976, The National Foundation–March of Dimes.
2. Committee on Fetus and Newborn: Guidelines for perinatal care, Evanston, Ill., 1983, American Academy of Pediatrics; and Washington, D.C., 1983, American College of Obstetricians and Gynecologists.
3. Committee on Fetus and Newborn, American Academy of Pediatrics: Level II neonatal units, Pediatrics **66**:810, 1980.
4. Committee on Nutrition of the Mother and Preschool child, Food and Nutrition Board: Nutrition services in perinatal care, Washington, D.C., 1981, Assembly of Life Sciences, National Research Council.
5. Poole, R.L., and Kerner, J.A., Jr.: Establishing a nutrition support team for an intensive care nursery, Nutr. Support Serv. **3**:35, 1983.
6. Dubowitz, L.M.S., and others: Clinical assessment of gestational age in the newborn infant, J. Pediatr. **77**:1, 1970.
7. Ziegler, E.E., Biga, R.L., and Fomon, S.J.: Nutritional requirements of the premature infant. In Suskind, R.M., editor: Textbook of pediatric nutrition, New York, 1981, Raven Press.
8. Widdowson, E.M.: Growth and composition of the fetus and newborn. In Assali, N.S., editor: Biology of gestation, vol. II, New York, 1968, Academic Press, Inc.
9. Heird, W.C., and others: Intravenous alimentation in pediatric patients, J. Pediatr. **80**:351, 1972.
10. Doelkel, R.D., and others: Clinical semistarvation: depression of hypoxic ventilatory response, N. Engl. J. Med. **295**:358, 1976.
11. Chandra, R.K.: Immunodeficiency in undernutrition and overnutrition, Nutr. Rev. **39**:225, 1981.
12. Abel, R.M., and others: Malnutrition in cardiac surgery patients, Arch. Surg. **111**:45, 1976.
13. Dobbing, J.: The later growth of the brain and its vulnerability, Pediatrics **53**:2, 1974.
14. Rosso, P., Hormazabal, J., and Winick, M.: Changes in brain weight, cholesterol, phospholipid, and DNA content in marasmic children, Am. J. Clin. Nutr. **23**:1275, 1970.
15. Dudrick, S.J., Wilmore, D.W., and Vars, H.M.: Long-term total parenteral nutrition with growth in puppies and positive nitrogen balance in patients, Surg. Forum. **18**:356, 1967.
16. Dudrick, S.J., and others: Long-term total parenteral nutrition with growth, development, and positive nitrogen balance, Surgery **64**:134, 1968.
17. Ziegler, M., and others: Route of pediatric parenteral nutrition: proposed criteria revision, J. Pediatr. Surg. **15**:472, 1980.
18. Kerner, J.A., Jr.: Indications for parenteral nutrition in pediatrics. In Kerner, J.A., Jr., editor: Manual of pediatric parenteral nutrition, New York, 1983, John Wiley & Sons, Inc.
19. Jewett, T.C., Jr., and Lebenthal, E.: Recent advances in gastrointestinal tract surgery in children. In Gluck, L., editor: Current problems in pediatrics, vol. 9, Chicago, 1978, Year Book Medical Publishers, Inc.
20. Dudrick, S.J., Copeland, E.M., III, and MacFadyen, B.V., Jr.: Long-term parenteral nutrition: its current status, Hosp. Pract. **10**:47, 1975.
21. Firor, H.V.: Technical improvements in the management of omphalocele and gastroschisis, Surg. Clin. North Am. **55**:129, 1975.
22. Stothert, J.C., Jr., and others: Esophageal atresia and tra-

cheoesophageal fistula: preoperative assessment and reduced mortality, Ann. Thorac. Surg. **28**:54, 1979.

23. Heird, W.C., and Winters, R.W.: Parenteral nutrition in pediatrics. In Schneider, H.A., Anderson, C.E., and Cowisin, D.B., editors: Nutritional support of medical practice, New York, 1977, Harper & Row, Publishers, Inc.

24. Filler, R.M.: Parenteral support of the surgically ill child. In Suskind, R.M., editor: Textbook of pediatric nutrition, New York, 1981, Raven Press.

25. Sunshine, P., Sinatra, F.R., and Mitchell, C.H.: Intractable diarrhea of infancy, Clin. Gastroenterol. **6**:445, 1977.

26. Gryboski, J., and Walker, W.A.: Parenteral nutrition. In Gryboski, J., and Walker, W.A., editors: Gastrointestinal problems in the infant, Philadelphia, 1983, W.B. Saunders Co.

27. Sinclair, J., and others: Supportive management of the sick neonate: parenteral calories, water, and electrolytes, Pediatr. Clin. North Am. **17**:863, 1970.

28. Cashore, W.J., Sedaghatian, J.R., and Usher, R.H.: Nutritional supplements with intravenously administered lipid, protein hydrolyzate, and glucose in small premature infants, Pediatrics **56**:88, 1975.

29. Mestyan, J., Jarai, I., and Fekete, M.: The total energy expenditure and its components in premature infants maintained under different nursing and environmental conditions, Pediatr. Res. **2**:161, 1968.

30. Anderson, T.L., and others: A controlled trial of glucose versus glucose and amino acids in premature infants, J. Pediatr. **94**:115, 1981.

31. Zlotkin, S.H., Bryan, M.H., and Anderson, G.H.: Intravenous nitrogen and energy intakes required to duplicate in utero nitrogen accretion in prematurely born human infants, J. Pediatr. **99**:115, 1981.

32. Kerner, J.A., Jr.: Caloric requirements. In Kerner, J.A., Jr., editor: Manual of pediatric parenteral nutrition, New York, 1983, John Wiley & Sons, Inc.

33. Kerner, J.A., Jr., editor: Manual of pediatric parenteral nutrition, New York, 1983, John Wiley & Sons, Inc.

34. Kerner, J.A., Jr.: Fluid requirements. In Kerner J.A., Jr., editor: Manual of pediatric parenteral nutrition, New York, 1983, John Wiley & Sons, Inc.

35. Fanaroff, M., and others: Insensible water loss in low-birth-weight infants, Pediatrics **50**:236, 1972.

36. Oh, W.: Fluid and electrolyte management. In Avery, G.B., Editor: Neonatology, pathophysiology, and management of the newborn, Philadelphia, 1981, J.B. Lippincott Co.

37. Friis-Hansen, B.: Changes in body water compartments during growth, Acta Paediatr. Scand. (suppl. 110) **46**:1, 1957.

38. Bell, E.F., and Oh, W.: Water requirement of premature newborn infants, Acta Paediatr. Scand. Suppl. **305**:21, 1983.

39. Hodson, W.A., and Truog, W.E.: Parenteral nutrition. In Hodson, W.A., and Truog, W.A., editors: Critical care of the newborn, Philadelphia, 1983, W.B. Saunders Co.

40. Wu, P.Y.K., and Hodgman, J.E.: Insensible water loss in premature infants, Pediatrics **54**:704, 1974.

41. Oh, W., and Karechi, H.: Phototherapy and insensible water loss in the newborn infant, Ann. J. Dis Child. **124**:230, 1972.

42. Marks, K.A., Friedman, Z., and Maisels, M.J.: A simple device for reducing insensible water loss in LBW infants, Pediatrics **60**:223, 1977.

43. Harkavey, K.L.: Water and electrolyte requirements of the very-low-birth-weight infant, Perinatal Press **6**:47, 1982.

44. Bell, E.F., and others: Effect of fluid administration on the development of symptomatic patent ductus arteriosus and congestive heart failure in premature infants, N. Engl. J. Med. **302**:598, 1980.

45. Stevenson, J.G.: Fluid administration in the association of patent ductus arteriosus complicating distress syndrome, J. Pediatr. **90**:257, 1977.

46. Goldberg, R.N., and others: The association of rapid volume expansion and intraventricular hemorrhage in the preterm infant, J. Pediatr. **96**:1060, 1980.

47. Brown, E.R., and others: Bronchopulmonary dysplasia: possible relationship to pulmonary edema, J. Pediatr. **92**:982, 1978.

48. Friis-Hansen, B.: Water distribution in the foetus and newborn infant, Acta Paediatr. Scand. Suppl. **305**:7, 1983.

49. Oh, W., Oh, M.A., and Lind, J.: Renal function and blood volume in newborn infants related to placental transfusion, Acta Paediatr. Scand. **56**:197, 1966.

50. Spitzer, A.R., Fox, W.W., and Delivoria-Papadopoulos, M.: Maximum diuresis—a factor in predicting recovery from respiratory distress syndrome and the development of bronchopulmonary dysplasia, J. Pediatr. **98**:476, 1981.

51. Miranda, L.E.V., and Dweck, H.S.: Perinatal glucose homeostasis: the unique character of hyperglycemia and hypoglycemia in infants of very-low-birth-weight, Clin. Perinatol. **4**:351, 1977.

52. Kerner, J.A., Jr.: Carbohydrate requirements. In Kerner, J.A., Jr., editor: Manual of pediatric parenteral nutrition, New York, 1983, John Wiley & Sons, Inc.

53. Chance, G.W.: Results in very-low-birth-weight infants (<1300 gm birth weight). In Winters, R.W., and Hasselmeyer, E.G., editors: Intravenous nutrition in the high risk infant, New York, 1975, John Wiley & Sons, Inc.

54. Jacobs, W.C., Lazzara, A., and Martin, D.J.: Parenteral nutrition in the neonate, Chicago, 1980, Abbott Laboratories, Hospital Products Division.

55. Sparks, J.W., and others: Parenteral galactose therapy in the glucose-intolerant premature infant, J. Pediatr. **100:**255, 1982.
56. Pribylora, J., and Kozlora, J.: Glucose and galactose infusions in newborns of diabetic and healthy mothers, Biol. Neonate **36:**193, 1979.
57. Simkims, R.A., and others: Development of gluconeogenesis from galactose by fetal rat liver explants in organ culture, Dev. Biol. **66:**353, 1978.
58. Benda, G.I., and Babson, S.G.: Peripheral intravenous alimentation of the small premature infant, J. Pediatr. **79:**494, 1971.
59. Vaucher, Y.E., Walson, P.D., and Morrow, G., III: Continuous insulin infusion in hyperglycemic, very-low-birth-weight infants, J. Pediatr. Gastroenterol Nutr. **1:**211, 1982.
60. Goldman, S.L., and Hirata, T.: Attenuated response to insulin in very-low-birth-weight infants, Pediatr. Res. **14:**50, 1980.
61. Brans, Y.W.: Parenteral nutrition of the very-low-birth weight neonate: a critical review, Clin. Perinatol. **4:**367, 1977.
62. Heird, W.C.: Total parenteral nutrition. In Lebenthal, E., editor: Textbook of gastroenterology and nutrition in infancy, New York, 1981, Raven Press.
63. Fischer, J.E.: Parenteral and enteral nutrition, Disease-a-Month **24:**23, 1981.
64. Hooley, R.A.: Parenteral nutrition—general concepts. Part II. Nutr. Support Serv. **1:**41, 1981.
65. Heird, W.C.: Panel report on nutritional support of pediatric patients, Am. J. Clin. Nutr. **34:**1223, 1981.
66. Snyderman, S.E.: The protein and amino acid requirements of the premature infant. In Jonxis, J.H.P., Visser, H.K.A., and Troelstra, J.A., editors: Metabolic process in the fetus and newborn infant, Baltimore, 1971, Williams & Wilkins.
67. Gaull, G.E., and others: Milk protein quantity and quality in low-birth-weight infants. III. Effects on sulfur amino acids in plasma and urine, J. Pediatr. **90:**356, 1977.
68. Rassin, D.K., Raiha, N.C.R., and Gaull, G.E.: Protein and taurine nutrition in infants. In Lebenthal, E., editor: Textbook of gastroenterology and nutrition in infancy, vol. 1, New York, 1981, Raven Press.
69. Kerner, J.A., Jr.: Protein requirements. In Kerner, J.A., Jr., editor: Manual of pediatric parenteral nutrition, New York, 1983, John Wiley & Sons, Inc.
70. Hornchen, H., and Neubrand, W.: Amino acids for parenteral nutrition in premature and newborn infants, use of mother's milk-adapted solution, J. Parent. Ent. Nutr. **4:**294, 1980.
71. Holt, L.E., Jr., and Snyderman, S.E.: The amino acid requirements of children. In Nyham, W.L., editor: Amino acid metabolism and genetic variation, New York, 1967, McGraw-Hill Book Co.
72. Fomon, S.J., and Filer, L.J., Jr.: Amino acid requirements for normal growth. In Nyham, W.L., editor: Amino acid metabolism and genetic variation, New York, 1967, McGraw-Hill Book Co.
73. Snyderman, S.E.: Recommendation for parenteral amino acid requirements. In Winters, R.W., and Hassel-Meyer, E.G., editors: Intravenous nutrition in the high risk infant, New York, 1975, John Wiley & Sons, Inc.
74. Ghadimi, H.: Newly devised amino acid solutions for intravenous administration. In Ghadimi, H., editor: Total parenteral nutrition: premises and promises, New York, 1975, John Wiley & Sons, Inc.
75. Seashore, J.H.: Metabolic complications of parenteral nutrition in infants and children, Surg. Clin. North Am. **60:**1239, 1980.
76. Heird, W.C., and others: Hyperammonemia resulting from intravenous alimentation using a mixture of synthetic L-amino acids: a preliminary report, J. Pediatr. **81:**162, 1972.
77. Poley, J.R.: Liver and nutrition: hepatic complications of total parenteral nutrition. In Lebenthal, E., editor: Textbook of gastroenterology and nutrition in infancy, New York, 1981, Raven Press.
78. Abitbol, C.L., and others: Plasma amino acid patterns during supplemental intravenous nutrition of low-birth-weight infants, J. Pediatr. **86:**766, 1975.
79. Pereira, G.R., and others: Hyperalimentation-induced cholestasis: increased incidence and severity in premature infants, Am. J. Dis. Child. **135:**842, 1981.
80. Sinatra, F.R.: Cholestasis in infancy and childhood, Curr. Prob. Pediatr. **12**(12):6, 1982.
81. Beale, E.F., and others: Intrahepatic cholestasis associated with parenteral nutrition in premature infants, Pediatrics **64:**342, 1979.
82. Vileisis, R.A., Inwood, R.J., and Hunt, C.E.: Prospective controlled study of parenteral nutrition–associated cholestatic jaundice: effect of protein intake, J. Pediatr. **96:**893, 1980.
83. Anderson, T.L., and others: A controlled trial of glucose versus glucose and amino acids in premature infants, J. Pediatr. **94:**947, 1979.
84. Kerner, J.A., Jr.: Fat requirements. In Kerner, J.A., Jr., editor: Manual of pediatric parenteral nutrition, New York, 1983, John Wiley & Sons, Inc.
85. Byrne, W.J.: Intralipid[R] or Liposyn[R]—comparable products? J. Pediatr. Gastroenterol. Nutr. **1**(1):7, 1982.
86. Holman, R.T., Johnson, S.B., and Hatch, T.F.: A case of human linolenic acid deficiency involving neurologic abnormalities, Am. J. Clin. Nutr. **35:**617, 1982.
87. Cooke, R.J., and Burckhart, G.J.: Hypertriglyceridemia during the intravenous infusion of a safflower oil–based fat emulsion, J. Pediatr. **103:**959, 1983.
88. Griffin, E.A., Bryan, M.H., and Angel, A.: Variations in

Intralipid tolerance in newborn infants, Pediatr. Res. **17:**478, 1983.

89. Dhanireddy, R., and others: Postheparin lipolytic activity and intralipid clearance in VLBW infants, J. Pediatr. **98:**617, 1981.

90. Zaidan, H., and others: Effect of continuous heparin administration on Intralipid clearing in very-low-birth-weight infants, J. Pediatr. **101:**599, 1982.

91. Penn, D., Schmidt-Sommerfeld, E., and Wolf, H.: Carnitine deficiency in premature infants receiving total parenteral nutrition, Early Hum. Dev. **4:**23, 1980.

92. Holman, R.T.: Essential fatty acid deficiency. In Holman, R.T., editor: Progress in the chemistry of fats and other lipids, vol. 9, Elmsford, New York, 1968, Pergamon Press, Inc.

93. Friedman, Z., and others: Rapid onset of essential fatty acid deficiency in the newborn, Pediatrics **58:**640, 1976.

94. Levy, J.S., Winters, R.W., and Heird, W.C.: Total parenteral nutrition in pediatric patients, Pediatr. Rev. **2:**99, 1980.

95. Hunt, C.E., and others: Essential fatty acid deficiency in neonates: inability to reverse deficiency by topical application of EFA rich oil, J. Pediatr. **92:**603, 1978.

96. Dolcourt, J.: Pediatric parenteral nutrition manual, Salt Lake City, 1983, Primary Children's Medical Center.

97. Gustafson, A., and others: Nutrition in low-birth-weight infants. II. Repeated intravenous injections of fat emulsion, Acta Paediatr. Scand. **63:**177, 1974.

98. Schreiner, R.L., and others: An evaluation of methods to monitor infants receiving intravenous lipids, J. Pediatr. **94:**197, 1979.

99. Starinsky, R., and Shafir, E.: Displacement of albumin-bound bilirubin by free fatty acids: implications for neonatal hyperbilirubinemia, Clin. Chim. Acta **29:**311, 1970.

100. Kerner, J.A., Jr., and others: Monitoring intravenous fat emulsions in neonates with fatty acid/serum albumin molar ratio, J. Parent. Ent. Nutr. **5:**517, 1981.

101. Andrew, G., Chan G., and Schiff, D.: Lipid metabolism in the neonate. II. The effect of Intralipid on bilirubin binding in vitro and in vivo, J. Pediatr. **88:**279, 1976.

102. Hertel, J., Tygstrup, I., and Anderson, G.E.: Intravascular fat accumulation after Intralipid infusion in the very low-birth-weight infant, J. Pediatr. **100:**975, 1982.

103. Dahms, B., and Halpin, T.C.: Pulmonary arterial lipid deposit in newborn infants receiving intravenous lipid infusion, J. Pediatr. **97:**800, 1980.

104. Pereira, G.R., and others: Decreased oxygenation and hyperlipemia during intravenous fat infusions in premature infants, Pediatrics **66:**26, 1980.

105. Askanazi, J., and others: Nutrition for the patient with respiratory failure: glucose vs. fat, Anesthesiology **54:**373, 1981.

106. Askanazi, J., and others: Effect of total parenteral nutrition on gas exchange and breathing patterns, Crit. Care Med. **7:**125, 1979.

107. Buzby, G.P., and others: Manipulation of TPN caloric substrate and fatty infiltration of the liver, J. Surg. Res. **31:**46, 1981.

108. Poole, R.L.: Electrolyte and mineral requirements. In Kerner, J.A., Jr., editor: Manual of pediatric parenteral nutrition, New York, 1983, John Wiley & Sons, Inc.

109. Committee on Nutrition, American Academy of Pediatrics: Sodium intake of infants in the United States, Pediatrics **68:**444, 1981.

110. Kerner, J.A., Jr., and Sunshine, P.: Parenteral alimentation, Semin. Perinatol. **3:**417, 1979.

111. Ziegler, E.E., and others: Body composition of the reference fetus, Growth **40:**329, 1976.

112. Kerner, J.A., Jr.: Metabolic complications. In Kerner, J.A., Jr., editor: Manual of pediatric parenteral nutrition, New York, 1983, John Wiley & Sons, Inc.

113. Leape, L.L., and Valaes, T.: Rickets in low-birth-weight infants receiving total parenteral nutrition, J. Pediatr. Surg. **11:**665, 1976.

114. Winslow, C., and others: Rickets in very-low-birth-weight infants: growth exceeding mineral intake, Clin. Res. **28:**897A, 1980.

115. Eggert, L.D., and others: Calcium and phosphorus compatibility in parenteral nutrition solutions for neonates, Am. J. Hosp. Pharm. **39:**49, 1982.

116. Poole, R., Ryp, C., and Kerner, J.A., Jr.: Calcium and phosphorus in neonatal TPN solutions, J. Parent. Ent. Nutr. **5:**580, 1981.

117. Venkataraman, P.S., Brissie, E.O., and Tsang, R.C.: Stability of calcium and phosphorus in neonatal parenteral nutrition solutions, J. Pediatr. Gastroenterol. Nutr. **2:**640, 1983.

118. Poole, R.S.: Problems with preparation of parenteral nutrition solutions. In Kerner, J.A., Jr.: Manual of pediatric parenteral nutrition, New York, 1983, John Wiley & Sons, Inc.

119. American Medical Association, Department of Foods and Nutrition: Multivitamin preparations for parenteral use; a statement by the Nutrition Advisory Group, J. Parent. Ent. Nutr. **3:**258, 1979.

120. Kerner, J.A., Jr.: Vitamin requirements. In Kerner, J.A., Jr., editor: Manual of pediatric parenteral nutrition, New York, 1983, John Wiley & Sons, Inc.

121. Moorhatch, P., and Chiou, W.L.: Interaction between drugs and plastic intravenous fluid bags, Am. J. Hosp. Pharm. **31:**149, 1974.

122. Howard, L., and others: Vitamin A deficiency from long-term parenteral nutrition, Ann. Int. Med. **93:**576, 1980.

123. Bhaka, J., Mims, L.C., and Roesel, R.A.: The effect of

phototherapy on amino acid solutions containing multivitamins, J. Pediatr. **96:**284, 1980.

124. Greene, H.L.: Vitamins in total parenteral nutrition, Drug Intel. Clin. Pharm. **6:**355, 1972.

125. Nutrition Reviews: Biotin deficiency as a complication of incomplete parenteral nutrition, Nutr. Rev. **39:**274, 1981.

126. Shenai, J.P.: Personal communication.

127. Howard, L., and others: Vitamin A deficiency from long-term parenteral nutrition, Ann. Int. Med. **93:**576, 1980.

128. Shenai, J.P., Stahlman, M.T., and Chytil, F.: Vitamin A delivery from parenteral alimentation solutions, J. Pediatr. **99:**661, 1981.

129. Shike, M., and others: Metabolic bone disease in patients receiving long-term parenteral nutrition, Ann. Int. Med. **92:**343, 1980.

130. Klein, G.L., and others: Infantile vitamin D–resistant rickets associated with total parenteral nutrition, Am. J. Dis. Child. **136:**74, 1982.

131. Dju, M.Y., Mason, K.E., and Filer, L.J.: Vitamin E in human fetuses and placentae, Etudes Neo-Natales **1:**49, 1952.

132. Bell, E.F., and Filer, L.J., Jr.: The role of vitamin E in the nutrition of premature infants, Am. J. Clin. Nutr. **34:**414, 1981.

133. Ansell, J.E., Kumor, R., and Deykin, N.: The spectrum of vitamin K deficiency, J.A.M.A. **238:**40, 1977.

134. Kerner, J.A., Jr.: Trace element requirements. In Kerner, J.A., Jr., editor: Manual of pediatric parenteral nutrition, New York, 1983, John Wiley & Sons, Inc.

135. Nutrition Advisory Group, American Medical Association, Department of Foods and Nutrition: Guidelines for essential trace element preparations for parenteral use, J.A.M.A. **241:**2051, 1979.

136. Thorp, J.W., and others: A prospective study of infant zinc nutrition during intensive care, Am. J. Clin. Nutr. **34:**1056, 1981.

137. Zlotkin, S.H., and Buchanan, B.E.: Meeting zinc and copper intake requirements in the parenterally fed preterm and full-term infant, J. Pediatr. **103:**441, 1983.

138. Wan, K.K., and Tsallas, G.: Dilute iron dextran formulation for addition to parenteral nutrition solutions, Am. J. Hosp. Pharm. **37:**106, 1980.

139. Kerner, J.A., Jr.: The transition from parenteral to enteral feedings. In Kerner, J.A., Jr., editor: Manual of pediatric parenteral nutrition, New York, 1983, John Wiley & Sons, Inc.

140. Feldman, E.J., and others: Effects of oral and venous nutrition on intestinal adaptation after small bowel resection in the dog, Gastroenterology **70:**712, 1976.

141. Kotler, D.P., and Levine, G.M.: Reversible gastric and pancreatic hyposecretion after long-term total parenteral nutrition, N. Engl. J. Med. **300:**241, 1979.

142. Greene, H.L., and others: Comparison of the adaptive changes in disaccharidase, glycolytic enzyme and fructose diphosphatase activities after intravenous and oral glucose in normal men, Am. J. Clin. Nutr. **28:**1122, 1975.

143. Alpers, D.H.: Protein synthesis in intestinal mucosa: the effect of route of administration of precursor amino acids, J. Clin. Invest. **51:**167, 1972.

144. Brady, M.S., Gresham, E.L., and Rickard, K.: Nutritional care of the low-birth-weight infant requiring intensive care, Perinatal Press **2:**125, 1978.

145. Lebenthal, E., Lee, P.C., and Heitlinger, L.A.: Impact of development of the gastrointestinal tract on infant feedings, J. Pediatr. **102:**1, 1983.

146. Feinstein, M.S., and Smith, C.A.: Digestion of protein by premature infants, Pediatrics **7:**19, 1951.

147. Ziegler, E.E., and others: Body composition of the reference fetus, Growth **40:**329, 1976.

148. Gross, S.J., and others: Growth and biochemical response of premature infants fed human milk or modified infant formula, N. Engl. J. Med. **308:**237, 1983.

149. Raiha, N.C.R., and others: Milk protein quantity and quality in low-birth-weight infants. I. Metabolic responses and effects on growth, Pediatrics **57:**659, 1976.

150. Fomon, S.J., and Ziegler, E.E.: Protein intake of premature infants: interpretation of data, J. Pediatr. **90:**504, 1977.

151. Rassin, D.K., and others: Milk protein quantity and quality in low-birth-weight infants. II. Effects of selected alphatic amino acids in plasma and urine, Pediatrics **59:**407, 1977.

152. Gaull, G.E., and others: Milk protein quantity and quality in low-birth-weight infants: III. Effects on sulfur amino acids in plasma and urine, J. Pediatr. **90:**348, 1977.

153. Rassin, D.K., and others: Milk protein quantity and quality in low-birth-weight infants. IV. Effects on tyrosine and phenylalanine in plasma and urine, J. Pediatr. **90:**357, 1977.

154. Schriener, R.L., and others: Lack of occurrence of lactobezoars with predominantly whey protein formulas, Am. J. Dis. Child. **136:**437, 1982.

155. Avery, G.B., and Fletcher, A.B.: Nutrition. In Avery, G.B., editor: Neonatology, Philadelphia, 1981, J.B. Lippincott Co.

156. Lebenthal, E., and Lee, P.C.: Development of functional response in the human exocrine pancreas, Pediatrics **66:**556, 1980.

157. Katz, L., and Hamilton, J.R.: Fat absorption in infants of birth weight less than 1300 grams, J. Pediatr. **85:**608, 1974.

158. Tantibhedhyangkul, P., and Hashim, S.A.: Medium chain triglyceride feeding in premature infants: effects on fat and nitrogen absorption, Pediatrics **55:**359, 1975.

159. Hernell, O., Blackberg, L., and Olivecrona, T.: Human milk lipases. In Lebenthal, E., editor: Gastroenterology and nutrition in infancy, New York, 1981, Raven Press.

160. Hanna, F.M., Navarette, D.H., and Hsu, F.A.: Calcium–fatty acid absorption in infants fed human milk and prepared formula simulating human milk, Pediatrics **45**:216, 1970.

161. Committee on Nutrition, American Academy of Pediatrics: Nutritional needs of low-birth-weight infants, Pediatrics **60**:519, 1977.

162. Antonowicz, I., and Lebenthal, E.: Developmental pattern of small intestinal enterokinase and disaccharidase activities in the human fetus, Gastroenterology **72**:1299, 1977.

163. MacLean, W.C., and Fink, B.B.: Lactose malabsorption by premature infants: magnitude and clinical significance, J. Pediatr. **97**:383, 1980.

164. Cicco, R., and others: Glucose polymers tolerance in premature infants, Pediatrics **67**:498, 1981.

165. Steichen, J.J., Gratton, T.L., and Tsang, R.C.: Osteopenia of prematurity: the cause and possible treatment, J. Pediatr. **96**:528, 1980.

166. Tsang, R.C.: The quandary of vitamin D in the newborn infant, Lancet **18**:1372, 1983.

167. Day, G.M., and others: Growth and mineral metabolism in very-low-birth-weight infants. II. Effects of calcium supplementation on growth and divalent cations, Pediatr. Res. **9**:568, 1975.

168. Greer, F.R., Steichen, J.J., and Tsang, R.C.: Calcium and phosphate supplements in breast milk–related rickets, Am. J. Dis. Child. **136**:581, 1982.

169. Shenai, J.P., Reynolds, J.W., and Babson, S.G.: Nutritional balance studies in very-low-birth-weight infants: enhanced nutrient retention rates by an experimental formula, Pediatrics **66**:233, 1980.

170. Okamoto, E., and Heird, W.C.: Feeding the low-birth-weight infant, Pediatr. Ann. **10**:37, 1981.

171. Glorieux, F.J., and others: Vitamin D metabolism in preterm infants: serum calcitriol values during the first five days of life, J. Pediatr. **99**:640, 1981.

172. Steichen, J.J., and others: Elevated serum 1,25-dihydroxyvitamin D concentrations in rickets of very-low-birth-weight infants, J. Pediatr. **99**:293, 1981.

173. Seino, Y., and others: Plasma active vitamin D concentration in low-birth-weight infants with rickets and its response to vitamin D treatment, Arch. Dis. Child. **56**:629, 1981.

174. Atkinson, S.A.: Calcium and phosphorus requirements of low-birth-weight infants: a nutritional and endocrinological perspective, Nutr. Rev. **41**:69, 1983.

175. Melhorn, D.K., and Gross, S.: Vitamin E–dependent anemia in the premature infant. I. Effects of large doses of medicinal iron, J. Pediatr. **79**:569, 1971.

176. Siimes, M.A., and Jarvenpaa, A.L.: Prevention of anemia and iron deficiency in very-low-birth-weight infants, J. Pediatr. **101**:277, 1982.

177. Committee on Nutrition, American Academy of Pediatrics: Relationship between iron status and incidence of infection in infancy, Pediatrics **62**:246, 1978.

178. Baltimore, R.S., Shedd, D.G., and Pearson, H.A.: Effect of iron saturation on the bacteriostasis of human serum: in vivo does not correlate with in vitro saturation, J. Pediatr. **101**:519, 1982.

179. Lundstrom, U., Siimes, M.A., and Dallman, P.R.: At what age does iron supplementation become necessary in low-birth-weight infants? J. Pediatr. **91**:878, 1977.

180. Phelps, D.L., and Rosenbaum, A.L.: The role of tocopherol in oxygen-induced retinopathy: kitten model, Pediatrics **59**:998, 1977.

181. Hittner, H.M., and others: Retrolental fibroplasia: efficiency of vitamin E in a double blind clinical study of preterm infants, N. Engl. J. Med. **305**:1365, 1981.

182. Hittner, H.M., and others: Retrolental fibroplasia: further clinical evidence and ultrastructural support for efficacy of vitamin E in the preterm infant, Pediatrics **71**:423, 1983.

183. Ehrenkranz, R.A., and others: Amelioration of bronchopulmonary dysplasia after vitamin E administration, N. Engl. J. Med. **299**:564, 1978.

184. Ehrenkranz, R.A., Ablow, R.C., and Warshaw, J.B.: Prevention of bronchopulmonary dysplasia with vitamin E administration during the acute stage of respiratory distress syndrome, J. Pediatr. **85**:873, 1979.

185. Phelps, D.L.: Vitamin E and retrolental fibroplasia in 1982, Pediatrics **70**:410, 1982.

186. Shojania, A.M., and Gross, S.: Folic acid deficiency and prematurity, J. Pediatr. **64**:323, 1964.

187. Heird, W.C., and Anderson, T.L.: Nutritional requirements and methods of feeding low-birth-weight infants. In Gluck, L., editor: Current problems in pediatrics, Chicago, 1977, Year Book Medical Publishers, Inc.

188. Al-Dahlan, J., and others: Sodium homeostasis in term and preterm infants. I. Renal aspects, Arch. Dis. Child. **58**:335, 1983.

189. Al-Dahlan, J., and others: Sodium homeostasis in term and preterm neonates, Arch. Dis. Child. **58**:343, 1983.

190. Roy, R.N., and others: Late hyponatremia in very-low-birth-weight infants (1.3 kg), Pediatr. Res. **10**:526, 1976.

191. Benda, G.I.: Modes of feeding low-birth-weight infants, Semin. Perinatol. **3**:407, 1979.

192. Schriener, R.L.: Continuous and bolus feeding techniques in the low-birth-weight infant: benefits and complications. In Report of 79th Ross Conference on Pediatric Research: Feeding the neonate weighing less than 1500 grams—nutrition and beyond, Columbus, Ohio, 1979, The Conference.

193. Murphy, M.: Guidelines for nasogastric residuals, Neonatal Network, April:35, 1983.

194. Egan, E.A.: Neonatal necrotizing enterocolitis. In Lebenthal, E., editor: Textbook of gastroenterology and nutrition in infancy, New York, 1981, Raven Press.

195. Krouskop, R.W., Brown, E.G., and Sweet, A.Y.: The relationship of feeding to necrotizing enterocolitis, Pediatr. Res. **8**:109, 1974.

196. Committee on Nutrition, American Academy of Pediatrics: Breastfeeding, Pediatrics **62**:591, 1978.

197. Fomon, S.J., Ziegler, E.E., and Vasquez, H.D.: Human milk and the small premature infant, Am. J. Dis. Child. **131**:463, 1977.

198. Davies, D.P.: Adequacy of expressed breast milk for early growth of preterm infants, Arch. Dis. Child. **52**:296, 1977.

199. Tyson, J.E., and others: Growth, metabolic response, and development in very-low-birth-weight infants fed banked human milk or enriched formula. I. Neonatal findings, J. Pediatr. **103**:95, 1983.

200. Gross, S.J.: Growth and biochemical response of preterm infants fed human milk or modified infant formula, N. Engl. J. Med. **308**:237, 1983.

201. Jarvenpaa, A.L., and others: Preterm infants fed human milk attain intrauterine weight gain, Acta Paediatr. Scand. **72**:239, 1983.

202. Chessex, P., and others: Quality of growth in premature infants fed their own mothers' milk, J. Pediatr. **102**:107, 1983.

203. Atkinson, S.A., Bryan, M.H., and Anderson, G.H.: Human milk feeding in premature infants: protein, fat, and carbohydrate balances in the first two weeks of life, J. Pediatr. **99**:617, 1981.

204. Gross, S.J., Geller, J., and Tomarelli, R.M.: Composition of breast milk from mothers of preterm infants, Pediatrics **68**:490, 1981.

205. Lemons, J.A., and others: Differences in the composition of preterm and term human milk during early lactation, Pediatr. Res. **16**:113, 1982.

206. Anderson, G.H., Atkinson, S.A., and Bryan, M.H.: Energy and macronutrient content of human milk during early lactation from mothers giving birth prematurely and at term, Am. J. Clin. Nutr. **34**:258, 1981.

207. Atkinson, S.A., Bryan, M.H., and Anderson, G.H.: Human milk: difference in nitrogen concentration in milk from mothers of term and premature infants, J. Pediatr. **93**:69, 1978.

208. Gross, S.J., and others: Nutritional composition of milk produced by mothers delivering preterm, J. Pediatr. **96**:641, 1980.

209. Anderson, D.M., and others: Length of gestation and nutritional composition of human milk, Am. J. Clin. Nutr. **37**:810, 1983.

210. Moran, J.R., and others: Epidermal growth factor in human milk: daily production and diurnal variation during early lactation in mothers delivering at term and at premature gestation, J. Pediatr. **103**:403, 1983.

211. Reid, B., Smith, H., and Friedman, Z.: Prostaglandins in human milk, Pediatrics **66**:870, 1980.

212. Lindberg, T., and Skuda, G.: Amylase in human milk, Pediatrics **70**:235, 1982.

213. Gross, S.J., and others: Elevated IgA concentration in milk produced by mothers delivered of preterm infants, J. Pediatr. **99**:389, 1981.

214. Goldman, A.S., and others: Effects of prematurity on the immunologic system in human milk, J. Pediatr. **101**:901, 1982.

215. Goldman, A.S., and others: Immunologic factors in human milk during the first year of lactation, J. Pediatr. **100**:563, 1982.

216. Yoshioka, H., Iseki, K., and Fujuta, K.: Development and differences of intestinal flora in the neonatal period in breast-fed and bottle-fed infants, Pediatrics **72**:317, 1983.

217. Narayanan, I., Prakash, K., and Gujral, V.V.: The value of human milk in the prevention of infection in the high-risk low-birth-weight infant, J. Pediatr. **99**:496, 1981.

218. Eyal, F., and others: NEC in the very-low-birth-weight infant: expressed breast milk feeding compared with parenteral feeding, Arch. Dis. Child. **57**:274, 1982.

219. Barlow, B., and others: An experimental study of acute neonatal enterocolitis: the importance of breast milk, J. Pediatr. Surg. **9**:587, 1974.

220. Atkinson, S.A., Radde, I.C., and Anderson, G.H.: Macromineral balances in premature infants fed their own mothers' milk or formula, J. Pediatr. **102**:99, 1983.

221. Chan, G.M.: Human milk calcium and phosphate levels of mothers delivering term and preterm infants, J. Pediatr. Gastroenterol. Nutr. **1**:201, 1982.

222. Committee on Drugs, American Academy of Pediatrics: The transfer of drugs and other chemicals into human breast milk, Pediatrics **72**:375, 1983.

223. Karp, T., and others: Nondiluted formula well tolerated by VLBW infants on enteral feeding, Pediatr. News August:36, 1983.

224. Olson, M.: The benign effects on rabbit's lungs of the aspiration of water compared with 5% glucose or milk, Pediatrics **46**:538, 1970.

225. Bergman, K.E., Ziegler, E.E., and Fomon, S.J.: Water and renal solute load. In Fomon, S.J., editor: Infant nutrition, Philadelphia, 1974, W.B. Saunders, Co.

226. Dancis, J., O'Connell, J.R., and Holt, L.E.: A grid for recording the weight of premature infants, J. Pediatr. **33**:570, 1948.

227. Lubchencho, L.O., and others: Intrauterine growth as estimated from liveborn birth-weight data at 24 to 42 weeks of gestation, Pediatrics **32**:793, 1963.

228. Moar, V.A., and Ounsted, M.K.: Growth in the first year of life: how early can one predict size at twelve months among small-for-dates and large-for-dates babies? Early Hum. Dev. **6**:65, 1982.

229. Harvey, D., and others: Abilities of children who were small-for-gestational-age babies, Pediatrics **69**:296, 1982.

230. Smith, F.R., and others: Plasma vitamin A retinol binding protein and prealbumin concentration in protein calorie malnutrition, Am. J. Clin. Nutr. **29**:1089, 1976.

231. Smith, M.F., Moldawer, L.L., and Bistain, B.R.: Trans-ferrins as a measure of the efficiency of parenteral and enteral nutrition, J. Parent. Ent. Nutr., vol. 1, 1977.

232. Horwood, S.P., and others: Mortality and morbidity of 500 to 1499 gram birthweight infants liveborn to residents of a defined geographic region before and after neonatal intensive care, Pediatrics **69**:613, 1982.

233. Bennett, F.C.: Neurodevelopmental outcome of premature/low-birth-weight infants. In Kelley V.C., editor: Practice of pediatrics, Philadelphia, 1983, J.B. Lippincott Co.

The Development of Food Patterns in Young Children

6

MIRIAM E. LOWENBERG

Food patterns in the United States show distinct cultural characteristics changing as life-styles change. Hurried small breakfasts, midmorning coffee breaks, and light lunches followed by heavy evening dinners show modern adjustments to change. In the home, snacking is known to have increased as television has become an integral part of the day and night activities of the American family. The current enthusiasm for behavioral control of food intake also points to a need to examine the day's program to learn when unneeded calories in food are taken.

At what age are food patterns formed? When does this learning begin? Those who have studied large numbers of children believe now that what happens during the first year of life as well as during the preschool years is of paramount importance. During the first 5 or 6 years of life it is undoubtedly easier to learn to like all foods than it will be later.

The young child is presently introduced early to hamburgers and french fries when families eat out; attesting to this is one quick-meal company's yearly sales—the highest in the restaurant industry. Eating out becomes a helpful respite for the young homemaker or working mother, and a pattern is established for the young child. When a mother hopes to establish a basic food pattern of meals enjoyed at home she must deal with the child's desire to eat out even though he or she only knows about it because other children talk about eating out.

When we examine our life-styles, however, we must admit that in modern America we may have many different meal patterns. There are inner-city patterns of poor or rich families, suburban patterns, and rural patterns of nonfarm and farm families. The rich and the poor have throughout the ages had different food patterns. Careful professional observers of young children eating in a group can often predict the home environment of an individual child.

Goals for the development of food patterns are the following:

1. Children should be able to eat in a matter-of-fact way sufficient quantities of the foods that are given to them, just as they take care of other daily needs. The preschool child who truly enjoys most foods but is able to eat without fuss those he doesn't especially like will be fortunate later.

2. Children should be able to manage the feeding process independently and with dispatch, without either unnecessary dawdling or hurried eating.

3. Children should be willing to try new foods in small portions the first time they are served to them and to try them again and again until they like or at least willingly accept them.

Social anthropologists point to various ways in

which children learn *cues* to fit into a social group. Anyone who is interested in guiding young parents or prospective parents must become analytical to determine which patterns produce healthy children and adults. We must also believe that it is possible to set up a home environment to foster the development of desirable food patterns in young children. Often an impersonal professionally trained outsider can point out to young parents how they can set up such an environment. It must be understood that food patterns begin to be formed from the day of an infant's birth. This reminds me of a healthy, happy young mother who telephoned from her hospital room to report the birth of a daughter 4 hours before. She said with joy that her baby had already tried to nurse; this mother, although still tired from the birth process, had already enjoyed the process of even feeble breast-feeding.

Those who are concerned about obesity as our chief problem of malnutrition are wisely pointing out that prevention as the preferred cure should begin early in infancy. A mother who gives her infant from birth the privilege of deciding and asserting that he or she has had enough food is well on the way to solving this problem. When an individual forms a pattern of quitting to eat at the first indication of satiety, it is believed that this encourages the food intake regulatory mechanism to continue to function. Of course, food that produces the growth of good body tissues must be provided so that more than calorie satiety is provided. This is an important part of early food patterning of a child. The food patterns established in a home, it must be emphasized, are reinforced by love of mother and father and, therefore, have far-reaching effects on lifetime patterns.

No one has ever phrased the functions of parents more aptly than did C. Anderson Aldrich and Mary Aldrich[1] 40 years ago when they said:

According to nature's plan then parents are meant to enter the feeding situation for three reasons:
    First, to provide the food,
    Second, to support a child's progress from simple to mature methods of eating, and

    Third, to make it easy for him to establish his own satisfying feeding habits.

Long ago another principle was observed* that we need to emphasize with parents. *It really is easier and quicker to change the food than it is to change the child.* For instance, young children often have trouble swallowing dry food, and when extra milk is added to thin their mashed potatoes they seem thankful. Such methods are explained in detail later in this chapter.

How can an adult know what foods children like? The answer lies in carefully observing young children while they are eating.

Table 6-1 on p. 186 gives approximate amounts of foods, learned from the study described below, that one can expect the average child to eat. *In no*

---

*For 12 years I observed 20 nursery schoolchildren eating their noon meals. Later, for 2 years these ideas were used in the daily feeding of 1000 children, mostly 18 months to 6 years of age, in two shipyard World War II nursery schools. My commission as chief nutritionist was to be in charge of the feeding and nutritional development. Feeding for the 9 hours at nursery school was carefully planned, and mothers and fathers were also advised and helped to feed their children at home.

Knowledge gained while studying the eating patterns and food preferences of the college nursery schoolchildren for 12 years was used to teach college students about feeding young children. All food was measured onto the child's plate before it left the kitchen serving area; second helpings and leftover foods were measured and recorded. For 1 school year, the adult who ate at a table with two or three children was asked to record each child's reaction to each food and to the menu as a whole. They were to record: was a food too dry? too tough? too acid to be easily eaten? Were there other characteristics that made the food unsuitable? Were the combinations of foods acceptable and liked by the children? As these criticisms came in daily, corrections were made in the menus and recipes for the foods. During the following year the corrected menus and specific foods were again studied, and further corrections were made. During this study each day, a chart was made of the amounts of each food to be served to each child. The head teacher confirmed that when the children's appetites were closely studied a child's specific food intake could be accurately judged. Most thoughtful mothers can do this.

The advice in this chapter is based on the ideas gained from this meticulous study as well as on extensive tests of these ideas.

way are these amounts to be used to force a certain amount of food on any specific child. If any child, however, habitually eats less than the amount in the chart, it is advised that the reasons for this be determined. As always, a particular child's food dislikes, his or her health condition, or specific family circumstances at the time need to be considered.

It has been found over the years that it is wise to serve a child less than he or she may eat rather than more. Modern behavioral conditioning theory confirms the belief that to help a child to be successful reinforces the behavior we hope to foster.

CULTURAL PATTERNS

In the United States many ethnic groups make up our population. Each ethnic food pattern, based on foods available and preferred, comes from the home country and is based firmly on tradition and often on long usage. Specific ways of cooking foods are always dependent on such factors as the fuel available, the time and the energy available for food preparation, as well as the primary interests and patience of the cook. We can appreciate the fact that the generous use of rye breads and fish in the Scandinavian countries is a result of the cool and short growing season, the long coastlines, and the Scandinavian people's knowledge of successful fishing. Even after such countries are able to import other foods, the preferred foods are still used as tradition dictates. The cause for the abundant use by Polynesian peoples of the coconut, tropical fruits and vegetables, and fish, abundant in tropical waters, is obvious.

The history of a people is written in their preferred foods. This explains why schoolchildren in North Dakota and in Georgia react radically differently to rice used as a vegetable. For instance, rice, which grew well in the American southern colonies from early colonial times, has become a preferred food in that part of the country. Rice, when first used in lunches in some schools in North Dakota, was rejected as an unfamiliar food. This must also

be recognized when we consider the special place of honor that the vegetable okra holds for those in the "deep South" of the United States. This vegetable is said to have been brought by slaves from Africa, and its preference has even withstood the memory of those sad journeys to which those slaves were subjected. Blends in Creole dishes could only occur where Spanish, French, black African, and American Indian influences came together.

During the latter part of the twentieth century most Americans have come to prize their cultural backgrounds, cultural foods, and differences in food patterns. In summary, two points should be emphasized. First, every ethnic diet must be based on nutritional adequacy, at least to some degree, for the group using it to survive. It has been pointed out that the very poor and food-deficient Irish people of the nineteenth century, who had an extremely limited diet, could scarcely have chosen any two foods as nutritionally adequate as buttermilk and potatoes. The nutritional adequacy for a desirable state of health may point, in some ethnic patterns, to a need for supplementation with some other foods. Adding other needed foods to this basic diet is often much easier than changing the *staple* food of a group. This, however, means that it is desirable to maintain the basic pattern with only the needed supplementation. American Indian children who have been taught to like the wild greens that their families eat, for instance, should be encouraged to follow these food patterns.

Second, children, who at an early age learn the cues of ethnic food patterns, should be allowed to make these patterns as permanent as possible in a new environment. A respect for differences in food patterns influences the way an individual views himself or herself as a worthwhile human being.

POSITIVE REINFORCEMENT

Experience with helping young children form desirable feeding patterns shows that the modern ideas of positive reinforcement of desirable behavior are sound. (For further discussion of behavior modification, see Chapter 14.) Some 40 years ago it was found that children developed desirable feeding patterns when they felt successful and when negative behavior was ignored. It is wise to make an effort to find out why a child does not like or does not readily eat a certain food or combination of foods. Often it is easy to change the food or menu.

Many ideas on how to help children eat successfully are discussed. The size of a child's portions is of paramount importance. When children are presented with less food than they normally eat they are allowed to accomplish the goal that the adult has set; they can then ask for second helpings. This allows them to receive adult approbation, which is a reward to them. However, if for some reason children cannot eat all the food that has been given to them, allowing them to set their own limit shows respect for them, and they can still feel successful. However, when a child restricts his or her food intake to much less than expected over a number of days, this merits investigating. Improving an environmental situation often corrects this low intake of food (see pp. 181-182 for specific suggestions).

HUNGER AND APPETITE

Food is taken into the body to satisfy the primal urge of hunger. According to the physiologist Dr. Anton J. Carlson,[2] there are two unpleasant sensations that are involved in what we call hunger. The first is a generalized weakness and restlessness all over the body, which is probably caused by a need for more sugar in the blood. The second is a definite localized sensation of pains of tension in the upper part of the stomach. These pangs of hunger are comparatively brief and are followed by periods when hunger pain is not felt. The infant and the young child are thought to have frequent and severe hunger pains. In the infant these sometimes are severe enough to cause an outcry as they awaken him or her from sleep. Infants' stomachs have

been observed to show feeble hunger contractions 1 hour after nursing and strong hunger contractions 2½ to 3 hours after a feeding. The length of time at which the stomach shows in this way that it is ready for food varies with the individual infant. In the young child of 2 to 5 years of age these hunger pains are somewhat less frequent or pronounced than in the young infant, but they are still quite definite. Normally, food taken into the body gives immediate pleasure to a child when it eases the pain of hunger. If nothing else interferes, food is associated with the easing of pain, and pleasure results from eating.

What is appetite and how does it differ from hunger? And what part does each play in food habits? Most authorities agree that although hunger is an unpleasant sensation, appetite is a pleasurable experience. Appetite is usually defined as the pleasant association of a food with past experiences with that food. Appetite, associated with the sight and odor of food, stimulates the flow of digestive juices and is, therefore, a vital part of good digestion, as has often been demonstrated in the clinic and laboratory.

Many people have searched diligently and long for foods that taste like those mother used to cook when they were children. No doubt her foods were good, but they were probably not incomparable. The remembered foods were eaten at times when the child was thoroughly happy, and, as a result, a strong appetite for them was created. As an individual grows older the zest for the same food may be lessened. There is only the memory of or the appetite for the former food. Appetites for certain foods are undoubtedly built up in children not only from the flavor, color, and texture of the food itself, but also from the many associations with the food.

It must be realized that to be hungry is normal for a young child. To be persistently nonhungry is decidedly abnormal. The child who is not hungry should be taken to a physician who will carefully assess his or her physical well-being (looking possibly for a chronic infection) and his or her daily habits. This child may not get enough brisk exercise in the open air or may need more sleep, a more regular diet pattern, sleep and rest, or a less stimulating environment.

If a child is in good health and is hungry, with a stomach calling urgently for food, food will be eaten to satisfy that urge rather than to satisfy whims. As has been so aptly said, hunger should control the child rather than the child, hunger. This fact may be taken advantage of in many ways. New foods in very small portions may be served at the time of the day when the child is hungriest. It should be remembered that for a young child a new food is a step in the dark; children are generally not as adventuresome as adults. If a child eats the new food when hungry, it will probably leave a pleasant sensation, and the next time this food is served it will be recognized as a friend. Children learn to like a food by tasting it time after time, even though the first tastes are but a few tiny bites.

SETTING UP A FOOD ENVIRONMENT

In helping parents to understand why children eat as they do, it is well to direct their attention to the fact that *behavior is caused*. When causes of behavior are understood, a food problem is on the way to being cured. When parents understand why children eat as they do, these parents can usually set up an environment that promotes a healthy appetite. Often an outside professional person can help a parent to discover these causes and to restructure the environment. Preparental education in which specific appetite problems are discussed can help prevent them. Part of this education must emphasize the requirements of a good food environment.

How does a parent set limits in helping a child develop desirable food patterns? The following are suggestions:

1. The mother as "gatekeeper" must recognize that the kinds of food available to the preschool child in the home are what she buys and provides. Many mothers need to be shown that, in

this, *she is really in command*. In a well-child clinic, a mother complained that her 3-year-old child was eating too many potato chips, yet she admitted that she was the one who bought them. Of course, other family members must cooperate in not having foods of this kind available.

2. Often parents must decide which of their own food patterns they want to pass on to their children. In discussing problems of preparation for parenthood, young people may need to be assured that they can change their own food patterns; sometimes they may even need to be helped to do this.

3. Feeding programs for groups of preschool children have proven again and again that the eating habits of young children can be repatterned under skilled guidance. This should give young parents added confidence.

DEVELOPMENTAL PATTERNS AND HOW TO USE THEM

Children develop for the most part in an orderly pattern—physically, emotionally, and psychologically.

Eating is always dependent on the abilities of the eater. For instance, when normal infants are born they are able to root for a nipple and to suck vigorously to ingest milk. When infants are given a chance to satisfy their hunger in this manner, they attain their first success in eating. As the mother discovers the child's hunger patterns and provides foods to satisfy hunger, she sets up the condition for successful eating.

DIFFICULTIES IN THE FORMATION OF GOOD FOOD HABITS AND WAYS OF AVOIDING THEM

When most infants are fed the first semisolid food, they will often spit it out rather violently—not because they do not want the food but because the motion of the tongue that they have used in sucking food into their mouth is the only motion that they know (see Chapter 4). Now they try this motion again, and the semiliquid cereal or food spatters everywhere. They must now learn an entirely new feeding technique. If they fail in the first efforts, a mother may be well spattered and naturally quite upset. Now they have met their first feeding disaster. To laugh at these efforts is also unwise because the infant learns to do this to make mother laugh. The mother should have prepared herself previously so that she could remain undisturbed by the incident.

Another difficulty enters into this situation—all the previous food has been liquid. Now, suddenly, here is a food with a new texture, besides having a flavor that is different from the usual, mildly sweet milk. Difficulties may be avoided by giving the infant minute amounts of the new food, well moistened and thinned by the familiar milk, until the new food is easily accepted. Weaning begins right here. The infant is being weaned away gradually from an exclusively fluid diet.

In this discussion weaning is used to mean a general process involving, as far as food is concerned, any change in food flavor, texture, consistency, temperature, or method of feeding. Many feeding difficulties arise because the changes are expected to take place *too abruptly* or because adults fail to realize how difficult some of these tasks are for the infant and the young child. A child can and will learn these new things, but neither the parent nor child should become upset over failures at first. Nor must the child come to the realization that the honors of the day are attained by spitting food out or by refusing it. The problem can be avoided by demonstrating the technique for spoon feeding.

At approximately 6 months of age, even before the first tooth appears, most infants make chewing movements with their gums. At this time infants should be given foods such as small strips of oven-dried toast, which offer a chance for chewing at the same time as they soften to allow easy swallowing. It has been observed that when an infant is not given a chance to chew at this time, trouble in mastering this skill may occur later.

When the infant begins to gain the muscular ability to pick up small particles using the thumb and forefingers, particles of soft green beans or peas can be fed (see Chapter 4 for a more detailed discussion of this). These efforts, along with reaching for the bottle and later holding it, are the infant's first efforts to learn to feed independently.

The stage of developing independence at 9 to 16 or 18 months of age can either be exciting or distressing for parents. If parents understand that exploring everything new is very important to an infant, they can encourage this exploration by providing new textures and flavors in foods; this allows an infant to discover what a food such as oatmeal feels like. At this stage many infants have learned to crawl out from their former sitting position or to walk. It is no longer satisfying to them to just look at something; they now want to examine it. The wise mother takes advantage of this new learning in providing a wide variety of food. She should not be discouraged at first if the child only feels a food before chewing it.

During the first year an infant has tremendous adjustments to make, only one of which is learning new foods and new methods of eating. In helping this infant to form good patterns, we will be most successful if thoughtful and understanding guidance is furnished in the following ways:

1. Introducing new textures and flavors gradually
2. Enlarging the child's experience with as many individual foods in as many different forms as possible
3. For the most part, feeding individual foods and not mixtures so that the infant may learn to appreciate foods for their own flavors and textures
4. Observing at what time of day the infant takes the new food most easily and giving it then
5. Being patient with the first efforts and allowing the infant to learn to feed himself or herself; offering help when the infant becomes too tired to finish the process easily

6. Being understanding of the infant's efforts in each new feeding process
7. Above all, securing the entire family's cooperation.

The high level of nutritive need of the first year of life is superceded by a slower metabolic rate and a slower rate of growth. Therefore, the child does not need as much food per unit of body weight as before. What is eaten and how it is eaten are now more important than how much is eaten. To watch a young child grow increasingly independent in feeding himself can be as thrilling for a parent as watching the taking of the first steps from chair to chair. Perhaps in no other area of development in young children is progress more individual. Each child should be allowed to try new skills over and over with no record of failures unless development is obviously too slow to show any progress.

When parents understand what children are telling them in the way they eat, rebellion against food can be lessened and future food refusals can be materially reduced. For instance, the realization that the 2-year-old child may have a sporadic appetite, which should not be the cause for undue alarm, may prevent the long-lasting influence of battles over food.

All of this may make the reader believe that we think that, in a family, only the meals for young children are important. This, of course, is not true. But in a happy family situation, priorities have to be individually determined. Sometimes children, who for some months have eaten at the family table, may suddenly be happier eating at their own small table with a parent nearby. Some mothers even find it possible to eat a quiet noon meal with the child at a small table.

SPECIFIC SUGGESTIONS FOR SETTING UP AN ENVIRONMENT TO FOSTER DESIRABLE PATTERNS OF EATING

Perhaps no arrangements for eating are more important than those that afford physical comfort to a child. Children should always feel secure on a sturdy, well-balanced chair with their feet well supported on the floor or otherwise. They should be able to reach their food on the plate easily without straining their muscles. This also provides a better opportunity to eat without the danger of spills. Dishes and utensils, as well as table arrangements, can foster success in eating. It is desirable to give the child sturdy and as nearly unbreakable utensils as possible so that spills and breaking utensils will not give a sense of failure. Also, it is important not to laugh at the child, because if parents laugh at a child's mistakes the child may gain an undue feeling of being the center of attention.

At the time when children's chairs are being purchased, these should be "tried on" (to fit the child's body) as clothing is. Some chairs, for instance, are designed to fit a child's torso and are much more comfortable than are perfectly straight chairs. Wise parents also prepare table surfaces and floors for children's spills. It can be observed that family restaurants have abundant patronage where children's spills are quietly and quickly handled by those serving the food.

Colorful table arrangements intrigue yound children and are worth the trouble to provide. When children have developed some skill in eating, they will appreciate eating from the family's best china. It has been found that confidence in a child's accomplishment is usually rewarded by care in handling prized possessions when the child is ready. It is easy to notice children who have had help in gaining skill in successful eating as one observes families eating together in restaurants.

Forks and spoons should be chosen for their suitability for young hands. The spoon, which is the first eating implement a child uses, should have a round shallow bowl and a blunt tip that allows the child to shove food from the plate. A handle that is blunt, short, and easily held in the child's palm is desirable. It must be remembered that at this age a child uses the hand as a mass of muscles. Only after 5 or 6 years of age is control of the finer muscles of the fingers accomplished. Forks with short, blunt tines are best adapted to the child's palm.

Some parents report, however, that their children enjoy sharper tines with which they can spear food. It must be remembered, however, that sharp tines can be dangerous.

Glasses that sit firmly on the table and are small enough for small hands to encircle have been observed to be the best for the hands of 2- to 4-year-old children. Small delicate handles on cups are difficult for small hands to maneuver.

The shape and weight of the dishes is also very important. The young child delights in pouring his or her own milk. Interesting, squat pitchers with broad handles from which the child can easily pour milk are recommended. Parents can be encouraged to experiment with the dishes and utensils for their children and to look for those that satisfy children's needs.

FOODS CHILDREN LIKE

Patient observing and long experience in feeding young children as well as in counseling parents have given me an insight into what children want in their food. When this point of view is combined with the knowledge of nutrients, children can be adequately and happily fed. The results of these observations are discussed on the following pages.

Menus

Simplicity in menus is a very important consideration. At the same time there must be variety to allow young children to learn to know many foods. Variety in foods is a good foundation for an adequate diet.

The following outline gives a general meal pattern that should satisfy nutrient needs in a hungry, preschool child.

A. Breakfast
  1. One high-protein food
     a. One egg *or*
     b. 2 oz of muscle meat *or*
     c. ¾ to 1 oz of cheese *or*
     d. ½ cup of cereal, cooked, *or*
     e. 1 cup of dry cereal with 4 to 6 oz milk
  2. Bread with butter or margarine (1 slice whole grain[2] or white enriched bread, plus 1 tsp butter)
  3. Milk, 6 to 8 oz
  4. Fruit—preferably one serving of citrus
     a. 4 oz of orange juice *or*
     b. ⅓ to ½ medium-sized grapefruit *or*
     c. 1 medium-sized orange
B. Noon meal
  1. One high-protein food (See breakfast for list of high-protein foods)
     a. 1 serving of a thick soup or stew *or*
     b. 1 serving of a casserole dish to a protein food in a starchy base
  2. Vegetables
     a. 1 cooked (see Table 6-1 for amounts)
     b. 1 raw (see Table 6-1 for amounts)
  3. Bread (1 slice whole grain[2] or enriched white bread with 1 tsp butter)
  4. Milk, 6 to 8 oz
  5. Dessert
     a. Simple dessert based on a combination of milk, eggs, and fruit *or*
     b. Serving of fruit
C. Evening meal
  1. One high-protein food
     a. 2 oz meat
     b. 1 oz cheese
     c. 1 egg
     d. or combinations of these and vegetables
  2. Vegetables
     a. 1 or 2 cooked
     b. 1 raw
  3. Bread and butter (1 slice whole grain[2] or enriched white bread with 1 tsp butter)
  4. Milk, 6 to 8 oz
  5. Dessert (see noon meal, dessert)
D. Snacks between meals or at bedtime
  These should provide some of the needed nutrients and be low in sugar and fat so that they do

not interfere with the appetite for the following meal—use, for example, any of the following:

1. Fruit juices with a cracker or a piece of bread *or*
2. Small pieces of fruit *or*
3. Small pieces of raw vegetables *or*
4. Small pieces of cheese with a small piece of bread or cracker

Combinations of Food

Most children eat most easily those foods with which they are familiar. It is advisable that a very small portion of a new food be introduced with a familiar and a popular food. If a child only looks at the new food or just feels or smells it at first, this is a part of learning to accept it.

Dry foods are especially hard for children to eat, as is discussed later in this chapter. In planning a menu, always carefully balance a dry food with one or two moist foods. For instance, it is wise to put a slice of meat loaf (relatively dry) with mashed potatoes and peas in a little cream sauce.

Combinations of sharp, rather acid-flavored foods with mild-flavored foods are popular with young children.

Ease of Manipulation

The ease of eating food with the unskilled and seemingly clumsy hands of a young child is very important. Many small pieces of foods such as cooked green peas or beans are difficult for a child to spoon up. These can be mixed with mashed potatoes to make for easier eating.

When a 2-year-old child eats a bowl of thin soup, many trials are made before it is finished. Although it is advisable to serve young children soups occasionally, one must realize that the process of spooning it is tiring. Two things may be done to make soup easier for a child to eat. It may be drunk from a cup, or the soup may be made slightly thicker so that it does not spill from the spoon easily. A prominent soup company promot-ed a two-way soup, after hiring me as a consultant. I suggested to the company that after a canned soup had been thinned, preferably with milk, it should be strained so that a child could spoon up the solid portion and drink the liquid. It is my belief that soup for children should be either spoonable or drinkable. Later, the child may have soup to be eaten with a spoon when he or she is able to manage a spoon without spilling its contents.

Many foods can be prepared so that a child can eat them with the fingers. Hard-cooked eggs may be served in quarters, cooked meat can be cut in small strips, and cooked green beans can be served as finger foods. Children have been observed to like oranges that have been cut in wedges (skin and all) much better than peeled and diced oranges.

Mixed-up salads, when there are layers of food to be eaten, are much more difficult to eat than simple pieces of raw vegetables with no salad dressing. This preference has also been observed in school lunches where very young schoolchildren are being fed. It is also wise to serve cottage cheese or similar foods separate from the lettuce leaf on a child's plate. Creamed foods served on tough toast are difficult for children to manage.

The size of the pieces of food for children must be given serious consideration. The problem of handling silverware and conveying food to the mouth at this early age is a greater task than many adults realize. Pieces of carrots that slide across the plate and are too small to remain on the fork while they are being lifted to the mouth or cubes of beets so large that they must be cut into bite-size pieces before being eaten exhaust the patience of a 2- or 3-year-old child. Most foods for these children should be served to them in bite-sized pieces. When the child is 4 years of age and older, the skills to cut up some foods may have been developed. If, however, much difficulty in managing is noticed, small pieces for the most part should be served, accompanied by occasional encouragement to cut up some foods. Canned pears and other soft fruits are usually easily cut into bite-size pieces.

Stringy spinach or tomatoes are a trial for anyone to eat. Much can be done with a handy pair of food shears in the kitchen to make these foods easier to eat. Finger foods such as pieces of lettuce or toast, which may be eaten with the fingers, should be used in meals where some of the foods are difficult to handle. Small sandwiches—that is, a large one cut into four squares—are popular with young children.

Texture

I have found it wise to serve one soft food (for easy eating), one crisp food (to allow easy chewing and enjoyment of the sounds in the mouth), and one chewy food (to use emerging chewing skills without having too much to chew) in each meal for young children.

Some children can fall into the habit of rejecting all foods of a certain texture; this limits the kinds of foods the child tries to eat. See p. 346 for suggestions on how to handle this problem.

Pieces of meat seem to be hard for a young child to eat; this explains why children often prefer hamburgers or frankfurters. Most children's meat can be served as ground meat. In fact, it was often found in nursery school feeding that thrice-ground meat was popular. This is true because the teeth of 2- or 3-year-old children do not grind meat as easily as adult teeth do. When parents want steaks, a roast, or a pot roast, the mother can cook a small portion of ground meat from the freezer for the young child. When ground meat is being cooked, it should be cooked only long enough for the color to change to brown. It should not be allowed to become dry with a hard crust, which is hard for a child to eat. Some children may prefer moderately rare meat, which is even more moist.

Flavor

In general, young children reject strong flavors. Many children, however, do seem to like pickles, some spicy sauces, and beer, which may seem to contradict this. In general, it has been found that children like food that is mildly salted, with about half as much salt as is used in adult recipes. Because some authorities now believe that all of us would profit by taking less salt, this may be a good health habit to foster (Chapter 10). In general, pepper and other sharp spices and acids such as vinegar on children's food should also be used sparingly.

Strong-flavored vegetables such as those belonging to the cabbage and onion family are more popular with young children when served raw. If these vegetables are cooked it is recommended that they be placed in an excessive amount of cooking water so that some of the strong flavor can be thrown away. Of course, water-soluble nutrients are thrown away by this process, but teaching children to eat these foods is most important at this time in their lives. A mild-flavored cream sauce also helps to make these vegetables more popular. In fact, this popularity was shown when some children in nursery school asked for very mild-flavored creamed onions after they had eaten dessert.

Because sharply tart fruits are often rejected by young children, such fruits should be diluted with those of mild flavor. Tart oranges were found to be popular when mixed with cooked peaches or bananas. The rule of one tart, one mild, and one crisp is a good one to follow. The crisp fruit may be small unpeeled pieces of apples.

In general, in helping children develop desirable food patterns, it is wise to keep the natural flavor of the food. This leads to the use of only small amounts of sugar. The use of a little honey is also recommended because this is sweeter than an equal amount of granulated sugar and less can be used.

Color

Children have a natural interest in color in their foods, and teaching them to appreciate the lovely fresh color of foods is a worthy aim. Young children are delighted when they may choose one of several different colored desserts. Green, orange, yellow, and pink are popular colors in food. Children in nursery schools rarely failed to comment on the food to which a tiny sprig of parsley had been

Fig. 6-1. Preschool children enjoy snacks that are colorful and can be fingerfed.

added or to notice bits of hidden color such as tomato, carrot, or parsley in sandwiches.

Cakes, cookies, and candies containing molasses, dried fruits, and nuts provide other nutrients in addition to calories. Natural fruit juices have more of the needed nutrients than sweetened, colored, and artificially flavored drinks. Because the water that fruit juices contain is also desirable for children, strong-flavored juices should be diluted, giving additional water to the child.

SPECIFIC FOOD PREPARATION

Children should be considered when the family plans meals. Many parents do, of necessity, vary their life-styles when they are raising their families, so the importance of food-patterning during this period is emphasized. Young children can be taught that as adults wear different clothes than children, so there also are adult-type foods and drinks. Children have been observed to prefer an orange or a serving of fruit to cherry pie that is being served to adults.

Foods can be made soft enough in texture for young children by adding extra milk to a dry, starchy food.

If the parents prefer strong-flavored vegetables, a small portion for the young child can be rinsed under the hot water faucet before it is served.

A young child may prefer food served at room temperature. In fact, preschool children often appear frightened by hot food. They also often stir hard ice cream until it is soupy and less sharply cold.

While the father serves dinner at the table, the mother may prefer to dish the preschool child's food in the kitchen. This can serve two purposes: (1) young children's hunger makes them impatient participants at a meal, so rapid service of food is desirable, and (2) the mother can easily regulate the amount of food served or can make any sudden changes. I have discovered that fathers sometimes have more difficulty serving small enough portions to a child than mothers do.

Table 6-1 has been devised from my many years of careful observations of how much the average child can eat easily. Some pediatricians who believe that children should not be forced to eat a specific amount of any food object to setting up such expectations in a chart. Yet mothers often need some help in the amount of food the *average* child can eat easily to get the needed nutrients.

Table 6-1. Food pattern for preschool children*

Food	Portion Size	Number of Portions Advised	
		Ages 2 to 4 Years	Ages 4 to 6 Years
Milk and Dairy Products			
Milk†	4 oz	3 to 6	3 to 4
Cheese	½ to ¾ oz	May be substituted for one portion of liquid milk	
Yogurt	¼ to ½ cup	May be substituted for one portion of liquid milk	
Powdered skim milk	2 tbsp	May be substituted for one portion of liquid milk	
Meat and Meat Equivalents			
Meat‡, fish§, poultry	1 to 2 oz	2	2
Egg	1	1	1
Peanut butter	1 to 2 tbsp		
Legumes—dried peas and beans	¼ to ⅓ cup cooked		
Vegetables and Fruits			
Vegetables		4 to 5 to include 1 green leafy or yellow‖	4 to 5 to include 1 green leafy or yellow
Cooked	2 to 4 tbsp		
Raw	Few pieces		
Fruit		1 citrus fruit or other vegetable or fruit rich in vitamin C	1 citrus fruit or other vegetable or fruit rich in vitamin C
Canned	4 to 8 tbsp		
Raw	½ to 1 small		
Fruit juice	3 to 4 oz		
Bread and Cereal Grains			
Whole grain or enriched white bread	½ to 1 slice	3	3
Cooked cereal	¼ to ½ cup		
Ready-to-serve dry cereals	½ to 1 cup	May be substituted for one serving of bread	
Spaghetti, macaroni, noodles, rice	¼ to ½ cup		
Crackers	2 to 3		

Fat				
Bacon	1 slice	Not to be substituted for meat		
Butter or vitamin A–fortified margarine	1 tsp		3	3 to 4
Desserts	¼ to ½ cup	As demanded by calorie needs		
Sugars	½ to 1 tsp		2	2

*Diets should be monitored for adequacy of iron and vitamin D intake.
†Approximately ⅔ cup can easily be incorporated in a child's food during cooking.
‡Liver once a week can be used as liver sausage or cooked liver.
§Should be served once or twice per week to substitute for meat.
‖If child's preferences are limited, used double portions of preferred vegetables until appetite for other vegetables develop.

Such goals may also prevent mothers from expecting their children to eat more than their children want. These average portion sizes may be too large for a new food, for a disliked food, or for a non-hungry child. Of course, the hungry child can have extra servings.

FOOD DISLIKES

It is safe to allow every person to have at least one or two food dislikes. Except for medically restricted diets, no one food has to be eaten. I am, of course, assuming that a family can afford a varied diet.

Some food dislikes, as has been previously discussed, have unusual causes. A woman reports that sugared oranges always have a flavor of castor oil to her, though she enjoys oranges without sugar. When she was young she was given doses of the then strong-flavored castor oil with sugared oranges to cover its flavor. Though she knows that she only imagines the castor oil flavor in the oranges, she says that even now she thinks ''What has been on my spoon, castor oil?'' The association of sugared oranges and castor oil has survived with her over many years.

Substitutions for liquid milk, which some children may dislike, can temporarily be made. Powdered milk (4 tbsp substituted for 8 oz of fluid milk) can be added to foods, and cottage or cheddar cheese can be used.

When children are in control of their appetite and hunger, they may refuse all foods. One cold, winter day in a nursery school when we were weary of preparing food for nonhungry children, we decided to give them a shock. On the usual array of dishes, we placed only 1 tbsp of vegetable meat stew in the soup bowl. No other food was in evidence in the entire dining room, no baskets of sandwiches, no pitchers of milk, no trays of dishes of desserts. When the children took one look, they at once exclaimed ''Where's our dinner? Is this all of our dinner?'' Rather slowly, second servings were brought in from the kitchen. The food records showed that more food was eaten that day than any day for several weeks before.

Telling a child that we know he or she doesn't like boiled potatoes and can have more green beans often encourages a good appetite. When a child, however, rejects many foods, as for example, all vegetables or all meat, it is well to investigate the reason for this, if possible. Adequate substitutions may need to be made. For instance, in hot summer weather, fruits can replace cooked vegetables in a child's diet if the family budget can tolerate the extra cost. This serving of fruit sometimes stimulates failing appetites.

At times the mother may need to seek professional help from someone who understands children both from closer observation of many children eating as well as from knowing the findings of research in the area.

In summary, the following can be emphasized:

1. Belief that changes can occur in a child's eating patterns is of primary importance. Eating is one of the pleasures of life. Fortunate is the individual who likes foods he or she needs to eat for the adequate nutrition of the body.

2. The goals set by someone when counseling parents about children's eating should be those that are easily accomplished. Success in following the advice of professional people promotes confidence and positively reinforces the child who succeeds in eating what is presented. When a food dislike is firmly established before the parent seeks help, it will probably not disappear suddenly; only gradual correction can be expected. Progress may not be consistent, and temporary failures to reach the goal must be expected. For instance, in helping a child to learn to eat coarse foods, a mother can freeze coarse-textured cooked vegetables (chunks, that is) in ice trays when she is trying to wean a child from eating only pureed vegetables. Increasing amounts of this coarser food can be added gradually to the child's vegetables.

3. When a child exhibits a strong food dislike, this should be accepted as a fact. Substitution for the missed nutrients often is the wisest plan. Often

a temporary release of pressure concerning eating a specific food causes the child to try it later. A mother who was looking at her 3-year-old son's noon meal food consumption record in a nursery school said "But he never eats eggs at home and this noon he had seconds!" That is exactly the reason why a mother enrolling a child is not asked about the child's food dislikes, only about the foods that make the child ill. Another mother said to her son as she looked at the records, "But you don't like turnips!" Whereupon her son answered, "Yours are black. They are white at nursery school. I like them white!" This leads to the next point.

4. Children are good judges of well-prepared food. Sometimes classes in food preparation for parents or prospective parents would be the best approach to handling children's food dislikes.

5. Sometimes the "war" over children's eating has become so sharp that withdrawing one of the combatants is the only solution to a battle over food. Someone other than the mother feeding the child temporarily may also be a solution to the problem.

6. Because children are usually rhythmic in all they do, it is advised that the satisfaction of their hunger should also be kept rhythmic. This means that meals served at the same time each day generally promote a good appetite. Fatigue, the most defeating factor in children's appetites, is thus avoided. I have found again and again that starving a child to get the child to eat does not promote good eating.

COMMON PROBLEMS

It should be remembered that healthy, hungry children will eat if they are given a calm atmosphere in which to eat. This is the first and most important consideration.

One of the most common problems, that of fatigue, has just been discussed. Only sympathy should be extended to the child who, eating at a tearoom in a large store after a morning's shopping, just looks at the food and cries when urged to eat. The child probably needs to rest more than he or she needs to eat.

When a child is regularly more hungry at a certain time of day than at other times, acceptance of this fact is wise. Perhaps the greater hunger at the evening meal is caused by having rested while watching a favorite television program before dinner. Sometimes healthy outdoor running, followed by a quiet rest, restores a lagging noontime appetite. It was found that nursery school food costs increased when the children played outdoors in a warm Iowa March after a cold and confining February.

Some of the earliest eating skills learned by a young child are those of chewing and swallowing. Each of these is accomplished to a great extent by trial and error. Some impatient parents worry over this slow progress.

Swallowing seems to be difficult for some children. They tend to swallow only after the food is thoroughly chewed and finely ground. In fact, some children hold food in the cheeks like chipmunks, and some children have been observed to have eaten all their dessert and still have the vegetable in their cheeks. The fact that some children apparently gain more enjoyment from filling their mouths full of food than from taking small mouthfuls makes learning to chew and swallow a bit complicated for them. These children may almost appear hopeless as they sit with packed mouths. Encouraging them to take small bites and to chew and swallow each mouthful has been successful in some cases.

No discussion of children's food problems would be complete without a discussion of the so-called vegetable war. Sometimes this may be created at first by a generally disgruntled parent who really wants to have the child reinforce his or her own belief that all vegetables are horrible.[1] Perhaps a father associates cooked vegetables with his mother with whom there was always a clash. It is fascinating to read in histories of American colonial times of husbands who refused their wives the money to buy seeds for green leafy vegetables because they considered these foods "fodder."

This was, of course, in the "previtamin days." This idea of fodder appears too often in the history of food patterns. Yet we also find in these histories stories of gathering wild greens for use during the so-called hunger weeks of spring when the food preserved for winter was either all gone or too spoiled to be used. It is also interesting to observe in tropical countries of Asia and Africa a vast array of what are to us strange-looking green leafy vegetables that are bought eagerly from native markets.

This rejection of some kinds of foods can easily be passed down from parents to their children. Sometimes a dislike for the usually popular milk can be directly accounted for in this way. The labeling of salads as "women's food" may also have caused some boys to reject them.

All of these influences, although subtle, are definitely effective in the development of food prejudices. Being branded as someone who does not like carrots often prevents a child who would like later to try them from doing so. When we begin to understand the basis of a food prejudice, we are on the way to counteracting it.

It can, however, be stated positively that many children do like well-cooked vegetables, and some raw vegetables are definitely well liked. Of course, we are assuming here that strong acrid odors and unpleasant flavors are not present in these cooked vegetables. When a person, coming in from outdoors and the fresh air, smells unpleasant cooking odors in a poorly ventilated kitchen, a prejudice may precede the actual meal. Sometimes better selection at the market of tender young root vegetables is necessary to prevent the unpleasant "woodiness" in root vegetables.

Another specific food problem concerns the child who is exceptionally fond of sweet foods. This often occurs because parents who are very fond of such food have patterned the child to be overfond of them. Sweet foods used as rewards or as special treats also reinforce the child's desire for sweets. The use of cake for a birthday celebration is too well grounded in American tradition to be uprooted, but we should recognize that when we present a child with a wonderful birthday cake, we are reinforcing the value of a sweet food. One child asked whether fruit cake (always served in his home at Christmas time) was Christ's birthday cake.

In no other area are family influences more strong than in food preferences. The association of mother's food and her love last over years and may supersede all outside influences. Studies have shown that of all meal patterns, Sunday dinner meal patterns change most slowly when a family moves to a new country. A father's influence on a child's food preferences was shown in one study in which children were found to dislike the foods that the father disliked.[3] The reason was that because mothers did not serve the food fathers disliked, these foods were unfamiliar to the children and they refused them when they were served later.

Modern mothers, buffeted by their children's faith in television advertisements for food as well as by the sweets offered in vending machines at school, sometimes lose faith in their role as the "home gatekeeper." They may need professional bolstering to reinforce their faith in themselves so that they actually do control the food in their homes and in their children's lives.

FACTORS THAT SHAPE FOOD PATTERNS IN YOUNG CHILDREN

Cristine M. Trahms

Nutrition educators have long been curious about the forces that shape food habits and consequently health status. It has also been generally accepted that patterns of food choices are developed early in life and that parents are influential in shaping food-related behaviors. The traditional manner of counseling parents has been to provide nutrition information and hope for a concomitant increase in knowledge and change in attitudes and behaviors related to nutrition and food choices. Guidance on shaping food-related behaviors has been primarily based on observation and common sense principles.

It is very difficult to define terms related to food behavior, such as food choices, food preferences, dawdling, and coaxing, and then to measure the intervening and confounding variables that may affect food behavior. Parents clearly no longer, if they ever did, have the single significant impact on the food choices of their young children.

Currently, the interaction of factors that shape food choices is being evaluated. These factors include nutrition attitudes and knowledge of parents and child-care providers, economic and social status of the family, ordinal position of the preschool child, siblings, peers, and media advertising. It is difficult but necessary to incorporate both an assessment of individual nutritional adequacy and an evaluation of food habits in an effort to assess the effect of food preferences on long-term health status.

In this section, some of these factors will be discussed in the light of recent research. This section is viewed as an afterword to Dr. Lowenberg's discussion of earlier research and the practical aspects of the development of the food habits of young children.

Factors that have recently been evaluated for the young child are texture, taste and familiarity of food, preferences of the child compared with those of parents and other significant adults, and interaction patterns of parents and children around food. The limitations of these reports are the usual limitatons found when dealing with a complex set of interacting factors. Thus sample size and biases of subsets of the general population, such as economic status and social and cultural background, limit the generalization of these results. However, these reports do point a direction for clinical practice and further research and suggest important considerations in developing multidimensional research models.

Food Preferences

As it is clearly very difficult to measure "attitudes" of young children, "preferences" are measured instead. Frequently selected foods are offered, and the children indicate their preferences on a hedonic scale. The number of foods offered is obviously limited by the age of the children. However, 3- and 4-year-old children have preferences for specific foods and are quite willing to indicate them.[4] Previous reports by a parent, usually the mother, plus food consumption information were considered to be the only reasonable measures of a child's food preferences. Sweetness and familiarity appear to be significant factors influencing food preferences for young children.[5]

It would seem that the food preferences of young children would be significantly influenced by the adults who provide their care and thus provide their food. Both mother and father appeared to influence a child's food preferences equally, possibly because of the high priority given to the father's preferences in the family menu.[6] Unrelated adults of the same subcultural group, i.e., day-care teachers, exert an influence equal to parents in development of food preference.[7]

Nutrition Knowledge of Caregiver

Nutrition knowledge of parents and other caregivers would seem to be an important factor to consider. However, it is not a clear-cut variable. The degree to which knowledge of nutrition is incorporated into family meal planning appears to be related to positive "attitude" toward self, problem-solving skills, and family organization in spite of a professed concern by all mothers interviewed about the total diet offered to young children and importance of mealtime with children.[8] The ordinal position of the preschool child in the family appears to influence choices of specific foods regardless of equivalent knowledge of nutrition between groups of mothers.[9] When preschool children were the youngest children in a family, mothers were found to be less susceptible to children's requests for new products. They were willing, however, to accommodate that preference when the preschool child was the oldest child in a family. Television was a major influence on the young child's preference for presweetened cereal.

Day-care teachers would, presumably, also have an impact on the development of food preference in young children. In a recent survey, day-care teach-ers reported that they knew little about nutrition, but they thought it was important.[10] Since young children are very responsive to early influences, the role of the day-care teacher in shaping positive food-related attitudes needs to be strongly supported by the nutrition community.

Influence of Family

In a recent review Hertzler[11] encouraged the development of a broader conceptual framework for studying children's food behavior and urged that the family unit be included in the research model.

The influence of the family unit on changing food-choice patterns to manage obesity has been reviewed.[12] Families are, as a unit, well-organized and supportive. Families also provide appropriate role models and reinforcements that are most likely to bring about appropriate food habit changes.

The child-parent interactions have an important influence on food consumption. There appeared to be differences between the interactions of thinner children and their mothers and fatter children and their mothers both in food and nonfood situations.[13] The thinner children and their mothers talked more with each other, ate less food and more slowly, and in general had a more positive, supportive relationship than the fatter children and their mothers. This type of study begins to look at the broader construct of family units as related to food and eating and needs to be further researched.

Obviously, children respond to the social environment when they make food choices for themselves. Birch, Zimmerman, and Hind[14] demonstrated that preferences for foods were enhanced when foods were offered as a reward or with brief positive social interactions with adults.

SUMMARY

In summary, for nutrition educators to maximize their influence on the health and well-being of young children, they must attend to the influences that shape the food preferences and eating patterns

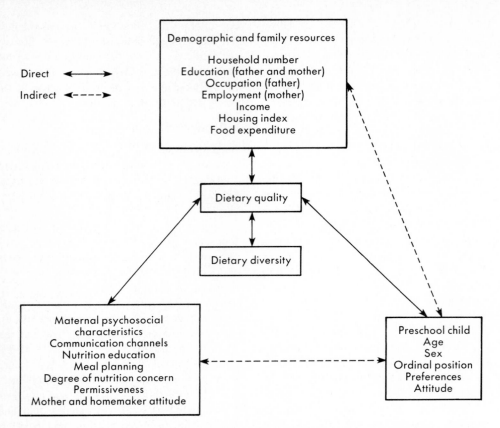

Direct ⟷

Indirect ⟵---▸

Demographic and family resources

Household number
Education (father and mother)
Occupation (father)
Employment (mother)
Income
Housing index
Food expenditure

Dietary quality

Dietary diversity

Maternal psychosocial
characteristics
Communication channels
Nutrition education
Meal planning
Degree of nutrition concern
Permissiveness
Mother and homemaker attitude

Preschool child
Age
Sex
Ordinal position
Preferences
Attitude

Fig. 6-2. Factors related to child's dietary status. (From Caliendo, M.A., and Sanjur, D.: J. Nutr. Ed. **10:**69, 1978.)

of young children. These influences are dynamic and multidirectional. Fig. 6-2 indicates one approach to describing these influences. Young children are shaped by their particular family unit in several ways. Effective nutrition work with young children and their families requires nutrition educators to forge strong ties with the social scientists.

To assist children to develop desirable food patterns, it is recommended that:

1. All foods should be well prepared and attractive in color, flavor, and texture, so that the child will feel friendly toward them and eat them happily. Children appreciate and enjoy an attractive plate and often comment on foods being "pretty"; they eat with greatest enthusiasm when there is a variety of flavors and textures in the meal.

2. The environment for eating should be suited to the abilities and comfort of the young eater. This includes appropriate tables and chairs as well as suitable dishes and implements for eating.

3. A child should be expected to have a good appetite and to be hungry when in good health physically and emotionally.

4. Appetite will be fostered if the child is happily excited over the fact that it is mealtime.

5. Pleasant associations with the food will be fostered if the meal can be eaten successfully with reasonable effort. A child should not become too tired physically before the meal has been eaten.

SUGGESTED LEARNING ACTIVITIES

1. During observation of a preschool feeding program, identify food preferences of the children.

2. Describe factors in the environment at mealtimes that influence children's food acceptance.

3. Discuss appropriate portions for 2- and 5-year-old children.

4. How can parents facilitate a child's acceptance of new textures?

5. Describe appropriate tables, chairs, and utensils for feeding utensils for young children.

6. If you were asked to provide a diet of 1000 kcal/day for a very overweight 2-year old boy (weight: 40 pounds, greater than 95th percentile; NCHS, height: 90th percentile), what factors would you need to consider in relation to the family unit and eating environment?

7. A 3-year-old girl is referred to you because she is a "picky" eater. Her mother is very concerned. The girl is at the 25th percentile for height and the 10th percentile for weight. Outline your assessment and intervention strategy.

8. If you were a nutrition consultant to a preschool that provides morning and afternoon snacks for the children and milk is provided at lunch even though children bring their own lunches,
   a. What easy, nourishing snacks that can be tied-in to activities for the children would you recommend?
   b. What basic concepts do you consider important in developing guidelines/in-service education for parents who prepare their children's lunches.

REFERENCES

1. Aldrich, C.A., and Aldrich, M.M.: Feeding our oldfashioned children, New York, 1946, Macmillan, Inc.
2. Carlson, A.J.: The control of hunger in health and disease, Chicago, Ill., 1916, University of Chicago Press.
3. Bryan, M.S., and Lowenberg, M.E.: The father's influence on young children's food preference, J. Am. Diet. Assoc. **34**:30, 1958.
4. Birch, L.L.: Preschool children's food preferences and consumption patterns, J. Nutr. Educ. **11**:189, 1979.
5. Birch, L.L.: Dimensions of preschool children's food preferences, J. Nutr. Educ. **11**:77, 1979.
6. Burt, J.V., and Hertzler, A.A.: Parental influence on the child's food preference, J. Nutr. Educ. **10**:127, 1978.
7. Birch, L.L.: The relationship between children's food preferences and those of their parents, J. Nutr. Educ. **12**:14, 1980.
8. Swanson-Rudd,J., and others: Nutrition orientations of working mothers in the North Central Region, J. Nutr. Educ. **14**:132, 1982.
9. Phillips, D.E., Bass, M.A., and Yetley, E.: Use of food and nutrition knowledge by mothers of preschool children, J. Nutr. Educ. **10**:73, 1978.
10. Gillis, D.E.G., and Sabry, J.H.: Daycare teachers: nutrition knowledge, opinions, and use of food, J. Nutr. Educ. **12**:200, 1980.
11. Hertzler, A.A.: Children's food patterns—a review. I. Food preferences and feeding problems. II. Family and group behavior, J. Am. Diet. Assoc. **83**:551, 1983.
12. Hertzler, A.A.: Obesity—impact on the faimly, J. Am. Diet. Assoc. **79**:525, 1981.
13. Birch, L.L., and others: Mother-child interaction patterns and the degree of fatness in children, J. Nutr. Educ. **12**:17, 1981.
14. Birch, L.L., Zimmerman, S.I., and Hind, H.: The influence of social-affective context on the formation of children's food preferences, J. Nutr. Educ. **13**:115, 1981.

Between Infancy and Adolescence

7

PEGGY L. PIPES
JANE MITCHELL REES

etween infancy and adolescence, changes in children's rates of growth, continuing maturation of fine and gross motor skills, and personality development influence not only the amounts of food consumed and the manner in which children consume food, but also those foods that are acceptable to them. Food habits, likes, and dislikes are established, some of which are transient, many of which form the base for a lifetime of food, and thus nutrient, intake. Environmental influences and parental behaviors reinforce or extinguish food-related behaviors.

NUTRITION PROBLEMS OF PRESCHOOL AND SCHOOL-AGE CHILDREN

Although clinical signs of malnutrition are rarely found in children in North America, there is evidence that there are children who are receiving diets that are inadequate in quantity and/or quality. The Ten-State Nutrition Survey and the Health and Nutrition Examination Survey indicated that nutrients most often consumed in less than recommended amounts by children are iron and vitamin B_6.[1,2] The Nationwide Food Consumption Study further identified that in addition to these nutrients, calcium and vitamin C are frequently consumed in less than recommended amounts.[3] Protein and riboflavin are most often consumed in excess of recom-

mended amounts. Nutritional status studies have shown that children from low-income families frequently are shorter than those from families with greater economic resources and have indicated that limited intakes of food may be compromising their growth potential. In some poverty-level populations groups of children have been identified that have shown both clinical and biochemical evidence of malnutrition. All preschool children are at risk for iron-deficiency anemia, which appears to be a greater problem in children of low-income families than in children of other groups. Dental caries as a result of excessive intakes of sweet foods, poor dental hygiene, and lack of dental care are common among all groups of children.

There are children who are receiving sufficient amounts of food, others who are consuming excessive amounts of food, and some who are receiving diets that are inadequate both in quality and quantity.

Ethnic and geographical variations in nutrient deficiency concerns have been found in various populations. Spanish-American children from migrant families in the south central and southwestern states have been noted to have a high incidence of biochemical and clinical signs of vitamin A deficiency. Clinical signs of rickets and biochemical evidence of inadequate intakes of protein, folate, iron, and ascorbic acid have been noted in some children of migrant families in Colorado.[4,5] Low intakes of niacin have been noted among Mexican-American children in California and Colorado.[5,6] Navajo Indian children in Montana were found to have low dietary intakes of calcium and vitamins A and C. Biochemical evidence of inadequate intakes of iron, vitamin A, and riboflavin was also noted.[7] White Mountain Apache children in Arizona were noted to have biochemical evidence of inadequate intakes of vitamins A and C.[8] School-age children from low-income families who had biochemical evidence of iron deficiency have been identified in Pennsylvania.[9] Biochemical evidence of riboflavin deficiency has been found in children from poverty groups in New York.[10] Biochemical evidence of vitamin B_6 deficiency has been reported in 9% of children studied in Virginia.[11]

Several studies have indicated that when nutrient intakes are calculated on the basis of nutrients per 1000 kcal consumed, they are similar at all economic levels.[12,13] Children from low-income families consume less food; therefore their total intake of nutrients and energy is less. Male family head employment status has been found to have an impact on average daily energy intake. Windham and others[12] found from analyzing data from the Nationwide Food Consumption Survey that family members in which the male head was employed averaged intakes of 165 kcal/day more than those in which the male head was unemployed. Female head employment status was not found to affect energy intake. Racial and geographical differences in the nutrient density of diets consumed were also noted. A lower calcium density was noted in the diets of Spanish and black groups than in other populations. The vitamin A density was lowest in the Spanish groups compared with other groups studied. The place of residence also influenced nutrient density of the diets consumed. Intakes of niacin, vitamin B_6, and C per 1000 kcal were lower in nonmetropolitan areas than in the central city and nonsuburban areas studied.[11]

The National Nutrition Status Study of preschool children conducted by Owen and others[13] found that black children consumed an average of 1 mg of iron/day more than white preschoolers at all ages. Cereal grains were the major contributors of iron. Vitamin C intakes were urelated to energy intakes, and children of parents who had more money to spend for food consumed greater amounts of ascorbic acid. Other studies have shown that vitamin A intake is also unrelated to energy intake.[14] A high percentage of school-age children in all studies have been found to be receiving multiple vitamin supplements. A decrease in use of supplements with age has, however, been noted.[15]

Mothers of 10% of the preschool children in a nutritional status study in the North Central Region of the United States reported that their children had conditions that required modification of the kinds or amounts of food consumed.[14] Compliance with dietary modifications necessary to control chronic diseases such as diabetes, celiac disease, allergies, and others is difficult in childhood. Children want to eat the same food as their peers and family. Teachers and friends are not always sympathetic with the need to restrict or modify intake of food. Restriction of several groups of foods such as may be necessary for children who have multiple allergies makes adequate energy intakes difficult. Thus children who must modify their intakes of food are at risk for nutritional deficits.

RESPONSIBILITIES OF FAMILIES FOR CHILDREN'S FOOD INTAKES

Children from infancy to adolescence depend on their parents for the selection of food they consume at home. As they grow older, have money to spend, attend school, and interact with larger numbers of individuals, the decisions as to their selection of food become increasingly their own. Since the preschool and the preadolescent periods are important in the formation of attitudes toward food, it is important that foods that supply the nutrients be available to children. Parents also need to understand and support children in their food-related behaviors so that food habits are formed that are conducive to an adequate nutrient intake. Children need some experiences in selection of food, yet parents need to set limits so that children eat foods that provide adequate amounts of nutrients.

Studies have repeatedly shown that it is usually the mother who is the gatekeeper, the person who decides which foods are to be purchased and how these foods are to be prepared. She makes the decision on the basis of the money available to be spent for food, the time she has to devote to food preparation, the foods that her family enjoys, her skills and interest in food preparation, her knowledge of nutrition, and the value she places on nutrient intake.

The educational level and nutrition knowledge of the mother influence the nutritional quality of the diet. Eppright and others[16] noted that as the nutrition knowledge of the mother increased, preschool children's intakes of calcium, iron, riboflavin, and ascorbic acid increased. They also found that nutrition knowledge was significantly related to positive attitudes toward meal planning and food preparation. Caliendo and others[17] found that the more positive mothers felt about meal planning, the importance of good nutrition for their children, and their roles as homemakers, the more likely were the children to receive good quality meals; the more discontent, nervous, and unhappy the mothers were with their roles as homemakers the lower was the dietary quality of the children's food intakes.

Parents often need help both in interpreting the nutrition information to which they have been exposed and in direction to valid sources of information. Sources of nutrition information vary among groups of parents. Low-income families reportedly receive their nutrition information from relatives and friends. Other families rely heavily on lay sources such as magazines, newspapers, books, radio, and television. Some of the information presented in these sources lack validity, and often conflicting information is presented in any two sources. In addition, advertising and merchandising often play on parents' emotional responses to suggestion and imply a false need for certain foods or supplements.

Convenience is another factor many mothers consider when they select food for their families. Working mothers may rely heavily on convenience food and fast-food establishments and have been known to leave the decision to the child as to which one he or she would like for dinner. Parents may need help in selection of convenience foods and combinations of other foods that, when served with them, provide a balanced nutrient intake and in how to plan other meals so that the daily intake is adequate when fast foods are consumed frequently. They may also need help in developing food preparation skills.

Mothers select and prepare foods that they believe their families will enjoy. Bryan and Lowenberg[18] found that 89% of mothers eliminated from the family menu or served infrequently those foods that their husbands disliked. In the study conducted by Eppright and others,[19] 81% of the mothers planned meals on the basis of their husbands' food likes and dislikes and 72% chose foods on the basis of the food likes and dislikes of other family members. Food likes and dislikes of children were considered by 58% of the mothers.

In addition, preschool children often accompany their mothers to the grocery store and request specific foods. In this situation, 68% of mothers have reported that they sometimes buy foods that are requested and 18% stated they always purchased the items. Sugar-coated cereal is the food most frequently requested.[3]

Peer group pressures also have an influence on the children's request for food and the mother's selection at the supermarket. Mothers who view candy, carbonated beverages, and potato chips as not of the best nutritional or economic value may purchase them simply because other children have them. Mothers may provide them for their children because they observe other parents using these foods as an expression of affection for their children.

FACTORS AFFECTING FOOD INTAKE

Provision of appropriate amounts and kinds of food does not ensure that children will consume foods that support an appropriate nutrient intake. Children imitate the models of food acceptance set for them. They learn to control concerned parents by the food they accept or reject. Emotional factors influence food acceptance and intake.

Parents and siblings provide a model of food acceptance and feeding behavior that children imitate. Laskarzewski and others[20] found a significant positive correlation between parent-child intake of calories, carbohydrate, saturated fats, and polyunsaturated fats in a study of parents and 6- to 19-year-old children. The correlation was greater for black than for white children. Food likes and dislikes of parents and older siblings are often passed on to younger children. It has been suggested that the older siblings exert an even greater influence by the models they set than do parents.[14] Unresolved conflicts about food intakes and feeding behavior may as a result be passed on to future children.

Food may be offered by parents, aunts, grandmothers, and others to show affection and to reward children for desired behavior; it is also often withheld for punishment. These nonnutritive uses of food lay the framework within which many attitudes about foods are formed and influence those foods that are acceptable to children. Foods withheld or used as rewards become desired foods; those that must be consumed to receive the more desired become less acceptable. Since many other reinforcers and punishers are effective with normal children, these uses of food are inappropriate. When food reinforcers are necessary to change behavior, careful consideration should be given both to the food used and the design of the program (see Chapter 14).

Attitudes of parents toward child rearing influence nutrient intake. Eppright[19] found permissiveness of parents in relation to eating to be negatively related to the nutritive value of food consumed by the children, adversely affecting all dietary components except fat. Less permissive mothers regulated to some degree the child's food intakes, and as a result children consumed greater amounts of protein, vitamins, and minerals. Sims and Morris[21] found that children of more affluent, nonauthoritarian mothers had higher intakes of calcium and ascorbic acid, whereas children of parents with authoritarian attitudes toward child rearing had higher intakes of calories, carbohydrates, iron, and thiamine.

Lack of structure to eating patterns, including meals and snacks, gives no opportunity for children to develop hunger. The frequency with which food is offered is therefore important (see Chapter 6). Knowledge that a more desired food such as a Popsicle is available after a meal is consumed may reduce a child's motivation to eat at the table.

The emotional environment at mealtime may influence food and nutrient intake. The dinner table is not the place for family battles or punitive action toward children. For eating to be successful, it should occur at a time and in a setting that is comfortable and free from stress and unreasonable demands. Lund and Burk[22] found that mealtime criticism about nonfood-related activities reduced the levels of food consumption and adversely affected intakes of vitamins A and C in 9- to 11-year-old children.

Parents concerned about children's food intake sometimes nag, urge, or even try to force their children to consume what they consider to be the appropriate kind or amount of food. The children soon learn that they can control many aspects of their parents' behavior by refusing to eat. As a result their food consumption may become so limited that growth is compromised and/or nutrient intakes quite limited. Helping parents identify what occurs in this situation and reassuring them about their children's development can alleviate their overconcern about their children's food intakes. As the pressure on children to eat is relieved, they usually increase their food intakes.

Parents themselves may interfere with children's food intakes when they make demands on them

Fig. 7-1. Children consume food successfully in a comfortable setting free from stress.

that are incompatible with eating. Parents may make such frequent demands on children related to proper use of utensils, position of the chair, and body posture that children do not have uninterrupted time to eat more than one or two mouthfuls. Such children become discouraged and frequently become engrossed in adjusting utensils and the position of the chair and fidgeting; consequently, they reduce their total food intakes. Helping parents ignore this behavior and focus conversation on nonmealtime activities can remedy this sitation. Making conversation with the children while they are eating can reinforce them for appropriate eating behavior and increase their food intake (Fig. 7-1).

Influence of Television on Children

In addition to the many familial, cultural, and psychosocial influences on children's food habits, mass media have an impact on children's requests for and attitudes toward food. Of the forms of mass media, television has the greatest impact on children because it reaches many children before they are capable of verbal communication.[23] Children spend more time in front of the television set than they do in any activity other than sleeping. Children from low-income families watch more television than do children from moderate- to high-income familes.[24] It has been estimated that the preschool child watches television for 26.3 hours per week, and 6- to 16-year-old children watch for 25 hours per week.[25] Television can be detrimental to growth and development by encouraging sedentary and passive activities, thus promoting a lifestyle that may lead to obesity.

Advertising and programs present models of behavior children may imitate. Advertisers attempt to use children to influence their parents' purchasing behavior. They present frequent cues for food and drink and often encourage consumption of a wide variety of sugared products.

Both parents and health care professionals have expressed concern about the effects of television programming and advertising on health practices of children. Groups have joined together and influenced regulations. Action for Children's Television, a national group formed in Boston, exerted sufficient pressure that vitamins and medicine are no longer advertised on children's television, appeals to children to ask parents for products are no longer common, and program hosts or characters in stories seldom advertise products. Because of the influence of this group, the National Association of Broadcaster's code authority issued new guidelines for advertising time on children's television. As of January 1976, 9.5 minutes per hour of commercial advertising is permissible. One can, therefore, anticipate that 15% of the hours spent watching television will be spent viewing commercials.[26] It is estimated that the average child watches 3 hours of television advertising per week, or 19,000 to 22,000 commercials per year.[27]

Kindergarten children often are unable to separate commercials from the program and frequently explain them as part of the program.[28] Younger school-age children (5 to 10 years of age) watch commercials more closely than do older children (11 to 12 years of age).[29] Older children are conscious of the concept of commercials, the purpose of selling, and the concept of sponsorship and are less likely to accept advertisers' claims without question. They perceive that television commercials are designed to sell products rather than entertain or educate. Children in second grade have been found to have a concrete distrust of commercials based on experiences with advertised products, and children in sixth grade have been found to have global mistrust of all commercials.[28]

Food manufacturers and fast-food establishments use the greatest percentage of advertising time on children's television. A 1975 study of children's programs on Saturday and Sunday in Boston revealed that 68.5% of the advertisements were for food,[26] of which 25% were for cereal, 25% were for candy and sweets, and 8% were for snacks and other food. Quick meals and eating places were the subjects of 10% of the advertisements. Only a few commercials were broadcast for milk, bread, or fruit. Advertisements for sugared cereals outnumbered those for unsugared cereals by a ratio of three to one.

It has been pointed out that certain attributes of food are promoted as being superior to others. The main characteristics presented positively are "sweetness," "chocolatey," and "richness."[30] Many food manufacturers, in other words, deemphasize the physiological need for nutrients and encourage selection on the basis of sweet flavor. Exposure to such messages may distort a child's natural curiosity toward other characteristics of food such as the fresh crispness of celery or apples.

Studies by Yankelovich[31] and by McNeal[32] indicate that children are influenced by commercials and consequently attempt to influence their parents' buying practices. In these studies it was also found that commercials for food have the strongest influence and that mothers are more likely to yield to requests for food than for other products. They have a greater tendency to respond to requests from older children but certainly do not completely ignore those of the younger children.[33] Highly child-centered mothers are less likely to buy children's favorite cereals than are mothers who are not as child centered.[34] Crawford, Hankin, and Huenemann[15] reported that two thirds of the mothers interviewed stated that food choices were influenced by television commercials by the time the child was 4 years of age.

Food-related behaviors of characters in television programs may also set an example for children. One study of prime-time television noted 5.31 food-related behaviors per program. The behaviors that involved more nutritious food were almost equal in number to those that involved nonnutritious food.[35]

Parents must set limits on their children's requests for advertised food and may need support in their efforts to do so. They may need guidance in principles of behavior modification (Chapter 13) and reassurance that it is to the child's advantage to learn that not all advertised products are a part of every child's meal pattern.

Other advertising also influences children's food requests. Box tops and prize offers lead to increased demand for and consumption of certain foods. Door-to-door sales of candy and cookies for charitable causes may adversely influence the distribution of the food dollar and encourage consumption of foods that provide sugar but few nutrients.

THE PRESCHOOL CHILD

During the preschool years rates of growth decrease and as a result appetites decrease. Children learn to understand language and to talk and ask for food. Development of gross motor skills permits them to learn to walk and seek food for themselves. Development of fine motor skills allows them to learn to feed themselves and to prepare simple foods such as cereal and milk and sandwiches. They learn about food and the way it feels, tastes, and smells. Preschool children learn to eat a wider variety of textures and kinds of food, give up the bottle, and drink from a cup. They demand independence and refuse help in many tasks in which they are not skillful, such as self-feeding. As they grow older they become less interested in food and more interested in their environment. They test and learn limits of behavior that are acceptable.

Self-feeding

Children learn to feed themselves independently during the second year of life. Spilling and messiness are marked during the first half of the year, but by their second birthday most children spill very little. Handedness is not established at 1 year of age. Children may grasp the spoon with either hand and may find when they try to fill the spoon that the bowl is upside down. The 15-month-old child will have difficulty scooping food into his or her spoon and bringing food to the mouth without turning the spoon upside down and spilling its contents because of lack of wrist control. By 16 to 17 months of age a well-defined ulnar deviation of the wrist occurs and the contents of a spoon may be transferred more steadily to the mouth. By 18 months of age the child lifts the elbow as the spoon is raised and flexes the wrist as the spoon reaches the mouth so that only moderate spilling occurs at this age, in contrast to earlier stages of self-feeding. By 2 years of age spilling seldom occurs.

Children are interested in how food feels and often prefer finger-feeding to spoon-feeding. Foods that provide opportunities for finger-feeding should be provided at every meal. Children not infrequently will place food in the spoon with their fingers and may finger feed foods commonly spoon fed, such as vegetables and pudding.

By 15 months of age children can manage the cup, although not expertly. They have difficulty in lifting and tilting a cup and in lowering it to a tray after drinking. The cup is tilted, using the palm, and often is tilted too rapidly. By 18 to 24 months of age the cup will be tilted by manipulation of the fingers.

Rotary chewing movements are refined in the second year and are well established by 2½ years of age.

Patterns of Food Intake

Few children pass through the preschool years without creating concern about their food intakes. Between 9 and 18 months of age a disinterest in food becomes apparent and lasts from a few months to a few years.[36] Food jags are common. Likes and dislikes may change from day to day and week to week. For example, a child may demand only boiled eggs for snacks for a week and completely reject them for the next 6 months. Rituals become a part of food preparation and service. Some children, for example, accept sandwiches only when they are cut in half, and when parents quarter the sandwiches the children may throw tantrums. Others demand that foods have a particular arrangement on the plate or that their dishes be placed only in certain locations on the table.

Appetites are usually erratic and unpredictable during this period. The child may eat hungrily at one meal and completely refuse the next. The evening meal is generally the least well received and is of the most concern to the majority of parents. It is possible that a child who has consumed two meals and several snacks has met his or her need for energy and nutrients before dinnertime; in this instance consumption of limited amounts of food may be appropriate. It is also important to

Fig. 7-2. Preschool children enjoy learning to self-feed.

Fig. 7-3. Preschool children refine their self-feeding skills as they grow older.

recognize that much social interaction occurs during the evening meal. This may be overwhelming for the preschooler who is learning not only to eat and interact at the same time but also to master the use of utensils as well as to eat harder-to-masticate foods.

Beal[36] and Eppright and others[19] report a high percentage of parental dissatisfaction with children's appetites and interest in food between 2 and 4 years of age. Concerns most frequently expressed are selection of a limited variety of foods, dawdling, limited consumption of fruits and vegetables, and consumption of too many sweets and too little meat. It is apparent that such problems are those of the parents' lack of insight into normal child development and, if properly managed, need not compromise a child's nutrient intake. Anticipatory guidance about children's food behavior is important for all parents, and intervention is imperative when battles are waged between parents and children about what is to be eaten.

Frequency of eating. Huenemann[37] has pointed out that we are raising a generation of nibblers. Nearly 60% of 3- to 5-year-old children eat more than three times a day.[38] They consume food an average of five to seven times per day, although ranges of three to fourteen times per day have been noted.[37] Crawford, Hankin, and Huenemann[15] found that by 6 years of age 50% of children ate five times per day. Eppright and others[39] noted that the frequency of food intakes was unrelated to nutrient intakes except when children consumed food less than four or more than six times a day. Children in this study who consumed food less than four times a day consumed fewer calories and less calcium, protein, ascorbic acid, and iron than average intakes of other children their age. Those who consumed food more than six times a day consumed more energy, calcium, and ascorbic acid than average intakes of children their age. Snacks have been noted to provide almost one fourth of the total calories, over one third of the total sucrose, and one fifth of the total calcium and ascorbic acid ingested by school-age children.[40]

Food preferences. Parents report that preschool

Fig. 7-4. Snacks are an important part of children's nutrient intake.

children enjoy meat, cereal grains, baked products, fruit, and sweets. They frequently ask for dairy products, cereal, and snack items such as cookies, crackers, fruit juice, and dry beverage mixes.[41] Food preferences during the preschool years seem to be for the carbohydrate-rich foods that are easier to masticate. Cereals, breads, and crackers often are selected in preference to meat and other protein-rich foods. The use of dry fortified cereals as a primary source of many nutrients is increasing.[15] Yogurt and cheese appear to be increasing in popularity among young children.

A concern of parents of many children between 1 and 3 years of age is that their children don't like and won't eat meat. In the description of their dissatisfaction, it may become apparent that the children do eat and enjoy chicken, frankfurters, and hamburger but refuse the more fibrous and harder-to-chew steaks and roasts. Foods have not yet been classified in relation to the pressure that must be applied to chew them well. Empirical observations, however, indicate that fibrous meats require the greatest pressure of any food consumed and may be difficult for the preschooler to eat. It may be important to focus parents' attention on the many softer, easier-to-chew meats and protein-rich foods that their children are consuming.

Food dislikes in childhood consistently include cooked vegetables, mixed dishes, and liver. Children accept raw vegetables more readily than they do cooked ones but often accept only a limited number. Acceptance of new foods appears to be age related. Owen and others[13] found that only 6% of the youngest but 18% of the oldest preschoolers in their study would flatly refuse a new food. Since familiarity with food is believed to influence its acceptance, new foods should be offered frequently, even though they have been previously refused.

Milk intakes are erratic and change with age. Beal[36] noted that a reduction in milk intake begins at approximately 6 months of age. Milk may be completely refused at times. Intakes of milk between ages 1 and 4 years approximate 1 to $2\frac{1}{2}$ cups per day. After this age, the total volume of milk consumed increases.

Patterns of Nutrient Intake

Both longitudinal and cross-sectional studies of nutrient and energy intakes of children have shown large differences in intakes between individual children of the same age and sex; some children consume two to three times as much energy as others.[15,42] After a rapid rise in intake of all nutrients during the first 9 months of life, reductions can be expected in the intakes of some nutrients as increases occur in intakes of others.

Sex differences in intakes of energy and nutrients have been noted by several researchers. In all studies males consumed greater quantities of food, thus greater amounts of nutrients and energy.

During the preschool years there is a decrease in intakes of calcium, phosphorus, riboflavin, iron, and vitamin A because of the omission of iron-fortified infant cereals in the diets of children, their reduction in milk intake, and their disinterest in vegetables. During this period children increase their intakes of carbohydrate and fat. Protein intakes may plateau or increase only slightly.[42] Between 3 and 8 years of age there is a slow, steady, and relatively consistent increase in intake of all nutrients. Since intakes of vitamins A and C are unrelated to energy intakes, greater ranges of intakes of these nutrients have been noted. Black preschoolers in California have been noted to have higher intakes of sodium than whites because of their frequent use of undiluted commercially prepared soups. They were found also to have greater energy intakes than whites between 2 and 4 years of age.[15]

Feeding Preschool Children

In spite of the reduction in appetite and erratic consumption of food, preschool children do enjoy food and gradually increase their average daily energy intakes. If simply prepared foods that provide a balance of nutrients are presented in a relaxed setting, children will consume an appropriate nutrient intake. Understanding and supportive help from parents and others who offer food to children lay the groundwork for the development of nutritionally sound and satisfying eating practices. Meals and snacks should be timed to foster appetite. Intervals necessary between meals and snacks may vary from one child to another; rarely can the clock be depended on to let one know appropriate intervals and times when it may be important for a child to eat.

Appetites may be satiated when energy needs are met, regardless of a child's need for nutrients. It is thus important that a food selection be provided that ensures that the foods consumed provide nutrients as well as calories. The food should be presented without comment and the child permitted to consume amounts that he or she desires without any conversation focused on what or how much is being eaten. Portions served should be scaled to the child's appetite (see Chapter 6). When the meal is over, food should be removed and the child should be permitted to leave the table.

Occasionally anxious or concerned parents need help with food sources of nutrients usually supplied by food refused and/or in establishing limits to preschooler's food intakes and feeding behavior. Of the commonly expressed concerns limited intakes of milk, refusal of vegetables and meat, eating too many sweets, and limited intakes of food appear to cause the most problems. It is important to recognize that 1 oz of milk supplies 36 gm of calcium, and many children receive 6 to 8 oz of milk on dry cereal daily. Although they consume only 1 to 2 oz at a time, their calcium intakes may be acceptable when they consume milk with meals and snacks. When abundant amounts of fruit juice or sweetened beverages are available, children may simply prefer to drink them rather than milk. Other dairy products can be offered when milk is rejected. Cheese and yogurt are usually accepted. Powdered milk can be used in recipes for soups, vegetables, and mixed dishes.

Parents' perceptions of children's dislike of meat may need to be clarified. If in fact preschoolers do consistently refuse all food sources of heme iron, their dietary intakes of iron should be carefully monitored. Parents concerned about children's excessive intakes of sweets may need help in setting limits on amounts of sweet foods they make available to their children. It may be important also to help them convey their concern and the need to set limits on the availability of these foods to other family members, day-care operators, and teachers.

When vegetables are consistently refused, wars between parents and children should not be permitted to erupt. Small portions (1 to 2 tsp) should continue to be served without comment and should be discarded if the child does not consume them. Preschool behavior modification programs that included token rewards when children consumed vegetables and another that provided education about specific vegetables served at mealtime have been found to increase children's acceptance and intake of them.[43,44]

If children's food intakes are so limited that their intakes of energy and nutrients are compromised, parents may need help in establishing guidelines so that the children develop appetites. They should offer food sufficiently often that children do not get so hungry that they lose their appetite, yet not so often they are always satiated. Intervals of 3 to 4 hours are often successful. Very small portions of food should be offered, and second portions should be permitted when children consume the foods already served. Attention should always be focused on children when they eat, and never when food is refused.

Group Feeding

Increasing numbers of children eat some of their meals outside the home. Preschool children of working mothers may be cared for and fed by babysitters or day-care workers. Kindergartens and preschools offer snacks and/or meals, and food experiences are often included as part of the learning exercises provided for children. Day-care centers are licensed by state agencies that mandate the meal pattern and types of snacks to be provided for the children and the percentage of the recommended daily allowances that must be included in the menus. The acceptance of foods presented will be influenced by the same factors that influence children's food intakes at home.

Breakfast may need to be provided for children who receive none at home. Snacks should be planned to complement the daily food intakes. Small portions of food should be served, and children should be permitted second servings of those foods they enjoy. Disliked or unfamiliar foods may be offered by the teaspoon, and the child's acceptance or rejection should be accepted without comment. Children who eat slowly will need to be served first and should be permitted to complete their meals without being rushed to other activities. Teachers should eat with the children without imposing their attitudes about food on them.

A new setting provides an opportunity for children to have exposure to many new foods. Day-care centers, kindergartens, and preschools can provide an important educational setting for both children and their parents. Children learn to prepare food, how food grows, how it smells, and what nutrients it contains. Parents learn through participation, observation, and in conversations with the staff. An organized approach to feeding children must include parents, teachers, and others who offer food to young children. Teachers and day-care workers can provide important information to parents about how children successfully consume food, the nutrients children need, and the foods that provide these nutrients. Parents offer important information to the centers about their children's food acceptance and needs. Each needs to be reinforced positively by the other for their efforts as they successfully provide food for children.

A study of 48 day-care and Head Start programs found that all participating children consumed appropriate intakes of nutrients. Total daily energy intakes were similar for all children regardless of whether one meal and one snack or two meals and two snacks were provided. In fact, when children consumed one meal and one snack, 82% of their energy intakes was provided, but when two meals and two snacks were provided, 84% of energy intakes was consumed in this setting.[45]

THE SCHOOL-AGE CHILD

The school-age period is one of more steady growth accompanied by few apparent feeding problems. A natural increase in appetite is responsible for normal increases in food intake. Because they spend their days at school, children adjust to a more ordered routine. They attempt to gain mastery in physical skills and expend energy in organized sports and games. They learn about food and

Fig. 7-5. Two 6-year-old girls whose birthdays are 1 week apart compare their height.

nutrition as part of their curriculum at school. They grow at their own genetically predetermined rate, and the differences in height of children in the 10th and 90th percentiles are visible and of concern to those who are small and/or are late maturers. They compare their size to that of their peers.

School-age children are not without food and nutrition concerns. Unresolved conflicts from the preschool years may persist. Children in their early school years often continue to refuse a food that touches another on the plate or to demand a special arrangement of dishes and utensils on the table. Likes and dislikes have been established but are not necessarily permanent; however, they may become so if parents are so convinced that children will refuse a food that they do not offer it to them or if a food dislike is discussed so frequently that children become fully patterned into their food idiosyncrasies.

Undernutrition may have serious consequences for the school-age child. Undernourished children become easily fatigued and are unable to sustain prolonged physical and mental effort and to fully participate in learning experiences. The risk of infection is greater. The child with limited nutrient reserves may, therefore, have frequent absences from school. Hopwood and Van Iden[46] examined physical growth and school performance over a 10-year period in school-age children in Ohio. They found that unacceptable patterns of growth were accompanied by scholastic underachievement. In addition, the longer an individual child grew at a less than expected rate, the less able he or she was to achieve success in school.

Breakfast is an important meal. Children will have to rise earlier to eat an unhurried and balanced meal and may have to prepare it themselves. Early morning school activities may make preplanning necessary. Some may find a glass of milk and fruit juice important before early sports activities. Studies have shown that when breakfast is consumed children have a better attitude and school record as compared with when it is omitted.[47] Politt, Leibel, and Greenfield[48] found that the effect of skipping breakfast on problem solving in 9- to 11-year-old well-nourished children was an adverse effect on accuracy of response in problem solving but a beneficial effect on immediate memory in short-term accuracy. The effect was attributed to a heightened arousal level, which in turn had a qualitative effect on cognitive function.

Actually most children do eat breakfasts that contribute at least one fourth of the recommended daily allowances.[49] A larger percentage of children in the lower grades eat breakfast than of those in the middle and the upper grades. Reasons for skipping breakfast have been reported to be "not hungry," "no time," "on a diet," "no one to prepare

food," "do not like food served for breakfast," and foods are "not available."[50] Morgan, Zabik, and Leville[49] found that children who consumed ready-to-eat cereals three or four times a week skipped breakfast less frequently than did children who ate non–ready-to-eat hot cereal.

It is important to recognize that symptoms of obesity and anorexia nervosa may appear during the school-age years in a study of dietary habits and attendant psychosocial factors. Intervention at this time is more likely to be effective than later when the disorders are fully developed.

As children explore the environment of school and peers they are likely to become influenced by these experiences. The credibility of parents is often questioned in the face of advice from teachers, peers, or peers' parents. The school-age child has more access to money, to grocery stores, and, therefore, to foods with questionable nutrient value.

Patterns of Food Intake

School-age children reduce the frequency of food consumption to four to five times per day on school days. They almost always want snacks after school, which they prepare themselves.[41] Although some increase the varieties of food they accept, many continue to reject vegetables, mixed dishes, and liver and the range of food they voluntarily accept may be small. Sugar contributes 24% to 25% of calories in the diets of school-age children. Milk is the primary contributor. Sweetened beverages, fruit, fruit juice, cakes, cookies, and other desert items are also significant contributors.[51]

A common difficulty for parents is finding a time when children are willing to sit down and eat a meal. They frequently are so involved with other activities that it is difficult to get them to take time to eat. Often they satisfy their initial hunger pangs and rush back to their activities and television programs, returning later for a snack. They may become so engrossed in television programs that they demand to eat in front of the television set. In

Fig. 7-6. School-age children may prefer television programs to meals.

fact, some families have yielded to the pressure to not miss a favorite television program and have moved the evening meal from the dining room table to trays in front of the television. It frequently has been observed that children in such families become so engrossed in the shows that they lose interest in their food.

Snacking between meals and while watching television is an important factor in the school-age child's nutrient intake and food habits. Parents can take advantage of urges to snack by planning and providing appropriate foods and discouraging children from responding to advertised suggestions that they ingest sweet foods.

Patterns of Nutrient Intake

Increases in size are accompanied by steady increases in intakes of energy and of all nutrients. By the school-age years most children have established a particular pattern of nutrient intake relative to their peers.[42] Although wide ranges of intake continue to be observed, those who consume the greatest amounts of food, thus energy and nutri-

ents, consistently do so, whereas those consuming smaller amounts of food maintain lesser intakes of food relative to their peers. Differences in intake between males and females increase gradually to 12 years of age and then become marked. Boys consume greater quantities of energy and nutrients than do girls.

School Meals

School feeding and nutrition education programs, when adequately implemented, provide not only important nutrients for children, but also an opportunity for them to learn to make responsible choices regarding dietary intake. Unfortunately, not all schools have provided well-prepared food or an optimum environment to encourage its acceptance. In some instances excessive food waste has been reported. In many instances schools have installed snack bars and/or vending machines that provide only sweet foods with high-energy and low-nutrient concentration that competed with the foods that would have provided a balance of nutrients. Factors believed to be responsible for food waste include unpalatability of the food, little choice in menus, children's low preference for vegetables, and the continuous availability of "junk food" in the school. Menus have been found to often provide insufficient iron and to offer no options for children who need to reduce their energy intakes to control obesity. Food waste has been found to be greater in elementary school programs than in high school programs. Less milk and a higher percentage of vegetables are returned than other foods.[52] Food handling has also influenced waste, on-site preparation, and service, resulting in the least food returns. Frozen preportioned and reheated lunches have been the least well accepted. Other factors believed to comprise children's food intakes include short lunch periods, long cafeteria lines, and a hurried, unsupervised atmosphere.

Successful programs have included students in menu planning and have prepared and served palatable, attractive food. Other programs have offered "fast foods" that comply with the National School Lunch Program (e.g., pizza, hamburger, milkshakes, and fruits).[53] Students have then had the option of selecting from the food available.

The fact that vending machines in schools, often viewed as money-makers for athletic and other school activities, have offered no choice but concentrated sources of sucrose has been a concern to many interested in dental health, control of obesity, and the development of sound food habits for all children. Sufficient concern has been created in some school districts that only machines that provide fruit, milk, nuts, and seeds have been made available to students. Sales have been found to initially decrease but ultimately to increase. One school discovered that they made a greater profit on apples than on chocolate bars.[54]

Since its inception in 1946, the school lunch program has been administered by the Department of Agriculture, which provides cash reimbursement and supplemental foods to feeding programs that comply with federal regulations. Federal regulations require that school lunches and breakfasts be sold at reduced prices or be given free to children of families that cannot afford to buy them. The lunch menus must be planned to meet the guidelines established for the National School Lunch Program. Table 7-1 shows minimum quantities of food required for the various age groups in a school lunch.

To provide variety and to encourage participation and consumption, schools are encouraged to provide a selection of foods. Senior high students may be permitted to decline up to two items. Students below the senior high level may decline up to two or only one item at the discretion of the local school food authority. Breakfast must include liquid milk, fruit or vegetable juice, and bread or cereal. Schools are encouraged to keep fat, sugar, and salt at moderate levels.

Current regulations require that schools devise a plan of student and parental involvement in the school lunch program. They may be included in such activities as menu planning, enhancing the eating environment, program promotion, and related student community support activities.

Foods sold in competition with school lunch in snack bars or vending machines must provide at least 5% of the recommended dietary allowances for one or more of the following nutrients: protein, vitamin A, ascorbic acid, niacin, riboflavin, thiamine, calcium, and iron. This regulation eliminates the sale of soda water, water ices, chewing gum, and some candies until after the last lunch period. It should also encourage the offering of more fruits, vegetables, and fruit and vegetable juices in places that compete with the school lunch.

Children who do not participate in the school lunch program generally bring a packed lunch from home. Studies have indicated that, compared with the school lunch, these meals provide significantly fewer nutrients other than calories.[55] Little variety is seen in the lunches since favorite foods tend to be packed and repacked and lack of refrigeration limits the kinds of foods that can be carried.

Although elementary schoolchildren are making more decisions regarding food selection, supervision and supportive guidance may be necessary at

Table 7-1 School lunch pattern—approximate per lunch minimums

Components	Minimum Quantities				Recommended Quantities for Group V: 12 Years and Older; 7-12†
	Group I: Age 1-2; Preschool	Group II: Age 3-4; Preschool	Group III: Age 5-8; K-3	Group IV: Age 9 and Older; 4-12	
Milk — Unflavored, fluid lowfat, skim or buttermilk must be offered*	¾ cup (6 fl oz)	¾ cup (6 fl oz)	½ pint (8 fl oz)	½ pint (8 fl oz)	½ pint (8 fl oz)
Meat or meat alternate (quantity of the edible portion as served)					
Lean meat, poultry, or fish	1 oz	1½ oz	1½ oz	2 oz	3 oz
Cheese	1 oz	1½ oz	1½ oz	2 oz	3 oz
Large egg	½	¾	¾	1	1½
Cooked dry beans or peas	¼ cup	⅜ cup	⅜ cup	½ cup	¾ cup
Peanut butter or an equivalent quantity of any combination of any of above	2 tbsp	3 tbsp	3 tbsp	4 tbsp	6 tbsp
Vegetable or fruit — 2 or more servings of vegetable or fruit or both	½ cup	½ cup	½ cup	¾ cup	¾ cup
Bread or bread alternate (servings per week) — Must be enriched or whole-grain—at least ½ serving‡ for group I or one serving‡ for groups II-V must be served daily	5	8	8	8	10

From Food and Nutrition Service, Department of Agriculture: National School Lunch Program Regulations, Nov. 16, 1982, Federal Register.

*If a school serves another form of milk (whole or flavored), it must offer its children unflavored fluid lowfat milk, skim milk, or buttermilk as a beverage choice.

†The *minimum* portion sizes for these children are the portion sizes for group IV.

‡Serving 1 slice of bread; or ½ cup of cooked rice, macaroni, noodles, other pasta products, other cereal product such as bulgur and corn grits; or as stated in the *Food Buying Guide* for biscuits, rolls, muffins, and similar products.

lunchtime. Children may give priority to activities other than eating, often rushing through their meals. They may prefer to do without meals rather than reveal the fact that they must receive reduced price or free lunches. Some may refuse to eat many foods on the menu. Disposable aluminum foil trays and plastic spoons are not easy implements for children to use.

Children and their parents may need guidance in the selection of food to be consumed. Overweight and obese children may find it necessary to gain willpower to refuse the gravies and sauces and ask for nonfat milk. As handicapped children enter the mainstream of education, careful planning with parents will be necessary to ensure that mealtimes at school provide appropriate foods as well as nutrients for these children.

Nutrition Education

Nutrition education during the school years is believed to be an important method of developing a nutritionally informed population, since the children are an impressionable and captive audience. Unfortunately nutrition is almost always a low priority to the educator. Few teachers have had basic nutrition information during their teacher training. Many have thought it to be a boring subject, difficult to integrate into an already crowded curriculum. Other reasons cited for ineffective nutrition education programs include lack of adequate research and resource materials and lack of specific curriculum guidelines that would be interdisciplinary and sequential.[56] Nutrition education activities have been a part of some programs of private sector groups, primarily the Dairy Council, and of some governmental agencies.

Because of concern that lack of adequate nutrition information was contributing to unwise food choices and to wasted food in the school lunch programs, Congress enacted the Nutrition Education Training Program in 1977. Administered by the Department of Agriculture, the program offered states grants to develop and implement a state nutrition education plan. Congress identified the following needs for this program in the NET legislation:[57]

1. The proper nutrition of the nation's children is a matter of highest priority.
2. The lack of understanding of the principles of good nutrition and their relationship to health can contribute to a child's rejection of highly nutritious foods and consequent food waste in school food service operations.
3. Many school food service personnel have not had adequate training in food service management skills and principles, and many teachers and school food service operators have not had adequate training in the fundamentals of nutrition or how to convey this information to motivate children to practice sound eating habits.
4. Parents exert a significant influence on children in the development of nutritional habits, and lack of nutrition knowledge on the part of parents can have detrimental effects on children's nutritional development.
5. There is a need to create opportunities for children to learn about the importance of the principles of good nutrition in their daily lives and how these principles are applied in the school cafeteria.

Funding for 1978 and 1979 was 50 cents per child, which was decreased to 30 cents per child in 1980 and to 10 cents per child in 1983.

However, during the program's most active phase, the states provided nutrition education for school lunch employees and teachers and developed curriculum guidelines and materials. As a result, classroom activities were developed in some schools that involved the cafeteria. Evaluation of these programs showed a strong positive impact on nutrition-related knowledge across several different curriculum-specific and standardized measures of knowledge. There was an increase in the number of children willing to select and taste new foods and in reported food preferences and food-related attitudes. However, the behavioral and attitudinal effects were neither as strong nor as consistent across grade levels as were the effect on knowledge. In grades 1 to 3 a positive impact was noted in self-reported measures of food preference and willingness of children to select unfamiliar fruits and vegetables when offered a choice during the school lunch.[58] In grades 4 to 6 children who participated in the programs were more willing to taste previously unfamiliar foods than were children who had not participated in the program. Although several programs noted a declined food waste, no strong program-related effects were noted on overall food waste.[58]

Other nutrition education programs have indicated that parental involvement in the nutrition education programs resulted in children who consumed a higher quality diet than in children in programs in which parents were not involved, an effect noted in kindergarten and the first grade but not in the upper grades.[59] The need to continue nutrition education programs is obvious. It is also important that we learn new methods of nutrition education that may have a greater impact on behavioral change in children.

As children prepare to enter adolescence, attitudes toward food will be well established. Between infancy and adolescence nutrients and energy provide compounds necessary for growth; reserves of some nutrients are accumulated that prepare children for stress and give preparation for the adolescent growth spurt into which they next enter. Knowledge of nutrition and attitudes toward food they acquire during this period provide a basis for the years when the decisions of food selection become theirs alone.

SUMMARY

Children between 1 year of age and the onset of puberty grow at a steady rate. They acquire many new skills, learn much about the environment in which they live, and test the limits of behavior the environment will accept. All these factors influence their food and, therefore, nutrient intake. Parents need to provide appropriate foods and support-

ive guidance so that food patterns that support an appropriate nutrient intake are developed. The nutrition knowledge of the mother positively influences children's nutrient intake. Advertising and television programs also affect children's requests for and acceptance of food.

School feeding programs provide an opportunity for nutrition education. That children acquire knowledge from nutrition education has definitively been provided. The behavioral effects of nutrition education appear to be grade related.

Although most children appear clinically to be well nourished, groups exist within our population with both clinical and biochemical evidence of malnutrition. Nutrients most often consumed in inappropriately limited amounts are iron, vitamins B_6 and C, and calcium.

SUGGESTED LEARNING ACTIVITIES

1. Assess the nutrient intake of a preschool child.
2. Observe a preschool feeding program and describe the feeding environment.
3. Describe factors that influence food acceptability in the preschool child.
4. Watch children's television for 1 hour and describe the food commercials presented during that hour.
5. Discuss with school-age children their interpretation of television commercials for food.
6. Describe appropriate snacks for school-age children.
7. Describe factors that influence foods acceptable to school-age children.
8. Plan a nutrition lesson for an elementary school class.
9. Plan a week's brown bag lunches for a school-age child that provide variety and are nutritionally appropriate.

REFERENCES

1. Abraham, S., and others: Dietary intake findings, United States, 1971-1974, DHEW Pub. No. (HRA) 77-1647,

Washington, D.C., 1977, Department of Health, Education and Welfare.

2. Centers for Disease Control: Ten-State Nutrition Survey, 1968-1970, DHEW Pub. No. (HSM) 72-8130-34, Washington, D.C., 1972, U.S. Department of Health, Education and Welfare, Health Services and Mental Health Administration.

3. Science and Education Administration: Nationwide Food Consumption Survey, 1977-1978, Preliminary Rep. No. 2, Food and nutrient intakes of individuals in 1 day in the U.S., Spring, 1977, Hyattsville, Md., 1980, U.S. Department of Agriculture.

4. Zee, P., Walter, T., and Mitchell, C.: Nutrition and poverty in preschool children, J.A.M.A. 213:739, 1970.

5. Larson, L.B., and others: Nutritional status of children of Mexican-American migrant families, J. Am. Diet. Assoc. 64:29, 1974.

6. Acosta, P.B., and others: Nutritional status of Mexican-American preschool children in a border town, Am. J. Clin. Nutr. 27:1359, 1974.

7. Van Duzen, J., Carter, J.P., and Vander Zwaag, R.: Protein and calorie malnutrition among preschool Navajo Indian children, Am. J. Clin. Nutr. 29:657, 1976.

8. Owen, G.M., and others: Nutrition survey of White Mountain Apache preschool children in nutrition, growth, and development of North American Indian children, Pub. No. (N.I.H.) 72-26, Washington, D.C., 1972, Department of Health, Education and Welfare.

9. Karp, R.J., and others: Iron deficiency in families of iron-deficient inner-city school children, Am. J. Dis. Child. 128:18, 1974.

10. Lopez, R., and others: Riboflavin deficiency in a pediatric population of low socio-economic status in New York City, J. Pediatr. 87:420, 1975.

11. Fries, M.E., Crisley, B.M., and Driskell, J.A.: Vitamin B_6 status of a group of preschool children, Am. J. Clin. Nutr. 34:2706, 1981.

12. Windham, C.T., and others: Nutrient density of diets in the USDA Nationwide Food Consumption Survey, 1977-1978. I. Impact of socioeconomic status on dietary density, J. Am. Diet. Assoc. 82:26, 1983.

13. Owen, G.M., and others: A study of nutritional status of preschool children in the United States, 1968-1970, Pediatrics 53:597, 1974.

14. Eppright, E.S., and others: Nutrition of infants and preschool children in the North Central Region of the United States of America, World Rev. Nutr. Diet. 14:269, 1972.

15. Crawford, P.B., Hankin, J.H., and Huenemann, R.L.: Environmental factors associated with preschool obesity, J. Am. Diet. Assoc. 72:589, 1978.

16. Eppright, E.S., and others: The North Central Regional study of diets of preschool children. II. Nutrition knowl-

edge and attitudes of mothers, J. Home Ec. 62:327, 1970.

17. Caliendo, M.A., and others: Nutritional status of preschool children, J. Am. Diet. Assoc. 71:20, 1977.

18. Bryan, M.S., and Lowenberg, M.E.: The father's influence on young children's food preferences, J. Am. Diet. Assoc. 34:30, 1958.

19. Eppright, E.S., and others: Eating behavior of preschool children, J. Nutr. Educ. 1:16, 1969.

20. Laskarzewski, P., and others: Parent-child nutrient intake interrelationships in school children ages 6 to 19: the Princeton School District Study, Am. J. Clin. Nutr. 33:2350, 1980.

21. Sims, L.S., and Morris, P.M.: Nutritional status of preschoolers, J. Am. Diet. Assoc. 64:492, 1974.

22. Lund, L.A., and Burk, M.C.: A multidisciplinary analysis of children's food consumption behavior, Technical Bulletin No. 265, St. Paul, 1969, University of Minnesota, Agricultural Experimental Section.

23. Somers, A.R.: Violence, television, and the health of American youth, N. Engl. J. Med. 294:811, 1976.

24. Reid, L.N., Bearden, W.O., and Teel, J.E.: Family income, TV viewing, and children's cereal ratings, Journalism Quarterly 57:327, 1980.

25. Television, 1976, North Brook, Ill., 1976, A.C. Nielson Co.

26. Barcus, F.E.: Weekend commercial children's television—1975, Newtonville, Mass., 1975, Action for Children's Television.

27. Choate, R.: Statement presented before the House Subcommittee on Communications of the Committee on Interstate and Foreign Commerce, U.S. House of Representatives, Washington, D.C., 1975, U.S. Government Printing Office.

28. Blatt, J., Spencer, L., and Ward, S.: A cognitive developmental study of children's reactions to television advertising. In Rubinstein, E.A., Comstock, G.A., and Murray, J.P., editors: Television and social behavior, vol. 4, Television in day to day life: patterns of use, Washington, D.C., 1972, U.S. Government Printing Office.

29. Ward, S., Levinson, D., and Wackman, D.: Children's attention to television commercials. In Rubinstein, E.A. Comstock, G.A., and Murray, J.P., editors: Television and social behavior, vol. 4, Television in day to day life: patterns of use, Washington, D.C., 1972, U.S. Government Printing Office.

30. Gussow, J.: Counternutritional messages of TV ads aimed at children, J. Nutr. Educ. 4:48, 1972.

31. Yankelovich, D.: Mothers' attitudes toward children's programs and commercials, Newtonville, Mass., 1970 Action for Children's Television.

32. McNeal, J.U.: An exploratory study of consumer behavior of children. In McNeal, J.U., editor: dimensions of com-

mercial behavior, New York, 1969, Appleton-Century-Crofts.

33. Wackman, D.B., and Ward, S.: Children's information processing of television commercial messages. Manuscript based on a symposium at the American Psychological Association Convention, Montreal, 1973. Cited in Sheikh, A.A., Prasad, V.K., and Rau, T.R.: Children's TV commercials: a review of research, J. Commun. **24:**126, 1974.

34. Berey, L.A., and Pollay, R.W.: The influencing role of the child in family decision making, J. Marketing Res. **5:**70, 1968.

35. Way, W.L.: Food-related behaviors on prime-time television, J. Nutr. Educ. **15:**105, 1983.

36. Beal, V.A.: On the acceptance of solid foods and other food patterns of infants and children, Pediatrics **20:**448, 1957.

37. Huenemann, R.L.: Environmental factors associated with preschool obesity. II. Obesity and food practices of children at successive age levels, J. Am. Diet. Assoc. **64:**489, 1974.

38. Lucas, B.L.: Nutrition in childhood. In Krause, M.V., and Mahan, L.K.: Food, nutrition, and diet therapy, ed. 7, Philadelphia, 1984, W.B. Saunders Co.

39. Eppright, E.S., and others: The North Central Regional study of diets of preschool children. III. Frequency of eating, J. Home Ec. **62:**407, 1970.

40. Frank, G.C., and others: Dietary studies of rural school children in a cardiovascular study, J. Am. Diet. Assoc. **71:**31, 1977.

41. Lamkin, G., Hielscher, M.L., and Janes, H.B.: Food purchasing practices of young families, J. Home Ec. **62:**598, 1970.

42. Beal, V.A.: Dietary intake of individuals followed through infancy and childhood, Am. J. Public Health **51:**1107, 1961.

43. Ireton, C.L. and Guthrie, H.A.: Modification of vegetable-eating behavior in preschool children, J. Nutr. Educ. **4:**100, 1972.

44. Harrill, I., Smith, C., and Gangever, J.A.: Food acceptance and nutrient intake of preschool children, J. Nutr. Educ. **4:**103, 1972.

45. Williams, S., Henneman, A., and Fox, H.: Contribution of food service programs in preschool centers to children's nutritional needs, J. Am. Diet. Assoc. **71:**610, 1977.

46. Hopwood, H.H., and Van Iden, S.S.: Scholastic under-achievement as related to sub-par physical growth, J. Sch. Health **35:**337, 1965.

47. Tuttle, W.W., and others: Effect on school boys of omitting breakfast, J. Am. Diet. Assoc. **30:**674, 1974.

48. Pollitt, E., Leibel, R.L., and Greenfield, D.: Brief fasting, stress, and cognition in children, Am. J. Clin. Nutr. **34:**1526, 1981.

49. Morgan, K.J., Zabik, M.Z., and Leville, G.A.: The role of nutrient intake of 5- to 12-year old children, Am. J. Clin. Nutr. **34:**1418, 1981.

50. Singleton, A., and Rhodes, J.J.: Meal and snacking patterns of students, J. Sch. Health **52:**529, 1982.

51. Morgan, K.J., and Zabik, M.E.: Amount and food sources of total sugar intake by children ages 5- to 12-years, Am. J. Clin. Nutr. **34:**404, 1981.

52. Jansen, G.R., and Harper, J.M.: Consumption and plate waste of menu items served in the National School Lunch Program, J. Am. Diet. Assoc. **73:**395, 1978.

53. Fast food staple for type A lunches, Sch. Food Serv. J. **31:**19, 1977.

54. Crawford, L.: Junk food in our schools: a look at student spending in school vending machines and concessions, J. Can. Diet. Assoc. **38:**195, 1977.

55. Emmons, L., Hayes, M., and Call, D.L.: A study of school funding programs. II. Effects on children with different economic and nutritional needs, J. Am. Diet. Assoc. **61:**268, 1972.

56. O'Donnell, N.L., and Alles, W.F.: School nurse demonstrates that mini-grant funding can improve elementary nutrition education, J. Sch. Health **5:**316, 1983.

57. GAO/CED: What can be done to improve nutrition education? Gaithersburg, Md., 1982, U.S. Government Accounting Office, Document Handling and Information Services Facility.

58. St. Pierre, R.G., and Rezmovic, V.: An overview of the national nutrition education and training program evaluation, J. Nutr. Educ. **14:**61, 1982.

59. Kirks, B.A., Hendricks, D.G., and Wyse, B.W.: Parent involvement in nutrition education for primary grade students, J. Nutr. Educ. **14:**137, 1982.

ADDITIONAL READINGS

Beal, V.A.: Nutritional intake of children. I. Calories, carbohydrate, fat, and protein, J. Nutr. **50:**233, 1953.

Beal, V.A.: Nutrition in a longitudinal growth study, J. Am. Diet. Assoc. **46:**457, 1965.

Beyer, N.R., and Morris, P.M.: Food attitudes and snacking patterns of young children, J. Nutr. Educ. **6:**131, 1974.

Birch, L.L., and others: Mother-child interaction patterns and the degree of fatness in children, J. Nutr. Educ. **13:**17, 1981.

Blakeway, S.F., and Knickrehm, M.E.: Nutrition education in the Little Rock school lunch program, J. Am. Diet. Assoc. **72:**389, 1978.

Breckenridge, M.E.: Food attitudes of 5-12 year old children, J. Am. Diet. Assoc. **35:**704, 1959.

Brown, M.L., and others: Diet and nutriture of preschool children in Honolulu, J. Am. Diet. Assoc. **57:**22, 1970.

Burke, B.S., and others: Calorie and protein intakes of children between 1 and 18 years of age, Pediatrics **24:**922, 1959.

Burke, B.S., and others: Relationships between animal protein, total protein, and total caloric intakes in the diets of children from one to eighteen years of age, Am. J. Clin. Nutr. **9:**729, 1961.

Caliendo, M.A., and Sanjur, D.: The dietary status of preschool children: an ecological approach, J. Nutr. Educ. **10:**69, 1978.

Clancy-Hepburn, K., Hickey, A.A., and Nevill, G.: Children's behavior responses to TV food advertisements, J. Nutr. Educ. **6:**93, 1974.

Crispin, S., and others: Nutritional status of preschool children. II. Anthropometric measurements and interrelationships, Am. J. Clin. Nutr. **21:**1280, 1968.

Driskell, J.A., and Price, C.S.: Nutritional status of preschoolers from low income Alabama families, J. Am. Diet. Assoc. **65:**280, 1974.

Dwyer, J.: Diets for children and adolescents that meet the dietary goals, Am. J. Dis. Child. **134:**1073, 1980.

Fryer, B.A., and others: Growth of preschool children in the North Central Region, J. Am. Diet. Assoc. **60:**30, 1972.

Galst, J.P., and White, M.A.: The unhealthy persuader: the reinforcing value of television and children's purchase-influencing attempts at the supermarket, Child. Dev. **47:**1089, 1976.

Juhas, L.: Nutrition education in day care programs, J. Am. Diet. Assoc. **63:**134, 1973.

Kerry, E., and others: Nutritional status of preschool children. I. Dietary and biochemical findings, Am. J. Clin. Nutr. **21:**1274, 1968.

Lambo, A.M.: Children's ability to evaluate commercial messages for food products, Public Health Rep. **71:**1060, 1981.

Lewis, C.E., and Lewis, M.A.: The impact of television commercials on health-related beliefs and behaviors of children, Pediatrics **53:**431, 1974.

Myers, M.L., Mabel, J.A., and Stare, F.J.: A nutrition study of school children in a depressed urban district, J. Am. Diet. Assoc. **53:**234, 1968.

Owen, G., and Lippman, G.: Nutritional status of infants and young children: USA, Pediatr. Clin. North Am. **24:**211, 1977.

Patterson, L.: Dietary intake and physical development of Phoenix area children, J. Am. Diet. Assoc. **59:**106, 1971.

Pollitt, E., Gersovitz, M., and Garziulo, M.: Educational benefits of the United States school feeding program: a critical review of the literature, Am. J. Public Health **68:**477, 1978.

Salz, K.M., and others: Selected nutrient intakes of free-living white children ages 6-19 years. The Lipid Research Clinic Program Prevalence Study, Pediatr. Res. **17:**124, 1983.

Diet and Hyperactivity

BETTY LUCAS

Over the last two decades, the terms *hyperactivity, hyperkinesis,* and *learning disability* have become commonly used in American homes, in classrooms, and in the mass media and printed media. Although the disorder is ill defined and poorly understood, it has been identified as one of the most common problems among school-age children in this country. An estimated 5% to 10% of schoolchildren are believed to be affected by hyperactivity. Males are affected more often than females; reported ratios from 3:1 to 9:1.[1,2]

A multitude of diagnostic terms have been used to describe the behavior and learning problems seen in these children—hyperkinetic syndrome, minimal brain dysfunction, learning disability, and others. The current preferred term is attention deficit disorder (ADD) with hyperactivity.[3] This difficulty with labels indicates the current uncertainty regarding etiology and the tendency to emphasize symptoms rather than the overall problem. It may be that the hyperactive child syndrome is really a group of varying disorders with different etiologies.

Using the diagnostic criteria of the American Psychiatric Association,[3] a child with this disorder would display for his mental and chronological age, inappropriate inattention, impulsivity, and hyperactivity. Signs must be observed by adults in the child's environment. Specific criteria for diagnosis include:

1. Inattention
2. Impulsivity
3. Hyperactivity
4. Onset before 7 years of age
5. Duration of at least 6 months
6. Not a result of schizophrenia, affective disorder, or mental retardation

Although a true diagnosis of hyperactivity is a result of assessment by medical and/or educational specialists, many children are often labeled hyperactive by less formal measures of behavior in the school or home. Regardless of the looseness of the diagnosis, the main focus of those involved with the child becomes treatment and management.

ETIOLOGY OF HYPERACTIVITY

A variety of causes of the attention deficit disorder have been proposed over the years, yet the etiology remains relatively unknown. It is quite possible that there may be various etiologies, with hyperactivity and its associated behaviors being the common expression.

Perinatal complications such as anoxia, toxemia, prematurity, and infection have long been suggested as causes, as have insults during the early years, including head injuries, seizures, toxic agents, or infections. There is some suggestion of a genetic component, with an increased family history of hyperactivity and learning disabilities in the identified children.[4,5]

Dietary factors have also been implicated as

215

causes of hyperactivity. One of the most well-known theories is that proposed by Feingold,[6] who identifies salicylate compounds and food additives as causes. Some experts also suggest that food allergy is highly correlated to the incidence of the syndrome, with basic foods such as milk, wheat, and egg being common culprits.[7] Of any foodstuff, sugar is most often pinpointed currently as a cause of hyperactivity and behavior disturbances, primarily in the popular media.

Other environmental factors that have been suggested in the etiology include exposure to fluorescent lights and heavy metals such as lead. An unstable home environment or poor emotional relationships can also cause a child to exhibit some of the symptoms of hyperactivity.

More recent evidence suggests a biochemical basis for the hyperactive child syndrome. Although a disorder in serotonin metabolism has been implicated in this disorder, subsequent research has not supported the association. However, studies of cerebrospinal fluid in children have provided evidence that the metabolism of the catecholamine dopamine may be involved in the mechanism.[8]

Concurrent research has also suggested that nutrients can modify behavior in humans much the same way that drugs do. Tryptophan as a seratonin precursor and tyrosine as a precursor of dopamine and norepinephrine given in controlled doses have demonstrated changes in mood and behavior.[9] This new information puts forth the possibility of treating neurological diseases with precursor nutrients, but whether this would be applicable to the attention deficit disorder is unknown.

In general, the etiology of hyperactivity continues to be a puzzle. Some of the proposed causes are mere associations without supportive data. Further investigations are needed to increase our understanding of the etiology of hyperactivity.

TREATMENT

The most widely used and accepted forms of therapy for hyperactivity are medication, behavioral management, and special education. Stimulant medication has been used for more than 40 years and its effectiveness is well documented.[10] The most commonly used drug is methylphenidate (Ritalin), with dextroamphetamine (Dexedrine) and pemoline (Cylert) used less frequently. Although the exact mechanism by which these drugs work is not fully understood, hyperactive children respond to the medication with reduction in such undesirable behaviors as motor restlessness, short attention span, and irritability. When the child is calmed down and is paying more attention, the assumption has been made that academic performance will improve. Recent evidence, however, suggests that stimulant drugs do not necessarily improve school learning and that long-term outcomes are no different from those of children who have no medication.[2,11]

For a long time it was believed that hyperactive children responded to stimulant medication paradoxically; i.e., their hyperactivity was reduced, and nonhyperactive children were thought to be stimulated by the drug. Newer studies, however, have demonstrated that both hyperactive and nonhyperactive children respond to stimulant medication similarly with decreased activity and improved cognitive performance.[12] Some specialists believe that long-term treatment of hyperactivity should emphasize behavior modification, parental counseling, and special school programs. Yet, stimulant medication continues to be the most common therapy.

Dietary treatments of the hyperactivity syndrome have become more popular in the last decade. Included in this group are diets that eliminate certain constituents (e.g., food additives, salicylate compounds, and sugar) and megavitamin therapy. These diets and megavitamin therapy are discussed in depth later.

STIMULANT MEDICATION AND ITS EFFECT ON GROWTH

One of the appeals of stimulant medication is its immediate dramatic effect with few toxic side effects. Anorexia is often noted as a side effect, but most authorities believe that this disappears or at least diminishes after a few weeks. Some weight loss is also initially reported, but generally it is believed to be transient. These assumptions have been supported by evidence that tolerance to stimulant drugs develops in the treatment of obesity.

Safer, Allen, and Barr[13] first reported in 1972 on the negative effects of stimulant medication on physical growth. They found that hyperactive children receiving dextroamphetamine and methylphenidate had suppressed weight gain and height increase as compared with established norms. A later study showed that long-term use of dextroamphetamine resulted in a highly significant suppression of growth in weight and height. Methylphenidate caused a less striking growth suppression and only when the dosage was 20 mg/day or more. Safer and Allen[14] reported that tolerance developed to the weight-suppressant effects of dextroamphetamine after 3 years, but a tolerance to its inhibition of height growth did not develop.

In a subsequent report Safer, Allen, and Barr[15] presented data demonstrating a growth rebound in children who discontinued medication during the summer. The growth rates were 15% to 68% above the expected increment for the age groups. These findings suggested that, in general, the degree of growth rebound is proportional to the degree of original drug suppression. Depending on the drug and dosage, however, a child may not be able to completely compensate in the summer for the growth suppression incurred during the school year.

Other reports have resulted in inconsistent findings.[16] Gross[17] reported growths in weight and height greater than expected after the children were receiving medication for more than 3 years. Although most investigations have dealt mainly with dextroamphetamine and methylphenidate, pemoline (Cylert) seems to have the same growth-suppressing effect.[18,19] Many of these studies had methodological problems such as inexact methods for growth measurements, inadequate controls, and outdated growth norms.

Mattes and Gittelman[20] recently reported on the growth of 86 hyperactive children who received methylphenidate for up to 4 years. Height was significantly decreased after 2 to 4 years of treatment but not after 1 year. Significant weight loss occurred from the first year of treatment. There was a significant relationship between dosage and decreased growth, and larger children had greater growth decrements. Although the magnitude of the drug effect was only about 2% of the variance in final height, the authors believed that growth should be monitored in these children receiving stimulant medication and dosage reductions considered in individual cases.

There appears to be considerable evidence that stimulant drugs moderately suppress growth in weight and also result in minor suppression of stature increase.[16] Higher doses seem to result in more growth suppression. Any diminished growth in the prepubertal child is apparently not evident in adulthood. However, the effects of treatment during puberty and adolescence is not known. Weiss and others[21] suggest discontinuing the use of stimulants for adolescents a year or two before closure of the epiphyses.

The mechanism by which stimulant medication inhibits growth is unclear. Theories that have been postulated include (1) decreased energy intake resulting from the anorexia, (2) inhibition of growth hormone secretion, (3) decreased production of somatomedin, (4) direct effect on bone and cartilage development, and (5) depressed blood prolactin levels.[16,18,22,23] For many of these proposed mechanisms, the data are conflicting and sketchy.

Two clinical case studies have documented the effect of stimulant drugs on nutrient and energy intakes.[24] In both boys, who were followed for 12 months, energy intakes were reduced when receiving medication, significantly so at higher levels. Methylphenidate appeared to have a less severe effect on energy intake than did dextroamphetamine. Increasing the drug dosage resulted in decreased kilocalorie levels (Fig. 8-1). This suggests that actual reduced food consumption and subsequent low energy intakes may explain the

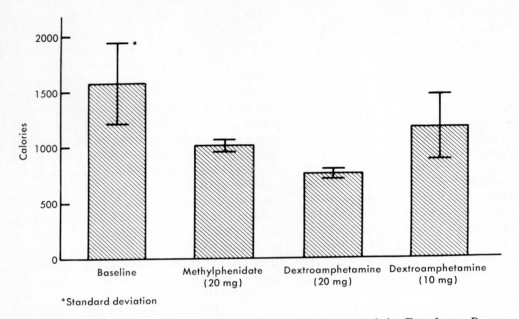

*Standard deviation

Fig. 8-1. Calorie intake of one subject during baseline and drug therapy periods. (From Lucas, B., and Sells, C.J.: Nutrient intake and stimulant drugs in hyperactive children, J. Am. Diet. Assoc. **70:**373, 1977.)

growth retardation in these children. However, it is quite possible that a combination of reduced energy intake and drug-induced endocrine abnormalities may be involved.

Numerous clinical observations indicate that hyperactive children receiving stimulant medication tend to present a variety of feeding problems. Families and school personnel often report pickiness, dawdling at mealtime, school lunches refused or returned home, and disinterest in food. Some children have been observed to consume large amounts of concentrated carbohydrates and other low-nutrient foods because parents are concerned that the child eat something. Because of their children's poor appetites and slow growth, families frequently resort to bribery, indulgence, and threats to induce them to eat. It is easy to understand how a preoccupation with food and eating can lead to frustration for parents and children, resulting in inappropriate behaviors and interac-

tions at mealtimes. When the children discontinue medication during vacations, dramatic increases in appetite and food consumption are often noted by parents.

Since it has been estimated that approximately 300,000 children in the United States are receiving stimulant medication,[25] it is reasonable to assume that a significant number of them may be at risk for suppression of optimal physical growth. For health professionals and educators working with these children, the efficacy of the medication should be assessed periodically using standard double-blind procedures. Frequent monitoring of height and weight is essential to follow longitudinal changes in growth.

As for practical dietary management, it is important to know the type of drug, dosage, and time of administration. Since the drug effect takes approximately 30 minutes to be clinically manifested, meals should be offered with or before the medication dose to take advantage of optimal appetite. The drug effect is usually minimal or absent after 4 to 6 hours, and energy-producing foods of high-nutrient density should be offered at that time. Each child should be evaluated individually with regard to drug administration, meal and snack routine, and appetite response. Coordinating the child's daily schedule is essential to provide optimal nutritional status and physical growth. Some families may benefit from counseling regarding specific feeding problems.

FOOD ADDITIVES

In recent years the idea that chemicals added to food can cause children to exhibit a variety of behavior patterns such as restlessness, irritability, and short attention span has become popular. One of the most well-known proponents of this idea was Benjamin Feingold, an allergist and the author of a popular book on the subject of diet and hyperactivity.[6] He proposed that the cause of hyperactivity is related to the intake of artificial colors and flavors. He correlated the increased incidence of hyperactivity and learning disabilities with increased use of these substances in our food supply over the past few decades.

As an allergist, Feingold developed this theory as an outcome of clinical work with allergy patients. Many patients were sensitive to aspirin, which contains salicylate. This then led to the elimination of natural foods containing salicylate. In addition, since many individuals were also allergic to tartrazine (a yellow dye), all artificial flavors and colors became suspect and were also eliminated.

It is worth noting that these artificial colors and flavors are widespread in our food supply. Of some 2800 intentional additives used in foods, approximately 2100 are flavorings and 31 are colors, most of which are synthetic.[26] Most concerns regarding additives center on safety issues and potential carcinogenicity. Two specific substances, however, apparently cause adverse physical reactions in sus-ceptible individuals. These are monosodium glutamate, which precipitates the Chinese restaurant syndrome, and tartrazine, which causes an allergic response in persons who are also sensitive to aspirin.[27,28]

The Feingold Diet

Feingold's thesis is that some individuals are genetically predisposed to react to these salicylate compounds and low molecular weight chemicals, but that the response is not an allergic reaction. An "innate releasing mechanism" is believed to be involved in the disturbance.[6]

The Feingold diet is based on eliminating all foods containing natural salicylates (box on p. 220), all artificial colors and flavors, and the preservatives butylated hydroxyanisole (BHA) and butylated hydroxytoluene (BHT). Besides foods, items also excluded are aspirin, toothpaste, cough syrup, vitamins, and most medications for children. The entire family is encouraged to follow the diet, rather than isolating the child. In most cases, more time and energy are required for menu planning, shopping, and food preparation. Reading labels is essential, and most mixed and prepared foods must be made from scratch. For many families this new emphasis on food constitutes a major change in their life-styles.

After a child responds positively to the Feingold diet for approximately 4 to 6 weeks, the natural fruits and vegetables are gradually reintroduced to the child's diet as tolerated. This is commonly referred to as the modified Feingold diet. Interestingly, most of the data on natural sources of salicylates are old and are based on less sophisticated techniques than are available today. More recent analysis of some of the foods prohibited in the Feingold diet have found no measurable levels of salicylate in grapefruit, lemons, oranges, tangelos, strawberries, and almonds.[29] Actual implementation of the Feingold diet is found to be varied in individual families. In some cases other food items such as sugar and milk are also restricted in the child's diet.

Food Containing Natural Salicylates

Almonds	Mint leaves
Apples	Nectarines
Cider and cider vinegars	Oranges
Apricots	Peaches
Blackberries	Prunes and plums
Cherries	Raspberries
Cloves	Strawberries
Cucumbers and pickles	Tea, all kinds
Currants	Tomatoes
Gooseberries	Oil of wintergreen
Grapes and raisins	
Wine and wine vinegars	

From Feingold, B.F.: Hyperkinesis and learning disabilities linked to artificial food flavors and colors. Copyright 1975, American Journal of Nursing Company. Reproduced with permission from the American Journal of Nursing, May 1975, vol. 75, no. 5.

A response rate of approximately 48% has been reported by Feingold.[6] He believed that most of the failure to respond to the diet was caused by poor compliance with the program. Feingold was criticized because of the lack of control studies, primarily subjective data, and failure to report findings in reputed journals. Despite these criticisms, the diet became popular with the general public.

The National Advisory Committee on Hyperkinesis and Food Additives was formed to deal with the issue. Their report was critical of the lack of double-blind controlled experiments on Feingold's theory.[30] Questions were raised as to how adoption of the diet affected family dynamics and interaction, whether suggestibility and expected improvements were factors, and whether ratings that were global and subjective rather than specific and objective were valid. Subsequently, the committee established guidelines for experimental studies to test the Feingold hypothesis.

Experiments on the Feingold Diet

Some initial reports showed marked improvement in children who were maintained on the Feingold diet.[31-33] In most instances, however, no control group or standardized objective ratings were used. In addition, the families knew they were trying the Feingold regimen.

One of the first double-blind controlled studies on the Feingold diet was conducted by Conners and others[34] with 15 children and two diets (the Feingold diet and a control diet). Some improvement in behavior was noted while the children were on the Feingold diet, but only teachers' ratings were significant. There was difficulty in disguising the different diets from the families, and there were inconsistencies in the findings when the diet order was changed.

The same investigators later reported on 16 hyperactive children who showed a minimum 25% improvement in behavior while on the Feingold diet. The children completed an 8-week double-blind challenge period in which they continued on the diet but were given specially prepared chocolate cookies with or without artificial color additives. The results showed no difference in behavioral parameters between challenge and placebo periods. Interesting findings, however, included indications that younger children were more susceptible to the challenge, and that a greater number of performance deficits were noted when measured 1 to 2 hours after ingestion of the cookies with the additives. A subsequent phase of the experiment showed some deterioration in behavior when parents rated younger children within 3 hours of the challenge, suggesting a transient pharmacological effect of the additives.[35]

A group of Australian investigators also considered the issue of possible time-limited effects. Using tartrazine as a challenge substance, they found no difference between challenge and placebo periods for the entire sample of 22 children. However, when they selected a subgroup of those children less than 8 years of age who showed a 25% improvement in behavior, there was a significant increase in symptoms immediately following the challenge.[36] Further replications of these findings are needed.

Harley and others[37] conducted a study with 36 school-age boys and 10 preschool boys by using the Feingold diet with a control diet. An ambitious study design included supplying all the food for the families weekly, as well as providing food for school snacks and parties. When evaluated by neurological, psychological, and behavioral parameters, the results showed no significant improvement in the school-age boys. Ratings of the preschoolers showed a positive response to the diet, but the sample size was small and only parents reported. In a subsequent phase of the study, nine of the original children who had shown some positive response to the diet were put through a challenge regimen for 9 weeks. This consisted of maintaining the Feingold diet and adding cookies or candy bars with or without the food color additives. No significant differences were noted between challenge and placebo, but one child did appear to respond with alterations in behaviors.[38]

In another study, comparison was made between the effect of the Feingold diet and use of stimulant medication.[39] Four different treatments were used for a week at a time: medication or placebo plus the diet with or without the additives. The ratings indicated some improvement with the Feingold diet, but stimulant medication was more effective than diet in decreasing hyperactive behaviors. On the other hand, teacher ratings suggested that the behavior was worse when the children were receiving placebo medication and the additives.

Weiss and others[40] studied 22 children 2½ to 7 years of age whose parents thought they were "super responders" to the Feingold regimen but who had not been diagnosed as hyperactive. In a double-blind trial, the children continued on the diet for 11 weeks but were challenged eight times with a carbonated beverage containing food color additives, receiving a placebo beverage the other days. Two children responded adversely to the additives when rated by parents and observers, one dramatically.

One of the criticisms of the controlled challenge study design is that the dose of additives has not been large enough to produce a response. Most of the studies have used 27 to 35 mg/day of mixed artificial colors in their challenge material—an amount that is supposed to represent an average intake for American children. Canadian researchers have recently suggested that the reaction to the additives may be related to dosage. Using a hospital clinical research unit, they challenged 40 children with 100 to 150 mg of the artificial colors and then measured response by a laboratory learning test rather than ratings.[41] The children's performance was significantly worse after receiving the challenge than after receiving the placebo, supporting the dose/response relationship. On the other hand, this information does not support Feingold's contention that even a single minor infraction of the diet causes a dramatic change in behavior. This study also suggests that laboratory learning tests may be a more sensitive measure of additive response than the behavior rating scales.

The nutritional adequacy of the Feingold diet was first assessed by Conners and others.[34] They found that the diet produced poorer nutrient intakes than the control diet but that it still met the recommended dietary allowances. Intakes of ascorbic acid were particularly low because of the exclusion of the natural salicylate-containing foods, many of which are excellent sources of this vitamin. In a later report, the modified Feingold diet (eliminating only artificial colors and flavors) was analyzed for nutrient adequacy.[42] Food records for 54 children were collected and calculated during baseline and diet periods. Mean intakes compared favorably with the recommended dietary allowances, and nutrient intakes did not change significantly while the subjects were on the Feingold regimen. The assumption might be made that the overall nutrient quality of the modified Feingold diet might be better than a control diet, since many foods containing the artificial flavors and colors are low nutrient–density items. A market survey in this study, however, showed that in each category of foods there were foods free of the additives that were of comparable nutritional quality to those foods excluded.

Overall, the controlled double-blind studies have not supported the Feingold diet as an effective therapy for hyperactivity.[43,44] The positive response that has been reported in uncontrolled studies and open trials is believed to be a placebo effect and/or the result of a significant change in the socioemotional environment of the child. It is certainly understandable that a family with a hyperactive child might expect a positive outcome from a diet that is relatively simple and without side effects. In addition, the focus on the dietary regimen may change the family setting, e.g., by bringing them together on a mutual project, giving positive attention to the hyperactive child, and lessening blame—changes that could result in a decrease in behaviors. The findings by one researcher that parents of children on the Feingold regimen were more rigid and controlling suggests that family structure and interaction may be critical in the use and success of the diet.[45]

On the other hand, evidence does exist that a small subgroup of hyperactive children benefit significantly from the diet. The research data suggest that the Feingold diet is effective for approximately 1 out of every 50 hyperactive children.[46,47] Although this calculated incidence of 2% is far from the 50% success rate reported by Feingold, it remains that some hyperactive children, perhaps 5% to 10%, will be dramatically improved on the regimen. The summary of a National Institutes of Health symposium on defined diets and hyperactivity states "The Panel believes the defined diets should not be universally used in the treatment of childhood hyperactivity at this time. However, the Panel recognizes that initiation of a trial of dietary treatment or continuation of a diet in patients whose families and physicians perceive benefits, may be warranted."[43]

Many unknowns remain regarding food additives and behavior in children. Although there is little need to replicate all of the previously cited studies, it is hoped that future investigations will shed more light on the issue. Areas deserving more research include the suggestion that preschool children are more susceptible, the question of whether there is an immediate pharmacological-related response, and the possibility of an additive dose/behavior relationship. Current interest and research in behavioral toxicology may provide new information in the future.

The Feingold diet has been tried, or is being currently used, by thousands of children in the United States. The nonprofit National Feingold Association has approximately 100 local associations, whose primary purpose is to assist families in adapting to the program. From a clinical management standpoint, care should be taken to do a comprehensive assessment of the hyperactivity in the individual child and to discuss the various management options with the parents. For those parents who wish to use the dietary approach and who believe that it works, the reality of improvement cannot and should not be denied regardless of the source(s) of that improvement. In addition, the modified Feingold diet, as long as it includes a wide variety of foods, can be quite adequate nutritionally. Positive effects may include improved nutrition for the entire family and more interest in the topic. Health professionals should take care, however, to counsel the family not to disregard the potential help provided by special education, behavioral management, and other therapy modalities that can combine appropriately with the diet.

MEGAVITAMIN THERAPY

The use of large doses of certain vitamins to treat hyperactivity and minimal brain dysfunction has become increasingly popular in recent years. Originating primarily from the popular press, lay groups, and some professionals, megavitamin therapy is loosely defined and varies a great deal in practice from individual to individual. It is also a component of "orthomolecular psychiatry," which is defined by Pauling[48] as "the achievement and preservation of mental health by varying the concentrations in the human body of subtances that are normally present, such as the vitamins." The basis of megavitamin therapy is that hyperactive children have biochemical imbalances and that these disturbances can be eliminated by the consumption of large amounts of certain vitamins.

Megavitamin therapy was first used to treat schizophrenia, using nicotinic acid.[49] Currently, proponents of this treatment recommend its use for a variety of disorders including hyperactivity, autism, mental retardation, and degenerative diseases. Suspecting vitamin deficiency as a cause of mental and behavioral problems is a result of existing nutritional knowledge on deficiency states. Classic examples are the neurological and mental changes noted in persons with niacin deficiency (pellagra) and thiamine deficiency (beriberi).

Most commonly, megavitamin therapy includes niacin, ascorbic acid, pyridoxine, and calcium pantothenate. On the other hand, personal clinical experience has indicated that children receiving megavitamin therapy may be taking a wide assortment of vitamin and/or mineral supplements with or without expert guidance.

Generally, established medical professionals have not supported the megavitamin theory of treatment. A task force report of the American Psychiatric Association concluded that the claims of megavitamin advocates have not been confirmed by well-controlled studies and that most of the data are anecdotal.[49] Similarly, a statement by the American Academy of Pediatrics[50] reported that "megavitamin therapy as a treatment for learning disabilities and psychoses in children, including autism, is not justified on the basis of documented clinical trials."

Two recent studies have tested megavitamin therapy using double-blind controlled studies. Arnold and others[51] reported on 31 children with minimal brain dysfunction who received either placebos or megavitamins during a 2-week trial. The megavitamin regimen was that advocated by Cott—1 gm of niacin, 1 gm of ascorbic acid, 100 mg of pyridoxine, 200 mg of pantothenate calcium, and 500 mg of glutamic acid, all twice daily. Parent and teacher behavior ratings taken before and after the trial showed no significant difference in the two groups. Only two children responded so well that stimulant medication was not considered necessary; they were both in the placebo group.

In an investigation by Kershner and Hawke,[52] 20 children with learning disabilities were put on a low-carbohydrate, high-protein diet and then given either megavitamins or placebos for 6 months. They were evaluated before and after this period with a combination of intellectual, school achievement, perceptual, and behavioral measures. Results showed no difference between the two groups and thus failed to support the claim that megavitamins are helpful to children with learning disabilities. Most of the children, regardless of their group, showed behavioral progress; this may be a result of the diet alone or it may be a placebo effect. Both of these studies were unable to support the theories advocated by the proponents of megavitamin therapy.

Potential dangers do exist from consuming large doses of vitamins, although the literature is not extensive and reports on children are relatively few. Toxicity from excess fat-soluble vitamins (A and D) has been documented.[53] Although these vitamins are not included in the standard megavitamin treatment, clinical experience reveals that some practitioners commonly recommend vitamins A and D or that families may, on their own initiative, include them in their regimen. Other biochemical complications that have been reported are the destruction of vitamin B_{12} by large amounts of ascorbic acid, hyperbilirubinemia and liver damage by large doses of nicotinic acid, and liver damage by large doses of vitamin B_6.[54,55] A case of severe vitamin A intoxication has been reported for a 4-year-old child who was receiving megavitamins for minimal brain dysfunction.[56] In another case, an 11-year-old boy who had been taking megavitamins for 4 years developed cholelithiasis, hepatitis, and thyroid dysfunction; he became well after a cholecystectomy and discontinuation of megavitamins.[57] Megavitamin therapy as an unfounded treatment for mental retardation is discussed in Chapter 12.

It is easy to understand why a family with a troubled child would respond to the appeal of megavitamin therapy. But too often it plays on the false hopes and guilt of the parents or provides a subject for blame. Some families can spend considerable money on vitamins and yet not deal with the basic problem related to the child's behavior.

There is no sound data to support the use of megavitamins with hyperactive children, yet the concept that some individuals may have increased needs for certain nutrients cannot be ignored. From a practical standpoint, the nutritional status of each child should be assessed and appropriate dietary intervention should be planned. In working with parents who choose to use megavitamins for their child, one needs to help them to recognize the practice as helpful, neutral, or harmful and to provide accurate information. At times counseling may be indicated to help families recognize and consider other treatment options.

SUGAR

Sugar (sucrose) has been implicated, mainly in popular books and anecdotal reports, as a causative factor in a multitude of diseases and disorders. Included in this group of disorders are diabetes, obesity, heart disease, and hypoglycemia, as well as mental and behavioral disorders such as hyperactivity, depression and psychoses. One practitioner believes that sugar is the most common food substance causing adverse behavior reactions in children.[58] In addition, parents, teachers, and school nurses report dramatic negative changes in some children after receiving a load of sugar. Anecdotal stories describe children "climbing the walls" the day after Halloween. All these reports, however, are subjective and are not based on controlled studies.

One popularly held theory is that undesirable behavior is the result of low or fluctuating blood glucose levels in some individuals. Langseth and Dowd[59] supported this theory in 1978 when they reported that nearly 75% of 261 hyperkinetic children had abnormal glucose tolerance curves following a 5-hour glucose tolerance test. Half of the curves were low and flat, similar to those seen in individuals with hypoglycemia. Lack of a control comparison group and controversy regarding glucose tolerance standards in children, however, make this data less conclusive. Other studies have not found abnormal glucose curves.[60] In another study, normal young adults were given a sugar solution (100 gm sucrose), saccharin solution, or water and completed a self-reported mood scale 20 minutes and 4 hours later. There were no significant mood changes in any of the groups, except the sugar group reported less anxiety after 4 hours.[61]

A report by Prinz, Roberts, and Hantman[62] suggested that there was a positive association between sugar consumption and destructive-aggressive behavior in 4- to 7-year-old children. The dietary data, however, were not adequately documented or analyzed. Rapoport[60] also studied sugar and behavior in 21 boys whose parents believed responded adversely to sugar. Behavior ratings, motor activity, memory, and blood levels were monitored for 5 hours after a double-blind challenge of glucose, sucrose, or saccharin. They found no significant effect of sugar on any of the behavioral measures in these children. Although many people believe that a high sugar intake will increase hyperactive behavior, Rapoport found the opposite. The children were less active and quieter after the sugar ingestion compared with those given the placebo. These results may be compatible with the theory that a high carbohydrate intake facilitates production of serotonin, or they may be the result of other unknown factors.

At this time the only direct cause/effect relationship between sugar and disease is the role of sugar in dental caries; no such relationship exists with other diseases. More well-designed investigations of the correlation between sugar intake and behavior are needed.

As a people, Americans consume large amounts of sugar, more than 100 lb per capita per year. It has been estimated that sugar represents approximately 24% of the average energy intake.[63] Many foodstuffs that are high in sugar are low in nutrients, and thus they dilute the nutrient quality of the diet. Indeed, reducing or eliminating sugar in the diet serves to improve the overall nutritional and dental health of both child and family. These positive changes in families' diets have been observed in personal clinical experience. The professional can reinforce the dietary changes while stressing the lack of data supporting a sugar/behavior association.

ALLERGY

Food allergies are known to produce respiratory, gastrointestinal, and/or skin manifestations in the susceptible individual. Some experts also believe that they cause behaviors commonly found in hyperactive children—excessive activity, lack of attention, and irritability.[7] True allergies are a result of the production of antibodies against specific proteins in the foods that the child eats. The most common food allergies are the proteins of milk, egg white, and wheat.

There have been reports indicating that hyperactive children have a higher incidence of food allergies and that they respond positively to an elimination diet, thus supporting a causal relationship between food allergies and hyperactivity.[7,64,65] A recent report suggests that a 7-day fast supplemented with an elemental formula can be a useful diagnostic procedure in determining those hyperactive children who are food hypersensitive by measuring an improved behavior response.[66] Some of these reports are subjective, however, and controversy exists regarding the validity and interpretation of the allergy tests used.

In cases in which food allergy is suspected, it is appropriate to obtain a thorough diagnosis by an expert clinician, including a double-blind food challenge.[67] However, there is no guarantee that behavioral symptoms will improve. Currently, no strong evidence is available to support a direct relationship between food allergy and hyperactivity; but the possibility that some children have adverse behavior reactions to food, whether they be immunological reactions or not, cannot be ruled out.

For a further discussion of food allergies, see Chapter 10.

SUMMARY

The role of diet in hyperactivity seems to produce more questions than answers. Although no sound data have definitively implicated dietary factors as causes or shown dramatic improvement as a result of diet treatment, not all the evidence is clear-cut. Studies of free-living populations have their design and control limitations; other investigations remain to be done.

The various proposed dietary treatments for hyperactivity have not been supported by documentation. It appears that a small percentage of children, however, may be susceptible to certain substances in foods (i.e., color and flavor additives), and it cannot be ruled out that some children might react to large amounts of commonly consumed foods. On the other hand, it remains difficult to ascertain the environmental and emotional aspects that may affect a child's behavior.

For the professionals working with these children and their families, it is important that an objective and comprehensive assessment and diagnosis be done initially. Children using stimulant medication should have their physical growth monitored frequently, and nutritional counseling should be available as needed.

When working with families who are using some of the dietary approaches (e.g., Feingold diet, megavitamins, sugar-free diet), remaining open-minded and objective is critical. In that way rapport can be maintained, and thus the professional continues to be a resource. For the individual child, the actual dietary practices should be assessed as to adequacy and rationale. Obviously, positive changes in the diet should be reinforced, such as decreasing sugar consumption or using more nutrient-dense foods. Practices that are undesirable or potentially harmful (such as some megavitamin doses) can be discussed with the family on a factual level and incorporated in any decisions to change. Lecturing or emotional appeals are usually not productive.

Hyperactive children tend to be very difficult to manage and hard to live with. Their families deserve a lot of credit for doing as well as they do in handling the symptoms and subsequent problems. It is certainly a relief to them, then, when a dietary treatment decreases the negative behaviors and makes their child more enjoyable and less stress-producing for the family. Despite whatever components were involved in the change, their success is real and should not be denied.

The years to come will no doubt bring more information and definitive answers to the questions posed by this topic.

SUGGESTED LEARNING ACTIVITIES

1. Prepare a talk for a parent group on the relationship of diet and hyperactivity.
2. Check a drug store or a health food store for vitamin and mineral supplements for children. Compare the nutrient dosage levels and the costs of the supplements.
3. Assess the nutritional status of a child who has been on long-term stimulant medication. What is his growth pattern? Is his appetite and nutrient intake appropriate?
4. Obtain a 3-day food record for a 7- to 9-year-old child. Modify the menus to fit the Feingold diet, making substitutions for food items eliminated. Determine nutrient adequacy of the modified diet.
5. Plan a list of snacks representing all food groups that would contain no sucrose but that would be acceptable to school-age children.

REFERENCES

1. Safer, D.J., and Allen, R.P.: Hyperactive children: diagnosis and management, Baltimore, 1976, University Park Press.
2. Weiss, G., and Hechtman, L.: The hyperactive child syndrome, Science **205:**1348, 1979.
3. American Psychiatric Association task force on nomenclature and statistics: Diagnostic and statistical manual of mental disorders, ed. 3, Washington, D.C., 1980, The Association.
4. Millichap, J.G.: The hyperactive child with minimal brain dysfunction, Chicago, 1975, Year Book Medical Publishers, Inc.
5. Wender, P.H.: Minimal brain dysfunction in children, New York, 1971, John Wiley & Sons, Inc.
6. Feingold, B.F.: Why your child is hyperactive, New York, 1974, Random House, Inc.
7. Crook, W.G.: Food allergy—the great masquerader, Pediatr. Clin. North Am. **22:**227, 1975.
8. Shaywitz, S.E., Cohen, D.J., and Shaywitz, B.A.: The biochemical basis of minimal brain dysfunction, J. Pediatr. **92:**179, 1978.
9. Wurtman, R.J.: Behavioral effects of nutrients, Lancet **1:**1145, 1983.
10. Eisenberg. L.: The clinical use of stimulant drugs in children, Pediatrics **49:**709, 1972.
11. Kolata, G.B.: Childhood hyperactivity: a new look at treatment and causes, Science **199:**515, 1978.

12. Weingartner, H. and others: Cognitive processes in normal and hyperactive children and their response to amphetamine treatment, J. Abnorm. Psychol. **89**:25, 1980.

13. Safer, D.J., Allen, R.P., and Barr, E.: Depression of growth in hyperactive children on stimulant drugs, N. Engl. J. Med. **287**:217, 1972.

14. Safer, D.J., and Allen, R.P.: Factors influencing the suppressant effects of two stimulant drugs on the growth of hyperactive children, Pediatrics **51**:660, 1973.

15. Safer, D.J., Allen, R.P., and Barr, E.: Growth rebound after termination of stimulant drugs, J. Pediatr. **86**:113, 1975.

16. Roche, A.E., and others: The effects of stimulant medication on the growth of hyperkinetic children, Pediatrics **63**:847, 1979.

17. Gross, M.D.: Growth of hyperkinetic children taking methylphenidate, dextroamphetamine, or imipramine/desipramine, Pediatrics **58**:423, 1976.

18. Dickinson, L.C., and others: Impaired growth in hyperkinetic children receiving pemoline, J. Pediatr. **94**:538, 1979.

19. Friedmann, N., and others: Effect on growth in pemoline-treated children with attention deficit disorder, Am. J. Dis. Child. **135**:329, 1981.

20. Mattes, J.A., and Gittelman, R.: Growth of hyperactive children on maintenance regimen of methylphenidate, Arch. Gen. Psychiatry. **40**:317, 1983.

21. Weiss, G., and others: Effect of long-term treatment of hyperactive children with methylphenidate, Can. Med. Assoc. J. **112**:159, 1975.

22. Shaywitz, S.E., and others: Psychopharmacology of attention deficit disorder: pharmacokinetic, neuroendocrine, and behavioral measures following acute and chronic treatment with methylphenidate, Pediatrics **69**:688, 1982.

23. Schultz, F.R., and others: Methylphenidate treatment of hyperactive children: effects on the hypothalamic-pituitary-somatomedin axis, Pediatrics **70**:987, 1982.

24. Lucas, B., and Sells, C.J.: Nutrient intake and stimulant drugs in hyperactive children, J. Am. Diet. Assoc. **70**:373, 1977.

25. Krager, J.M., and Safer, D.J.: Type and prevalence of medication used in the treatment of hyperactive children, N. Engl. J. Med. **291**:1118, 1974.

26. Lehman, P.: More than you ever thought you would know about food additives, FDA Consumer, Department of Health, Education and Welfare Pub. No. (FDA) 79-2115, Washington, D.C., 1979, U.S. Government Printing Office.

27. Nagy, M.: Monosodium glutamate and the "Chinese restaurant syndrome," J.A.M.A. **225**:1665, 1973.

28. Zlotlow, M.J., and Settipane, G.A.: Allergic potential of food additives: a report of a case of tartrazine sensitivity without aspirin intolerance, Am. J. Clin. Nutr. **30**:1023, 1977.

29. Aschoor, S., and Chu, F.S.: Analysis of salicylic acid and methyl salicylate in fruits and almonds, Personal communication, 1978.

30. The National Advisory Committee on Hyperkinesis and Food Additives: Report to the Nutrition Foundation, New York, 1975, The Nutrition Foundation, Inc.

31. Cook, P.S., and Woodhill, J.M.: The Feingold dietary treatment of the hyperkinetic syndrome, Med. J. Aust. **2**:85, 1976.

32. Brenner, A,: A study of the efficacy of the Feingold diet on hyperactive children, Clin. Pediatr. **16**:652, 1977.

33. Salzman, L.K.: Allergy testing, psychological assessment and dietary treatment of the hyperactive child syndrome, Med. J. Aust. **2**:448, 1976.

34. Conners, C.K., and others: Food additives and hyperkinesis: a controlled double-blind experiment, Pedriatrics **58**:154, 1976.

35. Goyette, C.H., and others: Effects of artificial colors on hyperactive children: a double-blind challenge study, Psychopharmacol. Bull. **14**(2):39, 1978.

36. Levy, F., and others: Hyperkinesis and diet: a double-blind crossover trial with a tartrazine challenge, Med. J. Aust. **1**:61, 1978.

37. Harley, J.P., and others: Hyperkinesis and food additives: testing the Feingold hypothesis, Pediatrics **61**:818, 1978.

38. Harley, J.P., Matthews, C.G., and Eichman, P.: Synthetic food colors and hyperactivity in children: a double-blind challenge experiment, Pediatrics **62**:975, 1978.

39. Williams, J.I., and others: Relative effects of drugs and diet on hyperactive behaviors: an experimental study, Pediatrics **61**:811, 1978.

40. Weiss, B., and others: Behavioral responses to artificial food colors, Science **207**:1487, 1980.

41. Swanson, J.M., and Kinsbourne, M.: Food dyes impair performance of hyperactive children on a laboratory learning test, Science **207**:1485, 1980.

42. Harper, P.H., Goyette, C.H., and Conners, C.K.: Nutrient intakes of children on the hyperkinesis diet, J. Am. Diet. Assoc. **73**:515, 1978.

43. National Institutes of Health Consensus Development Conference Summary: Defined diets and childhood hyperactivity, vol. 4, no. 3, Washington, D.C., 1982, The Institutes.

44. Wender, E.H., and Lipton, M.A., Chairmen, National Advisory Committee on Hyperkinesis and Food Additives: Final report to the Nutrition Foundation, New York, 1980, The Nutrition Foundation, Inc.

45. Feingold families found to be "rigid" in discipline, Nutrition Week, No. 20, Washington, D.C., May 19, 1983, Community Nutrition Institute.

46. Wender, E.: Food additives and hyperkinesis, Am. J. Dis. Child. **131**:1204, 1977.

47. Lipton, M.A., and Mayo, J.P.: Diet and hyperkinesis—an update, J. Am. Diet. Assoc. **83**:132, 1983.

48. Pauling, L: On the orthomolecular environment of the mind: orthomolecular therapy, Am. J. Psychiatry **131:**1251, 1974.
49. American Psychiatric Association task force on vitamin therapy: Megavitamins and orthomolecular therapy in psychiatry, Nutr. Rev. Suppl.**1:**44, 1974.
50. Committee on Nutrition, American Academy of Pediatrics: Megavitamin therapy for childhood psychoses and learning disabilities, Pediatrics **58:**910, 1976.
51. Arnold, L.E., and others: Megavitamins for minimal brain dysfunction: a placebo-controlled study, J.A.M.A. **240:**2642, 1978.
52. Kershner, J., and Hawke, W.: Megavitamins and learning disorders: a controlled double-blind experiment, J. Nutr. **109:**819, 1979.
53. Committee on Safety, Toxicity, and Misuse of Vitamins and Trace Minerals, National Nutrition Consortium: Vitamin-mineral safety, toxicity, and misuse, Chicago, 1978, American Dietetic Association.
54. White, P.L.: Megavitamin this and megavitamin that, J.A.M.A. **233:**538, 1975.
55. Winter, S.L., and Boyer, J.L.: Hepatic toxicity from large doses of vitamin B_3 (nicotinamide), N. Engl. J. Med. **289:**1180, 1973.
56. Shaywitz, B.A.: Megavitamins for minimal brain dysfunction: a potentially dangerous therapy, J.A.M.A. **238:**1749, 1977.
57. Wright, K: Personal communication, 1978.
58. Crook, W.G.: Personal communication, 1979.
59. Langseth, L., and Dowd, J.: Glucose tolerance and hyperkinesis, Food Cosmet. Toxicol. **16:**129, 1978.
60. Rapoport, J.L.: Methodology for asssessing effects of dietary substances in grade school children. In Lieberman, H.R., and Wurtman, R.J., editors: Research strategies for assessing the behavioral effects of foods and nutrients, Proceedings of a conference held at the Massachusetts Institute of Technology, Cambridge, Mass., 1982, Center for Brain Sciences and Metabolism Charitable Trust.
61. Brody, S., and Wolitzky, D.L.: Lack of mood changes following sucrose loading, Psychosomatics **24:**155, 1983.
62. Prinz, R.J., Roberts, W.A., and Hantman, E.: Dietary correlates of hyperactive behavior in children, J. Consult. Clin. Psychol. **48:**760, 1980.
63. Select Committee on Nutrition and Human Needs, U.S. Senate: Dietary goals for the United States, ed. 2, Washington, D.C., 1977, U.S. Government Printing Office.
64. Tryphonas, H., and Trites, R.: Food allergy in children with hyperactivity, learning disabilities and/or minimal brain dysfunction, Ann. Allergy **42:**22, 1979.
65. Rapp, D.J.: Does diet affect hyperactivity? J. Learning Disabilities **11:**56, 1978.
66. Hughes, E.C., and others: Food sensitivity in attention deficit disorder with hyperactivity (ADD/HA): a procedure for differential diagnosis, Ann. Allergy **49:**276, 1982.
67. May, C.D.: Diagnosis of hypersensitivity to food. In Committee on Nutrition, American Academy of Pediatrics: Pediatric nutrition handbook, Evanston, Ill., 1979, American Academy of Pediatrics.

Nutrition and the Adolescent 9

BETTY LUCAS
JANE MITCHELL REES
L. KATHLEEN MAHAN

The adolescent period is a unique stage in the process of growth and development. A rapidly changing time of "growing up," it is characterized by a wide variability in norms of growth, increasingly independent behavior, and the testing of adult roles. Adolescence lasts nearly a decade and has no specific beginning or end. This critical period of human development occurs at the physiological, psychological, and social levels. Changes do not occur simultaneously but at varying rates. Thus a teenager may have several ages at the same time—chronological, physical, psychological, and social. Although adolescence may be defined as the teenage years between 12 and 20, physical maturation and changes in nutrient requirements actually begin at younger ages and extend into the third decade.

Teenagers assume greater responsibility for decision making in their lives. Peer and social pressures ask them to choose between drinking or not drinking, smoking or not smoking. In contrast to younger children adolescents themselves most often determine their food intake. Their food choices are a reflection of various factors, including family eating patterns, peer influence, media, appetite, and food availability. Some of these factors can be positive for nutritional quality, and others may leave a lot to be desired.

PHYSICAL GROWTH AND PUBERTY

The velocity of physical growth in adolescence is second only to the rate of growth during infancy. Therefore, there is a high demand for calories and nutrients to support optimal growth. After the relatively latent growth period of childhood, adolescent growth is manifested by an increase in both cell number and size as well as in reproductive maturity. The end of adolescent physical growth is usually signaled by slowing of growth, completion of sexual maturation, and closure of the epiphyses of long bones. This is a general guide, however, and does not apply to other parameters of growth such as psychological and social development.

Up to approximately 9 years of age, males and females grow in height and weight at the same rate, with males slightly larger and heavier. The prepubescent growth period begins about 2 years earlier in females than in males. At this time females temporarily are taller and have a larger limb muscle mass than do males. As pubertal growth proceeds, the male develops more muscle and the skeleton enlarges, particularly in the shoulder region. In the female there is a smaller increase in muscle, but the pelvis rounds out and enlarges because of the deposition of fat. At the beginning of the prepubertal period, many children normally lay down excess fat. If a child has not been fat during earlier years, however, this fat will probably diminish gradually in 1 to 2 years.

The most rapid phase of adolescent growth is known as the growth spurt, and its highest point is called the peak. Growth velocity decelerates from birth until the pubertal growth spurt, at which time the increased growth velocity of a 14-year-old boy is comparable to that of a 2-year-old child. The average peak velocities of height and weight are shown in Table 9-1. It can be noted that although the peak velocity age occurs later in males, it is more intense and results in more tissue accumulation. Findings from the National Health Examination Survey suggest that American adolescents attain their peak height velocity earlier than do English adolescents: three quarters of a year earlier for boys and one quarter of a year earlier for girls.[1] The NHES data, however, are based on a cross-sectional study and cannot be interpreted as longitudinal data.

In females the height spurt signals the beginning of puberty, with pubic hair and breast development being the first notable changes. Menarche occurs at the end of the growth spurt, approximately 9 to 12 months after peak height velocity is attained.[2] The average age for menarche in the United States is about 12.8 years, although the normal range is 10 to 16 years of age.[3] The earlier the onset of menarche, the greater the peak velocity of growth and the less time that elapses between peak velocity and menarche. Early-maturing females do not necessarily become taller, but they do complete their growth spurts more quickly and at younger ages. Some studies indicate that these females have more subcutaneous fat, even from childhood years, and a greater predisposition to obesity.[4,5]

Frisch[6] has proposed the theory that a critical body weight and/or fat composition is necessary to achieve menarche. A minimal level of fatness needed for the onset of menstrual cycles is apparently 17% of body weight as fat, and about 22% of body weight as fat is minimal to maintain regular ovulatory cycles. This theory has been supported by epidemiological data as well as by observations of females with anorexia nervosa, ballet dancers, and well-trained athletes with minimal fat stores who develop amenorrhea or delayed menarche.[7,8] Others, however, have shown that this hypothesis is limited in its application to all adolescent females. Other factors determining onset or delay of menarche include skeletal development, strenuous physical activity, malnutrition, and stress.[9,10]

In males secondary sexual changes (pubic hair, voice changes, penis and testicular growth) indicate the beginning of the growth period. The height spurt occurs toward the end of the growth period. Males actually lose limb fat at the peak height velocity, probably because of testosterone action, whereas females maintain a positive balance of fat without loss of limb fat.

The stage of puberty is usually determined by using the standards of Tanner.[11] From a longitudinal examination of normal children, five stages of pubertal maturation were developed for each sex, beginning with stage 1, the prepubertal child, and ending with stage 5, adult sexual development. These standards of assessment are commonly used in clinical practice today.

Even though it is commonly assumed that full stature is attained by 18 to 20 years of age, data indicate that growth in length can continue for another decade. Results of longitudinal growth studies by Garn and Wagner[12] showed that from 17 to 28 years of age mean height increments were 1.2

Table 9-1. Average peak velocities of height and weight

	Height	Weight
Males		
Peak velocity	10.3 cm/year	9.8 kg/year
Peak velocity age	14.1 years	14.3 years
Females		
Peak velocity	9.0 cm/year	8.8 kg/year
Peak velocity age	12.1 years	12.9 years

Adapted from Tanner, J.M., Whitehouse, R.H., and Takaishi, M.: Arch. Dis. Child. **41**:454, 1966.

cm for females and 2.3 cm for males. This growth is believed to be primarily vertebral.

In relation to skeletal growth, it must be remembered that stature is not an indicative measure of skeletal mass. At 10 years of age approximately 80% of maximum stature has been attained, but only 50% of adult skeletal mass has been gained. Garn and Wagner[12] report that skeletal mass increases into the fourth decade, about 4% for males and 6% for females after 18 years of age. The continued increase in both skeletal length and mass indicates the need for ongoing calcium retention for a longer period than has been commonly accepted.

Development of sophisticated methodology has enabled the prediction of eventual adult height in children and adolescents. The data used include the Bayley tables[13] combined with the Greulich-Pyle skeletal atlas[14] to predict height based on present age, height, and bone age. In addition, Tanner and others[15] formulated an equation for adult height that is based on present height, bone age, and age at menarche for females, with allowance for midparent height.

Sex differences in body composition begin in infancy but are most dramatic by adolescence. Percent of lean body mass rises in adolescents, especially in males, who finish growth with 1.5 times the lean body mass of females. Studies of longitudinal growth parameters in males have shown that the peak increment in lean body mass coincides with peaks in height and weight and suggest that growth trends in height and lean body mass are more constant than trends in body weight.[16] Fat content is higher in the female after approximately the twelfth year, and by the end of the second decade, it is 1.5 to 2 times the male value. Correspondingly, the female has a lower percentage of body water than does the male. Because of these significant sex differences in the body composition of the adolescent, total body weight alone is not a valid measure with which to assess growth or to predict nutrient requirements.

Over the last century or more, growth records throughout the world have indicated secular trends in growth. These reports show that children are growing taller and weighing more with each generation. In addition, there has also been evidence for earlier sexual maturation, but this has stabilized in recent decades.[17] This early maturation is primarily responsible for children being taller and weighing more at one particular age. There is a shorter growth period and earlier cessation of growth. The eventual adult size has not, however, increased as dramatically. A 10-year-old boy in 1875 might have been only 50% of the way through his growth period, whereas a 10-year-old boy today might be 60% to 65% mature. Greulich[18] has compared growth parameters of American-born Japanese children in 1956 with data 15 years later and found little difference in heights and weights. This and other evidence suggests that growth trends have reached a plateau in developed countries in the past 30 to 40 years.

These factors of puberty—rapid physical growth, sexual maturation, and changes in appearance and body shape—have a significant impact on the adolescent's self-esteem, body image, and personality. Because of the wide variability of rates of growth and their timing, there are no "norms" for adolescent growth in conjunction with chronological age. Our culture does dicate some standards, variable although they may be, and adolescents continually compare themselves to these standards or to their peers. No other age group is as concerned and sensitive about their bodies or as devastated by criticism and comparison as are adolescents. This is particulary true of the obese adolescent and the early or late maturer. It is not unusual to find these adolescents with distorted body images making inappropriate food choices and thus compromising optimal growth.

ENERGY AND NUTRIENT REQUIREMENTS

Since no period of growth is less predictable than adolescence, nutrient allowances are only estimates and should not be applied to individuals. Indeed, most of the allowances have been extrapolated from data on young children and adults. Basically, the highest nutrient and energy demands occur at the peak velocity of growth, thus paralleling the growth rate. Requirements, then, should be determined by sex, age, stage of puberty, and current growth parameters.

Energy

Until the recent revision of the recommended dietary allowances, energy allowances were based on the average kilocalories for adolescent age groups (11 to 14 years of age, 15 to 18 years of age). It is obvious that those standards could not be appropriately applied to individuals with varying rates of growth. The current recommended dietary allowances use the same age groups, but include a range of kilocalories for each group and sex. Thus, the range of energy intake for 11- to 14-year-old females is 1500 to 3000 kcal; for 15- to 18-year-old males, it is 2100 to 3900 kcal;[19] These allowances represent an increase of 85% to 150% from minimun to maximun kilocalories.

One of the earliest studies of energy intakes, reported by Wait and Roberts in 1932, was based on studies of 52 females 10 to 16 years of age.[20] The variation in size and intake at any age is demonstrated by noting that the 12-year-old girls in this study ranged from 56 to 65 inches in height and from 79 to 149 pounds in weight. Their caloric intakes ranged from 1649 to 2925 kcal, an 80% difference between minimum and maximum values. These investigators first attempted to correlate caloric requirements with physiological age, accounting for maturation and growth rate. The function of physiological development in determining energy needs for adolescents is still sometimes ignored.

Heald, Remmell, and Mayer[21] compiled, from previous studies, caloric intake data on 2750 females and 2200 males between 7 and 20 years of age. For males, average caloric intakes increased steadily to 16 years of age, when the intake reached 3470 kcal, paralleling accelerated growth. From 16 to 19 years of age, caloric intake decreased by approximately 500 kcal. In females the rise in caloric intake increased to 12 years of age, when total kcal reached 2550, followed by a gradual decline to 18 years of age, when intakes averaged 2200 kcal. Although decelerated growth rate was probably the major factor in decreased caloric consumption, physical activity, which was not differentiated, may have been a factor.

In a longitudinal study conducted by Hampton and others,[22] there was great variation in caloric intakes from day to day for each individual, but more consistent intakes from week to week. According to body fat class, the lean females and average males consumed more kilocalories than did the other groups.

Age or weight alone is not a useful predictor of energy needs. Combinations of kcal/kg/age and kcal/kg/cm are more useful tools. Using a single measure, height in adolescents best expresses energy requirements because it usually correlates well with physiological development. Wait suggested 16 kcal/cm as a rough estimate of energy needs for females, and data from the longitudinal Child Research Council study give estimated intake percentiles of 10 to 19 kcal/cm for females and 13 to 23 kcal/cm for males, all healthy, growing adolescents 11 to 18 years of age.[23] Calculation of energy per median height from the recommended dietary allowances shows similar variance. An intake of 23.6 kcal/cm is estimated for an 11- to 14-year-old male consuming the maximum 3700 kcal; an intake of 7.4 kcal/cm is estimated for a 15- to 18-year-old female consuming the minimum 1200 kcal.[19]

Basically, little is known regarding actual energy requirements for adolescents. Physical activity and other life-style habits are key factors in considering needs. Adolescents may have widely varying and erratic caloric intakes and still continue to show optimal growth. It is possible that an internal mechanism exists for conserving energy in times of low intake or for eliminating excess energy.

Protein

Reports indicate that protein in the adolescent diet ranges from 12% to 16% of total energy intake.[21,22] Males consistently consume more total protein than do females. Although the highest recommended dietary allowance for adolescents is 56 gm of protein (for 15- to 18-year-old males), it is not unusual for intakes to be well over 100 gm/day. As with energy, total protein intake increases steadily in males up to approximately 16 years of age, whereas females have their highest intakes at 12 years of age.

Balance studies by Johnston[24] have helped define optimal needs. He found that a positive nitrogen balance was sustained only when the caloric requirement was satisfied and when 15% of total kilocalories was deprived from protein. In the current recommended dietary allowances, protein represents only 6.7% to 8.8% of kilocalories during adolescence.[19] Eating practices and food patterns of teenagers, however, usually result in higher protein consumption.

An important consideration is that a restricted energy intake during the rapid period of growth will compromise lean body mass accumulation and nitrogen retention despite a seemingly adequate protein intake. Without enough kilocalories, protein is used for energy instead of growth needs. This situation can occur in adolescents such as those dieting to lose weight or athletes attempting to make a specific weight class.

In the United States, reported intakes of protein usually exceed the recommended dietary allowances, a fact that leads some individuals to question whether persons living in the United States receive too much protein. Hegsted[25] has proposed that there is no strong evidence to support a substantial increase in protein requirements for adolescents. Similiarly, the FAO/WHO Expert Committee[26] recommends progressively decreasing levels of safe protein intakes from childhood to adulthood. The actual amount of protein intake will increase with growth, but the amount per kilogram decreases with age. However, some adolescents (e.g., those adhering to extreme reducing diets, those from lower socioeconomic classes, and those eliminating all animal products from their diets) are at risk for suboptimal intakes of protein.

Minerals

Calcium. Because calcium is absorbed more efficiently at lower levels of intake than at higher levels of intake, numerical recommendations have limited use. The amount of calcium needed to maintain a positive balance during growth is thought to be reflected by previous intake, explaining the absence of problems in areas of the world where the daily intake is a minimal 200 to 300 mg of calcium.

In the adolescent, calcium needs depend on growth velocity, bone structure and size, and absorption rate. Individual growth variability also influences calcium requirements; the unusually tall adolescent and the early maturer or late maturer will vary considerably in their needs. In relating calcium requirements to skeletal weight, the largest gains of dry weight occur in females between 10 and 14 years of age and in males between 12 and 16 years of age. Calcium retained as bone is approximately 100 mg/day in preschool years; however, this doubles for adolescent females and triples for adolescent males during peak periods of retention.[12] For example, a 14-year-old male may require 600 to 1200 mg of calcium/day, depending on absorption rates of 50% or 25%. The recommended dietary allowance of 1200 mg/day is thus designed to meet the needs of the adolescent who is growing at the fastest rate, and levels less than that may be quite adequate for some adolescents. Those adolescents who are at risk for limited calcium for growth are probably males with unusually rapid rates of bone growth, late-maturing females who are concerned with caloric restriction, and adolescents eliminating milk products from their diets. A low calcium/phosphorus ratio as a result of excess dietary phosphorus or a reduced calcium intake may also compromise optimal calcium status, but this is still a controversial issue. The intake of phosphorus-containing additives used in food processing may add 500 to 1000 mg of phosphorus/day above that found naturally in food.[27] Many of the foods that contain this added phosphorus, such as carbonated beverages, are popular with teenagers.

Iron. Iron is significant because it is frequently marginally adequate or deficient in adolescents. Although females are assumed to be most at risk, data from the HANES survey showed that the greatest prevalence of low hemoglobin and hematocrit levels was among boys.[28] The recommended dietary allowances for both sexes, 11 to 18 years of age, is 18 mg. Since most typical diet patterns in the United States provide approximately 6 mg of iron/1000 kcal, this allowance is not always reached by males and rarely by females. In a review of 12 studies with approximately 1300 females and 1000 males, the average iron intakes were 9.6 to 13.5 mg/day for females and 14.0 to 18.7 mg/day for males.[29]

The higher requirement for iron in adolescence is directly related to rapid growth, which is accompanied by increases in blood volume, muscle mass, and respiratory enzymes. Because of their increased need but often limited intake of iron, adolescents are, therefore, particularly susceptible to iron deficiency anemia.

Excretion of iron from physiological sources is insignificant with the exception of regular menstrual losses in the female. Hallberg and others[30] reported the mean blood loss during a period as 43.4 ml in all women, with smaller blood loss of 33.8 ml in 15-year-old females. Although iron loss will vary according to blood loss and length of normal menstrual cycle, it has been estimated that the iron loss is approximately 1.2 mg/day and that iron needs can be met if this amount is retained.[31]

There is little sex difference in iron requirements of children until females begin puberty, at which time their requirements are higher. By 15 years of age requirements for both males and females rise sharply. For the females this increase is directly related to menstrual losses. In the males the increase in tissue mass plus the rise in hemoglobin levels, which is probably caused by androgen activity, result in higher requirements. It has been suggested that boys growing at the 97th percentile may have iron needs greater than the recommended dietary allowances during their growth spurts.[32]

As with other requirements, chronological age is a poor predictor of iron needs. Daniel[33] has shown that differences in hematocrit values of males are more significant when correlated with sex maturity rating than when correlated with age. The same investigator demonstrated that iron intake increases consistently in both males and females as they progress in maturity stages. He found that intake was greater for males than for females at each maturity rating and that white adolescents had slightly greater intakes than did black adolescents. Following the same trend, iron stores, as measured by transferrin saturation, were consistently higher in males than in females but did not correlate with dietary intake of iron.[34]

Zinc. This mineral is an essential component in dozens of enzyme systems, including those that contribute to protein synthesis and bone mineralization. Zinc deficiency results in growth retardation, decreased taste acuity, sexual immaturity, anorexia, and impaired wound healing. Severe zinc deficiency was first described in Middle Eastern adolescent males who exhibited dwarfism and hypogonadism.[35,36] Their diets were high in phytate and fiber, which interfere with zinc absorption. Following treatment with zinc and an improved diet, these males showed increased growth and sexual maturation. As more information is acquired about the role and availability of zinc, it will become important to assess this nutrient in the diets of adolescents. In both sexes there is an increase in zinc retention that parallels the increase in lean body mass. In males, the requirement for growth apparently exceeds 400 μg/day.[37] The recommended dietary allowance for adolescents is 15 mg of zinc/day. Although there have been no studies on the zinc requirements of adolescents, increasing evidence suggests that this population is one of the groups most at risk for marginal intakes.[38]

Vitamins

Little satisfactory data are available to establish vitamin requirements for the adolescent, and most recommended amounts are extrapolated from other age groups. Although most needs are met by usual foods, mild vitamin deficiencies are not uncommon in this age group, resulting both from a poorly chosen diet and from the increased metabolic requirements during the growth spurt. In addition to identifying food sources of vitamins, the dietary assessment should also consider any supplements taken by the adolescent, especially large doses of the fat soluble vitamins A and D.

As with other nutrients, vitamin requirements are best correlated not with age but with growth demands. Using folate as an example, Daniel, Gaines, and Bennett[39] have shown that the sex maturity rating rather than age is a more significant factor associated with dietary intakes of folate. They found that males had higher intakes of folate than did females and that these values increased with maturity levels for both sexes. Plasma folate concentrations were, inversely, higher for females than for males, decreasing with maturity in both sexes. This paradox may represent the greater needs for folate during rapid cell growth, especially in males who may double their muscle mass during adolescence.

In summary, the energy and nutrient requirements of adolescents are directly related to the rate and stage of growth, the highest demand being at the peak velocity of growth. Care should be taken in interpreting common recommendations based on age groups and in comparing individuals to those standards.

FACTORS INFLUENCING FOOD INTAKE

The adolescent is not only maturing physically but is also progressing in social and pyschological parameters. He or she is striving to achieve the developmental tasks between childhood and adulthood. The changes and experiences each encounters affect his or her living pattern and, ultimately, his or her food intake and nutritional status.

Newly acquired independence and decision making result in adolescents spending more time outside the home, thus making independent food choices. It is not unusual for these choices to be made on the basis of sociability, enjoyment, and status, rather than on nutrient content. Activities of school, sports, part-time jobs, interest groups, and peer activities may result in the adolescent being away from home from early morning until after the evening meal. Adolescent life-styles and independence often result in irregular eating patterns such as skipped meals and increased frequency of snacks.

Body Image

Because of the multiple changes that are occurring simultaneously during this period of growth, adolescents are usually anxious and dissatisfied with their body images. This bodily overconcern is a normal preoccupation; that it may be distorted and unrealistic does not make it any less important to the adolescent. One study demonstrated this paradox well. It revealed that 70% of the females studied wanted to lose weight but that no more than approximately 15% were actually obese. On the other hand, 59% of the males wanted to gain weight, although only 25% were lower than average in fatness.[40]

Studies also indicate that adolescents are dissatisfied with their body dimensions. For males there is the desire for larger biceps, shoulders, chest, and forearms. Females, conversely, desire smaller hips, thighs, and waists.[40,41] Numerous clinical experiences with adolescents further document this phenomenon.

The body image is further influenced by advertising and mass media, which dictate the "in" look, clothing styles, and other elements of being accepted. In attempting to conform to cultural ideals, adolescents may compromise their own well-being, including optimal nutrient intake.

Perhaps the strongest influences on the adolescent are peer pressure and the desire to fit in. These influences may come from the immediate peer group or may include respected adults and national idols. This desire to be accepted may be manifested in such dietary practices as embarking on a weight-reducing scheme, espousing vegetarianism, indulging in alcohol, or altering diet to complement a muscle-building program. Any harmful results will depend on the practice and how it is carried out, but the initial decision to change is often the result of others' influence rather than health reasons.

Family

As adolescents move toward independence and autonomy, family influence on eating habits diminishes. The parental influence shifts from instructing to advising; the teen can "take it or leave it." Because of cognitive development, which allows teenagers to think in abstract terms and question parental rules, they question inconsistencies between what parents recommend and what they actually do, including eating habits. This can be very irritating to parents as their teens refuse to accept their word as given.

In a survey of adolescents, 77% believed that eating at least one meal a day with family members was important; however, 90% stated that their parents put more importance on the family meal than they did. Of the 23% who rated it as unimportant, the main reasons given were lack of time, apathy and indifference, and family conflict.[42]

Most teens and their families enjoy positive family relationships and are satisfied with how they get along.[43] However, for those who are not satisfied, poor family relationships can affect eating habits. Hinton and others[44] studied 140 adolescent girls and found that those who scored high on family relations had better diets. Those whose families were critical of their eating habits skipped more meals. Adolescents whose parents are authoritarian and rigid often use food as a vehicle to express rebellion against parental authority. This can lead to erratic and bizarre food practices such as binges, strong food aversions, food refusals, bizarre diets, fasting regimens, and missed meals. The same behavior can also be exhibited by teens with very permissive parents who are attempting to force their parents to set some limits on the teens' behaviors. Teens who eat with their families on a regular basis usually eat better and have more adequate diets.[45]

Peers

During adolescence the influence of peers becomes stronger as that of the family weakens. A study of 766 young adolescents showed that youth spent more than twice as much time with peers than with parents during a weekend.[46] Adolescents with poor parental relationships will be more susceptible to peer group control and influence over their behavior.[47] The peer group becomes a source of self-esteem and behavioral standards and appears to be even more important the greater the antagonism toward and emotional distance from parents. The peer group defines what is socially acceptable in terms of learning, dress, entertainment idols, language, and food and drink choices. Implied meanings of foods can be determined by the peer group.

Eating is an important form of recreation and socialization with friends; foods eaten usually need to meet the approval of the peer group. This can be a problem for teens with chronic illnesses that require diet modification, and they may face considerable social pressures and risk alienation and isolation by following the diet. In general, the peer group usually has a negative influence on the eating habits of adolescents and it seems that adolescents whose diets are poorest are those who eat alone or with their friends most of the time.

Media

Media consist of radio, films, television, magazines, newspapers, and books. The influence of media comes not only from its content but also from the advertising messages that usually accompany it.

From an economic standpoint adolescents are a unique and coveted market. Because they usually have an allowance or are earning money and yet do not have to pay for fixed expenses such as housing, food, or health care, they usually have more discretionary money to spend than their parents. Advertisers take advantage of the adolescent's need for self-esteem, desire to be attractive and popular, need to be accepted, and admiration of heroes and idols to sell their products. For example, television advertising aimed at youth depicts a life of fun, popularity, and success as associated with a particular soft drink.

It is estimated that children between 6 and 16 years of age watch about 24½ hours of television per week—an average of 3½ hours per day. This time decreases to about 2½ hours per day or 17½ hours per week for 17- to 18-year-old persons.[46,48] During this time they are exposed not only to the commercial advertising that accompanies the programming but also the nutritional messages from the programs themselves. In addition to observational learning during program watching, adolescents may attempt to emulate the behavior of their favorite stars and pick up cues regarding foods and eating.

Kaufman[49] analyzed the food-related messages in ten popular prime-time television programs. She found that 65% of the references to food in programs were to beverages and to sweets. Results showed that television program characters frequently snacked on foods of low-nutrient density, rarely ate a balanced meal, ate on-the-run, and used food primarily for the satisfaction of social and emotional needs.

Way[50] did a similar analysis of 101 hours of prime-time television programming. She found that there was an average of 7.67 food-related behaviors per hour of programming. Program characters (only the main characters were recorded) ate away from home about twice as often as at home. Overall, the number of food-related behaviors that involved more nutritious foods was almost equal to those involving less nutritious foods; however, the foods actually eaten by television characters were more often less nutritious, but the foods purchased,

requested, prepared, or served were most often more nutritious. Comedies more often showed behaviors involving less nutritious foods than did dramas.

Magazine reading increases during adolescence and the popular magazines become a source of information on food and nutrition. Among consumers in general, magazines have been found to be a main source of nutritional information.[51] Diet and nutrition articles from selected popular magazines were recently reviewed and unfortunately only one fourth of the sample magazines were rated as "generally reliable."[52] However, another review of popular magazine articles discussing weight control showed that in general the articles were fairly accurate, optimistic, supportive, and sympathetic. They conveyed the message that weight control is an individual responsibility that requires continual effort and that the outcome will most likely be positive.[53] This is a good message for adolescents to read in contrast to much of the advertising in these same magazines, which promotes rapid weight loss by questionable means. In summary there is a wide range in the quality of nutrition information in popular magazines that adolescents read, and the nutrition professional should try to educate the adolescent in basic methods for evaluating the reliability of articles.

Fast Foods

The presence of fast food both in fast-food restaurants and vending machines has increased tremendously within the past decade. This rapidly growing industry is having a large impact on the American diet and eating patterns, including those of adolescents.

Story[45] describes fast-food restaurants as having a great appeal for adolescents for several reasons. Fast-food restaurants are a prime employer of adolescents and provide a socially acceptable and casual place to "hang out" with friends. The food is inexpensive and convenient, and the service is fast. Ordering requires a minimum of decision making, and the food offered is the kind adolescents like, is in a standard and familiar form, and can be eaten without utensils or plates. In short, fast foods fit the adolescent's life-style.

In general fast foods tend to be calorically dense; high in fat, sugar, and sodium; and low in fiber, vitamin A, ascorbic acid, and folate. Therefore if they form the mainstay of an adolescent's diet, they could have a negative impact on the diet's nutritional value. Whether they do or do not depends on the frequency with which they are consumed and the nutritional value of the fast-food selections. For example, if the adolescent chooses servings from the salad bars, which are increasing in popularity, the nutrient contributions of a fast-food meal will most likely be improved. If the limitations and potential problems of excessive fast-food intake are explained to teens, they can then make more appropriate selections from fast foods that will build to an overall nutritionally sound diet.

REPORTED INTAKES AND EATING PATTERNS

Intakes of adolescents tend to be more variable than those of younger children or adults for the various reasons mentioned previously. Over the years studies have indicated that adolescent diets are lowest or deficient in calcium, iron, ascorbic acid, and vitamin A.[22,54,55] Because females often reduce their energy intakes, they are most at risk for suboptimal intakes.[56] On the other hand, it is not uncommon for the same proportion of adolescents, primarily males, to exceed the recommended allowances for these same nutrients.

Meal Skipping and Snacking

Teenagers generally have the reputation of being meal skippers, and this is documented by reports as well as by numerous clinical interviews. Breakfast and lunch are the meals usually missed.[57,58] According to the 1977-1978 Nationwide Food Consumption Survey (NFCS), 19% of teenage girls and 11% of teenage boys (12 to 18 years of age) missed breakfast.[59] On the other hand, teenagers tend to eat often, and snacking is characteristic of the adolescent life-style. However, even though adolescents in general eat more frequently than adults, this snacking behavior is not so different from that of adults. From the NFCS it was found that 56% of teenagers (12 to 18 years of age) ate four or more times in the day as compared with 46% of the adults (19+ years of age).[59]

The NFCS also reported on the snacking patterns of 1424 adolescents. Almost half of the snacking occurred in the evening with less in the afternoon and the smallest proportion in the morning. The peak periods for snacks were from 8 PM to 10 PM (27% of snacking occasions) and 2 PM to 4 PM (20% of snacking occasions.)[60] Generally, adolescents eating less than three times a day have poorer diets than those eating more frequently.[22]

The snacking habits of teenagers have long been maligned, with parents and professionals alike being concerned about the "empty-calorie" foods being consumed. Various studies, however, have shown that this between-meal eating contributes significantly to the total nutrient intake.[22,61,62] The most limiting nutrients provided by snacks are vitamin A, calcium, and iron; low intakes of these nutrients also occur in the overall adolescent diet. Thus, although the nutrient density of snacks is less than that of meals, snacks make a significant contribution to meeting total daily nutritional needs.[62] Observation, on the other hand, shows that some teenagers consume large amounts of high-calorie, low-nutrient snack foods. The most frequently reported snack item for teenagers in the NFCS was soft drinks.[60] Given the choices available from vending machines, school stores, and neighborhood grocers, it is not unusual for the adolescent to end up with a snack that is high in kilocalories, sucrose, fat, and/or salt but that provides minimal nutrients. This combination of frequent snacks and sucrose consumption is significant in the high incidence of dental caries in adolescence.

Irregular eating patterns, common during adolescence, are especially prevalent in middle and late adolescence.[58,63] This pattern reflects an increasing need for independence and time away from home. Although there are exceptions, adolescents who eat regular meals and snacks tend to have better nutrient intakes than do irregular eaters. Rather than stressing regular meals and omission of snacks, teens and their families should be directed into choosing nutritious snacks and having quality foods convenient and available for snacks and "quick" meals.

Nontraditional Eating Patterns

Adolescents are going through a period of development in which they are forming values and testing their newly acquired independence, which may be manifested in unusual eating patterns for a variety of reasons. The obese teenager may try the latest reducing diet with hopes of a quick cure and the young athlete may ingest protein supplements and vitamins in the hopes of improving his or her performance. Both individuals are subject to nutrition misinformation, the end results of which may vary from being harmless to a situation in which growth is compromised.

Some young people may adopt nontraditional eating patterns such as vegetarianism or "natural" foods. Motivation for these dietary changes may include asserting independence, a particular philosophy or religion, an ecological or environmental concern, rebellion against parents, pressures to conform or fit a cultural ideal, or a genuine interest in health. Any detrimental effects of these dietary practices on the optimal nutritional status of adolescents will depend on the particular diet, the volume and variety of foods it includes, and the length of time it is practiced. Specific nutrients likely to be at risk in vegetarian and other nonmeat diets are discussed in Chapter 11.

Fad diets for weight reduction are often tried by adolescents and can be detrimental to their nutritional intake and health. These diets or diet products are attractive to teens if they are dissatisfied with their bodies and yearn for miraculous transfor-

mations. Adolescents' vulnerability and anxiety about their physical appearance make them easy prey for promoters of special diets and diet supplements.

NUTRITIONAL CONCERNS

Eating Disorders

Eating disorders account for a large number of nutritional concerns during adolescence. The physical symptoms of teenagers with the disorders range on a spectrum from the skeleton-like thinness of the terminally starving person with anorexia nervosa to the hugely overfat condition of the morbidly obese person (100% above ideal body weight), as shown in Fig. 9-1. Although it is easy to focus on the outward appearance of these conditions, the underlying psychological characteristics must also be studied to fully understand the development and treatment of eating disorders. Drawing on the information about human development as applied to eating habits described in previous chapters of this book is very helpful in this regard.

From infancy, interaction with first the mother and the father and then an expanding environment influences the child's development according to the particular characteristics of the individual. In families in which interactions are disturbed, eating habits are among the patterned behaviors that are vulnerable to maladjustment.[64] If the needs of the child are misinterpreted throughout childhood by parents and caregivers, a severe distortion of the eating function may be built up by the time the child reaches adolescence. This is particularly true in the case of individuals whose inherent characteristics predispose them in some way to an eating problem.[65]

Parents of adolescents with eating disorders have been found to be intrusive in the lives of their children with the result that the children have not been free to develop autonomy. Children and parents are enmeshed in a system of overdependence, which is destructive. The families are rigid in their approach to life, unable to foster creativity in problem solv-

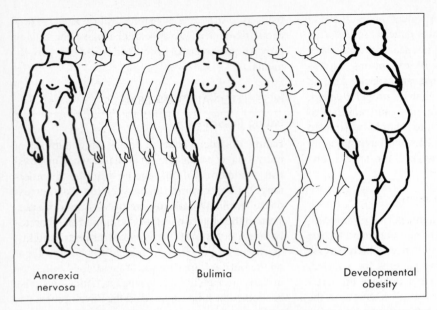

Fig. 9-1. The spectrum of eating disorders. Underlying psychologic characteristics are held in common, whereas physical conditions vary across the spectrum. (From Rees, J.M.: Eating disorders. In Mahan, L.K., and Rees, J.M., editors: Nutrition in adolescence, St. Louis, 1984, The C.V. Mosby Co.)

ing among their children. They, in fact, demonstrate a lack of ability to resolve conflicts, attempting instead to ignore serious problems.[66]

Within this family milieu children are unable to develop into normal independent beings. Maladaptive eating behaviors will be among the outstanding manifestations of developmental problems for certain adolescents. It is thought that misuse of food (rather than other psychosomatic problems such as alcoholism) is the mode of expression in families in which food, weight control, or fitness is emphasized in some way.[66]

The rapid development of body image during adolescence accounts for a great amount of the psychological component of eating disorders in some teenagers. Adolescents along the spectrum are generally unable to view themselves without distortions, their problems being similar to those of all adolescents as described earlier but to an exaggerated degree.[65,67]

Obesity. Obesity is probably the most common nutritional and general health problem among adolescents in developed countries. Although the incidence is not known, estimates of obesity range from 10% to 20%. In numbers this represents more than 10 million adolescents in the United States. Realistically, the prognosis for these teenagers is poor—80% of them will remain obese as adults[68] and be resistant to treatment. This is an important fact to consider in helping obese adolescents set realistic goals.

As in adults, obesity in teenagers is seldom an isolated problem but is combined with social and psychological difficulties. It is not a moral issue, nor is it a simple medical problem. Many health care workers have found that it is a mistake to equate obesity solely with overeating and to treat the adolescent with an inspirational lecture accompanied by a diet.

Characteristics. Although there is no typical

obese adolescent, certain physical characteristics seem to persist. These include rapid weight gain in the first year of life, earlier maturation, earlier menarche, a highly endomorphic physique, and advanced bone age.[69,70] This is especially true for those who have been obese through the growing years.

The physiological processes that are associated with long-term overweight have been operative for over a decade in many obese adolescents. Their overweight status is often maintained by fat cell hypertrophy and hyperplasia,[71] increased lipoprotein lipase levels,[72] decreased thermogenetic potential,[73-75] and inherent genetic traits.[76] The longer the overweight status has persisted, the more difficult it will be to overcome these processes since they affect the body's use of energy in a way that has now been described in the ''set point'' theory.[77] Theoretically the ''set point'' is defended by the channeling of energy to maintain a certain rather narrow range of body weight. It is, therefore, difficult to achieve the energy deficit necessary to decrease body fat. At present decreasing dietary energy intake and increasing energy output through activity are the only means for accomplishing this deficit.

Since adolescents are, in general, sensitive about their bodies, obese teenagers are especially affected by the social rejection and derogatory attitudes in our culture. In our society, which admires and merchandises slimness, obese teenagers are under constant pressure to change their bodies to conform with social norms. Monello and Mayer[78] have shown that obese girls have traits in common with other minority groups, such as obsessive concern (with overweight and food), passivity, withdrawal, self-contempt, and actual discrimination. In reality obesity does affect attractiveness, popularity with the opposite sex, ability to obtain a job, college acceptance, and other practical life situations. These teenagers may experience so much humiliating rejection and poor self-esteem that they become socially isolated.[79] In addition, their consistently low level of activity requires less energy. This

combination of emotional and environmental factors often leads to more severe obesity. A vicious circle ensues whereby food and eating may be the only outlets for frustration and depression (Fig. 9-2).

Food practices and activity patterns. In considering the food practices of obese adolescents, one should remember that they may not be consuming excessive energy. Studies have shown that the energy intakes of some obese adolescents are equal to or lower than those of nonobese adolescents.[22,80,81] There is a tendency for obese teenagers to eat less frequently and to skip more meals, especially breakfast. Expressions such as ''I'm not hungry in the morning'' and ''Eating breakfast makes me sick'' are common. Often an accompanying pattern is the frequent or continuous eating from after school until late in the evening.

Another major factor is the inactivity of obese adolescents as compared with normal weight adolescents. This has been demonstrated by activity records and motion picture sampling.[80,81,82] Since inactivity is often accompanied by reduced energy intake, it is not surprising that inactivity is a strong predictor of a poor-quality diet.[56] It is not hard to imagine why body-sensitive overweight teenagers decline to participate in sports and activities that make them feel awkward, embarrassed, and exhausted. In addition, many obese adolescents are eliminated from participation in organized sports because of poor performance. Because they expend less energy they may eat less than normal weight adolescents and yet still gain weight or at least maintain their weight. This seeming self-denial without results often causes feelings of frustration and hopelessness in the individual.

Treatment. It has been estimated that the odds against an overweight adolescent becoming an average weight adult are 28 to 1.[83] Despite these discouraging statistics there is a large demand for adolescent weight control programs from parents, teachers, health professionals, and teenagers themselves. Adolescence can certainly be a critical period of influence in the establishment of positive

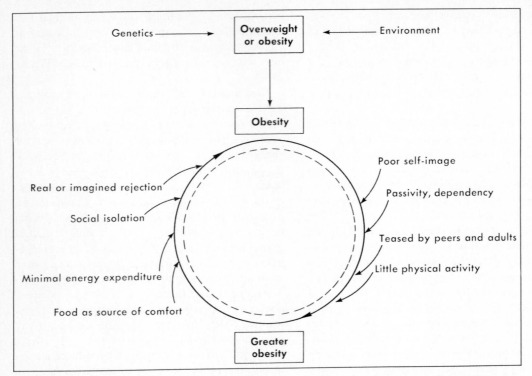

Fig. 9-2. Factors that contribute to obesity. (Courtesy Betty Lucas, Clinical Training Unit, Child Development and Mental Retardation Center, University of Washington, Seattle, Wash.)

health attitudes and practices. On the other hand, not recognizing the complex make-up of the obese adolescent or establishing unrealistic treatment plans can subject both the adolescent and the helping professional to feelings of failure and discouragement.

In most cases conventional methods such as rigid diets and/or parental control have produced poor results. Anorectic drugs are usually contraindicated because of their ineffectiveness and because of the potential of abuse. Jejunoileal bypass surgery has not been considered a reasonable option because of its postoperative morbidity and unknown effects on growth. For those sexually mature adolescents, however, who are morbidly obese and have not been successful in previous reducing attempts, gastric bypass has been shown

to be an effective treatment method without the complications of jejunoileal surgery.[84]

A less invasive treatment is the protein-sparing modified fast,[85] which has been tested in hospital settings with a liquid preparation[86] and lean meats as the protein source.[87] Either of these radical methods should be used to treat sexually mature adolescents only if life-threatening complications develop and if a change in environment for the adolescent is assured following dismissal from the hospital. Neither will lead to long-term maintenance of a lower weight without an altered eating pattern and life-style that are supported by family and health professionals.

Behavior modification techniques are being used increasingly in the treatment of adult obesity. This therapy can be useful in working with teenagers, but success will depend on the motivation, maturity, and family support of the adolescents. Programs that have included physical activity and behavioral components as well as diet have demonstrated more success, but few long-term follow-up studies have been done.[88] A behavioral approach alone seems to have limited application to the situation of the obese adolescent.[89]

Assessment. To determine the best therapeutic approach for the obese adolescent, a myriad of factors must be considered. One clinical assessment tool that addresses the complexity of the problem is shown on p. 244. By assessing these factors, preferably through an interdisciplinary team process, a treatment approach can be planned to meet the needs of the individual.

Those adolescents who have poor self-esteem, who are significantly depressed, and who are dependent and immature will generally require intensive counseling before they can deal with the weight problem. Those individuals who are more motivated and relatively unencumbered by the severe psychological aspects will probably have success with a program that includes dietary guidance, physical activity, behavioral components, and supportive counseling. Reports indicate that such a combined approach can be effective, both in clinical and in school settings.[90-92]

Clinical management. Successful treatment of the obese adolescent usually involves more than one health professional and requires an understanding of adolescent development as well as skills in counseling. The ideal program incorporates decision making by the adolescent and is realistic in its time frame.

Goals for treatment must acknowledge the adolescent's pubertal stage. For those in their growth spurts, weight can be maintained or slowly increased over time, allowing for changes in the ratio of lean body mass and fat. Both teenagers and parents must understand that weight gain is expected in periods of growth. For those who have completed their growth spurts, the plan will probably include actual weight reduction by loss of fat.

From a practical aspect, most obese adolescents will benefit from nutrition education because they have tried various types of diets or have acquired misinformation regarding obesity. Too often they are not aware of the basic concepts of energy balance (consumed versus expended). They may have the idea that a "calorie" is only negative and undesirable. They should learn about the psychological processes involved in body weight gain, maintenance, and loss. Rather than being talked to or given information to read, these adolescents will respond best if information is given by a supportive counselor and they are included in activities and problem solving. Keeping food records, assessing their activity patterns, trying new recipes, calculating energy values, analyzing popular fad diets, or checking labels at the supermarket give adolescents a feeling of responsibility and accomplishment. The professional can help them to focus on food behaviors they would like to change gradually at their own speed, as well as to consider alternatives for handling such food-oriented situations as holidays or snacks. They should, in all cases, be encouraged to make their own decisions. Role playing is often an effective tool in this regard.

Physical exercise is often given little credit in the treatment of obesity in general. For the adolescent, activity should be encouraged and reinforced as a permanent aspect of his or her life-style. In many cases it provides an alternative to eating as well as a means to increase energy expenditure with or without restriction of energy intake. Regular exercise yields positive changes in body composition, such as decreases in body weight and relative fat and increases in lean body mass, as well as cardiovascular benefits.[93]

It is vital to encourage activities that the teenager enjoys. The activities should be relatively inexpensive and feasible and should have potential for continuing on into adulthood. Popular activities include bicycling, swimming, skating, walking, running, and tennis. For the significantly obese, care should be taken to assess the teenager's abilities and to program a slow, consistent increase in

Clinical Assessment of Eating Disorder

Motivation

Desire to lose weight
Goals
Insight

Family Characteristics

Eating disorders
Other diseases
Natural or other parent

Parental Attitude Toward Weight Problem

Role of food in family
Perceptions of weight problem
Attempts to intervene

Social Relationships

Friends
School
Social life and activities
Social skills
Teasing

Growth and Adiposity

Weight history
Maturation stage
Body fatness
Growth velocity
Age

Mental Function

Psychological testing
School performance

Emotional/Psychological Status

Depressed
Locus of control
Body image
Self-esteem
Oral expression
Coping skills
Compulsiveness

Eating Behavior

Control over food intake
Meal pattern
Bizarre eating habits
Knowledge of nutrition
Nutritional adequacy

Medical Data

Clinical findings
Thyroid status

Physical Activity

Exercise and frequency
Family activity patterns
Hobbies and interests
Personal feeling about activity

Developed by Mahan, L.K., and Rees, J., Adolescent Clinic and Child Development Mental Retardation Center, University of Washington, Seattle.

exercise. Actual fitness testing has been used in clinical settings to plan realistic exercise programs for obese adolescents and to engage their interest and motivation. This testing includes strength, flexibility, endurance, and cardiorespiratory function. The steps of assessing fitness levels and planning subsequent activity programs are outlined on p. 245.

Although psychotherapy alone has not been rec-

ommended, teenagers with significant weight problems will be able to make changes only when they are presented within the context of a therapeutic relationship. Counseling techniques developed within the social sciences along with dietary and fitness strategies developed in the physical sciences must be used.[94] Group treatment is commonly used for many adolescent difficulties, including obesity. It may range from intensive treatment in a summer

Fitness: Testing and Planning Improvement Programs

1. a. Have client sit quietly and relax for 3 to 5 minutes.
   b. Take pulse for 10 seconds.*
   c. Record *resting heart rate (RHR):* _____
2. a. Find intensity of exercise required to reach *training heart rate (THR)*† immediately after exercise. THR for teens: 20 to 22 beats/10 seconds.
      Stop with the exercise that achieves 20 to 22 beats/10 seconds. This is the exercise to use initially in the improvement program.

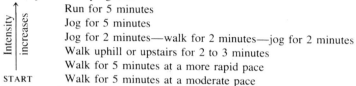

Run for 5 minutes
Jog for 5 minutes
Jog for 2 minutes—walk for 2 minutes—jog for 2 minutes
Walk uphill or upstairs for 2 to 3 minutes
Walk for 5 minutes at a more rapid pace
START   Walk for 5 minutes at a moderate pace

   b. Monitor pulse return toward RHR after each exercise level—it should be below 16 beats/10 seconds by 5 minutes.

   _____   _____   _____   _____
   Immediate _____→ 1 minute _____→ 2 minutes _____→ 5 minutes _____→

3. *Improvement program:* To maintain THR for 15 minutes 4 to 5 days/week:
   a. Work with client to design an individualized program that is comfortable for him/her.
   b. Plan 5-minute warmup—move at level below the level that maintains THR.
   c. Exercise at intensity that maintains THR.
   d. 5-Minute cool down—back to warmup speed—client should not sit or lie down immediately.
   e. Use a combination of exercise levels and types, if necessary.
   f. If the client is ill, he/she should begin after illness at lower intensity and return slowly to intensity achieved before illness.
4. a. Retest every 3 to 4 weeks.
   b. Increase intensity of exercise to maintain THR.
   c. Client can increase time spent doing the exercise by 5-minute increments, up to 30 minutes.
   d. When client has reached jogging level and maintained it for 6 to 8 weeks, increase THR to 22 to 25 beats/10 seconds.
   e. Client can use any aerobic activities (e.g., jogging, bicycling, skating, dancing) or combinations that the client prefers.

Developed by Scott, B., and Rees, J., Adolescent Program, University of Washington, Seattle.
*10-Second time segment is easiest to measure and use.
†*Maximum heart rate* (MHR): ≈ 200 beats/minute for persons under 20 years of age (Cumming, G.R., Everatt, D., and Hastman, L.: Bruce treadmill test in children: normal values in a clinic population, Am. J. Cardiol. **41**:69, 1978). THR is 60% of MHR for persons with poor initial fitness, 75% of MHR for persons who are fit (i.e., 60% of 200 = 120 beats/minute = 20 bests/10 seconds [20 to 22 beats/10 seconds for normal variation]).
Note: Contraindications for testing and initiating fitness program will be revealed by routine medical history and physical examination.

Fig. 9-3. Adolescent and nutritionist discuss management of weight control.

camp to weekly sessions in a school or clinical setting. Groups will vary according to their general goals, their leaders, and their members. The specific goals of group sessions may include the acquisition of nutrition information, the use of behavior modification tools, physical activity, social skills improvement, emphasis on a positive image, and the development of peer relationships. Success by group treatment cannot be measured by weight loss alone, but also by evaluating psychosocial parameters. For some adolescents, willing attendance at group sessions, initiating a conversation, or reporting a personal achievement to the group will be a big step. The group leader plays a critical role. He or she should have an understanding of adolescent development in general, an awareness of the varying complexity of the obese teenager, and skills in group process. Camps and other groups that provide only for short-term weight loss are detrimental and should be avoided.

The obese adolescent should be individually assessed whether one-to-one therapy or group therapy is used, because although some common char-

acteristics exist, there is no typical overweight teenager. Programs may vary with the individual, but in all cases attention should be given to the adolescent's diet, activity, and feelings. This concept has been developed as a teaching tool in one area (Fig. 9-4).

Outcome. Because of the poor prognosis for many obese teenagers to achieve ideal weight, the professional working with them should help them avoid setting unrealistic goals or believing that they can accomplish the impossible. For these individuals obesity should be considered a chronic condition, and treatment goals should include working toward the adolescent's acceptance of the idea of lifelong weight control. Once this concept can be maturely accepted, goals of ongoing modification of eating patterns and activity patterns can be emphasized.

Despite poor prognosis and lack of long-term success of obesity treatments, program efforts for obese adolescents usually yield positive changes, although they may be small and difficult to measure. But for the individual teenager, these effects

BE SIZEWISE
Don't Lose
Your Balance.

Feelings

Learn to know and
like yourself

Have realistic goals
for yourself

Don't substitute food for
love and companionship

Build satisfying relationships with your family
and friends

Get help for problems you
can't cope with alone

Activities

Do interesting things—
quiet as well as energetic

Take time to relax
everyday

Don't let eating be
your only recreation

Do some strenuous
activity every day

Share active and quiet
time with friends

Nourishment

Be good to your body—
give it what it needs

Don't starve or
stuff yourself

Know what's in the
food you eat

American Heart Association of Washington
4414 Woodland Park Avenue North
Seattle, Washington 98103

Fig. 9-4. © American Heart Association of Washington.

can be significant by enhancing his or her present situation and/or by providing information and skills that can be put into practice at a later time.

Anorexia nervosa. Anorexia nervosa is an eating disorder with serious underlying developmental and psychological disturbances. It occurs most commonly among females, and the symptoms are usually manifested in adolescence. The initial symptoms include amenorrhea, weight loss, compulsive physical activity, and dietary restriction. In many cases, everyday events or remarks critical of their bodies appear to precipitate the weight loss. It may seem to be a response to real or imagined obesity. Initially, the weight goals may be reasonable, but with success these individuals are reinforced both externally and internally to continue losing weight. When weight goals are reached, new lower ones may be established. Dieting becomes a primary focus of the lives of those with anorexia nervosa, described by Bruch[65] as "a relentless pursuit of thinness."

Anorexia is actually a misnomer for this disorder. Patients do not lack hunger, but rigidly deny and control it. As outlined by Bruch,[65] a pattern of denial occurs—denial of thinness, hunger, fatigue, and personal effectiveness.

Characteristics. The disorder may be characterized by progressive and/or significant weight loss and avoidance of any "fattening" foods. They may alternate "binge" eating with dieting. These young women are usually very clever at concealing their gorging of food, self-induced vomiting, and heavy use of laxatives. There is a dramatic increase in hyperactive behavior and compulsive exercise patterns. The hyperactivity may begin as routine physical exercise but may increase, as the disorder progresses, to compulsive jogging and calisthenics, denying the need for adequate rest, even to the inability to sit down for more than a moment. Of significance is the fact that the physical activity is usually done alone.

These individuals are often preoccupied with food and will prepare high-calorie dishes for their families but limit themselves to a taste or nothing.

Aspects of nutrition are also of great interest to them, and in fact most are more knowledgeable of nutrition than their peers. However, this nutrition knowledge may be distorted, and the individual may be unable to practically conceptualize the information. The bizarre eating habits of individuals with anorexia nervosa may be well hidden, so that family and friends often deny any problems and do not seek help until the disorder becomes severe.[95]

Psychodynamic features of the anorexia nervosa syndrome include a distorted body image, fear of physical maturation and adulthood, and a tremendous dependence/independence conflict. Even when the disorder has progressed to the point of emaciation, these anorectic women will deny reality, insisting that they are normal or even overweight. The apathy and preoccupation with food combined with a lack of ability to think coherently, which is described in starving individuals, can be recognized as being superimposed on the disturbed personality of the starving anorectic person. There is a pattern of doing exceptionally well academically by setting high goals and studying excessively, but withdrawing from peer relationships in preference for a self-imposed isolation. Their ability to function realistically in a school or work setting, however, may be significantly compromised. Family histories of patients with anorexia nervosa reveal psychopathology among families, as well as a higher prevalence of obesity and anorexia nervosa. Some evidence also suggests an increased incidence of perinatal complications in these individuals.[96] Classically, the family is very achievement oriented and successful at economic, social, and academic levels, but parents may experience significant hidden marital discord. The parents' need to control and the anorectic person's need to please form a basic conflicted relationship that demands resolution for the patient with anorexia nervosa.

It is well to remember that not all individuals with anorexia nervosa exhibit the classical characteristics. Approximately 5% to 10% are male; some cases are not manifested until later adulthood; and other cases do not show dramatic weight loss or all the common psychological behaviors. In a recent report males as well as females who were referred to an endocrinology clinic for growth retardation had been severely restricting food intake out of fear of fatness.[97] These atypical cases may not be readily diagnosed, but they require approximately the same treatment.

In recent years, there have been numerous studies of the metabolic and endocrine abnormalities often associated with the nutritional crisis of this disorder, focusing primarily on pituitary and hypothalamic function.[98,99] Hormonal secretion patterns have been shown to be essentially those of the prepubertal state. Hypothalamic function and physical symptoms such as edema, postural hypotension, bradycardia, and hirsutism parallel those seen in other cases of starvation. At this time it appears these alterations are the effects rather than the cause of the voluntary starvation.[67]

With the continual weight loss and semistarvation, the nutritional status of these individuals deteriorates. Fluid and electrolyte imbalances can result from induced vomiting and purging. Long-term debilitation results in death in a small percentage of cases.

Treatment. Treatment and management of anorexia nervosa is varied. Most programs include nutritional, medical, and psychiatric support. Although early intervention may prevent a nutritional crisis, cases of severe debilitation require hospitalization and refeeding. It is not unusual for the patient to sabotage treatment attempts by hiding food, performing surreptitious exercise, or attaching weights to her body before stepping on the scale. But with support, a positive response can usually be developed. Satisfactory weight gain by a patient in an institution cannot be interpreted as success. Although it is essential that the underlying developmental problems be resolved, a hospital stay and subsequent weight gain can be the first stage of a comprehensive program.

One of the most comprehensive treatment programs has been developed by Crisp[100] in England.

The in-patient program includes an initial psychiatric assessment, a refeeding program with bed rest, and ongoing individual and family psychotherapy. Emphasis is placed on the psychological environment, which is accepting and supporting of the patient. After attaining normal weight, the patient is allowed more freedom while ongoing counseling is provided in the hospital setting.

Behavior modification, in which weight gain is required to earn certain privileges or activities, has been used with some initial success.[101] This method of therapy has been criticized for its lack of long-term evaluation and its focus on only tangible measures.[102] Critics believe that it tends to undermine the patient's individuality, which is essential for ultimate treatment success. In a recent study, 81 patients were randomly assigned either to behavior modification therapy or to the standard hospital therapy. No significant difference in weight gain was found between the two groups after 35 days.[103] Many experts, however, believe that behavior modification techniques can be usefully incorporated into eclectic treatment protocols.[104]

Long-term individual and family psychotherapy is the basic component of treatment. A high success rate has been reported by Minuchin[105] if patients and their families are treated within 1 year of the onset of the syndrome.

Assessment. A thorough knowledge of anorexia nervosa is necessary for the identification and assessment of teenagers with this disorder. Taking a history using the assessment guidelines on p. 244 will enable the professional to decide whether the patient is just beginning to physically manifest the disorder, is near or at a crisis, or is in the recovery period.[67] Weight-for-height proportion along with the presence or absence of signs of significant starvation will be an important indication of the physical state. Food habits, exercise patterns, use of laxatives, diuretics, and induced vomiting, as well as distorted beliefs about body image and food intake, must be explored. Patient and family psychological assessments are necessary to establish the degree of disturbance in perceptions and relationships as well as the ability to respond within the bounds of a therapeutic relationship.[106]

Clinical management. The nutritional component of management will vary greatly depending on the stage of the disorder. If the patient is not at a physical crisis point the goal will be to help her establish a psychotherapeutic relationship and to provide nutritional guidance within the context of the patient's ability to respond. During a crisis, refeeding will be managed in a manner that blends with the overall philosophy of the in-patient program. It is usually possible to obtain sufficient cooperation from patients so they can take food by mouth.[107] A concentrated fluid dietary preparation may be prescribed as medicine if other food is refused. Invasive procedures such as parenteral or enteral nourishment are reserved for life-threatening states. Following a crisis or in the event a crisis is avoided, the patient will need guidance in developing realistic nourishment and exercise patterns as well as an understanding of physiological needs.[95]

Outcome. Common features of anorexia nervosa are the strong resistance to treatment and the high incidence of relapse or partial recovery. Some of these patients will manifest varying degrees of the symptoms in adulthood. Very few follow-up evaluations have been conducted on the long-term outcome of the various treatment modes used for anorexia nervosa. Hsu, Crisp, and Harding[108] in England reported on the outcome of a follow-up study of 100 patients. The time lapses ranged from 4 to 8 years after the initial clinic visit. All but 12 of the patients had been involved in refeeding programs and/or psychotherapy. Using the criteria of near-normal weight, regular menstruation, and satisfactory psychosexual and psychosocial adjustments, 48% had a good outcome. Poor outcome was associated with longer duration of illness, lower body weight during illness, onset at a later age, presence of vomiting, compulsive overeating, anxiety when eating with others, poor social adjustment in childhood, and disturbed parental relationships. The low mortality (2%) in these severely ill

patients supports the use of weight gain and psychotherapy. Though follow-up criteria have been inconsistently used by researchers, a compilation of results reported from 1954 to 1978 indicate that though weight-for-height proportion improved in about three fourths of the patients described, menstrual cycles were often unsatisfactorily maintained and psychosocial maladjustment was common.[109] Health care professionals should watch for symptoms (often well disguised) in vulnerable individuals and attempt to intervene early. Whether the person with anorexia nervosa is treated as an in-patient or an out-patient, the goals of management include: (1) maintaining a positive nutritional state, (2) achieving physical and developmental maturation, and (3) providing therapy for the patient to work out underlying conflicts and emotional disorders.

Bulimia. Bulimia, referring to the gorging and vomiting first described in anorexia nervosa, is now recognized as a separate syndrome in the spectrum of eating disorders. Although there is still some discussion about how the term should be used, it is most frequently applied to the practice of gorging/bingeing (eating excessive amounts of food) combined with self-induced vomiting and/or abuse of diuretics and laxatives in individuals who nevertheless maintain normal weight. It will be used in that way in this chapter. Bulimarexia is the name given to the disorder in which body weight is excessively decreased by voluntary starvation, i.e., the gorging and vomiting seen in the anorexia nervosa syndrome. Bulimia has been reported to affect 19% of college women,[110] with speculation among health care professionals working with this population that it actually may affect an even greater number.

Unfortunately, there is a growing practice among normal teenagers to use vomiting as a form of weight control. It may be socially reinforced on athletic squads or when groups of adolescents or young people such as college students live together. Although this is not a practice to be encouraged, it is not classified as bulimia unless it is an obsession, which signifies interrupted development.

Bulimia is at present thought to arise under similar patterns of familial disturbance as anorexia nervosa.[111] Bulimic persons may have previously been obese or have experienced classical anorexia nervosa. They are often older than the average anorexic person when seen for treatment.[112,113]

Characteristics. Physically, bulimic persons are usually near normal weight for their height. This attests to the fact that they retain sufficient nourishment to sustain themselves though vomiting and purging frequently. Individuals may, for example, follow the practice of vomiting only snack-type foods that they have eaten following regular meals. Bulimic persons differ in the practices they follow. In fact, some will define eating one cookie as a binge because of their distorted attitudes about foods and their physiological needs. They experience dental problems, swollen parotid glands, and irritation of the throat as the result of exposure of unprotected tissues to acidic vomitus.[113] Rectal bleeding may be caused by excessive use of laxatives. Electrolyte imbalances and the development of fistulas in the esophagus are more rare and serious consequences requiring hospitalization.[112]

Psychological characteristics most prominently seen are an overriding sense of guilt and linkage between self-worth and the ability to maintain a body size close to the "ideal."[112-115] The preoccupation with these issues and the physical activities of eating and ridding herself of the food fill the day of the bulimic person to the extent that it interferes with her ability to succeed in an educational or professional setting.[116] Nevertheless, the bulimic person will often appear to be very attractive and to lead a busy and successful life as compared with her peers. Bulimic persons are prone to problems of impulse control including abuse of drugs and alochol, shoplifting, and outbursts of anger.[113] Bouts of bingeing and vomiting are often attempts to deal with unwanted feeling states.[112]

Treatment

Assessment. Learning from the bulimic person the true nature of her practices, ideas, and goals related to food intake and its effect on her body constitute an assessment on which to base treatment. With some individuals this will require sev-

eral vistis, whereas others may welcome disclosure to rid themselves of guilt. A physical examination is necessary to detect any truly significant symptoms and to assure those of normal physical status that they have done no permanent damage to themselves. A psychological assessment will be necessary to determine the nature of the personality disorder.[116]

Clinical management. An electrolyte imbalance requires aggressive management, usually in a hospital setting. Otherwise, key changes in bulimic behaviors will be facilitated by skillful techniques on the part of the nutrition counselor in conjunction with individual and family psychotherapy. Guilt is often alleviated by the opportunity to discuss specific practices. If a great deal of anxiety is provoked by discussion of dietary habits in detail, it is best to postpone direct intervention until the individual is ready. It is usually unworkable to attempt to control vomiting and lose weight at the same time although many bulimic persons will declare these goals on entering treatment. To succeed, cessation of vomiting must be a primary goal. Following the realization that she can control her vomiting, the bulimic person will gradually be able to control her eating. Because the behavior is commonly based on faulty ideas about physiological needs, the chance to learn within a trusting relationship allows her to formulate new concepts about foods.[116] Cognitive restructuring techniques have been used with good results.[117] These methods can also be applied to facilitate her adoption of goals regarding weight for height, which are more reasonable in terms of her natural physiological makeup. Weight-for-height standards should be presented without an authoritarian stance to the bulimic person who exhibits readiness. A range of weights for a particular height such as those available by including the 25th through the 50th percentile of the HANES detailed tables[1,118,119] should always be used to demonstrate the wide range that is normal. The speed at which cognitive and behavioral goals can be accomplished will be determined by the gains bulimic persons make in psychotherapy. Successful psychotherapeutic group treatment protocols have incorporated all elements mentioned above.[115-117]

Outcome. Although it is too soon after recognition of bulimia as a disorder to have long-term follow-up data, improvement in both psychological and physical states of bulimic persons in treatment have been reported.[115-117] Incorporation of strategies directed toward the nutritional and developmental aspects of the disorder based on experience with anorexia nervosa appears to be an important aspect of positive outcome seen to date.

Pregnancy in Adolescence

Although the overall birth rate in the United States is declining, this is not the case for the adolescent age group. During the last two decades, the rate of pregancy among 15- to 19-year old girls has decreased, but since the number of teenage girls has nearly doubled, the number of live babies born has not changed.[120] On the other hand, birth rates among females under 15 years of age continue to rise at an alarming rate. In addition, out-of-wedlock births have increased among adolescents; it is estimated that 85% of births to those 15 years old or younger and 23% of births to 19-year-old girls are illegitimate.[120] Another particular concern is the trend of young teenagers to have more children, have them closer together, and have more unwanted and out-of-wedlock births.[121]

Teenage mothers have more complications during pregnancy and give birth to a higher percentage of stillborn infants and low birth weight infants. Also, their infants have higher rates of neonatal and infant mortality.[122] The American Academy of Pediatrics[120] states that an increase in low birth weight infants and preeclampsia are the two major complications related to the teenage pregnancy itself. The incidence of births of babies weighing less than 2500 gm is significantly higher among all adolescents, but especially among those who give birth before they are 15 years of age.

Recent data suggest that gynecological age, or time interval since menarche, is a better base of comparison for high incidence of births of low birth weight infants than is chronological age.[123] Low gynecological age (2 years or less) is associated with a higher incidence of births of low birth weight infants.

Some of the adverse effects of teenage pregnancy are believed to be related to socioeconomic status and other environmental factors that are difficult to isolate. In a recent study by Zuckerman and others,[124] pregnancy outcomes were compared between adolescent and nonadolescent women independent of numerous health and social differences. The only statistically significant difference between the two groups was that infants of adolescent mothers weighed 94 gm less than infants of nonadolescent mothers. The authors[124] demonstrated that several health and social factors (including low pregnancy weight gain, low prepregnant weight, and marijuana use during pregnancy), but not adolescent status itself, were associated with adverse infant outcome.

The pregnant teenager characteristically does not receive early prenatal care, thus increasing her risk for a poor outcome. A subsequent pattern of dropping out of school and thus decreasing future employability, having no financial independence, and often having little emotional support all create a poor psychosocial milieu for the adolescent.

Females are particularly at nutritional risk when pregnancy occurs before their own growth is completed, mainly before 17 years of age. In addition their nutrient stores may be minimal at the time of conception because of poor eating habits and dieting attempts. For the young, early-maturing female, pregnancy is an extra demand on a body that is still growing rapidly and that has not reached skeletal maturation.

Studies indicate that many pregnant adolescents receive inadequate amounts of nutrients (primarily iron, calcium, calories, and vitamin A) and that they have lower biochemical values.[125] The multiple nutrient demands of adolescent growth and pregnancy, combined with a poor food intake, do not predict an optimal outcome of pregnancy. Generally, the nutrient needs of pregnant adolescents are estimated by adding the recommended dietary allowances for pregnancy to the allowances for 15- to 18-year-old females (Table 9-2)[126]. These nutrient levels may be an overestimation for some individuals, depending on changes in nutrient absorption, hormonal alterations, or decreased physical activity. But unless the adolescent is obviously mature, the additive allowances of adolescence plus pregnancy are probably the best guides in planning diets for this group. Each individual should be assessed for current intake and life-style. Many pregnant girls decrease their levels of physical activity and thus may not require all the calories allowed. Iron and folic acid needs are increased substantially during pregnancy; these

nutrients are often found marginally in adolescent diets. A prenatal supplement, therefore, is usually standard practice to cover the increased needs.

For many young teenagers, it may be normal and appropriate for weight gain to exceed 25 or 30 pounds, especially if the women are average weight or underweight.[127,128] One study reported the average term weight gain of 80 adolescents to be 37 pounds, with females of younger chronological and gynecological age gaining less than older, more mature females.[128] In addition, some data suggest that although these young women lose weight easily in the postpartum period, their weight usually stabilizes at a higher level than their prepregnant weight.[128] These two trends, more

Table 9-2. Estimates of dietary needs for pregnant teenagers

Nutrient	Recommended Intake for Nonpregnant Teenagers, 15-18 Years*	Recommended Increment for Adult Pregnancy	Recommended Intake for Pregnant Teenagers, 15-18 Years
Energy (kcal/kg)	38	5	43
Protein (gm/kg)	0.8	0.4	1.2
Calcium (gm)	1.2	0.4	1.6
Phosphorus (gm)	1.2	0.4	1.6
Iron (mg)	18	0‡	18‡
Magnesium (mg)	300	150	450
Iodine (μg)	150	25	175
Zinc (mg)	15	5	20
Vitamin A (μg RE)	800	200	1,000
Vitamin D (μg)	10	5	15
Vitamin E (mgαTE)	8	2	10
Ascorbic acid (mg)	60	20	80
Niacin (mEq)	14	2	16
Riboflavin (mg)	1.3	0.3	1.6
Thiamin (mg)	1.1	0.4	1.5
Folacin (μg)	400	400	800
Vitamin B_6 (mg)	2.0	0.6	2.6
Vitamin B_{12} (μg)	3.0	1.0	4.0

From Worthington-Roberts, B.S.: Nutritional needs of the pregnant adolescent. In Worthington-Roberts, B.S., Vermeersch, J., and Williams, S.R., editors: Nutrition in pregnancy and lactation, ed. 2, St. Louis, 1981, The C.V. Mosby Co.; developed from Food and Nutrition Board: Recommended dietary allowances, Washington D.C., 1980, National Academy of Sciences, National Research Council.

*The reference girl weighs 55 kg and stands 163 cm tall.

‡Supplemental iron is recommended.

prenatal weight gain and a higher postpartum weight, seem to indicate continued physical growth and maturation during the pregnancy.

Pregnant teenagers are just as likely as other teenage girls to have patterns of meal-skipping, poor snacks, overconcern about weight, and limited food choices. Professionals working with pregnant girls to improve nutritional status and the subsequent pregnancy outcome should be cognizant of the patients' life-styles and habits as they affect eating behavior.

The psychosocial factors imposed on the pregnant adolescent can cause her to be in a situation where she is alone, has no emotional support, has little or no money to buy food, and does not seek prenatal care. A team of health care providers with expertise in multiple areas is best suited to meet her needs. In the last decade or more, comprehensive programs have been developed that include prenatal care, nutritional guidance, psychological counseling, family planning, continued schooling, and parenting and infant care. In practical terms, however, programs such as these are not found consistently in all localities and they generally struggle for financial and program support. This type of program, if available in a community, however, no doubt is the most appropriate resource to optimize the outcome for both the teenage girl and her baby.

Sports and Athletics

Participation in a variety of physical activities is enjoyed by most adolescents. This may range from the organized, competitive sport and daily training to weekend skiing and bicycle trips. Regardless of the type of sport, optimal nutrition is a basic requisite for training and maintaining good physical performance. It is probably not coincidental that Olympic gold medal winners come from those countries with a high level of nutritional status.

As with the nonathlete, the diet of the athlete must supply optimal amounts of energy, protein, water, fat, carbohydrates, vitamins, and minerals. Energy will be needed for growth plus extra expended energy. In most situations appetite will be the guide for food intake. The specifics of nutrient needs and problem areas are dealt with in Chapter 12.

Despite the influence of good nutrition, dietary practices alone cannot be counted on for super powers or to supply the "winning edge." It is not unusual for adolescent athletes to emulate the professional star, including following a "winning" diet or accepting an endorsement of a food supplement. Adolescents competing in sports in which minimal body fatness is desired, e.g., gymnastics, wrestling, distance running, and ballet, may compulsively control food intake and lose weight to an unhealthy and dangerous degree.[129] Coaches and trainers, who work closest with the athlete, may also allow or encourage undesirable dietary practices because of their lack of nutrition expertise or their hope that the practice will improve performance. Many dietary practices relating to foods included or excluded in the athlete's diet are often based on psychological reasons or superstitions rather than on physiological and nutritional soundness.

Ideally, more nutrition education should be available to coaches, trainers, and others who greatly influence the young athlete. A study demonstrated that physical education students who had a college nutrition course scored higher than those who received nutrition information from parents and coaches.[130] Because adolescents are developing lifelong eating habits, it is desirable that those adults guiding them should reinforce positive dietary practices.

Substance Use and Abuse

Tobacco, alcohol, and marijuana are the substances most used and abused by the adolescent age group.[131] Hard, or addictive, drugs are used by a smaller percentage of teenagers. The use of these substances present significant problems in the public health, social, and family spheres.

Alcohol. Increased attention has been given to the problem of alcohol consumption in adolescents. The decision to drink or not to drink is made in the teen years. It has been reported that more than 90% of high school students have had at least some experience with alcohol by 18 years of age, and most have their first exposure under parental supervision between 12 and 15 years of age.[132] Currently, alcohol use among females is almost as high as among males.

Alcoholism or "problem drinking" in the adolescent age group has been difficult to define, because most definitions and classifications of alcoholism have been based on adult males. In most cases adolescent drinkers are identified by higher rates of alcohol-related problems such as school difficulties, psychological problems, and arrests and/or delinquency. Young people tend to drink less regularly than do adults, but they consume larger amounts at a time (i.e., binge drinking).[133]

The degree of nutritional risk for drinking adolescents depends on the frequency and amount of their alcohol consumption. It is known that alcohol has deleterious effects on nutritional status in more than one way. First, the alcoholic beverage, which has almost no nutritional value, displaces food that provides nutrients for growth. The B vitamins, especially thiamine and niacin, are needed for alcohol metabolism in the liver. Ethanol provides energy, at 7 kcal/gm, but significantly dilutes the nutrient content of the diet, making the individual at risk for nutritional deficiencies. In addition, continued alcohol consumption has a direct toxic effect on the gastrointestinal mucosa, interfering with digestion and absorption.[134] This adverse effect occurs independently of the malabsorption that can result from alcoholic cirrhosis. The nutrients most likely to be deficient are pyridoxine, folic acid, thiamine, and vitamin B_{12}. In many cases of chronic alcoholism, the malnutrition that exists is a result of both an inadequate diet and the alcohol's direct action on the gut.

For the pregnant adolescent who consumes alcohol, there is the risk of producing a child with fetal alcohol syndrome.[134] More subtle effects on the offspring may be caused by the alcohol itself or by the combination of alcohol and a marginal diet.

Nutritional status evaluations of adolescents should not neglect the area of alcohol consumption. Some individuals may initially withhold this information, in which case the interviewer should adopt a nonthreatening approach. Those adolescents who have significant alcohol problems obviouwly need comprehensive programs of counseling and rehabilitation, but it is appropriate that nutritional therapy and education be a component of such treatment. Programs for education and prevention of alcohol-related problems are needed, starting at the elementary school level.

Drugs. Drug use by teenagers may run the gambit from caffeine to illegal narcotic drugs. The kind of drug as well as its frequency of use or abuse will determine the detrimental effects on nutritional status and overall health.

Caffeine. Carbonated beverages provide most of the caffeine in teenage diets, but coffee and tea are also contributors. Soft drinks were the most frequently reported snack items in the Nationwide Food Consumption Study.[60] Although moderate amounts of caffeine can have positive stimulant effects, larger amounts can result in nervousness, agitation, gastric distress, and sleep problems. Because food habits in adolescence set the stage for adult eating patterns, teenagers should be encouraged to use caffeine-containing beverages in moderation. Although the soft drink industry is now making caffeine-free beverages available, these beverages may still displace milk, fruit juice, and other fluids that provide nutrients.

Marijuana. Marijuana is a substance often used by many adolescents as an alternative to alcohol. Although it is illegal, it is readily attainable and socially accepted in many peer groups. Controversy exists as to its harmful effects compared with other drugs, especially when used infrequently. The more detrimental effects are seen with heavy, long-term use.[135]

Marijuana causes changes in mental sensations and alters perceptions of time and space.[135] Sensory organs are affected, with an increased appetite and enjoyment of eating, especially sweets, reported by users.[136] Whether this is a direct effect of marijuana or an environmental effect is not clear. No specific marijuana-nutrient interaction has been identified, but little research has been done in this area.

Although many people believe that moderate marijuana use is benign, the social milieu of purchasing and using an illegal substance can have serious consequences for an adolescent. In addition, the marijuana may be contaminated with toxic substances or laced with addictive drugs such as heroin to ''hook'' a user on harder drugs.

Hard drugs. Included in this category are heroin, cocaine, PCP, morphine, and LSD. Although used by a small percentage of adolescents, these are the addictive drugs that are routinely abused by their users. Their use in adolescence is associated with a downward life-style—poor school performance or drop-out, deteriorating family interactions, isolation, and illegal activities such as theft to obtain money to purchase the drug.

Drug abusers are faced with a multitude of problems because of their habit, including poor health and nutrition. Their nutritional status is often negatively affected because of (1) money used for drugs instead of food, (2) depressed appetite, (3) irregular life-style and eating habits, (4) hepatitis and other infectious diseases that cause anorexia and increased need for nutrients, and (5) simultaneous use of alcohol or other drugs.[137]

A comprehensive drug treatment program is almost always needed to help the young person get free of the drug dependency and regain control of his or her life. Good nutrition is certainly an important part of that treatment. A nutritional assessment will identify the critical areas and provide information for counseling and educating the adolescent regarding food choices for optimal health.

Acne

Problems of poor complexion, blackheads, and pimples are dreaded by all adolescents of both sexes. Many experience these problems to some degree during puberty, and a small percentage are affected by a full-blown case of the clinical disease, acne vulgaris. Although teenage acne is subject to fads and fallacies regarding cause and treatment, there is nothing mysterious about this phenomenon. Acne is not caused by eating chocolate, french fries, or carbonated beverages, despite popular thought to the contrary. The sebaceous glands of the skin are under hormonal control, chiefly that of androgens; thus the rapid acceleration and increase of hormone production are directly related to the skin changes.

There is no rationale for recommending a specific diet in the treatment of acne, although any food that seems to be aggravating for an individual should be limited. Medical treatment of acne vulgaris involves both topical and systemic medications. Retinoic acid (a vitamin A acid) is sometimes used as a topical agent in difficult cases, but its use requires physician supervision.[138] Large doses of vitamins, however, will not alleviate the symptoms of acne and may lead to toxicity of fat-soluble vitamins. Recent studies have suggested that zinc supplementation improves severe acne. A level of 135 mg of oral zinc daily (the RDA is 15 mg/day) reduced the mean acne score by 85%.[139] The mechanism for this zinc response is unknown; further studies are indicated.

In preventing or lessening the symptoms of acne, a basic diet providing optimal nutrients will help ensure healthy skin, but again, specific foods should not be eliminated unless they are suspect for the adolescent. An optimal diet combined with good skin care will not prevent the superficial signs of acne but will help lessen the severity of the symptoms.

COUNSELING AND NUTRITION EDUCATION

Adolescents in the United States are not experiencing the dire results of malnutrition, despite the fact that some of them do not receive optimal nutrition.

This realization is significant when considering methods and approaches to nutrition counseling and education for this age group.

According to Piaget's theory of cognitive development, 11 years of age and beyond is the formal operations period.[140] At this stage, there is expansion of abstract thinking and deeper understanding of scientific and hypothetical processes. The concept of nutrients functioning at biochemical levels can be grasped, yet knowledge as to wise food choices may be overshadowed by peer and social influences.

Counseling

Providing nutritional counseling to adolescents can be challenging, frustrating, and rewarding. Counselors who work with adolescents must be aware of the developmental stages of adolescence, including the physical, social, and emotional. A positive aspect in working with many teenagers is their built-in interest in nutrition, even though their information sources may not be completely reliable.

Establishing rapport with the adolescent is a first priority, one that often takes time and patience. Past experiences with adults may make it difficult for the adolescent to initially trust the helping professional. Emphasis on making the adolescent comfortable, showing a genuine interest in him or her as a person, and allowing flexibility in the session will result in more productive counseling. A wide variety of counseling approaches can be successful, depending on the characteristics of client and counselor, but either extremes of "authority figure" or "buddy" are not likely to work.

Initial assessment should be made as to whether dietary practices are beneficial, neutral, or harmful. The positive aspects of a dietary regimen can be emphasized. Reinforcement can certainly be given to the adolescent who has decreased consumption of concentrated carbohydrates and packaged snack items in favor of more fruits, vegetables, and whole grains.

In the case of unhealthy dietary patterns, concrete supportive data are more likely to be accepted by questioning adolescents than are superficial answers. The pregnant teenager will more likely accept the idea of an optimal weight gain if she understands the various components of weight gain and why each is essential for a healthy baby. Likewise, the overweight adolescent may be willing to give up a fad diet if the counselor helps him or her analyze its nutritional quality and long-term consequences.

The counseling relationship should encourage the adolescent to participate mutually with the counselor in setting goals, although the professional will need to make sure the goals are reasonable and attainable. Specific counseling techniques are described in detail in other sources,[94] but the following guidelines can assist the professional in working with the adolescent:

1. **Supportive counseling.** This should be provided on a consistent basis and is often long-term.
2. **Setting realistic goals.** These may include specific goals for weight change (gain, loss, or maintenance), changes in activity, or altering food-related behaviors. Goals should be short-term and developed in a gradual but progressive manner.
3. **Positive reinforcement.** Initially this will be provided by the counselor and others supportive to the adolescent. Eventually the adolescent will be taught to reinforce himself or herself.
4. **Patience.** This requires the counselor to accept periods of silence, to listen actively, and to reassess after a period of regression. Too often the professional is ready to give up and conveys this to the adolescent as failure.

Because some adolescents do not seek health care through established avenues, successful nutrition counseling and education have been demonstrated by rap sessions and team efforts in free clinics, youth centers, and other places accepted by the adolescents.[141,142] An initial appeal to their desire to be healthful persons will help in establishing a good rapport.

Implications for Nutrition Education

A survey of over 1300 high school students revealed that nutrition was a subject of relatively low interest compared with other areas of health for reasons such as boring subject matter, repetition of material learned earlier, learning "useless" facts, and superficial presentation.[143] Despite reports showing that teenagers are concerned about weight and growth,[41,144] this survey reported the lowest response of knowledge regarding weight loss and gain. In addition, female high school graduates with previous home economics courses incorporating foods and nutrition do not necessarily demonstrate better nutrition knowledge, attitudes, and practices than those without such courses.[145]

This information reveals a definite need for innovative nutrition education approaches to the adolescent. Leverton[146] points out some positive aspects in reaching adolescents: (1) they get hungry, (2) they like to eat, (3) they want energy, vigor, and the means to compete and excel in whatever they do, and (4) they have many good food habits that were established in childhood. Primary assets such as these yield access points to reach the adolescent at his or her own level of interest and readiness. By respecting the adolescent's ideas about food, it is easier for the health professional to emphasize the positive aspects and to build on them.

In addition to their roles in the family, adolescents also have significant roles as students and consumers. At school, a well-designed nutrition curriculum incorporated with relevant subjects can provide a base of knowledge. In a larger sense the school can be a nutrition laboratory, providing practical experience not only in science and health classes, but also in the lunchroom and at the vending machine. As consumers, teenagers are increasing their power in the marketplace but are also the targets of sophisticated advertising. To make rational food choices, they need practical information about food labeling and purchasing, nutrient density of foods, and how to analyze advertisement messages.

Because today's teenagers are generally more sophisticated and knowledgeable, they will usually respond to nutrition information in terms of growth and development, even in physiological parameters. With respect to future parenthood, it is obvious that the female should have an understanding of the impact of long-term nutrition on the outcome of pregnancy. However, since the father's food preferences are the most influential factor in family food choices, appropriate nutrition education for the male adolescent is just as vital.

Practical experience has shown that visual aids or other media developed specifically for adolescents lead to stimulating discussion and an increased interest in many areas of nutrition. Some novel and successful attempts at getting a nutritional message across to teenagers have included the use of a fantasy comic format and a radio/television media campaign using prizes and contests.[147,148] Newer techniques used in the classroom include computer-assisted learning programs and the use of games and tournaments that emphasize team effort.[149] Many of these efforts have been primarily experimental, however, reaching only a limited audience. One would hope that in the future appropriate program planning would support the use of innovative educational techniques to provide nutrition knowledge and concepts to all adolescents.

It should be remembered that food is only one part of the exciting and rapid journey to adulthood, and that nutrition education can be incorporated along with many aspects of adolescents' life-styles and at various stages of readiness. In completing their own growth and maturity, adolescents are nearing the time when they will influence and make decisions regarding the food habits and nutritional status of the next generation.

SUGGESTED LEARNING ACTIVITIES

1. Analyze a typical menu from two different fast-food establishments for energy and major nutrients. What deficiencies and excesses exist? How would you correct them?

2. Ann is 14 years of age and pregnant. What other information would you need (i.e., physiological, environmental, social, emotional) to adequately counsel her regarding nutrition for an optimal pregnancy?

3. Obtain 5-day food records from three adolescents. Assess the records in terms of frequency of eating, meals skipped, types of snacks chosen, times of day eaten, and location eaten. How do these data compare with the NFCS reports?

4. Perform a fitness test on an overweight adolescent. Working with the individual, design a program of appropriate aerobic activities to maintain the training heart rate.

5. Prepare a 40-minute talk on eating disorders for a high school health class, including the concepts of nourishment, activities, and feelings.

6. Review several magazines popular with teenagers and young adults. What is the focus of the health-nutrition-diet articles? What image(s) do the advertisements convey?

7. Prepare a talk for a wrestling team and coach regarding the critical nutritional factors needed for both good health and optimal performance.

REFERENCES

1. Height and weight of youth 12-17 years, Vital and Health Statistics, Series 11, No. 124, Washington D.C., 1973, Department of Health, Education and Welfare, U.S. Government Printing Office.
2. Marshall, W.A., and Tanner, J.M.: Variations in pattern of pubertal changes in girls, Arch. Dis. Child. **44**:291, 1969.
3. McMahon, B.: Age at menarche, DHEW Pub. No. (HRA) 74-1615, Supt. of Documents, Washington, D.C., 1973, U.S. Government Printing Office.
4. Hammar, S.L., and others: An interdisciplinary study of adolescent obesity, J. Pediatr. **80**:373, 1972.
5. Garn, S.M., and Haskell, J.A.: Fat thickness and developmental status in childhood and adolescence, Am. J. Dis. Child. **99**:746, 1960.
6. Frisch, R.E.: Critical weight at menarche, initiation of the adolescent growth spurt, and control of puberty. In Grumbach, M., Grave, G., and Mayer, F., editors: Control of the onset of puberty, New York, 1974, John Wiley & Sons, Inc.
7. Frisch, R.E., Wyshak, G., and Vincent, L.: Delayed menarche and amenorrhea in ballet dancers, New Engl. J. Med. **303**:17, 1980.
8. Vandenbroucke, J.P., van Laar, A., and Valkenburg, H.A.: Synergy between thinness and intensive sports activity in delaying menarche, Br. Med. J. **284**:1907, 1982.
9. Crawford, J., and Osler, D.: Body composition at menarche: the Frisch-Revelle hypothesis revisited, Pediatrics **56**:449, 1975.
10. Ellison, P.: Skeletal growth, fatness, and menarcheal age: a comparison of two hypotheses, Hum. Biol. **54**:269, 1982.
11. Tanner, J.M.: Growth at adolescence, ed. 2, Oxford, 1962, Blackwell Scientific Publications Ltd.
12. Garn, S.M., and Wagner, B.: The adolescent growth of the skeletal mass and its implications to mineral requirements. In Heald, F.P., editor: Adolescent nutrition and growth, New York, 1969, Meredith Corp.
13. Bayer, L.M., and Bayley, N.: Growth diagnosis, Chicago, 1959, University of Chicago Press.
14. Greulich, W.W., and Pyle, S.I.: Radiographic atlas of skeletal development of the hand and wrist, ed. 2, Stanford, Calif., 1959, Stanford University Press.
15. Tanner, J.M., and others: Prediction of adult height from height, bone age, and occurrence of menarche at ages 4 to 16 with allowance for mid-parent height, Arch. Dis. Child. **50**:14, 1975.
16. Parizkova, J.: Growth and growth velocity of lean body mass and fat in adolescent boys, Pediatr. Res. **10**:647, 1976.
17. Wyshak, G., and Frisch, R.E.: Evidence for a secular trend in age of menarche, New Engl. J. Med. **306**:1033, 1982.
18. Greulich, W.W.: Some secular changes in the growth of American-born and native Japanese children, Am. J. Phys. Anthropol. **45**:553, 1976.
19. Food and Nutrition Board: Recommended dietary allowances, ed. 9, Washington, D.C., 1980, National Academy of Sciences, National Research Council.
20. Wait, B., and Roberts, L.J.: Studies in the food requirement of adolescent girls. I. The energy intake of well-nourished girls 10 to 16 years of age, J. Am. Diet. Assoc. **8**:209, 1932.
21. Heald, F.P., Remmell, P.S., and Mayer, J.: Caloric, protein, and fat intakes of children and adolescents. In Heald, F.P., editor: Adolescent nutrition and growth, New York, 1969, Meredith Corp.
22. Hampton, M.C., and others: Caloric and nutrient intake of teenagers, J. Am. Diet. Assoc. **50**:385, 1967.
23. Beal, V.A.: Nutritional intake. In McCammon, R.W., editor: Human growth and development, Springfield, Ill., 1970, Charles C. Thomas, Publisher.

24. Johnston, J.A.: Protein requirements of adolescents, Ann. N.Y. Acad. Sci. **69**:881, 1958.

25. Hegsted, D.M.: Current knowledge of energy, fat, protein, and amino acid needs of adolescents. In McKigney, J., and Munro, H., editors: Nutrient requirements in adolescence, Cambridge, Mass., 1976, MIT Press.

26. Report of a Joint FAO/WHO Ad Hoc Expert Committee: Energy and protein requirements, World Health Organization Technical Series No. 522, FAO Nutr. Meet. Ser. No. 52, Geneva, 1973, World Health Organization.

27. Committee on Nutrition, American Academy of Pediatrics: Calcium requirements in infancy and childhood, Pediatrics **62**:826, 1978.

28. Abraham, S., Lowenstein, F.W., and Johnson, C.L.: Preliminary findings of the first health and nutrition examination survey, United States, 1971-1972: Dietary intake and biochemical findings, Washington, D.C., 1974, Department of Health, Education and Welfare.

29. Bowering, J., Sanchez, A.M., and Irwin, M.I.: A conspectus of research on iron requirements of man, J. Nutr. **106**:985, 1976.

30. Hallberg, L., and others: Menstrual blood loss—a population study, Acta Obstet. Gynecol. Scand. **45**:320, 1966.

31. Frenchman, R., and Johnston, F.A.: Relation of menstrual losses to iron requirements, J. Am. Diet. Assoc. **25**:217, 1949.

32. Hepner, R.: General discussion of adolescent nutrient requirements and recommended dietary allowances. In McKigney. J., and Munro, H., editors: Nutrient requirements in adolescence, Cambridge, Mass., 1976, MIT Press.

33. Daniel, W.A.: Hematocrit: maturity relationship in adolescence, Pediatrics **52**:388, 1973.

34. Daniel, W.A., Gaines, E.G., and Bennett, D.L.: Iron intake and transferrin saturation in adolescents, J. Pediatr. **86**:288, 1975.

35. Prasad, A.S., Halstad, J.A., and Nadimi, M.: Syndrome of iron deficiency, dwarfism, and geophagia, Am. J. Med. **31**:532, 1961.

36. Prasad, A.S., and others: Biochemical studies in dwarfism, hypogonadism, and anemia, Arch. Intern. Med. **111**:407, 1963.

37. Sanstead, H.H.: Zinc nutrition in the United States, Am. J. Clin. Nutr. **26**:1251, 1973.

38. Greenwood, C.T. and Richardson, D.P.: Nutrition during adolescence, World Rev. Nutr. Diet. **33**:1, 1979.

39. Daniel, W.A., Gaines, E.G., and Bennett, D.L.: Dietary intakes and plasma concentrations of folate in healthy adolescents, Am. J. Clin. Nutr. **28**:363, 1975.

40. Huenemann, R.L., and others: A longitudinal study of gross body composition and body conformation and their association with food and activity in a teenage population: views of teen-age subjects on body conformation, food and activity, Am. J. Clin. Nutr. **18**:325, 1966.

41. Dwyer, J., and others: Adolescent attitudes toward weight and appearance, J. Nutr. Educ. **1**(2):14, 1969.

42. Haugen, D.L.: The relationship of family meals to food habits and attitudes of youth in Minnesota, plan B, master's paper, Minneapolis, 1981, University of Minnesota.

43. Steinberg, L.D.: Understanding families with young adolescents, Chapel Hill, N.C., 1980, Center for Early Adolescence, University of North Carolina.

44. Hinton, M.A., and others: Eating behavior and dietary intake of girls 12- to 14-years-old, J. Am. Diet. Assoc. **43**:223, 1963.

45. Story, M.: Adolescent life-style and eating behavior. In Mahan, L.K., and Rees, J.M.: Nutrition in adolescence, St. Louis, 1984, The C.V. Mosby Co.

46. Santrock, J.W.: Adolescence, Dubuque, Iowa, 1981, Wm. C. Brown Group.

47. Muuss, R.E., editor: Adolescent behavior and society: a book of readings, ed. 3, New York, 1980, Random House, Inc.

48. Ruben, A.M.: Television usage, attitudes, and viewing behaviors of children and adolescents, J. Commun. **21**:355, 1977.

49. Kaufman, L.: Prime-time nutrition, J. Commun. **30**:37, 1980.

50. Way, W.L.: Food-related behaviors on prime-time television, J. Nutr. Educ. **15**:205, 1983.

51. Walker, M.A., and Hill, M.M.: Homemaker's food and nutrition knowledge, practice, and opinions, Home economics research report, No. 39, Washington, D.C., November 1975, U.S. Department of Agriculture, Agricultural Research Service.

52. Hudnall, M.: American Council on Science and Health Survey: how popular magazines rate on nutrition, ACSH News Views, 3(1):1, 1982.

53. Parham, E.S., Frigo, V.L., and Perkins, A.H.: Weight control as portrayed in popular magazines, J. Nutr. Educ. **14**:153, 1982.

54. Lee, C.J.: Nutritional status of selected teenagers in Kentucky, Am. J. Clin. Nutr. **31**:1453, 1978.

55. Schorr, B.C., Sanjur, D., and Erickson, E.C.: Teenage food habits, J. Am. Diet. Assoc. **61**:415, 1972.

56. MacDonald, L.A., Wearring, G.A., and Moase, O.: Factors affecting the dietary quality of adolescent girls, J. Am. Diet. Assoc. **82**:260, 1983.

57. Hodges, R.E., and Krehl, W.A.: Nutritional status of teenagers in Iowa, Am. J. Clin. Nutr. **17**:200, 1965.

58. Huenemann, R.L., and others: Food and eating practices of teenagers, J. Am. Diet. Assoc. **53**:17, 1968.

59. Science and Education Administration: Nationwide Food Consumption Survey, 1977-1978, Preliminary Rep. No.

2, Food and nutrient intakes of individuals in 1 day in the U.S., Spring, 1977, Hyattsville, Md., 1980, U.S. Department of Agriculture.

60. Pao, E.M.: Eating patterns and food frequencies of children in the United States, Hyattsville, Md., 1980, U.S. Department of Agriculture, Human Nutrition, Science and Education Administration, Consumer Nutrition Center.

61. Thomas, J.A., and Call, D.L.: Eating between meals: a nutrition problem among teenagers? Nutr. Rev. **31**:137, 1973.

62. McNutt, K.W., and McNutt, D.R.: Nutrition and food choices, Chicago, 1978, Science Research Associates, Inc.

63. Greger, J.L., Divibliss, L., and Aschenbeck, S.K.: Dietary habits of adolescent females, Ecol. Food Nutr. **7**:213, 1979.

64. Kintner, M., Boss, P.G., and Johnson, N.: The relationship between dysfunctional family environments and family member food intake, J. Marriage Fam. **43**:633, 1981.

65. Bruch, H.: Eating disorders, New York, 1973, Basic Books, Inc., Publishers.

66. Minuchin, S., Rosman, B.L., and Baker, L.: Psychosomatic families: anorexia nervosa in context, Cambridge, Mass., 1978, Harvard University Press.

67. Rees, J.M.: Eating disorders. In Mahan, L.K., and Rees, J.M.: Nutrition in adolescence, St. Louis, 1984, The C.V. Mosby Co.

68. Abraham, S., and Nordsieck, M.: Relationship of excess weight in children and adults, Public Health Rep. **75**:263, 1960.

69. Seltzer, C.C., and Mayer, J.: Body build and obesity: who are the obese? J.A.M.A. **189**:677, 1964.

70. Heald, F.P., and Hollander, R.J.: The relationship between obesity in adolescence and early growth, J. Pediatr. **67**:35, 1965.

71. Sjöström, L.: Fat cells and body weight. In Stunkard, A.J., editor: Obesity, Philadelphia, 1980, W.B. Saunders Co.

72. Schwartz, R.S., and Brunzell, J.D.: Increased adipose-tissue lipoprotein-lipase activity in moderately obese men after weight reduction, Lancet **1**:1230, 1978.

73. Sims, E.A.H.: Experimental obesity, dietary-induced thermogenesis and their clinical implication, Clin. Endocrinol. Metabl. **5**:377, 1976.

74. Elliot, J.: Blame it all on brown fat now, J.A.M.A. **243**:1983, 1980.

75. DeLuise, M., Blackburn, G.L., and Flier, J.S.: Reduced activity of the red-cell sodium-potassium pump in human obesity, New Engl. J. Med. **303**:1017, 1980.

76. Foch, T.T., and McLearn, G.E.: Genetics, body weight and obesity. In Stunkard, A.J., editor: Obesity, Philadelphia, 1980, W.B. Saunders Co.

77. Keesey, R.E.: A set-point analysis of the regulation of body weight. In Stunkard, A.J., editor: Obesity, Philadelphia, 1980, W.B. Saunders Co.

78. Monello, L.F., and Mayer, J.: Obese adolescent girls: an unrecognized "minority" group? Am. J. Clin. Nutr. **13**:35, 1963.

79. Tobias, A.L., and Gordon, J.B.: Social consequences of obesity, J. Am. Diet. Assoc. **76**:338, 1980.

80. Johnson, M.L., Burke, B.S., and Mayer, J.: Relative importance of inactivity and overeating in the energy balance of obese high school girls, Am. J. Clin. Nutr. **4**:37, 1956.

81. Stefanik, P.A., Heald, F.P., and Mayer, J.: Caloric intake in relation to energy output of obese and nonobese adolescent boys, Am. J. Clin. Nutr. **7**:55, 1959.

82. Bullen, B.A., Reed, R.B., and Mayer, J.: Physical activity of obese and nonobese adolescent girls appraised by motion picture sampling, Am. J. Clin. Nutr. **14**:211, 1964.

83. Stunkard, A.J., and Burt, V.: Obesity and the body image. II. Age at onset of disturbances in the body, Am. J. Psychiatry **123**:1443, 1967.

84. Soper, R.T., and others: Gastric bypass for morbid obesity in children and adolescents, J. Pediatr. Surg. **10**:51, 1975.

85. Lindner, P.G., and Blackburn, G.L.: Multidisciplinary approach to obesity utilizing fasting modified by protein-sparing therapy. Obesity/Bariatric Med. **5**:198, 1976.

86. Brown, M.R., and others: A high-protein, low-calorie liquid diet in the treatment of very obese adolescents: long-term effect on lean body mass, Am. J. Clin. Nutr. **38**:20, 1983.

87. Grace, E., Dietz, W., and Emans, S.J.: Protein sparing modified fast in morbidly obese adolescents (abstract), J. Adolesc. Health Care **4**:211, 1983.

88. Coates, T.J., and Thoresen, C.E.: Treating obesity in children and adolescents: a review, Am. J. Public Health **68**:143, 1978.

89. Brownell, K.D., Kelman, J.H., and Stunkard, A.J.: Treatment of obese children with and without their mothers: changes in weight and blood pressure, Pediatrics **71**:515, 1983.

90. Seltzer, C.C., and Mayer, J.: An effective weight control program in a public school system, Am. J. Public Health **60**:679, 1970.

91. Christakis, G., and others: Effect of a combined nutrition education and physical fitness program on the weight status of obese high school boys, Fed. Proc. **25**:15, 1966.

92. Stanley, E.J., and others: Overcoming obesity in adolescents, Clin. Pediatr. **9**:29, 1970.

93. Moody, D.L., and others: The effects of a jogging program on the body composition of normal and obese high school girls, Med. Sci. Sports **4**:210, 1972.

94. Rees, J.M.: Nutritional counseling for adolescents. In Mahan, L.K., and Rees, J.M.: Nutrition in adolescence, St. Louis, 1984, The C.V. Mosby Co.

95. Crisp, A.H.: Anorexia nervosa: let me be, New York, 1980, Grune & Stratton, Inc.

96. Halmi, K.A., and others: Pretreatment evaluation in anorexia nervosa. In Vigersky, R.A., editor: Anorexia nervosa, New York, 1977, Raven Press.

97. Pugliese, M.T., and others: Fear of obesity: a cause of short stature and delayed puberty, New Engl. J. Med. **309:**513, 1983.

98. Casper, R.C., Davis, J.M., and Pandey, G.N.: The effect of the nutritional status and weight changes on hypothalamic function tests in anorexia nervosa. In Vigersky, R.A., editor: Anorexia nervosa, New York, 1977, Raven Press.

99. Vigersky, R.A., and others: Anorexia nervosa: behavioral and hypothalamic aspects, Clin. Endocrinol. Metabol. **5:**517, 1976.

100. Crisp, A.H.: A treatment regime for anorexia nervosa, Br. J. Psychiatry **112:**505, 1965.

101. Stunkard, A.J.: New therapies for the eating disorders, Arch. Gen. Psychiatry **26:**391, 1972.

102. Bruch, H.: Perils of behavior modification in treatment of anorexia nervosa, J.A.M.A. **230:**1419, 1974.

103. Eckert, E.D., and others: Behavior therapy in anorexia nervosa, Br. J. Psychiatry **134:**55, 1979.

104. Pertschuk, M.: Behavior therapy: extended followup. In Vigersky, R.A., editor: Anorexia nervosa, New York, 1977, Raven Press.

105. Rosman, B., and others: A family approach to anorexia nervosa: study, treatment, and outcome. In Vigersky, R.A., editor: Anorexia nervosa, New York, 1977, Raven Press.

106. Garfinkel, P.E., and Garner, D.M.: Anorexia nervosa: a multidimensional perspective, New York, 1982, Brunner/Mazel, Inc.

107. Drossman, D.A., Ontjes, D.A., and Heizer, W.D.: Anorexia nervosa, Gastroenterology **77:**1115, 1979.

108. Hsu, L.K.G., Crisp, A.H., and Harding, B.: Outcome of anorexia nervosa, Lancet **1:**61, 1979.

109. Hsu, L.K.G.: Outcome of anorexia nervosa, Arch. Gen. Psychiatry **37:**1041, 1980.

110. Halmi, K.A., Falk, J.R., and Schwartz, E.: Binge eating and vomiting: a survey of a college population, Psychol. Med. **11:**697, 1981.

111. Garner, D.M., Garfinkel, P.E., and O'Shaughnessy, M.: Clinical and psychometric comparison between bulimia in anorexia nervosa and bulimia in normal weight women. In: Understanding anorexia nervosa and bulimia, Report of the fourth Ross conference on medical research, Columbus, Ohio, 1983, Ross Laboratories.

112. Anderson, A.E.: Anorexia nervosa and bulimia: a spectrum of eating disorders, J. Adolesc. Health Care **4:**15, 1983.

113. Pyle, R., Mitchell, J.E., and Eckert, E.D.: Bulimia: a report of 34 cases, J. Clin. Psychiatry **42:**60, 1981.

114. Boskind-Lodahl, M., and White, W.C.: The definition and treatment of bulimarexia in college women—a pilot study, J. Am. Coll. Health Assoc. **27:**84, 1978.

115. White, W.C., and Boskind-White, M.: An experiential-behavioral approach to the treatment of bulimarexia, Psychother. Theory Res. Pract. **18:**501, 1981.

116. Willard, S.G., Anding, R.H., and Winstead, D.K.: Nutritional counseling as an adjunct to psychotherapy in bulimia treatment, Psychosomatics **24:**545, 1983.

117. Fairburn, C.: A cognitive behavioral approach to the treatment of bulimia, Psychol. Med. **11:**707, 1981.

118. National Center for Health Statistics: Weight by height and age for adults 18-74 years; United States. Vital and health statistics. Series 11, No. 208, Health Services and Mental Health Administration, Washington, D.C., 1979, U.S. Government Printing Office.

119. Mahan, L.K., and Rosebrough, R.: Physiological basis for nutritional requirements and assessment of nutrient needs for adolescent health. In Mahan, L.K., and Rees, J.M.: Nutrition in adolescence, St. Louis, 1984, The C.V. Mosby Co.

120. Committee on Adolescence, American Academy of Pediatrics: Statement on teenage pregnancy, Pediatrics **63:**795, 1979.

121. Trussell, J., and Menken, J.: Early childbearing and subsequent fertility, Fam. Plann. Perspect. **10:**209, 1978.

122. Committee on Maternal Nutrition, Food and Nutrition Board: Maternal nutrition and the course of pregnancy, Washington, D.C., 1970, National Academy of Sciences, National Research Council.

123. Zlatnik, F.J., and Burmeister, L.F.: Low "gynecologic age": an obstetric risk factor, Am. J. Obstet. Gynecol. **128:**183, 1977.

124. Zuckerman, B., and others: Neonatal outcome: is adolescent pregnancy a risk factor?, Pediatrics **71:**489, 1983.

125. Weigley, E.S.: The pregnant adolescent, J. Am. Diet. Assoc. **66:**588, 1975.

126. Worthington-Roberts, B.S.: Nutritional needs of the pregnant adolescent. In Worthington-Roberts, B.S., Vermeersch, J., and Williams, S.R., editors: Nutrition in pregnancy and lactation, ed. 2, St. Louis, 1981, The C.V. Mosby Co.

127. Hassan, H.M., and Falls, F.H.: The young primipara: a clinical study, Am. J. Obstet. Gynecol. **88:**256, 1964.

128. Meserole, L.P., and others: Prenatal weight gain and postpartum weight loss patterns in adolescents, J. Adolesc. Health Care **5:**21, 1984.

129. Smith, N.J.: Excessive weight loss and food aversion in athletes simulating anorexia nervosa, Pediatrics **66:**139, 1980.

130. Cho, M., and Fryer, B.A.: Nutritional knowledge of collegiate physical education majors, J. Am. Diet. Assoc. **65**:30, 1974.

131. Bachman, J.G., Johnston, L.D., and O'Malley, P.M.: Smoking, drinking, and drug abuse among high school students: correlates and trends, 1975-1979, Am. J. Public Health **71**:59, 1981.

132. Morrissey, E.R.: Alcohol-related problems in adolescents and women, Postgrad. Med. **64**:111, 1978.

133. National Institute on Alcoholism and Alcohol Abuse: Technical Support Document to the Third Special Report to the U.S. Congress on Alcohol and Health, Washington, D.C., 1978, Department of Health, Education and Welfare.

134. Roe, D.A.: Alcohol and the diet, Westport, Conn., 1979, Avi Publishing Co.

135. Committee on Drugs, American Academy of Pediatrics: Marijuana, Pediatrics **65**:652, 1980.

136. Brown, J.: Diet and the new drugs: eating habits of some drug users, Ecol. Food Nutr. **2**:21, 1973.

137. Frankle, R., and Christakis, G.: Some nutritional aspects of "hard" drug addiction, Dietetic Currents, Ross Timesaver **2**:July/August, 1975.

138. Esterly, N.B., and Furey, N.L.: Acne: current concepts, Pediatrics **62**:1044, 1978.

139. Michaëlsson, G., Juhlin, L., and Vahlquist, A.: Effect of oral zinc and vitamin A in acne, Arch. Dermatol. **113**:31, 1977.

140. Robinson, N.M., and Robinson, H.B.: The mentally retarded child, ed. 2, St. Louis, 1976, McGraw-Hill Book Co.

141. Frankle, R.T., and others: The door, a center of alternatives: the nutritionist in a free clinic for adolescents, J. Am. Diet. Assoc. **63**:269, 1973.

142. Erhard, D.: Nutrition education for the "now" generation, J. Nutr. Educ. **2**:135, 1971.

143. Dwyer, J.T., Feldman, J.J., and Mayer, J.: Nutritional literacy of high school students, J. Nutr. Educ. **2**:59, 1970.

144. Deisher, R.W., and Mills, C.A.: The adolescent looks at his health and medical care, Am. J Public Health **53**:1928, 1963.

145. Schwartz, N.E.: Nutritional knowledge, attitudes, and practices of high school graduates, J. Am. Diet. Assoc. **66**:28, 1975.

146. Leverton, R.M.: The paradox of teenage nutrition, J. Am. Diet. Assoc. **53**:13, 1968.

147. Mapes, M.C.: Gulp: an alternate method for reaching teens, J. Nutr. Educ. **9**:12, 1977.

148. Alexson, J.M., and DelCampo, D.S.: Improving teenagers' nutrition knowledge through the mass media, J. Nutr. Educ. **10**:30, 1978.

149. Wodarski, L.A., and others: Teaching nutrition by teams-games-tournaments, J. Nutr. Educ. **12**:61, 1980.

ADDITIONAL READINGS

Brasel, J.: Factors that affect nutritional requirements in adolescents. In Winick, M., editor: Nutritional disorders of American women: current concepts in nutrition, New York, 1977, John Wiley & Sons, Inc.

Cheek, D.B.: Body composition, hormones, nutrition and adolescent growth. In Grumbach, M.M., Grave, G.D., and Mayer, F.E.: Control of the onset of puberty, New York, 1974, John Wiley & Sons, Inc.

Huenemann, R.L., and others: Teenage nutrition and physique, Springfield, Ill., 1974, Charles C Thomas, Publisher.

Ikeda, J.: For teenagers only: change your habits to change your shape, Palo Alto, 1978, Bull Publishing Co.

Nutrition for athletes: a handbook for coaches, Washington, D.C., 1971, American Association for Health, Physical Education, and Recreation.

Pipes, T.V., and Vodak, P.A.: The Pipes fitness test and prescription, Los Angeles, 1978, J.P. Tarcher, Inc.

Special Concerns of Dietary Intake during Infancy and Childhood

10

Common concerns related to food and nutrient intake during infancy and childhood include excessive energy intakes, food allergies, dental caries, and lactose malabsorption. Diets of children who modify their food intakes to control these conditions often need to be monitored for adequacy of nutrient intakes. In addition, parents and professionals frequently have questions about the long-term effects of nutrient intakes during childhood. These special concerns will be discussed in this chapter.

ENERGY BALANCE AND OBESITY

Obesity is a frequent concern in clinics that serve adolescents. Lack of success in achieving sustained weight reduction of obese adolescents has focused attention on identifying children at risk and motivating families to alter life-styles and environmental and psychosocial factors that contribute to the development of this condition.

Obesity is a major health hazard predisposing the affected adult to a greater risk of hypertension, cardiovascular disease, diabetes, gallbladder disease, and degenerative joint disorders than persons of normal weight. Obese adolescents face discrimination at college entrance, and obese adults are discriminated against in job placement and advancement.[1] Obese adolescents have been observed to exhibit psychosocial difficulties. They frequently have distorted body images and low

self-esteem and may become socially isolated. They have been described as leading a "Cinderella-like" existence.[2]

Many obese children become obese adolescents and adults. Abraham and Nordsieck[3] found that 80% of females and 86% of males who were overweight at 10 to 13 years of age were overweight 20 years later. Retrospective investigations have shown that approximately 30% of the obese adults had a history of juvenile obesity.[4] Data from the United States Health Examination Study showed that three fourths of those classified as obese between 6 and 11 years of age were classified as obese 3 to 4 years later.[5] Early-onset obesity is more severe and resistant to treatment than is obesity acquired later in life.[6]

Approximately 5% to 10% of school-age children and 10% to 15% of adolescents are obese. Limited data exist on obesity in preschoolers. One study in Manhattan suggested an incidence of greater than 13%.[7]

Definition

Obesity is defined as an excessive deposition of adipose tissue. It differs from overweight, which implies only weight in excess of average for height. Overweight can result from increased lean body mass, adipose tissue, or both. Forbes[8] has suggested that there may be two types of obesity in childhood and adolescence: one type characterized by increased lean body mass in addition to fat, a tendency for tallness, advanced bone age, and a history of overweight since infancy; and another type with no increase in lean body mass, normal bone age and height, and weight gain in the mid-childhood or late childhood years.

Weight greater than 20% of normal for height is one criterion that has been used to define obesity. Such standards, although they show trends for populations, are not applicable to individual children. The use of weight standards tends to underestimate fatness in children less than 6 or 7 years of age and frequently overestimates adiposity in adolescents.[9] Diagnosis of grossly obese children is easily made by visual inspection. Recognition of less severely obese children versus those who are overweight because of increased muscle mass requires measurements that give indications of body composition. Identification of children who are overfat and are settled into patterns of growth indicative of future obesity requires that measurements of body composition be included in health examinations, just as other measurements of growth are obtained. As described in Chapter 1, standards for tricep fatfold measurements with calipers have been published for all age groups. Use of these measurements to define greater than normal increases in adipose tissue of infants and children as they grow older will aid in identifying children for whom preventive measures should be applied.

Etiological Factors

Studies of rats and other animals have definitively shown that, in animals, genes carrying obese traits are transmitted to offspring. Mayer[10] has described many genetic obesities including a hereditary hypoglycemia syndrome and a genetically controlled spontaneous degeneration of the hypothalamus.

Definition of human genetic obesities has been more difficult because of the mixed racial heritage of most individuals and the many environmental factors known to contribute to obesity that cannot be controlled in studies. The high incidence of obesity among parents of obese children and the fact that early-onset obesity appears to be almost intractable lead one to believe that hereditary factors are important. Studies have shown that 60% to 70% of obese adolescents have one or both obese parents,[11,12] and 40% of obese adolescents have obese siblings. Other studies have found that less than 10% of children of average-weight parents are obese.[13]

Seltzer and Mayer[14] studied weight patterns of different body types. Using Sheldon's somatotypes they described obese adolescent females as more endomorphic and less ectomorphic than nonobese adolescent females. Inherited body type may predispose children to obesity.

Inactivity is another factor known to be operative in the etiology of obesity. Obese adolescents and school-age children are less active than are those of normal weight. Most become obese by ingesting calorie intakes equivalent to or less than their peers. Activity patterns are acquired in childhood. Children learn to enjoy those activities in which their families and peers engage. Parents who enjoy hiking, swimming, and sports often teach their children to engage in and enjoy these physical activities. Parents who spend their hours at home urging their children to be still so that they can watch television or read reinforce inactivity and sedentary living.

As discussed in Chapter 1, there are indications that excessive weight gains during critical periods of development may result in deposition of excessive numbers of adipose cells with which individuals will live for their entire lives. Later reductions in weight result in reduction of the size of the adipose cells, not the number.[15] Questions have been raised as to the validity of this hypothesis.[16,17] It is, however, an interesting speculation that could provide an explanation for the difficulties encountered in efforts to effect weight reductions in those with juvenile-onset obesity.

Several researchers have reported increased birth weights of obese children compared with children of normal weight.[18,19] Others have found no differences in birth weights of the two groups of children.[20,21] Fisch, Bilek, and Ulstrom[22] found that infants who were extremely obese at birth tended toward normal weight at 4 and 7 years of age but that an unusually high percentage retained their stocky physiques. Children who were very obese at 4 and 7 years of age tended to have had stocky physiques at birth. By 7 years of age, however, they were joined in their obese and overweight status by several children who had normal physiques at birth.

Infant feeding practices have been implicated as a factor in the etiology of obesity in childhood. Authorities initially suggested that bottle-fed infants are more likely to be overfed than are breast-fed infants. They also suggested that the addition of semisolid foods in the early weeks and months of life might result in excessive intakes of energy. The hypotheses have been invalidated. Yeung and others[23] found more obese breast-fed than bottle-fed infants in a longitudinal study of 316 infants followed from birth to 18 months of age. The introduction of semisolid foods before or after 2 months of age was not related to fatness at 6 months of age. Obese infants consumed significantly more energy than lean infants. Dubois, Hill, and Beaton[24] found the age at which semisolid foods were introduced was slightly later in obese than in normal weight infants. This lack of relationship between mode of milk feeding or the age of introduction of semisolid foods and the development of obesity has also been observed by other researchers in Europe, Canada, and the United States.[25-28]

Sveger[27] found that only 4 of 23 obese and none of 26 overweight infants remained so at 4 years of age. Poskitt and Cole[28] noted an incidence of 2.5% obesity and 11% overweight in a study of 203 4- to 5-year-old children. Three of five obese children were obese as infants; however, only one in nine obese infants became obese preschoolers. A study in a Swedish urban community found that only 10% of obesity in 7-year-old children could have been predicted from observations of weight gain during infancy.[29] Most obese infants do not become obese children and/or adults. There is a

"channeling tendency for obesity from infancy that becomes stronger with increasing age, and intervention to prevent obesity is appropriate at any age."[30]

Interestingly, retrospective studies of obese adolescents have shown that a large percentage of them had feeding problems in infancy, and some had even been hospitalized for failure to gain weight. Seven of ten mothers of obese adolescents studied by Hammer and others[2] reported seeking advice about feeding their children during infancy at least six times. Seven of the ten obese adolescents had had allergic reactions to food in late infancy and early childhood. Massengale[31] found that 28% to 30% of 92 obese adolescents had histories of feeding problems in the first year of life. Two children had had pyloric stenosis, and eight had been hospitalized for poor weight gain or dehydration.

Psychosocial factors and parent-child interactions are important factors that may contribute to obesity in childhood. The obese child is often an only child or the youngest child and frequently the result of an unwanted pregnancy. These children are often given food and material objects instead of love and the opportunity to have experiences that lead to the development of coping skills.[32] Anxious and insecure parents frequently overfeed children as expressions of their concern and love. They usually measure their success as parents by the amount of food their children eat and by how much weight they gain. As previously discussed, children who are reinforced for eating learn that eating pleases their parents; as a result food habits may be established that are conducive to obesity.

Food may be used to reward a desired behavior, to comfort an unhappy or frustrated child, or to compensate for a handicap or problem. These nonnutritive uses of food teach children to rely on food to compensate for emotional and social difficulties, a pattern that may continue throughout a lifetime.

Psychological trauma has been observed to be another factor associated with the onset of obesity. Bruch[33] noted that fear of hospitalization was associated with the onset of obesity in some children. Kahn[34] found a history of separation from their mothers in 32% of 72 obese children under 12 years of age. Fourteen of the children had experienced rapid weight gains that began shortly after the separations.

Differences have been noted in the incidence of obesity among children from the lower and higher socioeconomic groups. Garn, Clark, and Guire[35] reported, from analysis of data compiled during the Ten-State Nutrition Survey of 1968-1970 and the Preschool Nutrition Survey conducted by Owens and associates, that after the first few years of life and into adolescence the children of the poorest group were leaner and the children of the affluent group were fatter. The higher the socioeconomic status, the greater the amount of adipose tissue. Females were fatter than males at all ages at comparable income levels. White children had more adiposity than blacks. In adults the relationship between fatness continued in males but reversed for females. Low-income female adults were fatter than those who had greater economic resources.

They reevaluated the socioeconomic influences on adiposity with data from the Tecumseh, Michigan, Community Health Survey. Again they found low-income preadolescent males and females to be leaner than their higher income peers during the first examination. When the same individuals were reevaluated 18 years later, the low-income children had become fatter than their high-income peers.[35a]

Prevention

Regardless of its cause, obesity results when energy intakes exceed energy needs for growth, maintenance, and activity. Its manifestation is usually the result of small excesses of calorie intakes over expenditure for a period of weeks, months, or years. By monitoring rates of growth and deposition of adipose tissue, children can be identified who are accumulating more fat than would be anticipated, and measures to increase activity and/or decrease caloric intakes can be effected.

Adolescents often make their own decisions about what and when they eat. Counseling must be directed to the teenagers themselves. Parents control the food available to younger children, create the environment that influences their acceptance of food, and can influence energy expenditure by the opportunities they create for physical activity for their children. It may be important to explore first with parents their reason for encouraging children to consume amounts of food that result in rapid weight gain. Some parents may not recognize that their expectations for the quantity of food they encourage their children to consume are excessive and that the ''chubby'' child is not necessarily the healthy child.

Parents may need help in developing appropriate parenting skills. They may need to learn how to respond to hunger and other needs of their infants or how to interact with their children. They may need help in identifying ways to help their children develop initiative and to cultivate friends and outlets in the community.[32]

The activity pattern of both the child and the family should be explored; it may be important to help parents find ways of increasing their child's level of activity. Parents who live in apartments often reinforce sedentary activities to reduce the noise level and complaints from neighbors. Those who live in one-family dwellings may have limited space for activities for children. City park departments, preschools, and schools frequently have programs that offer opportunities for increases in children's activities.

It is important to remember that the range of appropriate energy intakes at any given age is large. Overweight children and children with familial trends to obesity may need fewer calories than their peers. Griffith and Payne[36] found that normal weight 4- to 5-year-old children of obese parents expended 1174 kcal/day as compared with 1508 kcal/day expended by children of the same size and age of normal weight parents. It was interesting that children of normal weight parents expended twice as much energy in physical activity as did those of obese parents. Families of children with a familial tendency to obesity may need help

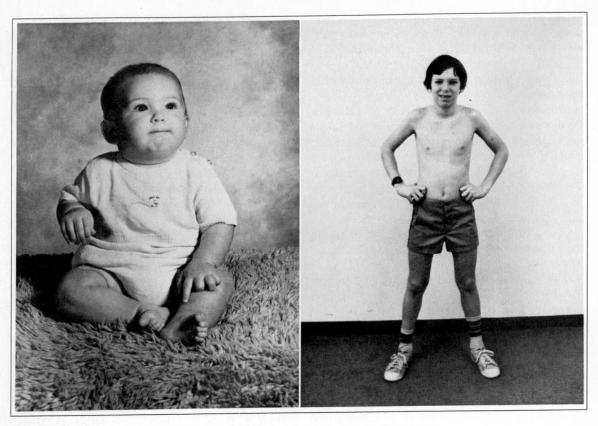

Fig. 10-1. An overweight infant who became a lean, well-proportioned adolescent.

in identifying the kinds and amounts of food that provide an energy intake that will support normal growth and weight gain.

Nutrition counseling should be family oriented and based on normal nutrition, emphasizing foods that provide a balance of nutrients as well as appropriate calorie intakes. Families will need to realize that efforts are directed at reduction in rates of weight gain and are not intended to effect weight loss. They must recognize that the food available and the models set for their child will determine the child's response to efforts to control weight gain. Family meals may need to be modified to include fewer fried foods, less gravy, and fewer rich desserts. Parents and siblings may have to modify

their own eating practices to set appropriate examples. Teachers, baby-sitters, and day-care workers should be alerted to and included in programs designed to control weight. Food experiences at school may need to be modified to exclude corn dripping with butter and chocolate cupcakes so frequently provided for special occasions. Low-calorie snacks such as raw fruits and vegetables can be provided instead of cookies, candy, and hot dogs. The use of food as reinforcers can be modified. Comparative energy values of snack foods are shown in Table 10-1.

Parents and children will need help in planning for parties and special occasions. Some children delete 50 kcal/day from their planned diet and have

Table 10-1. Approximate energy value of common snack foods offered young children

Food	Portion Size	kcal	Food	Portion Size	kcal
Cheese cubes	¼ oz	25	Homogenized milk	3 oz	60
Hard-boiled egg	½ medium	36	Chocolate milk	3 oz	80
Frankfurter, 5″ by ¾″	1	133	Cauliflower buds	2 small	2
Pretzel, 3″ by ½″	1	20	Green pepper strips	2	2
Potato chips	10	114	Cucumber slices	3 large	2
Popcorn with oil and salt	1 cup	41	Cherry tomato	each	3
Bread stick, 4½″	1	38	Raw turnip slices	2	5
Saltines	1	12	Dill pickle, large	⅓	5
Graham cracker	2 squares	55	Apple wedges	¼ medium apple	20
Animal cracker	1	11	Banana	½ small	40
Brownie, 3″ by 1″ by ⅞″	1	97	Orange wedges	¼ medium orange	18
Chocolate cupcake	1	51	Orange juice	3 oz	35
Vanilla wafer	1	18	Grape juice	3 oz	60
Yogurt, plain	¼ cup	40	Lemonade	3 oz	40

From Adams, C.F.: Nutritive value of American foods in common units, Agriculture Handbook No. 456, Washington D.C., 1975, U.S. Department of Agriculture.

a calorie savings account that permits them to participate in the refreshments. Some prefer to have very special food. For example, one child has a "very special glass of water and gingersnap" for his preschool snack. No other child is permitted a similar snack.

If the child is grossly obese, a very slow rate of weight reduction may be attempted; however, linear growth should be frequently monitored. Clinical experience of the author has indicated that in grossly obese preschool and school-age handicapped children, a weight reduction of 2 pounds per month did not affect linear growth. Others, however, have reported that restricted calorie intakes did modify linear growth. Wolff[37] noted children who lost 2% or more of their weight per month grew in length at a less than expected rate. Children who (1) lost less than 2% of their body weight, (2) did not lose, or (3) gained weight grew at a rate faster than expected.

Knittle[7] reported that children on a protein-sparing modified fast diet may experience a transient slowed rate of growth but that height/age 6 months after weight reduction will not be affected. The multiplicity of factors in the etiology of childhood obesity indicates that a multidisciplined approach may be necessary. The team might consist of a psychologist or behaviorist, a physician, and a dietitian/nutritionist.

CASE STUDY

The 2½-year-old daughter of a single parent seen at the Child Development and Mental Retardation Center at the University of Washington at the request of her local pediatrician needed evaluation and therapy from several professionals. The child was visibly obese. Her weight plotted above the 95th percentile, her length between the 25th and 50th percentiles, her weight/height over the 95th percentile.

During the nutrition interview it was reported that she was obviously overfat at 4 months of age. By 14 months of age her mother and grandmother became concerned. When she was 2 years of age, she was often upset because she was "fat." Her mother tried offering her low-calorie foods. She, however, often gorged and sneaked food. The child by diet history was consuming 1500 to 1700 kcal/day, 75 to 85 kcal/kg, 16 to 18 kcal/cm of height. A diet supplying 850 kcal (9 cal/cm) was prescribed.

Fig. 10-2. A previously obese child and her mother exercise as part of a program to control the child's weight.

The mother and child lived with the mother's male friend and his father. The child was often cared for by her grandmother, and there was no coordination of efforts to control her food or energy intake.

The mother's friend, a rehabilitated drug addict, frequently told the child she was a ''fatty'' and ugly and then gave her food to keep her quiet. The child's mother did not want to move to her parents' home and doubted that she could ''make it'' on her own.

The following 3 months the child lost 2 kg. Her linear growth proceeded in channel. Often when she came to the clinic she was very reluctant to be weighed, stating ''I not a fatty; I not ugly.'' Play therapy for the child and therapy sessions for the mother as well as nutrition counseling were incorporated into the monthly visits.

The child's mother applied for and received a scholarship to a junior college, which carried a monthly stipend, and was able to move to her own apartment and enroll the child in a preschool program that included a variety of daily physical activities. When she had lost 3 kg her weight/height plotted below the 95th percentile, and her suggested energy intake was increased to 10.5 kcal/cm/day (950 to 1000 kcal/day) with a goal of weight maintenance. However, she began to gain weight.

It soon became apparent that each episode of weight gain was associated with psychosocial problems of the mother and that only the continuing counseling and play therapy made implementation of the plan for maintaining a normal weight possible. Even today, as a school-age child, her diet and weight gains must be carefully monitored. She is, however, no longer classified as obese. Continuing support has been necessary to maintain the gains toward prevention of future obesity.

Parents and their children need continuing support as they implement programs to prevent obesity and face incredible responses from other members of society. Well-meaning merchants and bankers who provide sweets for children should be encouraged to honor parents' requests to provide nonfood items as alternatives. Neighbors, relatives, and other children's parents should support weight-control programs.

As children grow older, they must learn to exercise willpower in refusing amounts of food that result in a positive energy balance. The children themselves should receive positive reinforcement

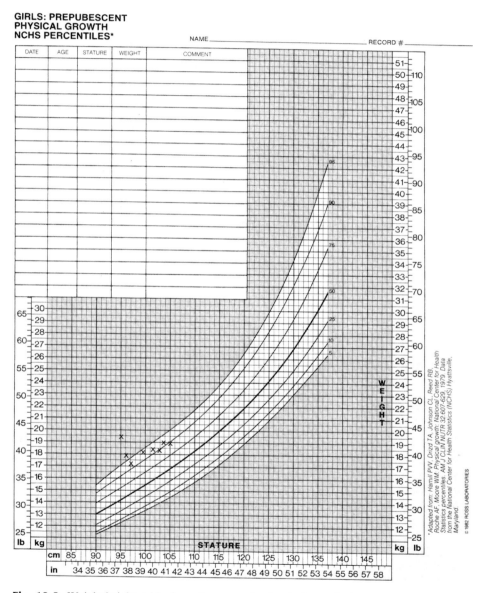

Fig. 10-3. Weight/height grid of an obese preschooler during and after nutrition counseling and psychosocial intervention.

for control of weight gain. They need continuing support, education, and understanding as they grow older. An 8-year-old boy who has been on a weight control program since obesity and was reversed at 27 months of age expressed the difficulties encountered on such a program. He stated during a recent clinic visit, "It's really hard to control my weight. I'm often hungry. I can't eat as much as the other boys, and my food is different from that of the other children in my class. I don't want to get fat, but I don't like being different." He, however, understands his program and knows he will receive the guidance and support he desires from his family as he assumes control of his own food selection and management of weight control.

FOOD ALLERGIES IN INFANCY AND CHILDHOOD

The most common chronic condition affecting children is allergies. There is no agreement as to the prevalence of food allergies in infants and children. Various investigators have reported incidences that range from 0.3% to 38%, the incidence reported varying with the criteria used for diagnosis and the population studied.[38] It is known that the incidence of food allergies is greatest during infancy. Children whose parents have allergic reactions to food are at a greater risk of having food allergies than are others.

Allergic Responses to Food

Manifestations of allergy result from antigen antibody reactions. Any tissue in the body can be the site of an immune reaction. Reactions may occur in several sites in the same individual in response to a single allergen. Allergic responses to food result in a variety of symptoms that include rhinitis, diarrhea, vomiting, malabsorption, abdominal pain, urticaria, eczema, irritability, and hyperactivity. Symptoms are not specific for any food or for allergies alone. They mimic those of other clinical conditions.

Reactions may occur immediately after a food is eaten (usually within 2 hours) or may be delayed, occurring within 4 to 72 hours. Both types of responses may be observed in the same child but to different foods. The type of reaction experienced by different children may vary when the same food is ingested. The immediate reaction is thought to be caused by antigenic properties of intact protein, the delayed reaction by antigenic properties of compounds formed during digestion.

The frequency and severity of symptoms may be influenced by psychological and physiological stress, quantity of food consumed at one time, and frequency a food is ingested. Anxiety and worry are known to cause symptoms after ingestion of a food that can be consumed with no problem in the absence of psychological stress. Allergic reactions to nonfood items such as pollens during hay fever season may cause allergic symptoms to foods that are normally nonallergenic. Reactions may be cumulative. A food consumed irregularly without any effect may cause symptoms when eaten regularly. Overindulgence in a food that can be consumed in small amounts without problem may cause allergic reactions.

Any food is potentially allergenic. Investigators do not agree on the most important food allergens. However, milk, wheat, eggs, and corn are consistently listed as the most allergenic foods. Other foods to which children are often allergic include chocolate, oranges, soy, legumes, rice, fish, beef, pork, and chicken.[39] Food additives such as flavorings and colors are other items that often cause allergic reactions. Diagnosed allergy to one food item often implies allergy to all food in its botanical group. For example, a child allergic to apples is often also allergic to pears.

The allergenicity of food may be reduced by cooking or processing. For example, some individuals allergic to fresh cow's milk tolerate evaporated milk. Others allergic to a raw fruit or vegetable may eat it without reaction when it is cooked.

Diets used in diagnosis. The variability of symptoms makes diagnosis of allergy a challenge for physicians. Skin tests may identify some food allergens but are generally considered unreliable. Diagnoses are made from dietary histories coupled with parents' perception of symptomatic responses to food, food diaries in combination with records of careful observations of symptoms, and elimination diets.

Detailed dietary histories give the physician indications of the foods and amounts commonly consumed. During the interview parents are questioned as to whether they suspect any food of causing symptoms. Parents appear to report immediate reactions well but often are unaware of foods that cause delayed reactions.

Food diaries are often requested. The parents are asked to record every food (including condiments) the child consumes for 1 week and to note every symptom the child manifests each day during that time (see box below). Careful scrutiny of such records gives the physician clues about which foods to suspect.

If dietary histories and/or diaries indicate specific foods that appear to be allergenic to the child,

Diet/Symptom Diary*

Name _____ Starting Date _____

DAY	1	2	3	4	5	6	7
Breakfast Morning snacks Drinks							
Symptoms							
Medicine							
Lunch Afternoon snacks Drinks							
Symptoms							
Medicine							
Dinner Evening snacks Drinks							
Symptoms							
Medicine							

From Bierman, C.W., and Furukawa, C.T.: Pediatr. Rev. **3:**213, 1982. Copyright American Academy of Pediatrics, 1982.
*List amounts of foods and drinks consumed; symptoms: severity and time; medications dosage and time given.

these foods are restricted from the diet for 1 week or longer. If improvement occurs, suspect foods are reintroduced and the child is observed for symptoms to confirm the diagnosis. If no improvement is noted, more severe restricted elimination diets are prescribed.

If an adverse reaction to specific foods is suspected, a double-blind challenge with the suspect foods is often used to confirm the diagnosis. Foods believed to cause allergic reactions are eliminated from the diet during the period of observation. When the individual is free of symptoms, capsules are filled with a dry form of the food to be tested. Wet foods are freeze-dried and powdered. Older children can generally be persuaded to swallow the capsule. For children younger than 6 years of age, the wet or dry food is masked in other foods consumed. Capsules are given by someone unaware of their contents, and the child remains under continuous surveillance in a hospital or office setting so that definitive observations can be made. If no reaction is noted, repeated challenges using increasingly larger doses of the dry food are conducted until the child consumes 8 gm of the dry food. If no symptoms occur, a placebo control is not necessary. In case of doubt, capsules of glucose are administered and observations for symptoms continue.[40]

Elimination Diets. When medical histories and food diaries fail to identify allergens and food allergies are still suspected, diets are often used as a diagnostic tool. Diets that eliminate two or three foods believed to have a high index of probability for sensitization are usually started first. In children older than 2 years of age, milk, chocolate, and cola are suggested to be eliminated first. Mothers are requested to keep a symptom score for 2 weeks before and during the 2-week trial diet for comparison. If improvement on the trial diet is indefinite, the diet is maintained for an additional 2 weeks. If the diet results in positive improvement of symptoms, single foods are introduced by an open visible or double-blind oral provocative challenge to see if symptoms recur. If no improvement occurs,

a new diet deleting corn and wheat may be tried; eggs and legumes may be eliminated next.[38]

If the "probability" multiple-elimination diet does not identify foods to which the child is allergic, an extensive elimination diet may be used. These diets restrict all but a very few foods. The foods included are those that have been proved to produce no reaction in most children. The Rowe cereal-free elimination diet as shown in the box on p. 275 is very restrictive but must be carefully followed if food allergens are to be identified. Recipes are provided so that there can be some variability in the child's menu.[41] The diets are followed for periods of 1 week to several months. If there is remission of symptoms, new foods are added at intervals of 5 to 7 days and the child is observed for reactions. If no change in symptoms is noted, a new elimination diet is designed.

A chemically defined product made from crystalline amino acids, glucose oligosaccharides, safflower oil, and recommended vitamins and minerals has been used as an elimination diet. Use of such a regimen until symptoms disappear may be difficult if children spend much of their time away from home and are exposed to food often.[42]

Dietary Management of Children with Food Allergies

When foods to which a child is allergic have been identified, they are eliminated from the diet. This may cause no difficulty if the child is allergic to only one food, particularly if it is not often mixed with others. When food allergies are multiple and/or include foods basic to culturally accepted diets such as milk, wheat, and eggs, however, parents may need help in identifying hidden sources of the food, finding acceptable substitutes, including where these may be purchased, methods of preparation, and menu planning. They must learn to read ingredient statements on labels to avoid hidden sources of allergens and may need to use cookbooks prepared for individuals with allergies.[43,44]

Cereal-free Elimination Diet (Rowe)

Tapioca	Apricots
White potatoes	Grapefruit
Sweet potatoes or yams	Lemon
Soybean potato bread	Peaches
Lima bean potato bread	Pineapples
Soy milk (Mull-Soy)	Prunes
	Pears
	Cane or beet sugar
Lamb	Salt
Chicken, fryers, roosters,	Sesame oil (not Chinese)
and capon (no hens)	Soybean oil
Bacon	Willow Run oleomargarine
Liver (lamb)	Gelatin (Knox's) with flavoring of allowed fruits and juices
Peas	White vinegar
Spinach	Vanilla extract
Squash	Lemon extract
String beans	Corn starch–free baking powder
Tomatoes	Baking soda
Artichokes	Cream of tartar
Asparagus	Maple syrup or syrup made with sugar flavored with maple
Carrots	
Lettuce	
Lima beans	

From Rowe, A.H.: Food allergy: its manifestations and control and the elimination diets, Springfield, Ill., 1972, Charles C Thomas, Publisher. Courtesy Charles C Thomas, Publisher, Springfield, Illinois.
NOTE: This diet was revised in 1970.

Parents should have instructions about the foods their children can consume as well as those that must be avoided. The child who is allergic to cow's milk is often offered a soy milk. Some children, however, are allergic to soy and/or the corn syrup that many manufacturers add to these products. Commercially manufactured or homemade meat-base formulas prepared according to a recipe devised by Rowe and Rowe[41] may offer acceptable substitutes for infants. Formulas constructed of pure amino acids (Nutramigen, Pregestimil) may be required for some infants. These formula are rarely acceptable to older infants and children.

Corn is extremely difficult to avoid. Corn starch is present in salad dressing, most sauces, many puddings and baking mixes, and a large number of other commercially prepared foods. Corn syrup is an ingredient that many manufacturers use in candy, sugar-coated cereals, and formula products.

If wheat is eliminated from the diet, alternate grains for baking must be found. Soy, rice, rye, and potato flours are often acceptable but require special recipes and a sizeable investment of the mother's time in food preparation. Commercially prepared pure rye and rice bread are available but cannot be found in many communities.

Table 10-2. Food selection in food allergy

Restricted Foods	May be Listed on Label	Foods to Avoid	Substitutes
Milk	Casein	Cheese	Mocha mix
	Caseinate	Cottage cheese	Coffee Rich
	Whey	Ice cream, yogurt	Soy formulas (Isomil, Pro Sobee)
	Lactalbumin	Creamed soups and sauces	Tofu
	Sodium caseinate	Butter and some margarines	Milk-free baked goods (often french bread)
	Lactose	Baked goods made with milk	
	Nonfat milk solids	Some "nondairy" products	Nut milk*
	Cream	Candy (creams and milk chocolate)	Coconut milk
	Calcium caseinate	Custards and puddings	Supplement for calcium + vitamin D
Egg	Albumin	Many baked goods	Egg-free baked goods*
	Egg whites	Egg noodles	Spaghetti
	Egg yolks	Custards, pudding	Rice
		Mayonnaise, some salad dressings	Some egg substitutes* (read label)
		Hollandaise sauce	
		Meringues	
		Some egg substitutes	
		Some batter-fried foods	
Wheat	Flour (enriched)	Baked goods made with wheat flour	Wheat-free breads, crackers (rice, cakes, special breads)
	Wheat germ	Crackers	Certain cold cereal (corn, barley)
	Wheat bran	Macaroni	Oatmeal or cream of rice
	Wheat starch	Spaghetti	Corn pasta*
	Gluten	Noodles	Bean threads
	Food starch	Gravies, thickened sauces	Rice
	Vegetable starch	Fried food coating	Corn tortillas
	Vegetable gum	Baking mixes	Popcorn
		Soy sauce	Wheat-free cereal crumbs for "breading"
		Hot dogs with wheat filler	
		Batter-fried foods	Thickeners: cornstarch, rice flour, tapioca
		Some sausages	Flours: rye, rice, potato
Soy	Soy flour	Soy sauce	Nut milk
	Soybean oil	Teriyaki sauce	Coconut milk
	Vegetable oil	Worcestershire sauce	
	Soy protein	Tuna packed in vegetable oil	
	Soy protein isolate	Tofu	
	Textured vegetable protein (TVP)	Baked goods or cereals that may include soy	
	Vegetable starch	Soy nuts	
	Vegetable gum	Soy infant formulas (Isomil, Pro Sobee)	
		Many margarines	

From Adams, E.J., and Mahan, L.K.: Nutritional care in food allergy and food intolerances in Krause, M.V., and Mahan, L.K.: Food, nutrition, and diet therapy, ed. 7, Philadelphia, 1984, W.B. Saunders Co.
*Products available from Ener-g Foods, 6901 Fox Avenue South, P.O. Box 24723, Seattle, Wash.

Table 10-2. Food selection in food allergy—cont'd

Restricted Foods	May be Listed on Label	Foods to Avoid	Substitutes
Corn	Cornmeal Corn starch Corn oil Corn syrup (solids) Corn sweetener Corn alcohol Vegetable oil Vegetable starch Vegetable gum Food starch	Some baked goods Corn tortillas (chips, tacos) Popcorn Some cold cereals Corn syrup Pancake syrup Many candies Some baking powder	Flour tortillas Thickeners: wheat, potato, or rice flour Beet or cane sugar Maple syrup or honey Baking soda and cream of tartar
Chocolate	Cocoa Cocoa butter	Candy Baked goods Colas	Carob products
Beef	Shortening Lard Gelatin	Soups Gravies, sauces Hot dogs Cold cuts	Pure vegetable shortening Turkey hot dogs
Pork	Shortening Lard	Bacon Sausage Hot dogs Baked beans, soups made with pork	All-beef hot dogs, cold cuts Vegetarian baked beans Pure vegetable shortening

If eggs must be omitted, products containing eggs, including noodles, mayonnaise, and many ice creams, puddings, and baked products, are also eliminated. Recipes for baking without eggs are needed as well as commercial sources of ice cream and bread not glazed with egg.

Table 10-2 gives suggestions for food selection in food allergy, including alternate names of the restricted foods, foods to avoid, and possible substitutes.

The rotation diet. Some clinicians believe that individuals who are sensitive to multiple foods may develop sensitivity to food and beverages previously tolerated if they are eaten too frequently. For these individuals, a 4-day rotation diet is planned so that no food is eaten more often than every 4 days. In most instances menus are provided so that parents can have the appropriate foods for each day

on hand. The rigidity and monotony of this diet makes it difficult for children to follow.[45]

Monitoring Nutrient Intake

Children with food allergies have potential areas of nutritional concern. Allergic reactions of the immediate type may make eating an aversive experience and cause children to reduce the number and quantity of foods they voluntarily consume. Malabsorption secondary to food allergies may increase nutritional deficits. In addition, parents anxious about the adequacy of an allergic child's food intake or response to a specific food convey that concern to the child who may use acceptance or rejection of food to control his or her parents' behavior. The monotony of the very restrictive diets may discourage children from consuming appropriate amounts of food. Energy and nutrient intakes of children with multiple food allergies should be carefully monitored. Diets of children who are allergic to milk should be monitored for calcium and vitamin D; diets of those allergic to citrus fruits should be monitored for vitamin C. The adequacy of intakes of the B vitamins should be checked when one or more cereal grains are limited.

Children often spontaneously recover from food allergies by 5 years of age. Foods to which a child is allergic should be singly introduced and the child observed for symptoms as he or she grows older. If allergic reactions to food continue, both parents and children need continuing support as they exercise willpower in refusing allergenic foods and select a combination of foods to support appropriate nutrient intakes.

CARBOHYDRATE

Dietary intakes of carbohydrate influence the development or control of dental caries. Children who have low lactase levels may find it necessary to limit their intakes of the carbohydrate lactose.

Dental Caries

Dental caries, one of the most common nutritional diseases, affects children at all ages and income levels. As with other tissues, nutrition plays an important role during development in the acquisition of sound teeth and the surrounding structures that hold them and in the later susceptibility of the teeth to caries. Once the tooth has erupted, the composition of the diet, the presence of acid-producing bacteria, and the buffering capacity of the saliva interact and result in the control or development of dental caries. Calcified dental tissues, unlike the long bones, which are subject to constant remodeling and repair, do not have the ability to repair themselves. Tooth destruction by decay is permanent.

Etiology. Dental plaque, a prerequisite for dental caries, has been described as a sticky, gelatinous mixture that contains water, salivary protein, des-

quamated cells, and bacteria.[46] The plaque bacteria, using energy derived from the catabolism of dietary carbohydrate, synthesize several toxic substances including enzymes that have the potential to degrade the enamel and dentin and are precursors of acidic fermentation products. *Streptococcus mutans* appears to be the primary bacteria. These acids and enzymes cause demineralization of the hydroxyapatite of the enamel followed by proteolytic degradation and demineralization of the enamel and dentin. It has been proposed that when the acidic environment falls below 5.5, cariogenic bacteria[7] invade the tooth and caries results. The saliva, the pH of which is 6.5 to 7.0, acts as a buffer and provides mechanical cleansing of the teeth.

Sugar. It has been well documented from animal studies and studies of humans in institutions and of outpatients when intakes of sugar could be controlled that sucrose is the most cariogenic carbohydrate and that the incidence of caries can be reduced when the intakes of sucrose are reduced.[46-51] Glucose is thought to be the next most cariogenic sugar, and maltose, lactose, and fructose have been found to have equal effect.[52]

Starch can also cause the production of large amounts of plaque acid because the carbohydrate, once attacked by salivary amylase, is broken down into sugar and is attacked by plaque bacteria.

It appears that the cariogenicity of sucrose is related to the high energy of hydrolysis of the covalent bond between the molecules of glucose and fructose. This energy is used by cariogenic bacteria to synthesize, among other compounds, extracellular polysaccharides, which are considered important factors in the etiology of dental caries. The polysaccharides may be absorbed on the crystal surface in the enamel, promote growth of cariogenic and other bacteria, act as inflammatory agents, and provide material for the formation of simple cariogenic monosaccharides and bacteria.[52]

The presence of sucrose, or even the total amount of sucrose in the diet, may not be the determining factor in the incidence of dental caries. An often-quoted study in an institution for the mentally handicapped in Sweden showed that the more important factors were the frequency with which the sugar is consumed and the adhesiveness of the food to the teeth.[53] The researchers who conducted this 5-year study showed that the consumption of sticky candy between meals produced a high increase in the incidence of dental caries, whereas the increase in incidence of dental caries from the addition of sugar-sweetened water at mealtime was small. When sucrose was fed in chocolate or bread, an intermediate increase in the incidence of caries was noted. Other studies have not supported these findings. Many researchers have found no difference between meal eating habits of caries-free and caries-prone individuals.[54,55]

Snacking at bedtime is especially effective in increasing dental caries. Reduction of the flow of saliva, which occurs during sleep, reduces the natural cleansing mechanism and permits greater fermentation of cariogenic material.[56] It has been proposed that the ingestion of foods that alter the buffering capacity of the saliva (e.g., milk and fats, which form a protective oily film on the tooth surface) may offer some protection for the teeth.[57,58]

Nursing bottle syndrome. A characteristic pattern of decay in infants and young children of all the upper and sometimes the lower posterior teeth, known as nursing bottle syndrome, is often observed in children who are given sweetened liquid by bottle at bedtime or who breast-feed frequently when they sleep with their mothers.[59,60] As children suck, the tongue protrudes slightly from the mouth, covering the lower front teeth. Liquids are spread over the upper and lower posterior teeth. Sucking stimulates the flow of saliva, which washes the debris from the teeth and promotes the secretion of compounds that buffer the acids in the plaque. When children are awake they swallow the liquid quickly. However, if they fall asleep, sucking stops and the salivary flow and buffering are reduced. The sweetened liquid pools around the teeth not protected by the extended tongue, and the bacterial plaque has contact with the carbohydrates during the hours of sleep.

Infant formulas, fruit juice, human milk, and cow's milk consumed when infants are falling asleep may cause this decay. To prevent this dental destruction it has been suggested that infants be held when feeding and burped and put to bed as soon as they fall asleep.[61]

Population difference in the incidence of dental caries. Some children appear to be more susceptible to dental caries than others. A study of Japanese, Hawaiian, and white children living in Hawaii showed that Hawaiian children were more affected by dental caries than were Japanese or white children and that the impact of sweet snacks between meals was greater on Hawaiian than on Japanese or white children.[62] In Detroit, Michigan, white children were found to have a much higher caries prevalence than blacks, but no difference was noted in caries prevalence in Columbia, South Carolina, between the races.[63]

Control. The less frequently foods are consumed and the less ability the foods have to adhere to the teeth, the more positive will be the outlook for control of dental caries. That fluoride can reduce the incidence of dental caries has been definitively proved (Chapter 2). It suppresses sugar metabolism by bacteria, makes enamel more resistant to acid, and stimulates remineralization of the teeth. A fluoridated water supply is an important approach to the prevention of dental caries. Other approaches to ensuring adequate fluoride that are under investigation include sodium fluoride capsules that can be chewed and swallowed, the use of an aerosol that causes fluoride-containing organisms to adhere to the teeth and enhances fluoride uptakes by the plaque and enamel, and the use of a small device attached to the teeth that releases fluoride at a predetermined rate for at least 6 months.[64]

Dietary control continues to be a most important and effective approach to the control of dental caries. The frequency of eating breads, rolls, and cereals has not been associated with an increase in dental caries, whereas the frequency of the consumption of candy and gum has been shown to increase the number and incidence of dental caries.[54] Cookies, cakes, pies, and candies have been shown to cause profound falls in pH of the plaque. It is interesting that the researchers found that the more acid-carbonated beverages depress the pH less than apple and orange juice.[65]

A study of 147 junior high school students' snacking patterns in relation to caries production showed chocolate candy to be the most carious snack food selected. Children who consumed fruit drinks, cookies, or apples at bedtime and between meals had a significant caries increment during the year studied. No carious lesions developed in 47 children who had higher intakes of fruit juice and oranges and lesser use of sugar-sweetened chewing gum than the other children. As the amount of spending money a child had increased, the frequency of snacking increased.[66]

Researchers have studied the cariogenicity of foods in rats by noting the caries experience after food comes in contact with the teeth for a designated period and in human beings by noting changes in the plaque pH before and immediately after a food is eaten. The box below shows foods that cause the plaque pH to fall below 5.5 and are considered to be cariogenic.[67,68]

Certain foods do not cause the plaque pH between the teeth to fall to levels at which demineralization will occur. These foods have a relatively high protein content with basic amino acids, a

---

A Partial List of Foods Which Cause the pH of Human Interproximal Plaque to Fall Below 5.5

Apples, dried	Gelatin, flavored dessert
Apples, fresh	Grapes
Apple drink	Milk, whole
Apricots, dried	Milk, 2%
Bananas	Milk, chocolate
Beans, baked	Oatmeal, instant cooked
Beans, green, canned	Oats, rolled
Bread, white	Oranges
Bread, whole wheat	Orange juice
Caramel	Pasta
Carrots, cooked	Peanut butter
Cereals, nonpresweetened	Peas, canned
Cereals, presweetened	Potato, amylose
Chocolate, milk	Potato, boiled
Cola, beverage	Potato chips
Cookies, vanilla sugar	Raisins
Corn flakes	Rice, instant cooked
Corn starch	Sponge cake, cream filled
Crackers, soda	Tomato, fresh
Cream cheese	Wheat flakes
Doughnuts, plain	

From Schachtele, C.F.: Nutr. News **42**:13, 1982. Courtesy Nutrition News, National Dairy Council.

moderate fat content, a strong buffering capacity, a high mineral content including calcium and phosphorus, and a pH greater than 6.0. They also stimulate saliva flow. Meats, nuts, and cheese have been found to be noncariogenic. In fact, they may have a beneficial effect when consumed with other foods. Cheddar cheese has been observed to block caries formation caused by sweet snacks when sweets and cheese are eaten alternately.[69]

Children should be taught to select foods that provide the essential nutrients and to limit their consumption of cariogenic foods. It is important that they learn to include noncariogenic protective foods in their snacking patterns, especially when sucrose-containing foods are included in the menu. The important between-meal snacks can be carefully planned to contribute nutrients without creating an oral environment conducive to tooth decay. Sweet foods as dessert items should be consumed as infrequently as possible within the framework of acceptability to the child and family.

Lactose Malabsorption and Intolerance

Low levels of activity of intestinal lactase, the enzyme that hydrolyzes lactose, the carbohydrate in milk to glucose and galactose, have been reported in 60% to 100% of nonwhite and 0% to 35% of whites in the world's postweaning population. The response of individuals with lactase deficiency to the ingestion of milk varies. Some manifest no symptoms. Others experience symptoms of flatulence, bloating, and cramping and may have diarrhea a few hours after milk is ingested. The amount of milk that must be consumed at one time to produce symptoms ranges from less than 240 ml to 1000 ml. Many persons who have lactase deficiency are not intolerant to lactose or to milk. Adults and older children with low lactase levels have usually consumed milk in infancy and early childhood without symptoms. The etiology of the low lactase activity is unknown. It has been hypothesized that it may be caused by a genetic factor with delayed expression. Others believe that the ability to hydrolyze lactose may be related to ecological changes in populations exposed to dairying for the past thousands of years.[70]

It has been estimated that 70% of black American adults and 10% to 15% of white Americans have a limited ability to hydrolyze lactose.[71] There is evidence that the onset of diminished levels of lactase occurs in childhood and adolescence. Paige, Bayless, and Graham[72] found that 20% of black elementary schoolchildren refused at least half of the milk in their type A lunch. Of those who were classified as non–milk drinkers, 77% had evidence of low lactase levels when a lactose tolerance test was performed.

Lactose malabsorption. Unaffected individuals hydrolyze and absorb ingested lactose in the small intestine. If lactase activity is low, only a portion of the sugar will be hydrolyzed. Undigested lactose remains in the lumen of the intestine and has a hyperosmolar effect, drawing large amounts of fluid into the gut. As the sugar is transported to the ileocecal region and first part of the colon, it is attacked by the bacterial flora. Bacterial fermentation of lactose causes the production of carbon dioxide, hydrogen, and low molecular weight acids that interfere with the reabsorption of fluids and electrolytes. The increased fluid load and products of bacterial fermentation cause the symptoms of bloating, flatulence, and abdominal cramping. Diarrhea may also result.

Tests for disaccharide malabsorption. The most accurate way to confirm deficiency of a disaccharidase is measurement of the enzyme activity in the mucosa by a biopsy of the small intestine. Low lactase activity is diagnosed when there is less than 2 units of lactase activity/gm of wet mucosa.[73] Ratios of sucrase to lactase activity are also used to identify low lactase activity. Ratios of sucrase to lactase greater than 4:1 are indicative of diminished lactase activity.[74]

A more commonly used but less satisfactory test for disaccharide malabsorption is a carbohydrate tolerance test. The individual in a fasting state is given 2 gm of carbohydrate/kg of body weight dissolved in water. Blood glucose determinations are obtained while fasting and at half-hour intervals for 2 hours. Normal response to a lactose tolerance test is a rise of 25 mg/100 ml or more from a fasting state.[75] False-positive results indicative of lactose malabsorption may be found in as many as 25% of normal subjects because of delayed gastric emptying.[76] Lactase deficiency is confirmed when symptoms of incomplete digestion of carbohydrate occur.

Calloway, Murphy, and Bauer[77] have shown that lactose-intolerant individuals have elevated concentrations of hydrogen in their breath after consuming lactose and have suggested that measurements of breath hydrogen are ideally suited for mass screening.

Arvanitakis and others[78] have shown measurements of $^{14}CO_2$ expired 2 hours after the ingestion of isotopically labeled lactose to be a sensitive test for lactase deficiency in adults. The use of an isotope, however, prohibits its use with children.

Lactose intolerance. Three types of lactose intolerance have been identified. Cases of congenital deficiencies of lactase in infancy have been described in which diarrhea continued as long as lactose was consumed but subsided when the carbohydrate was excluded from dietary intake.[79] Some of these affected infants develop normal lactase activities within months, suggesting temporary intestinal injury or delayed development of the enzyme.[80] Others have been described as having a rare inborn error of metabolism. Lactase is missing from birth throughout life even though the histology of the mucosa is normal.[81]

Deficiencies of all disaccharidases may occur secondary to diseases that damage the mucosal wall of the intestine, such as occurs in untreated celiac disease and may occur following a viral or bacterial gastrointestinal infection when diarrhea is prolonged.[82,83] Lactase deficiency is commonly more severe than deficiencies of the other disaccharidases. Lactase is the last enzyme to return to normal activity after recovery. Protein malnutrition may result in a temporary deficiency of sugar-splitting enzymes.[83] Children with kwashiorkor often

have severe diarrhea that improves when lactose is deleted from dietary intake. There have been reports of lactose intolerance in patients treated with antibiotics for long periods.[84] Secondary lactase deficiencies are usually temporary, and normal levels of lactase activity return in most persons when the disease is controlled. Offending sugars, however, should be omitted until treatment has effected a solution to the basic problem.

The other form of lactose intolerance found in many healthy populations is commonly acquired with age, being found infrequently in children under 3 years of age. The prevalence of lactose malabsorption and intolerance increases with age and varies among ethnic groups. It was found that 29% of 116 black children 13 to 59 months of age had lactose malabsorption but only 18% had symptoms when lactose was ingested.[85] Other studies have shown 11% of 4- to 5-year-old, 50% of 6- to 7-year-old, and 72% of 8- to 9-year-old black children to be lactose intolerant.[86]

Reports also indicate that Mexican-American and Indian populations have a high incidence of lactase deficiency. In a study of 282 Mexican-American children Wateki, Weser, and Young[87] documented that 18% of 2- to 5-year-old and 56% of 10- to 14-year-old children were lactose intolerant. Studies of American Indian children have shown an increase in the incidence of lactose malabsorption from 20% in 3- to 5-year-old children to 70% in 13- to 19-year-old children.[88]

Lactose malabsorption is almost nonexistent in white preschoolers. An incidence of 30% in adolescence has been suggested.[89] Lebenthal, Antonowicz, and Schwachman,[90] after reviewing 172 intestinal biopsies of New England whites 6 weeks to 50 years of age, found no case of low lactase activity below 5 years. After 5 years of age, two groups were identified: 24.6% had low lactase levels, and the remainder had lactase levels equal to those in the first 3 years of life.

Several studies indicated that lactose malabsorption might play a role in the symptoms of children with recurrent abdominal pain. However, Wald and others[91] found clear symptoms of lactose malabsorption after lactose ingestion in only 1 of 40 children with the problem, and they question if lactose malabsorption plays an important role in the majority of children with recurrent abdominal pain.

Effect on nutrient bioavailability. When lactose remains unsplit and is not absorbed, there is obviously a loss of calories from this nutrient. The percentage of intake lost is unknown and probably unimportant unless milk provides the major portion of the child's food intake. No differences have been found in nitrogen balance among lactose-tolerant and lactose-intolerant adults who consumed milk or lactose-free milk when energy intakes were considered[92]

Effect on milk intake. Bowie[93] found nitrogen absorption depressed but retention similar in children with lactose-induced diarrhea who were fed milk in contrast to a disaccharide-free diet. Fat absorption was similar on both regimens. Calcium, magnesium, and phosphorus absorption have been reported to be unaffected by lactose intake in lactose-intolerant persons as compared with lactose-tolerant persons. Lactose intolerance does not indicate intolerance to milk. Affected individuals often consume small amounts of milk without exhibiting symptoms. Some who experience bloating, cramping, and flatulence do not associate the symptoms with milk consumption. The production of symptoms depends on the amount of lactose consumed at one time. Reddy and Pershad[94] have shown that if given in small quantities, lactase-deficient individuals may consume as much as 1 quart of milk per day without symptoms. Stephenson and Latham[95] found that many lactose-intolerant individuals could consume 15 to 30 gm of lactose (1¼ to 2½ cups of milk) at a time with only mild symptoms of abdominal discomfort. Ice-cold milk and milk consumed without food seem to cause greater discomfort than milk consumed with food and milk consumed at room temperature.[96]

Intakes of milk have been shown to be similar in several lactase-sufficient and lactase-deficient schoolchildren. No differences were found in milk intakes of lactose-tolerant and lactose-intolerant black children at ages 13 to 59 months, 6 to 7 years, and 8 to 9 years.[85,86] Likewise, no differences were noted in the amounts of milk consumed by lactose-tolerant and lactose-intolerant Mexican-American children.[87] Stephenson, Latham, and Jones[97] found in a study of children in grades 1 to 6 from two schools that racial groups exhibited no differences in milk consumption. Students consumed an average of 6 oz. of milk at school and reported drinking an average of 3 glasses of milk per day.

Paige, Bayless, and Dellinger[96] have shown that lactose-intolerant elementary schoolchildren who refused more than half of the milk provided by the school lunch had a maximum blood sugar rise of 12.3 mg/100 ml, whereas the lactose-intolerant children who drank over half of the milk provided had a maximum blood sugar rise of 18.4 mg/100 ml. When given a lactose tolerance test, it appeared that some lactose-intolerant children had sufficient levels to hydrolyze moderate amounts of milk sugar. The blood sugar rise of lactose-intolerant individuals after a lactose challenge may define children who can consume moderate amounts of milk without problems.

Milk is an important source of protein, calcium, riboflavin, and vitamin A, and fortified milk is also a source of vitamin D in the diets of many children. Membership in a racial group known to have a high incidence of lactose intolerance in older children and adults is no indication for limitation of milk in children who do not manifest symptoms. Children who manifest symptoms should be encouraged to consume dairy products in which lactose has been fermented (e.g., yogurt, buttermilk, and cheese). Small amounts of milk may be well tolerated when consumed with meals. Lactose-free milks or milks treated with lactase are commercially available for children in whom symptoms are severe. Some children, however, have reported symptoms when whole, lactose-free, or lactose-hydrolyzed milk was consumed.[98] Lactose is added to many prepared foods. Parents of children with lactose intolerance should be directed to read labels carefully so that additional loads of lactose can be avoided. Diets of all children who limit their intakes of milk should be carefully monitored for vitamin D and calcium, and supplements should be prescribed if appropriate.

DIETARY FATS

Intakes of cholesterol and saturated fatty acids and food habits established in childhood are believed by some to be important factors in the development of coronary artery disease. In 1970 a subcommittee of the Inter-Society Commission for Heart Disease Resources recommended changes in the dietary patterns of all age groups.[99] This commission recommended that calorie intakes be adjusted to achieve and maintain normal weight and that cholesterol intakes not exceed 300 mg/day. The group urges that dietary fat contribute less than 35% of the total calories and that fat calories be equally divided among saturated, monounsaturated, and polyunsaturated sources. These recommendations were endorsed by the United States Senate Select Committee on Nutrition in 1977.[100] Both the Department of Agriculture and the U.S. Surgeon General's office reinforced these recommendations in subsequent publications.[101,102] Other groups and researchers have not considered dietary modification during infancy and childhood appropriate.[103-106] Many investigators have stressed the experimental nature of dietary intervention, the lack of knowledge about the effects of long-term ingestion of diets rich in polyunsaturated fats, and the expense of such changes in dietary patterns. Others have hypothesized that cholesterol may be an essential nutrient in infancy.[107]

Hyperlipidemia

Both cholesterol and triglycerides in the plasma are derived from two sources, dietary intake and endogenous synthesis in the liver and intestines. Dietary cholesterol is absorbed in proportion to the amount consumed. Increases in intakes reduce only partially endogenous synthesis. Endogenous triglycerides are synthesized from carbohydrate, fatty acids, and a variety of two-carbon fragments.

All plasma lipids, cholesterol, triglycerides, and phospholipids are transported in the blood bound to protein, which solubilizes them. Four macromolecule families of plasma lipoproteins are found in the blood. *Chylomicrons* transport the major portion of dietary triglyceride. *Very low-density lipoproteins* (pre-β-lipoproteins) transport endogenous triglyceride. *Low-density lipoproteins* (β-lipoproteins) transport one half to two thirds of the total plasma cholesterol. *High-density lipoproteins* transport cholesterol and phospholipids. Low-density lipoprotein cholesterol is transported primarily to peripheral tissue, including the smooth muscle of the arterial intima. High-density lipoprotein cholesterol travels through the capillary bed of peripheral tissue and acquires redundant-free cholesterol. It is ultimately carried to the liver, where it is released and excreted.[108] Low-density lipoproteins appear to damage the arteries; high-density lipoproteins are beneficial. The ratio of low-density lipoprotein cholesterol to high-density lipoprotein cholesterol has been found to be a good predictor for coronary heart disease.[109]

Cholesterol concentrations that are lower in cord blood than in maternal blood rise after infants are fed. Infants fed human milk or cow's milk have higher serum cholesterol concentrations than those fed formulas containing soy or corn oil at 6 months of age. These differences are modified when other foods are added to the diet. At 1 year of age differences in serum cholesterol levels between infants fed cow's milk or formula with unsaturated fatty acids and a variety of other food disappear. Total protein, total fat, and cholesterol intakes all correlated with total serum lipoprotein cholesterol and serum low-density lipoprotein cholesterol at 1 year of age.[110]

Several researchers have found that infants fed similarly after weaning from formula or breast milk have similar cholesterol concentrations in the preschool years.[111-113] They have concluded that earlier hypotheses based on studies with rats and pigs, which indicated that a cholesterol challenge in early infancy might be important in establishing a mechanism for low cholesterol levels in adults, are not applicable to humans.

Researchers in Louisiana studied changes in serum cholesterol concentrations in the early years (Table 10-3). They found serum cholesterol concentrations rose dramatically in the first 2 years of life. Low-density lipoproteins account for the major increase during the first year. However, a slow but progressive rise in high-density lipoproteins occurs.[114]

Other researchers in Ohio have noted no change in plasma lipid or lipoprotein levels between 6 and 11 years of age and a trend for plasma cholesterol levels to decline between 12 and 17 years of age (Table 10-4).[115] However, the Louisiana study found that during adolescence race/sex specific changes in serum cholesterol occur. They found a decrease in high-density lipoprotein serum cholesterol levels accompanied by an increase in low-density lipoprotein serum cholesterol in white males between 10 and 16 years of age. High-density lipoprotein cholesterol levels declined in black males of the same age though not as dramatically. They experienced a slight drop in low-density lipoprotein cholesterol. Declines were noted in high-density lipoprotein cholesterol levels with almost no change in low-density lipoprotein cholesterol in both black and white females between 9 and 14 years of age. The ratio of mean serum low-density lipoprotein cholesterol/high-density lipoprotein cholesterol rose dramatically in white boys beginning at 11 years of age, but it remained unchanged in black adolescent males and black and white adolescent females.[116] After 24 years of age, there is a progressive rise in total cholesterol for the next 30 years.

It should be noted that some studies have determined serum and others have determined plasma lipoprotein levels. It is important that one recognize that serum levels are higher than plasma levels in interpreting or comparing values. When recognizing this, the Louisiana and Ohio studies are in good agreement.[117]

The Louisiana study found that cholesterol levels in the first year were the most predictive factors studied of subsequent cholesterol levels. Of the children at the 90th and 10th percentiles in the first year, 45% persisted at their respective levels in the second year. Children of parents with high serum cholesterol levels are 2.57 times more likely to have serum cholesterol levels greater than the 95th percentile.[114]

Table 10-3. Serum lipoprotein cholesterol and triglycerides by age, Bogalusa Heart Study, 1973-1974, mean (95th percentile)

		Cholesterol				
Age	N*	Total	α-*	β-†	Pre-β†	Triglycerides†
Birth	419	70 (103)	36(60)	30(50)	4(12)	40 (54)
6 months	312	135 (185)	51(88)	74(111)	10(25)	92 (169)
1 year	291	145 (193)	53(81)	83(121)	9(25)	82 (158)
2½-5½ yrs	694	157 (198)	60(90)	91(129)	6(18)	63 (113)
5-14 yrs	3446	165 (215)	69(104)	89(130)	8(22)	69 (126)

From Berenson, G.S., and others: Lipids **14**:91, 1979.
*Nonfasting included in total numbers; numbers vary slightly for each variable.
†Fasting samples only.

Table 10-4. Mean and (SD) cholesterol (TC), triglyceride (TG), high (C-HDL) and low (C-LDL) density lipoprotein cholesterol (mg/dl) in 927 fasting school children

| Age | Male subjects | | | | | | | | | | Female subjects | | | | | | | | | |
| | White | | | | | Black | | | | | White | | | | | Black | | | | |
	No.	TC	TG	C-HDL	C-LDL	No.	TC	TG	C-HDL	C-LDL	No.	TC	TG	C-HDL	C-LDL	No.	TC	TG	C-HDL	C-LDL
6-7	50	158	50	56	94	17	158	49	60	93	39	161	71	49	101	16	168	55	57	104
		(21)	(16)	(11)	(21)		(31)	(15)	(15)	(26)		(16)	(35)	(9)	(19)		(15)	(14)	(11)	(15)
8-9	45	158	57	56	92	18	172	48	62	103	40	162	70	53	98	21	176	56	62	104
		(20)	(25)	(10)	(18)		(29)	(14)	(13)	(23)		(21)	(28)	(11)	(19)		(22)	(20)	(8)	(23)
10-11	60	164	58	56	98	20	171	58	63	99	70	161	72	51	98	22	160	69	53	99
		(31)	(20)	(10)	(29)		(27)	(20)	(9)	(29)		(25)	(24)	(10)	(21)		(22)	(36)	(10)	(20)
12-13	78	160	65	55	96	28	167	59	55	102	56	161	73	52	98	32	168	69	56	102
		(24)	(29)	(15)	(22)		(38)	(21)	(13)	(39)		(25)	(24)	(10)	(20)		(25)	(28)	(13)	(24)
14-15	57	155	69	48	96	23	156	60	53	95	56	151	72	50	91	21	166	60	56	102
		(29)	(29)	(10)	(27)		(22)	(22)	(10)	(17)		(21)	(27)	(10)	(19)		(18)	(18)	(11)	(19)
16-17	68	155	78	48	94	13	145	63	50	86	65	159	72	55	93	12	152	62	54	89
		(24)	(39)	(10)	(22)		(19)	(18)	(12)	(18)		(24)	(33)	(12)	(22)		(24)	(19)	(10)	(30)
6-11	155	160	55	56	95	55	167	52	62	98	149	161	71	51	99	59	168	60	58	102
		(25)	(21)	(11)	(24)		(29)	(17)	(12)	(26)		(22)	(28)	(10)	(20)		(21)	(27)	(10)	(20)
12-17	203	157	70	51	96	64	159	60	54	97	177	157	72	52	94	65	164	65	56	100
		(25)	(33)	(12)	(23)		(30)	(21)	(12)	(29)		(24)	(28)	(11)	(21)		(23)	(24)	(12)	(24)

From Morrison, J.A., and others: Pediatrics **62**:990, 1978. Copyright American Academy of Pediatrics, 1978.

Studies have suggested that 5% of the children in the United States have serum cholesterol levels greater than 200 to 220 mg/100 ml. It appears that these individuals will maintain their elevated levels throughout childhood and into adulthood, and they are considered at risk of developing coronary artery disease.[114,118] As they grow older they will be joined by others who enter the ranks of the at risk population.

Etiological Factors in Atherosclerosis

Cardiovascular disease, considered epidemic in the western world, is responsible for more deaths in the United States than all other causes together. Atherosclerosis is responsible for more than 50% of the deaths resulting from cardiovascular disease.

Atherosclerosis is a major specific type of arteriosclerosis, involving primarily the large elastic and medium-sized arteries. Lipids similar to those circulating in the blood accumulate on the intima of the arteries, to which an accumulation of connective tissue and various blood products are added, and plaques result. Several complications such as hemorrhage, thrombosis, or ulceration can occur in the atherosclerotic lesion and transform plaques into rough, complicated lesions. The plaques narrow the lumen of the arteries and may produce a deficiency of blood flow to some degree. They set the stage for complete occlusion.[119]

Fatty flecks and streaks are present by 3 to 5 months of age in the aortas of all children of all populations. As children age, the number and size of the streaks increase.[120] Studies of animals have suggested that dietary intakes of cholesterol and fatty acids determine whether the fatty deposits are reabsorbed, remain, or develop into atherosclerotic plaques.[121,122]

The average extent of intimal involvement is small in the first 10 years of life. After the first decade the extent of the intimal surface involved by fatty streaks increases rapidly. The lipid in the juvenile fatty streak is predominantly intracellular. There is minimal connective tissue. Black children have more extensive fatty streaks than do children of other ethnic groups. Females have more extensive streaking than do males. This is true in all populations studied, regardless of the incidence of atherosclerosis. After 25 to 29 years of age differences appear. Fatty streaks progress through continued lipid accumulation and lead to plaque formation. These fatty streaks contain much of their lipid in the form of extracellular accumulations in areas where intact cells are scanty. An increase in extracellular components of connective tissue also becomes apparent. Fibrous plaques then appear in a significant number of cases.

Autopsies of soldiers who died in the wars in Korea and Vietnam revealed a striking incidence of atherosclerotic plaques in males in their early twenties. Of 300 males killed in Korea, 77% were found to have evidence of atherosclerosis, ranging from minimal thickening to complete occlusion of one or more of the main artery branches.[123] Studies of Japanese natives undertaken at the same time revealed no cases in which plaque caused over 50% luminal narrowing. The amount of lipid in the plaques was less in the Japanese than in soldiers from the United States. The researchers concluded that diet was the primary source of the lipid.[124]

Autopsies of soldiers killed in Vietnam revealed a lesser but significant incidence of atherosclerosis. Of the casualties autopsied during this war 45% were found to have atherosclerosis, but only 5% had gross evidence of coronary artery involvement.[125]

A group of pathologists cooperating in the International Atherosclerosis Project examined 25,000 aortas and coronary arteries collected at autopsy in 14 countries. They found more extensive involvement in white men than in white women. Sex differences were not present in black populations.[126] Although the group found that the severity of atherosclerosis was associated with total energy intake derived from fat and the serum cholesterol concentrations in populations, they found no conclusive data that showed a relationship between atherosclerotic lesions and serum lipids and diets of individuals within populations. Their studies showed that the amount of lipid in the intima of the coronary artery of young adults predicted the extent of advanced lesions that occurred in later life in the same population.[127]

Risk factors associated with atherosclerosis. The major risk factors include elevated serum levels of low-density lipoprotein cholesterol, cigarette smoking, hypertension, obesity, sedentary lifestyle, and a family history of heart disease. All risk factors have been found to be independent and continuous variables. There is no arbitrary serum cholesterol level at which the risk of developing cardiovascular heart disease is increased. As the serum cholesterol level is increased, the risk for atherosclerosis increases. Also, the risk of developing atherosclerosis increases as the number of risk factors increases. Two or three risk factors increase the risk for atherosclerosis in an exponential manner.[127] For example, the obese individual with a moderately elevated serum cholesterol level who has hypertension and smokes cigarettes has a higher risk of developing atherosclerosis than the person who has a more elevated serum cholesterol level but is lean, active, and does not smoke.

That elevated serum low-density lipoprotein cholesterol and low serum high-density lipoprotein cholesterol concentrations are risk factors in the etiology of coronary artery disease is well documented. Populations that consume diets rich in cholesterol and saturated fats have higher serum cholesterol concentrations and higher incidences of and mortality rates from premature coronary heart disease than populations that consume diets low in cholesterol and saturated fat. The risk of developing premature atherosclerotic heart disease increases in any population group as the serum cholesterol concentration rises.[127] The Framingham study showed that the risk of myocardial infarction for men 30 to 49 years of age increased five times if cholesterol levels were greater than 260 mg/100 ml as compared with less than 220 mg/100 ml.[128]

Effect of dietary intervention. It has been proved that dietary alterations can reduce serum lipids.

Reduction in intakes of dietary cholesterol reduces serum lipids from 5% to 8%. Reductions in intakes of saturated fats accompanied by increases in intakes of polyunsaturated fats and reductions in cholesterol can reduce the serum cholesterol by 24%.[105] It has not been possible, however, to establish relationships in individuals between dietary consumption of fat and cholesterol and serum cholesterol levels.

Friedman and Goldberg found that 3-year-old children who had followed low-cholesterol, low–saturated fat diets from birth had serum cholesterol levels of 145 ± 4 mg/100 ml as compared with 154 ± 1/100 ml in children who had consumed the standard western diet.[113] Witschi and others[129] effected a 10% reduction in serum cholesterol levels in 3 weeks in free-living adolescents who followed dietary instructions. Stein and others[130] used dietary intervention to reduce serum cholesterol levels 14% in 229 adolescent males who lived in a boarding school in South Africa.

Morrison and others[131] found few significant correlations between dietary lipid and lipoprotein levels in 10-year-old children. However, children in the top quartiles for serum cholesterol ingested more total fat, more saturated fat, and less polyunsaturated fat than those in the lowest quartile. Another study found no significant correlation between mean daily intakes of total calories, total fat, and sugar and serum cholesterol levels.

Anderson, Lifschitz, and Friis-Hansen[132] found a direct correlation between intakes of saturated fat and an inverse relation between the ratio of polyunsaturated to saturated fatty acids of the diet with serum cholesterol levels during infancy. However, they found no relationship between intakes of fat and serum lipid levels in 3- to 4-year-old children.

McGandy and others[133] reduced calories from fat from 39% to 34%, reduced cholesterol consumption from 720 to 380 mg/day, and increased the dietary P/S ratio from .2 to 1.2 in children 12 to 18 years of age. Boys whose initial serum cholesterol was 200 mg/100 ml experienced a reduction of 15%. However, those whose initial serum cholesterol was 199 mg/100 ml or less experienced a reduction of only 8.3%. Stein and others[134] found that a high dietary plasma/serum ratio reduced total and low-density lipoprotein cholesterol but did not affect high-density lipoprotein levels in normal and hypercholesterolemic children and adolescents.

It has been hypothesized that diet has little to do with the magnitude of risk factors.[135] Others have suggested that diets of all those studied contained excessive amounts of fat, cholesterol, and calories.[136] Still others believe that genetic control predominates in determining the magnitude of the risk factors, including intakes of cholesterol and saturated fats.[127]

Potential difficulties of dietary intervention. Several potential problems have been suggested from the consumption of diets low in cholesterol and rich in polyunsaturated fatty acids. Fomon[107] has hypothesized that such diets in infancy may interfere with myelination of the brain because they do not contain preformed cholesterol. Schubert[106] has pointed out tht increases in intakes of polyunsaturated fatty acids increase the requirement of vitamin E. Other suggested consequences of the use of diets high in polyunsaturated fatty acids are increased incidences of gallstones and cancer of the colon.[137,138]

Many questions remain unanswered. Although there is a proven relationship between serum cholesterol and dietary intakes of fat in populations, no association has been found between dietary habits and serum lipid levels or coronary lesions in individuals within populations. It remains to be proved if reductions in serum lipid concentrations can delay the onset of atherosclerosis. The variability in response of individuals to dietary fat is as yet unexplained, although there is a large body of data that suggests genetic control. There are those who believe that serum lipid disorders originate in childhood and that food habits developed during that time should be patterned to acceptance and selection of diets low in cholesterol and saturated fats and rich in polyunsaturated fats.[139] Others

believe that efforts directed toward prevention of atherosclerosis should be focused on the adolescent and young adult.[120] Still others think that dietary intervention should be directed only to susceptible individuals.[139]

There is no difference of opinion that dietary intervention is appropriate for individuals in whom hyperlipoproteinemia has been identified or who have proven coronary artery disease. All agree that obesity and overweight should be discouraged at all ages. The Committee on Nutrition of the American Academy of Pediatrics[140] recommends screening of children older than 2 years of age who are at risk because of a family history of hyperlipoproteinemia with at least two serum cholesterol measurements. If high-density lipoprotein cholesterol is not the cause of an elevated serum cholesterol, they recommend that the child be treated with diet and/or drugs. For other children who are not at risk, they recommend a varied diet with selections from each of the major food groups and that the trend to decrease consumption of saturated fat and cholesterol be followed with moderation.

Dietary factors other than fats have been shown to influence cholesterol levels. For example, fiber, especially pectin, has a hypocholesterolemic effect. The source of dietary protein has also been shown to be a factor. It is apparent that until many questions are answered recommendations for modification of dietary intakes of fat and cholesterol should be individualized to the needs of each child and family.

SALT INTAKE

Essential hypertension, another risk factor in cardiovascular heart disease, is also a major health problem affecting 20% of adults over 40 years of age. Epidemiological studies have suggested that as with hyperlipidemia, genetic and environmental factors interact to determine an individual's susceptibility to the disorder. Salt has been implicated as one factor that may play a role in the etiology of hypertension.

Success in reducing blood pressure in hypertensive patients with the low-sodium rice diet designed by Kempner caused some researchers to hypothesize that excessive salt intakes could cause hypertension. Dahl[141] became so convinced that salt intakes were important in the development of hypertension that he devoted his life to this research. He studied the effect of salt intakes on thousands of rats, the effect of reduced sodium intake on hypertensive patients, and the relationship of sodium intakes to the incidence of hypertension in populations.

Evidence from Animal Studies

Meneely and others[142] induced hypertension in rats by mixing salt with their food and allowing them to consume as much water and food as they wished. They studied six groups of rats, each of which was fed an increasing amount of salt, and found that as sodium chloride intakes increased, elevations in blood pressures increased. Hypertension developed early in those animals who consumed the highest salt intakes. Although increases in blood pressure of groups of animals were related to the level of salt intakes, individual variations within groups were noted. They later fed diets that included extra amounts of salt to three groups of older animals who had been maintained on the basic food throughout their lives. Elevation in blood pressure did occur, but increases were always less than those of the young animals who ate the same rations.[143]

Dahl and others[144] found that in unselected rats, blood pressure increases in response to high salt intakes ranged from none to gradually increasing blood pressures, including the malignant phase. Some rats died from hypertension within a few months. There was no increase in blood pressure in one fourth of the animals in response to increased salt ingestion. The other animals developed increases in blood pressure that were associated with increasing morbidity and mortality.

In successive generations, rats were inbred and a strain of rats genetically susceptible to salt was developed. It was found that increased salt intakes

of these animals during the first 12 to 13 months after weaning produced hypertension that was sustained regardless of later reductions in sodium intakes. Control rats fed low-sodium mixtures developed no hypertension.[145] Dahl, Heine, and Tassinari[146] concluded that salt intakes in infancy and early childhood may be more critical than those in later life to persons genetically determined to be responsive to salt intakes. In 1963 they fed commercially prepared salted infant foods to those rats bred to be genetically sensitive to salt. Five of seven rats developed hypertension, whereas none of the seven control rats who were fed low-sodium diets developed the disorder. At that time they suggested that there may be groups of human infants with similar genetic potentials who are at risk for induced hypertension from salt intakes in early life. They advocated reductions in salt intakes in infancy.

Srinivasan and others[147] found the systolic and diastolic blood pressure levels increased in spider monkeys that were fed salt and salt-sucrose diets as compared with the levels of monkeys fed a control diet. A greater rise was noted in blood pressure of those fed the salt-sucrose diet. They suggested a potentiating effect of sucrose on sodium-induced hypertension.

Studies of Populations

Dahl[141] studied five population groups whose lifetime salt intakes varied from 4 to 26 gm/day and found that as average salt intakes increased the incidence of hypertension increased.

Gleibermann[148] reviewed studies of 27 populations. Sodium intakes had been estimated by urinary excretion of sodium for 24 hours in some and by estimated salt intakes in others. Her statistical analysis of these studies suggested a direct relationship between salt intakes and blood pressure across population lines.

Oliver, Cohen, and Neel[149] found that blood pressure in Yanomamo Indians who add no salt to their diets failed to increase with age but remained low throughout life.

The relationship of salt intakes of individuals to

blood pressure has not been established. Dahl and Love[150] found fewer hypertensive adults among those who salted foods lightly than among those who salted foods heavily.[150] Researchers in the Framingham study were unable to find a correlation between salt intake and blood pressure.[151] Prior and others[152] and Miall[153] found no relationship between salt intakes and blood pressure of individuals in two Polynesian groups and in a Welsh community.

Whitten and Stewart[154] studied two groups of black males, one fed a low level of salt, the other a high level of salt starting at 3 months of age. They found no difference in blood pressure levels of the two groups at 8 months or 8 years of age.

Schierf and others[155] found no correlation between sodium excretion and blood pressure in 20- to 40-year-old men in Heidelberg, Germany. Pietinen, Wong, and Altschul[156] found a correlation between sodium excretion and blood pressure of 20- to 40-year-old volunteers who had first-degree relatives who were hypertensive but no correlation between sodium excretion and blood pressure of individuals with no family history of hypertension.

Very high intakes of salt have been noted to increase blood pressure in individuals. Normotensive adults were noted to have an increase in blood pressure when fed 800 mEq/day.[157] A diabetic male became hypertensive consuming 700 mEq/day. His blood pressure returned to normal, consuming only 85 mEq/day.[158]

It appears that some individuals are very sensitive to intakes of salt whereas others experience no effect.

Levels and Effects in Infants and Children

During the first year of life intakes of sodium increase as infants consume more milk; the increase is more rapid as they begin to consume semisolid foods. In response to concern about the quantity of salt added to commercially prepared infant foods, in 1971 a subcommittee of the Food Protection Committee of the Food and Nutrition Board reviewed the studies and concluded that although the level of salt added to infant foods was not harmful, neither was it beneficial. The subcommittee recommended that the level of salt added to infant foods be reduced and that the upper limit of salt added be 0.25%.[159] However, concern continued until the addition of salt to commercially prepared infant foods was discontinued by all manufacturers.

Many parents make their own infant foods from a variety of foods prepared and seasoned for the family. Studies of semisolid infant foods prepared by 36 mothers showed that they contain 1005% more salt than commercially prepared infant foods.[160]

The sodium intake of infants is relatively low when human milk and commercially prepared infant foods are consumed, relatively high when cow's milk and table foods are eaten. As the transition is made to table foods, salt intakes will reflect family food habits and cultural patterns.

The use of convenience foods and the popularity of fast-food establishments for feeding children past infancy have given the food industry a major role in determining salt intakes of children.[161]

It appears that salting habits are unrelated to a taste threshold or an inborn taste for sodium chloride. Lauer and others[162] studied three groups of children 11 to 16 years of age whose blood pressures were average, less than the 5th percentile, or equal to or greater than the 95th percentile. They found no difference in salt threshold or preference in the three groups.[135]

Fomon, Thomas, and Filer[163] studied the acceptance of salted and unsalted foods by 4- to 7-month-old infants. They found that infants accept equivalent amounts of salted and unsalted foods. It appears that a taste for salt is acquired, not inborn.

Sodium is an essential nutrient. It functions in the maintenance of water and acid base balance and the regulation of blood volume. It regulates cell membrane and capillary permeability and is a constituent of tissues. It is estimated that total body sodium increases from 240 mEq in the 3.3-kg newborn to 3100 mEq in a 70-kg adult. Requirements are determined by the individual's needs for growth and by losses from the skin and in the urine and stools.[164] Needs for growth are estimated to be 0.5 mEq/kg/day during the first 3 months, 0.2 mEq/kg/day from 3 to 6 months, 0.1 mEq/kg/day from 6 to 12 months, and less than 0.1 mEq/kg/day after the first year. Skin losses depend on the ambient temperature. Stool losses are independent of intake, averaging 5% to 10% in the first year. Because of the variability of losses, Fomon[165] suggests an advisable intake of 8 mEq/day from birth to 4 months of age, 6 mEq/day from 4 to 24 months of age, and 8 mEq/day from 24 to 36 months of age.

Humans adapt to a wide range of sodium intake by varying excretion in relation to intake and nonrenal losses. The Committee on Nutrition of the Academy of Pediatrics[141] has stated that safe limits for normal children appear to be between 8 and 100 mEq/day. They have recommended that moderation be practiced in the trend to decrease sodium intakes of children. Dietary therapy should be individualized for children with identified hypertension and those with family histories of hypertension who may or may not derive benefits from reductions in sodium intakes. It is important to remember that iodized salt is a major source of iodine in the United States. Intakes of children who consume low-sodium diets should be carefully monitored for iodine. A palpable goiter has been noted in two adolescent females whose family had adopted a low-sodium dietary intake because of diagnosed hypertension in the father.

SUMMARY

Obesity, hypertension, and hyperlipoproteinemia are all risk factors for cardiovascular disease, as well as other disorders. The multiple etiologies of all three conditions have made it difficult to define the role nutrient intake plays in the etiology of such problems. Dietary intervention is appropriate for children who are overweight or obese or who have diagnosed hyperlipoproteinemia or hypertension.

It has been suggested for the remainder of the population of children that moderation be practiced in the trend to reduce sodium and saturated fat and cholesterol intakes.

Diets of children that must be modified because of food allergies or lactose intolerance should be carefully monitored for the adequacy of nutrient intake. Reducing sucrose intake combined with using noncariogenic foods at snacktime are effective in reducing the incidence of dental caries.

SUGGESTED LEARNING ACTIVITIES

1. Plan a week's menu for a 5-year-old girl who weighs 21 kg and is 109 cm tall that would maintain her weight.
2. Investigate and report on physical activities that are developmentally appropriate to increase energy expenditure for 2- and 8-year-old girls.
3. Describe how you would counsel the parents of an obese 8-month-old male.
4. Plan a week's menu for a child who is allergic to milk, wheat, eggs, fish, beef, and chocolate. Calculate the energy and nutrients in the menu.
5. Investigate sources in your community of rice flour, potato flour, and other products that can be used in the diet of a child allergic to wheat, rye, and oats.
6. Prepare a class for preschool children on snacks that are noncariogenic.
7. Investigate and report on the races in which one could expect to find a relatively high incidence of postweaning lactose intolerance.
8. Describe children at risk of hyperlipoproteinemia. How would one counsel parents of these children?
9. Investigate the salt content of fast-food menu items.

REFERENCES
Obesity
1. May, J.: Overweight causes, cost, and control, Englewood Cliffs, N.J., 1968, Prentice-Hall, Inc.

2. Hammar, S.L., and others: An interdisciplinary study of adolescent obesity, J. Pediatr. **80**:373, 1972.

3. Abraham, S., and Nordsieck, M.: Relationship of excess weight in children and adults, Public Health Rep. **75**:263, 1960.

4. Mullins, A.G.: The prognosis in juvenile obesity, Arch. Dis. Child. **33**:307, 1958.

5. Zack, P.M., and others: A longitudinal study of body fatness in childhood and adolescence, J. Pediatr. **95**:126, 1979.

6. Lloyd, J.K., Wolff, O.H., and Whelen, W.S.: Childhood obesity, a long-term study of height and weight, Br. Med. J. **2**:145, 1961.

7. Knittle, J.L., and others: Childhood obesity. In Suskind, R.M.: Textbook of pediatric nutrition, New York, 1981, Raven Press.

8. Forbes, G.B.: Lean body mass and fat in obese children, Pediatrics **34**:308, 1964.

9. Weil, W.B.: Current controversies in childhood obesity, J. Pediatr. **91**:175, 1977.

10. Mayer, J.: Some aspects of the problem of regulation of food intakes and obesity, N. Engl. J. Med. **274**:610, 1966.

11. Angel, J.L.: Constitution in female obesity, Am. J. Phys. Anthropol. **7**:433, 1949.

12. Rony, H.: Obesity and leanness, Philadelphia, 1940, Lea & Febiger.

13. Gurney, R.: The hereditary factor in obesity, Arch. Intern. Med. **57**:557, 1936.

14. Seltzer, C.C., and Mayer, J.: Body build and obesity—who are the obese? J.A.M.A. **189**:677, 1964.

15. Knittle, J.L.: Obesity in childhood: a problem of adipose tissue development, J. Pediatr. **81**:1048, 1972.

16. Widdowson, E., and Shaw, W.T.: Letters to the editor: full and empty fat cells, Lancet **2**:905, 1973.

17. Ashwell, M., and Garrow, J.S.: Letters to the editor: full and empty fat cells, Lancet **2**:1036, 1973.

18. Shukla, A., and others: Infantile overnutrition in the first year of life: a field study of Dudley, Worcestershire, Br. Med. J. **4**:507, 1972.

19. Sveger, T., and others: Nutrition, overnutrition, and obesity in the first year of life in Malmo, Sweden, Acta Paediatr. Scand. **64**:635, 1975.

20. Wolff, O.H.: Obesity in childhood: a study of the birth weight, the height, and the onset of puberty, Q. J. Med. **24**:109, 1955.

21. Heald, F.P., and Hollander, R.J.: The relationship between obesity in adolescence and early growth, J. Pediatr. **67**:35, 1965.

22. Fisch, R.O., Bilek, M.K., and Ulstrom, R.: Obesity and leanness at birth and their relationship to body habitus in later childhood, Pediatrics **56**:521, 1975.

23. Yeung, D.L., and others: Infant fatness and feeding practices: a longitudinal assessment, J. Am. Diet. Assoc. **79**:531, 1981.

24. Dubois, S., Hill, D.E., and Beaton, G.H.: An examination of factors believed to be associated with infantile obesity, Am. J. Clin. Nutr. **32**:1997, 1979

25. Gagnan, G., and others: Subcutaneous fat and nutrition in the first year of life, Nutr. Rep. Intern. **19**:541, 1979.

26. Ferris, A.G., and others: The effect of feeding on fat deposition in early infancy, Pediatrics **64**:397, 1979.

27. Sveger, T.: Does overnutrition or obesity during the first year affect weight at age four? Acta Paediatr. Scand. **67**:465, 1978.

28. Poskitt, E.M.E., and Cole, T.J.: Do fat babies stay fat? Br. Med. J. **1**:7, 1977.

29. Mellbin, T., and Vuille, J.C.: Physical development at 7 years of age in relation to velocity of weight gain in infancy with special reference to incidence of overweight, Br. J. Prev. Soc. Med. **27**:225, 1973.

30. Committee on Nutrition, American Academy of Pediatrics: Nutritional aspects of obesity in infancy and childhood, Pediatrics **68**:880, 1981.

31. Massengale, O.N.: The obese adolescent observations on etiology management prevention, Clin. Pediatr. **4**:649, 1965.

32. Hertzler, A. A.: Obesity—impact of the family, J. Am. Diet. Assoc. **79**:525, 1981.

33. Bruch, H.: Obesity in childhood. III. Physiologic and psychologic aspects of food intake of obese children, Am. J. Dis. Child. **59**:739, 1940.

34. Kahn, E.J.: Obesity in chidlren: identification of a group at risk in a New York ghetto, J. Pediatr. **77**:771, 1970.

35. Garn, S.M., Clark, D.C., and Guire, K.E.: Growth, body composition and development of obese and lean children. In Winick, M., editor: Childhood obesity, New York, 1975, John Wiley & Sons, Inc.

35a. Garn, S.M., Hopkins, P.J., and Ryan, A.S.: Differential fathers of low income boys and girls, Am. J. Clin. Nutr. **34**:1465, 1981.

36. Griffith, M., and Payne, P.R.: Energy expenditure in small children of obese and nonobese parents, Nature **260**:698, 1976.

37. Woff, O.H., and Lloyd, J.K.: Obesity in childhood, Proc. Nutr. Soc. **32**:195, 1973.

Food allergies

38. Crawford, L.V., and Herrod, H.G.: Allergy diets for infants and children, Curr. Prob. Pediatr. **11**:1, 1981.

39. Speer, F.: Management of food allergy. In Speer, F., and Dockhorn, R.J.: Allergy and immunology in children, Springfield, Ill., 1973, Charles C Thomas, Publisher.

40. May, C.D., and Bock, S.A.: A modern clinical approach to food hypersensitivity, Allergy **33**:166, 1978.

41. Rowe, A.H., and Rowe. A.: Food allergy, its manifestations and control and the elimination diets: a compendium, Springfield, Ill., 1972, Charles C Thomas, Publisher.

42. Hughes, E.C.: Use of a chemically defined diet in the diagnosis of food sensitivities and the determination of offending foods, Ann. Allergy **40**:393, 1978.

43. Williams, M.L.: Cooking without recipes for the allergic child, Blue Bell, Pa., 1981, Tri-Cor, Inc.

44. Frazier, C.A.: Coping with food allergy, New York, 1974, Quadrangle/The New York Times Book Co., Inc.

45. Gerrard, J.W.: Food allergy, Springfield, Ill., 1980, Charles C Thomas, Publisher.

Carbohydrate and dental caries

46. Nizel, A.E.: Nutrition in preventive dentistry: science and practice, ed. 2, Philadelphia, 1983, W.B. Saunders Co.

47. Guggenheim, B., and others: The cariogenicity of different dietary carbohydrates tested on rats in relative gnotobiosis with a streptococcus-producing extracellular polysaccharide, Helv. Odontol. Acta **10**:101, 1966.

48. Frostell, G., Keyes, P.H., and Larson, R.H.: Effect of various sugars and sugar substitutes on dental caries in hamsters and rats, J. Nutr. **93**:65, 1967.

49. Harris, R.: Biology of the children of Hopewood House, Bowral, Australia, observations on dental caries experience extending five years (1957-1961), J. Dent. Res. **42**:1387, 1963.

50. Templeman, A.J.: The dietary control of dental caries, Aust. Dent. J. **9**:163, 1964.

51. Jay, P.: The role of sugar in the etiology of caries, J. Am. Dent. Assoc. **27**:293, 1940.

52. Makinen, K.K.: The role of sucrose and other sugars in the development of dental caries: a review, Int. Dent. J. **22**:363, 1972.

53. Gustafson, B.E., and others: The Vipeholm dental caries study: the effect of different levels of carbohydrate intake on dental caries in 436 individuals observed for five years, Acta Odontal. Scand. **11**:232, 1954.

54. Bagramian, R.A., and others: Diet patterns and dental caries in third grade U.S. children, Commun. Dent. Oral Epidemiol. **2**:208, 1974.

55. Martinsson, T.: Socio-economic investigation of school children with high and low caries frequency. III. A dietary study based on information given by children, Odont. Rev. **23**:93, 1972.

56. Palmer, J.D.: Dietary habits at bedtime in relation to dental caries in children, Br. Dent. J. **130**:288, 1971.

57. Weiss, M.E., and Bibby, B.G.: Effects of milk on enamel solubility, Arch. Oral Biol. **11**:49, 1966.

58. Williams, W.L., Broquist, H.P., and Snell, E.E.: Oleic acid and related compounds on growth factors for lactic acid bacteria, J. Biol. Chem. **170**:619, 1947.

59. Tass, E.N.: Is bottle feeding of milk a factor in dental caries? J. Dent. Child. **29**:245, 1962.

60. Finn, S.B.: Dental caries in infants, Curr. Dent. Concepts **1**:35, 1969.

61. Gardner, D.E., Norwood, J.R., and Eisenson, J.E.: Atwill breastfeeding and dental caries, J. Dent. Child. **13**:186, 1977.

62. Hankin, J.H., Chung, C.S., and Kau, M.C.W.: Genetic and epidemiologic studies of oral characteristics in Hawaii's schoolchildren: dietary patterns and caries prevalence, J. Dent. Res. **52**:1079, 1973.

63. Bagramian, R.A., and Russell, A.L.: Epidemiologic study of dental caries experience and between meal eating patterns, J. Dent. Res. **52**:342, 1973.

64. Mirth, D.B., and Bowen, W.H.: Chemotherapy antimicrobials and methods of delivery in microbial aspects of dental caries. In Stiles, H.M., and others, editors: Microbial aspects of dental caries, Washington, D.C., 1976, Information Retrieval.

65. Edgar, W.M., and others: Acid production in plaque after eating snacks: modifying factors in food, J. Am. Dent. Assoc. **90**:418, 1975.

66. Clancy, K.L., and others: Snack food intakes of adolescents and caries development, J. Dent. Res. **56**:568, 1977.

67. Bowen, W.H., and others: A method to assess cariogenic potential of food stuffs, J. Am. Dent. Assoc. **100**:677, 1980.

68. Schachtele, C.F., and Jensen, M.B.: Human plaque pH studies: estimating the cariogenic potential of foods, Cereal Food World **26**:14, 1981.

69. Schachtele, C.F.: Changing perspectives on the role of diet in dental caries formation, Nutr. News **42**:13, 1982.

Lactose malabsorption and intolerance

70. Simoons, F.J.: The geographic hypothesis and lactose malabsorption, a weighing of the evidence, Dig. Dis. **23**:963, 1978.

71. Rosenweig, N.S.: Diet and intestinal enzyme adaptation: implications for gastrointestinal disorders, Am. J. Clin. Nutr. **28**:684, 1975.

72. Paige, D.M., Bayless, T.M., and Graham, G.G.: milk programs: helpful or harmful to Negro children? Am. J. Public Health **62**:1486, 1972.

73. Protein Advisory Group of the United Nations: Low lactase activity and milk intake, N.Y. P.A.G. Bull., vol. II, no. 2, Spring 1972.

74. Johnson, J.D., Kretchmer, N., and Simons, F.J.: Lactose malabsorption: its biology and history, Adv. Pediatr. **21**:197, 1974.

75. Ament, M.E.: Malabsorption syndromes in infancy and childhood, J. Pediatr. **81**:685, 867, 1972.

76. Newcomer, A.D., and McGill, D.B: Lactose tolerance test in adults with normal lactase activity, Gastroenterology **50**:340, 1966.

77. Calloway, D.H., Murphy, E.L., and Bauer, D.: Determination of lactose intolerance by breath analysis, Am. J. Dig. Dis. **14**:811, 1969.

78. Arvanitakis, C., and others: Lactase deficiency—a comparative study of diagnostic methods, Am. J. Clin. Nutr. **30**:1597, 1977.

79. Levin, B., and others: Congenital lactose malabsorption, Arch. Dis. Child. **45**:173, 1970.

80. Burke, V., Kerry, K.R., and Anderson, C.M.: The relationship of dietary lactose to refractory diarrhea in infancy, Aust. Paediatr. J. **1**:147, 1965.

81. Holzel, A.: Sugar malabsorption due to deficiency of disaccharidase activity and of monosaccharide transport, Arch. Dis. Child. **42**:341, 1967.

82. Plotkin, G.R., and Isselbacher, K.J.: Secondary disaccharidase deficiency in adult celiac disease (non tropical sprue) and other malabsorption states, N. Engl. J. Med. **271**:1033, 1964.

83. Chandrasekaran, R., and others: Carbohydrate intolerance in infants with acute diarrhea and its complication, Acta Paediatr. Scand. **64**:483, 1975.

84. Bowie, M.D., Brinkman, G.L., and Hansen, J.D.L.: Acquired disaccharide intolerance in malnutrition, J. Pediatr. **66**:1083, 1965.

85. Paige, D.M., and others: Lactose malabsorption in preschool black children, Am. J. Clin. Nutr. **30**:1018, 1977.

86. Garza, C., and Scrimshaw, N.S.: Relationship of lactose intolerance to milk intolerance in young children, Am. J. Clin. Nutr. **29**:192, 1976.

87. Wateki, C.E., Weser, E., and Young, E.A.: Lactose malabsorption in Mexican children, Am. J. Clin Nutr. **29**:19, 1976.

88. Caskey, D.A., and others: Effects of age on lactose malabsorption in Oklahoma native Americans as determined by breath H_2 analysis, Am. J. Dig. Dis. **22**:113, 1977.

89. Committee on Nutrition, American Academy of Pediatrics: The practical significance of lactose intolerance in children, Pediatrics **62**:240, 1978.

90. Lebenthal, E., Antonowicz, I., and Schwachman, H.: Correlation of lactase activity, lactose tolerance and milk consumption in different age groups, Am. J. Clin. Nutr. **28**:595, 1975.

91. Wald, A., and others: Lactase malabsorption in recurrent abdominal pain of childhood, J. Pediatr. **100**:65, 1982.

92. Calloway, D.H., and Chenoweth, W.L.: Utilization of nutrients in milk and wheat-based diets by men with adequate and reduced abilities to absorb lactose. I. Energy and nitrogen, Am. J. Clin. Nutr. **26**:939, 1973.

93. Bowie, M.D.: Effect of lactose-induced diarrhea on absoprtion of nitrogen and fat, Arch. Dis. Child. **50**:363, 1975.

94. Reddy, V., and Pershad, J.: Lactase deficiency in Indians, Am. J. Clin. Nutr. **25**:114, 1972.

95. Stephenson, L.S., and Latham, M.C.: Lactose intolerance and milk consumption: the relationship of tolerance to symptoms, Am. J. Clin. Nutr. **27**:296, 1974.

96. Paige, D.M., Bayless, T.M., and Dellinger, W.S.: Relationship of milk consumption to blood glucose rise in lactose intolerant individuals, Am. J. Clin. Nutr. **28**:677, 1975.

97. Stephenson, L.S., Latham, M.C., and Jones, D.V.: Milk consumption by black and by white pupils in two primary schools, J. Am. Diet. Assoc. **71**:258, 1977.

98 Paige, D.M., and others: Lactose hydrolyzed milk, Am. J. Clin. Nutr. **28**:818, 1975.

Fats

99. Atherosclerosis Study Group and Epidemiology Study Group of the Inter-Society Commission for Heart Disease Resources: Primary prevention of the atherosclerotic diseases, Circulation **42**:A-55, 1970.

100. Select Committee on Nutrition and Human Needs, United States Senate: Dietary goals for the United States, ed. 2 Washington, D.C., 1977, U.S. Government Printing Office.

101. United States Department of Agriculture and United States Department of Health, Education and Welfare: Nutrition and your health: dietary guidelines for Americans, Pub. No. 79-55071, Washington D.C., 1979, U.S. Government Printing Office.

102. Surgeon General's report on health promotion and disease promotion and disease prevention: health people, Pub. No. 55071, Washington, D.C., 1979, U.S. Government Printing Office.

103. Committee on Nutrition, American Academy of Pediatrics: Childhood diet and coronary heart disease, Pediatrics **49**:305, 1972.

104. Mitchell, S., and others: The pediatrician and atherosclerosis, Pediatrics **49**:165, 1972.

105. North, A.F.: Should pediatricians be concerned about children's cholesterol levels? Clin. Pediatr. **14**:439, 1975.

106. Schubert, W.K.: Fat nutrition and diets in childhood, Am. J. Cardiol. **31**:581, 1973.

107. Fomon, S.J.: A pediatrician looks at early nutrition, Bull. N.Y. Acad. Med. **47**:569, 1971.

108. Lewis, B.: Normal and abnormal lipid metabolism in children, Postgrad. Med. J. **54**:181, 1978.

109. Gordon, T., and others: High-density lipoprotein as a protective factor against coronary heart disease, Am. J. Med. **102**:707, 1977.

110. Farris, R.P., and others: Influence of milk source on serum lipids and lipoproteins during the first year of life, Am. J. Clin. Nutr. **38**:42, 1982.

111. Friedman, G., and Goldberg, S.J.: Concurrent and subsequent serum cholesterols and breast- and formula-fed infants, Am. J. Clin. Nutr. **28**:42, 1975.

112. Glueck, C.J., and others: Plasma and dietary cholestrol in infancy: effects of early low or moderate dietary cholesterol intake on subsequent response to increased dietary cholesterol, Metabolism **21**:1181, 1972.

113. Hodgson, P.A., and others: Comparison of serum cholesterol in children fed high, moderate, or low cholesterol milk during neonatal period, Metabolism **25**:739, 1976.

114. Berenson, G.S., and others: Serum high-density lipoprotein and its relationship to cardiovascular disease risk factor variables in children—the Bogalusa Heart Study, Lipids **14**:91, 1979.

115. Morrison, J.A.: Lipids and lipoproteins in 927 school children, ages 6 to 17 years, Pediatrics **62**:990, 1978.

116. Berenson, G.S., and others: Dynamic changes of serum lipoproteins in children during adolescence and sexual maturation, Am. J. Epidemiol. **113**:157, 1981.

117. Morrison, J.A.: Personal communication.

118. deGroot, I., and others: Lipids in school children, aged 6-17: upper normal limits, Pediatrics **60**:437, 1977.

119. Strong, J.P., and others: Pathology and epidemiology of atherosclerosis, J. Am. Diet. Assoc. **62**:262, 1973.

120. McMillan, G.C.: Development of arteriosclerosis, Am. J. Cardiol. **31**:542, 1973.

121. Armstrong, M.L., Warner, E.D., and Connor, W.E.: Regression of coronary atheromatosis in rhesus monkeys, Circ. Res.**27**:59, 1970.

122. Wissler, R.W., and others: Atherogenesis in the cebus monkey, Arch. Pathol. **74**:312, 1962.

123. Enos, W.F., Holmes, R.H., and Beyer, J.C.: Coronary disease among United States soldiers killed in action in Korea, J.A.M.A. **152**:1090, 1952.

124. Enos, W.F., Beyer, J.C., and Holmes, R.H.: Pathogenesis of coronary disease in American soldiers killed in Korea, J.A.M.A. **158**:912, 1955.

125. McNamara, J.J., and others: Coronary artery disease in combat casualties in Vietnam, J.A.M.A. **216**:1185, 1971.

126. Geer, J.C., and others: Histologic characteristics of coronary artery fatty streaks, Lab. Invest. **18**:565, 1968.

127. Hatch, F.T.: Interactions between nutrition and heredity in coronary heart disease, Am. J. Clin. Nutr. **27**:80, 1974.

128. Dawber, T.R., and others: The epidemiology of coronary heart diseases: the Framingham inquiry, Proc. R. Soc. Med. **55**:265, 1962.

129. Witschi, J.C., and others: Family cooperation and effectiveness in a cholesterol lowering diet, J. Am. Diet. Assoc. **72**:384, 1978.

130. Stein, E.A., and others: Lowering of plasma cholesterol levels in free-living adolescent males: use of natural and synthetic polyunsaturated foods to provide balanced fat diets, Am. J. Clin. Nutr. **28**:1204, 1975.

131. Morrison, J.A., and others: Parent child association at upper and lower ranges of plasma cholesterol and triglyceride levels, Pediatrics **62**:468, 1978.

132. Anderson, G.E., Lifschitz, C., and Friis-Hansen, B.F.: Dietary habits and serum lipid during the first four years of life, Acta Paediatr. Scand. **68**:165, 1979.

133. McGandy, R.B.: Adolescence and the onset of atherosclerosis, Bull. N.Y. Acad. Med. **47**:590, 1971.

134. Stein, E.A., and others: Changes in plasma lipid and lipoprotein fractions after alteration in dietary cholesterol polyunsaturated, saturated, and total fat in free-living normal and hypercholesterolemic children, Am. J. Clin. Nutr. **35**:1375, 1982.

135. Connor, W.E., and Connor, S.L.: The key role of nutritional factors in the prevention of coronary heart disease, Prev. Med. **1**:49, 1972.

136. Gotto, A.M., and Scott, L.: Dietary aspects of hyperlipidemia, J. Am. Diet. Assoc. **62**:617, 1973.

137. Sturdevant, R.A.L., Pearce, M.L., and Dayton, S.: Increased prevalence of cholelithiasis in men ingesting a serum cholesterol–lowering diet, N. Engl. J. Med. **288**:24, 1973.

138. Rose, G., and others: Colon cancer and blood cholesterol, Lancet **1**:181, 1974.

139. Breslow, J.L.: Pediatric aspects of hyperlipidemia, Pediatrics **62**:510, 1978.

140. Committee on Nutrition, American Academy of Pediatrics: Toward a prudent diet for children, Pediatrics **71**:78, 1983.

Salt and hypertension

141. Dahl, L.K.: Salt and hypertension, Am. J. Clin. Nutr. **25**:231, 1972.

142. Meneely, G.R., and others: Chronic sodium chloride toxicity in the albino rat. II. Occurrence of hypertension and a syndrome of edema and renal failure, J. Exp. Med. **98**:71, 1953.

143. Meneely, G.R., and Ball, C.O.T.: Experimental epidemiology of chronic sodium chloride toxicity and the protective effect of potassium chloride, Am. J. Med. **25**:713, 1958.

144. Dahl, L.K., and others: Effects of chronic excess salt ingestion: modifications of experimental hypertension in

the rat by variations in the diet, Circ. Res. **22**:11, 1968.

145. Dahl, L.K.: Effects of chronic excess salt feeding induction of self-sustaining hypertension in rats, J. Exp. Med. **114**:231, 1961.

146. Dahl, L.K., Heine, M., and Tassinari, L.: High salt content of Western infants' diet: possible relationship to hypertension in the adult, Nature **198**:1204, 1963.

147. Srinivasan, S.R., and others: Effects of dietary sodium and sucrose on the induction of hypertension in spider monkeys, Am. J. Clin. Nutr. **33**:561, 1980.

148. Gleibermann, L.: Blood pressure and dietary salt in human populations, Ecology Food Nutr. **2**:143, 1973.

149. Oliver, W.J., Cohen, E.L., and Neel, J.V.: Blood pressure, sodium values, and sodium related hormones in the Yanomamo Indians: a "no-salt" culture, Circulation **52**:146, 1975.

150. Dahl, L.K., and Love, R.A.: Etiologic role of sodium chloride intake in essential hypertension in humans, J.A.M.A. **164**:397, 1957.

151. Dawber, T.R., and others: Environmental factors in hypertension. In Stamler, J., Stamler, R., and Pullman, T.N.: The epidemiology of hypertension, New York, 1967, Grune & Stratton, Inc.

152. Prior, I.A.M., and others: Sodium intake and blood pressure in two Polynesian populations, N. Engl. J. Med. **279**:515, 1968.

153. Miall, W.E.: Follow up study of arterial pressure in the population of a Welsh mining valley, Br. Med. J. **2**:1204, 1959.

154. Whitten, C.F., and Stewart, R.A.: The effect of dietary sodium in infancy on blood pressure and related factors, Acta Paediatr. Scand. Suppl. 279, 1980.

155. Schierf, G.L., and others: Salt and hypertension data from the "Heidelberg Study," Am. J. Clin. Nutr. **33**:872, 1980.

156. Pietinen, P.I., Wong, O., and Altschul, A.M.: Electrolyte output, blood pressure, and family history of hypertension, Am. J. Clin. Nutr. **32**:997, 1979.

157. Murray, R.H., and others: Blood pressure responses to extremes of sodium intake in normal man, Proc. Soc. Exp. Biol. Med. **159**:432, 1978.

158. McQuarrie, I., Thompson, W.H., and Anderson, J.A.: Effects of ingestion of sodium and potassium salts on carbohydrate metabolism and blood pressure in diabetic children, J. Nutr. **11**:77, 1936.

159. Filer, L.J.: Salt in infant foods, Nutr. Rev. **29**:27, 1971.

160. Kerr, C.M., Reisinger, K.S., and Plankey, F.W.: Sodium concentration of homemade baby foods, Pediatrics **62**:331, 1978.

161. Committee on Nutrition, American Academy of Pediatrics: Sodium intake of infants in the United States, Pediatrics **68**:444, 1981.

162. Lauer, R.M., and others: Blood pressure, salt preference and relative weight, Am. J. Dis. Child. **130**:493, 1976.

163. Fomon, S.J., Thomas, L.N., and Filer, L.J.: Acceptance of unsalted strained foods by normal infants, J. Pediatr. **76**:242, 1970.

164. Sperotto, G.: Sodium chloride in pediatrics. In Moses, C., editor: Sodium in medicine and health, Baltimore, Md., 1980, Reese Press.

165. Fomon, S.J.: Infant nutrition, Philadelphia, 1974, W.B. Saunders Co.

ADDITIONAL READINGS
Obesity

Brownell, K.D., and Kaye, F.S.: A school-based behavior modification, nutrition education, and physical activity program for obese children, Am. J. Clin. Nutr. **35**:277, 1982.

Crawford, P.B., and others: An obesity index for six month old children, Am. J. Clin. Nutr. **27**:706, 1974.

Dine, M.S., and others: Where do the heaviest children come from? A prospective study of white children from birth to 5 years, Pediatrics **63**:1, 1979.

DuPart, R.H., and others: The prevalence of obesity and thinness in children from a lower socioeconomic population receiving comprehensive health care, Am. J. Clin. Nutr. **33**:202, 1980.

Ferris, A.G., and others: The effect of diet in weight gain in infancy, Am. J. Clin. Nutr. **33**:2635, 1980.

Huenemann, R.L.: Environmental factors associated with preschool obesity. I. Obesity in six month old children, J. Am. Diet. Assoc. **64**:480, 1974.

Huenemann, R.L.: Environmental factors associated with preschool obesity. II. Obesity and food practices of children at successive age levels, J. Am. Diet. Assoc. **64**:488, 1974.

Lloyd, J.K., and Wolff, O.H.: Childhood obesity, a long term study of height and weight. Br. Med. J. **2**:145, 1961.

Mack, R.W., and Kleinhenz, M.E.: Growth, calorie intake, and activity levels in early infancy: a preliminary report, Hum. Biol. **46**:345, 1974.

Rolland-Cachera, M.F.: Adiposity indices in children, Am. J. Clin. Nutr. **36**:178, 1982.

Shenker, I.R., Fisichelli, V., and Lang, J.: Weight differences between foster infants of overweight and non-overweight foster mothers, J. Pediatr. **84**:715, 1974.

Spahn, U., and others: Overnutrition and obesity in childhood as a potential risk for chronic degenerative disease in later life, Bibl. Nutr. Dieta. **31**:61, 1982.

Whitelaw, A.: Infant feeding and subcutaneous fat at birth and at one year, Lancet **2**:1098, 1977.

Winick, M., editor: Childhood obesity, New York, 1975, John Wiley & Sons, Inc.

Allergy

Bahna, S.L.: Control of milk allergy: a challenge for physicians, mothers, and industry, Ann. Allergy **41**:1, 1978.

Bierman, C.W., and Furukawa, C.T.: Food allergy, Pediatr. Rev. **3**:213, 1982.

Crook, W.G.: Food allergy—the great masquerader, Pediatr. Clin. North Am. **22**:227, 1975.

Dannaeus, A., Johansson, S.G.O., and Foucard, T.: Clinical and immunological aspects of food allergy in children. II. Development of allergic symptoms and humoral immune responses to foods in infants of atopic mothers during the first 24 months of life, Acta Paediatr. Scand. **67**:497, 1978.

Freedman, B.J.: A diet free from additives in the management of allergic disease, Clin. Allergy **7**:417, 1977.

Fries, J.H.: Chocolate: a review of published reports of allergic and other deleterious effects, real or presumed, Ann. Allergy **41**:195, 1978.

Gerrard, J.W., and others: Cow's milk allergy: prevalence and manifestations in an unselected series of newborns, Acta Paediatr. Scand. Suppl. 234, 1973.

Goldstein, G.B., and Heiner, D.C.: Clinical and immunological perspective in food sensitivity, a review, J. Allergy **46**:270, 1970.

Kuitunen, P., and others: Malabsorption syndrome with cow's milk intolerance, Arch. Dis. Child. **50**:351, 1975.

McCarty, E.P., and Frisk, O.L.: Food sensitivity: keys to diagnosis, J. Pediatr. **105**:645, 1983.

Miller, J.B.: Hidden food ingredients, chemical food additives, and incomplete food labels, Ann. Allergy **41**:93, 1978.

Minford, A.M.B., MacDonald, A., and Littlewood, J.M.: Food intolerance and food allergy in children, Arch. Dis. Child. **57**:742, 1982.

Pratt, E.L.: Food allergy and food intolerance in relation to the development of good eating habits, Pediatrics **21**:642, 1958.

Shacks, S.M., and Heiner, D.C.: Allergy to breast milk, Clin. Immunol. Allergy **2**:121, 1982.

Speer, F.: Multiple food allergy, Ann. Allergy **34**:71, 1975.

Speer, F.: Food allergy, the 10 common offenders, Am. Fam. Physician **13**:106, 1976.

Carbohydrate and dental caries

Abbey, L.M.: Is breast feeding a likely cause of dental caries in young children? J. Am. Dent. Assoc. **98**:21, 1979.

Brown, A.T.: The role of dietary carbohydrate in plaque formation and oral disease, Nutr. Rev. **33**:353, 1975.

Enwonwu, C.O.: Role of biochemistry and nutrition in preventive dentistry, J. Am. Soc. Prev. Dent. **4**:6, 1974.

Evaluation of the caries-producing ability of human foods, Nutr. Rev. **36**:249, 1978.

McBean, L.D., and Speckmann, E.W.: A review: the importance of nutrition in oral health, J. Am. Dent. Assoc. **89**:109, 1974.

Newbrum, E.: The role of food manufacturers in the dietary control of caries, J. Am. Soc. Prev. Dent. **4**:33, 1974.

Newbrum, E.: Sugar and dental caries: a review of human studies, Science **217**:418, 1982.

Sheiham, A.: Sugar and dental decay, Lancet **1**:282, 1983.

Sreenby, L.M.: Sugar and human dental caries, World Rev. Nutr. Diet. **40**:19, 1982.

Lactose malabsorption and intolerance

Dahlqvist, A., and Lindquist, B.: Lactose intolerance and protein malnutrition, Acta Paediatr. Scand. **60**:488, 1971.

Food and Nutrition Board: Background information on lactose and milk intolerance, a statement of the Food and Nutrition Board Division of Biology and Agriculture, National Academy of Sciences, National Research Council, May 1972.

Gallagher, C.R., Molleson, A.L., and Caldwell, J.H.: Lactose intolerance and fermented dairy products, J. Am. Diet. Assoc. **65**:418, 1974.

Hijazi, S., El-Khateeb, M., and Abdulatif, D.: Lactose malabsorption in Jordanian infants and young children, Acta Paediatr. Scand. **70**:759, 1981.

Maclean, W.C., and Graham, G.G.: Evaluation of a low-lactose nutritional supplement in malnourished children, J. Am. Diet. Assoc. **67**:558, 1975.

McGill, D.B., and Newcomer, A.D.: Primary and secondary disaccharidase deficiencies, Prog. Gastroenterol. **2**:392, 1970.

Simoons, T.J.: Perspectives on milk drinking and malabsorption of lactose, Pediatrics **59**:98, 1977.

Fat and cardiovascular disease

Crawford, P.B., and others: Serum cholesterol of 6-year-olds in relation to environmental factors, J. Am. Diet. Assoc. **78**:41, 1981.

Glueck, C.J., and Morrison, J.A.: Relationship of pediatric nutrients to lipids, lipoproteins, and ultimate risk of atherosclerosis, Pediatr. Ann. **10**(11)45, 1981.

Knieiman, T.J., West, C.E., and Hautvast, J.G.A.J.: Infant and child nutrition: the effect on serum lipids and the consequences in later life, Bibl. Nutr. Dieta. **31**:131, 1982.

Laver, R.M., and others: Coronary heart disease risk factors in school children: the Muscatine Study, Pediatrics **86**:797, 1975.

Morrison, J.A., and others: High and low density lipoprotein cholesterol levels in hypercholesterolemic school children, Lipids **14**:99, 1979.

Nestel, P.J., Posyer, A., and Boulton, T.J.C.: Changes in cholesterol metabolism in infants in response to dietary cholesterol and fat, Am. J. Clin. Nutr. **32**:2177, 1979.

Shekelle, R.B.: Diet, serum cholesterol, and death from coronary heart disease: the Western Electric Study, New Engl. J. Med. **304**:65, 1981.

Turner, R.W.D.: Perspectives in coronary prevention, Postgrad. Med. J. **54:**141, 1978.

Van Biervliet, J.P., and others: Plasma apoprotein and lipid patterns in newborns: influence of nutritional factors, Acta Paediatr. Scand. **20:**851, 1981.

Salt and hypertension

Faust, H.S.: Effect of drinking water and total sodium intake on blood pressure, Am. J. Clin. Nutr. **35:**1459, 1982.

Swales, J.D.: Dietary salt and hypertension, Lancet **1:**1177, 1980.

Tobian, L.: The relationship of salt to hypertension, Am. J. Clin. Nutr. **32:**2739, 1979.

Weinsier, R.L.: Overview: salt and the development of essential hypertension, Prev. Med. **5:**7, 1976.

Vegetarian Diets for Children

11

CRISTINE M. TRAHMS

Using plant foods as the primary source of nutrients in the diet is not a new concept, but it is a fairly recent phenomenon in the United States.

In the past many religious groups have strongly advocated the importance of a meat-free diet, and this practice continues today. Traditionally, religious groups chose to be vegetarian for reasons of moral purity and/or food sanitation. The general populations of many countries have also long been vegetarian or near vegetarian, not necessarily by choice but because of limited food availability. The availability of food choices and the adequacy of the total food supply are often not considered as influences when the adequacy of a vegetarian diet is discussed. The practice of eating meat does not inherently ensure good health, just as the practice of not eating meat does not ensure poor health. The interrelationships of nutrition, health, social mores, and food choices are very complex. The exclusion of one food source or food group does not necessarily swing the pendulum of health or nutritional adequacy in either the positive or the negative direction. Therefore when discussing vegetarianism—the concept of non–meat eating—one must consider other factors carefully.

Generally, a "vegetarian" is considered an individual who chooses to not eat meat, poultry, or fish, and a "vegan" (pure vegetarian) is an individual who chooses to not eat any animal products at all. However, people do not base their food choices or life-styles on tidy categories. Therefore, many people who call themselves vegetarians, may in fact eat meat as often as once per week or twice per month. On the other hand, people may choose extremely rigid diets that forbid them yeast and honey or they may avoid the use of wool, leather, or cotton because they are considered animal products. In this chapter a vegetarian will be considered a person who has chosen to omit meat, poultry, and fish from his or her food intake pattern, and a vegan will be considered a person who has chosen to eat only plant foods (i.e., no animal products). However, the commonly used labels of lacto-vegetarian, lacto-ovo-vegetarian, new vegetarian, and the like are generally confusing to the nutrition counselor in practice. Individuals seldom make their personal food choices based on the accepted categories. It seems, then, most reasonable to work with individuals to evaluate foods as sources of nutrients rather than to "force" labels on individual food patterns. This method of evaluation also provides a reasonable basis for nutrition education.

HEALTH ADVANTAGES AND DISADVANTAGES

Recent work with population subgroups has indicated that there are health advantages to the vegetarian food pattern. Much of this work has centered on adults in industrialized countries and specialized subgroups of the population that have made additional life-style changes in addition to omitting meat from their food patterns. It was found that some of the advantages of vegetarianism include lower total body weight,[1] decreased incidence of cancer of the colon,[2] lower blood lipid levels,[3] and decreased incidence of osteoporosis.[4]

In general, factors such as abstinence from smoking and alcohol, great interest in exercise, and/or seclusion from the rest of society must be considered as potential intervening or modifying variables for religious subgroups.

Much of the work that points out the disadvantages of a vegetarian diet has been conducted in third world countries, where the total amount of food and the food choices available are very limited. Thus, many of these people would probably not choose to be vegetarians, but they have no alternative. Energy deficit and lack of food to provide specific nutrients must be considered when interpreting these reports. In this country the negative impact of a vegetarian diet has also been reported. Often young adults become overzealous in following specific teachings or omitting specific foodstuffs from their food patterns. One classic example of overzealousness is the Zen macrobiotic followers, who felt that tea and brown rice were the way to ultimate purity of body and soul. Even the leaders of the group warned against this extreme practice and encouraged a more moderate food intake pattern that included grains, legumes, fruits, and vegetables. The health disadvantages of the vegetarian diet have been documented primarily among those people who have chosen the vegan (pure vegetarian) diet. In general, the more restricted the pattern of food choices, the more likely that individual is to be at high nutritional risk. (The same can be said for popular weight-reduction formats.) Young children and pregnant women, who are generally considered to be at high nutritional risk, are thought to be particularly vulnerable to food intake patterns that limit the quantity or the kinds of food for consumption.

INDIVIDUALS WITH SPECIAL NEEDS

In the few sketchy reports on the outcome of the pregnancies of women who were vegans or vegetarians, there appear to be no detrimental effects to the mother or the offspring if the mother chooses a food pattern that provides the required nutrients in appropriate quantities to support the pregnancy. Hardinge and Stare[1] included several pregnant vegetarian women in one of their early nutritional status reports. The food intake patterns and calculated nutrient intakes were grouped with those of other adults, but they appeared adequate. The infants were reported to be of normal birth weight. Thomas, Ellis, and Diggory[5] reported on the health of vegans during pregnancy, comparing 14 vegans (28 pregnancies) and 18 control subjects (41 pregnancies). There were no differences in rates of stillbirths, toxemia, or anemia between the groups. There were also no differences in the birth weights of the infants. Few (3%) of the women who were vegan took iron supplements during pregnancy. They also breast fed their infants more frequently and for longer periods than did the control mothers. No data on weight gain during pregnancy were reported. Another report found no differences in birth weights between the vegetarian children (both extensive and limited food group avoidances) and the control children.[6]

It has been well documented that young children can indeed grow normally on diets comprised entirely of cereal proteins if the diets are carefully formulated. Knapp and others[7] rehabilitated 102 malnourished male infants 5 to 14 months of age and then offered nine different formulations that were isocaloric (100 kcal/kg) and contained 2 gm of protein/kg. The children fed soybean, rice, cottonseed, cottonseed and rice, cottonseed and peanut, rice and soybean, soybean and peanut, or cow's milk formulas all demonstrated equivalent nitrogen retention. In crossover studies, the children fed wheat plus lysine, rice and cottonseed, and peanut and rice formulas grew at rates equivalent to those of children fed cow's milk. The children fed only peanut formulas did not retain as much nitrogen as did the children fed cow's milk, and the children fed only rice formulas did not grow as well as did the children fed cow's milk. It should also be noted that although the growth curves were equivalent, the children fed cow's milk diets demonstrated smoother growth curves. Recent reports have indicated that deficits in height and weight may occur among young children on vegan diets in the United States.

Young vegan children were significantly shorter (p <0.001) and lighter (p <0.005) than were age- and sex-matched vegetarian children and control children.[8] Dwyer and others[9] suggested an environmental influence on the size of young children. When adjusted for midparental height, 61% of 119 preschool vegetarian children were less than the 20th percentile for height. In another report, 72 white children less than 5 years of age living at home were longitudinally measured using a standardized technique.[6] Thirty-four children had parents who consumed macrobiotic diets, 12 were members of yoga groups, 12 were Seventh-Day Adventists, and 14 had no group affiliation. Almost all (96%) of the children had been or were still being breast fed. The vegetarian children younger than 2 years of age showed mean weight and length velocities that were lower than the Harvard norms, whereas those of the older vegetarian children were comparable with the Harvard norms.

Recently, the growth patterns of 142 vegetarian and 228 nonvegetarian schoolchildren were compared.[10] The two groups of children demonstrated differing growth patterns. It appeared that the more limiting the food choices, the more growth was affected. In general, length was more affected than weight although measurements were generally within normal limits. Evaluation of food intakes suggested that protein intakes for these children were adequate and energy intakes were less than the accepted recommendations. It would appear that, again, the availability of adequate nutrients to the individual child was a more significant factor than the beliefs of the parents and the concommitant prescribed food pattern.

Young children consuming diets consisting only of plant foods seem to be at greater risk for nutritional deficiencies related to intakes of protein, calcium, total energy, essential fatty acids, riboflavin, and possibly vitamins B_{12} and D. This is in part related to family food choice patterns and in part to the individual preferences of the child who may or may not eat the foods that are offered. An example of nutritional risk caused by limited food choices is the young child who was offered a grain beverage called kokoh consisting of rice, sesame seeds, and oats in a reasonable protein complement. However, the quantities offered to the child or that the child was willing to take did not provide adequate nutrients to support normal growth. In some cases, the deficiencies were severe and prolonged enough to cause death.[11] The young infant being exclusively breast fed by a mother who has a marginal or definite vitamin B_{12} deficiency may have an increased risk of deficiency. Older children who consume diets severely restricted in animal foods may also be at risk if the choices of foods available to them are severely restricted and exclude all animal foods.

Young children in developing countries who are breast fed but whose diets are not supplemented with additional foods may suffer adverse nutritional effects after 4 to 6 months of age, especially if they are weaned to a cereal gruel or other form of predominantly vegetarian diet. However, in these cases it must be remembered that other factors (e.g., poor sanitation and poor health care) may be important variables.

Reports of cases in the United States describe the severe malnutrition of one young child fed no animal products and no cereals,[12] a striking case of kwashiorkor of a young child on a vegan diet,[13] several cases of kwashiorkor among infants whose parents were vegetarian,[14] and poor weight gain in children fed cereal-base formulas.[15] In another report,[16] four infants who were fed "cult" diets were severely malnourished when seen by health care workers. Apparently the infants were fed restricted quantities of kokoh (a grain and cereal beverage) and limited quantities of other foods. Although the nutritional data presented in the report are sketchy, it would appear that the nutrient limitation was quantity of food rather than quality of food. All of the children were rehabilitated (e.g., growth increased) on vegetarian or near vegetarian diets within a few months. Unfortunately, legal intervention was necessary to change family food management patterns for the benefit of the children. In all of these reports, the number of children evaluated was very small and long-term observations on growth or nutrient intake were not made, but the questions these reports raise are disturbing.

Calculation of nutrient intakes of preschool children has shown that children whose diets excluded all animal products consumed significantly less total protein, fat, calcium, and riboflavin (p<0.01) than did vegetarian children and control children.[17] Intakes of iron and calcium were also calculated at lower than acceptable levels. Ten children on Zen macrobiotic diets were described as being at the 40th percentile for height and weight.[18] Nutrient intakes were calculated as less than optimal, that is, less than 60% of the recommended dietary allowance for most nutrients except calcium and riboflavin, which were even lower.

Recently, evaluation of intakes of a small number of children with a mean age of 4 years, consuming different types of vegetarian diets suggested that these patterns were reasonable when compared with the dietary goals for the United states for carbohydrate, fat, protein, sodium, and cholesterol. Some children had intakes limited in iron and in vitamins D and B_{12}.[19]

Recent reports indicate that infants and preschool children may also be at risk for vitamin D deficiency if they are consuming diets restricted in animal products. An increase in clinical identification of rickets has recently been reported in older infants[20] who demonstrated the classic symptoms of growth failure, listlessness, delayed motor development, and abnormal gait. Bony deformity was evident on further investigation. The children received little or no cow's milk or formula and no vitamin D supplements. Not all of the children were vegetarian or vegan. However, healing occurred with dietary changes in all cases. Of 52 children on macrobiotic diets 88% had vitamin D intakes of less than 100 IU/day[21] compared with vegetarian children, of whom only 18% had vitamin D intakes this low. Although five children had pathological findings related to bone mineralization, roentgenograms did not indicate rickets. Clinically, only three children demonstrated signs (bowed legs) that could possibly be attributed to vitamin D deficiency. The serum calcium and serum phosphorous levels of both the children on macrobiotic diets and the vegetarian children were within normal limits. Eight of the children on macrobiotic diets and two of the vegetarian children had elevated serum alkaline phosphatase levels.

Young breast-fed infants whose mothers are vegan may be at risk for vitamin B_{12} deficiency. Case reports cite growth failure and other clinical signs of vitamin B_{12} deficiency in infants who were breast fed by vegan women.[22,23] Apparently, these infants required more vitamin B_{12} than could be supplied by the breast milk of women with marginal vitamin B_{12} stores. The status of zinc nutriture in these children has not been evaluated to date. It would seem that zinc may be a limiting nutrient in some very restricted food patterns.

FACTORS INFLUENCING THE INTAKES OF YOUNG CHILDREN

The young child depends on caregivers to provide adequate foods as sources of nutrients. Food preferences are demonstrated early in life, and this may also affect adequacy of intake. The older infant and toddler with rigid food preferences despite adequate food availability may be at risk for deficits of specific nutrients.

The young child on a food intake pattern comprised totally or primarily of plant proteins may have problems obtaining an adequate intake of energy if the volume of food required to meet energy needs is large. Often a legume milk (commercially prepared or home prepared with a sufficient energy concentration) will provide an easily ingested volume of protein, energy, and other nutrients for the young child.

In addition to volume, texture may also influence the adequacy of the intake of the young child on a vegetarian diet. Many foods that contain adequate quantities of protein must be texture modified for the young child, for instance, beans (legumes) must be well cooked and mashed or pureed. Even rice must be mixed with liquid and mashed for the infant. Whole grain breads may not be well chewed by the young child, and consequently the nutrients may not be well absorbed. The same is true for nuts and seeds, dried fruits, and some vegetables.

PROTEIN NEEDS OF YOUNG CHILDREN

Protein utilization is affected by a variety of factors, including quality and quantity of ingested protein, percent of calories as fat, total energy intake, biological variation of the individual, and growth and maintenance needs (e.g., age and nutritional state). Calculating protein utilization, and consequently protein needs, is a complex undertaking because many of the relationships are not clearly defined and/or are extremely difficult to measure.

Much work is being done to document protein utilization among young children and the ability of vegetable protein diets to maintain growth and nitrogen balance for young children or to rehabilitate them from malnutrition or illness. The infectious process is a confounding variable that is difficult to quantitate, and it affects the utilization of nutrients.

Many combinations of grain and legume proteins have been evaluated in terms of maintenance of nutritional health or the rehabilitation of malnourished children in developing countries. Evaluation of a macaroni product containing 60% corn

(maize), 30% defatted soy flour, and 10% wheat germ indicated nutritional recuperation in both the experimental and control groups of children.[24] The protein quality of most common grains and legumes consumed by young children in Mexico was evaluated.[25] Combinations of corn and soy in ratios of 80:20 and 90:10 had highest protein quality. Combinations of corn and beans (50:50) and wheat and beans (50:50) were better than single sources of corn, wheat, or beans but were not significantly different from each other.

A CSM (68% corn, 28% defatted soy flour, 5% nonfat dry milk) infant food demonstrated that a small percentage of protein from animal foods enhances the value of a food product as a sole source of nutrients for young infants. This formulation promoted nitrogen retention similar to that of casein.[26]

A soybean protein textured food (soy protein isolate) with added egg albumin and wheat gluten has a protein quality of about 80% of that of milk. Children required 138 mg of nitrogen from the soy food as compared with 97 mg of nitrogen from milk to maintain nitrogen equilibrium.[27] This food was readily accepted by the children.

The question of lysine fortification of wheat products and long-term improvements in the growth of children dependent on this cereal for almost all of their protein intake remains an elusive question. For very young infants, it may be that wheat protein is inadequate to maintain normal growth and development.[28]

Fat absorption in young children depends on levels of dietary protein intake.[29] Very low protein intakes with adequate energy intakes are detrimental to maximum fat absorption and may ultimately increase total energy requirements. Children on diets containing 5% or more of energy as protein (FAO/WHO recommendation) showed improvement of apparent fat absorption as protein intakes increased.

All this information on relative biological value or utilization of protein is interesting, but in this country few if any children must exist on a single food that, in turn, must supply all or the majority of nutrients. The young formula-fed infant is the exception. Formulations of infant food must be done very carefully to meet the rigorous nutrient requirements to support normal growth and development.

Choosing Protein Foods for Young Children

It is important that the protein sources offered to young children be appropriately combined so that the pattern of amino acid intake will be adequate to support normal growth and development. Careful attention to combining plant proteins in the best proportion for optimal utilization is a must. Appetites of young children fluctuate widely on a day-to-day basis, making it important that all foods eaten provide nutrients rather than calories only.

In combining plant proteins, not only must foods that supplement the most limiting amino acids of each other be combined, but they should be combined in specific proportion for the most efficient utilization of protein. The ratio is specific for each combination. Examples of satisfactory combinations include the following: (1) ¾ cup of dry rice with ¼ cup of dry beans; (2) ¾ cup of dry rice with 1 cup milk or ¼ cup of milk powder; and (3) 3¼ cup of wheat flour with ¼ cup of soy grits and ½ cup of sesame seeds. Complementation of proteins is also a useful and practical way to enhance the value of foods readily accepted by young children. One can easily accomplish this by adding a small amount of soy grits while oatmeal is being cooked or by adding wheat germ, soy flour, or dry milk to muffins, pancakes, cookies, and breads. The simple method called the Cornell Triple Rich Flour Formula developed at Cornell University complements the proteins of baked products. According to this formula, before any flour is put into the measuring cup the following should be measured into the bottom of the cup: 1 tbsp of soy flour, 1 tbsp of dry milk, and 1 tsp of wheat germ. The cup is then filled with flour.

Preschool children are in the process of developing their individual food patterns and are not amenable to eating foods because they are good protein sources. The difficulty of encouraging young children to eat a sufficient volume of legumes, grains, seeds, and nuts in forms that they can easily digest and encouraging them to eat foods in a precise proportional relationship is very great. For young children without dairy foods or eggs in their diets it is difficult to provide sufficient quality and quantity of proteins and an adequate amount of calories to support adequate growth.[17]

ENERGY NEEDS OF YOUNG VEGETARIAN CHILDREN

It is possible that the volume of food required to meet the energy needs of young children may interfere with adequate intakes. This is especially true for those children who are offered foods without modification of texture. In most studies, the foods offered to children were texture modified into beverages with constant energy per unit of volume so that the children could easily ingest the required volume to meet energy needs. This theoretical or research strategy may not be appropriate for the practical application of foods as sources of nutrients for this age group.

Energy intake should be adequate to promote growth in channel on acceptable growth charts. As for any child, parental size should be considered when evaluating the growth of children.

MEETING THE NUTRIENT NEEDS OF YOUNG VEGETARIAN CHILDREN

Protein and energy needs of young children must be stated as a dyad to provide guidelines for the relative adequacy of these dietary components. This dyad should include some factors for individual variation in energy, for the possibility that these needs may to some degree be independent of protein needs, and for the degree of adaptation of expenditure to suit intake or vice versa. Examples of recorded food intakes of vegan, vegetarian, and nonvegetarian children that show the variety of foods and general quantities needed to provide reasonable intakes of nutrients are given in Table 11-1.

Table 11-1. Recorded 1-day intakes of young children

Food	Portion Size	Food	Portion Size
Child No. 1 (Aged 12 Months)—Inadequate Vegan Intake		**Child No. 3 (Aged 13 Months) —Vegetarian Intake**	
Oatmeal, cooked	½ cup	Milk, whole	9 oz
Raisins	1 tsp	Cereal	
Yellow squash, cooked	½ cup	Cornmeal, dry	¼ cup
Apple	1 medium	Wheat germ	3 tbsp
Oatmeal, cooked	1 cup	Milk	¼ cup
Yams, cooked	½ cup	Apple	1 tbsp
Pudding		Soybeans, cooked	1 cup
Apple cider	1 cup	Apricot, dried	2 halves
Arrowroot flour	1 tsp	Apple	½ medium
No supplements		Potato, baked	½ small
TOTAL ENERGY INTAKE	610 kcal	Tomato	1 small
TOTAL PROTEIN INTAKE	12 gm	Cheddar cheese, grated	¼ cup
		Soy oil	2 tsp
Child No. 2 (Aged 14 Months)—Better Vegan Intake		Milk	9 oz
		Milk	9 oz
Kokoh	1¼ cup	No supplements	
Rice	½ cup	TOTAL ENERGY INTAKE	1280 kcal
Sweet rice	¼ cup	TOTAL PROTEIN INTAKE	66 gm
Whole oats	⅛ cup		
Sesame seeds	⅛ cup	**Child No. 4 (Aged 12 Months)—Nonvegetarian Intake**	
Wakame	½ tsp		
Squash	⅓ cup	Peach, canned	½
Whole wheat noodles	½ cup	Link sausage	2
Miso soup		Toast, white	½ slice
Miso	1 tsp	margarine	½ tsp
Scallions	1 tsp	Egg yolk	1
Onion	1 tsp	2% Milk	8 oz
Kokoh	1¼ cup	2% Milk	8 oz
Nori	1 piece	Veal	50 gm
Cauliflower	¼ cup	Cracker	1
Aduki beans, cooked	⅓ cup	Rice, cooked	½ cup
Watercress	1 sprig	Tomato	¼ medium
Brown rice Kayu (1:5)	1¼ cup	2% Milk	8 oz
Squash, cooked	¼ cup	2% Milk	8 oz
Apple, baked	2 tbsp	Supplement: Poly-vi-sol	6 ml/day
Raisins	1 tsp	TOTAL ENERGY INTAKE	1020 kcal
No supplements		TOTAL PROTEIN INTAKE	58 gm
TOTAL ENERGY INTAKE	1140 kcal		
TOTAL PROTEIN INTAKE	35 gm		

Table 11-2. Key nutrients to consider when choosing food patterns

If These Foods are Excluded	Then These Nutrients are Limited	Replace With These Foods
Meat, fish, poultry	Protein, iron, energy, zinc, folate, vitamin B_{12}, thiamine, essential fatty acids	Milk, dairy products, grains, legumes
Milk, dairy products	Protein, energy, calcium, vitamin B_{12}, vitamin D, riboflavin	Legumes, soy milk (fortified), dark green vegetables
Grains	Protein, iron, niacin, riboflavin, zinc, fiber	Legumes, dairy products
Legumes	Protein, iron, zinc, calcium, fiber	Grains, dairy products
Fruits	Vitamin A, vitamin C, fiber, folate	Vegetables
Vegetables	Vitamin A, vitamin C, fiber, folate	Fruits

A model proposed by Payne[30] suggests that an adequate, safe protein/energy ratio in young children is close to 5%. Since most cereal grains seem to provide protein levels close to this, energy deficit rather than protein deficit may be the cause of protein/energy malnutrition in children in developing countries.

Many nutrient needs can be met by careful planning and by including foods that are equivalent sources of specific nutrients. Table 11-2 defines foods as sources of nutrients and the foods that can be exchanged to provide the equivalent nutrients. This scheme may be used not only by vegetarians but also by those who have specific food likes and dislikes or by those who for some other reason feel the need to restrict the variety of choices in their food intake patterns.

COUNSELING THE VEGETARIAN FAMILY

The word *vegetarian* has a specific nuance or value system attached to it for each person who has chosen to apply that label to himself or herself. The health care professional in the counseling role should carefully examine his or her own biases and, whether they are negative or positive, try to approach the family or household as open-mindedly as possible.

It seems reasonable that one should first ask the family to describe the foods regularly included and excluded in the family's diet and the individual's

diet (Chapter 2). A recent survey of women in Seattle indicated the importance of this approach.[31] Less than 50% of the persons who described themselves as vegetarians never ate meat, 30% ate meat once or twice per month, and nearly 10% ate meat as often as once per week.

Every food pattern that a person chooses has some positive aspects, which should be defined and reinforced. Clinical experience would indicate that a counseling/supportive role is much more effective than a directive (e.g., argumentative) approach. People can, in fact, adequately meet their nutrient needs in a wide variety of ways, and the individual variability or standard deviation of needs is quite wide.

For the infant and young child linear growth and rate of weight gain can be used as indices of appropriate energy intake. The mother of an exclusively breast-fed infant should be questioned about the adequacy of her own intake and should be advised of all the usual guidelines regarding adequate fluid, protein, calcium, and energy to maintain health and support lactation.

Some provisions should be made to ensure that the breast-fed infant receives adequate supplies of iron, vitamin B_{12}, and vitamin D. Recent evidence[32] indicates that iron in breast milk is well absorbed by the infant, so if the mother's diet provides adequate amounts of iron the needs of the infant should be met. Vitamin B_{12} may be a concern, especially if the mother's levels are low or if she has chosen a vegan diet. A supplement or additional food choices may be necessary to provide adequate quantities of this nutrient. There is, however, some evidence[33] that fermented soy products (e.g., tempeh and miso) may be "contaminated" during the fermentation process, thus providing a reasonable source of vitamin B_{12} for those persons who regularly consume the products. Vitamin D may also be a concern for those infants who receive minimal exposure to the sun. Again, options such as foods containing vitamin D or supplements (either synthetic or natural, e.g., cod liver oil) can be presented to the family. Usually, if the need for the particular nutrient can be clearly documented the parents are willing to reexamine their philosophical basis for making food choices and a reasonable decision and/or compromise can be reached for the ultimate nutritional welfare of the child.

When breast-feeding is not feasible, the infant needs to receive adequate quantities of a properly prepared formula. This can be a commercial soy formula or a cow's milk formula, but it must provide adequate quantities of critical nutrients such as protein, calcium, iron, energy, and vitamins B_{12}, A, and D. It has been demonstrated[34] that fortified soy formulas can promote normal growth and development in infants. Less work has been done on evaluation of the nutrient properties of grain milks. Reports[11,13,15-16] indicating poor growth in young children consuming grain milks were complicated by the inappropriate dilution and volume of milk offered to the children. Grain and legume blends formulated into milks and appropriately supplemented certainly have the potential of meeting the needs of young children, but none are currently available in the United States.

Home-prepared infant formulas with a cow's milk or goat's milk base and supplemented with calcium, yeast, lactose, and other vitamin and mineral preparations are not advised. These types of formula are susceptible to errors in measurement and dilution; thus they put the infant at risk for excess of specific nutrients and potential renal solute problems.

Home-prepared soy milk supplemented with vitamin B_{12} can provide an appropriate base for the child who also consumes a wide variety of other foods. One family in our clinical experience prepared soy milk for the children. The soy milk was supplemented with crystalline vitamin B_{12}, and the hulls and pulp of the soy remaining after milk preparation were carefully used in mixed dishes and baked goods. Tofu (soy cheese) was used frequently in mixed dishes. The children enjoyed all these foods and drank adequate quantities of the milk with enthusiasm, particularly if it was flavored with vanilla and served ice-cold.

Many adolescents and young adults who choose vegetarian or semivegetarian food patterns are concerned with their own health and the nutrition that is basic to it. Often their food choices are based, at least in part, on political and philosophical convictions. These people need information and supportive counseling to make sound health decisions as well as the political or philosophical statement of their choice.

Young adolescents who are not yet emancipated from the nuclear family may use food selection as a means of establishing independence. In this situation parents must remain flexible, tolerant, and interested in the adolescent's convictions regarding food choices. When there is little understanding, the food pattern can quickly become another point of intense family conflict. It must be remembered that an unusual food pattern is not necessarily a harmful food pattern. The parents and the adolescent need guidance to discern the difference. Any direct criticism of food choices may be considered personal criticism, so counseling must be supportive. It should reinforce the positive aspects of the chosen food pattern and consider the energy and nutrient needs required for growth, development, and physical activity. Nonjudgmental discussion of alternatives and a mutual decision-making process among health care worker, adolescent, and parent can guide adolescents in making healthful and responsible food choices (see Table 11-3).

In addition to the food guide (Table 11-4), the following point should be kept in mind when counseling a family that has chosen to become vegetar-

Table 11-3. Combinations of food for vegetarian diets

Food	Ingredients
Oatmeal, cooked	¾ cup of cooked oatmeal with 2 tsp of soy grits, ⅓ cup of milk
Scalloped potatoes	½ cup of potatoes, ½ cup of milk
Macaroni and cheese	½ cup of cooked macaroni, 3 tbsp of grated cheese
Rice pudding	½ cup of cooked rice, ¼ cup of milk
Peanut butter sandwich on whole wheat bread	½ tbsp of peanut butter, 1 slice of bread
Tortillas with beans	2 tortillas, ¼ cup of cooked beans
Whole wheat and soy muffin	2 tbsp of whole wheat flour, 1 tsp of soy flour, 1 tbsp of milk
Sesame and oatmeal cookies	1 tbsp of oatmeal, 1 tbsp of whole wheat flour, 1½ tsp of sesame, ½ tbsp of milk

Table 11-4. Vegetarian food guide

Food Group	Portion Size	Number of Portions		
		Pregnant	2 to 3 Years	4 to 6 Years
Breads, cereals, pasta	1 slice of bread	6	3	3
	⅓ cup of granola			
	¾ cup of cooked cereal			
	1 biscuit, muffin			
	1 tbsp of wheat germ			
	¾ cup of cooked rice			
Protein foods				
Legumes, meat analogues	1 cup of cooked beans	¾	⅛	¼
	¼ cup of peanut butter			
	6 oz of tofu			
Nuts and seeds	3 tbsp	1	⅛	¼
Dairy Products				
Milk	1 cup of milk, yogurt	4	2-3	2-3
	1 oz of cheese			
	4 tbsp of cottage cheese			
Eggs		1½	1	1
Fruits and vegetables	1 cup, raw	5-6	2	3
	½ cup, cooked			
	½ cup of juice			
Extra foods	No requirement (recommendation)			

Modified from Smith, E.B.: J. Nutr. Educ. **7**:109, 1975.

ian: the goal of the health care professional is the same as when counseling a nonvegetarian family, i.e., to promote good health through reasonable food choices. Responsibilities would include the following:

1. To support the individual and the family in every positive aspect of the chosen food pattern

   a. By being nonjudgmental about the stated reasons for specific food choices

b. By recognizing the wide variety of food choices that are appropriate to maintain good health

c. By understanding the food taboos and food preferences and the reasons for them

2. To evaluate the food intake of a specific family member, identifying those nutrients might be at risk for deficient intake because of food choices or food preparation methods

a. By helping the family recognize the differing needs of infants, young children, adolescents, adults, pregnant women, and sedentary individuals

b. By working with the individuals to identify food as sources of nutrients

3. To encourage the family members to purchase foods that provide the most nutrients for the money

a. By encouraging the evaluation of foods for their nutrient content, packaging, and processing

b. By encouraging the use of simple foods, whole grains, fresh fruits, and vegetables

c. By encouraging the use of cooking methods that conserve nutrients

SUMMARY

The more restrictive food choices become, the more difficult it is to plan a nutritionally adequate diet. Vegetarian diets that include prudently chosen plant foods and a reasonable amount of dairy foods are adequate to support normal growth and development for people of all ages, including young children and pregnant and lactating women. These recommendations are supported by a recent position paper from the American Dietetic Association.[35] General recommendations to support an adequate nutritional intake for vegetarians and vegans include:

1. Use of a variety of fruits and vegetables
2. Use of whole grain breads and cereals
3. Limitation of foods that are high-energy, low-nutrient density

4. Provision of adequate quantities of the limiting nutrients iron, calcium, folate, zinc, and vitamin B_{12} either by appropriate food choices or fortified food supplements

5. Use of an appropriately supplemented cow's milk formula or soy formula for infants who are not breast fed

6. Use of a suitable supplement or daily exposure to sunlight to provide adequate vitamin D

Robertson, Flinders, and Godfrey[36] have compiled a helpful manual that includes recipes for those who choose nonmeat food patterns.

SUGGESTED LEARNING ACTIVITIES

1. Plan a menu for a 2-year-old vegetarian boy who weighs 10 kg. He is unwilling to consume beans of any kind. His mother is unwilling to offer more than 1 cup of milk or yogurt per day because "it causes phlegm."

2. Outline teaching objectives and a food pattern for a young woman with a 6-month-old infant who is at the 25th percentile for length and weight. The mother prefers to avoid all animal products. The infant is totally breast fed. The mother plans to continue breast-feeding until the infant is 1 year of age.

3. Judy is a 4-year-old girl enrolled in the Head Start Program. She has been labelled "anemic" on the entrance physical examination. Her weight/stature is at the 10th percentile. Her mother is strongly opposed to all supplements. The family is vegan. Outline a plan for the family and for the classroom.

4. A mother of 2 young children (5 and 6 years of age) has recently become "vegetarian" and is adjusting her cooking habits and the family food pattern. Her children are "picky eaters" in both the variety and the quantity of food they are willing to consume. She feels that they may have lost weight on the vegetarian diet. Suggest how she can provide appropriate intakes for her children.

REFERENCES

1. Hardinge, M.G., and Stare, F.J.: Nutritional studies of vegetarians. I. Nutritional, physical, and laboratory studies, J. Clin. Nutr. **2**:73, 1954.
2. Burkitt, D.P.: Epidemiology of cancer of the colon and rectum, Cancer **28**:3, 1971.
3. Sacks, F.M., and others: Plasma lipids and lipoproteins in vegetarians and controls, N. Engl. J. Med. **292**:1148, 1975.
4. Ellis, F.R., Scura, H., and Ellis, J.W.: Incidence of osteoporosis in vegetarians and omnivores, Am. J. Clin. Nutr. **25**:555, 1972.
5. Thomas, J., Ellis, F.R., and Diggory, P.L.C.: The health of vegans during pregnancy, Proc. Nutr. Soc. **36**:46A, 1976.
6. Shull, M.W., and others: Velocities of growth in vegetarian preschool children, Pediatrics **60**:410, 1977.
7. Knapp, J., and others: Growth and nitrogen balance in infants fed cereal proteins, Am. J. Clin. Nutr. **26**:586, 1973.
8. Trahms, C.M., and others: Restriction of growth and elevated protoporphyrin in children deprived of animal protein, Clin. Res. **25**:179, 1977.
9. Dwyer, J.T., and others: Preschoolers on alternate lifestyle diets, J. Am. Diet. Assoc. **72**:264, 1978.
10. Dwyer, J.T., and others: Growth in ''new'' vegetarian preschool children using the Jenso-Bayley curve fitting technique, Am. J. Clin. Nutr. **37**:815, 1983.
11. Shinwell, E.D., and Gorodisches, R.: Totally vegetarian diets and infant nutrition, Pediatrics **70**:582, 1982.
12. Erhard, D.: The new vegetarians, Nutr. Today **8**:4, 1973.
13. Berkelhamer, J.E., and others: Kwashiorkor in Chicago, Am. J. Dis. Child. **129**:1240, 1975.
14. Chase, H.P., and others: Kwashiorkor in the United States, Pediatrics **66**:972, 1980.
15. Robson, J.R.K., and others: Zen macrobiotic dietary problems in infancy, Pediatrics **53**:326, 1974.
16. Roberts, I.F., and others: Malnutrition in infants receiving cult diets: a form of child abuse, Br. Med. J. **1**:296, 1979.
17. Trahms, C.M., and Feeney, M.C.: Evaluation of diet and growth of vegans, vegetarian, and nonvegetarian preschool children, Fed. Proc. **34**:675, 1975.
18. Brown, P.T., and Bergan, J.G.: The dietary status of ''new'' vegetarian, J. Am. Diet. Assoc. **67**:455, 1975.
19. Dwyer, J.T., and others: Nutritional status of vegetarian children, Am. J. Clin. Nutr. **35**:204, 1982.
20. Rudolf, M., and others: Unsuspected nutritional rickets, Pediatrics **66**:72, 1980.

21. Dwyer, J.T., and others: Risk of nutritional rickets among vegetarian children, Am. J. Dis. Child. **133**:134, 1979.
22. Higginbottom, M.C., and others: A syndrome of methylmalonic aciduria, homocystinuria, megaloblastic anemia and neurologic abnormalities in a vitamin B_{12} deficient breast fed infant of a strict vegetarian, N. Engl. J. Med. **299**:317, 1978.
23. Lampkin, B.C., and Saunders, E.F.: Nutritional vitamin B_{12} deficiency in an infant, J. Pediatr. **75**:1053, 1969.
24. Beghin, I., and others: Assessment of biological value of a new corn-soy-wheat noodle through recuperation of Brazilian malnourished children, Am. J. Clin. Nutr. **26**:246, 1973.
25. Valencia, M.E., and others: Protein quality evaluation of corn tortillas, wheat flour tortillas, pinto beans, soybeans, and their combinations, Nutr. Rep. Int. **19**:195, 1979.
26. Graham, G.G., and others: Dietary protein quality in infants and children. IX. Instant sweetened corn-soy-milk blend, Am. J. Clin. Nutr. **26**:491, 1973.
27. Bressani, R., and others: Protein quality of a soybean protein textured food in experimental animals and children, J. Nutr. **93**:349, 1967.
28. Vaghefi, S.B., and others: Lysine supplementation of wheat proteins: a review, Am. J. Clin. Nutr. **27**:1231, 1974.
29. MacLean, W.C., and others: Effect of the level of dietary protein intake on fat absorption in children, Pediatr. Res. **11**:774, 1977.
30. Payne, P.R.: Safe protein-calorie ratios in diets: the relative importance of protein and energy intake as causal factors in malnutrition, Am. J. Clin. Nutr. **28**:281, 1975.
31. Johnston, P.K.: Infant feeding among Seventh-Day Adventists, unpublished master's thesis, Seattle, 1979, University of Washington.
32. Saarinen, U.M., and Siimes, M.A.: Iron absorption from breast milk, cow's milk, and iron supplemented formula, Pediatr. Res. **13**:143, 1979.
33. Liem, I.T.H., and others: Production of vitamin B_{12} in tempeh, a fermented soybean food, Appl. Environ. Microbiol. **34**:773, 1977.
34. Fomon, S.J., and others: Requirements for protein and essential amino acids in early infancy: studies with soy-isolate formula, Acta Paediatr. Scand. **62**:33, 1973.
35. American Dietetic Association: Position paper on vegetarian approach to eating, J. Am. Diet. Assoc. **77**:61, 1980.
36. Robertson, L., Flinders, C., and Godfrey, B.: Laurel's kitchen: a handbook for vegetarian cookery and nutrition, Berkeley, 1976, Nilgiri Press.

Nutritional Considerations for Children in Sports

12

BONNIE WORTHINGTON-ROBERTS

Interest in sports and physical fitness has increased dramatically among children and adolescents. No longer is athletic competition and training restricted to boys in varsity team sports. Much enthusiasm has developed among women, and individual sports have gained in popularity among girls and boys of all ages. In general, this interest in athletic performance is viewed as beneficial to the health of our youth. This is true when the intensity of involvement is not excessive and when sensible health maintenance practices are encouraged.

Health maintenance for growing athletes is multifaceted, including attention to diet and nutrition. Primary objectives include the following:

1. Relaxed, supportive, loving home environment
2. Sufficient (but not excessive) training or athletic practice
3. Sufficient sleep
4. Adequate food and fluid
5. Appropriate medical attention for disease prevention and injury management
6. Support and encouragement in the face of error or defeat

The area of diet is unfortunately filled with super-

stition and myth about "optimum practices." Special diets or foods are sometimes advocated, and the use of supplements is frequently recommended. Often scientific proof is lacking to support special diets or supplement programs. Instead, however, the enthusiasm of the trainer may be more than adequate to motivate compliance. Very few studies have been undertaken on nutritional needs of *growing* athletes. Most published research has dealt with adolescents who agreed to be studied while training for specific sports. Data on normal, moderately active children may also be considered in determining nutritional recommendations for athletes (see Chapter 9).

CALORIES

Sports activities differ widely in the amount of energy required to support them (Table 12-1). In general, however, a child in sports requires a greater caloric intake than does the sedentary youngster. Whereas the average 10-year-old boy may expend between 2000 and 2800 kcal/day, the majority of boys this age who are running great distances or exerting themselves in other physical activities may expend an additional 300 to 700 kcal/day. The caloric needs of preadolescent girls are similar to those of boys for moderate and heavy exercise. In adolescence, however, when boys become relatively larger, their total daily needs in

This chapter is adapted from Worthington-Roberts, B.S.: Diet and athletic performance. In Contemporary developments in nutrition, St. Louis, Worthington-Roberts, B.S., editor: 1981, The C.V. Mosby Co.

Table 12-1. Approximate energy cost of various exercises and sports as estimated for adults

Sport or Exercise	Total Calories Expended/Minute of Activity	Sport or Exercise	Total Calories Expended/Minute of Activity
Climbing	10.7-13.2	Rowing—cont'd	
Cycling		97 strokes/minute	11.2
5.5 mph	4.5	Running	
9.4 mph	7.0	Short distance	13.3-16.6
13.1 mph	11.1	Cross-country	10.6
Dancing	3.3-7.7	Tennis	7.1
Domestic work		Skating, fast	11.5
Bed making	3.5	Skiing	
Dusting	2.5	Moderate speed	10.8-15.9
Ironing	1.7	Uphill, maximum speed	18.6
Cleaning floors	3.5	Squash	10.2
Football	8.9	Swimming	
Golf	5.0	Breaststroke	11.0
Gymnastics		Backstroke	11.5
Balancing	2.5	Crawl	14.0
Abdominal exercises	3.0	Walking	
Trunk bending	3.5	2 mph	2.5
Arms swinging, hopping	6.5	3 mph	3.5
Rowing		5 mph	5.5
51 strokes/minute	4.1	Watching television	1.5
87 strokes/minute	7.0	Wrestling	14.2

Modified from Nutrition for athletes: a handbook for coaches, Washington, D.C., 1971, American Alliance for Health, Education and Recreation.

all circumstances become greater. By adulthood, women expend approximately 10% less than men, assuming physical conditioning and training regimens are comparable. Extensive training decreases energy expenditure in both males and females; the trained individual burns about 7% less energy than the nontrained person to complete any specified task. The size of the individual, the level of training, and the type of sports activity engaged in are major factors determining total daily caloric needs (Fig. 12-1).[1-5]

Since very young children are now participating in athletic events, which in some cases are quite demanding, Torún, Chew, and Mendoza[6] measured 47 preschool children (17 to 45 months of age) under basal metabolic conditions and while

participating in various exercises. In all situations, preschool children required more kilocalories per unit of body weight than did adults (Table 12-2). Freedson and others[7] examined 6- and 7-year-old children and reported similar observations. In addition, however, these workers found that males expended 11% to 16% more energy than females in completing treadmill running tests at slow, medium, and fast speeds. Although there are no satisfactory guidelines for calculating energy costs of activities for children, Torún, Chew, and Mendoza[6] propose the following strategy for estimating the energy expenditure of preschool children in time-motion studies: (1) use the energy costs of activities that have been measured in children whenever available, and (2) use 1.2, 2, and 2.5

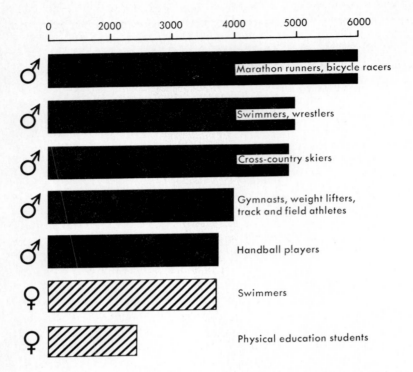

Fig. 12-1. Typical daily calorie expenditure of athletes training for various sports. (Data from Saltin, B.: Fluid electrolyte and energy losses and their replenishment in prolonged exercise; and from Rogozkin, V.A.: Some aspects of athlete's nutrition. In Parizkova, J., and Rogozkin, V.A., editors: Nutrition, physical fitness, and health, Baltimore, 1978, University Park Press.)

Table 12-2. Comparison of energy expenditure of preschool children with those of adult men and women (kcal/kg/min)

Activity	Children	Adult Men	Adult Women
Basal metabolism	38	18	17
Lying down, awake	44	20	21
Sitting quietly, playing, or sedentary work	47	22	22
Walking leisurely on level ground	71	64	53
Walking uphill and downhill	87	83	77
Walking rapidly at a grade	98	85	—
Leisure ride on tricycle or bicycle	75	58	58
Climbing stairs	94	—	—

Data from Torún, B., Chew, F., and Mendoza, R.D.: Nutr. Res. **3:**401, 1983.

times the child's basal metabolism for sedentary, light, and moderately heavy activities, respectively, or use the values determined in adults per unit of body weight multiplied by 2 for sedentary activities and by 1.2 for all other activities.

Besides being used for basal metabolism and physical activity, calories are required to support normal growth. Growing athletes, therefore, demand somewhat more calories per kilogram of body weight than those athletes who are mature. During adolescence (especially for boys), when growth rate is extremely rapid, the caloric needs may be very great. The consequence of insufficient calorie ingestion may be a lack of sufficient energy to perform optimally in sports events, and in some cases growth may be impaired. The most frequently encountered nutrition problem among athletes is failure to consume sufficient food energy. This may be related to an overcommitted life-style, a disorganized or poverty-stricken background, or an overaggressive effort to limit body fatness.

In general, the athlete's greatly increased caloric expenditure automatically increases the appetite, with the result that he or she ingests more food. Although it is unlikely that an athlete in heavy physical training will gain too much weight, caloric intake greater than the daily expenditure is not recommended, as it results in unnecessary fat deposition with subsequent increased work load to the heart. The increased caloric requirements are best met by increasing food intake across the board, without significantly altering the proportions of the micronutrients or macronutrients of the diet. There are no known "special" food sources that supply "extra reserves of energy" that are not provided by other foods with the same nutrients.

Energy Sources

The immediate source of energy for muscle work is adenosine triphosphate (ATP), which is formed in muscles largely by metabolism of carbohydrates and fats. It can be metabolized rapidly to meet the needs of sudden episodes of activity in intensive short-term exercise. Since ATP is metabolized without the use of oxygen, the reaction is classified

as anaerobic. This type of reaction is important during strenuous exercise, when the heart and lungs cannot deliver oxygen quickly to the muscles. If energy is needed for more than brief spurts, the high-energy compound in muscles, called phosphocreatine (PC), can almost instantaneously provide the energy required to regenerate ATP. Within a matter of minutes of vigorous exercise, however, the small stores of ATP-PC are used up, and then the body must turn to another source of energy to regenerate the ATP-PC system.[5,8,9]

Glycogen is the second energy source for muscles. It is stored in limited amounts in muscle cells and can be metabolized within the muscle cells to restore ATP. This activity is carried out primarily in the absence of oxygen; thus it is also classified as anaerobic. The level of glycogen storage in skeletal muscles is modified to some degree by dietary composition. It is possible to load muscles with unusually high levels of glycogen by adherence to a specially designed nutrition program used in conjunction with proper conditioning. The principles of glycogen loading and the available data on its effectiveness and safety are discussed on pp. 335-336.

As prolonged exercise gradually depletes the stores of ATP-PC and muscle glycogen, the body increasingly resorts to another source of energy. This last type of fuel comes from the aerobic metabolism of carbohydrates (glucose) and fats (Fig. 12-2). In most children, a considerable amount of stored fat is available, but its slow rate of metabolism makes it a less efficient source of quick energy. For reasons that are not presently clear, fat does not seem to be available to maintain performance at very high intensities of muscle work (i.e., 60% to 70% VO_2 max*). Neither the supply of free fatty acids exogenous to active muscle[10] nor the endogenously available muscle triglyceride[11] can fully replace the essential role of carbohydrates. It is true, however, that the highly

---

*VO_2 max is a term used to express the percentage of maximum oxygen consumption of a working individual; work physiologists use this term to express the severity of a specific type of work or exercise.

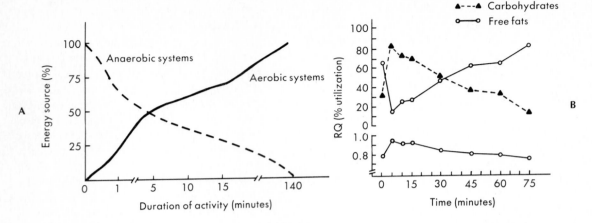

Fig. 12-2. A, Variation in energy over time. **B,** Changes in the respiratory quotient (*RQ*) or oxygen and carbon dioxide, indicating a shift in the utilization of carbohydrates and fats by the working muscles. (**A** modified from Matthew, D.K., and Fox, E.L.: The physiologic basis of physical education and athletics, Philadelphia, 1971, W.B. Saunders Co. **B** modified from Costill, D.: Scientific approach to distance running, Los Altos, Calif., 1979, Tafnews Press.)

conditioned competitor works long hours in conditioning activities to improve oxygen-burning capacity. With intensive training, athletes can significantly increase their efficiency in utilizing fatty acids and ketones as energy sources.[12,13] This is particularly important for endurance events in which glycogen usage may be partially spared as fat is burned. In sports activities requiring much endurance, glucose metabolism makes a minor contribution to total energy needs.

Fig. 12-3 summarizes the predominant energy systems required in the more common physical activities. The relative contributions of the anaerobic and aerobic systems to the overall energy requirement differ markedly with the time and intensity of the specific activity to be performed. With an intense burst of energy, like a tennis serve, the energy is provided anaerobically and supplied almost exclusively by the stored high-energy phosphates, ATP and CP. As the duration of the activity increases, energy from lactic acid plays a much more important role. As the intensity of the activity diminishes somewhat and the duration extends to between 1½ and 4 minutes, dependence on energy

from the phosphate stores decreases while energy release from aerobic reactions becomes more important. After 4 minutes of continuous exercise, an activity becomes more dependent on aerobic energy. In a cross-country ski race or a marathon, the body is powered almost exclusively by the energy from aerobic reactions.

Carbohydrate is widely recognized as the most readily available source of energy. The simple sugars from digested carbohydrate are absorbed from the small intestine and are taken by means of the bloodstream to the liver; here fructose and galactose are largely converted to glucose, which reenters the bloodstream for transport to body tissues, particularly brain and skeletal muscle. A fairly small amount of circulating glucose is converted to glycogen for storage in liver and muscle. The importance of glycogen is viewed as substantial when athletic involvement extends over long periods. Carbohydrate administration during competitive efforts may prevent the premature depletion of liver glycogen stores and improve endurance performance.[14] With provision of a high-carbohydrate diet, long-distance cyclists have ridden farther,[15]

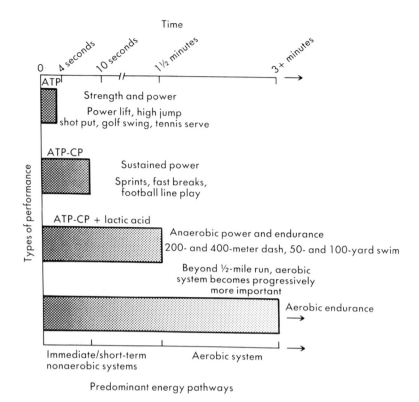

Fig. 12-3. Classification of activities based on duration of performance and the predominant energy pathways. (Modified from McArdle, W.D., Katch, F.I., and Katch, V.L.: Exercise physiology, Philadelphia, 1981, Lea & Febiger.

long-distance cross-country skiers have raced faster,[16] long-distance canoeists have paddled faster,[17] and soccer players have scored more goals in the latter parts of games.[18] Availability of carbohydrate is a major limiting factor, and its ingestion during performance or in conjunction with prior exercise recovery plays an important role in the total well-being of the athlete.

PROTEIN

For many years, it has been generally believed that physical activity does not significantly increase the need for dietary protein.[19,20] Recent data suggest,

however, that protein metabolism *may* change somewhat during endurance exercise or rigorous weight training. The earlier view that skeletal muscle functions as a fairly inert protein reservoir is no longer tenable. Evans and others[21] reported a substantial decrease in the rate of protein synthesis during exercise. They estimated that *protein can provide up to 5.5% of the total caloric cost of exercise*.

The continual flux of amino acids between muscular tissue and nonmuscular tissue, particularly the liver and kidney, supports the view that proteins play a role in the generation of energy. During periods of stress, glucocorticoids are released from the adrenal cortex to cause amino acid mobilization from muscle. The amino acids that originate from muscle can be used by the liver as gluconeogenic precursors. The elevated flux of amino acids to the liver originates from the skeletal muscle in two ways. The circulating glucocorticoids can accelerate muscle protein breakdown to augment hepatic gluconeogenesis.

In addition to their role in gluconeogenesis, amino acids contribute to whole body energy metabolism. During rest, and to a greater degree during exercise, there is significant interorgan flux that results in the redistribution of amino acids from one tissue to another. In 1971, Felig and Wahren[22] found that during exercise alanine far exceeds all other amino acids in the net release from muscle. Because alanine makes up only about 11% of the free amino acids in skeletal muscle, this would mean that alanine synthesis increases tremendously during exercise. Felig[23] explained this elevated alanine synthesis in what he described as the glucose-alanine cycle. Pyruvate carbon, derived either from glucose or from other amino acids, is transmitted to alanine using nitrogen donated by the branched chain amino acids. Alanine is thus able to serve an important carrier function for the transport of amino groups, in a nontoxic form, from skeletal muscle to liver. Although serum alanine from skeletal muscles has been found to increase during exercise, branched chain amino acids are selectively taken up by exercising muscles. Alanine from the skeletal muscles eventually reaches the liver where it is reconverted to glucose by means of gluconeogenesis. Presumably, the alanine nitrogen, which originally was derived from the branched chain amino acid molecule, is transferred to the urea cycle in the liver, where it is eventually excreted. Elevated urea levels have been observed during exercise in experimental animals as well as in human subjects.[24-26]

The alpha-ketoacid, which results from the glucose-alanine cycle during exercise, can be converted irreversibly to acetyl CoA, which ultimately provides high-energy fuel to meet metabolic demands. The oxidative potential of this cycle led recent investigations toward a more extensive account of the relationships between branched chain amino acids and muscle amino acids and their role in exercise. The prediction that a greater than tenfold increase in oxygen consumption is common in working muscle supports the theory that branched chain amino acid oxidation occurs in working muscle.[22]

Of the three branched chain amino acids, only leucine can be completely degraded in muscle to carbon dioxide, after transamination and decarboxylation. Therefore, only leucine can supply a considerable fraction of the muscle's energy during exercise. Dohm, Hecker, and Brown[27] have found that a substantial amount of energy can come from leucine oxidation in exercising rats. During exercise in human subjects, leucine oxidation rates have been found to increase by 240% while leucine flux decreased by 21%.[28] This means that protein synthesis decreased significantly. Therefore, *the elevated efflux of hepatic amino acids can be made available to muscle as an energy source without an increase in muscle protein breakdown.*

According to Evans and others[21] and Evans, Wright, and Phinney,[28] protein may provide up to 5.5% of the total caloric cost of exercise. Unlike carbohydrates and fats, leucine is a nonrenewable source of energy in that it is an essential amino acid. Evans, Wright, and Phinney[28] have estimated that 853 mg of leucine is oxidized during a 2-hour ride on a cycle ergometer at 55% of VO_2 max. This represents almost 90% of the current estimated leucine requirement. Because essential amino acid requirements have been determined only for resting humans, a reevaluation of minimum daily requirements should be considered for physically active humans.

In addition to using amino acids for energy (to a limited extent), the athlete who is training and/or competing may demand greater amino acid retention when muscles are being developed and blood volume is increasing. Increases in lean body mass, enzymatic protein, myoglobin, and hemoglobin are typical effects of training that may temporarily require greater protein utilization.[20] Athletes who develop proteinuria, hemoglobinuria, or myoglobinuria as a result of prolonged intense exercise may also require higher levels of protein until these conditions subside. Overall, the increase in protein need is easily accommodated through common food selections.

Sweating does not significantly increase the need for protein in the athlete. Sweating as a result of vigorous physical activity does increase nitrogen loss, and this may amount to 600 mg after 2 hours of strenuous exercise by the mature man.[19] If this activity lasts for 4 hours in 1 day, the nitrogen lost through sweat would be about 1.2 gm; replacing this loss through dietary sources would require an extra 7.5 gm of protein, an amount obtained in three or four bites of meat.

The performing athlete, like everyone else, must replace nitrogen losses incurred each day. The child and adolescent must go one step further and provide sufficient nitrogen (as dietary protein) for physical growth. Precise data are unavailable on protein requirements of either the mature adult who is developing his muscle mass or the growing child or adolescent who is engaged in a muscle development program. Obviously their needs are measurably greater than those of comparable persons not engaged in rigorous physical conditioning.

Table 12-3 provides a liberal estimate of protein requirements for the rapidly growing, tall, adolescent male athlete. To begin with, the 70-kg adult male loses approximately 4 gm of nitrogen/day through the urine, feces, and skin; this level of nitrogen is equivalent to approximately 25 gm of protein.[19] Obviously, there is individual variation that could conceivably (according to available data) increase the protein needs of some adults by about 30%. This estimation increases protein needs from 25 to 32.5 gm/day. Allowing for 4 hours of strenuous exercise with consequent sweat losses of nitrogen, an additional 7.5 gm of protein is required, or a total of 40 gm of protein/day for the 70-kg male. If muscle mass is being markedly

Table 12-3. Liberal estimate of daily protein need for the large, rapidly growing male athlete with a developing muscle mass

Basis for Need	Protein (gm)
Replacement of nitrogen lost through urine, feces, skin, and other sites (for 70-kg male)	24.5
Provision of 30% extra protein for individual variation (for 70-kg male)	7.5
Replacement of nitrogen lost through sweat during 4 hours of strenuous exercise (for 70-kg male)	7.5
Coverage of increased protein need of growing muscle mass (for 70-kg male)	7.5
Coverage for extra protein associated with rapid growth in adolescence (liberal estimate)	10.0
Extra protein allotment for the exceptionally large male (liberal estimate)	10.0
Provision of extra protein to cover that burned during rigorous endurance events or weight training	12.0
TOTAL	79.0

Data obtained in part from Durnin, J.V.G.A.: Protein requirements and physical activity. In Parizkova, J., and Rogozkin, V.A., editors: Nutrition, physical fitness, and health, Baltimore, 1978, University Park Press; and Evans, W.J., and others: Protein metabolism and endurance exercise, Phys. Sports Med. **11**:53, 1983.

increased, an extra 7 to 8 gm of protein might be added to the requirements, but only during the phase of active muscle building. If one liberally estimates an extra 10 gm of protein/day for the rapidly growing adolescent boy, the total daily protein requirement now should be approximately 55 to 60 gm. For those young males who are exceptionally large and/or engaged in endurance sports or demanding weight training, the protein needs may be greater. Even if the needs were to reach 80 gm/day, this amount is readily obtained through ingestion of ordinary foods (Table 12-4).

The majority of athletes tend to consume more

Table 12-4. Protein content of representative American foods

Food	Portion Size	Protein (gm)
Milk	1 cup	8
Hamburger patty, broiled	3 oz	23
Egg	1	7
Yogurt	1 cup	8
Steak	3 oz	20
Cheddar cheese	1 oz cube	7
Chili con carne	1 cup	19
Chicken drumstick	1	12
Tuna	3 oz	24
Peanut butter	1 tbsp	4
Whole wheat bread	1 slice	3
Spaghetti (noodles only)	1 cup	5
Minestrone soup	1 cup	5

Table 12-5. Representative levels of protein intake associated with varying levels of calorie intake

Calorie Intake	Calories Derived From Protein		Protein Intake (gm)	
	10%	15%	10%	15%
2000	200	300	50	75
2500	250	375	65	94
3000	300	450	75	113
3500	350	525	88	132
4000	400	600	100	150
4500	450	675	113	169
5000	500	750	125	187
6000	600	900	150	225
7000	700	1050	175	263

protein than the estimated requirement. It is known, for example, that most common diets provide 10% to 15% of calories from protein. It follows, then, that with high-calorie diets substantial amounts of protein may be readily obtained (Table 12-5). Athletes emphasizing high-protein foods may consume even higher levels of protein each day.

An obvious question is whether excessive protein consumption improves in any measurable way the short- or long-term performance of athletes. In one investigation, the effect of protein supplements was assessed in 32 male competitors.[29] Sixteen of the men were given a protein supplement as they proceeded through the basic training program in Marine Officer Candidate School. Physical performance was evaluated in all subjects before, during, and after the program. Both the supplemented and nonsupplemented groups significantly improved their physical performance scores from program onset to program termination, but no significant difference was observed between the groups.

Fig. 12-4. Weight training program for adolescent boys may increase their protein requirements to some extent. Weight training should be discouraged during the prepubescent period.

Therefore, most growing athletes consume more protein than can be effectively used for maintenance or growth. Consequently, a portion of each day's protein supply is used for energy or is stored as fat with the nitrogen waste being excreted in the urine. Although this high protein intake is generally not hazardous, it is usually expensive and it promotes loss of appetite and sometimes diarrhea. Production of excessive nitrogen waste always increases fluid requirements, so that efficient urinary excretion of this waste is achieved. For the athlete at risk for dehydration, this latter observation clearly suggests some cause for concern.

VITAMINS

Vitamins are obviously required for health and are essential for optimal physical performance. However, the attitude has unfortunately developed that the more of a good thing one gets, the better. Few controlled studies have been conducted on athletes to assess vitamin needs and effects of supplements. The limited available data support small increases in demand for B vitamins based on their roles in many biochemical reactions that make energy available for muscle work. In general, however, the higher the energy expenditure of the athlete, the higher the calorie and vitamin intake. It is important to recognize that daily B vitamin needs may be met by consumption of a balanced American diet, even when needs are slightly increased by regular high-energy expenditure in physical performance. Whether *excessive* intake of vitamin supplements contributes effectively to improved performance is a matter open to much debate. Controlled investigations do not support their ''nutritional'' merit, but the placebo effect cannot be ignored.

Several studies have been undertaken to assess the value of vitamin E supplements for athletes.[30,31] Sharman[30] studied two groups of adolescent swimmers who were provided daily with either 400 mg of α-tocopherol acetate or placebos in addition to their normal diets. The swimmers were studied for 6 weeks, and all were involved in daily swimming workouts and supportive exer-

cises. Before and after the supplementation program, a variety of anthropometric measurements were recorded and performance was tested by evaluation of cardiorespiratory efficiency and motor fitness. Although training was found to significantly improve the performance of swimmers in both experimental groups, vitamin E did not produce any obvious benefits.

In a later study by Lawrence and others,[31] two groups of well-trained competitive swimmers were observed. The first group was given 90 IU of α-tocopherol acetate/day for 6 months, whereas the second group was given placebos. A swimming endurance test was given before the start of the supplementation and after 1, 2, 5, and 6 months. No difference in swimming endurance was observed between the two groups during the 6 months. A comparable study on a younger, less trained group of competitive swimmers again revealed that vitamin E supplementation did not affect swimming endurance.

The effect of vitamin C supplementation has also been studied by several investigators. Bailey and others[32] observed 40 young males, 20 of whom were classified as trained and the remainder as untrained. Performance on various treadmill tests was recorded before and after a 5-day ingestion of 2 gm of ascorbic acid/day or placebos. The purpose of the study was to determine if vitamin C had any effect on oxygen uptake and ventilatory adjustment in trained and untrained subjects before, during, and after exercise. The results provided no indication that ascorbic acid supplementation improved performance in any measurable way.

Vitamin B_{15} or pangamic acid is widely used by amateur and professional athletes because they believe it lowers blood lactic acid, stabilizes blood sugar during exercise, and reduces the effects of fatigue. This substance is actually not a vitamin at all but a mixture of calcium gluconate and N.N-Dimethylglycine. Russian studies suggest that use of this substance promotes increased oxygen efficiency, but these investigations were not properly controlled. Several American studies support the claims of reduced lactic acid and increased performance, but others show no measurable effects. It may be that further studies are justified, but for the time being it is illegal to sell vitamin B_{15} as a dietary supplement or a drug.[33,34]

Vitamin supplements are not generally recommended for several basic and important reasons. First, excess water-soluble vitamins cannot be stored in the body effectively and thus are rapidly excreted in the urine when tissue saturation occurs. Second, the fat-soluble vitamins are retained and stored in the body, and daily high-potency supplements of vitamin A and/or vitamin D are known to be toxic and sometimes fatal. Third, a balanced diet containing more than approximately 1800 kcal/day should provide satisfactory levels of all vitamins. Only the person surviving on "junk foods" or existing on a very restricted regimen might find the diet inadequate in its vitamin content.

MINERALS

The most significant effect of exercise on mineral nutrition is the loss of electrolytes through sweat. In general, sweat contains approximately 20 to 30 mEq (460 to 690 mg) of sodium/liter, so when sweating is excessive, losses up to 350 mEq (8050 mg) may occur each day in the acclimated adult male. This amount may be greater in the nonacclimated individual, and in either case it is great enough to disturb fluid and electrolyte homeostasis.[2]

Observations of children during strenuous running show that children under 12 years of age sweat less but stay cooler.[35] Apparently, younger children have a better ratio of surface area to weight than do older children and adults, and thus they are able to dissipate heat more effectively without as great a fluid loss. Young children, therefore, exhibit less risk of dehydration and electrolyte imbalance than adolescents and adults. This situation does not mean, however, that attention to fluid replacement should be overlooked in this population.

Salt can be replaced on a regular basis by salting foods to a satisfying taste. Use of salt tablets is generally unnecessary, and sometimes they may even cause gastrointestinal disturbances resulting from fluid movement into the gut. If rates of water loss exceed 5 to 10 pounds in a given contest or workout, some consideration might be given to specific salt replacement.[8] Adding salt to the normal diet may adequately cover needs but use of *dilute* salt-containing fluids may also be considered. Commercially available electrolyte drinks are pleasantly flavored and may be diluted since most are more concentrated than they need to be for greatest effectiveness and comfort. Since thirst alone may not prompt sufficient water intakes during intense competition and/or extreme heat, regularly scheduled periods for fluid replacement should be part of any athletic training program.

Attention to potassium and magnesium replacement may be more important than consideration of sodium needs. The amount of these minerals lost through sweat is negligible when environmental temperature is mild and exercise level is moderate. Under conditions of moderate to extreme heat, however, potassium losses may be considerable if exercise is heavy and prolonged. Liu, Borowski, and Rose[36] recently described a patient with bouts of carpopedal spasm after exercise. The patient played six hours of tennis daily, swam, and sunbathed. She was found to have hypomagnesemia. After receiving magnesium supplements, her symptoms abated and her serum magnesium normalized. Lane and others[37] and Lane and Cerda[38] assessed potassium and sodium balance in volunteer runners performing in a hot climate with high humidity. Estimated losses of potassium tended to exceed the daily level of intake recommended for healthy Americans, especially in persons who were poorly acclimated. Costill, Cote, and Fink[39] reported somewhat different findings in eight men examined during two 4-day exercise-dietary regimens. When the men consumed either a control or a low-potassium diet, significant diminishment in total body potassium content was not observed.

Similarly, Dressendorfer and others[40] studied the plasma mineral levels in 12 male marathon runners during a 20-day road race. The runners consumed an unrestricted, isocaloric diet that averaged 4800 kcal/day (range 4100-5600). All subjects maintained normal plasma mineral levels without using mineral supplements during the 312-mile road race. These latter reports[39,40] suggest that there is no need for trained athletes to take salt pills, special electrolyte solutions, or mineral supplements. It seems reasonable, however, to emphasize to sports enthusiasts the value of high-potassium foods (Table 12-6). Electrolyte beverages may also be provided if they are *palatable, hypotonic,* and *balanced* in their content of glucose, chloride, sodium, and potassium.

Iron is another mineral of major importance for maintenance of optimal condition in the athlete. Adequacy of iron status is now known to significantly affect endurance and physical performance.[41,42] Iron is presently available in limited amounts in the American diet; this limited supply is a major concern for menstruating girls, premenopausal women (pregnant and nonpregnant), and rapidly growing adolescent boys whose needs are greater than other members of the population.[43]

Research on iron deficiency in animals and humans indicates that inadequate iron intake results in loss of strength and endurance, easy fatigability, shortening of attention span, loss of visual perception, and compromised learning ability.[44,45] The iron-deficient athlete, therefore, should be identified and should be provided with iron supplements and dietary counseling on useful food sources of iron. Female athletes using the intrauterine device are especially good candidates for iron supplements, because excessive menstrual blood loss often occurs when the device is used.[46] Most sensibly, however, prevention of iron deficiency is a better approach than treatment of the problem once established; thus general dietary guidelines for athletes should emphasize iron-rich foods of both animal and vegetable origin. When the self-selected diet appears inadequate to fulfill daily needs for

Table 12-6. Potassium content of common foods

Food	Portion Size	Potassium (mg)
Banana	1 small	370
Orange	1 small	200
Grapefruit	½ medium	135
Potato	1 2¼" diameter	407
Tomato	1 small	244
Carrot	1 large	341
Celery	1 small inner stalk	68
Beef steak	½ lb	325
Chicken breast	3½ oz (uncooked)	350
Salmon	3½ oz (uncooked)	399
Bread, white	1 slice	20
Bread, whole wheat	1 slice	63
Milk, whole	½ cup	176
Cheese, American	1 oz	23

iron, a low-level supplement may then be worthwhile in the maintenance of satisfactory long-term iron status.

It should be noted, however, that a phenomenon exists, called *sports anemia, runner's anemia,* or *pseudoanemia*.[47,48] This condition has been reported in some athletes, especially those involved in long-distance running or swimming or those who are subjected to recurrent trauma (e.g., football players and boxers). Suggested causes of sports anemia include inadequate iron intake, decreased intestinal absorption of iron, blood loss, expansion of blood volume, intravascular hemolysis caused by onset of heavy training and trauma, resulting in hemoglobinuria, and inadequate dietary protein intake. However, few of these causes have been studied in depth in athletes.

One definition of sports anemia is the presence of clinical anemia (hemoglobin below 12 gm/100 ml in females, 14 gm/100 ml in males) in an athlete who is usually experiencing a decline in athletic performance. Such a definition, however, may not be entirely satisfactory, because in recent years the generalization regarding the optimal hemoglobin concentration has been challenged in several studies. Although some investigators believe that optimal hemoglobin concentration for athletes may be at the upper end of the normal range, others support the concept that sports anemia is a normal physiological adaptation that should provoke no concern.

In support of the concept that sports anemia is normal, Yoshimura[49] believes the evidence from Japan indicates that sports anemia is caused by increased destruction of red blood cells (RBCs), which is a result of an increase in fragility. He cites evidence suggesting that the spleen releases a hemolyzing factor during exercise. He also quotes studies indicating that the destruction of RBCs allows the protein from the hemoglobin to be used to "promote growth or hypertrophy of muscles and regeneration of new and strong RBCs."

A scheme of adaptation that is easier to study relates oxygen transport to hematocrit and blood viscosity.[47] As the hematocrit (or hemoglobin)

increases, the oxygen-carrying ability of the blood improves. The optimum hematocrit for carrying oxygen would be 100%, but the viscosity of the blood also increases with an increasing hematocrit. As the blood becomes thicker, it becomes more difficult to pump. Therefore, the hematocrit should be at a level that combines an optimum oxygen-carrying capacity and viscosity. Crowell and Smith[50] determined that a hematocrit of 40% is optimal for oxygen transport. This roughly corresponds to a hemoglobin in the range of 13 to 14 gm/100 ml. Guyton, Jones, and Coleman[51] suggest that the "borderline anemia state" is optimal for oxygen transport and that the factors governing RBC production are fine tuned to meet the daily stresses athletes impose on their bodies. If one supports this hypothesis, guidelines for diagnosis of sports anemia would be compatible with those outlined in the box below.

Support for the belief that sports anemia may indeed by physiological is provided by Dressendorfer, Wade, and Amsterdam[52] who observed marathon runners during a 20-day road race. RBC count, blood hemoglobin concentration, and relat-

---

Guidelines for the Diagnosis of Sports Anemia

Hemoglobin Concentration in Men and Women

	Normal Range	Approximate Population Mean
Men	14-18 gm/100 ml	16 gm/100 ml
Women	12-16 gm/100 ml	14 gm/100 ml

Suggested Criteria for Sports Anemia and Suboptimal Hemoglobin Concentration

	Sports Anemia	Suboptimal Hemoglobin Concentration
Men	< 14 gm/100 ml	< 16 gm/100 ml
Women	< 12 gm/100 ml	< 14 gm/100 ml

Modified from Pate, R.R.: Phys. Sports Med. **11**:115, 1983.

ed hematological factors were recorded in 12 young men during a 312-mile run. The RBC and hemoglobin levels decreased significantly (Fig. 12-5), and the runners became marginally anemic during the race. Running speeds, however, were not adversely affected, and no abnormal clinical signs (other than rare instances of hematuria) were noted. The investigators suggest that a sudden increase in long-distance running mileage above the regular training level may cause sports anemia, a functional pseudoanemia that, in mild cases, does not impair endurance performance.

In a similar study, Frederickson, Puhl, and Runyan[53] examined indices of iron status in female high school cross-country runners during and after the competitive season. The runners experienced sports anemia in that their hemoglobin concentrations and packed RBC volumes declined signifi-

cantly during the first week of training (Fig. 12-6). Between weeks 1 and 8 of the season, the runner's hemoglobin concentrations and packed RBC volumes gradually returned to preseason values while the serum iron and percent transferrin saturation showed steady but nonsignificant declines (Fig. 12-6). By the end of the detraining period, all the iron indices had returned to initial values (except total iron-binding capacity). The authors suggest that in young women the *recovery from* sports anemia may impose a demand on body iron reserves and that it would be prudent to assess iron status as well as hematological indices in such women before and during aerobic training.

Others have found that mild anemia is not harmful to performance. Studies in Norway[54] on students found no relationship between hemoglobin and maximal oxygen uptake after correcting for body size in mild anemia or low normal hemoglo-

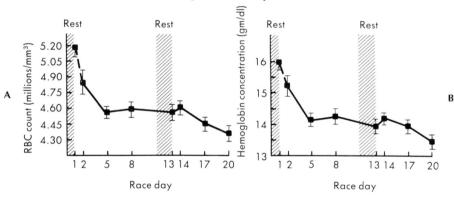

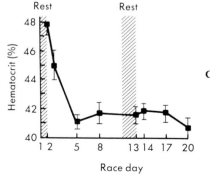

Fig. 12-5. Red blood cell concentration (**A**), hemoglobin concentration (**B**), and hematocrit reading (**C**) during 312-mile race held over 20 days. Values are means ($\pm$ S.E.M.) (*vertical bars*) for 12 marathon runners. (Modified from Dressendorfer, R.H., Wade, C.E., and Amsterdam, E.A.: Development of pseudoanemia in marathon runners during a 20-day road race, J.A.M.A. **246**:1215, 1981.)

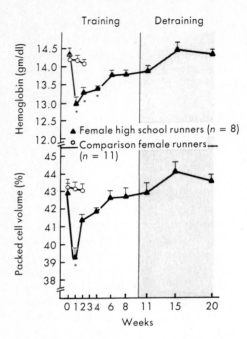

Fig. 12-6. Mean hemoglobin concentration and packed cell volume of runners and comparison subjects. Vertical lines indicate ± S.E.M. (Modified from Frederickson, L.A., Puhl, J.L., and Runyan, W.S.: Effects of training on indices of iron status of young female cross-country runners, Med. Sci. Sports Exercise **15**:271, 1983.)

bin.[55-59] Coted, Dabbs, and Elwood[60] found no difference in ventilation or heart rate in subjects with hemoglobin values between 8 and 15 gm/100 ml.

But more severe anemia is clearly associated with retarded oxygen delivery to tissues. Several studies in rats and humans support this belief.[61-63] Anemic subjects have been found to demonstrate increased anaerobic metabolism during exercise, prolonged recovery times after performing standardized work loads on a bicycle ergometer, decreased maximum aerobic power, and elevated peak exercise heart rates and lactate levels following exercise.

Diagnosis of sports anemia is based on the his-tory of athletic participation and the exclusion of other forms of anemia. A complete blood cell count is recommended along with an RBC count. (The RBC count is usually normal in sports anemia.) Serum iron and iron-binding capacity should be obtained to rule out iron deficiency as a cause. After the less common causes of anemia such as folic acid deficiency, vitamin B_{12} deficiency, thalassemia, and chronic disease have been eliminated, it is possible to determine the haptoglobin level immediately before and after a workout. A drop in the haptoglobin level implies that hemolysis has occurred and supports mechanical destruction of RBCs as a contributor to the anemia, although one cannot be sure it is the only cause.[47]

After being diagnosed as having sports anemia, many athletes ask about the usefulness of supplemental iron, even when they have been told that their iron level is normal. There is little evidence that additional iron in a nondeficient person will lead to increased RBC production.[64-66] If all other causes of anemia have been eliminated and sports anemia is diagnosed, no treatment is believed to be necessary.

It should be remembered, however, that true iron deficiency may be identified in athletes and when treated may lead to improvement in their performance. High-risk individuals should be monitored for change in iron status and provided appropriate dietary or supplementation guidelines when deemed appropriate. The incidence of iron deficiency in an otherwise healthy group of athletes is significant.[67-70] Since iron deficiency is know to be the most common specific nutrient deficiency among Americans, attention to its presence should not be ignored, even if sports anemia may not require aggressive management.

A worthwhile note regarding iron is that "conservation" is occasionally noted in the female competitor of menstrual age.[71-80] Menarche reportedly is delayed in young women who are actively involved in physically demanding athletics (Fig. 12-7).[81] Secondary amenorrhea is known to result from rigorous exercise as well as excessive weight

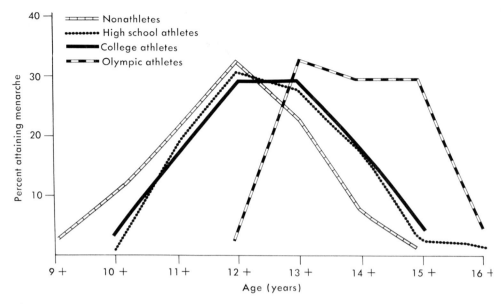

Fig. 12-7. Relative distributions of ages at menarche in nonathletes and athletes at different competitive levels. The athletes attained menarche significantly later than did the nonathletes, and the Olympic athletes attained menarche significantly later than did the high school and college athletes. (From Malina, R.M., and others: Age at menarche and selected menstrual characteristics in athletes at different competitive levels and in different sports, Med. Sci. Sports **10**:218, 1978).

loss leading to establishment of a low percentage of body fat. Although many young athletes with amenorrhea have low body weights, no obvious association between fatness and menstrual regularity has been observed among athletes. Theoretically, amenorrhea may ultimately improve the iron status of the competitor. It is uncertain, however, whether ongoing suppression of the normal female menstrual pattern produces any lasting harm to the health and reproductive performance of such women.

The major concern derived from recent observations is that ongoing amenorrhea in mature women may simulate menopause as far as the bony skeleton is concerned. Cann[82] observed 25 amenorrheic patients, 19 to 49 years of age, and found that all demonstrated significant bone loss, as measured by a quantitative computed tomographic technique for assessing vertebral mineral content. The total group of 25 women had a mean of 28% less bone mass than 45 age-matched control subjects. Not all the women with amenorrhea developed the condition as a result of athletic participation, but bone loss in women with amenorrhea for whatever cause was similar. The lingering question that is still unanswered is "Are some young female athletes in danger of developing early osteoporosis?" There is also concern over the effects of prolonged hypoestrogenism on the genitourinary and vascular systems.

If amenorrhea in young women leads to bone loss or other adverse consequences, there will be a need to carefully examine the contributing factors. There is a consensus that active women need not significantly change their life-styles and eliminate exercise. That alone might provide additional stress that would contribute to menstrual irregularity. As more information is accumulated, it should be reported in such a way that it ultimately will enhance the health care provided to women. It is definitely premature, at best, to recommend that women abandon exercise programs that offer positive contributions to self-image and stress management and probably assist in the *prevention* of osteoporosis.

WATER

Attention to daily water requirements is of major importance to athletes of all calibers.[1-5,8,9] Water is obviously needed as the supporting medium in which all body reactions occur. In addition, it is extremely important in body temperature regulation; excessive heat generated by exercise must be dissipated, and this is done most effectively through the evaporation of sweat. This mechanism fails to function effectively, however, if the water supply is inadequate to meet the needs of the sweat glands.

A well-conditioned athlete who exercises in high temperatures will voluntarily drink more fluid. Some conscientious attention to water needs must be maintained, however, because creation of a water deficit of approximately 3% of total body water is associated with deterioration in performance in both males and females. Individuals in prime physical condition can function effectively until body water equal to 4% to 5% of body weight is lost; at this point, athletic performance clearly deteriorates. The conscientious athlete never allows a deficit of this degree to develop.[14]

It should be noted, however, that although children can acclimatize to exercise in the heat, the rate of their acclimatization is slower than that of adults. Therefore, the child needs more exposure to the new climate to sufficiently acclimatize. Whatever the circumstance, children frequently do not instinctively drink enough fluids to replenish fluid lost during prolonged exercise and may become gravely dehydrated. A major consequence of dehydration is an excessive increase in body tempera-

ture during exercise. For a given level of dehydration, children are subject to a greater increase in core temperature during exercise than are adults. Clinically, the dehydrated child is more prone to heat-related illness than the fully hydrated one.[83]

According to the American Academy of Pediatrics,[83] children with the following conditions are at a potentially greater risk of heat stress: obesity, febrile state, cystic fibrosis, gastrointestinal infection, diabetes insipidus, diabetes mellitus, chronic heart failure, caloric malnutrition, anorexia nervosa, sweating insufficiency syndrome, and mental deficiency. The parent, the coach, and the clinician should be especially careful about monitoring children with these conditions who choose to participate in rigorous physical activities.

Negative fluid balance is commonly noted in competitive wrestlers attempting to "make weight." Aggressive efforts to quickly lose pounds may involve induced sweating and spitting as well. Vaccaro, Zauner, and Cade[84] observed college wrestlers in an effort to assess dehydration and rehydration before competition. Body weight, hematocrit values, and plasma protein concentration were determined at the normal state, at weight certification, and just before competition. Results of analysis confirmed that wrestlers cannot regain in 5 hours all the fluid lost in the process of "making weight." Thus they enter most wrestling matches in a relative state of dehydration.

Dehydration is known to produce undesirable changes in several physiological processes; these changes ultimately compromise physical performance and health (box, above). The American Medical Association's guidelines for weight management in young wrestlers should be the foundation for practice of coaches and trainers (box, p. 329).

CASE STUDY: Dehydration and Pulmonary Embolism in a High School Wrestler*

A 16-year-old high school wrestler had flu-like syndrome with fever, nausea, weakness, and myalgia 2 days

*Data from Croyle, P.H., Place, R.A., and Hilgenberg, A.D.: J.A.M.A. **241:**827, 1979.

Food Restriction and Fluid Deprivation and Dehydration Produce the Following:

1. Decreased muscular strength
2. Decreased work performance
3. Decreased plasma and blood volumes
4. Decreased cardiac function
5. Decreased oxygen consumption
6. Impaired thermoregulatory processes
7. Decreased kidney blood flow
8. Depletion of liver glycogen stones

American Medical Association's Guidelines for Weight Management in Young Wrestlers

1. 7% to 10% body fat is desirable for the wrestler.
2. The wrestler should participate in a 6-week intensive training and conditioning program with no regard for his weight.
3. Weight at the end of this period is to be his minimum effective weight for competition and certification.
4. Any effort to maintain a weight below this would be a hardship on the body.

---

before a match. He lost 3.5 kg to "make weight" for the match and fell to an opponent he had easily defeated earlier. He was dyspneic for 30 minutes after his fall. He lost 2.5 kg by sweating and fluid restriction before another match 4 days later. He became exhausted in the second period and was pinned; cyanosis was noted and oxygen administered. The next day his physician heard a heart murmur and hospitalized the boy. Most clinical indices appeared to be normal at admission. A third heart sound was heard, and an ECG showed tachycardia with right axis deviation. A systolic murmur was heard 12 hours later, and premature ventricular beats appeared; left scapular pain was reported. Hypotension and cyanosis with severe chest pain were evident the following day. A total cardiopulmonary bypass was performed; large amounts of embolic material of varying ages were removed from both pulmonary arteries. There is presumptive evidence that dehydration before a match helped to increase blood viscosity and venous stasis, which, combined with lower extremity trauma, led to asymptomatic deep vein thrombosis and massive pulmonary embolism.

FIBER

Fiber in foods is now well recognized as a valuable component of the diet of human beings. Even though the human gastrointestinal tract is incapable of effective digestion and absorption of this material, it serves beneficial roles in the gut by promoting normal motility and regulating the rate and character of digestive/absorptive processes. Because fiber does remain in the gut along with fluid, which it may retain, it may add to body weight at a time when the athlete would prefer to be at a low, healthy state. In addition, it may be broken down, to some degree, by bacteria in the large bowel. This may involve the production of gas, which may disturb the feeling of optimal readiness for precise athletic competition. On occasion, therefore, it may behoove the competior to use moderation in cónsumption of fiber before weigh-in or actual competition.

ALCOHOL

Some adolescent athletes have the mistaken notion that moderate alcohol consumption improves their performance.[85] In fact, ethanol cannot be used as an energy source for exercise; it does not influence maximal oxygen consumption during exercise nor does it affect anaerobic energy expenditure through sources such as ATP and PC. In addition, alcohol is a depressant to the central nervous system, it accentuates fatigue by increasing the production of lactate, it slows the reaction time, it interferes with reflexes, and it destroys coordination. Overall, the effect of alcohol on physical performance appears to be negative on all counts; decreased performance has been reported thus far in tests of dynamic balance, visual tracking, arm steadiness, body sway, and various other psychomotor tasks. It is interesting to note, however, as did one high school alcoholic, that the sensation promoted by alcohol was deceptively positive. One student stated the following in a recent interview:[85]

I would drink before going to school, and I'd get to physical education class rarin' to go. But the coordination wasn't there. I *felt* I could perform better, but it was all in my head. In reality, I really performed worse.

"HEALTH FOODS" AND THE VEGETARIAN DIET

A wide variety of foods are presently available to consumers in the United States. Most of these foods provide some valuable contributions of nutrients along with the ever-present calories. Some foods are better than others in the amounts of nutrients provided within a given calorie allotment. Ingestion of an array of basic foods may allow for establishment and maintenance of health. No foods carry magical properties that make them especially effective in promotion of optimal physical performance.

It is generally wise to be leery of advertisements that tout the value of a new "health food." Often such products are quite expensive and provide nothing more than can normally be obtained from a balanced diet. The typical athlete usually consumes a sizable number of calories each day. The majority of such individuals consequently obtain their required nutritional support through food sources in the daily menu. Consequently, supplements are entirely unnecessary, with the exception of the several circumstances referred to in this text.

But still one sees in the local "health-maintenance establishment" an array of products advertised for "the athlete." None has been found to actually improve athletic performance. The characteristics of some of these "ergogenic agents" are given in Table 12-7. Although the established scientific merit of these substances is clearly in doubt, the placebo benefit may be substantial.

The vegetarian diet can support good health, providing that basic pitfalls are avoided (see Chapter 11). Satisfactory nonmeat sources of iron, calcium, vitamin B_{12}, zinc, protein, and calories must be selected. Combining vegetable proteins so that they complement each other is especially important for the strict vegetarian athlete. Since most vegetables provide calories in a more dilute form than do animal materials, the athlete must be careful about meeting calorie needs so that growth will be maintained along with energy level for athletic competition.

Table 12-7. Characteristics of selected "ergogenic agents"

I. Bee Pollen

A. Composition

Bee pollen is a mixture of bee saliva, plant nectar, and pollen (the male germ cells of flowering plants). Traditionally, the pollen is brushed off the back legs and pollen basket of worker bees forced to enter the hive through a portal partially obstructed by a wire mesh. But with the increasing popularity of pollen as a health food, this means of pollen collection has proved inadequate to meet demand. Instead, tons of bee pollen are now being produced after direct collection from hives.

The pollen material is sold either as loose powder, compressed into tablets of 400-500 mg with or without other nutritional supplements, or as capsules.

Manufacturers' data suggest that after removal of the water, the protein varies from 10%-36% with an average of 20%; the essential amino acid content is reasonably high. Simple sugars, such as those in honey, make up 10%-15% of the content, and in addition to small quantities of fats, pollen contains significant amounts of minerals, such as potassium, magnesium, phosphorus, calcium, copper, and iron. Some vitamins are also present including thiamine, riboflavin, niacin, pantothenic acid, ascorbic acid, biotin, and carotenes.

B. Problems Claimed to be Helped by Product

A vast body of literature, especially in the lay press, has extolled the curative properties of pollen in diseases ranging from colitis, premature aging, and renal disease to skin blemishing and weight loss. A flier from a local health food store claims that "pollen has a dramatic effect upon mental perception in athletic performance. In documented clinical trials, IQs of children have been doubled and resistance to stress has been increased significantly in both animals and humans. Experiments by French doctors suggest that pollen contains both antibiotic and growth factors."

C. Proven Assets of Product

Scientific literature on the composition and healthful properties of bee pollen is almost nil, and evidence defining health benefits is entirely anecdotal.

D. Adverse Side Effects of Use (Especially in Large Amounts)

A recent report describes three patients who experienced systemic reactions after ingesting bee pollen. Another patient was reportedly treated after suffering an anaphylactic reaction from ingestion of bee pollen for remedy of his allergic rhinitis. In most of the cases, the specific allergen causing the problem derived from a plant pollen contaminating the bee pollen.

Since bee pollen contains nucleic acids, high intakes are not recommended for those individuals predisposed to gout or who have signs of renal disease.

E. Other Comments

Taken as a supplement, it appears that bee pollen might provide a satisfactory nutritional contribution to the diet of an individual who cared to pay the price for the product.

II. Brewer's Yeast

A. Composition

Brewer's yeast is the nonfermentative, nonextracted yeast of the botanical classification *Saccharomyces* and is derived as a by-product from the brewing of beer and ale. It is generally sold in dry form since the fresh form spoils readily.

A suitable daily portion of the dried yeast is 1-2 tbsp (15-30 ml) and may be mixed in vegetable drinks such as tomato juice, cooked cereals, flavored instant breakfast drinks, gravies, meat loaf, and various sauces.

If there is a choice of product, one that is "debittered" should be selected. Tablets are also available for those who prefer a more convenient and palatable form of the product.

Continued.

Table 12-7. Characteristics of selected "ergogenic agents"—cont'd

B. Problems Claimed to be Helped by Product

Brewer's yeast is promoted as a natural potent source of protein, vitamins, minerals, and nucleic acids; consequently, athletes have used it as an energy food.

Claims for its usefulness in diabetes are related to its content of GTF-chromium. In fact, one investigation showed that a group of elderly subjects provided with brewer's yeast (rich in available chromium) gained significant improvement in glucose tolerance and serum cholesterol levels compared with torula yeast (low in chromium).

C. Proven Assets of Product

Brewer's yeast is used primarily as a rich supplemental source of B vitamins, although it is also a good source of fair quality protein, with a minimum of 35% crude protein. When irradiated with ultraviolet light, it provides vitamin D.

It is rich in chromium and selenium, minerals that are limited in the diets of some Americans. Chromium is present in an organic form (glucose tolerance factor) that is much more beneficial to the body than the inorganic form of the mineral.

D. Adverse Side Effects of Use (Especially in Large Amounts)

Since brewer's yeast is rich in nucleic acids, individuals susceptible to gout should be cautious in their use of the product.

Systemic saccharomyces yeast infections have resulted from daily oral ingestion of viable organisms in brewer's yeast. As a supplement, it is important to make sure the yeast is dead.

III. Ginseng

A. Composition

Ginseng is the root of the ginseng plant and is sold in capsules, extract, instant powder, paste, tea (sometimes made with leaves), and whole root.

Ginseng's growing popularity is attributed to pharmacologically active agents that exert stimulant action. Ginseng cointains peptides, steroids, and many unidentified substances that appear responsible for its stimulant effect. Nevertheless, some commercial ginseng products are devoid of these active agents. Others may be "spiked" with synthetic products and drugs. In addition, most of the ginseng sold in the United States may be derived from a North American plant related to the original *Panax schinseng* plant. Though little work has been done, evidence indicates that extracts from the original plant may not have the same pharmacological effects as extracts from related plants.

B. Problems Claimed to be Helped by Product

Ginseng is claimed to be a general tonic for digestive troubles, impotence, and overall lack of vitality.

C. Proven Assets of Product

Reports of effectiveness are largely anecdotal. The amounts consumed (1 tsp or 5 gm) are too small to contribute much in the way of nutrients. Recently, however, extracts from ginseng root powder were shown to have cholesterol-lowering effects in birds. This effect has been attributed to saponins (ginsenosides) in ginseng.

D. Adverse Side Effects of Use (Especially in Large Amounts)

In China, doses of ginseng up to 50 gm have been tested, and 2-3 gm is considered the amount needed to elicit behavioral stimulation. However, recently, what has become known as the Ginseng Abuse Syndrome has been associated with use of the herb. With doses as low as 3 gm, hypertension and neurological symptoms such as insomnia, nervousness, feelings of depersonalization, confusion, and depression have been reported. Also, skin eruptions, edema, and diarrhea are seen. Abrupt withdrawal of ginseng may lead to hypotensive crises.

Table 12-7. Characteristics of selected "ergogenic agents"—cont'd

Ginseng has been reported to produce a physiological estrogen-like effect on the vaginal mucosa, mastalgia with diffuse mammary nodularity in postmenopausal women, and, experimentally, stimulation of corticotropin secretion and altered RNA hepatic metabolism. After a bilateral oophorectomy, one research team observed a notable vaginal effect in a patient ingesting an unstated amount of Romanian ginseng only 2 weeks per month. A 72-year-old woman experienced vaginal bleeding and a moderate estrogen effect after ingesting one tablet daily of a Swiss-Austrian geriatric formula containing 200 mg ginseng of an unspecified source.

IV. Protein supplements

A. Composition

Protein supplements are available as liquids, powders, and tablets. They contain either all the essential amino acids to make a "high quality" protein or only specific amino acids.

B. Problems Claimed to be Helped by Product

Products are often promoted to improve physical performance, assist in weight reduction, or build skeletal muscles.

C. Proven Assets of Product

Most Americans consume far more protein than they can use; excess protein can be converted to fat that the body eventually can burn. No evidence exists that athletes or physically active people require protein in excess of levels normally required by adolescents or that extra protein improves physical performance.

D. Adverse Side Effects of Use (Especially in Large Amounts)

Excess protein can lead to ketosis, dehydration, tendency for gout, and increased urinary excretion of calcium.

V. Royal jelly

A. Composition

Royal jelly is a milky white substance produced by worker bees to nourish the queen bee. Queen bees differ from worker bees: they are about twice the size, they live up to 8 years (about 40 times longer than worker bees), and they lay about 2000 eggs per day (female worker bees are infertile).

While the egg of the queen starts out like all the others, the royal jelly fed to this bee is the basis for the difference that develops during the growth state.

Royal jelly is sold in capsule form as a nutritional supplement, but it is also an ingredient in certain expensive cosmetics.

B. Problems Claimed to be Helped by Product

The implication of promoters of royal jelly is that it will do as much for humans as it does for queen bees—it will increase size, longevity, and fertility. Although it is a rich source of certain B vitamins (like pantothenic acid), it has not been shown to possess any recognizable preventive, therapeutic, or rejuvenating characteristics.

C. Proven Assets of Product

None known.

D. Adverse Side Effects of Use (Especially in Large Amounts)

None reported.

Continued.

Table 12-7. Characteristics of selected "ergogenic agents"—cont'd

VI. Wheat germ

A. Composition

Wheat germ is the embryo of the sprouting part of the wheat seed. It constitutes only 2.5% of the kernel and is the source of wheat germ meal and wheat germ oil.

Wheat germ meal is low in fiber, high in fat and vitamin E, and fairly rich in protein (minimum 25% crude protein). Defatted wheat germ is the product that remains after removal of part of the oil from the meal; it contains at least 30% crude protein, but is much lower in vitamin E than regular wheat germ meal.

The defatting process is desirable, however, in that the fat decomposes readily and markedly reduces the shelf-life of the product. The label indicates whether the germ is defatted.

Wheat germ is a good source of calories, essential fatty acids, proteins, minerals, vitamin E, and the B vitamins.

B. Problems Claimed to be Helped by Product

Wheat germ and its oil are on the list of popular ergogenic foods. A well-known athletic trainer with good academic credentials published experiments that led him to propose the benefit of wheat germ in improving physical performance. His findings received considerable attention. However, other researchers have been unable to reproduce his work or show evidence that wheat germ or its oil improves physical performance. This same athletic trainer also claimed to have isolated from wheat germ a compound, octacosanol, that provides energy and builds endurance. Recently, octacosanol has become available as a single supplement. It is a solid white alcohol extracted from wheat germ, but again the criticisms raised against wheat germ also apply to its components.

C. Proven Assets of Product

Wheat germ meal is used chiefly as a livestock feed, although some of it is now used as a human nutritional supplement. Wheat germ oil is used primarily as a rich vitamin E supplement for humans and animals. It can be added to many kinds of foods, such as bread, cookies, cereals, and milkshakes.

D. Adverse Side Effects of Use (Especially in Large Amounts)

None reported.

NUTRITIONAL PREPARATION FOR ATHLETIC PERFORMANCE

Short-Term Events

Before a short-term athletic contest a general well-balanced diet should be consumed. Immediately before the competition, muscular work should be limited, so that muscle sources of energy will be plentiful. Between several scheduled short-term events, time should be allowed to replenish these energy sources (e.g., ATP, PC, and glycogen) and clear the by-products of anaerobic metabolism (e.g., lactic acid). An adequate supply of carbohydrate and water should be available throughout the day. Fruit juices are popular with many athletes, but some prefer complete liquid meals or other easily digested foods. A sensation of lightness may be promoted by restriction of high-fiber foods, such as the following:

1. Whole grains (e.g., cereals, breads, and other derivatives)
2. Dried peas and beans
3. Nuts and seeds
4. Fruits, especially raw with skins

5. Vegetables, especially raw with skins, stems, and seeds.

6. Bran

Avoidance of high-fat foods, which demand long-term digestion, will also support a feeling of readiness. The following is a list of representative high-fat foods:

1. Butter and margarine
2. Cream, sour cream, ice cream, mayonnaise, gravy, and salad dressings
3. Meats, especially fried or fatty
4. Creamed dishes
5. Most cheeses and cheese dishes
6. Pastry
7. Bacon and sausage
8. Chocolate

Gas-forming foods should be minimized in the diet if gas formation is disturbing or distracting to the athlete. Gas-forming foods include the following:

1. Melons
2. Sulfur-containing vegetables such as cabbage, cauliflower, radishes, brussels sprouts, turnips, onions, rutabagas, green peppers, dried peas and beans, lentils, apples, corn, and avocados
3. Others (different for each person)

Long-Term Events

Preparation for lengthy competitive activities involves attention to the same basic nutrition principles encountered in other circumstances. In addition, sensible eating practices on the day of the event should be followed. On the morning of the competition high-bulk foods and fatty foods should be avoided, and choices should be made from available carbohydrate sources. In preparing for a lengthy afternoon competition, a light lunch that is low in residue and fatty foods should be taken at least 2½ hours before the starting time. Foods that are satisfying to the individual should be selected.

In choosing high-carbohydrate foods for consumption on competition day, effort should be made to avoid those that are too concentrated in form. Such foods include honey, glucose syrups, and high-sugar/high-electrolyte beverages. Such concentrated solutions, when present in the gut, may provoke the movement of water from body tissues into the gut lumen to balance the osmotic condition; this phenomenon may be associated with abdominal discomfort and diarrhea, which may aggravate poor gastric function already present in the nervous athlete. Diluted, sweetened fruit juices or fruit-flavored drinks are tolerated better than are more concentrated products. Caffeine-containing beverages (e.g., cola drinks) are of questionable merit because of their initial ability to act as stimulants followed by a tendency to produce depression in young athletes. Individuals who are particularly sensitive to caffeine may develop adverse central nervous system and cardiovascular effects as well as ringing in the ears, insomnia, gastric irritation, and diuresis. The diuretic effect of caffeine may not only increase risk of dehydration, but it may also bring on the urge to urinate at a critical point during the athletic competition.

Some athletes in recent years have used the glycogen-loading diet to maximize muscle glycogen stores for moderate to long-term activities.[86-90] Since the readily available anaerobic energy sources in muscle cells are exhausted within 5 minutes (or less) of heavy physical activity, a substantial store of glycogen is very useful, since enough oxygen cannot be supplied to muscle to meet energy needs through metabolism alone. Glycogen stores support an increase in anaerobic energy production just when it is needed. An example of the value of extra muscle glycogen is provided in Fig. 12-8: the work times of men on bicycle ergometers were markedly increased as muscle glycogen stores were augmented.

Glycogen stores can be greatly increased by adherence to a high-carbohydrate regimen during the week preceding competition. For some athletes a high-carbohydrate diet has proved successful for improving performance when moderate to long-term energy support is demanded. the glycogen-

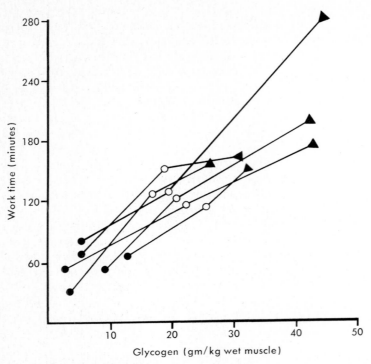

Fig. 12-8. Relationship between initial muscle glycogen content in quadriceps femoris and work time in six subjects on bicycle ergometers with the same relative load three times each with 3-day intervals. Diets before exercise: (1) mixed (*open circle*), (2) carbohydrate free (*closed circle*), and (3) carbohydrate rich (*triangle*). (Redrawn from Bergstrom, J., and Hultman, E.: Nutrition for maximal sports performance, J.A.M.A. **221**:999, 1972.)

loading diet was developed as a follow-up to data originally collected by Swedish physiologists. These workers conducted studies of muscle glycogen content during the course of a week of controlled dietary intake (Fig. 12-9). It was found that on a normal diet, the average concentration of glycogen in muscle tissue was approximately 1.75 gm/100 gm of muscle. After 3 days on a diet limited largely to fat and protein, the glycogen level fell to 0.6 gm/100 gm of muscle. When the diet was reversed to include large amounts of carbohydrate, the level increased to 3.5 gm/100 gm muscle. The same studies demonstrated that if the specific muscle was exercised strenuously to specifi-

cally deplete it of glycogen while on a low-carbohydrate diet, the subsequent institution of a high-carbohydrate diet caused the glycogen in the muscle to rise to 4.7 gm/100 gm in the exercised muscle. This Swedish work thus demonstrated that glycogen stores could be practically tripled through diet modification in conjunction with a program to first deplete then replete muscle glycogen content.

The glycogen-loading diet as it traditionally is prescribed involves 6 days of attention to dietary manipulation, as illustrated in Fig. 12-10. If the athletic event is to be held on Saturday, one starts on the preceding Sunday evening or early Monday

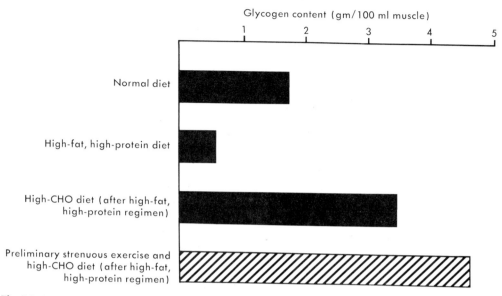

Fig. 12-9. Effect of dietary composition on muscle glycogen content on endurance athletes. *CHO,* Carbohydrate. (From Bergstrom, J., and Hultman, E.: Nutrition for maximal sports performance, J.A.M.A. **221**:999, 1972. Copyright 1972, American Medical Association.)

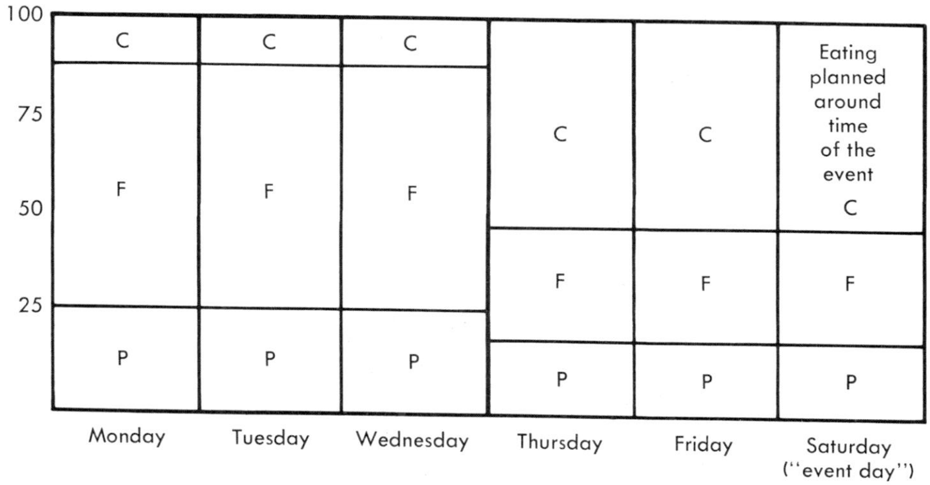

	Monday	Tuesday	Wednesday	Thursday	Friday	Saturday ("event day")
100	C	C	C			Eating planned around time of the event
75				C	C	
50	F	F	F			C
25				F	F	F
	P	P	P	P	P	P

Fig. 12-10. Diagrammatic representation of daily dietary composition of an athlete following the strict glycogen-loading routine. *C,* Carbohydrate; *F,* fat; *P,* protein. (In some cases, Wednesday's routine may be like Thursday's and Friday's if a shorter depletion period is specified.)

Definitions of Terms Describing Glycogen Depletion

Bonking—running out of liver glycogen, which causes hypoglycemia, dizziness, shakiness, and confusion. An athlete can recover from a bonk by eating immediately.

Hitting the wall—running out of muscle glycogen with the development of fatigue. The athlete usually cannot come back or continue, even if he or she eats some carbohydrate.

---

morning by consuming a diet that is rich in protein and fat, with carbohydrate representing only approximately 10% of the daily calories. After several days of this depletion phase, most athletes find that they tire easily and perform suboptimally during practice sessions. On the third day, the high-protein, high-fat regimen is replaced by a high-carbohydrate diet. Carbohydrate-rich foods are emphasized in this period, but protein and fat may still be consumed at reasonably normal levels. Some athletes have used flavored beverages that are rich in glucose to supply part of the carbohydrate needs. A new commercial product called Gatorade 280* is sold for carbohydrate loading, and trial data suggest that it works quite well.[91] The cost, however, is substantial so consideration of this factor is recommended before planning a carbohydrate-loading routine.

Adherence to the glycogen-loading diet requires dedication on the part of the athlete, particularly during the first phase, when carbohydrate intake is rigorously restricted. During this time, the specified diet is significantly different from that usually consumed. The fatigued feeling that often develops during this period may prove frustrating and discouraging to the athlete in training. Consequently, it is wise to use the glycogen-loading regimen with

considerable discretion; it probably should not be undertaken for every competition during the season, but should be reserved for those few occasions when special preparation is clearly in order. It has been shown, in fact, that it is impossible to attain extremely high muscle glycogen storage at more frequent intervals than a few weeks, even if the program is carefully followed. At other times, the athlete may prefer to emphasize the high-carbohydrate aspect of the diet for 3 to 4 days preceding competition. This is obviously much easier to accomplish, because the several days of fatigue associated with the high-fat, high-protein depletion phase may then be avoided. In fact, recent research has shown that levels of glycogen storage close to that achieved with the full depletion/loading regimen can be reached with just a high-carbohydrate diet and rest.[92]

A recent finding of considerable interest is that moderate caffeine consumption before an endurance event may allow for a moderate delay in the use of muscle glycogen stores.[93-96] This effect appears to be related to the role of caffeine in elevating plasma-free fatty acids. Studies conducted in both rats and humans have revealed delays in development of exhaustion when caffeine is provided in moderate doses before physical performance. Although use of this stimulant may be attractive to competitors involved in endurance sports, the potential dangers of excessive caffeine consumption should be carefully considered.

Just how safe the glycogen-loading diet is remains to be confirmed through continued observation.[97,98] Glycogen retains water, and both sub-

---

*Gatorade 280 provides 280 calories and 70 gm of carbohydrate in a 12-oz serving. It contains maltodextrin as a carbohydrate source, sucrose, citric acid, and artificial apple flavor. It is fortified with 30% of the RDA for vitamins C, B_1, and B_2 to enhance the metabolism of carbohydrate. Its proposed advantages over a traditional pasta diet are that it is less bulky, is isotonic, and leaves less residue in the intestine before exercise.

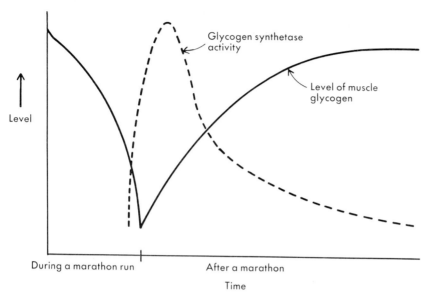

Fig. 12-11. Changes in muscle glycogen concentration and in muscle glycogen synthetase activity during and after a marathon run.

stances may be deposited in muscle to such an extent that a feeling of heaviness and stiffness may be experienced. The weight increase caused by water retention may reduce the ability of the athlete to take up oxygen maximally. Based on individual case studies, fears have been raised that it may cause cardiac arrhythmias, raise serum triglyceride levels, and destroy muscle fibers by the excessive glycogen storage. Little definitive proof has been found to support these fears.[90,99] Recently, however, an Oregon State University researcher reported observation of cardiac arrhythmias during the depletion of the carbohydrate-loading regimen in four healthy male runners.[100] This scientist suggests that the diet causes the skeletal muscles to rob from the heart muscle, using the glycogen the heart should be using. He suggests that marathon runners skip the glycogen-depletion phase if carbohydrate loading is attempted.

The onset of exhaustion is thought to reflect depletion of glycogen stored in the muscles and liver. The terms *bonking* and *hitting the wall* are often used (box, p. 338). When muscle glycogen is depleted, muscle contraction fails. When liver glycogen is depleted, the blood glucose level falls, causing exercise-induced hypoglycemia, which impairs the functioning of the nervous system, muscular tissue, and RBCs.

When the skeletal muscle is depleted of glycogen, glycogen synthetase activity increases (Fig. 12-11). This enzyme stimulates the synthesis of glycogen, a process that begins soon after rigorous activity ceases. The time required for glycogen repletion depends on the intensity of the exercise that was undertaken and the amount of carbohydrate that is consumed in the diet. Even when carbohydrates provide 90% of the calories, 46 to 48 hours are required to restore muscle glycogen to preexercise levels after exhaustive exercises.[101] Restoration rates appear to vary; some athletes are not able to restore muscle glycogen on a high-carbohydrate diet, even after a 5-day rest. At least one study suggests that consumption of a complex carbohydrate diet, as opposed to a diet rich in simple carbohydrates, promotes a higher level of glycogen repletion by 48 hours after exercise.[102]

The Pregame Meal

Many superstitions exist in our society about which foods to consume before competition. In reality, there is no magic formula that is clearly indicated for every person. Since individuals differ with regard to food preferences, psychological crutches, and digestive response to stress, a variety of food items and eating schedules may support good preparation. Still, a few basic comments about sensible eating in the hours just preceding the scheduled event are appropriate:

1. The diet should include familiar foods that the athlete believes "will make him win."
2. Energy intake should be sufficient to prevent hunger and faintness during the period of competition.
3. The foods chosen should be relatively easy to digest, so that the stomach and upper gut are empty at the time of competition.
4. Fluid intake should be sufficient to maintain an optimal level of hydration throughout the day.
5. Gas-forming foods should be selected with discretion and should be avoided if they pose problems for the athlete.
6. Meals should not be skipped entirely, because the overall performance capacity of the athlete may ultimately suffer.

At times the liquid pregame meal may be chosen as a sound alternative to other available options. Commercial products such as Sustagen, Sustacal, and Ensure provide a palatable high-carbohydrate, high-calorie, high-fluid pregame diet. These products typically provide sufficient amounts of fat and protein to promote satiation and palatability, but the fluid character of the meal allows for its easy passage through the stomach and small intestine. Aside from these characteristics, a liquid diet has no particular advantage that warrants its serious consideration as a diet of choice. If the team or athlete accepts such a preparation and believes that it optimizes status before competition, then certainly it may be justifiably selected as a sound, nutritious pregame diet.

A common practice of part-time athletes is consuming "quick-energy foods" (candy, honey, and concentrated sugar drinks) 20 to 30 minutes before a sports event. This may actually impair their performance. Eating such concentrated sugars increases plasma insulin, which in turn inhibits the utilization of free fatty acids by the muscle. Another objection of quick energy foods is that the osmotic effect of concentrated sugars may cause retention of fluids in the gastrointenstinal tract. The athletes may experience nausea, stomach cramps, and, during endurance events, dehydration. A dilute sugar solution (2% or less) can be safely consumed periodically during an endurance sport and helps to restore fluids lost and to maintain blood sugar levels. In fact, once an athlete begins to exercise, periodic ingestion of dilute glucose solutions does not significantly increase the plasma insulin concentration.

One final comment about pregame preparation relates to a recent observation that the alkalotic state may improve the performance of middle-distance runners.[103] Six trained middle-distance runners were studied after ingestion of sodium bicarbonate ($NaHCO_3$) or a placebo such as calcium carbonate ($CaCO_3$) to determine the effect of an acute metabolic alkalosis on the time it took to run an 800-meter race. In the alkalotic state subjects ran faster (2.9 seconds), and the corresponding postexercise values for blood lactate concentration and extracellular hydrogen ion (H^+) levels were higher than in the control conditions, suggesting an increased anaerobic energy contribution. These results support the speculation that the increase in extracellular buffering following $NaCHO_3$ ingestion facilitated H^+ efflux from the cells of working muscle, thereby delaying the decrease in intracellular pH and postponing fatigue. It was concluded that the ingestion of $NaHCO_3$ (300 mg/kg/body weight) by middle-distance runners before an 800-meter race had an ergogenic effect. However, since this practice was also accompanied by minor acute gastrointestinal distress, the potential usefulness of this practice remains to be evaluated.

WEIGHT MANAGEMENT

Adjustment of body weight is sometimes necessary to prepare an athlete to perform optimally in certain sports. Neither weight loss nor weight gain is easily achieved, and both adjustments require appropriate early planning so that goals may be reached within a *reasonable* period.[104] Weight that is lost or gained represents mainly fat and muscle; ideally, weight that is lost should consist mostly of fat, whereas weight that is gained should consist predominantly of muscle and its associated fluid. Major changes of this sort do not occur overnight, especially in the absence of physical activity. Planning well in advance of the scheduled competition is an absolute must; any sound program in weight management must emphasize rigorous physical training, not just diet. Only when this philosophy is practiced will one satisfactorily meet and maintain weight gain or weight loss goals. Last-minute attention to weight modification may compromise both the health and performance of the athlete.

Three components are vital to the success of any organized weight management program. First, sufficient time should be allowed; in most cases, a maximum rate of gain of 0.5 to 1 kg of muscle mass/week should be anticipated. Weight loss at a rate of 1 kg/week is usually the desired rate; never should this rate exceed 2 kg/week. Second, all special diets or food plans for weight management should fulfill all nutritional needs, including those for protein, vitamins, and minerals. Vitamin, mineral, and protein supplements are thus not required, although occasionally iron supplements may be justifiably recommended for women of reproductive age. Third, weight management programs are ideally supervised by individuals other than the head coach. This duty is best delegated to a team nutritionist, physician, trainer, or assistant coach.

During the season of scheduled competitions, some sports (e.g., wrestling) require that preevent body weight be recorded. Weight at this time can be minimized without harm to the athlete by avoidance of salty foods, which promote excessive water retention, and by reduction in intake of dietary fiber, which may linger in the gut lumen and provide unneeded weight. Water intake should not be compromised during this period, and efforts to promote dehydration as a means of "making weight" (e.g., vomiting, spitting, exercising in plastic suits, sauna bathing, and using diuretics and cathartics) should never be undertaken.

Recent studies provoking much concern report that some young athletes go to incredible extremes to lose body weight or maintain it at an acceptable low level.[105-108] This is especially evident in the individual whose basal metabolic rate is low to moderate and whose typical level of body fat is well above 10% of total body weight. To maintain a body composition of 5% fat requires considerable training and dietary self-control for the majority of athletes, male or female. Since females normally support a much higher body fat content, however, the effort required in training and diet is often tremendous. Unfortunately, some athletes place so much emphasis on achievement of minimum body fatness that starvation diets and demanding training schedules are undertaken. Such practices may ultimately adversely affect endurance, physical growth, and psychological stability.

Excessive weight loss and food aversion similar to that seen in anorexia nervosa is a problem among some seriously committed young athletes. This pathological aversion to food and fatness differs from anorexia nervosa in that male and female athletes appear to be at equal risk, the affected athlete is usually recognized relatively early, and the emotional stresses leading to the weight loss are not usually deep-seated or chronic, but are short-term concerns that respond well to counseling. According to Dr. N. Smith,[109] "the athlete at greatest risk of abusive weight loss is typically a serious student and outstanding athlete with unrealistic goals who

Table 12-8. Percentage body fat in a group of Junior Olympians by event

Event Category	Percent Body Fat (Males)	Percent Body Fat (Females)
Middle-distance runs	7.3	12.5
Mile walk	9.9	15.1
Sprints and hurdles	8.4	13.4
Throws	13.9	22.0
Jumps and vaults	8.5	12.9
Gymnastics and diving	8.4	14.8
Wrestling	9.7	—

Data from Throland, W.G., and others: Med. Sci. Sports Exerc. **13**:332, 1981.

fears failure to meet the high expectations of coaches, parents, and friends.[11]

Most successful athletes do not function optimally at very low levels of body fatness. Many recent studies have examined the physical and physiological characteristics of various types of elite athletes. Several of these studies have focused on children and thus provide some reference for the concerned parent, coach, or health care provider. Thorland and others[110] examined boys and girls (15.2 to 18.6 years of age) who were participating in the Junior Olympics (Table 12-8); percent body fatness ranged between 7.3% and 13.9% for the boys and between 12.5% and 22% for the girls. Mayers and Gutin[111] looked at elite prepubertal male cross-country runners; percent body fatness ranged from 14.0% to 18.6%. Sady and others[112] recorded the body composition and physical dimensions of 9- to 12-year-old experienced wrestlers; mean percent body fatness for the wrestlers was 13.3%, a level nearly 30% higher than that found in more mature wrestlers and almost twice that recommended by the American College of Sports Medicine (7%).

Attempts to increase body weight are also undertaken by athletes desirous of improving performance. This practice is most commonly encountered in the United States among young men playing football. A variety of diets have been used in this effort, but essentially what is needed is sufficient calories and protein to support tissue deposi-

tion. Somewhat larger portions of basic foods may provide what is needed. Alternatively, nutritious high-calorie snacks may be added to the diet. Diets that are rich in saturated fats and cholesterol should be avoided. Vitamin and protein supplements serve no useful purpose in the overall plan.

Increases in body weight ideally result from creation of lean body mass instead of fat. Increasing muscle mass can only result from muscle work. An intake of approximately 2500 extra calories is needed to acquire 0.5 kg of muscle tissue. The addition of 750 to 1000 kcal/day to a regular diet will provide the energy needs for gaining 0.5 to 1 kg/week as well as for the increased energy output of the muscle-training program. Specific details of a muscle development program should be geared to the age and condition of the athlete. Progress should be assessed at regular intervals by measuring fatfold thickness and body weight, reviewing dietary practices and problems, and judging psychological and emotional status. Excessive deposition of body fat may indicate that the muscle-training program requires modification.

SUMMARY

Common sense clearly should prevail in assessing the nutritional needs of the growing athlete. Sufficient calories must be consumed to support growth and activity. Fluid and electrolytes lost during practice or competition must be replaced to avoid the consequences of dehydration and electrolyte imbalance. Protein, vitamin, or mineral supplements are generally unnecessary, but occasionally an iron supplement may serve to correct iron deficiency or maintain iron balance in adolescent boys and girls. Weight management efforts should be approached sensibly, without focus on achieving minimal weight through promotion of fluid loss. Eating before competition should be scheduled to avoid retention of undigested food material in the gut at the time of the event. Foods that are easy to digest should be selected with avoidance of unnecessary fat, fiber, and gas-forming fruits and vegetables. No special diet is recognized as clearly the ticket to success. However, if ingestion of a certain food provides a psychological edge, selection of it must be considered potentially advantageous.

SUGGESTED LEARNING ACTIVITIES

1. Investigate the use of nutrient supplements by the high school football athlete in your community.
2. Plan a glycogen-loading diet for a long-distance runner.
3. Write a menu for three pregame meals.
4. Plan a diet for a 14-year-old 75-kg male who needs to lose 10 pounds to make the wrestling team.
5. Prepare a talk on nutrition for a junior high school basketball team.

REFERENCES

1. Astrand, P., and Rodahl, K.: Textbook of work physiology, New York, 1970, McGraw-Hill Book Co.
2. Saltin, B.: Fluid, electrolyte and energy losses and their replenishment in prolonged exercise. In Parizkova, J., and Rogozkin, V.A., editors: Nutrition, physical fitness, and health, Baltimore, 1978, University Park Press.
3. Rogozkin, V.A.: Some aspects of athlete's nutrition. In Parizkova, J., and Rogozkin, V.A., editors: Nutrition, physical fitness, and health, Baltimore, 1978, University Park Press.
4. American Alliance for Health, Physical Education and Recreation: Nutrition for athletes: a handbook for coaches, Washington, D.C., 1971, The Alliance.
5. Bobb, A., Pringle, D., and Ryan, A.J.: A brief study of the diet of athletes, J. Sports Med. Phys. Fitness **9**:255, 1969.
6. Torún, B., Chew, F., and Mendoza, R.D.: Energy costs of activities of preschool children, Nutr. Res. **3**:401, 1983.
7. Freedson, P.S., and others: Energy expenditure in prepubescent children: influence of sex and age, Am. J. Clin. Nutr. **34**:1827, 1981.
8. Matthews, D.K., and Fox, D.K.: The physiologic basis of physical education and athletics, Philadelphia, 1971, W.B. Saunders Co.
9. Smith, N.J.: Food for sport, Palo Alto, Calif., 1976, Bull Publishing Co.
10. Ziegler, K.L., and others: Muscle metabolism during exercise in man, Trans. Assoc. Am. Physicians **81**:266, 1968.
11. Carlson, L.A., Ekelund, L., and Froberg, S.O.: Concentrations of triglycerides, phospholipids, and glycogen in skeletal muscle and of free fatty acids and beta-hydroxy-butyric acid in blood in man: response to exercise, Eur. J. Clin. Invest. **1**:248, 1977.
12. Hendriksson, J.: Human skeletal muscle adaptation to physical activity, Unpublished data, Karolinska Institute, Stockholm.
13. Saltin, B., and others: The nature of training response: peripheral and central adaptations to one-legged exercise, Acta Physiol. Scand. **96**:289, 1976.
14. Ryan, A.: Round table–balancing heat stress, fluids and electrolytes, Phys. Sports Med. **3**:43, 1975.
15. Brooke, J.D., Davies, G.J., and Green, L.F.: The effects of normal and glucose syrup work diets on the performance of racing cyclists, J. Sports Med. Phys. Fitness **15**:257, 1975.
16. Karlsson, J., and Saltin, B.: Diet, muscle glycogen and endurance performance, J. Appl. Physiol. **31**:203, 1971.
17. Green, L.F., and Bagley, R.: Ingestion of glucose syrup drink during long distance canoeing, Br. J. Sports Med. **6**:125, 1972.
18. Muckle, D.S.: Glucose syrup ingestion and team performance in soccer, Br. J. Sports Med. **7**:340, 1973.
19. Durnin, J.V.G.A.: Protein requirements and physical activity. In Parizkova, J., and Rogozkin, V.A., editors: Nutrition, physical fitness, and health, Baltimore, 1978, University Park Press.
20. Consolazio, C.F., and others: Protein metabolism of intensive physical training in the young adult, Am. J. Clin. Nutr. **28**:29, 1975.
21. Evans, W.J., and others: Protein metabolism and endurance exercise, Phys. Sports Med. **11**:53, 1983.
22. Felig, P., and Wahren, J.: Amino acid metabolism in exercising man, J. Clin. Invest. **50**:2703, 1971.
23. Felig, P.: The glucose-alanine cycle, Metabolism **22**:179, 1973.

24. Lemon, P.W., and Mullin, J.P.: Effect of initial muscle glycogen levels on protein catabolism during exercise, J. Appl. Physiol. **48**:624, 1980.

25. Decombaz, J., and others: Biochemical changes in a 100-km run: free amino acids, urea, and creatinine, Eur. J. Applied Physiol. **41**:61, 1979.

26. Refsum, H.E., and Stromme, S.B.: Urea and creatinine production and excretion in urine during and after prolonged heavy exercise, Scand. J. Clin. Lab. Invest. **33**:247, 1974.

27. Dohm, G.L., Hecker, A.L., and Brown, W.E.: Adaptation of protein metabolism to endurance training: increased amino acid oxidation in response to training, Biochem. J. **164**:705, 1977.

28. Evans, W.J., Wright, E.D., and Phinney, S.D.: The effects of submaximal exercise on whole body leucine metabolism, Med. Sci. Sports Exerc. (In press.)

29. Rasch, P., and others: Protein dietary supplementation and physical performance, Med. Sci. Sports Exerc. **1**:195, 1969.

30. Sharman, I.: The effects of vitamin E and training on physiological function and athletic performance in adolescent swimmers, Br. J. Nutr. **26**:265, 1971.

31. Lawrence, J.D., and others: Effects of tocopherol acetate on the swimming endurance of trained swimmers, Am. J. Clin. Nutr. **28**:205, 1975.

32. Bailey, D.A., and others: Effect of vitamin C supplementation upon the physiological response to exercise in trained and untrained subjects, Int. J. Vitam. Nutr. Res. **40**:435, 1970.

33. Gray, M.E., and Titlow, L.W.: The effect of pangamic acid on maximal treadmill performance, Med. Sci. Sports Exerc. **14**:424, 1982.

34. Gray, M.E., and Titlow, L.W.: B$_{15}$: myth or miracle? Phys. Sports Med. **10**:107, 1982.

35. Barnes, L.: Preadolescent training: how young is too young? Phys. Sports Med. **7**:114, 1979.

36. Liu, L., Borowski, G., and Rose, L.I.: Hypomagnesemia in a tennis player, Phys. Sports Med. **11**:79, 1983.

37. Lane, H.W., and others: Effect of physical activity on human potassium metabolism in a hot and humid climate, Am. J. Clin. Nutr. **31**:838, 1978.

38. Lane, H.W., and Cerda, J.J.: Potassium requirements and exercise, J. Am. Diet. Assoc. **73**:64, 1978.

39. Costill, D.L., Cote, R., and Fink, W.J.: Dietary potassium and heavy exercise: effects of muscle water and electrolytes, Am. J. Clin. Nutr. **36**:266, 1982.

40. Dressendorfer, R.H., and others: Plasma mineral levels in marathon runners during a 20-day road race, Phys. Sports Med. **10**:113, 1982.

41. Finch, C.A., and others: Iron deficiency in the rat: physiological and biochemical studies of muscle dysfunction, J. Clin. Invest. **58**:447, 1976.

42. Sproule, B.J., Mitchell, J.H., and Miller, W.F.: Cardiopulmonary physiological responses to heavy exercise in patients with anemia, J. Clin. Invest. **39**:378, 1960.

43. Committee on Nutrition of the Mother and Preschool Child: Iron nutriture in adolescence, Washington, D.C., 1976, Department of Health, Education and Welfare.

44. Leibel, R.L.: Behavioral and biochemical correlates of iron deficiency, J. Am. Diet. Assoc. **71**:398, 1977.

45. Worthington-Roberts, B.S.: Suboptimal nutrition and behavior in children. In Worthington-Roberts, B.S., editor: Contemporary developments in nutrition, St. Louis, 1981, The C.V. Mosby Co.

46. Worthington-Roberts, B.S., and Doan, R.: Nutrition and family planning. In Worthington-Roberts, B.S., Vermeersch, J., and Williams. S.R.: Nutrition in pregnancy and lactation, ed. 2, St. Louis, 1981, The C.V. Mosby Co.

47. Williamson, M.R.: Anemia in runners and other athletes, Phys. Sports Med. **9**:73, 1981.

48. Pate, R.R.: Sports anemia: a review of the current research literature, Phys. Sports Med. **11**:115, 1983.

49. Yoshimura, H.: Anemia during physical training (sports anemia), Nutr. Res. **28**:251, 1970.

50. Crowell, J.W., and Smith, E.E.: Determinant of the optimal hematocrit, J. Appl. Physiol. **22**:501, 1967.

51. Guyton, A.C., Jones, C.E., and Coleman, T.G.: Circulatory physiology: cardiac output and its regulation, Philadelphia, 1973, W.B. Saunders Co.

52. Dressendorfer, R.H., Wade, C.E., and Amsterdam, E.A.: Development of pseudoanemia in marathon runners during a 20-day road race, J.A.M.A. **246**:1215, 1981.

53. Frederickson, L.A., Puhl, J.L., and Runyan, W.S.: Effects of training on indices of iron status of young female cross-country runners, Med. Sci. Sports Exerc. **15**:271, 1983.

54. Vellar, O.D., and Hermansen, L.: Physical performance and hematological parameters with special reference to hemoglobin and maximal oxygen uptake, Acta Med. Scand. Suppl. **522**:1, 1971.

55. Edgerton, V.R., Bryant, S.L., and Gillespie, C.A.: Iron deficiency anemia and physical performance and activity of rats, J. Nutr. **102**:381, 1972.

56. Astrand, P.O.: Experimental studies of physical working capacity in relation to sex and age, Copenhagen, 1952, E. Munksgaard.

57. Kjellberg, S.R., Ruhde, U., and Sjostrand, T.: The amount of hemoglobin (blood volume) in relation to the pulse and heart volume during work, Acta Physiol. Scand. **19**:152, 1950.

58. Sjostrand, T.: Volume and distribution of blood and their significance in regulating the circulation, Physiol. Rev. **33**:202, 1953.

59. Von Dobeln, W.: Maximal oxygen intake, body size, and

total hemoglobin in normal man, Acta Physiol. Scand. **38**:193, 1957.

60. Cotes, J.E., Dabbs, J.M., and Elwood, P.C.: Iron deficiency anemia: its effect on transfer factor for the lung (diffusing capacity) and ventilation and cardiac frequency during submaximal exercise, Clin. Sci. **42**:325, 1972.

61. Anderson, H.T., and Barkve, H.: Iron deficiency and muscular work performance: an evaluation of the cardiorespiratory function of iron deficient subjects with and without anemia, Scand. J. Clin. Lab. Invest. Suppl. **114**:1, 1970.

62. Davies, C.T., Chukweumeka, A.C., and Van Haaren, J.P.: Iron deficiency anemia: its effect on maximum aerobic power and responses to exercise in African males 17-40 years, Clin. Sci. **44**:555, 1973.

63. Gardner, G.W., Edgerton, V.R., and Barnard, R.J.: Cardiorespiratory, hematological and physical performance responses of anemia subjects to iron treatment, Am. J. Clin. Nutr. **28**:982, 1975.

64. de Wijn, J.F., de Jongste, J.L., and Mosterd, W.: Hemoglobin, packed cell volume, serum iron, and iron-binding capacity of selected athletes during training, Nutr. Metab. **13**:129, 1971.

65. Pate, R.R., Maguire, M., and Van Wyk, J.: Effects of dietary iron supplementation on hemoglobin concentration and iron stores of female athletes, Med. Sci. Sports Exerc. **10**:38, 1978.

66. Pate, R.R., Maguire, M., and Van Wyk, J.: Dietary iron supplementation in women athletes, Phys. Sports Med. **7**:81, 1979.

67. Schoene, R.B., and others: Iron repletion decreases maximal exercise lactate concentrations in female athletes with minimal iron-deficiency anemia, J. Lab. Clin. Med. **102**:306, 1983.

68. Clement, D.B., and Asmundson, R.C.: Nutritional intake and hematological parameters in endurance runners, Phys. Sports Med. **10**:37, 1982.

69. Falsetti, H.L., and others: Hematological variations after endurance running with hard- and soft-soled shoes, Phys. Sports Med. **11**:118, 1983.

70. Hunding, A., Jordal, R., and Paulev, P.: Runner's anemia and iron deficiency, Acta Med. Scand. **209**:315, 1981.

71. Malina, R.M., and others: Age at menarche and selected menstrual characteristics in athletes at different competitive levels and in different sports, Med. Sci. Sports Exerc. **10**:218, 1978.

72. Feicht, C.B., and others: Secondary amenorrhea in athletes, Lancet **2**:1145, 1978.

73. Wentz, A.C.: Body weight and amenorrhea, Obstet. Gynecol. **56**:482, 1980.

74. Baker, E.R.: Menstrual dysfunction and hormonal status in athletic women: a review, Fertil. Steril. **36**:691, 1981.

75. Calabrese, L.H., and others: Menstrual abnormalities, nutritional patterns, and body composition in female classical ballet dancers, Phys. Sports Med. **11**:86, 1983.

76. Speroff, L., and Redwine, D.B.: Exercise and menstrual function, Phys. Sports Med. **8**:42, 1980.

77. Schwartz, B., and others: Exercise-associated amenorrhea: a distinct entity? Am. J. Obstet. Gynecol. **141**:662, 1981.

78. Lutter, J.M., and Cushman, S.: Menstrual patterns in female runners, Phys. Sports Med. **10**:60, 1982.

79. Caldwell, F.: Menstrual irregularity in athletes: the unanswered question, Phys. Sports Med. **10**:142, 1982.

80. Vandenbroucke, J.P., van Laar, A., and Valkenburg, H.A.: Synergy between thinness and intensive sports activity in delaying menarche, Br. Med. J. **284**:1907, 1982.

81. Frisch, R.E., and others: Delayed menarche and amenorrhea of college athletes in relation to age at onset of training, J.A.M.A. **246**:1559, 1981.

82. Cann, C.: Personal communication, 1982.

83. American Academy of Pediatrics: Climatic heat stress and the exercising child, Phys. Sports Med. **11**:155, 1983.

84. Vaccaro, P., Zauner, C.W., and Cade, J.R.: Changes in body weight, hematocrit and plasma protein concentration due to dehydration and rehydration in wrestlers, J. Sports Med. Phys. Fitness **16**:45, 1976.

85. Alcohol and athletes, Phys. Sports Med. **7**:39, 1979.

86. Astrand, P.: Diet and athletic performance, Fed. Proc. **26**:1772, 1967.

87. Astrand, P.: Nutrition and physical performance, World Rev. Nutr. Diet. **16**:59, 1973.

88. Bergstrom, J., and Hultman, E.: Nutrition for maximal sports performance, J.A.M.A. **221**:999, 1972.

89. Forgac, M.T.: Carbohydrate loading—a review, J.A.M.A. **75**:42, 1979.

90. Moore, M.: Carbohydrate loading: eating through the wall, Phys. Sports Med. **9**:97, 1981.

91. Tufto, D., and Hefnawy, M.: Pasta vs. Gatorade, Food Engineering **54**:10, 1982.

92. Costill, D.L.: Carbohydrate-loading without depletion, Runner's World, August, 1978.

93. Costill, D.L., and others: Effects of elevated plasma free fatty acids and insulin on muscle glycogen usage during exercise, J. Appl. Physiol. **43**:695, 1977.

94. Hickson, R.C., and others: Effects of increasing plasma free fatty acids on endurance, Fed. Proc. **36**:450, 1977.

95. Rennie, M.J., Winder, W.W., and Holloszy, J.O.: A sparing effect of increased plasma fatty acids on muscle and liver glycogen content in exercising rat, Biochem. J. **156**:647, 1976.

96. Costill, D.L., Dalsky, G.P., and Fink, W.J.: Effects of caffeine ingestion on metabolism and exercise performance, Med. Sci. Sports Exerc. **10**:155, 1978.

97. Mirkin, G.: Carbohydrate loading: a dangerous practice, J.A.M.A. **223:**1511, 1973.

98. Nelson, R.A., and Gastineau, C.F.: Nutrition for athletes. In Craig, T.T., editor: The medical aspect of sports, Chicago, 1974, American Medical Association.

99. Blair, S., and others: Blood lipid and ECG responses to carbohydrate loading, Phys. Sports Med. **8:**69, 1980.

100. Leklem, J.: Personal communication.

101. Piehl, K.: Time course for refilling of glycogen in human muscle fibers following exercise-induced depletion, Acta Physiol. Scand. **90:**297, 1974.

102. Costill, D.L., and others: The role of dietary carbohydrates in muscle glycogen resynthesis after strenuous running, Am. J. Clin. Nutr. **34:**1831, 1981.

103. Wilkes, D., Gledhill, N., and Smyth, R.: Effect of acute induced metabolic alkalosis on 800-m racing time, Med. Sci. Sports Exerc. **15:**277, 1983.

104. Smith, N.J.: Gaining and losing weight in athletes, J.A.M.A. **236:**149, 1976.

105. Peterson, M.S.: Nutritional concerns for the dancer, Phys. Sports Med. **10:**137, 1982.

106. Cohen, J.L., and others: Exercise, body weight and professional ballet dancers, Phys. Sports Med. **10:**92, 1982.

107. Niinimaa, V.: Figure skating: what do we know about it? Phys. Sports Med. **10:**51, 1982.

108. Croyle, P.H., Place, R.A., and Hilgenberg, A.D.: Massive pulmonary embolism in a high school wrestler, J.A.M.A. **241:**827, 1979.

109. Smith, N.J.: Excessive weight loss and food aversion in athletes simulating anorexia nervosa, Pediatrics **66:**139, 1980.

110. Thorland, W.G., and others: Body composition and somatotype characteristics of Junior Olympics athletes, Med. Sci. Sports Exerc. **13:**332, 1981.

111. Mayers, N., and Gutin, B.: Physiological characteristics of elite prepubertal cross-country runners, Med. Sci. Sports Exerc. **11:**172, 1979.

112. Sady, S.P., and others: The body composition physical dimensions of 9- and 12-year-old experienced wrestlers, Med. Sci. Sports Exerc. **14:**244, 1982.

Nutrition and Feeding of Children with Developmental Delays and Related Problems

13

PEGGY L. PIPES
ROBIN PRITKIN

Approximately 3% of the population of infants and children are developmentally delayed. A very small percentage of those so affected can be expected to be institutionalized; the remainder will function in the free-living population in their natural homes, in foster homes, or in group homes. It is thus important that health care professionals be alerted to potential problems of nutrient intake and that efforts be made to prevent or alleviate problems amenable to therapy.

DEFINITION OF DEVELOPMENTAL DELAYS

The term *developmentally delayed* includes a wide range of ability from persons so handicapped that there is no head control to those who function in the mildly retarded range who can learn and, as adults, operate in a self-sufficient and productive manner. The etiologies of developmental delays are multiple and include genetic and biological anomalies and psychosocial and environmental factors that interact to determine the level of function. Activity patterns range from immobility to hyperactivity, motor skills from absence of suck and head control to well-coordinated children, and behavior from apathy to disruptive behavior. Therefore, no generalizations can be made about developmentally delayed children and their problems of feeding and

nutrient intake. However, among populations of developmentally delayed individuals, reasons for concern about feeding and nutrient intake frequently are found.

NUTRITIONAL NEEDS OF THE DEVELOPMENTALLY DELAYED CHILD

Developmentally delayed children require the same nutrients as any individual. There are, however, no dietary standards applicable to groups of developmentally delayed children. Many of these children, although not all, are growth retarded because of a genetic or biological defect.[1] Syndromes with which growth retardation is associated include Down's syndrome, Prader-Willi syndrome, trisomy 13 and 18, de Lange's syndrome, Hurler's syndrome, Turner's syndrome, Silver's syndrome, Williams' syndrome, and others.[2] Body composition may differ from that of the normal child. Isakkson[3] found reduced body cell mass in children with both spasticity and athetosis caused by atrophy of skeletal muscles resulting from disease and low levels of physical activity. Reduced cell mass may reduce requirements for essential nutrients as well as calories. On the other hand, a reduced cell mass may result from a lifetime of limited nutrient and calorie intakes.

Commonly reported parental and professional concerns relating to handicapped children's food and nutrient intakes include the following:

1. Slow growth in length and lack of appropriate weight gain
2. Excessive weight gain in relation to gains in length
3. Obesity
4. Iron deficiency anemia
5. Refusal of the child to consume specific foods and/or groups of foods
6. Refusal of the child to progress in feeding behavior when developmentally ready
7. Pica
8. Bizarre feeding patterns
9. Lack of appetite
10. Excessive appetite
11. Gagging, vomiting, or rumination
12. Food allergies
13. Limited fluid intake
14. Constipation
15. Abnormal motor patterns that affect the child's ability to consume food
16. Inability or unwillingness of the child to finger-feed and/or to self-feed
17. Limited attention span at mealtime
18. Disruptive behavior at mealtime

There have been few studies of nutrient intake or feeding problems of developmentally delayed children. Data collected in diagnostic and evaluation centers give indications of common problems. Studies in institutions have given criteria on which estimates of appropriate energy intake may be made. Investigations of children with abnormal motor patterns have suggested problems in achieving appropriate nutrient intakes of children with cerebral palsy. The effects of anticonvulsants on the need for vitamin D and folate have been researched. There have been isolated reports of efforts to control obesity, behavior modification in relation to acceptance of specific textures of food, and the acquisition of self-feeding skills. One diagnostic and evaluation center reported that the most frequent inadequacies of nutrient intake were of ascorbic acid, iron, fluoride, and high-quality protein. Another center found an incidence of 21.3% overweight, 15% underweight, 7.7% bizarre feeding habits, 13.0% inadequate nutrient intake, and 30.6% feeding problems in 500 patients.[4]

Difficulties in weight control are often clustered in specific syndromes. Obesity is commonly a problem in children with Down's syndrome, Prader-Willi syndrome, Carpenter's syndrome, Cohen's syndrome, and Laurence-Moone-Biedl syndrome. Underweight is frequently noted in children with athetoid cerebral palsy, hyperactivity, and behavior problems.

Underweight children with limited energy intakes also commonly have limited intakes of several nutrients because of the limited volume of food they consume. Inadequate intakes of vitamins A, C, and D and folate have been noted to be the most frequent problems.[4]

Measurements of Physically Handicapped Children

Evaluating the adequacy of a child's nutrient and energy intake includes assessment of physical growth. This means the child must be accurately weighed and measured and the data plotted on growth charts (Chapter 1). However, difficulties may be encountered in securing and interpreting the date for children who have developmental delays.

Accurate measurements of linear growth may be impossible to secure for children who have contractures and/or cannot stand. Roche[5] suggests using crown rump length or sitting height. The measurements however, cannot be considered accurate when a child's trunk or torso is affected. To estimate linear height Manenica and others[6] have investigated the applicability of measurements of arm span for children with spina bifida, and Gleason[7] has used tibia length for boys with Duchenne's muscular dystrophy.

Using a control group of normal children, Manenica and others[6] found a correlation of arm span to linear height. They found that a normal arm span/height ratio of 1:1 provides a simple approximation technique. Arm span measurements are made with an anthropometer, a stainless steel detachable rod approximately 7 feet long with etched gradations to 0.1 cm and one movable sleeve. The arm span has been defined as "the greatest distance between the outstretched fingers of the right and left hand with the arms and forearms extended horizontally sidewards and the back pressed against a flat surface."[8] To secure this measurement, the subject stands in the erect position with arms outstretched (Fig. 13-1). The fixed end of the anthropometer is held by one individual at the tip of the subject's middle finger of one hand, while another individual positions the sleeve at the tip of the middle finger of the subject's other hand. The subject is then told to stretch his or her arms, and the movable sleeve is adjusted to the maximum arm span.[9] This method was developed by K. Manenica, nutritionists, and M. Hurlich, physical anthropologist.

Estimation of linear length and height using tibia length had higher standard errors because of the dynamics of relative tibial length. However,

though less accurate than arm span, this measurement was believed to provide useful information for individuals who had contractures in the arms and had previously been mobile.[7]

Tibia length is defined as the distance between the medial tibial epicondyle to the medial malleolus.[10] To measure tibia length, subjects are seated with their feet resting as flat on the floor as possible. The top of the right tibia is located by palpating downward from the medial condyle of the femur to the zone of articulation between the femur and the tibia. This point is marked at the closest approximation to the highest point of the medial condyle of the tibia, which is buried. The tip of the medial malleolus is easily identified and marked. The distance between these two points is measured with a sliding anthropometer. This method was developed by C. Gleason, nutritionist, and M. Hurlich, physical anthropologist (Fig. 13-2). Height is estimated from the equation[7]:

$$\text{Height (cm)} = 3.54 \times \text{tibial length} + 32.23.$$

Though more data are needed on normal children to establish standards, arm span can be used to

Fig. 13-1. Arm span is measured from the tip of one middle finger to the other.

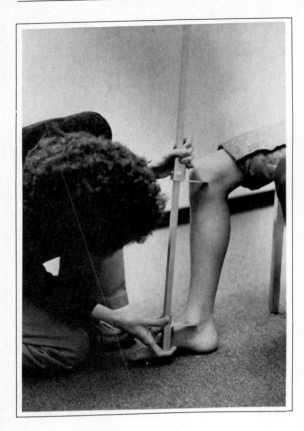

Fig. 13-2. Tibia length measurement.

estimate linear height for children who cannot stand and tibia length can be used for children with contractures in their arms.

Some classifications of handicapped children show normal growth, whereas others with congenital or metabolic disorders are associated with significant growth deviation. Researchers realize that the growth standards for normal children are not applicable for individuals with some handicapping conditions and that there is a need for syndrome specific reference data. Growth curves have been developed for children with dysplasia congenita, and pseudoachondroplasia and for children with Down's syndrome from birth to 3 years of age.[9,11]

These growth grids should be used when measurements of these children are plotted. For other children who have developmental delays, the rates of gain in height and weight as well as weight/height percentiles and midarm circumference and triceps fatfold measurements over time provide useful information. The professional interpreting this data should have knowledge of specific syndromes associated with growth retardation.

Nutritional Studies

Children with cerebral palsy generally grow in both height and weight at rates less than normal. Weight, however, may be greater than that of normal children of the same height. Leamy[12] found calorie intakes of institutionalized children with cerebral palsy to be considerably below the recommended amounts and suggested that a cyclic phenomenon occurred. The disease restricts growth, and the calorie intake then further limits increases in size. Ruby and Matheny[13] found mouth area involvement closely associated with poor food intake and believed that the extent of mouth involvement and poor growth were generally parallel.

Bone age delays have been reported, indicating less than optimal intakes of nutrients. Hammond, Lewis, and Johnson[14] reported a range of 19 to 35 months delay, Leamy,[12] a range of 1.4 to 47.4 months delay, and Ruby and Matheny,[13] an average of 19.3 months delay in bone age.

Studies of free-living populations of children with cerebral palsy have shown acceptable intakes of nutrients other than iron.[15] Dietary intakes of less severely retarded children have been found to be markedly higher in all nutrients except vitamins A and C than intakes of the more severely delayed children. The energy value of the diets are influenced by the children's ability to self-feed. Children with motor involvements and mental retardation severe enough to interfere with their ability to feed themselves tend to consume fewer calories than do those who are able to self-feed.[14]

Caliendo, Booth, and Moser[16] found that 31%

of a population of 3.1- to 9-year-old children consumed less than 70% of the recommended daily allowance for iron from food. However, when those who took supplemental iron were excluded, only 21% of the subjects consumed less than 70% of the recommended daily allowance for iron. Most of the serum ferritin values were within the normal range. Older children with relatively good feeding skills, as assessed by the mother, were likely to have higher serum ferritin levels.

Pica, an eating disorder commonly found in institutionalized retarded individuals but found also in the free-living population, has been shown to result in malabsorption of zinc and iron. Danford, Smith, and Huber[17] found individuals with pica had low plasma zinc and measures of iron status even though they received adequate dietary intake of minerals.

Socioculturally developmentally delayed school-age children have been shown to consume less protein, iron, thiamine, and fewer kilocarlories than nonretarded children of the same age and sex from low-income families. Intakes of iron, calcium, and ascorbic acid were less than recommended in the developmentally delayed children.[18]

Energy Requirements

Culley and Middleton[19] and Culley and others[20] have reported that institutionalized retarded children who are ambulatory have energy requirements similar to those of normal children if height is used as a standard for estimating calorie needs. Because many of the children in their study had short stature, their calorie requirements were less than those of other children the same age. They found that only when motor dysfunction becomes severe enough to cause children to be nonambulatory does it reduce the calorie requirement per centimeter of height significantly. Pipes and Holm[21] have reported that children with Prader-Willi syndrome have reduced energy requirements per centimeter of height as compared with energy requirements of normal children. Mertz and others,[22] on the other

hand, reported that a group of emaciated children in an institution for the mentally handicapped had energy requirements in excess of those of normal children. Even though such children consumed calorie intakes recommended for their ages, they remained emaciated.

Children with spasticity (hypertonia) frequently become overweight for their heights, consuming low-calorie intakes for their ages. Eddy, Nicholson, and Wheeler[23] studied one female with spasticity, an obese 16-year-old quadriplegic, and found her to have a basal energy expenditure of that of a person half her body weight. The girl was confined to a wheelchair; her total energy expenditure was estimated to be 1270 to 1370 kcal/day.

Children with athetosis (mixed pattern of too much and too little tone) consume greater numbers of calories than do those with spasticity and are less likely to become obese because they are able to engage in greater amounts of activity. Some children with athetosis expend energy constantly in involuntary movements. Researchers have found that basal energy expenditures of children with athetosis are similar to those of normal children and that the energy cost of activity depends on the child's capacity for muscular work. As levels of activity reach limits, acitivity becomes costly and uneconomic.[23]

The activity patterns of developmentally delayed children are often less than those of their peers because of low muscle tone, immobility, or general disinterest in their environments. This inactivity limits their energy expenditures and therefore energy requirements. Grogan and Ekvall[4] found levels of 7 kcal/cm of height necessary to produce weight reduction in children with myelomeningocele. Children with cerebral palsy who have decreased levels of activity have been noted to need 10 kcal/cm of height, whereas those with normal or increased levels of activity need 15 kcal/cm of height.

Recommendations for energy intakes of developmentally delayed children must be individualized. Because physical growth of handicapped children frequently deviates from the norm, kcal/cm of height may prove to be a more useful reference on which to base estimated needs than kcal/kg of body weight.

Drug/Nutrient Interrelationships

Anticonvulsant drugs prescribed to control seizures increase a child's need for vitamin D and alter folate metabolism. Evidence of vitamin D deficiency has been found in both institutionalized patients and outpatients treated with anticonvulsant drugs for longer than 6 months for control of seizures. It was found that serum calcium levels were normal or low, serum phosphate levels were low, and serum alkaline phosphatase levels were elevated.[24] Plasma 25-OHD levels have been found to be low but levels of 1,25-OHD normal.[25] Cases of rickets and osteomalacia confirmed by roentgenograms have been reported.[26-29] All drugs commonly used to control seizures have been implicated. The incidence of abnormalities increases with duration of therapy. Multiple drug regimens cause the most problems. The drugs do not affect intestinal absorption of vitamin D. It appears that they increase the catabolism and excretion of vitamin D and its biologically active products. They also have a direct inhibitory effect on calcium transport and bone metabolism.[30]

Lifshitz and Maclaren[26] reported an incidence of rickets of 7% in residents younger than 15 years of age in an institution for the mentally handicapped who had received long-term anticonvulsant therapy. All residents of the institution had received diets providing adequate amounts of calories, protein, fat, calcium phosphate, and supplemental vitamins. Their intakes of vitamin D_2 approximated 800 to 1200 IU/day. Rickets was diagnosed in nonambulatory children with spasticity who had lived indoors most of their lives and who had had infrequent exposure to sunlight, had had frequent chronic infections, and had received combinations of anticonvulsant medications. Rickets healed rapidly, usually with doses of 6000 IU of vitamin D_2 or with 50 units of 25-OHD$_3$ given orally.

Lifshitz and Maclaren[26] also found that residents who received phenobarbital alone had decreased serum calcium levels but no alterations in serum phosphorus levels as compared with children who received no medication. Those who received phenytoin alone had no detectable alterations in serum calcium and phosphorus levels but had increased alkaline phosphatase activity as compared with the control subjects. Combinations of anticonvulsant medications, however, had highly significant effects on concentrations of serum calcium, phosphorus, and alkaline phosphatase, producing marked drops in serum calcium and phosphorus levels.

Silver and others[27] found that institutionalized adolescents who received anticonvulsants, who had frequent exposure to sunlight, and whose intakes of vitamin D averaged 85 IU/day had serum calcium levels that were not significantly different from those not receiving anticonvulsants; however, serum phosphorus levels were lower and serum alkaline phosphatase levels were elevated as compared with control subjects. Increases in phosphate levels resulted from intakes of 3000 IU of vitamin D_3, which also led to radiological evidence of healing in those children with diagnosed rickets. They found no case of rickets resistant to treatment with vitamin D.

Although many children consume anticonvulsants without biochemical or clinical evidence of rickets or osteomalacia, most of those who take the drugs have significant derangement of mineral metabolism. Serum 25-OHD levels have been found to be 40% to 70% lower than normal values, bone mass 10% to 30% lower than normal values.[30]

Amounts of vitamin D necessary to prevent deficiency and rickets in children receiving anticonvulsant therapy appear to vary depending on the number of anticonvulsant drugs, the dosage the child receives, and the duration of therapy in addition to the pattern of mobility and exposure to sunlight.[28] Hahn[30] suggests an intake of 10,000 IU of vitamin D/week in patients who have been receiving therapy for 6 months or longer, adjusted on the basis of individual response. Silver and others[27] believe that an intake of 3000 IU/week for children who are exposed to sunlight would be preventive. Rickets recurred in a 14-year-old girl receiving phenobarbital who had recovered from rickets and maintained an intake of 600 IU of vitamin D_2/day when phenytoin was added to the phenobarbital she was receiving daily. An intake of 1200 IU of vitamin D_2/day prevented recurrence.[31] It is obvious that children who receive anticonvulsants should be given larger doses of vitamin D than those who receive no anticonvulsants. It has been suggested that such children be monitored biochemically on a regular basis.[26]

Drug-induced disturbances of folate metabolism have been found in a significant number of patients receiving anticonvulsants. Low serum folate levels accompanied by a fall in red cell folate and cerebrospinal folate levels have been reported in 33% to 90% of patients studied.[32] Megaloblastic anemia is reported to occur in 0.5% to 0.75% of epileptic patients. The symptoms are usually associated with phenytoin therapy but can occur with phenobarbital or primidone therapy.[33] There appear to be two effects of the drugs on folate metabolism. The anticonvulsants interfere with incorporation of thymidine into DNA and can therefore increase folate requirements. Also they may increase the activities of enzymes that catabolize folate or may increase activities or metabolic pathways in which folate is essential.[34] Administration of folate has been reported to precipitate seizures or increase seizure frequency in some patients treated with anticonvulsants. In most patients no effect has been noted.[35]

Yeast tablets given as a natural source of folate to epileptic, mentally retarded patients showed that folate deficiency caused by anticonvulsants could be corrected within 3 months without effect on seizures.[36] Chien and others[37] have suggested that there may be some folate-sensitive patients and some folate-insensitive patients and that folate should be administered with caution. They describe the effect of an intravenous infusion of folate on an 18-year-old girl treated with phenytoin and phenobarbital who showed electroencephalographic evidence of seizures followed by tonic and clonic seizures after the intravenous administration of 14.4 mg of folate. In the same study there were no reactions to the infusion of 75 mg of folic acid in seven other patients. Although the amounts infused seem large, one might encounter such levels of intake in individuals who are receiving megadoses of vitamins.

Long-term anticonvulsant therapy may be associated with other vitamin deficiency states. Clinical evidence of cardiac beriberi and subclinical ascorbic acid deficiency has been noted in a 28-month-old black girl who allegedly was receiving a full diet in a nursing home and was receiving phenobarbital, phenytoin sodium (Dilantin), and primidone (Mysoline).

Megavitamin Therapy

For many years there have been claims that megadoses of vitamins and minerals will increase the intelligence of children who are developmentally delayed.[39,40] Evidence supporting the claims have been scant and unconvincing and not much attention has been focused on this therapy.[41] However, Harrell and others[42] reported in 1981 that 16 children who were developmentally delayed experienced gains in IQ with megavitamin therapy. Those children who experienced the greatest gains were those with Down's syndrome. Attention was again focused on the use of nutrients. Many parents became very hopeful that help was available for their children and requested help in following the megavitamin regimen.

Testing the hypothesis replication of the Harrell study has been undertaken in several clinical settings using a double-blind control design. The studies were conducted on both school-age children and adults with Down's syndrome. In no instance has the vitamin supplement increased intelligence, motor performance, or communicative abilities of the individuals involved.[43,46] However, some who offer the supplements for sale continue to offer false hope at considerable expense to families of affected children.

FEEDING THE DEVELOPMENTALLY DELAYED CHILD

Planning for feeding developmentally delayed children implies that recommendations for intakes of energy, nutrients, and textures of food as well as expectations for the acquisition of self-feeding skills must be individualized for each child. Some children may have oral, fine, and gross motor, language, and personal/social development that is proceeding at a less than normal rate. Others may also have physical anomalies that imply the need for special equipment to sustain sitting posture to eat and adaptation of utensils to self-feed.

It is important to recognize that many of the problems of nutrient intake in developmentally delayed children are preventable. Guidance and support for parents as they select foods for their children that provide the nutrients they need and create an environment in whcih the child learns to consume foods in a manner appropriate for his or her developmental level are important. Guidance may need to be provided as to the appropriate stages at which to change the textures of food, to expect the child to feed himself or herself, and the degree of messiness to expect when a child is self-feeding.

Factors that Influence Food Intake

Because of the many factors that interact to determine the food available to and accepted by the developmentally delayed children, concerns about food and nutrient intake and feeding rarely result from a single cause; many factors must be considered. An understanding of those factors that contribute to problems of food intake is important in planning for feeding of such children.

Developmentally delayed children experience the same responses to parental anxiety about their food intake as any child and in a like manner can control their parents by their acceptance or rejection of food. Most normal preschoolers reduce their intakes of milk and vegetables, go on food jags, and have brittle and unpredictable appetites. It is not unreasonable to expect that developmentally delayed children will present the same food-related behaviors. There may be, in addition, difficulties in feeding developmentally delayed children that are not encountered with normal children.

Developmental level. Delays in motor development may result directly or indirectly in an inappropriate nutrient intake. The development and sequence of acquisition of feeding behaviors of delayed children proceed in the same orderly predictable sequence as that of normal children. The chronological age at which the developmental stages will occur, however, is not predictable, and wide ranges will be seen both in the timing at which stages occur and in the ultimate developmental level of function of delayed children. Abnormal motor and behavioral patterns may interfere with the sequence of development and acquisition of feeding skills.

Failure to recognize developmental readiness may result in failure of parents to provide children with appropriate stimuli. Parents who are unaware of their children's potential often do not encourage them to progress in the oral motor skills of eating and gross and fine motor skills of self-feeding. Children may be offered strained foods when they are capable of masticating food with a more mature texture; parents may feed the children when they have the ability to learn to feed themselves.

Readiness to accept solids is demonstrated blatantly in normal children and is difficult to ignore. They reach for food and bring it to their mouths. Clues as to readiness for this step in handicapped children may be very subtle, and, as a result, the stage is often ignored. Parents also may not realize the importance of the introduction of solids at the proper time. When parents decide it is time for children to learn to eat table food, conflicts may occur between children and their parents that may be sufficient to appreciably reduce the children's nutrient and caloric intakes. Such children may refuse to eat at all or may skillfully spit out lumps while sucking and swallowing the soft, strained foods.[47]

Parents have reported restraining their children and forcing them to accept foods with texture. For example, one mother stated that it took four adults to hold her 10-year-old child who was developmentally 4 years of age when she attempted to make the transition from strained to table food. The child eventually accepted the foods but later accepted only small amounts of very soft food and lost weight.

It is important to recognize that some children are hypersensitive in the oral area. It may be important for an occupational, physical, or speech therapist to institute a program to normalize sensation before plans for presenting more textured foods to the child (Fig. 13-3).

Children so delayed that they are unable to feed themselves depend on other people. Feeding the infant is a culturally defined maternal role, but feeding a handicapped child over a period of many years may become a tedious process that interferes with other activities several times a day. Some parents may become so overwhelmed with such a schedule that they continue feeding soft foods that do not support developmental progress; others may cease their efforts at feeding their children before the children consume sufficient food. Achieving self-feeding skills may appreciably increase nutrient intake, self-confidence, and self-image. Scales[48] describes an experience in teaching a 13-year-old severely retarded child to feed himself. With this learning the boy gained 9 lb in 6 weeks. A marked improvement in social behavior was noted.

Children whose delays in motor development are such that they lack the ability to learn to walk must be moved by their caregivers. The more weight the children gain, the more difficult they become to lift, move, and care for. Parents and caregivers of such children have expressed concern about the difficulties that may be created for them when chil-

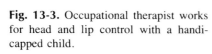

Fig. 13-3. Occupational therapist works for head and lip control with a handicapped child.

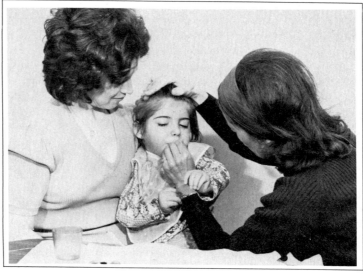

dren grow and gain weight and have been known to limit inappropriately the amounts of food they feed. Obesity must be prevented, but children should have the advantage of nutrient and energy intakes that support the best possible growth and development for them. Parents may need information and counseling in methods of moving and caring for their children and in accepting their needs for increased amounts of nutrients and energy.

Abnormal oral-motor patterns and muscle tone. Problems in sucking and swallowing and in the coordination of these functions with breathing can potentially be life threatening and may require that a child be fed in alternative ways such as gavage or gastrostomy feeding. In addition to demonstrating pathological oral motor patterns, i.e., oral patterns that are never observed as part of the normal developmental sequence, a child may show primitive oral patterns with the retention of primitive oral reflexes. These immature, primitive patterns can make the acquisition of mature feeding skills difficult. For example, a child who sucks reflexively when food is placed in the mouth cannot learn to chew until this reflexive bahavior is integrated and more isolated movements of lips, tongue, and jaw are developed.

Abnormalities in overall muscle tone can exacerbate problems in oral control. Many pathological oral patterns are seen in association with specific types of abnormal muscle tone and are frequently exacerbated by the tonal abnormalities. A tongue thrust may be seen as part of increased extensor tone throughout the body. With extension of a child's head, the tongue thrust can be exaggerated. Poor lip closure and an open mouth position are frequently seen in the child with a hypotonic face and body. Asymmetry in the distribution of muscle tone can be observed in jaw deviation toward the more involved side during chewing or during opening of the mouth for spoon insertion.[49]

Abnormal oral motor patterns resulting in a lack of control of the tongue, lips, and cheeks or lack of coordination of swallowing and breathing can make eating a difficult and prolonged event requir-

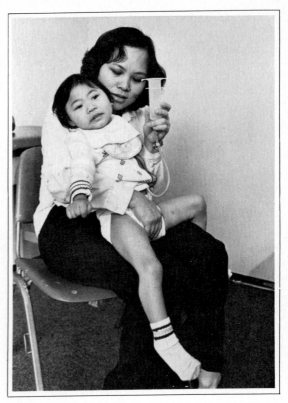

A

Fig. 13-4. A, Oral motor problems in some children make gavage feeding necessary for normal growth and development.

ing patience on the part of the child and the feeder. The amount of food lost from the mouth may be appreciable and may cause inadequate intake of nutrients. Children so affected require the skills of occupational, speech, and physical therapists to achieve motor patterns necessary for feeding.

For some infants with abnormal muscle tone and abnormal oral patterns or for infants with structural defects, gavage feeding may be necessary to ensure adequate nutritional intake. Problems with increased tactile sensitivity in the oral area may become apparent when the transition from nonoral to oral feeding begins. Techniques can be used to prepare the child for oral feeding even during the

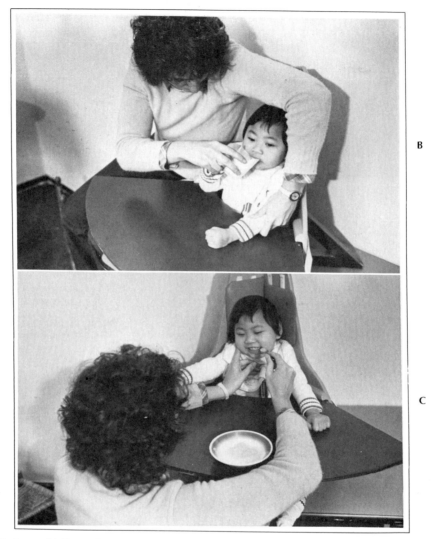

Fig. 13-4. cont'd. B and **C,** Even though gavage feeding is necessary, therapy is needed to foster the development of eating and drinking skills so normal eating patterns will be achieved in the future.

period when the child is predominantly fed by tubes. Oral intervention techniques used by occupational, physical, and speech therapists designed to maintain normal oral-tactile sensitivity should be continued during this period.[50]

The association between sensations in the mouth and sensations in the stomach can be maintained by using a pacifier during tube feedings.[51] For the toddler or older child who is receiving gastrostomy feedings, the hunger-satiation cycle may be established by normalizing the volume at each gastrostomy feeding to approximate the normal mealtime schedule. Thus, a gastrostomy-fed child who receives six equal-volume feedings per day might have the schedule changed to three larger gastrostomy "meals" and three smaller gastrostomy "snacks." This feeding schedule would approximate that of a normal child and would help the developmentally delayed child experience hunger and satiation while still maintaining the necessary caloric intake per day.

Termination of prolonged tube feeding is often followed by a difficult and sometimes lengthy adjustment period. A child who has been fed by tubes for a long period may have missed the critical or sensitive period for the introduction of solid foods.[47] Preparation before initiating oral feeding while the child is still being fed by tubes and the use of an interdisciplinary team of professionals to combat problems during the adjustment period may ease this transition.

Primitive oral reflexes. The full-term infant is normally born with a variety of well-established oral reflexes making the infant fully equipped to take in nourishment. Bosma[52] cites research showing that the human fetus can develop a functional swallow by 12.5 weeks gestation and sucking behavior by 14 weeks gestation. Many premature babies have extremely weak, inefficient sucks at birth. With increasing maturation, strength of suck, endurance, and rhythmicity of sucking improves. Some premature babies, however, require intervention to establish more mature feeding behavior. Tactile and proprioceptive facilitation techniques used by occupational and physical therapists or nurses in special care nurseries have resulted in better weight gain, faster transition from nasogastric feedings to bottle feedings, and more sustained sucking ability in premature infants.[51,53]

In a child who has feeding difficulties, the evaluation of individual primitive oral reflexes may provide some insight into the nature of the feeding difficulty. Ingram,[54] however, believes that merely testing oral reflexes provides little information about the individual's feeding abilities other than the presence of basic reflex arcs. Rather, Ingram states that one needs to consider how the primitive reflexes are integrated with breathing, adaptive feeding behavior, and vocalizations to adequately assess a child's feeding problems.

Protective oral reflexes. The gag and cough reflexes are oral reflexes that do not become integrated with increasing maturation but remain as protective reflexes throughout an individual's life. These reflexes serve to open the air passage when it is blocked or is in danger of being blocked. A cough reflex is a violent expiratory effort preceded by a preliminary inspiration; the accessory muscles of expiration are brought into action as air is noisily expelled. When related to food, the stimulation is the presence of food or liquid in the laryngeal vestibule that must be expelled so that it does not enter the lungs. The gag reflex is an involuntary attempt to vomit to remove food from the oral cavity that is in danger of traveling into the airway. When the soft palate is stroked or pressure is applied to the posterior wall of the pharynx or the posterior half of the tongue, there is an arching of the tongue, mouth opening, head extension, and facial grimacing.[55] Intense gagging may induce a vomit response.

In normal development the gag reflex is frequently elicited when a baby puts a toy far into the mouth. Oral play helps the child to accommodate to a variety of sensations and aids in the normal reduction in the intensity of the gag reflex. Through oral exploration, the infant experiences a variety of textures, temperatures, shapes, and sizes that may lay the groundwork for future learning. Frequently, the parent of a child with feeding problems will report that the child never participated in this normal mouthing stage of development. This fact should make the professional aware of a potential problem with a hyperreactive gag reflex.

Treatment for hypersensitivity to oral and tactile stimulation is a gradual, careful program of increasing the sensory experiences. The program is carefully graded according to the child's response because overstimulation could cause negative emotional and behavioral reactions or further increases in abnormal muscle tone that might interfere with feeding to a greater extent than the original problem. The therapeutic techniques used by occupational, physical, and speech therapists to normalize facial and oral sensitivity, therefore, are varied according to the individual child's reactions and needs.[56]

The gag reflex can also be inhibited or sensitized (increased) by physiological and psychological factors. A physiological sensitization may occur when a person is not feeling well, is dizzy, or is emotionally upset. The normal reaction to these feelings is to avoid eating. If food were to be offered or forced, the reaction might well be a gag. Fear of choking resulting from a previous incident may cause a gag response to the sight of a particular food. This behavior usually receives attention from adults, who frequently do not persist in offering the undesirable food. Children with these sorts of behavioral responses often severely restrict the variety of food textures in their diet, resulting in further sensory deprivation and increased oral sensitivity. A graded oral tactile stimulation program under the direction of a pediatric occupational, physical, or speech therapists would be indicated.

Positioning of children. The position of the child during feeding is of prime importance.[50,56] Proper positioning considers the child as a whole—the relationship of the head position to the body as well as the overall body position. Frequently a child's feeding difficulties can be greatly improved just by changes in the child's position during meals. Normalization of the child's muscle tone through positioning may minimize abnormal oral movement patterns and increase the child's voluntary oral control.

Head position is especially important for children who have swallowing difficulties or who do not have a normally responsive gag or cough response. The child should never be fed with the head or body tipped backwards in a position often referred to as a "bird-feeding" position. In this position normal swallowing and tongue control are impaired, and the child is in danger of aspirating food into the lungs or choking. Food in the lungs may lead to pneumonia or other respiratory difficulty. The head should be upright or slightly flexed forward (5° to 10°). The body should be upright, or if support is needed for head and trunk, within 30° of vertical.[57]

Children with feeding problems, especially those with abnormal muscle tone are often difficult to position. It is essential that a pediatric occupational or physical therapist assess each child and recommend appropriate positioning. A consistent effort should be made to follow through with these techniques. Adapted positioning during mealtimes should be comfortable for both the child and the caregiver and enable communication and interaction.

Fig. 13-5 demonstrates some feeding positions that may be prescribed by occupational and physical therapists. Each position incorporates basic principles of appropriate, therapeutic positioning.[49,50,57] The head is in good alignment with the body, and the mouth is in the midline. With the head in line with the body or slightly flexed forward, abnormal head extension or pushing backward can be inhibited. In some children, pushing back with the head is not caused by increased extensor tone but rather is a compensatory behavior that reflects a lack of ability to stabilize the head in an upright position. Proper head support can normalize abnormal tone or provide stability if needed.

The position of the arms is related to and influences head and trunk control. When the arms and shoulders pull backward, the head also tends to tilt backward and overall muscle tone increases. The shoulders and arms should be held forward and oriented toward the midline of the body. This forward position of the arms can be achieved by the manner in which the child is held near the feeder's body or by rolled towels or cushions placed behind the child's shoulders in the child's chair. Some children learn to stabilize their arms forward by grasp-

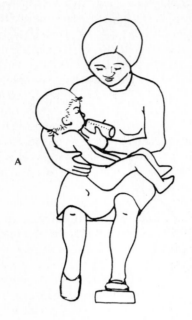

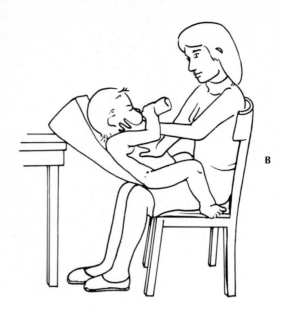

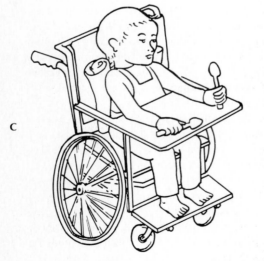

Fig. 13-5. A, A young infant or child can be fed while being held in someone's lap. The head is in line with the body, with the arms forward. With the left knee raised, hip flexion can be maintained. **B,** By using a firm wedge, a young child can be fed while facing the feeder. The legs are abducted and flexed, which inhibits extension. The feeder's hands are freed to assist with jaw control. **C,** Rolls can be inserted into a wheelchair to provide temporary trunk support and help keep the arms forward and toward the midline.

ing the far end of the wheelchair tray or supporting themselves with both elbows on the table.

Trunk stability is essential as the trunk provides the base on which to achieve good head and arm control. If the child is unable to sit independently, support should be provided through the use of a back rest or support provided by the feeder. If the child falls sideways, lateral supports can be provided through adaptations built into a wheelchair or through supportive cushions. Chest straps may be helpful for the child with minimal trunk control who falls forward. It would be preferable, however, to find a chair with a slight backward tilt to allow gravity to assist with trunk control.

The position of the hips and legs affects trunk control and thus influences the position of the rest of the body. Extension at the hips can increase tone throughout the body and cause extension of the head and mouth opening. Stiffness or spasticity in the legs can cause the legs to pull together narrowing the child's sitting base and impairing the postural adjustments needed for sitting balance. Adequate leg separation can be provided by a pommel placed between the child's legs to widen the base of support.

The hips should be flexed to a 90° neutral position. If the hips tend to extend, causing the child's hips to slip forward in the chair, greater than 90° of hip flexion can be provided by adding a wedge to the child's chair with the larger edge under the child's knees. Often just a seatbelt firmly fastened across the hips can keep the hips in a normal neutral positon and provide a better base for trunk control. Finally, good stability at the feet can be achieved through a foot rest allowing the feet to be flat and flexed at the ankle.

Proper positioning during mealtime supports the child's highest level of oral motor control. The relationship between the child's gross motor level at rest and during eating must be considered. The ability to independently control head or trunk positon may deteriorate when a child is asked to eat or self-feed. Mealtime should not be the time to make the child work on better head and trunk control.

Rather, adapted positioning should reinforce the child's motor level while fostering better oral and feeding skills.

In addition to the type of static positioning used during meals, the environment and the placement of the food or spoon can influence the child's feeding skills. If the spoon and foods are presented above eye level, the child may tilt the head backward to orient toward the food and thus reinforce an extension pattern. Presenting the food in the middle, from a low angle, will encourage slight head flexion and symmetry. Withdrawal of the spoon can also influence head position. If the spoon is lifted up and scraped against the upper front teeth, the head will tend to tilt backward and lip control will be impaired. Placing the container or plate of food at the side may encourage the child to turn sideways and increase asymmetry. By placing the food in front of the child, a symmetrical midline position can be encouraged.

Screening children to determine the primary concerns and the criteria for referral was discussed in Chapter 2. The foregoing information should prove useful in improving the quality of food intake when therapy services are not immediately available. It is important to use a problem-solving approach that includes ideas and feedback from the child and the caregiver. The rationale for any suggestions should be thoroughly explained and expectations for follow-through must be reasonable. It may take more time to feed a child in the desired position, especially at first. It may be suggested that the new techniques be used toward the beginning of the meal for a short time then increasing the amount of time as both the child and the caregiver become used to the techniques. Consideration of the child's and the caregiver's comfort, feelings, and opinions is likely to yield good results. Changes in motor control may be slow to develop, but the quality of the daily feeding experience has great impact on the ultimate skills that will develop.

A few children who have abnormal oral motor patterns have difficulty ingesting fluids. As a result, their intakes of liquids are very limited and they remain at risk for dehydration. Fluid intakes of such children should be carefully monitored. Heavily salted foods such as bouillon and commercially prepared soups should be avoided, as should high intakes of other nutrients that obligate water.

Management of Feeding

The diversity of concerns about the food and nutrient intake of handicapped children and the many factors that affect children's level of function and food acceptance imply that the skills of several disciplines may be necessary to effect solutions to concerns about food and nutrient intake and in setting priorities for therapy for individual children. The occupational, physical, and/or speech therapist will be called on to provide therapy for children with abnormal motor tone. The dentist will cupboards have been necessary to control obesity in such children. Food-related behaviors of such children cannot be altered by behavior modification methods.

Behaviors. Children may have inappropriate nutrient intakes and food habits because of learned behavior. Children learn from the model set for them by their parents, peers, and relatives. If examples of poor food habits are set, the children will imitate them. It is very difficult to retrain developmentally delayed children who have learned to reject many foods or groups of foods as a result of parental example.

The behavior pattern and attention span of children affect their calorie and nutrient needs and consumption. Hypoactivity reduces energy expenditure and needs. Lack of planned activity and stimulation for such children often results in boredom and in children spending their days seeking and consuming excessive amounts of food.

Hyperactive children never appear to be quiet and expend much energy in their numerous activities. The attention span of hyperactive children may be limited at the dinner table as in other activities, resulting in very small intakes of food at one time. It may be important to offer hyperactive children frequent small feedings of high nutrient content.

Disruptive and inappropriate behaviors of children make mealtime an unpleasant experience both for the children and the family and can result in inappropriate food intakes. Children quickly learn that behaviors such as throwing food or utensils, stuffing the mouth, spitting out food, and whining generally attract parental attention. In an effort to deal with disruptive behavior, many parents try different kinds of tactics. For one meal they may cajole the child into stopping the undesirable behavior, for another they may spank, and for another they may laugh at the child's activity. Since these responses usually occur on an intermittent basis depending on the mood of the parents at the time the disruptive behavior occurs, the effect for the child is one of intermittent positive reinforcement (Chapter 14). Many parents find it effective to remove the child from the table as soon as disruptive behavior occurs. The child should go to his or her room or to another room in the house where he or she does not receive adult attention until the meal is over. The child then does not receive food (except water) until the next meal is served.

Just as disruptive behaviors are discouraged, it is important to positively reinforce a child's appropriate mealtime behaviors. In this way the child learns the alternative behaviors that parents consider desirable.

Constipation. Constipation is not an unusual problem in children with developmental delays, especially in those who are hypertonic or hypotonic. The infrequent passage of feces or the passage of unduly hard dry fecal matter can result from a variety of causes, such as lack of muscle tone in the intestine or duodenal wall, excessive fatigue, anxiety, inappropriate dietary intake, or failure to establish a routine bowel pattern. When children are constipated, there will usually be complaints of stomachache, distention, swelling of the abdomen, or frank discomfort and pain.

It is possible that increasing the amount of fluid and roughage in the diet may be useful for treating children who are constipated. Parents should also observe for individual food stimuli. In some instances it may be important to limit milk intake to 1 pint/day. Prunes and prune juice are also frequently helpful.

Appetite. Lack of appetite as a result of central nervous system damage in some children has been reported. These children never express hunger, and some mothers of such children have stated that setting alarm clocks is an aid in reminding them to feed. Children so affected are rarely pleased by any food and limit the volume of food they consume. The children's unresponsiveness to parental efforts at feeding results in a lack of reinforcement for parents. This lack of positive interplay between parent and child may result in lack of satisfaction in each and may adversely affect the parents' motivation to continue helping the child consume food and the child's motivation to consume appropriate energy and nutrient intakes.

Damage to or developmental defects of the hypothalamus can result in insatiable appetites in children. Children so affected may sometimes gorge, steal food, or eat animal food. Extreme measures such as locking refrigerators and kitchen correct dental caries and malocclusions. A professional who is proficient in behavior modification techniques may be required to change behavior. It is possible that correction of these problems may lead to solutions of concerns about nutrient intake. Parents may, however, need help in planning appropriate foods for their children.

Parents of handicapped children are especially vulnerable to those who sell vitamin supplements and who often promise a cure or improvement. Attempts to coerce children to swallow 75 to 80 vitamin and mineral pills per day have been reported by parents. Careful evaluation of the children's nutrient intakes may alleviate parental concern that dietary insufficiencies are causing the problem.

Parents need to have realistic expectations about the child's potential for physical growth. It is not possible to increase a child's height beyond his or her genetic potential; it is possible to increase a child's weight for height. Parental concern about a child's slow rate of growth may create anxiety about the volume of food the child is consuming. Counseling about expectations and growth response to food intake is important.

The daily use of high-protein, high-calorie drinks that contain raw eggs should be discouraged. Sweetman and others[58] have described biotin deficiency in an 11-year-old mentally retarded male who consumed a drink with two raw eggs daily for 5 years. Clinical manifestations were alopecia totalis and an erythematous, exfoliative dermatosis.

Overindulgences are common among those who are responsible for the care of the handicapped, and such children frequently receive large amounts of preferred high-carbohydrate, sweet foods. As with anyone, it is difficult to design a food intake pattern that will provide necessary amounts of essential nutrients and maintain weight gain in growth channel if many of the foods consumed supply only carbohydrate and fat and few other nutrients. It may be important to help parents find ways of expressing affection other than in feeding and to make them aware of why they offer the foods they do.

Identifying readiness to progress. Assessing children's developmental levels of function and their readiness to progress in eating and self-feeding is necessary to define reasonable expectations for parents and caregivers. Parents often need help in accepting their children's handicaps and in recognizing their potential to progress.

It is important that changes in food and feeding behavior be effected when the children are developmentally 6 to 7 months of age, when they demonstrate readiness to self-feed and to use a cup. Table 13-1 defines important developmental landmarks and suggested food appropriate for changes in feeding behavior.

Early intervention programs can aid in preventing later problems of food and nutrient intake.

Table 13-1. Developmental stages of readiness to progress in feeding behaviors

Developmental Landmarks	Change Indicated	Examples of Appropriate Foods
Tongue laterally transfers food in the mouth Voluntary and independent movements of the tongue and lips Sitting posture can be sustained Beginning of chewing movements (up and down movements of the jaw)	Introduction of soft, mashed table food	Tuna fish; mashed potatoes; well-cooked mashed vegetables; ground meats in gravy and sauces; soft diced fruit such as bananas, peaches, pears; liverwurst; flavored yogurt
Reaches for and grasps objects with scissor grasp Brings hand to mouth	Finger-feeding (large pieces of food)	Oven-dried toast, teething biscuits, cheese sticks, peeled Vienna sausage (food should be soluble in the mouth to prevent choking)
Voluntary release (refined digital grasp)	Finger-feeding (small pieces of food)	Bits of cottage cheese, dry cereal, peas, etc.
Rotary chewing pattern	Introduction of more textured food from family menu	Well-cooked chopped meats and casseroles, cooked vegetables and canned fruit (not mashed), toast, potatoes, macaroni, spaghetti, peeled ripe fruit
Approximate lips to rim of the cup Understands relationship of container and contained	Introduction of cup Beginning self-feeding (messiness should be expected)	Food that when scooped will adhere to the spoon, such as applesauce, cooked cereal, mashed potatoes, cottage cheese
Increased rotary movement of the jaw Ulnar deviation of wrist develops	More skilled at cup and spoon feeding	Chopped fibrous meats such as roast and steak Raw vegetables and fruit (introduce gradually)
Walks alone	May seek food and get food independently	Food of high nutrient value should be available
Names food, expresses preferences; prefers unmixed foods Goes on food jags Appetite appears to decrease		Balanced food intake should be offered (child should be permitted to develop food preferences without parents being concerned that they will last forever)

Pipes and Holm[59] found that an early intervention program for families with children who have Down's syndrome that emphasizes developmental readiness to progress in feeding as well as an appropriate nutrient and energy intake reduced the incidence of most of the excesses and limitations of energy and nutrient intake in the children 6 years later. The program did not, however, eliminate the susceptibility of parents to the spiel of persons selling nutrient supplements.

Assessment of problems and suggested solutions. Efforts at prevention of problems of nutrient intake are not always successful. Frequently expressed concerns about food and nutrient intake of delayed children, factors that need to be assessed, and suggestions for solution are provided in Table 13-2.

Text continued on page 369.

Table 13-2. Assessment of concerns about foods and nutrients

Symptom	Assessment	Action and/or Counseling Suggestions
Lack of appetite	What is child's total food and nutrient intake?	Counsel with parents about child's needs and help them obtain needed food
	Is some essential nutrient consumed in insufficient amounts?	Provide only between-meal snacks of high-nutrient content at intervals that will not interfere with appetite at mealtime
	Is child receiving adequate amounts of food at other meals without having to eat large amounts?	Serve very small portions
	Is the food properly prepared?	Provide child with a quiet period before mealtime to prevent weariness
	Is child's rate of growth normal in spite of his or her apparent lack of appetite?	Reinforce child's acceptance of food with social reinforcement
	Is child reinforced?	Do not reinforce with food
	When he or she is eating? (appropriate)	Eat with child to provide a model
	When he or she is not eating? (inappropriate)	Refer the emotionally deprived child to the nurse or social worker
	Is child receiving too many snacks? (inappropriate)	
	Is child too weary to eat at mealtime?	
	Is child attending to eating or is his or her attention diverted at mealtime?	
	Is child psychologically deprived?	
Refuses specific groups of foods	Is food properly prepared?	Continue offering very small portions of foods refused
	Has child had previous experiences with the foods?	Reinforce foods accepted with foods child likes
	Does child have a model (parents, teacher, peers, etc.) who eats these foods?	Provide a model for child by eating the foods
		Provide guidance in food preparation for children
Inappropriate feeding behavior:	What started the behavior?	All inappropriate behaviors should be ignored even if it is necessary to remove child from feeding situation
Throwing	What follows the behavior?	
Gorging	Is child reinforced?	
Stuffing food in the mouth	Is child punished?	All attempts at appropriate eating should be encouraged through social reinforcement and food the child likes
Will not sit at the table	Is child ignored?	

Continued.

Table 13-2. Assessment of concerns about foods and nutrients—cont'd

Symptom	Assessment	Action and/or Counseling Suggestions
Refuses to eat table food; insists on strained food	Has child had experience with table food? Has it been offered and refused? Has child eaten table food previously but refuses it currently? How is child positioned for feeding? Can he or she sit upright? Has a critical stage of development been ignored? Is child delayed so that strained foods are appropriate for his or her stage of motor development? Can child bite or chew? Is child hypersensitive in and/or around the mouth?	Consult with occupational, physical, or speech therapist regarding positioning, development, and hypersensitivity Seat child in upright sitting position (using props if necessary) If child demonstrates readiness: Choose a food the child enjoys and place it between back molars (watch your fingers) Offer crunchy foods such as arrowroot biscuits, melba toast, crackers (be careful of foods that splinter, such as graham crackers)
Will not bite	Does child have a hypersensitive gag reflex? Does child have dental caries or malocclusion? Can child close the mouth? Has child been offered foods that require biting? Can child breathe through the nose?	Offer easy-to-bite foods such as arrowroot biscuits and melba toast Manually assist child in closing the jaw Provide social reinforcement when child takes a bite
Does not chew with a rotary motion	Is child delayed so that only munching or sucking is appropriate? Can child lateralize the tongue? Has child been offered foods that require chewing? Is child hypersensitive or hyposensitive? Are foods offered that are too tough to chew?	Consult an occupational, physical, or speech therapist regarding lateralization of the tongue and sensitivity Model for child by demonstrating chewing Manually move the jaw in chewing motions Encourage chewing with social reinforcement and with foods child likes
Refuses harder-to-chew foods	Is hypertonia or hypotonia preventing development of oral motor skills? Does child have dental caries? Is child sufficiently delayed that hard-to-chew foods are inappropriate for him or her?	Consult with occupational, physical, or speech therapist about oral motor skills; stimulate area around the lips and mouth before feeding as directed Consult about dental caries Give small bites; reinforce with social reinforcement and foods child likes

Problem	Assessment	Intervention
	Is there too much in child's mouth at one time for him or her to chew anything adequately?	
	Has child had experience with harder-to-chew foods?	
Lack of self-feeding	What cues of readiness to self-feed does child demonstrate?	If ready:
	Can child bring hand to mouth?	Behavior modification (i.e., putting the child through the motions of feeding, phasing out assistance)
	Can child hold the spoon?	Reinforce child's attempts to:
	Is child so delayed that self-feeding is inappropriate?	Hold spoon
	Can child sit either unsupported or propped in an upright position?	Put spoon in dish
	Do adults interrupt when child begins to make efforts to self-feed?	Bring spoon to the mouth
	Does child have behavior incompatible with self-feeding?	Close the lips around the spoon
	Physiologically, does child have any spasticity?	Return spoon to dish
	Behaviorally, does child throw food, utensils, etc?	
	Is child receiving attention by not feeding himself or herself?	
	Is child controlling parents by not feeding himself or herself?	
	Is child offered foods that will stick to the spoon?	
	Is child attending to eating or is he or she distracted by others in the environment?	
Lean for height	Is child receiving sufficient amounts of food?	Family should keep a food record if there is concern about amounts of food and frequency of eating
Weight loss	Is child receiving sufficient calories?	Feed more frequently; small feedings
Failure to gain adequate weight	Is some essential nutrient consumed in inappropriate amounts?	Provide high-caloric snacks of high-nutrient value, such as milkshakes or peanut butter or fruit on crackers or bread
	How frequently is child given food?	Counsel with parents regarding appropriate feedings for the child
	At school?	Reinforce with activities, not with food
	At home?	
	Does child eat on a regular schedule?	
	What is the family body type?	

Continued.

Table 13-2. Assessment of concerns about foods and nutrients—cont'd

Symptom	Assessment	Action and/or Counseling Suggestions
Failure to gain adequate weight	Does child have an illness or disease contributing to the lack of weight gain? Vomiting or diarrhea? Other chronic illness? What is child's history of weight gain Has child always been lean? Has child recently lost weight Is there sufficient food available to child? Is food presented to child in a manner appropriate for his or her level of function and self-help skills?	
Overweight	What is child's activity pattern? What foods does child have available at home? How has child's pattern of overweight been achieved? Has child gained weight recently? Is child currently gaining weight in the same channel, and is overweight a result of earlier feeding experiences? How does the family feel about child's weight? Is child reinforced for eating? What is child's activity level? What is child's snacking pattern?	Offer nonfat milk instead of whole milk, unsweetened fruit instead of desserts Limit fried foods, gravies, and sauces Provide low-calorie snacks Feed child on a schedule; discourage indiscriminate snacking Limit the number of desserts, cookies, candy, and other sweets offered Increase portion size of vegetables, meat, and fresh fruits; decrease portion size and number of servings of breads, potatoes, cereals, and fatty foods Reinforce with activities, not with food Help the family find ways of increasing child's level of activity Direct efforts at a reduction in the rate of weight gain, not a weight loss
Obesity	Assess as above	Weight reduction diet planned to effect weight loss of no more than 2 lb/month Counsel with all who offer food to child in the weight reduction program Plan physical activities daily in any manner compatible with the child's level of function Provide continuing support for parents and children as the program progresses

Developmentally delayed children frequently experience failure in their many efforts. It is therefore important that any plan to modify a child's food intake pattern be designed so that success is obtainable and so that the child and the parents are reinforced for each gain, however small. Adequate nutrition is important for every child to achieve his or her physical, mental, and emotional potential. Delayed and physically handicapped children should have the advantage of a nutrient intake that can support well-being, optimal growth, and development. Solutions to difficulties in attaining such goals may be complex and may require a multidisciplined approach.

SUMMARY

Children who are developmentally delayed are vulnerable to the same problems of nutrient intake as other children. The incidence of feeding and nutrition problems appears to be greater than in the normal population, and they are often more severe. The etiology of nutrition problems in developmentally delayed children often involves motor abnormalities and/or delays, infantilism, and lack of attention to critical periods of development. Therefore an interdisciplinary approach to intervention is appropriate. Specific syndromes are associated with undernutrition; others with obesity.

SUGGESTED LEARNING ACTIVITIES

1. Describe factors that must be addressed in evaluating the nutrient intake of a 3-year-old child with athetoid cerebral palsy.
2. Describe syndromes associated with mental retardation also associated with growth failure.
3. Define the nutritionist's role in early intervention programs for developmentally delayed children.
4. How would you respond to parents of a developmentally delayed child who were considering megavitamin therapy?

5. How would you determine an appropriate energy intake for a 14-month-old girl with Down's syndrome?
6. Observe a school lunch program in a school for special education. What motor problems of feeding do you observe? What adaptive equipment is being used to facilitate self-feeding?
7. To experience the effect of head position on eating, try to chew or swallow semisolid foods with your head tilted backward, try to drink with your head tilted backward.
8. To experience the effects of the position of the body on the head and on feeding ability, try to eat with your hips slid forward in the chair without your feet touching the ground.

REFERENCES

1. Garn, S.M., and Weir, H.F.: Assessing the nutritional status of the mentally retarded, Am. J. Clin. Nutr. **24**:853, 1971.
2. Smith, K.W.: Growth and its disorders, Philadelphia, 1977, W.B. Saunders Co.
3. Isaksson, B.: The nutritional needs of disabled children. In Blix, G., editor: Nutrition in preschool and school age, Symposium of the Swedish Nutrition Foundation, VII, Stockholm, 1969, Almqvist & Wiksell Forlag A.B.
4. Palmer, S., and Ekvall, S.: Pediatric nutrition in developmental disorders, Springfield, Ill., 1978, Charles C Thomas, Publisher.
5. Roche, A.F.: Growth assessment of handicapped children, Diet. Curr. **6**:25, 1970.
6. Manenica, K., and others: Evaluating growth and obesity in the child with meningomyelocele. [Submitted for publication.]
7. Gleason, C.: Nutritional assessment of boys with Duchenne's muscular dystrophy, unpublished master's thesis, Seattle, 1982, University of Washington.
8. Berke, A.R., and Wilmore, J.H.: Evaluation and regulation of body build and composition, Englewood Cliffs, N.J., 1974, Prentice-Hall, Inc.
9. Horton, W.A., and others: Growth curves for height for diastrophic dysplasia, spondyloepiphyseal dysplasia congenita, and pseudoachondroplasia, Am. J. Dis. Child. **136**:316, 1982.
10. Zorab, P.A., Prime, F.J., and Harrison A.: Estimation of height from tibia length, Lancet **1**:195, 1963.
11. Cronk, C.E.: Growth of children with Down's syndrome, birth to age 3 years, Pediatrics **61**:564, 1978.
12. Leamy, C.M.: A study of the food intake of a group of

children with cerebral palsy in the Lakeville Sanitorium, Am. J. Public Health **43:**1310, 1953.

13. Ruby, D.O., and Matheny, W.D.: Comments on growth of cerebral-palsied children, J. Am. Diet. Assoc. **40:**525, 1962.

14. Hammond, M.I., Lewis, M.N., and Johnson, E.W.: A nutritional study of cerebral palsied children, J. Am. Diet. Assoc. **49:**196, 1966.

15. Karle, I.P., Blehler, R.E., and Ohlson, M.A.: Nutritional status of cerebral-palsied children, J. Am. Diet. Assoc. **38:**22, 1961.

16. Caliendo, M.A., Booth, G., and Moser, P.: Iron intakes and serum ferritin levels in developmentally delayed children, J. Am. Diet. Assoc. **81:**401, 1982.

17. Danford, D.E., Smith, J.C., and Huber, A.M.: Pica and mineral status in the mentally retarded, Am. J. Clin. Nutr. **35:**958, 1982.

18. Wilton, K.M., and Irvine, J.: Nutritional intakes of socio-culturally mentally retarded children vs. children of low and average socioeconomic status, Am. J. Ment. Defic. **8:**79, 1983.

19. Culley, W.J., and Middleton, T.O.: Calorie requirements of mentally retarded children with and without motor dysfunction, J. Pediatr. **75:**380, 1969.

20. Culley, W.J., and others: Calorie intake of children with Down's syndrome (mongolism), J. Pediatr. **66:**772, 1965.

21. Pipes, P., and Holm, V.: Weight control of children with Prader-Willi syndrome, J. Am. Diet. Assoc. **62:**520, 1973.

22. Mertz, E.T., and others: Protein malnutrition in mentally retarded children. In Food and Nutrition Board: Meeting protein needs of infants and children, Pub. No. 843, Washington, D.C., 1961, National Academy of Sciences, National Research Council.

23. Eddy, T.P., Nicholson, A.L., and Wheeler, E.F.: Energy expenditures and dietary intakes in cerebral palsy, Dev. Med. Child Neurol. **7:**377, 1965.

24. Kruse, R.: Osteopathien bei antiepileptischer. Langeitherapie (Vorlanfige Meheilung) Monat sch. Kinderheilko **116:**378, 1968. Cited in Borgstedt, A.D., and others: Long-term administration of antiepileptic drugs and the development of rickets, J. Pediatr. **81:**9, 1972.

25. Jubiz, W., and others: Plasma 1,25-dihydroxyvitamin D levels in patients receiving anticonvulsant drugs, J. Clin. Endocrinol. Metab. **44:**617, 1977.

26. Lifshitz, F., and Maclaren, N.K.: Vitamin D–dependent rickets in institutionalized mentally retarded children receiving long-term anticonvulsant therapy. I. A survey of 288 patients. J. Pediatr. **83:**612, 1973.

27. Silver, J., and others: Prevalence and treatment of vitamin D deficiency in children on anticonvulsant drugs, Arch. Dis. Child. **49:**344, 1974.

28. Medlinsky, H.L.: Rickets associated with anticonvulsant medication, Pediatrics **53:**91, 1974.

29. Borgstedt, A.D., and others: Long-term administration of anti-epileptic drugs and the development of rickets, J. Pediatr. **81:**9, 1972.

30. Hahn, T.J.: Bone complications of anticonvulsants, Drugs **12:**201, 1976.

31. Teotia, M., and Teotia, S.P.S.: Rickets precipitated by anticonvulsant drugs, Am. J. Dis. Child. **125:**850, 1973.

32. Norris, J.W., and Pratt, R.F.: Folic acid deficiency and epilepsy, Drugs **8:**366, 1974.

33. Reynolds, E.H.: Folate metabolism and anticonvulsant therapy, Proc. R. Soc. Med. **67:**6, 1974.

34. Chanarin, I.: Effects of anticonvulsant drugs. In Botez, M.I., and Reynolds, E.H., editors: Folic acid in neurology, psychiatry, and internal medicine, New York, 1979, Raven Press.

35. Hommes, O.R., and others: Convulsant properties of folate compounds: some considerations and speculations. In Botez, M.I., and Reynolds, E.H., editors: Folic acid in neurology, psychiatry, and internal medicine, New York, 1979, Raven Press.

36. Eastham, R.D., Jancan, J., and Cameron, J.D.: Red cell folate and macrocytosis during long-term anticonvulsant therapy in non-anemic mentally retarded epileptics, Br. J. Psychiatry **126:**263, 1975.

37. Chien, L.F., and others: Harmful effect of megadoses of vitamins: electroencephalogram abnormalities and seizures induced by intravenous folate in drug treated epileptics, Am. J. Clin. Nutr. **28:**51, 1975.

38. Klein, G.L., and others: Multiple vitamin deficiencies in association with chronic anticonvulsant therapy, Pediatrics **60:**767, 1977.

39. Turkel, H.: Medical amelioration of cytogenic anomalies, Brooklyn, N.Y., 1971, Copen Press.

40. Williams, R.J.: Let's pursue nutrition to heal and prevent, Fam. Week. p. 4, April 25, 1076.

41. American Academy of Pediatrics Policy Statement, News and Comment, August 1981.

42. Harrell, R.J., and others: Can nutritional supplements help mentally retarded children, Proc. Natl. Acad. Sci **78:**574, 1981.

43. Smith, G.F., and others: Failure of vitamin/mineral supplementation in Down's syndrome, Lancet **2:**41, 1983.

44. Ellis, N.R., and Tomporowski, R.D.: Vitamin/mineral supplements and intelligence of institutionalized mentally retarded adults, Am. J. Ment. Defic. **88:**211, 1983.

45. Weathers, C.: Effects of nutritional supplementation of IQ and certain other variables associated with Down's syndrome, Am. J. Ment. Defic. **88:**214, 1983.

46. Bennett, F.C., and others: Vitamin and mineral supplements in Down's syndrome, Pediatrics **72:**707, 1983.

47. Illingworth, R.S., and Lister, J.: The critical or sensitive period with special reference to certain feeding problems in infants and children. J. Pediatr. **65**:839, 1964.

48. Scales, H.E.: The application of operant conditioning to establish self-help feeding patterns in two mentally retarded children, unpublished Master of Nursing thesis, Seattle, 1966, University of Washington.

49. Connor, F.P., Williamson, G.G., and Siepp, J.M., editors: Program guide for infants and toddlers with neuromotor and other developmental disabilities, New York, 1978, Teachers College Press.

50. Morris, S.E.: The normal acquisition of oral feeding skills: implications for assessment and treatment, New York, 1982, Therapeutic Media, Inc.

51. Measel, C.P., and Anderson, G.C.: Nonnutritive sucking during tube feedings: effect on clinical course in premature infants, J.O.G.N. Nurs. **8**(15):265, 1979.

52. Bosma, J.F.: Structure and function of the infant oral and pharyngeal mechanisms. In Wilson, J., editor: Oral motor function and dysfunction in children, Chapel Hill, N.C., 1977, University of North Carolina, Division of Physical Therapy.

53. Leonard, E.L., Trukowski, L., and Kirkpatrick, B.V.: Nutritive sucking in high-risk neonates after perioral stimulation, Phys. Ther. **60**:299, 1980.

54. Ingram, T.T.S.: Clinical significance of infantile feeding reflexes, Devel. Med. Child Neurol. **4**:159, 1962.

55. Radtke, S.: Feeding reflexes and neural control. In Wilson, J., editor: Oral motor function and dysfunction in children, Chapel Hill, N.C., 1977, University of North Carolina, Division of Physical Therapy.

56. Mueller, H.: Facilitating feeding and prespeech. In Pearson, P.H., and Williams, C.E., editors: Physical therapy services in the developmental disabilities, Springfield, Ill., 1972, Charles C Thomas, Publisher.

57. Mueller, H.: Feeding. In Finnie, N.R.: Handling the young cerebral palsied child at home, New York, 1975, E.P. Dutton & Co., Inc.

58. Sweetman, L., and others: Clinical and metabolic abnormalities in a boy with dietary deficiency of biotin, Pediatrics **68**:553, 1981.

59. Pipes, P.L.: Feeding children with Down's syndrome, J. Am. Diet. Assoc. **77**:277, 1980.

ADDITIONAL READINGS

American Dietetic Association: Infant and child nutrition: concerns regarding the developmentally disabled, J. Am. Diet. Assoc. **78**:443, 1981.

Crosley, C.J., Chee, C., and Berman, P.H.: Rickets associated with long-term anticonvulsant therapy in a pediatric outpatient population, Pediatrics **56**:52, 1975.

Finnie, N.R.: Handling the young cerebral palsied child at home, New York, 1975, E.P. Dutton & Co., Inc.

Gauge, A.L., and Ekvall, S.W.: Diets of handicapped children: physical, psychological, and socioeconomic correlations, Am. J. Ment. Defic. **80**:149, 1975.

Greecher, C.P., Colen, I.T., and Ballentine, F.V.N.: Survey of nutritional problems encountered in children with neuromotor disorders, J. Parent. Ent. Nutr. **4**:490, 1980.

Hahn, T.J., and others: Serum 25-hydroxycalciferol levels and bone mass in children on chronic anticonvulsant therapy, N. Engl. J. Med. **292**:550, 1975.

Morris, S.E.: Prespeech and language programming for the young child with cerebral palsy, Milwaukee, Wis., 1975, Curative Workshop of Milwaukee, 9001 W. Watertown Plank Rd., Milwaukee, WI 53226.

Ottenbacher, K., Bundy, A., and Short, M.A.: The development and treatment of oral-motor dysfunction: a review of clinical research, Phys. Occup. Ther. Pediatr. **3**(2):1, 1983.

Scherzer, A.L., and Tscharnuter, I.: Early diagnosis and therapy in cerebral palsy, New York, 1982, Marcel Dekker, Inc.

Springer, N.S., and Fricke, N.L.: Nutrition and drug therapy for persons with developmental disabilities, Am. J. Ment. Defic. **80**:317, 1975.

Tolman, K.G., and others: Osteomalacia associated with anticonvulsant drug therapy in mentally retarded children, Pediatrics **56**:45, 1975.

Management of Mealtime Behaviors

14

SALLY M. O'NEIL

It is apparent that parent/child interactions are important determinants of children's acceptance of food and attitudes toward eating. They often are responsible for difficulties presented to health professionals. Parents, anxious about their children's nutrient intakes, sometimes urge, nag, or pressure children to eat, and children often assume control of the feeding environment. The battle for control may become so intense that the children's nutrient intakes may be compromised. The conflict may result in a variety of problems including failure to thrive and overweight or obesity. Difficulties in achieving adequate nutrient intakes because of inappropriate parent/child interactions during the preschool and early school years have been observed clinically in children who have histories of allergies and oral motor difficulties during infancy and in children who are overweight and obese. Inappropriate parent/child interaction is that which, in the struggle for control over child behavior, results in high levels of tension and parental reinforcement of child behaviors that interfere with adequate nutrient intake. Children may be inadvertently reinforced for disruptive activities (e.g., tantrums and throwing food) as well as for eating exceedingly large amounts of food.

Parent/child interaction is a complex reciprocal process. Events occur in sequence on an interaction continuum between parents and children in which each response to an action can become the cause of future behaviors. It is by this interactive process that both parents and children learn new behaviors. The interactive process includes parents' expressions of attitudes, values, interests, beliefs, and their caregiving behavior as well as children's individual growth patterns, learning potential, and ability to incorporate increasingly complex experiences into their current stages of thinking and functioning.[1] Behavior is both the cause and effect of other behaviors. All parent/child interactions are both elicited by the child and impinge on the child. For instance, the cries of an infant who is hungry can become the stimulus for the mother to respond by feeding the infant.

The purpose of this chapter is to focus on parent/child behaviors, to examine their effects on feeding and nutrition, and to explore methods of changing behavior, which in turn may effect changes in food intake patterns.

BASIC CONCEPTS IN BEHAVIOR ASSESSMENT AND MANAGEMENT

Behaviorists have determined that behaviors are increased, maintained, or decreased by the consequences that immediately follow them.[2] These consequences can be reinforcing or punishing. Since reinforcers and punishers are defined from an individual's point of view, what may be reinforcing to one person may not be to someone else; the determination of what is reinforcing or punishing is made by the effect of a particular consequence on the behavior that preceded it. To be a reinforcer, a consequence must increase the behavior that it follows.

Reinforcers are of two types: positive and negative. Positive reinforcement is a consequence in which something desirable to the subject is added or applied to his or her environment as a result of a specific behavior. A smile, praise, hug, food, and money are examples of positive reinforcers. Negative reinforcement, on the other hand, is a consequence in which something aversive or unpleasant is subtracted, that is, removed or terminated. For example, a person who is annoyed by loud static on the radio may turn down the volume or turn off the radio. The silence, or absence of static, is a negative reinforcer for turning off the sound, and the person is likely to do it again if static recurs. All reinforcers must increase the behavior that they follow. The important distinction between these two concepts is that in positive reinforcement something pleasant is added as a consequence and in negative reinforcement something unpleasant is removed as a consequence.

Punishers decrease the behaviors that they follow. They are defined operationally in two ways. One definition includes consequences in which something aversive is added or applied, such as a spanking. This is generally called *punishment*. The second definition includes those consequences in which a positive reinforcer is removed, for example, the withholding of adult attention (ignoring) during a child's temper tantrum or withholding eye contact when someone else is talking. This is generally called *extinction*.

Interaction Processes Between Positive and Negative Reinforcement and Punishment

To examine positive and negative reinforcement and punishment as interactive processes, it is important to analyze the various parts of interaction. Peterson[3] has suggested that one way to do this effectively is to consider interaction in terms of A (antecedent events), B (behavior), and C (consequences).[4] Consider the following example in which the ABC analysis is used. A mother takes her preschool son into a grocery store. The child immediately begins to ask for candy, then whines and cries when the mother refuses to give him any candy. After several minutes of loud crying and repeated looks from other shoppers, the mother gives the child a piece of candy. The child immediately stops crying.

A diagrammatic analysis of this situation is presented below. From this analysis one would correctly conclude that in giving her child candy the mother had reinforced her child for crying. Also, because he was reinforced, it is highly likely that the child will repeat this behavior during future trips to the grocery store. The consequence that the mother received when she gave the candy was one of negative reinforcement because the crying ceased after the mother gave the child the candy. By giving candy, she terminated something that was aversive to her—the child's crying. In this interaction both mother and child were reinforced for their behaviors. The child was positively reinforced (candy was added) for crying, and the mother was negatively reinforced (crying was removed) for giving the candy. Both are likely to repeat their behaviors next time.

What if, in a similar situation, the mother decided to ignore the child? What would the mother's consequences be if ignoring stopped the crying? As before, her consequence is that of negative reinforcement if she successfully stops the crying. Because the mother will be negatively reinforced for whatever she does that stops the crying, she may be reinforced for being inconsistent: giving

A (antecedent)	B (child's behavior)	C (consequence)
1. Entering grocery store	2. Asks for candy	3. Mother refuses
	4. Cries and yells	5. Mother gives candy
	6. Stops crying	

Child Behaviors at Mealtime

Noneating Behaviors	Meals Observed 1	2	3	4	5	6
Arguing						
Complaining						
Crying						
Hitting						
Noncomplying						
Not sitting at table						
Teasing						
Yelling						
Pouting						
Whining						
Moving hands nonpurposefully						
Talking back						
Throwing food or utensils						
Spitting						
Gagging						
Refusing certain foods						

Eating Behaviors						
Using fingers for finger foods						
Using utensils appropriately						
Sitting at table						
Accepting variety of foods						
Socializing as appropriate						
Complying to requests						

Parent Behaviors at Mealtime

Antecedents to Child Behaviors	Meals Observed 1	2	3	4	5	6
Commanding						
Requesting						
Questioning						
Prompting verbally						
Physically assisting						
Interrupting						
Positioning child appropriately						
Presenting food appropriately						
Presenting appropriate utensils						

Consequences of Child Behaviors						
Commenting positively						
Commenting negatively						
Ignoring						
Touching						
Spanking						
Yelling						
Arguing						
Laughing						
Using same tone of voice						
Talking irrelevantly						

candy one time, ignoring the child the next, and perhaps spanking another time.

It is easy for parents to become trapped in their responses to their children's behaviors and thus become unable to see those aspects of their interactions that are ineffective for both of them. It becomes important for parents to consider how they would like to respond most consistently to their child in the light of the behaviors they would like their child to learn. Parents have to consider their child's stage of development and reinforcers that fit his or her particular stage and personality. In addition, they have to be aware of the effects of the child's behavior on themselves. This is no small task, and it seems to become especially important around mealtimes. Since nutrition, socialization, and intense family interactions seem to converge in this event, it is no wonder that so many clinical issues arise around mealtime behaviors.

Assessment of Mealtime Behaviors

Initial assessment consists of identifying the patterns of parent/child mealtime behaviors. The observation checklist on the opposite page is a useful recording guide that pinpoints problem behavior as well as desirable behaviors. This tool can be used by professionals who are recording their direct observations or by parents who are recording the mealtime behaviors of themselves and their children. Behaviors can be tallied for each meal.

Once problem behaviors are identified, the most frequent eating and noneating behaviors and their consequences can be identified in ABC sequences. Parents are helped to identify those child behaviors that they wish to change as well as the appropriate eating behaviors that they wish to foster in their children. The next step is to determine appropriate consequences for all the behavior categories.

As we noted earlier, parents generally behave toward their children (reinforce, punish, or ignore) in certain ways because of the reinforcement they receive from their children. For instance, they may reinforce a crying child with a cookie because they know this will stop the crying. Thus the parent is negatively reinforced for giving the child the cookie. Frequently, to help parents change the consequences they provide their children, it is necessary to look at the reinforcers parents are getting for their own behavior. One way to do this is to help them identify the subsequent child behavior step to the ABC pattern. For parents to alter their antecedent cues to the child, they must be aware of these behaviors and their part in the entire ABC pattern.

The brief case studies that follow illustrate a variety of parent/child ABC patterns that relate to mealtimes.

1 Laura refuses to drink milk.

A	B	C
1. Mother pours milk into glass	2. Child starts crying	3. Mother says, "Drink your milk"
	4. Child cries	5. Mother removes milk and gives child soda
	6. Child stops crying and drinks soda	

In this instance the mother was negatively reinforced. She successfully terminated the crying by giving the child soda, which, in turn, positively reinforced the child's crying when milk was presented to her.

2 Billy, a toddler, writes his own menu.

A (mother)	B (child)	C (mother)
1. Presents applesauce to toddler in highchair	2. Cries and whines, points to the refrigerator	3. "What do you want?"

B (child)—cont'd	**C (mother)—cont'd**
4. Cries, points to cupboard	5. "Do you want a cracker?" Gives him a cracker
6. Cries, points to cupboard and refrigerator	7. "What do you want? Here is some cereal."
8. Cries, points to refrigerator	9. "No you can't have ice cream."
10. Child screams	11. "OK, here is some ice cream."
12. Stops crying	

In this situation the child keeps his mother going in circles in an effort to stop his crying. A management plan was developed with her in which she would leave the room and when the child would stop crying she would return and praise him for eating so nicely. The ABC looked like this:

A (mother)	**B (child)**	**C (mother)**
1. Presents applesauce to toddler in highchair	2. Cries, points to cupboard	3. Leaves room (can see child but he can't see her)
	4. Slowly stops crying, starts eating applesauce	5. Returns and says "My, what a big boy!"
	6. Child laughs and keeps on eating	

3 John, a school-age child who has a hearing impairment, wanders at mealtimes.

A (parents)	**B (child)**	**C (parents)**
1. Announce dinner	2. Sits at table with parents	3. Talk to each other, ignore child
	4. Gets up and wanders around house	5. Yell, "Come back here, John."
	6. Approaches dining room	7. Ignore John
	8. Wanders away from dining room	9. "Come here, John." Father goes and leads him to table
	10. John sits and looks at food	11. Ignore John
	12. John leaves table	

In discussing this ABC with John's parents they decided that they had been reinforced by John's absence at the table since, before that time, he had had tantrum behavior at the table. They believed that he should eat with them, but it was more comfortable to eat without him and to feed him later. A management program was developed with them in which they agreed to reinforce him for sitting at the table, using signing as well as verbal praise, and to try to include him in the general conversation. A subsequent ABC looked like this:

A (parents)	**B (child)**	**C (parents)**
1. Announce dinner	2. John sits at table, starts eating	3. Talk and sign to John
	4. Leaves table	5. Ignore John
	6. Approaches table	7. Talk and sign to John, discussing day's events
	8. Sits down, starts to eat	9. Eat, yet continue to socialize with John
	10. John talks, signs, eats, and remains seated during meal	

The importance of antecedents. Although consequences are important in maintaining behaviors, the antecedent events frequently tell a child or parent that certain behaviors will be reinforced. As discriminative stimuli, antecedents set the occasion for reinforcers. For example, when the mother in case 1 poured the milk, the child knew that if she cried at that time she would be likely to get soda instead.

Frequently, in an attempt to get control of such a situation this parent may have suggested as she poured the milk, "You have to drink milk, you will not get soda this time." However, the child cries anyway, even louder and longer than before. To terminate the crying the parent generally gives in and replaces the milk with soda. Instead of discouraging the child, the parent has only made the discriminative stimulus even stronger by adding the verbal reminder when pouring the milk.

Another example of important antecedents is demonstrated in case 4.

4 Suzi, a preschooler, uses cues supplied by her mother to control her mother's behavior.

A	B	C
Meal 1		
1. Mother presents food	2. Child eats	3. Mother sits with book, does not talk to child
Meal 2		
1. Mother presents food	2. Child gags and spits up food	3. Mother attends, cleans up child, then finishes feeding her the meal

In assessing this situation, it was found that Suzi did not vomit every meal. Yet somehow she was getting cues as to when to vomit. In an attempt to further identify these cues, the mother's meal preparation was observed as part of the antecedent behavior. Surprisingly, the typical ABC pattern for vomiting and nonvomiting meals looked like this:

A	B	C
Vomiting meal		
1. Preparing lunch, mother says, "Suzi, you have carrots today. I hope you don't vomit them."	2. Child starts eating, then gags and vomits carrots	3. Mother attends, cleans her up, and feeds her the rest of the meal
Nonvomiting meal		
1. Preparing lunch, mother says, "Oh good, Suzi, you have macaroni today."	2. Eating well	3. Mother sitting with book, ignoring Suzi

For the vomiting meal mother was cuing Suzi to the fact that if she vomited she would get attention, be cleaned up, and be fed her lunch. For the nonvomiting meal no such cue was given, so Suzi ate her lunch as expected. These ABC patterns were discussed with the mother, and a strategy was developed in which she would not read at mealtime, would reinforce Suzi for eating by talking with her at mealtime, and would only provide antecedent verbal cues such as in the nonvomiting meal. A later ABC pattern looked like this:

A	B	C
1. "Suzi, we have egg sandwiches today."	2. Child eats, smiles, and talks to mother	3. Mother attends to Suzi by smiling and conversing

ADDITIONAL CONCEPTS IN BEHAVIOR MANAGEMENT

There is no doubt about the importance of food as an effective reinforcer for most people. Since it meets a basic biological need, it is considered to be a primary reinforcer. Secondary reinforcers such as affection, praise, and touch are said to derive their reinforcing qualities from having been paired with food during the early infant period. Later, money becomes reinforcing when used to buy a wide variety of reinforcers such as food, shelter, clothing, and other desirable items. Food is a potential reinforcer for a wide variety of activities; it is frequently paired with or follows attendance at outings, movies, sports, and social events.

The decision to use food as a reinforcer is made after a careful assessment process in which a variety of reinforcers are tried. Reinforcers are *individualized,* as discussed earlier. What may be reinforcing for one individual may not be for another, depending on biophysiological factors within an individual and his or her history of experiences.

For some children social praise may be reinforcing, for others food may be reinforcing. For still others neither social praise nor food is reinforcing, and parents must seek other kinds of reinforcers. Children who have developmental delays may not be able to use the usual things that most children find reinforcing. Because of sensory deficits or problems in neuromuscular development and/or because experiences have been limited, these children may need specialized reinforcers such as vibration, flickering lights, or even music. The point here is that an effort must be made to determine what kind of reinforcers is effective for any given individual. In some instances food is the only reinforcer with which a child can learn appropriate behaviors. If this is the case, food should be used and other reinforcers (e.g., affection and praise) can be paired with it until they also become reinforcing for this particular individual and food no longer needs to be used.

When it has been determined that food will be the most effective reinforcer for a particular child, several considerations are important. The first factor is the kind of food to use. Again, this should be individualized according to the child's tastes, and care should be taken to use food with high-nutrient value whenever possible. In many instances potato chips and candy are used when raisins or cheese might be just as effective. Any food reinforcement should be considered as part of the total nutrient and caloric intake for the child.

Another factor to consider is the timing of food reinforcers. If one is concerned that the child eat adequate meals, training programs that use food reinforcers should not immediately precede a meal. Likewise, if success in the training program is important, a program using food reinforcers should not directly follow a meal. Any individual may become satiated by food unless adequate time has elapsed between intervals of food intake.

Satiation can also occur when too much of the same food is given. If particular foods are used during a training program, they should not be available to the child at any other time of the day to ensure maximum effectiveness of the reinforcer. For instance, a child may be given a dish of ice cream daily at home. If a decision is made to use a dish of ice cream in a program at school, the ice cream should no longer be available at home.

Another factor to consider when using food reinforcement is the pairing of another potential reinforcer with food. Because it is important for the child to be able to use other reinforcers, it is necessary to provide reinforcers such as praise at the same time that food is given. After it is determined that the combination of food and praise is reinforcing to the child, the food can be given less frequently, whereas praise will still be provided every time the desired behavior occurs. The food is gradually eliminated, and praise will have become a reinforcer for the child.

Consistency is another important factor in applying reinforcers. As children learn an increasing variety of behaviors, they learn about new and different reinforcers. Food and feeding habits may be incorporated into behavioral repertoires designed to gain adult attention. Throwing utensils and/or food may cause a variety of interesting adult reactions. A parent may laugh at one such incident, respond with anger at another, and at a third may feed the child in exasperation. In the effort to keep up with the child, parents may respond inconsistently, depending on their mood at the time. Consistency means that desirable behaviors generally are reinforced, whereas undesirable behaviors are not reinforced and may even be punished. What is important is that the child knows what desirable behaviors are expected by his or her parents and, in turn, what consequences can be expected for certain behaviors.

When food intake is the major concern, experience has indicated that reinforcers other than food are more effective for managing feeding behaviors. For instance, if a child must be on a special diet for a biological reason such as allergy, parents and professionals usually become concerned that the child may not eat adequate amounts of acceptable foods. In this instance the child receives mixed messages if he or she is reinforced with food yet perceives that the parents will not allow certain other foods. The child quickly learns that by refusing foods that are allowed he or she can gain a great deal of attention and may even receive the forbidden foods as parents become upset by the child's refusal to eat. The use of nonedible reinforcers such as outings, toys, and games following meals generally helps to refocus the parents' and child's attention to other activities.

TEACHING SELF-FEEDING BEHAVIORS

In addition to the use of reinforcement, *shaping* and *fading* techniques are useful procedures for teaching new behaviors and skills. Both of these procedures are useful for teaching feeding behaviors and are frequently used by parents and professionals.

Shaping is the reinforcement of successive approximations to a desired behavior. In this pro-

cedure the behavior is broken down into its component steps. The type and number of steps are determined by the task to be learned. The first step is reinforced; when that step is learned, the next step is added and the reinforcement is shifted to the second step in the chain of responses that lead to the desired behavior.

Teaching spoon-feeding by shaping

1. Desired behavior: independent spoon-feeding
2. Changing steps in child responses:
   a. Child looks at spoon
   b. Child moves hand toward spoon
   c. Child touches spoon
   d. Child picks up spoon
   e. Child puts spoon in dish
   f. Child scoops food
   g. Child brings food to mouth
   h. Child takes food off spoon
   i. Child returns spoon to dish
3. Reinforcement: bites of food or other reinforcers as each step is accomplished

Fading is a different procedure in that the entire behavior is used each time for reinforcement. Instead of requiring the child's responses to proceed through several steps, the trainer's cues are changed as the child's skill develops. For example, the trainer holds the child's hand around the spoon and puts the child through the motions of scooping food onto the spoon, bringing the spoon to the mouth, and returning the spoon to the dish. As the child gradually assumes independent movement, physical assistance is decreased and the trainer only provides assistance as needed to complete the task. The number and type of trainer cues needed depends on the task to be learned and the abilities of the child.

Teaching spoon-feeding by fading

1. Desired behavior: independent spoon-feeding
2. Steps:
   a. Holding child's hand around spoon, scoop food, bring arm, hand, and spoon *to* mouth. Allow child to take food off spoon in mouth, then (still holding child's hand around spoon) return spoon to dish.

b. Holding child's hand around spoon, bring it *toward* mouth and allow child to complete movement to mouth if possible. Assist through rest of cycle.

c. Assist child in holding spoon and scooping food. By touching arm slightly, provide cues that assist child in completing movement to mouth. Also by touches, assist child in returning spoon to dish.

d. Provide only as much assistance as child needs to pick up spoon, scoop food, move spoon to mouth, and return to dish.

The actual number of steps delineated for any given individual depends on the developmental level and skill that the individual possesses before using either of these procedures.

GENERAL CONSIDERATIONS IN THE USE OF BEHAVIOR MANAGEMENT TECHNIQUES

Behavior modification is generally easy to use as a method of therapeutic intervention. The difficulties lie in the behavioral analysis, which is necessary to pinpoint specific behaviors and their consequences. Frequently, the relationships between behaviors and their consequences (particularly when two or more persons are involved) are difficult to discover, and care must be taken to delineate them with accuracy and reliability. Behavior is not simple and becomes increasingly complex when viewed within a framework of human interaction. Yet to try to remedy behaviors in isolation is to treat them outside the context of their everyday occurrence. This, in turn, leads to unsuccessful programs.

The preceding examples have been assessed by direct observation of mealtime behaviors, yet there are more complex situations that would preclude direct observation or that would be greatly altered by the presence of an observer. In-home videotaped recordings (if available to the professional) frequently work well for these situations. Parents are usually quite willing to allow several meals to be videotaped to pinpoint difficulties. These tapes are analyzed according to their ABC patterns. Important segments of tape are then played back to the parents, who frequently are able to discover the problems themselves. Frequently, this is an impetus for them to discuss their feelings and concerns about the situations and to generate alternative ways of behaving with their children.

Professionals must be concerned about all the possible effects of the techniques before implementing them and should secure assistance while learning the procedures involved. Collaboration of nutrition, nursing, and other disciplines will assist in continually refining observation and recording techniques and management procedures. Successful programs require that the role of each discipline in the analysis, program design, and implementation be well defined.

During nutrition and feeding evaluation, observations of parental and child behaviors by two or more disciplines can help to identify more reliably the cause of a specific problem. Programs should be designed jointly with parents by a member of one discipline primarily relating to the family. Changes in physical growth, nutrient intake, and behavior should be monitored on an interdisciplinary basis to direct attention to both psychosocial (behavioral) and physical parameters.

SUMMARY

Feeding and nutrition problems during childhood may result from inappropriate parent/child interactions. Behavior management programs when adequately implemented can resolve the problems presented. Observations of parent/child interactions give clues as to the antecedent to the behavior and the reinforcers that cause it to continue. Reinforcers used in behavior management programs must be individualized for each client. If food is used as a reinforcer, the program and nutrient intake should be carefully monitored to ensure that it does not compromise the child's nutritional status.

SUGGESTED LEARNING ACTIVITIES

1. Observe a child eating a family meal. What cues do parents give the child to eat? Identify positive and negative reinforcers parents consciously or unconsciously use.
2. How would you identify appropriate foods as reinforcers for a child who needed a behavior management program?
3. Describe feeding problem behaviors for which a behavior management program would be appropriate.
4. Define factors that should be monitored to ensure that a child's nutritional status is not compromised when a behavioral management program is planned to change a child's feeding behavior.
5. Design a behavior management program to effect an increase in textures of food acceptable to a developmentally delayed child.

REFERENCES

1. O'Neil, S.M., McLaughlin, B.N., and Knapp, M.B.: Behavioral approaches to children with developmental delays, St. Louis, 1977, The C.V. Mosby Co.
2. Bijou, S.W., and Baer, D.M.: Child development: readings in experimental analysis, New York, 1967, Appleton-Century-Crofts.
3. Peterson, L.W.: Operant approach to observation and recording, Nurs. Outlook **15:**28, 1967.

ADDITIONAL READINGS

Aquas, W., Kazden, A.E., and Wilson, J.T.: Behavior therapy: toward an applied clinical science, San Francisco, 1979, W.H. Freeman & Co., Publishers.

Becker, W.C.: Parents are teachers: a child management program, Champaign, Ill., 1971, Research Press.

McLaughlin, B.N.: Learning and social behavior, New York, 1971, The Free Press.

O'Neil, S.M.: Behavior analysis of feedback among family members. In Miller, J., and Janosick, E., editors: Theory and practice of family health, New York, 1978, McGraw-Hill Book Co.

Patterson, G.R.: Application of social learning to families, Champaign, Ill., 1974, Research Press.

Sears, R.R., Maccaby, E.E., and Levin, H.: Patterns of child rearing, New York, 1957, Row, Peterson & Co.

Yule, W., and Caur, J., editors: Behavior modification for the mentally handicapped, Baltimore, 1980, University Park Press.

Glossary

allergen Substance that causes an altered response of cells and as a result symptoms of allergy

allergy Hypersensitive state caused by the interaction of an allergen with an antibody

anorexia Lack of appetite

antibody Protein synthesized in response to an antigenic stimulus

antigen Any substance that produces an immune response as a result of contact with the tissue; hypersensitivity may result

alopecia totalis Complete loss of hair

amenorrhea Absence or abnormal stoppage of the menses

amylase Enzyme that catalyzes the hydrolysis of starch to glucose

anaerobic Occurring in the absence of oxygen

anoxia Lack of oxygen in the tissues or body

assessment Critical analysis of the status or quality of a condition

asymmetry Dissimilarity in corresponding parts or organs on opposite sides of the body that are normally alike

atonic Lacking normal tone or strength

"bird-feeding" Feeding an individual with his or her head thrown back

bonding Development of a close emotional tie to another individual or to a newborn infant

botulism Food poisoning caused by the toxin produced by *Clostridium botulinum*

bulimia Gorging and vomiting

bronchopulmonary dysplasia Disorder characterized by hypoxia, hypercardia, and oxygen dependency; a computation of hyaline membrane disease

calcitonin Hormone secreted by the thyroid gland that is concerned with the regulation of calcium ions in the blood

casein Principal protein of milk

cholestatic jaundice Jaundice caused by arrest of the flow of bile

cm Abbreviation for centimeter

colic Acute abdominal pain

colostrum First milk secreted by the mammary gland after parturition

congenital Existing at, and usually before, birth

creatinine Anhydride of creatine, formed largely in the muscles by irreversible and nonenzymatic removal of water from creatine phosphate; the amount excreted in the urine is an index of muscle mass and may be used as a measure of basal heat production

Down's syndrome Congenital condition caused by trisomy 21, a chromosomal abnormality; characterized by a small, anteroposteriorly flattened skull, short flat-bridged nose, epicanthus, short phalanges, widened space between the first and second digits of hands and feet, and moderate to severe mental retardation

enteral By way of the intestine

epiglottis Structure that covers the entrance to the larynx

epilepsy Condition characterized by paroxysmally recurring impairment or loss of consciousness, involuntary excess or cessation of muscle movements, psychic or sensory disturbances, and perturbation of the autonomic nervous system

erythematous Redness of the skin caused by congestion of the capillaries

evaluation Judgment of the value of that which is being assessed

exfoliative Falling off in scales or layers

extension Movement that brings the members of a limb into or toward a straight condition

extensor Any muscle that extends a joint

flexed Bent or put into a state of being bent

gag reflex Elevation of the soft palate and retching elicited by touching the back of the tongue or the wall of the pharynx

gastroschisis Congenital fissure of the abdominal wall

gavage Feeding by insertion of a stomach tube through the mouth into the stomach

glia Supporting tissue of brain and the spinal cord

HANES Abbreviation for Health and Nutrition Examination Survey, a nutritional status survey of the United States' population, conducted on a 2-year cycle

Heimlich maneuver Technique for removing foreign matter from the trachea of a choking victim

hemoglobin Oxygen-carrying pigment of the erythrocytes

heparin Anticoagulant; it inhibits coagulation by preventing conversion of prothrombin to thrombin

hyponatremia Subnormal blood sodium concentration

hydroxyproline Proline to which a hydroxyl group has been added; found in the structural protein collagen

hyperactivity Abnormally increased activity

hyperkinesis Abnormally increased mobility or activity

hyperplasia Increase in cell number; increase in the number of normal cells

hypersensitivity Abnormally increased sensitivity

hypertension Elevation of blood pressure above normal

hypertonia Condition of excessive tone, tension, or activity

hypertrophy Increase in cell size

hypocalcemia Reduction of blood calcium below normal

hyponatremia Deficiency of sodium in the blood

hypotonia Condition of abnormally diminished tone, tension, or activity

immunity Protection against invasion by infectious agents because of the presence of antibody or reactivity of antibody-forming cells and of phagocytic cells

intestinal atresia Complete occlusion of the intestinal tract

ketones Compounds derived from the oxidation of a secondary alcohol

kg Abbreviation for kilogram

kilocalorie Amount of heat required to raise the temperature of 1 kg of water $1°$ C

kwashiorkor Protein deficiency disease occurring in children

laryngeal Of or pertaining to the larynx—the muscular and cartilaginous structure at the top of the trachea and below the root of the tongue and the hyoid bone

lateralization Moving from one side to the other

linoleic acid Essential fatty acid; a polyunsaturated fatty acid with 2 double bonds and 18 carbon atoms

marasmus Form of extreme undernutrition

maturation Stage or process of becoming fully developed

mechanical ventilation Mechanically supplying oxygen through the lungs

megaloblastic anemia Type of anemia characterized by an increased level of megaloblasts, which are primitive nucleated red blood cells much larger than the mature erythrocytes

megavitamin therapy Treatment of disease with massive doses of vitamins

menarche Beginning of the menstrual function

myelin Fatty substance forming a sheath around certain nerve fibers

myelinization Taking on of myelin by nerve cells

myoglobin Iron-protein complex in muscle that acts as a store of oxygen

neonatal Pertaining to the newborn

neuronal Pertaining to one or more nerve cells

neutrophil Cell that stains easily with neutral dye

occiput Back part of the head

omphalocele Hernia of the naval

osteomalacia Inadequate mineralization of the organic matrix of the bones, resulting in skeletal deformities and fractures

osteopenia Insufficiency of bone resulting from reduced production or increased breakdown of bone

parenteral Injection of substances into the body through any route other than the alimentary tract

patent ductus arteriosus Open lumen in the ductus arteriosus after birth causing recirculation of arterial blood through the lungs

pharynx Muscular and membranous tube extending from the oral cavity to the esophagus

pincer grasp Grasp of small object with the thumb and index finger

prehension Act of seizing or grasping

prenatal Before birth

proprioceptive facilitation Promotion or hastening of receiving stimulations within the tissues of the body

prothrombin Protein in blood plasma needed for blood clotting

pica Abnormal craving to consume unusual articles such as clay, chalk, laundry starch, and dirt

Prader-Willi syndrome Syndrome characterized by small genitals, mental retardation, and obesity; affected individuals have an abnormal craving for food

raking grasp Grasp of objects by raking with palm of the hand

reflex Sum total of any particular involuntary activity

reflux Backward or return flow

self-esteem Satisfaction in oneself

sepsis Infection in the blood stream

slough Dead tissue in or separated from living tissue

solute Substance dissolved in a solution

spasticity State of increase over the normal tension of a muscle, resulting in continuous increase of resistance to stretching

supraorbital Situation above the bone cavity that contains the eyeball

tactile Pertaining to the sense of touch

tactile sensitivity State or quality of being unusually responsive to touch

tongue thrust Moving the tongue through the lips when swallowing, normally associated with suckling in infants less than 4 months of age; an abnormal reflex in some individuals with motor coordination difficulties

tracheoesophageal fistula Abnormal tube-like passage in the esophagus often connecting the trachea and distal esophagus

vegan Vegetarian who excludes all animal protein from the diet

volvulus Intestinal obstruction caused by twisting of the bowel

whey Residue of milk remaining after the curd and cream have been removed

Index